A HISTORY OF PREACHING
IN BRITAIN AND AMERICA

A HISTORY
OF PREACHING

IN BRITAIN AND AMERICA

Including the Biographies of
Many Princes of the Pulpit and the
Men who influenced them

PART TWO

By F. R. Webber

Northwestern Publishing House
Milwaukee, Wisconsin

TABLE OF CONTENTS

Contents

CHAPTER I

PRE-REFORMATION SCOTLAND

A N ACCOUNT of the Celtic Church has been given in Part One of this work, and it is not necessary to repeat it at this place. Many important facts have been brought to light in recent years by careful historians, and there is no reason to declare nowadays that the history of the great Celtic Church is but a tangle of contradictory legends. Historians of a certain school of thought have been ready enough to persuade us that such is the case, and to assure us that any study of Celtic Christianity is but a waste of effort. The great majority of people believe that every movement worthy of notice had its origin in Mediterranean lands. The Celtic Church did not begin with the Greeks and Romans, but was quite distinct from Grecian and Latin Christianity in almost every respect. Painstaking men, trained in careful historical research, have gone to original sources, and have not been content to base their conclusions upon such speculative writers as Bede, Adamnan, Ailred of Rievaulx, Gildas and William of Malmesbury. The Venerable Bede and those who followed him had but an imperfect understanding of Celtic Christianity. They interpreted the doctrines, customs and forms of government of the Celtic Church in language with which their Latin readers were familiar. This idle speculation, garbling of history, to say nothing of a readiness to accept absurd legends as historical facts, led to the confusion that has been mentioned. Modern research has gone far in making Celtic Christianity free from idle speculation and baseless legends.

The influential Celtic Church, with its Pictish and Gaidhealic branches, flourished in Scotland from 397 A.D. to 1109 A.D., a period of 712 years. During this time much of Scotland was evangelized, and the tireless Celtic missionaries pushed on into Ireland, England, Wales, Cornwall and the Northern Islands, as well as establishing important centers in Switzerland, Italy, Germany and even Iceland and Scandinavia. Advocates of prelacy, both Roman Catholic and Protestant, have not been too eager to give the Celtic

Church the credit that it deserves, but in their efforts to establish an unbroken apostolic succession in the British Isles, they would have us believe that the Latin Church was there from the beginning. There is no proof, either documentary or archaeological, that any permanent work was established in Scotland before the days of St. Ninian the Celt, who founded his great missionary center *Candida Casa* at Whithorn, in southwestern Scotland between 397 and 400 A.D. Legends of Donald King of Scots and St. Servanus are wholly fictitious. To make the assertion that Palladius visited Scotland in 431 A.D. is merely to overlook the fact (intentionally or else out of ignorance), that whenever early writers speak of the "Scots," they refer to the people of what is now called Ireland. All careful historians are agreed upon this fact. "When Scotia, or the land of the Scots, is spoken of by writers in the early centuries of Christianity, they refer not to the country now called Scotland, but to Ireland. The concurrence of evidence on this point is so complete and distinct that it would be a waste of words to refer to individual authorities. The writings of Bede and Adamnan, the letters of the popes and fathers during the eighth and ninth centuries, and all the historical vestiges referring to portions of the earth so obscure in these ages, are quite distinct in their reference to Ireland."[1]

Christianity of the Latin type was introduced into England in 597 A.D. with the coming of St. Augustine of Canterbury. This was 200 years after St. Ninian began his far-reaching work in Scotland.[2] Latin Christianity spread slowly northward, but the Celtic Church and the Church of Rome remained entirely independent of one another, as far as Scotland was concerned, until after 842 A.D. On that date Kenneth Mac Alpin, a Gaidhealic Celt, assumed the throne at Fortrenn. A slow union of the Pictish and the Gaidhealic branches of the Celtic race began at that time. The Gaidheals had their own church, and in Kenneth's day it had begun to show a friendly attitude toward Rome. A

---

[1]. J. H. Burton, *The History of Scotland* (Edinburgh, 1867), vol. I, p. 208.

[2]. See Archibald B. Scott, *The Pictish Nation, its People and its Church* (Edinburgh, 1918).

gradual transition took place. The Celtic Church, which had refused for centuries to conform to Rome in doctrine, practice and forms of church government, did not yield finally until long after Kenneth Mac Alpin's day.

The final surrender was hastened by a remarkable woman, Queen Margaret. She was a daughter of Edmund Ironside, and of a Bavarian princess, and she had married Malcolm, King of Scotland. She had been educated by Lanfranc, archbishop of Canterbury, and had become a devout Roman Catholic. The marked difference between the teachings and customs of the Celtic Church and those of her own Church, grieved her, and she sought to persuade the Celtic leaders to conform. On one occasion she urged them to celebrate Holy Communion more frequently. The Celts replied that their regard for Holy Communion was very high, but they feared that frequent participation in the Sacrament might lead men to receive it unworthily.

Queen Margaret and her chaplain, Turgot, a Benedictine monk, called the attention of the Celts to many other points of difference between their church and that of Rome. The Celts observed the Lenten season, but they began their observance with the first Monday in Lent, rather than with Ash Wednesday. It was not the custom in the Celtic Church to celebrate Holy Communion on Easter Day. The Celtic Communion liturgy differed from that of Rome, for the Celts seem to have followed the Gallican order of service. The Celts did not keep the Lord's Day with the same strictness as did the Latin Church of Queen Margaret's day, for after the church service was over, certain recreations were permitted on Sunday afternoon. The Celts had made certain concessions in regard to the prohibited degrees of Leviticus 20, permitting the marriage of a man to his brother's widow, under certain conditions. The difference in the date of Easter had long been a burning issue, and the Synod of Whitby had attempted to settle it, yet the Celtic Church was not unanimous in conforming to the Roman Catholic method of reckoning Easter.

Queen Margaret and her chaplain called together the Celtic leaders on several occasions, endeavoring to persuade them to conform to Rome in these matters.   Here the queen showed much more tact and patience than had been the case at the Synod of Whitby, when Wilfrid, a Celt who had conformed to Rome, charged his former companions with barbarous heresies.   Four centuries later Queen Margaret attempted to win them by persuasiveness.

"What then?" asked Queen Margaret of the Celtic Christians.   "Shall all who are sinners refuse to partake of that holy mystery?   No one in that case ought to partake, for none are free from the stain of sin.   The Apostle's words must manifestly, according to the judgment of the Fathers, have another meaning. . . . He means that a man eats and drinks judgment to himself who fails to distinguish by faith the body of our Lord from ordinary food, and who . . . without confession and penitence, approaches these sacred mysteries. . . . We who, having made confession of our sins many days before, are chastened with penitence, worn with fastings and cleansed from our sins by alms and tears, approach the Table on the day of our Lord's Resurrection in the catholic faith and partake of the flesh and blood of the immaculate Lamb, not to our condemnation but for remembrance of our sins and salutary preparation for eternal blessedness."[3]

While these words indicate Queen Margaret's Roman Catholic position, yet, as Dr. MacEwen shows,[4] nothing is said about Rome, the pope, archbishops or bishops.   The Celtic Christians had their own form of religion, which had been evangelical in the days of St. Ninian and his immediate successors.   They had their own form of church government, which knew nothing of submission to a foreign pontiff, neither were there diocesan bishops among the Celts, nor archbishops.   Writers of garbled history and superficial annotators have jumped at the conclusion that the Celtic Church, merely because it flourished in pre-Reformation times, must have been in fellowship with Rome, with the Latin form of church government, as well as the teachings of the Latin Church.   This was certainly not the case.   The

---

[3]. A. R. MacEwen, *A History of the Church in Scotland* (London, 1913), vol. 1, p. 159.
[4]. *Op. cit.*, p. 159.

Latin Church had a large part in the evangelization of Central, Western and Southern Europe, but insofar as the British Isles are concerned, the Celtic Church was the pioneer.

Queen Margaret died in 1093, and her three sons, Edgar, Alexander and David, reigned successively for the next 56 years. During the time of Queen Margaret and her sons, diocesan episcopacy was established in Scotland. St. Andrews, Glasgow, Dunkeld, Moray, Aberdeen, Ross, Caithness, Dunblane and Brechin were given diocesan bishops of the Latin type. The few Celtic training centers and smaller communities that had survived the raids of the Vikings who had undertaken their extermination, were reorganized as monasteries. Thus it is that the mission of St. Augustine of Canterbury extended its influence northward until, after some five or six centuries the dominion of the Celtic Church was succeeded by that of the Roman Church. The Church of the Gaidheals, one branch of the Celtic Church, was the first to yield to Rome. The Pictish Church, another branch of Celtic Christianity, resisted much longer, but at last they yielded after the Gaidheals had absorbed some of their centers of influence and the Vikings had destroyed many others.

It is most unfortunate that superficial authorities make it appear that Scotland was Roman Catholic from the beginning, for by so doing they rob the powerful Celtic Church of the credit that is due her. For over 700 years she did her full share toward the spread of Christianity, and there is no reason why this important branch of Northern Christianity should not be given her just credit for the things that she accomplished. The facts that have been brought to light during the past century entitle her to unreserved praise. Historians who are content merely to rewrite the statements of Bede, Adamnan, Ailred and others of that school, have been slow to recognize the importance of the Celtic Church's work. "In every effort to get at the facts through such sources as these," says Burton, "there is a rather unequal struggle with the powerful and compact literary organization to carry back into remote times the

evidence that the bishop of Rome exercised supreme authority over all the Christian Church."[5]

The Angles and Saxons invaded the British Isles, coming at first as allies and later as enemies intent upon remaining as colonists. Even more distress was caused by the
Viking raiders who endeavored to bring about a systematic
destruction of Celtic Christianity by plundering and burning
the many training and missionary centers of the Brito-Picts,
the Iro-Picts and the Gaidheals.

The Celtic Church produced a number of great missionary preachers, but after the last of these men died, we
find no preacher of first rank until the appearance of John
Wyclif (c. 1324-1384). Wyclif was an excellent preacher
himself, and he trained groups of men called "poor preachers," and sent them out to declare evangelical truths to the
people. They came to be known as Lollards, a name that
seems to have been borrowed from the Lollards of Continental Europe. These men were trained to expound the
Scriptures without adorning the truth of God's Word with
elaborate allegories and legends. They denounced sin in
emphatic terms, whether it were found among the people or
among their priests. They urged all to repent and to believe
on the Lord Jesus. In 1382, twenty-four of Wyclif's teachings were declared to be heretical, and Parliament ordered
the arrest of the "poor priests" or Lollards.

The movement was not suppressed, however, for the
teaching of these men, known as Lollardism, found its way
into Scotland. In 1406 or 1407 a Lollard named James
Resby, a follower of John Wyclif, came to Scotland and
preached to the people the doctrines that he had learned
from his reading of Wyclif's translation of the Bible. He
was charged with heresy and burned at Perth. John Bower,
who edited and enlarged Fordun's Chronicle about forty
years after Resby's death, says of him:

"Resby . . . was charged with forty heresies, of which
the first was that the pope is not actually vicar of Christ
(non est de facto Christi vicarius), the second that he is
no pope nor vicar of Christ unless he is holy (nullus est papa
nec Christi vicarius nisi sit sanctus). His other heresies

[5]. J. H. Burton, Op. cit., vol. I, p. 41.

were similar or worse. Such errors, which were culled from the heresies of John Wyclif, arch-heretic, are still maintained in Scotland by some Lollards and are cautiously guarded, at the prompting of the devil, by men to whom stolen waters are the most pleasant and concealed bread the sweetest. Those who have once been stained and rooted in the school of this most accursed doctrine scarcely or never come to the unity of the faith. Rarely if ever do I remember to have seen such men falling asleep in the Lord in Christian fashion. And no wonder, since they publicly and privately slander the flock of the Lord and the pope, being worshippers of antichrist. . . . They destroy the sacrament of penance, weakening oral confession, attempting to erect shadows into royal palaces, not believing with the heart unto righteousness, rousing the disgust of Holy Mother Church by their idle philosophy and rationalism and by breaking the unity of the faith."[6]

In 1425 the Scottish Parliament directed the bishops to make a search for all persons holding Lollard views; and all candidates for the degree of Master of Arts at St. Andrews University were obliged to take an oath: "Ye shall swear that ye will defend the Church against the insults of the Lollards, and that ye will resist with all your power whosoever adheres to their sect." The Lollards were not suppressed, and toward the end of the same century a number of lairds and ladies from Kyle and Cunningham were charged with teaching that images and relics ought not to be worshipped; that after the consecration the bread remains bread; that there is a universal priesthood that includes every faithful believer; that the pope is not St. Peter's successor; that it is not lawful to forbid a priest to be married; that God alone, not the pope, can forgive sin; that prayers ought not to be offered to the Virgin Mary; that the Christian is not obliged to believe all that the doctors of the Kirk have written.[7]

---

[6]. Scotichronicon, XV, 20, quoted by A. R. MacEwen.

[7]. For the thirty-four points of heresy, see John Knox, *Historie of the Reformation* (1790), p. 63ff.

In 1431 a Bohemian physician named Peter Craw came to Scotland and lived at the cathedral town of St. Andrews. He was a follower of Wyclif and a man of eloquence, and before long "the town began to ring with his teaching." He declared that the people should have the Bible in their own language, and he denied transubstantiation and purgatory. Craw was charged with heresy, declared guilty and burned at the stake.[8]

Efforts to suppress the reformed teachings led to nothing, and the people met by night in private homes behind closed shutters. Manuscript copies of Wyclif's translation of the Bible were brought out, read, expounded and discussed, and the old teachings were compared with the new. About the year 1525 other books found their way into Scotland. They were brought into the ports of Dundee, Leith and Montrose by seafaring men who had brought them from the Continent. The printing press had been invented, and copies of Tyndale's Bible and the writings of Luther and his associates were smuggled into Scotland. They came hidden in packing cases or wrapped in bales of cotton and wool. The bishops declared Tyndale's translation to be faulty, and Luther's writings were pronounced heretical. The fact that these books were forbidden awakened the curiosity of the people, and many were eager to obtain copies of them, and thus the teachings of the reformers spread throughout Scotland. In the stately homes of lairds and nobles, in the thatched dwellings of humble cotters, in the *dachaidh* of the Highlander, people gathered to hear the reading of these books, and before long all Scotland was discussing the new teachings.

In 1525 the Scottish Parliament passed a law declaring that "No manner of person, stranger, that happens to arrive with their ship within any part of this realm, bring with them any books or works of said Luther, his disciples, servants or deputies, or rehearse his heresies, etc., under the pain of escheating of their ships and goods, and putting of their persons in prison."[9] In 1527 this act was amended to include residents of Scotland as well as strangers.

---

[8]. John Knox, *Op. cit.*, p. 63.
[9]. Thomas M'Crie, *Life of John Knox* (Edinburgh, 1812), p. 38.

The execution of Patrick Hamilton in 1528 caused nation-wide excitement. Hamilton was a promising young man of 25, well educated and a great-grandson of King James II. He was tried for heresy and burned at the stake,[10] and when word of his death spread throughout Scotland, the people were eager to know just what things this young man had preached, and why so prominent a man should have been executed. The details of his religious beliefs were passed from person to person by word of mouth, and it was not long until every shire in Scotland was familiar with the story.

A friar named William Arithe,[11] who had preached boldly at Dundee and at St. Andrews, inveighing against the sins of the bishops and the greed of the lesser clergy, was silenced. Patrick Hepburn[12] preached against the same sins, and was forced to flee to England for sanctuary. Alexander Furrour[13] was imprisoned for seven months because of his outspoken condemnation of the sins of the day. Alexander Seaton, "a black friar of good learning and estimation," preached sin and grace throughout an entire Lenten season. He was called to account for his deviations from the older teachings, and he fled to England. "Alexander Seaton remained in England, and publicly (with great praise and comfort of many) taught the Gospel in all sincerity certain years."[14] Then there was David Stratoun,[15] a layman, who was burned in Edinburgh in 1534 for his religious beliefs. Thomas Forret,[16] or Forrest, preached the doctrines of the Reformation every Sunday to his congregation at Dollar. He compiled a catechism and taught the people the chief parts of Christian doctrine. He was burned with four others in 1540. Sir John Borthwick,[17] a Lutheran theologian, was charged with preaching heresy, excommunicated and burned in effigy at St. Andrews in 1540.

---

[10]. John Knox, *Op. cit.*, pp. 65-72.
[11]. *Ibid.*, pp. 72-73.
[12]. *Ibid.*, p. 73.
[13]. *Ibid.*, p. 73.
[14]. *Ibid.*, p. 76.
[15]. Thos. M'Crie, *Op. cit.*, p. 379.
[16]. *Ibid.*, pp. 379-80.
[17]. *Ibid.*, pp. 387-388.

Others were executed during this period. Thomas M'Crie has cited a number of such examples.[18]

During the 162 years that elapsed between the death of Wyclif and the first public appearance of John Knox, there were few preachers of first rank. Patrick Hamilton was a man of great religious zeal, but his career was cut short when he was but 25 years of age, and we have but a few particulars by which to judge his preaching. We are assured by John Knox and others that Hamilton was a young man of great courage, zeal and fluency of speech. His summary of the relation of Law and Gospel shows that he had grasped the basic principles of that difficult subject. George Wishart was another man who would have become a great preacher had he lived, but his execution at the age of 33 years cut short his career. He, too, was a man of great courage and zeal, and his contemporaries speak in highest terms of his preaching. Thomas Forret, Henry Forrest, Alexander Alesius, Thomas Williams and a number of other such men were faithful preachers of evangelical truth at the end of the pre-Reformation period, and of these Forrest and Alesius lived to see the new movement definitely established. With a few rare exceptions the period between Wyclif and Knox was an interval in which humble men, here and there, kept the light of evangelical truth burning. In many cases their very names have been forgotten, nevertheless each man, however obscure, did his humble share in making possible the new era that was to begin in the year 1547 A. D.

Walter Mylne (1476-1558)

Walter Mylne, or Mill, was a priest at Lunan in Angus. We hear of him first when he paid a visit to Germany and became acquainted with the teachings of the Reformation. He returned to Scotland, and in the days of Cardinal Beaton he began to preach the doctrines of the Reformation. He was charged with heresy and ordered to appear for trial, but he fled and remained in concealment until it appeared that the matter had been forgotten. Then he began to preach publicly and to meet with friends of the new teach-

---

[18]. Thos. M'Crie, *Op. cit.*, pp. 379-388.

ings in their homes. He was declared an outlaw and ordered burned at the stake wherever found.

In 1558, in the days of Bishop Hamilton, of St. Andrews, Mylne was arrested at Dysart, Fifeshire. He was confined in the castle at St. Andrews, and then brought before a court composed of bishops, abbots and doctors. Eighty-two years of age, weak and in poor health, his friends feared that he would not survive the ordeal of the heresy trial. He appeared before the ecclesiastical court, and when given an opportunity to answer the charges brought against him, he delivered a ringing sermon in which he denounced error and set forth the teachings of the reformers. The bishops condemned him to die at the stake, but the sympathy of the townspeople was so strong that they closed their shops on the day of his execution and refused to lend assistance in any manner to the bishops. No judge was found willing to pass the sentence of death upon him, and the archbishop was compelled to order one of his own household servants to do this for him. Mylne was burned on August 28, 1558, and at the stake he addressed the people, declaring among other things: "As for me, I am fourscore and two years old, and cannot live long by course of nature; but a hundred better shall rise out of the ashes of my bones. I trust in God I shall be the last that shall suffer death in Scotland for this cause."

Thomas Forret (c. 1490-1540)

Thomas Forret, sometimes confused with Henry Forrest, was born toward the close of the fifteenth century at Logie, Fifeshire. After his elementary education he went to Cologne and studied there. Upon his return to Scotland, he became a canon regular at Inchcolme. He read the writings of St. Augustine and became convinced that the only pardon from sin is through the blood of Jesus Christ alone. He preached this boldly to his congregation at Dollar, Clackmannanshire, where he was vicar.

In those days only the Greyfriars and Blackfriars preached in Scotland. Ordinary vicars were not supposed to preach. The friars complained to the local bishops that the Vicar of Dollar "showed the mysteries of the Scriptures to the vulgar people in English." The bishop sent for Forret and agreed to permit him to preach, but advised him to confine himself to "one good Epistle or one good Gospel" each Sunday. Forret replied that he had never found an evil Epistle or Gospel in the Scriptures, and asked his bishop to tell him just which were good and which he considered ill. To this the bishop replied that he knew neither the Old Testament nor the New.[19] The people in a country as far away as Cornwall are said to have a proverb: "He knows nothing about the New Testament and still less about the Old, like the Bishop of Dunkeld."

Thomas Forret preached with great boldness every Sunday. He compiled a Catechism, and instructed his people in the chief parts of Christian doctrine. He preached against indulgences. He made it his rule to memorize three chapters of the Latin Bible each day, so as to be able to answer his adversaries. He was not molested for about ten years, but after he attended the marriage of another vicar, he was arrested, charged with preaching heresy, and burned with four others, in 1540.[20]

Henry Forrest (c. 1500-1553)

Henry Forrest was born about the year 1500, probably in Linlithgow, Scotland. In 1518 the name of a Henry Forrest appears among the students of Glasgow University, and in 1526 a Henriccus Forrest is listed among those at St. Leonard's, St. Andrews. He became a Benedictine friar, and became the owner of a copy of the New Testament, which the Scottish sailors brought into the country from time to time.

About the year 1553 he declared that Patrick Hamilton had died a martyr to the true faith. He went to confession, and when questioned, he expressed his honest opinion in regard to Patrick Hamilton and his death. For this, and for his unauthorized possession of an English New Testament, he was imprisoned by the bishop, and finally burned.

---

[19]. See D. Calderwood, *Historie of the Kirk of Scotland,* Thompson ed. (Edinburgh, 1842-49), vol. I, pp. 124-128.

[20]. D. Calderwood, *Op. cit.,* pp. 124-128.

Whether Forrest preached his beliefs publicly, or expressed them privately is not clear. The chief source of information is John Knox,[21] and his account of the career of Forrest is not very detailed. Calderwood[22] seems to have based his account upon that of Knox.

Alexander Alesius (1500-1565)

Alexander Alane, or Alesius,[23] was born in Edinburgh in 1500. He was educated at St. Andrews. He studied the writings of Luther so as to be able to answer the Lutherans of Scotland. In 1527 he was appointed to admonish Patrick Hamilton, and if possible to reclaim him from the Lutheran teachings that he had learned in Germany. Instead of winning Hamilton, Alane was himself won over to Lutheranism.[24]

In 1529 Archbishop Beaton invited Alane to deliver a sermon at the synod meeting at St. Andrews. Alane preached in Latin, urging the clergy to live in chastity, and to be diligent in their calling. Some of his statements caused Beaton to suspect him of Lutheranism, and he was confined to prison for a year. Some of his fellow canons released him and provided him with funds to flee to Germany. He arrived in Cologne in 1533 in time to see two men burned for heresy. From there he went to Wittenberg, where he became well acquainted with Luther and his associates, who changed his name to Alesius. In 1530 he signed the Augsburg Confession. In 1535 he went to England, lectured for a time at Cambridge, and then practiced medicine in London. While in England he preached the doctrines of the Reformation. Summoned before the Archbishop of Canterbury, he declared that a Sacrament must be of divine origin, and must convey remission of sins. Later he returned to Germany, taught for three years at Frankfurt-on-Oder, and then went to Leipsic.

Alesius was a close friend of Melanchthon, and he accepted the unstable doctrinal position of Melanchthon,

---

21. John Knox, *Historie of the Reformation* (1790), p. 63.
22. D. Calderwood, *Historie of the Kirk of Scotland* (Edinburgh, 1842-49), vol. I, pp. 96-97.
23. See Spottiswoode, *Historie of Church and State in Scotland* (London, 1655), p. 66.
24. See D. Calderwood, *Historie of the Kirk of Scotland* (Edinburgh, 1842-49), vol. I, pp. 93-96.

which reflected itself at times in his preaching. He was a
man of diligence, and in addition to his preaching he published a number of theological works. These fall into three
classes: exegetical, dogmatic and controversial. Of his
seven exegetical writings mention might be made of *In
aliquot Psalmos* (1550); *De utilitate Psalmorum* (1542);
In Evangelium Johannis (1553); and *In omnes Epistolas
Pauli*. Of his several works on dogmatics the more important are: *De Scripturis legendis in Lingua materna*
(1553); *De autoritate Verbi Dei* (1542); *Ad Scotorum
Regem contra Episcopos* (1542); *Contra calumnias Cochlaei*
(1551); and *Responsio ad Jacobum V Regem* (1554). His
controversial works include some seventeen titles, and of
these perhaps the best known are *De justificatione contra
Osiandrum* (1552), and *Contra Michaelem Servetum* (1554).
About 30 of the works of Alexander Alesius have survived.
Several standard reference works describe him as a Scottish
Lutheran, although his doctrinal position, due to Melanch-
thon's influence, is not without its weaknesses.

Patrick Hamilton (c. 1503-1528)

Patrick Hamilton was born about the year 1503 at Stane-
house, Lanark, Linlithgow. He was a son of Sir Patrick
Hamilton, and his mother was a grand-daughter of King
James II. In 1517 he was appointed to a titular abbacy of
Ferne, Rosshire. He went to Paris, attended the University
there, and was graduated in 1520. Following this, he went
to Louvain University, and studied with Erasmus. He re-
turned to Scotland in 1522 and studied at St. Andrews with
John Major who had just begun his work at that university.
In 1524 he was made a member of the faculty of arts at St.
Leonard's, St. Andrews, teaching languages, philosophy and
church music.

In 1526 he urged his friends and students to read Tyndale's New Testament. This translation had been condemned as heretical, and, because of the displeasure of
Beaton, Patrick Hamilton was obliged to flee to the Continent. He went to Germany, met Luther, and spent some
time with him. He attended Marburg for a time.

Hamilton returned to Scotland in 1527, declaring himself a Lutheran. Whether he was ordained or not is uncertain, but he began to preach whenever the opportunity afforded, and attracted many because of his learning and eloquence. In 1528 he was invited to take part in a conference and to discuss certain evils that had crept into the Church. During this lengthy conference, Hamilton expressed himself candidly on justification by faith alone, the distinction between Law and Gospel, the inability of man to merit salvation because of his works, the needlessness of the intercession of the saints and the right of the Christian to read and interpret the Scriptures for himself. The council declared him guilty of heresy, and he was tried and executed.

The eloquence and fiery zeal of Patrick Hamilton had attracted the attention of many; and the fact that this young man of but 25 years of age, when given time to consider the matter and recant, after having been found guilty of heresy, spent this time in preaching the doctrines of the Reformation — made a deep impression upon many. His execution caused a demand for copies of Tyndale's New Testament, which was being brought in by sailors, and it was not long until the teachings of the Reformation were being discussed far and wide in Scotland.

The account of Patrick Hamilton's life is given in great detail, and a number of his theological writings are included in John Knox's *Historie*.[25] Here, for example, is Hamilton's summary of the relation of Law and Gospel: [26]

"The Law saith, pay thy debt.
The Law saith, thou art a desperate sinner.
The Law saith, thou shalt die.
The Gospel saith, Christ hath paid it.
The Gospel saith, thy sins are forgiven thee.
The Gospel saith, be of good comfort, thou art saved.
The Law saith, make amends for thy sin.
The Law saith, the Father of Heaven is wroth with thee.
The Law saith, where is thy righteousness, goodness and satisfaction?

[25]. John Knox, *Historie of the Reformation* (1790), pp. 65-72.
[26]. *Ibid.*, p. 68.

> The Law saith, thou art bound and obliged unto me, the devil and hell.
> The Gospel saith, Christ hath made it for thee.
> The Gospel saith, Christ pacified Him with His blood.
> The Gospel saith, Christ is thy righteousness, goodness and satisfaction.
> The Gospel saith, Christ hath delivered thee from them all."

Hamilton's *Patrick's Places, or Common Places,* a Latin treatise on the distinction between Law and Gospel, was translated from the Latin and published by John Frith, and is included in Richmond's *Fathers of the English Church.* Biographies include Lorimer's *Patrick Hamilton, the First Preacher and Martyr of the Scottish Reformation* (1857), and William Dallmann's *Patrick Hamilton* (1918).

George Wishart (c. 1513-1546)

George Wishart was one of the early Scotsmen whose preaching cost him his life. Of his early history not much is known. He was born about the year 1513, probably at Pittarrow, near Montrose, and he is said to have been graduated from King's College, Aberdeen. In the year 1538 a man named George Wishart was master of the grammar school at Montrose, and taught his students the Greek New Testament, which seems to have been an innovation as far as Scotland is concerned. In 1539 a "George Wischarde, a Scotsman," was cited for heresy in Bristol, England, and was charged with having denied that the merit of Jesus Christ is imputed to the believer. This Wischarde was taken to Canterbury and there he recanted.

About the year 1539 it is known that Wishart went to Germany and Switzerland, where he remained for about three years. In 1543 he returned to England, and we find him at Corpus Christi College, Cambridge, for one Emery Tilney, one of his students, gives us a description of him as "a man of tall stature, polde-headed, and on the same a round French cappe of the best; judged of melancholick complexioun, by his physiognomie; black-haired, long-bearded, comelie of personage, weill spokin after his countrie of Scotland; courteous, lovelie, glade to teache, desirous to learne, and was well travelled."[27]

In 1544 he returned to Scotland and preached at Dundee, Kyle, Haddington and elsewhere. Not only did he preach against some of the teachings of the Roman Church, but he had the unfortunate habit of predicting the death of prominent church leaders — a thing which caused him to be suspected of plotting against Cardinal Beaton and others. His preaching influenced John Knox, then a school-master, and Knox became his bodyguard for a time, protecting him with a two-handed sword.[28] In 1545, after a sermon at Haddington, he was arrested and imprisoned in the castle at St. Andrews. Eighteen charges of heresy were brought against him, most of which he denied emphatically. A detailed account of his trial is given by Calderwood.[29] Among the charges were: denying the authority of the lord governor; denial that there are seven Sacraments; denial of the Real Presence; denial of the freedom of the will; denial of purgatory and a number of similar accusations. He was declared guilty and burned at the stake in 1546.

Calderwood declares that he was a good preacher, "singulairlie learned in divinitie and humane sciences."[30] He seems to have considered himself a prophet, and it is possible that his outspoken predictions of the sudden death of several churchmen of high rank had something to do with his execution. He is not to be confused with George Wishart (1599-1671), a leader of the prelatic faction in the Scottish Kirk.

"He did grow and advance in godly knowledge," says John Knox, "joined with fervency and integrity of life, and he was in admiration of many. The zeal of God's glory did so eat him up, that he could not long continue to remain there,[31] but returned to his country, where the bright beams of the true light, which by God's grace was planted in his heart, began most abundantly to burst forth, as well in

---

[27]. David Calderwood, *Historie of the Kirk of Scotland* (Edinburgh, 1842-49), vol. I, p. 185.
[28]. David Calderwood, *Op. cit.*, vol. I, p. 195.
[29]. *Ibid.*
[30]. *Ibid.*, vol. I, p. 186.
[31]. In Germany.

public as in secret."[32]   Accounts of Wishart are to be found in John Knox's *Historie of the Reformation* (1790); in W. Cramond's *The Truth about George Wishart* (1898); in C. Roger's *Memoirs of George Wishart* (1876); in Thos. M'Crie's *Life of John Knox* (1841); and in numerous Scottish histories and accounts of the martyrs.

Thomas Guillaume

Thomas Guillaume, or Williams, was the man whose preaching first awakened in John Knox an interest in the teachings of the reformers. Guillaume was born at Athelstoneford, in East Lothian. He became a member of the Dominican order, and rose to a position of eminence. The writings of the reformers came into his hands, and he severed his connection with the Black Friars. At that time the Regent Arran was inclined toward the reformed views, and Thomas Guillaume came into his favor, and was welcomed at the court. Later, when the Regent Arran began to waver, Guillaume was dismissed from the court and went to England.

Thomas Guillaume was an eloquent preacher, and during the days of his favor at court, his expositions of the Scriptures attracted much attention and served to introduce many people to the teachings of the reformers.

John Rough (c. 1510-1557)

John Rough, who was among the first to discover the qualities of leadership of John Knox, was born about 1505 or 1510 A. D. He was educated at St. Leonard's College, St. Andrews. At the age of 17 he left the home of his parents and entered a monastery at Stirling. He made two visits to Rome, and affirmed "that he had been twise at Rome, and there had seen plainlie with his own eyes, which he had heard many times before, namelie, that the pope was the verie Antichrist; for he had seen him carried on men's shoulders, and the false-named Sacrament borne before him, yitt more reverence givin to him than to that which they computed to be their God."[33]

---

[32]. John Knox, *Historie of the Reformation* (1790), pp. 65, 66.
[33]. D. Calderwood, *Historie of the Kirk of Scotland* (Edinburgh, 1842-49), vol. I, p. 254.

By the year 1543 John Rough had acquired considerable local fame as a preacher; and the Regent Arran, who was friendly to the reformed cause at that time, appointed him chaplain. Rough and Thomas Guillaume, (Williams), did not hesitate to preach boldly against the evils of their day. When the Regent Arran wavered in regard to the cause of the reformers, the preaching of John Rough proved displeasing to him, and Rough was dismissed. From the royal court Rough went to Kyle, where the influence of the Lollards had prepared the way for him, and there in Ayrshire he began to proclaim the new teachings.

After the slaying of Cardinal Beaton, Rough cast his lot with the group of people, sincere and otherwise, who had retired to the castle at St. Andrews for safety. He became chaplain to this group, and expounded the Scriptures to them each day. One day a frail, mild-mannered schoolmaster, with several of his pupils, came to the castle. He was John Knox, 42 years of age, whose friendship for George Wishart had caused him to be suspected. Rough listened to Knox as he lectured to his pupils, and he attended the public catechizations conducted by Knox in the nearby parish church. He was impressed by Knox's great learning, his fluency of speech, and above all by his doctrinal assurance. The manner in which the unassuming schoolmaster verified his theological principles by means of clear Scripture verses, and the absence of allegorical and legendary material made a deep impression upon Rough. He urged Knox to become his associate, and to assist him in preaching to the people in the castle. John Knox had, until this time, given but little thought to preaching, and he pleaded with Rough that no man should presume to preach unless he had been properly called.

John Rough considered this matter carefully, he examined the Scriptures, and he discussed it with the people who made up his congregation in the chapel of the castle. Rough grasped an important Christian truth that had escaped so many people, and that is not evident to many to this day. He came to the conclusion, on the basis of Scripture, that the call to preach has its basis in the universal priesthood of all true believers, and is extended by a local congregation. It is not conferred by a bishop, or a synod, neither is it dependent upon a group of ordained clergymen, nor upon a self-perpetuating "representative Church." Rough came to the conclusion that the mixed congregation that assembled daily in the castle, had the right, by virtue of the Christian believers among them, to call John Knox as associate pastor, and to authorize him to preach. In this he set forth a truth so ably expressed in the Smalcald Articles in these words: "Wherever there is a true church, the right to elect and ordain ministers necessarily exists."[34] One day, when the congregation had assembled for worship, John Rough addressed Knox publicly, calling upon him to preach, and he gave proper form to the call by asking the congregation to declare publicly that they had extended the call.

John Rough went to England not long after this incident, and he was not present at St. Andrews when the French invaded the town, captured the castle and carried away its occupants as prisoners. The Protector Somerset assigned him to Carlisle, Berwick and Newcastle. In 1553 Edward VI died and Mary Tudor came to the throne. Rough sought safety in Friesland, where he and his wife supported themselves by knitting caps and gloves. In 1557 they were no longer able to obtain yarn, and they returned to England. There Rough became acquainted with a group who held reformed views, and who met secretly for worship. He became their chaplain. The authorities learned of the presence of this group of people, and of Rough's preaching, through a seceder. Rough was arrested, charged with heresy and confined for a time in Newgate. Shortly before Christmas of the same year he was tried, declared guilty and burned at the stake in Smithfield Market.

Rough seems to have left but scanty literary remains. Of the two men whose preaching assisted John Knox in forming his religious views, Knox assures us that Thomas Guillaume was the more learned of the two, but that in his preaching John Rough was "simple and vehement against all impiety." Rough was a faithful, evangelical preacher,

---

[34]. *Smalcald Articles* (1537), II, 2, 67.

setting forth his religious beliefs with conviction, yet without pretending to be a man of deep scholarship. His plain, practical sermons proved attractive to the congregation in the castle, among whom were John Knox and his schoolboys. Scotland owes him a debt in more ways than one. It was John Rough who called the attention of the Scots to the fact that it is not a bishop and not an assembly of clergymen, but the local congregation of Christian believers, in whom is invested the right to call a man into the ministry. In later years, when tyrannical kings, arrogant bishops, patrons and heritors, sought to take away that sovereign right from the Christian congregation, and with the aid of the civil courts to "settle men by intrusion," the old truth so clearly stated by John Rough was not forgotten. Men gave their lives for that principle, disruptions were caused, but in the course of time that truth became firmly established in Scotland. The Scottish people owe a debt to Rough in yet another way, for it was he who realized the worth of John Knox, and who did much to persuade that famous reformer to lay aside the schoolmaster's books and rod, and to take upon himself the perilous task of leading the Reformation movement in Scotland.

John Carswell (fl. 1550-1570)

Partly to pre-Reformation days and partly to the period that followed belongs John Carswell, a man of distinguished scholarship and an influential preacher. Little is known of his early days except that he was a monk of Iona, then rector of Kilmartin in Argyllshire. Like others of his time, his early preaching did not go much beyond the condemnation of profanity, which was so common among the people of his time, and sermons in which he rebuked the clergy for their covetousness and their infrequent preaching. His study of the Scriptures led him to a realization of salvation by grace through faith. He seems to have had a thorough knowledge of both English and Gaelic, for later he translated John Knox's prayer book into the Gaelic language. Long after his death a translation of Calvin's Catechism, often attributed to him, was published.

The queen appointed him titular bishop of the Isles, and then bishop of Argylle and the Isles. He accepted, much to the displeasure of the Assembly. Carswell was far beyond the average of his day in the matter of scholarship, and his influence in the Highlands and the Isles was hardly equalled by any of his contemporaries.

Preaching was much neglected in pre-Reformation times. There were preaching friars, of course, but too often their efforts were no better than John Carswell's early preaching. They were content to condemn the evils of their day: drunkenness, profanity, theft, immorality and cruelty. In Perth, in 1543, a merchant named Robert Lamb, interrupted a preaching friar. Holding up an English Bible, Lamb asked the friar why he did not preach salvation by grace, and without the intercession of the saints. He was silenced, and later he was hanged outside the city together with four friends who held similar opinions. There seems to have been no attempt to translate the Scriptures into the Scoto-English of the Lowlands. If Bibles existed in Gaelic, the language of the Highlands and the Isles, such copies were rare, and were usually in manuscript form. It was only when copies of the English translations of the Scriptures became known in Scotland that men began to preach the evangelical doctrine of salvation by grace through faith.

CHAPTER II

THE PERIOD OF THE REFORMATION

JAMES V, King of Scotland, died in 1542. He was a nephew of Henry VIII of England, and he might have accepted the Reformation except for the fact that he had married Mary of Guise, who was a staunch Roman Catholic. When James V died, his infant daughter, later to be known as Mary Queen of Scots, inherited the throne. The question of regency arose. Cardinal Beaton attempted to act in this capacity during the infancy of Queen Mary, but he was unsuccessful. The regency was conferred upon the Earl of Arran, at that time friendly toward the reformed movement. Henry VIII of England had hopes of uniting the kingdoms of England and Scotland, and he sought to bring about an engagement between Queen Mary and his own son Edward, later known as Edward VI. The Scots seemed ready to accept this arrangement, and papers were drawn up and dispatched to England. Through the influence of Mary of Guise, mother of the young queen, and of Cardinal Beaton, and through the timidity of the Regent Arran, negotiations were finally broken off, and the queen was betrothed to the dauphin of France. The Regent Arran renounced his Protestant views publicly in the church at Stirling.

The Reformation meanwhile was making steady progress. In 1542 the Scottish Parliament passed an act permitting all persons to read the Scriptures in the vernacular. Although strongly opposed by the bishops, this law was enacted, and it was not long until "the Bible was to be seen on every gentleman's table; the New Testament was almost in every one's hands."[1] Friends of the new movement became bolder; books of the reformers of continental Europe were circulated without fear, and books written by Scottish authors began to appear. Clergymen throughout Scotland began to preach the new doctrines, and converts were made daily.

---

[1]. John Knox, *Historie of the Reformation* (1790), p. 34.

Mary of Guise and Cardinal Beaton were determined to stamp out the new movement, and there were times when Scotland was threatened with civil war. Assistance came from England, and as one town after another accepted Protestantism, it was seen that the efforts of Mary of Guise and Cardinal Beaton were destined to fail. So rapidly did the new movement grow that by the year 1560 the Scottish Parliament enacted laws abolishing the jurisdiction of the pope, prohibiting the celebration of the Mass after the Roman Catholic manner, and repealing all enactments that had favored Rome and restricted the Protestants.

In 1546 an incident occurred that cannot be defended. Cardinal Beaton had done his utmost to check the reformed movement, and tales began to be told throughout Scotland that he had given his consent to the hanging of four men because they ate a goose on Friday. Other rumors were heard: that Beaton had been implicated in the death of a young mother who was drowned because of her refusal to offer her prayers in the old manner, and that Beaton was planning the execution of certain influential men of Fifeshire who were known to hold Protestant views. These reports, whether they be true or false, aroused great indignation in Scotland. On May 29, 1546, a group of men confronted Cardinal Beaton in St. Andrews castle and assassinated him. The immediate cause of this act was the execution of a young Scotsman named George Wishart, a brother of the laird of Pittarrow. Possessed of great eloquence and persuasiveness, Wishart had preached in several parts of Scotland, expounding the new teachings. He was charged with having preached heresy, and burned at the stake in 1546. This aroused the people, and the assassination of Beaton soon followed. John Knox has attempted to excuse the executioners of Cardinal Beaton on the ground that it was the act of a just God who had lost patience with Beaton because of his persecutions. Today such an act as the slaying of Beaton would not be upheld by any thoughtful Christian. Granting that Beaton himself had caused men to be executed for what he considered heresy, yet the old adage still holds, namely that two wrongs do not constitute a right. Every man is entitled to a fair trial by his peers, and no group of men, however great the provocation, is justified in resorting to lynch-law, even though their victim be a tyrant.

The men who slew Beaton took refuge in the castle at St. Andrews, and in the reaction that followed the death of the cardinal other Protestant leaders fled to the same place for safety. Among these refugees was a middle-aged schoolmaster named John Knox. He was not one of the men who killed Beaton, and he was in no manner implicated in the plot other than his effort to justify the murder as the act of an outraged God. His coming to the castle at St. Andrews was one of the turning points of the Scottish Reformation. Hitherto many men of prominence had become associated with the movement, but no powerful leader had yet appeared. George Wishart might have become such a leader, had his career not been cut short by his execution. Few of the mixed gathering of Protestants who had entrenched themselves in the castle suspected on that misty spring morning in 1547 that the mild-mannered, 42-year-old tutor who sought admission to the stronghold was to become, almost overnight, the great leader before whose stormy eloquence two nations were soon to tremble.

The group of refugees in the castle was, as has been said, a mixed one. Some were men who were blameless, but whose outspoken defense of the new teachings had reached the ears of those who were determined to stamp out the reformed doctrines. Others in the castle were mere adventurers who sought to further their political ambitions by casting their lot with a movement that seemed to be gaining in popular favor. Still others were the men who had slain Cardinal Beaton without giving him the benefit of due process of law. John Knox, at least, was allowed a certain amount of freedom, for he seems to have moved about without molestation.

In connection with the castle in the village of St. Andrews was a chapel, and within its walls a friar named John Rough was accustomed to preach daily. Rough had once been chaplain to the Regent Arran. He was a faithful man, but without any conspicuous gifts of leadership, although his quiet expositions of the Scriptures proved attractive to the people within the castle. Rough had accepted the teachings of the reformers, and to the best of his ability he proclaimed them to his mixed congregation. He enjoyed a brief period of local fame, but his place in history is due to the fact that it was he who was among the first to discover the potential leadership of John Knox.

Among others in the castle at St. Andrews was Henry Balnaves, who had held the office of secretary of state during the early days of Arran's regency. Balnaves had been born of a poor family in Kirkaldy, and while yet a mere boy he had paid a visit to the Continent. There was a free school at Cologne, and he succeeded in entering it and receiving a good education. While there he became acquainted with the teachings of the Reformation. Upon his return to Scotland, he became an attorney, then a member of the Scottish Parliament and a member of the Court of Sessions. King James V recognized his superiority and gave him a part in the management of public affairs. Balnaves became a staunch friend of the reformers, and his fearless defense of their teachings caused him to be looked upon with disfavor after the Regent Arran had abandoned the Protestant party. For his own safety Balnaves joined the group who held the castle.

On July 31, 1547, the French captured the castle, made prisoners those within it and razed the entire building.

John Knox (1505-1572)

John Knox, the greatest of the Scottish reformers, was an obscure tutor for the first 42 years of his life. While listening to a sermon in the chapel of St. Andrews castle, he was called upon to preach, and he fled from the church in tears.

Knox was born at Haddington, not far from Edinburgh, of humble parentage. The year 1505 is usually given as the date of his birth, although a few modern historians insist that 1515 is the correct date, and that it was some other John Knox whose name is found among the students of Glasgow University in the year 1522. There is little doubt that he studied at Glasgow, where John Major was one of his teachers. He studied Aristotle's rhetoric and logic and Aquinas's canonical law. Some years later he studied Greek and Hebrew, and it is known that he was familiar with the French and Italian languages. When John Major went from Glasgow University to St. Andrews, there is reason to believe that Knox followed him,[2] but why his name does not appear among the graduates of either university has puzzled historians, for Knox was a man of exceptional learning. It is possible that he may have had some misgivings when asked, when given his degree, to take the century-old anti-Lollard oath.

About the year 1530 Knox was ordained, but instead of becoming a parish priest or a monk, he chose to become a notary, or clerk of canonical law, as well as tutor to the sons of noblemen. His conversion to Protestantism was gradual. Some of his friends became converts to the teachings of the reformers, and while Knox did not accept the new views at first, yet he began to urge more practical methods of study. For this he was suspected of secret heretical views. Next he began to express himself in regard to the evils of the day, and while this was not done publicly, yet the word of it reached Cardinal Beaton, who had resolved to suppress the new teachings wherever they might be found. Upon learning of Beaton's displeasure, Knox fled to the southern part of Scotland, and finally declared himself a Protestant. For this he was pronounced a heretic and deposed from the priesthood. He had been a diligent student of Augustine, and various statements of Augustine led him to study the Bible, but whether it was the Vulgate or the Tyndale translation has never been determined. He was especially moved by the 17th chapter of St. John, and he became more thoroughly convinced that the new teachings were correct.

Knox was influenced by the preaching of Thomas Guillaume and of John Rough, but perhaps the greatest impression was made upon him in 1544 by the preaching of George Wishart. Two years later Knox became Wishart's body-guard, and although a small, frail man, Knox provided

---

[2]. A. F. Mitchell, *The Scottish Reformation* (Edinburgh, 1900), p. 79.

himself with a two-handed sword with which to protect Wishart,[3] after an attempt had been made on his life at Dundee. When Wishart was seized by his enemies, Knox drew his sword, but Wishart merely said: "Nay, return to your bairns, and God bless ye; ane is sufficient for a sacrifice."[4]

After Wishart's execution, Knox went to St. Andrews, then a village of 4000 people. There was a castle in the village, and within it were a number of Protestants who had withdrawn to the castle for safety. Among those who had barricaded themselves in the castle were lairds and nobles, priests and monks who had accepted the new views, others who had become Protestants for political reasons, and even the murderers of Beaton, who had been assassinated after the execution of George Wishart. Knox and his pupils joined the group of Protestants in the castle, and there he continued to teach his schoolboys. If the castle at St. Andrews resembled Moy, Auchallader and scores of others that still exist wholly or in part, it could not have been a spacious affair; and Knox's lectures and catechizations must have been overheard by the others who moved about through the building. Probably for the sake of greater quiet and privacy, Knox began to conduct his daily catechizations in the parish church nearby. The townspeople learned of it, and they came to listen to the catechizations.

John Rough was, as has been stated, chaplain to the people living in the castle, and he expounded the Scriptures to them daily. Rough was faithful and courageous, but he realized quickly enough that Knox was much superior to him in learning. He urged Knox to assist him in preaching to the people in the castle, but Knox declined, insisting that he had no right to preach because he had never been called. He did not believe that his ordination had conferred upon him the right to preach. Rough discussed the matter with his congregation, and it was agreed by all that John Knox should be called to preach. Rough, as we have shown, was convinced that the right to call a pastor is not

---

[3]. D.Calderwood, *Historie of the Kirk of Scotland* (Edinburgh, 1842-49), vol. I, p. 195.
[4]. *Ibid.*

vested in a bishop or a group of clergymen, but in the Christian congregation. At the close of a sermon one day, John Rough looked squarely at Knox and addressed him in the following words:

"Brother, ye shall not be offended, albeit that I speak unto you that which I have in charge, even from all those that are here present, which is this: In the name of God and of His Son Jesus Christ, and in the name of those that presently call you by my mouth, I charge you that ye refuse not this holy vocation, but that, as ye tender the glory of God, the increase of Christ's Kingdom, the edification of your brethren, and the comfort of me, whom ye understand well enough to be oppressed by the multitude of labours, that ye take upon you the public office and charge of preaching, even as ye look to avoid God's heavy displeasure, and desire that He shall multiply His graces with you." Then, turning to the congregation, Rough said, "Was not this your charge to me, and do ye approve this vocation?" Every one present said, "It was; and we approve it."[5] It was then that John Knox arose and fled from the chapel in tears. Knox himself says that "his countenance and behaviour, from that day till the day that he was compelled to present himself in the public place of preaching, did sufficiently declare the grief and trouble of his heart; for no man saw any sign of mirth from him, neither had he pleasure to accompany any man for many days together."[6]

Knox's distress was not due to an unwillingness to preach the Word, much less was it due to any misgivings that he might have had in regard to the validity of the call. "In common with all the original reformers," says his distinguished biographer, "he rejected the order of episcopal ordination, as totally unauthorized by the laws of Christ; nor did he even regard the imposition of the hands of presbyters as a rite essential to the validity of orders, or of necessary observance in all circumstances of the Church. . . . I will not say that our reformer utterly disregarded his early ordination in the Popish Church, although, if we may credit the

---

[5]. Thos. M'Crie, *Life of John Knox* (Edinburgh, 1812), p. 47.
[6]. John Knox, *Historie of the Reformation* (1790), p. 68.

testimony of his adversaries, this was his sentiment; but I have little doubt that he looked upon the charge which he had received at St. Andrews as principally constituting his call to the ministry."[7]

The chaplain of the castle church, John Rough, was not allowed to defend the new teachings without opposition. In the little village of St. Andrews there was a university, to say nothing of an abbey. John Annand, principal of St. Leonard's College, challenged the reformed teachings, and he proved more than a match for John Rough. Knox came to his assistance. When Principal Annand quoted the fathers and the authority of the Church, Knox declared that the Latin Church had become corrupted, and a "synagogue of Satan, and the head thereof, called the pope, to be that man of sin of whom the Apostle speaks."[8] John Knox offered to prove these things in writing, but the townspeople urged him to ascend the pulpit and give all of them an opportunity to hear his proofs. Knox agreed to preach on the following Sunday. The sermon was delivered not in the chapel of the castle, but in the parish church.

Taking Daniel 7, 24-25 as his text, Knox declared that the four animals represent the Babylonian, Persian, Grecian and Roman empires, and out of the last arose the papacy. He cited parallel passages in the New Testament, declaring that the Roman pontiff is Antichrist. Under three heads — life, doctrine and laws, he reviewed the history of the papacy, and especially the attitude of the popes toward justification, holy days, fasting and marriage. Many men of prominence were present, including John Major and other members of the university faculty, the sub-prior of the abbey and a large number of canons and friars. The first sermon of John Knox revealed that power of popular eloquence that was to play so important a part in the Scottish Reformation. His hearers were astonished at his daring polemics, as well as at his learning.

As a result of the sermon, Knox and Rough were asked to appear before a convocation of learned men from the

---

[7]. Thos. M'Crie, *Op. cit.*, pp. 48-49.
[8]. *Ibid.*, p. 51.

university and the abbey, and debate the points of difference. Knox defended his position with skill, and his opponents blundered when one of them made the rash assertion that the Holy Ghost did not come upon the Apostles until after the Epistles had been written. Having accomplished nothing at the convocation, the adversaries of Knox and Rough drew up what Cornish Methodists of today would call "the plan." This was a schedule by which the clergymen of the district were to preach in rotation at a given church. The clergy of the university and the abbey appeared in turn at the parish church, making it impossible for Knox and Rough to preach there. However, they continued to preach daily in the chapel of the castle, and in the few weeks into which all these events were crowded, many of the people of St. Andrews became converts to Protestantism.

A French fleet appeared in the harbor late in June, 1547, and a month later the castle surrendered. Rough chanced to be in England at the time, but Knox and the others who were in the castle, were captured. For twenty months Knox was made to toil as a galley slave. Once, when their ship was anchored in the Loire near Nantes, an image of the Virgin, wrought of wood, was brought out and the prisoners were asked to give it reverence. Knox flung it through a port-hole, remarking, "she is licht enough, let her lairn to swim." Again, when they were at anchor off the coast of Scotland, between Dundee and St. Andrews, they could see the spires of the latter town. Knox was ill at the time, but when his friend James Balfour asked him whether he knew the place, he declared, "Yes, I know it well; for I see the spire of that place where God first opened my mouth in public to His glory; and I am fully persuaded, how weak soever I now appear, that I shall not depart this life till my tongue shall glorify His godly name in the same place." While chained in the ship, Knox wrote a confession of faith which he managed to send to his friends in Scotland, urging them to preserve the reformed teachings regardless of any efforts that might be made to cause them to do otherwise. In February, 1549, Knox was released, and made his way to England.

When Knox reached England, he found that Henry VIII had died, and his son, Edward VI, a young boy, was ruling in his stead, with Edward Seymour, also known as the Protector Somerset, acting as regent. Peter Martyr, Martin Bucer, Paul Fagius and Emanuel Tremellius had been given important places at Cambridge and Oxford so that they might influence the future clergymen of England; and other men who held reformed views were sent throughout the country on preaching missions. Knox's preaching ability was known to the English reformers, and he was sent to Berwick, where he preached the new doctrines for two years. In 1551 he went to Newcastle-on-Tyne, where he spent the next two years. Shortly after his removal to Newcastle he was made one of the chaplains to Edward VI. There were six of these men, selected from among the clergy "accounted the most zealous and ready preachers of that time." As chaplain he visited London from time to time, and when the Edward VI *Prayer Book* was revised in 1552, Knox succeeded in excluding the mention of a Real Presence, and he protested against a rubric which called for kneeling on the part of the communicant when receiving the Sacrament. A certain Dr. Weston, in a disputation with Latimer, declared: "A runnagate Scot did take away the adoration or worshipping of Christ in the Sacrament, by whose procurement that heresy was put into the last Communion book; so much prevailed that one man's opinion at the time."[9] Knox preached daily, and his vehement testimony against the evils of the day attracted wide attention.

The English government, under which he enjoyed protection, was not a stable one. King Edward VI was a mere boy, precocious, but subject to the wishes of a group of counsellors who can hardly be considered assets to the Reformation movement. The Protector Somerset (Edward Seymour), professed great loyalty to the reformers, but he craved political power, and did not hesitate to behead his own brother Thomas, when the latter's political ambitions seemed to threaten the Protector's prestige. The Duke of Northumberland was a man of great influence, but his

---

[9]. Fox, p. 1326, quoted by M'Crie, *Op. cit.,* p. 68.

intense zeal for the Protestant cause was but a cloak to hide his desire to seize control of the government. Thoroughly "without conscience and without fear" as the dying Henry VIII had declared him to be, Northumberland's scheming brought about the execution of the Protector Somerset, uncle of the boy-king, and Northumberland's own appointment as Protector. The early death of the boy-king had further tragic results. He induced the unwilling Lady Jane Grey, a young girl of 17, to marry his son, and then, much against her will he placed her upon the throne. Like her cousin Edward VI, she was precocious far beyond her years, and she would have made an excellent queen, and a strong supporter of the reformed leaders. However, Mary Tudor, daughter of Henry VIII, raised an army and met the troops of Northumberland near London. Northumberland was defeated and later beheaded. Queen Jane was charged with treason because of the fact that she had accepted a throne, even though it had been forced upon her much against her will. After a reign of but nine days she and her husband were beheaded in the Tower, in 1553.

Mary Tudor was proclaimed queen in July of the same year, and for a short time Knox was allowed to preach without molestation throughout Buckinghamshire and Kent. However, his friends feared for his safety under the new government, and induced him to flee to France, early in the year 1554. Knox paid a visit to Geneva, where John Calvin was at the height of his influence. He found the city filled with visitors from a number of European countries. They had come either to consult with Calvin, or else to find refuge from persecution in their own lands. Calvin was greatly pleased with the talents and the religious views of Knox, and a friendship was formed that remained unbroken until the death of the Genevan reformer a decade later. Through Calvin's influence Knox was made pastor of a congregation of English and Scottish refugees at Frankfurt-am-Main. This congregation had agreed to adopt the form of worship of the Genevan Church. However, Dr. Cox, who had been preceptor to Edward VI, and who had come to Frankfurt with a few others, insisted that the English liturgy be used.

In the dissension that followed, Knox showed prudence and moderation, consulting with other reformers, including John Calvin. He preached a sermon on the subject which offended the liturgical group within the congregation, and their reply was to accuse Knox of high treason against the emperor of Germany, his son, and Queen Mary of England, quoting statements that he had made several years before in England. Upon the advice of friends, Knox withdrew from Frankfort, and from 1555 to 1559, after a visit to England and Scotland, he was one of the pastors of a congregation of refugees in Geneva.

John Knox returned to Scotland in 1559, and found the reformed cause in a critical condition, due to the determination of the queen regent and her prelates to suppress the Protestant movement. Knox visited Dundee and then Perth, and at the latter place he preached a sermon against the mass. After the congregation had departed, a priest uncovered the altar and proceeded to say mass. A few who had loitered in the church spread the word. A crowd quickly collected, tore down the altar and destroyed the images in the church. Then, marching to the monasteries of the Greyfriars, the Black Friars and the Carthusians, they reduced these to ruins. Knox condemned these acts, but he received the blame, and armed conflict was narrowly averted. Against the advice of his friends, he preached at St. Andrews, and with the same results. The people returned to the church, stripped it of its ornaments and pulled down the monasteries. The excitement spread, and within a few weeks altars and images were destroyed in the churches and monasteries were razed at Crail, Cupar, Lindores and Stirling, and then at Linlithgow, Edinburgh and Glasgow. The queen regent marched upon Edinburgh with an army, and the Protestants took up a position near Cragingate, on Calton Hill. The queen regent decided to sign a treaty by which the Protestants were granted freedom of worship.

John Knox undertook a preaching tour which included much of Scotland. His vehement eloquence attracted great gatherings of people wherever he went, and his exposition of the reformed teachings caused large numbers of people

to cast their lot with the new movement. In 1560 Calvinistic
Protestantism became the recognized religion in Scotland,
Knox and five others drawing up the confession of faith.

We cannot follow in detail the events that followed.
Knox became pastor of St. Giles's Church, the most important place of worship in Edinburgh, at that time a town of
about 25,000 inhabitants. He preached there twice on Sunday and three times during the week to congregations that
overflowed the building. In 1561, Mary Queen of Scots
ascended the throne at the age of 19 years. Knox became
her most powerful opponent, not hesitating to rebuke her
actions in stern language. In his thunderous sermons he
denounced all women rulers, especially Mary Tudor of England, and by implication, Mary Queen of Scots. One of his
most famous sermons, known nowadays as "The Source and
Bounds of Kingly Power,"[10] was preached in Edinburgh in
1565. Lord Darnley, whom the Scottish queen had married
that year, was offended by the sermon and ordered Knox
cast into prison. He was soon released, and spent the remaining years of his life in Edinburgh, preaching, catechizing and directing the affairs of the Kirk.

Knox preached the Law with terrible force, and he
preached the Gospel as well, from his strict Calvinistic viewpoint. Dr. W. M. Taylor says that Knox believed firmly in
the Trinity, in the Atonement and in the mediation of the
Lord Jesus Christ. "Luther did not proclaim the doctrine
of Justification by Faith more energetically than he; and in
every appeal he made to his fellow men, they were sure to
see that Jesus was in the midst." Knox prepared his sermons with care, but it is an unfortunate thing that he did
not find time to write them either before or after preaching
them, with the exception of the one already mentioned.
Sermons exist that have been attributed to him,[11] but it is
probable that these were taken down by reporters. Based
upon his own statements, his preaching was expository. He
was a man of emphatic convictions, and his zeal for the
reformed cause often led him to use language that might

[10]. *Select Practical Writings of John Knox* (Edinburgh, 1845), pp.
264-311.
[11]. *Op. cit.*, pp. 229-252.

be looked upon today as intemperate, especially when he characterized his religious opponents. He had a gift of popular eloquence that has often been compared to that of Luther. James Melville's account of one of Knox's last sermons has been reprinted again and again. He tells us that Knox, at the age of 66, was so frail that it was necessary for two servants to assist him to the pulpit. After Knox had preached for half an hour, Melville, who was taking down the sermon, declares that he himself became so moved that he could no longer write. Although very weak at first, yet "ere he had done with his sermon, he was so active and vigorous that he was like to ding that pulpit into blads and flee out of it."[12]

Knox taught that "there is no other name by which men can be saved but that of Jesus, and that all reliance on the merits of others is vain and delusive; that the Saviour having by His one sacrifice sanctified and reconciled to God those who should inherit the promised kingdom, all other sacrifices which men pretend to offer for sin are blasphemous; that all men ought to hate sin, which is so odious before God that no sacrifice but the death of His Son could satisfy for it; that they ought to magnify their heavenly Father, who did not spare Him who is the substance of His glory, but gave Him up to suffer the ignominious and cruel death of the cross for us; and that those who have been washed from their former sins are bound to lead a new life, fighting against the lusts of the flesh, and studying to glorify God by good works."[13]

Dargan says of him: "Small of stature and frail of body, like Calvin, he was far more vehement and excitable than the reserved Frenchman. His eye gleamed and his frame worked with the inward power of his convictions, and his mastery of his audience was that of the born speaker. The first sermon at St. Andrews, when he attacked the papacy, showed his coming power, and the far later one in the same place, when he defied Archbishop Hamilton's threats and put aside the warnings of his friends to urge

[12]. *Diary of James Melville* (Edinburgh, 1844), p. 26.
[13]. Thos. M'Crie, *Op. cit.*, pp. 125-126.

the immediate reformation of worship, was a triumph of brave and powerful preaching."[14]   Of the many biographies of John Knox, the 579-page work of Dr. Thomas McCrie has never been equalled.

John Knox's *First Book of Discipline* left a lasting impression upon Scotland.   In it he declares Jesus Christ to be the one Head of the Church, and His Gospel is to be preached and His Sacraments administered in every kirk. No man is to preach until he has been called in an orderly way by the congregation.   Each congregation is self-governed, and is to have equal representation in the presbytery, the synod and the General Assembly.   In the General Assembly all men were to have equal rights, and for several years they did not have so much as a president.   In 1567 the new organization became the State Church of Scotland, but with the distinct understanding that in all matters of doctrine, administration of divine ordinances, election, admission, suspension and discipline of pastors, the Kirk must be supreme.

Mary Queen of Scots sought for years to overthrow these principles, but Knox withstood her resolutely, and at times he opposed her face to face.   He stood firm even when other leaders yielded, and when Erskine, Winram, Spotswood, Willock, Carswell and others made concessions, Knox stood alone, waging battle for the freedom of the Kirk from State interference.   Queen Mary coaxed, flattered, wept, raged, threatened, but John Knox could not be moved, neither did the queen or any of her nobles dare lay hands upon him.   When bishops were suggested, Knox protested vehemently, declaring that evangelical teachings seldom flourish in an atmosphere of prelacy.   He succeeded in causing twenty pages to be incorporated in the Statute Books of Scotland, declaring Jesus Christ to be the only Head of the Kirk, that His teachings must forever be proclaimed without restriction in Scotland, and that the Kirk must be forever supreme in all spiritual matters.   Thus the principles which he set forth in the *First Book of Discipline* became

---

[14]. E. C. Dargan, *A History of Preaching* (New York, 1905-12), vol. I, p. 521.

embodied in the laws of Scotland, where they remain to this day. Not only did this frail, sickly little man cause the tyrants of his day to fear him, but he established principles of religious freedom that have been the directing force in his own land for four centuries, and in all other lands to which Scotsmen have migrated. When James VI came to the throne he was a young child, but as he grew up he did his utmost to substitute prelacy for the democratic form of church government that John Knox had established. Bishops were forced upon the people from time to time, and the State sought to restrict the religious freedom for which Knox was responsible. Resolute Scotsmen defended their liberties, and at Rullion Green, at Drumclog, at Ayrsmoss and at Bothwell Brig, men died that these liberties might be perpetuated. They died on the scaffold, they died by the hands of assassins and they died on the field of battle, but neither despotic kings nor scheming politicians of Kirk and State could make Scotland forget the fiery words of the frail little pastor of St. Giles's Kirk.

Knox wrote *Epistles* (1554); *Admonition* (1554); *On prayer* (1554); *On affliction* (1556); *The First Blast of the Trumpet against the Monstrous Regiment of Women* (1558); *On Predestination* (1591); and his great *History of the Reformation of Religion in the Realm of Scotland,* 5 volumes (1560-86). The standard edition of his collected *Works,* 6 volumes (1846-64), was edited by D. Laing. There are a number of good biographies of John Knox, but perhaps the best is Thomas M'Crie's *Life of John Knox* (1811), of which several revised editions appeared. Other biographies of recognized merit are P. Hume Brown's *John Knox, a Biography,* 2 volumes (1895); J. Glasse's *John Knox, a Criticism and an Appreciation* (1905); and Edwin Muir's *John Knox* (1929). Andrew Lang's *John Knox and the Reformation* (1905), is a well-written book, but undue attention is given to incidents that are not favorable to the great reformer. Other biographies are: F. McCunn, *John Knox* (1895); Taylor Innes, *John Knox* (1905); K. Hewat, *Makers of the Scottish Church* (1920); J. C. Carrick, *John Knox and his Land* (1902); James Stalker, *John Knox, his Ideals and Ideas* (1904); W. M. Taylor, *John Knox* (1885); and *David Buchanan, Life of John Knox* (1664). Biographies have been written by Lord E. Percy (1907); D. Macmillan (1905); P. Lorimer (1875); and others.

John MacAlpine (c. 1505-1577)

John MacAlpine, known among the reformers of Central Europe, as MacBee or Maccabeus, was born about the year 1505 in Scotland. He came of an excellent family, and there is every reason to believe that he was of the notable Clan Alpine. Not only do old records state this,[15] but his name would seem to verify it. The word *Mac* in the Gaelic, means "son of"; thus MacAlpine would suggest that he was a descendent of the clan that played so important a part in Scottish history. As such, he was entitled to the green and violet tartan of the Alpines. He received an excellent education, and he attended one of the universities. He entered a monastery and in 1532 he became prior of the Dominican community at Perth. Luther's writings were being circulated in Scotland, and MacAlpine became familiar with the writings of the German reformer. A copy of Tyndale's Bible came into his possession, and he began to question some of the old teachings and to defend the doctrines emphasized by the reformers. In 1534 has was summoned for trial because of his Lutheran views.[16] He left the priory, fled to England and made the acquaintance of Miles Coverdale, whose sister-in-law he married.

MacAlpine's interest in Luther's teachings led him to visit Germany in order to continue his studies at Cologne and Wittenberg. At the latter place he became a friend of Luther and his associates; and the big Scotsman, wearing his *feileadh-mhor* and *sporran*, amused Luther, who named him MacBee, and then Maccabeus. However, the Germans soon learned that MacAlpine was a forceful preacher, and a man without fear. He learned the German and Danish languages, and in 1542 he became professor in Copenhagen

---

[15]. *"Reliquerat is, qui ex nobili et antiqua Macalpinorum in Scotia familia ortum trahebat,"* — Gerdes III, p. 417.

[16]. John Knox, *Historie of the Reformation* (1790), p. 97.

University and one of the Danish king's chaplains.[17]   He
was one of the four men who translated the Bible into the
Danish language. This Bible was published in folio in the
year 1550.

MacAlpine was an eloquent preacher and in his later
years he was able to declare the reformed teachings in English, Gaelic, Danish and German. He became one of the
leaders of Lutheranism in Denmark, and did much to persuade that country to accept the Reformation. In 1552, together with Plade, he published a work in which the errors
of Osiander were made known. MacAlpine published several
theological works in the Latin language, of which *Enarratio
in Deuteronomium,* (1563), may be mentioned.

William Harlow (c. 1500-c. 1575)

One of the friends and helpers of John Knox was William Harlow of Edinburgh. He was born about the beginning of the sixteenth century, and in his earlier years he
was a merchant tailor in Edinburgh. He became acquainted
with the teachings of the reformers, and he had a desire to
preach. Calderwood says that "he went to England and
preached for some time as a Deacoun, according to the corrupt custom of that Kirk."[18]   On the other hand, the same
historian says of him, "he was not verie learned, yitt his
doctrine was plaine and sound, and worthy of commenda-
tioun."[19]   At this time Edinburgh was a town of about
25,000 inhabitants, and there was but one church, St. Giles's,
whose seating capacity was about 3000. West of the town
was another church called St. Cuthbert's, or the West Kirk.
William Harlow returned to Scotland, after having preached
for a time in England, and he was made pastor of St.
Cuthbert's.[20]

When John Knox was forced to go into exile, it fell to
the lot of William Harlow to encourage the people to stand
firm until the return of their leader. In 1559 the queen
regent issued a proclamation forbidding any person to preach

---

[17]. D. Calderwood, *History of the Kirk of Scotland* (Edinburgh,
     1842-49), vol. I, p. 96.
[18]. D. Calderwood, *Op. cit.,* vol. I, p. 303.
[19]. *Ibid.*
[20]. Thos. M'Crie, *Op. cit.,* pp. 115, 237.

or administer the Sacraments without the express consent of the bishops. William Harlow, Paul Methven, John Christison and John Willock were summoned to stand trial at Stirling for preaching and celebrating Holy Communion according to the reformed faith. When they did not appear they were declared to be outlaws, and all persons were warned not to give them shelter or assistance under penalty of disloyalty to the crown.

William Harlow was not a learned theologian, nor was he one of the greatest preachers of his time. He labored faithfully, first in England, then in Ayrshire, and then in other parts of Scotland, where he "continued to preach in different parts of the country with great fervour and diligence."[21] He deserves mention because it was he, at a critical time in the history of the Scottish Reformation, who was able to keep the people steadfast during the exile of their great leader John Knox.

John Willock (c. 1512-1585)

John Willock, a preacher of great influence and an able assistant to John Knox, was born in Ayrshire early in the sixteenth century. He attended Glasgow University and became a friar at Ayr. About the year 1541 he went to London, where he was pastor of St. Catherine's church and chaplain to the Duke of Suffolk, father of Lady Jane Grey, who was Queen of England for nine days. It is possible that it was he who accompanied her to the scaffold on Tower Hill, when Mary Tudor seized the throne by force and beheaded the unfortunate young Queen. After Mary seized the throne, Willock fled to the Continent, where he was a practicing physician for a few years in Emden.

In 1558 he ventured back to England and became pastor of St. John's church in Ayr, but his Protestant preaching caused him to be charged with heresy, but for some reason the sentence against him was never enforced. In 1559, when the Queen regent took the city of Edinburgh and John Knox was driven out, it was John Willock who became interim pastor at St. Giles' church. In 1562, for some reason

---

[21]. Thos. M'Crie, *Op. cit.*, p. 115.

that has never been made clear, Willock left Scotland and went to Loughborough, Leics., where he became pastor of a congregation.

An eminent authority says, "Willock was not inferior to Knox in learning, and though he did not equal him in eloquence and intrepidity, he surpassed him in affability, in moderation and in address; qualities which enabled him sometimes to maintain his station and to accomplish his purposes when his colleagues could not act with safety or success." [22]

For a while John Willock served as superintendent of the Glasgow district. This office was in no respect similar to that of a bishop. In the Scottish Kirk of those days there were four kinds of office-bearers, as Thomas M'Crie, the careful historian, points out.[23] The first was the pastor, whose duty it was to preach the Gospel and administer the Sacraments. Then there was a teacher or doctor, who interpreted the Scriptures and answered the claims of the errorists whether in the kirk, the school or the university. Then there was the ruling elder, whose duty it was to assist the pastor in exercising doctrinal and ecclesiastical discipline in the congregation. Then there was the deacon, whose duty it was to minister to the poor and to exercise oversight of the revenues of the congregation. It was found that an extra-congregational office-bearer was necessary in order to supply congregations without a pastor. Devout men of fair education were appointed to read the Scriptures and lead the prayers of such vacant congregations, and these men are called readers. If they were especially well qualified, they were permitted to add a few simple exhortations to the Scriptures that they read, and such men were known as exhorters. Then it was found necessary, in those unsettled days, to relieve certain pastors of congregational duties and allow them to become missionaries-at-large. They were given a certain city or district, and they organized new congregations, preached in places where vacancies occurred, supervised the work of lay-readers and exhorters, and in

---

[22]. Thos. M'Crie, *Op. cit.*, p. 115.
[23]. Thos. M'Crie, *Op. cit.*, p. 211.

some cases conducted visitations. John Willock was such a superintendent, and the office that he held bore no resemblance to that of a bishop; but rather was it a position that combined the duties of a missionary-at-large and what is known in some denominations as a circuit visitor. Willock's memoir is contained in Wodrow's *Biographical Collection* (1834-35).

John Craig (c. 1512-1600)

Another impressive preacher of post-Reformation Scotland was John Craig, who was born about the year 1512 in Craigston, Flodden. After his education at St. Andrews University he tutored for two years, and then became a Dominican monk. In 1536 he went to England and from there to Rome. He became a teacher in Bologna, and master of the novices in a Dominican convent.

Craig read John Calvin's *Institutes,* and became convinced that the Roman Church contained doctrinal errors. Because of this he was imprisoned for a time, but in 1559, after the death of the Pope, the people threw open the prison and he was released, and went to Vienna. In 1560 he returned to Scotland, was ordained, and preached with great acceptability in St. Magdalene church, Cowgate, Edinburgh, and at Holy Rood. When John Knox died, Craig became one of the leaders of the Scottish Kirk. After the death of Lord Darnley, the young husband of Mary Queen of Scots, Mary straightway prepared to marry Bothwell. John Craig refused to publish their banns. In 1580 he helped draft the National Covenant. In 1580, King James VI, then but 14 years of age, appointed John Craig a court preacher, a position which he retained until his death.

As a preacher, John Craig had something of the fearlessness and candor of John Knox, and at all times he was faithful in proclaiming the teachings of the Scottish reformers, and in expounding the Scriptures to the people. Although hardly a theologian of first rank, yet he preached the truths of the Scriptures to the best of his ability.[24] Craig compiled part of the *Second Book of Discipline,* and

---

[24]. See Thos. M'Crie, *Life of John Knox* (Edinburgh, 1813), pp. 236-240.

he wrote *The King's Confession* (1580), *A Short Sum of the Whole Catechism* (1581) and *A Form of Examination before Communion* (1590). An account of his life and influence is to be found in Thomas M'Crie's biography of John Knox, volume 2, pp. 53-57.

Christopher Goodman (c. 1520-1603)

Another eloquent Scottish preacher of post-Reformation days was a man who was not a Scotsman by birth, but by adoption. Christopher Goodman was born in Chester, England, about the year 1520. He was graduated from Brasenose College, Oxford, in 1541; and in 1547 he was senior student at Christ Church, Oxford, and in 1549 a proctor. He was also made Lady Margaret professor of divinity.

In 1554 he went to the Continent, and a year later he joined John Knox at Geneva; and at the request of the latter he became his associate pastor. Knox, at that time, was serving a congregation of refugees. Goodman shared Knox's dislike for women rulers, and in 1558 he delivered a sharp dissertation on the subject. When Knox returned to Scotland in 1559, he begged Goodman to follow him, which he did. Goodman became minister of Ayr in 1559, and in 1560 he was translated to St. Andrews. In 1566 he was appointed chaplain to Sir Henry Sidney, of Ireland; and in 1570 he was given the congregation at Alford, Cheshire. A year later his opponents deprived him of Alford, and he was sentenced to be beaten with rods because of his outspoken nonconformity.

Dargan says of him: "He was highly esteemed as a preacher, but, like his greater friend and colleague, he had a sharp tongue and a vehement spirit that often hurt more than they helped."[25] Two surviving works of Goodman are: *How far Superior Powers ought to be Obeyed* (1558), and *A Commentary upon Amos*.

David Ferguson (c. 1525-1598)

David Ferguson was born in Dundee about the year 1525. Accounts of his early life vary. His opponents

---

[25]. E. C. Dargan, *A History of Preaching* (New York, 1905-12), vol. I, p. 524.

termed him a cobbler, and again a glover. Little is known of his schooling, but some time before the year 1563 he began to preach in Dunfermline. It was a rough place, but through his preaching many were led to repent and turn to their Saviour. In 1567 he went to Rosyth, and in 1574 to Cumnock and Beith. He preached before the Assembly in 1571, and urged that the wealth that had belonged to the Roman Catholic Church be used to build new churches and schools, rather than to alienate it to the private use of the nobility. John Knox, just before his death, thanked the Lord that such men as David Ferguson had been raised up to continue the work of reform in the Scottish Church. Ferguson was chosen moderator in 1573. He was often selected to present matters of the Assembly to the King.

David Ferguson was noted for his wit as well as for his deep piety. He was on cordial terms with King James VI, and on one occasion when the King suggested bishops for Scotland, Ferguson agreed that it might be a good idea, provided every clergyman be made a bishop, and all equal in authority; but "if ye set up ten or twelve loons over honest men's heads to knock us down, and give them in rent more thousands than honest men has hundreds, we will never be content. We are Paul's bishops, Christ's bishops: hold us as we are."[26] While David Ferguson indulged in flashes of wit, yet in the main he was serious, and preached Law and Gospel with courage and with great spiritual conviction.

James Lawson (1538-1584)

As death approached, John Knox selected a young clergyman of exceptional ability as his successor at St. Giles' church, Edinburgh. This man was James Lawson. He was born in 1538 at Perth, and received his preliminary education in Perth grammar school, after which he attended St. Andrews University. After his graduation he became tutor to a private family, and spent some time in Continental Europe, where he studied the Hebrew language. In 1567 or 1568 he became professor of Hebrew in St. Andrews

---

[26]. John Row, *History of the Kirk of Scotland* (Edinburgh, 1842), p. 419.

University, and has the distinction of being the first man to teach Hebrew in Scotland. In 1569 he became sub-principal of King's College, Aberdeen, and pastor of Old Machar Church. The Scottish people have often encouraged such a combination of teaching and pastoral work, so that the men who teach students of theology are in direct touch themselves with the current problems of parish work.

James Lawson soon became one of the leaders of the Protestant clergy in his part of Scotland. In 1572 John Knox called him to Edinburgh and urged him to become pastor of St. Giles' church. Knox was so ill that he had to be carried to the church, and one of the last acts before his death was to assist in the installation of his chosen successor. Lawson proved to be a faithful pastor and "a man of singular learning, zeal and eloquence," [27] but due to his misguided zeal he was considered somewhat intolerant at times.

In 1584 he preached with considerable fire against parliamentary meddling in the affairs of the Kirk. This irritated some of the officials, and a warrant was issued for his arrest. It was a case similar to that of Richard Whyting, when Henry VIII gave his famous order: "Richard Whyting to be given a trial, and to be hanged, drawn and quartered on Tor Hill." Lawson's death was a foregone conclusion, but he succeeded in fleeing to London, and nothing was done to punish him. He was a courageous preacher, tending at times to go to extremes in his condemnation of things that he considered wrong, and his candor often made enemies. However, he deserves a place among the men whose zeal made possible the Scottish Reformation.

Andrew Melville (1545-1622)

Greater in every way than any of these able associates of John Knox was Andrew Melville. This exceptional preacher and fearless, judicious leader, more than any other man, had qualifications to take Knox's place when Knox died. Melville was born at Baldovy, Montrose, Scotland, where his father was laird of Baldovy. He was educated in the grammar school at Montrose and in St. Mary's College,

---

[27]. Melville's *Diary*, p. 33.

St. Andrews, from which he was graduated with very high honors in 1564. He went to Paris the same year, with a letter of introduction expressed in superlatives, testifying as to his consummate scholarship. There he studied Latin, Greek, Hebrew and Philosophy. He was able to deliver orations in Greek. In 1566 he became regent in St. Marceon College, Poitiers, at the same time studying civil law. Upon Beza's recommendation he was made teacher of Latin at Geneva. During his five years at that place he studied theology with Beza. He returned to Scotland in 1574, to the great regret of his Genevan associates.

Melville became principal of Glasgow University, at that time in a languishing condition. So ably did he direct its affairs that the class rooms were soon filled to overflowing. His work there is almost without parallel in the history of education. He taught Theology, Greek, Hebrew, Old and New Testament Exegesis, Moral Philosophy, Natural History and Mathematics, and distinguished himself in every subject. So great was his fame as a teacher that the reputation of the University became world-wide. Even the alumni came back in numbers and enrolled as beginners, merely to be able to say that Andrew Melville had been their teacher. Finally students had to be turned away because of the crowded condition of the university. From a languishing school, Glasgow became so famous that "there was no place in Europe comparable to Glasgow for good letters during these years."[28]

Not only was Andrew Melville a superb teacher and executive, but he was a brilliant preacher as well. He preached regularly, and was easily the most influential clergyman of his day. A controversy in regard to church government had arisen in the Scottish Kirk, as to whether it should be ruled by the presbytery or by bishops. In the former case, a local congregation was governed by the pastor and the kirk-session (vestry). Next above them was the presbytery (conference), composed of both pastors and lay representatives. Then came the synod, and finally the

---

[28]. Quoted by Thos. M'Crie, *Life of Andrew Melville*, 2 vols. (Edinburgh, 1819), vol. I, p. 75.

general assembly. The governing power lay in the presbytery. In the prelatic form of government, the power was
in the hands of the bishop. The idea of prelacy was
repugnant to Melville, and he expressed his dislike for it in
emphatic terms. He was pastor of Govan church for three
years, while head of the university. He was a powerful
champion of the Scottish Reformation, and a determined
opponent of the scheme of King James VI to force the
episcopate upon the Scottish people.

Andrew Melville was among the first to declare that
πρεσβύτερος and 'επίσκοπος are words that denote the same
office in the New Testament Church. His strong convictions
and his eloquent controversial preaching drew multitudes
to his church. As time went on, he went farther than the
New Testament, and declared that government by the
presbytery is alone God-pleasing, that bishops must be
abolished, and complete parity of the clergy established. He
was unable to accept the idea that the form of church government is not specified in detail in the Scriptures. It has
been said that "Knox made Scotland Protestant, but Melville
made it Presbyterian."[29]

In 1580 Melville was made principal of St. Mary's
College, St. Andrews. In 1581 the government abolished
the episcopacy and Melville triumphed. He had declared
emphatically that the State has no right to interfere with the
spiritual affairs of the Kirk, and he looked upon the abolish-
ment of the prelacy as the righting of a great wrong. In
1583 the King and his party had their revenge, and Melville
was charged with treason and compelled to flee to England.
In 1597 he was deprived of St. Andrews, and in 1606 he was
imprisoned in the Tower of London, and for a time denied
all visitors and even writing materials. With a bit of metal
he covered the walls of his prison with beautiful inscriptions.
The pretext for his imprisonment was a Latin couplet which
he had composed after attending a highly ritualistic service
in the Chapel Royal. He was released from the Tower in
1610 and allowed to go into exile in Sedan, where he taught
theology for 12 years.

---

[29]. W. M. Taylor, *The Scottish Pulpit* (New York, 1887), p. 98.

Melville knew no fear. When summoned before King James he said: "Sir, as divers times before I have told you, so now again I must tell you, there are twa kings and twa kingdoms in Scotland. There is King James, the head of the Commonwealth, and there is Jesus Christ, the King of the Church, whose subject James VI is, and of Whose Kingdom he is not a king, nor a lord, nor a head, but a member. . . . We will yield to you your place, and give you all due obedience; but again I say, you are not the head of the Church; you cannot give us that eternal life which we seek for, even in this world, and you cannot deprive us of it. Permit us then freely to meet in the name of Christ, and to attend to the interests of that Church of which you are the chief member."[30]   Melville knew that these words might have cost him his life, but he felt it his duty to utter them.

Andrew Melville was pastor of a congregation for but three years, although he preached frequently throughout his life, and was famous both for his eloquence and for his thoughtful expository teachings. It was his preaching, and his famous declaration to James VI that convinced the people that "there are twa kings and twa kingdoms in Scotland."

"Though he was not himself, for any length of time a preacher, he must have preached through them for years after he had been driven into exile. Even yet there come from his words sparks enough to kindle our souls into eager loyalty to Christ, and that is greatness, wherever and howsoever it may be manifested."[31]   Melville's works were published after his death, but his nephew's *Autobiography and Diary* is more widely known as a valuable source of early post-Reformation Scottish history. It was published in 1829.

Once Andrew Melville addressed a group of noted Englishmen at Hampden Court, and the impression that he made upon them gives one an idea of his manner of speaking, for "he gave himself up to all his native fire and vehemence, and astonished the English nobility and clergy with a torrent of bold, impassioned, impetuous eloquence, to

---

[30]. J. Melville, *Diary*, pp. 276-278.
[31]. W. M. Taylor, *The Scottish Pulpit* (New York, 1887), p. 79.

which they were altogether strangers."[32]   Dr. Thomas
M'Crie's *Life of Andrew Melville,* 2 volumes, ranks very
highly among religious biographies.

John Davidson (c. 1549-1603)

John Davidson was born about the year 1549 at Dunfermline, Fifeshire. He entered St. Leonard's College, St.
Andrews, in 1567. After completing his college course, he
was elected regent, or assistant teacher, and at the same time
he continued his theological studies. He became acquainted
with John Knox shortly before the death of the latter, and
was influenced deeply by the teachings and the courage of
the famous reformer.

In 1570 he wrote a poem which offended the Regent
Morton, and was imprisoned for it. Upon his release he
sought safety for three years on the Continent. It is said
that when Morton was facing death, he sent for Davidson,
begged his forgiveness, and declared that he himself had
become convinced that salvation is to be found in the atoning
work of Jesus Christ alone.

Meanwhile, in 1579, John Davidson had become pastor
of the congregation at Liberton, near Edinburgh, where the
boldness of his preaching attracted wide attention. In 1582
he had an encounter with James VI, in which Davidson expressed himself in a fearless, but rather blunt manner in
regard to the monarch's efforts at the restoration of prelacy.
He did not hesitate to preach with the same bluntness to
increasing multitudes; and his friends, alarmed at his
plainness of speech, contrived to remove him from so near
Edinburgh. In 1582 he was authorized by the Assembly
to pronounce the sentence of excommunication against the
archbishop of Glasgow; after which his friends urged him
to go to London for a time for his own safety. In 1590 he
preached before the King, and so outspoken was he that
James VI inhibited him for a time.

In 1595, when the Spanish invasion was feared, Davidson was asked to preach before the 400 members of the

---

[32]. Thos. M'Crie, *Life of Andrew Melville* (Edinburgh, 1819), vol. 2,
pp. 66-67.

General Assembly. At his own request, a day of national humiliation and prayer was set apart. For an hour John Davidson preached the Law in all its severity, basing his admonition on the 13th and the 34th chapters of Ezekiel. The scene that followed is said to be without precedent, for the members of the Assembly were so overcome that their audible weeping made it necessary for Davidson to cease preaching for a short time. After they had composed themselves somewhat, Davidson turned to St. Luke 12, 22, and preached the Gospel for another hour. At the conclusion of his sermon, the moderator asked the Assembly to enter into a new covenant with Christ the King, and with the exception of one man, the 400 rose to their feet, raised their right hands and pledged themselves to Jesus Christ, the Head of the Church.

In 1596, urged by friends who feared for his safety, John Davidson went to Prestonpans, in East Lothian, where he built a new church, a school and a manse at his own expense.

John Davidson was blunt of speech, and even rude at times, and entirely fearless. Gifted with a depth of spiritual fervor far beyond that of most men, and with a power over his hearers that has seldom been equaled, his friends overlooked his plainness of speech; while his enemies feared him and never dared to carry out the threats against his life that had been made on more than one occasion.

Robert Bruce (1554-1631)

Robert Bruce of Kinnard was born in 1554, and was a son of Sir Alexander Bruce of Airth, an eminent baron of an old Scottish family. After his education at St. Andrews, he studied law in Paris, returned to Scotland and prepared to enter the legal profession. However, he had no peace. His conscience accused him. Although he had led an upright life insofar as his outward conduct was concerned, yet he saw himself a sinner of the vilest kind. He says, "I cried God's mercy for the merits of Christ; yea, I appealed even to His mercy, purchased to me by the blood, death and passion of Christ." Feeling an urgent call to preach, he gave up all thought of the law and went back to St. Andrews and

studied theology with Andrew Melville. Urged by Melville
to succeed James Lawson at Edinburgh as pastor of St. Giles
Church, where John Knox had once been pastor, he declined.
Continuing his theological studies, he contented himself by
gathering groups of students about him and expounding the
Scriptures to them.[33]

In 1587, at the age of 33, he was called to a church in
Edinburgh. The same year, and before his ordination, he
was chosen moderator of the General Assembly, and is said
to have been the youngest man ever elected to that position.
He was moderator again in 1592. For a time he was in the
good graces of the King, but when he opposed the King's
efforts to establish bishops over the Kirk, he was imprisoned
in 1596 and then banished from Edinburgh. Twice was he
allowed to return, only to be banished again in 1600 and in
1620. Shortly before his death he was permitted to return
to the family estate at Kinnard. He became pastor of
Larbert parish, and died at the age of 77, with his Bible
opened before him, and his finger on Romans 8, 38-39.

Robert Bruce was a man of superlative gifts, for his
contemporaries went so far as to declare that no man since
the days of the Apostles had ever preached with such
power.[34] It was a sermon preached by Robert Bruce at
Forgan that changed the opinions of Alexander Henderson
and set him to searching the Scriptures. Henderson, who
had been an advocate of prelacy, became a leader of the
group who sought to maintain the rule of the presbytery.

Bruce was a man of distinguished appearance and manner, of high social standing, and a leader of men. In his
nine brief years at St. Giles Church, Edinburgh, he rose to
national prominence. As a preacher, no man was his equal.
He was one of those exceptional men whose preaching has
the power to change the lives of many. Had it not been for
the miserable conceit of James VI, who could tolerate no
man who did not share his views, Bruce's preaching and
leadership might have transformed all Scotland. On one
occasion, when banished to Inverness, he looked upon it as

---

[33]. James Melville, *Diary*, p. 148.
[34]. E. C. Dargan, *A History of Preaching,* 2 vols. (New York,
1905-12), vol. 2, pp. 23-24.

a divine call to a new field of opportunity. So great was his fame that people were drawn from afar, and crowded any church in which he preached. His sermons were thoroughly Scriptural, and the doctrine of the grace of God in Christ was always paramount. He was a master of clear exposition and forceful English, and in the matter of persuasiveness he may be numbered among the most effective preachers of any age.

A number of sermons survive, and they reveal Robert Bruce's manner of preaching. *Sermons upon the Sacrament of the Lord's Supper, Preached in the Kirk of Edinburgh* (c. 1590) and *The Way to True Peace and Rest, XVI Sermons Preached in Edinburgh* (1617), are both in the dialect known as Old Scots. Other surviving volumes are: *Sermons Preached in the Kirk of Edinburgh* (1591); *Sermons Reprinted from the Original Editions of 1590 and 1591*, with an account of his life by R. Wodrow, edited by Dr. William Cunningham (1843); and *Robert Bruce's Sermons on the Sacrament, Done into English, with a Biography*, edited by J. Laidlow (1901). The difficulties that led to his banishment from Edinburgh are described in *Robert Bruce: Narrative Concerning his Troubles in the Year 1600* (1827). An account of his life and preaching may be found in D. Macnicol's *Robert Bruce* (1907), and in Principal Cunningham's *Life and Sermons of the Rev. Robert Bruce*.

Robert Rollock (1555-1598)

Robert Rollock was born about the year 1555 at Powis, near Stirling. After finishing the grammar school of Stirling, he entered St. Salvator's College, St. Andrews, in 1574. In 1578 he was made regent, and in 1580 examiner of arts, and in 1580 director of the arts faculty of his college. He continued his theological studies meanwhile. In 1583 he was made regent of the newly founded college which became Edinburgh University, and in 1585 he was appointed first principal of this university. Two years later he was made professor of theology.

In those days the people of Edinburgh were in the strange habit of assembling in New Church, Dr. Blaikie tells

us, and sitting there in idleness.[35]   Rollock thought that such
an opportunity for spiritual instruction should not be overlooked, and in 1587 he began to preach to these people at
seven in the morning — an unusual thing in Edinburgh.   So
helpful were Rollock's expositions of the Scriptures, and so
well impressed were the people, that they urged him to
become a pastor as well as head of the university.   He
agreed with some reluctance, and became a preacher of
unusual power, expounding the Scriptures in so deeply
spiritual a manner that the people flocked to the church at
the early hour of 7 a.m., week after week, and were greatly
benefited.

In 1598 he became pastor of Upper Tolbooth, Edinburgh.
He was "a man of good conversation and a powerful
preacher,"[36] but unfortunately he died at the age of 44, after
a very fruitful period of eleven years in the pulpit at Upper
Tolbooth and at Magdalen (Greyfriars) Kirks.

Principal Rollock published a number of works.   Among
these are commentaries on a number of the Psalms, on the
Book of Daniel and on John, Romans, Corinthians, Galatians,
Ephesians, Colossians, Thessalonians and Hebrews.   His
Select Works, edited by W. Gunn, were published in 1844-49.
A life of Rollock, attributed to George Robertson and Henry
Charteris, was reprinted in 1826.   A good account of Rol-
lock's life was published in 1884.   Dr. Wm. G. Blaikie was
its author.

---

[35]. W. G. Blaikie, The Preachers of Scotland from the Sixth to the
Nineteenth Century (Edinburgh, 1888), pp. 74-75.

[36]. David Calderwood, Historie of the Kirk of Scotland (Edinburgh,
1842-49), vol. 5, p. 732.

CHAPTER III

THE DAYS OF THE COVENANTERS

WHEN JOHN KNOX died in 1572, James VI, a boy five years of age, was the nominal king of Scotland, having succeeded his mother, Mary Queen of Scots, who had been forced to abdicate in 1567. At the age of twelve, James VI began to take a lively interest in politics. He was an arrogant, conceited lad, wholly without a sense of honor, slovenly and superficial; and most of these faults remained with him throughout his inglorious career as king of Scotland and later of England. As he grew older his arrogance led him to lay great stress upon a fictitious quality that he called his "king craft," which rendered his judgments, in his own estimation, all but infallible. He obtained a smattering of theology, and by virtue of this fact he felt himself fully qualified to dictate to the leaders of the Kirk.

Shortly after the death of John Knox, a violent controversy broke out. The great majority of the Scottish people were thoroughly tired of prelacy, and anxious to preserve the more democratic form of government in which the local congregation had a right to call its own pastor and regulate its own internal affairs without interference on the part of a bishop. A minority, including King James VI, his nobles and his bishops, were eager to restore a Protestant form of episcopacy. The reason for this difference of opinion is not difficult to discover. A careful authority declares: "Fully half the wealth of Scotland was in the hands of the clergy, and the greater part of it in the hands of a few. Avarice, ambition and secular pomp were widespread. A vacant bishopric or abbacy called forth powerful competitors, who contended for it as for a petty kingdom." [1] The same authority tells us that such vacancies were often taken by force, that benefices were bought and sold without shame, and pluralism existed — an abuse by which one clergyman might hold several profitable livings at the same time and neglect them all.

---

[1]. Thos. M'Crie, *Life of John Knox* (Edinburgh, 1812), p. 25.

During the lifetime of John Knox, these evils were held in check to a great degree, but after his death it was discovered that not all the men who had declared themselves Protestants were worthy men. They had renounced the Roman Church, but there were a number of nobles and former church dignitaries who were reluctant to see half the wealth of Scotland turned over to the common people, who could administer the property of the churches and the former abbeys as they saw fit. Selfish interests were at stake. The king and his nobles, and the former bishops, believed that they should be given full control of this valuable property. Knox's form of church government seemed too democratic to them, and the king, the nobles and the former bishops dreamed of a form of government somewhat like that of England, where the Roman Catholic doctrines had been renounced, but the old form of church government retained.

Two forms of church government were destined to struggle for supremacy in Scotland, and this bitter controversy was to continue for generations. The king and his followers demanded that the Kirk be ruled by Protestant bishops, and these in turn were to be ruled by the government. It was to be a prelatic State Church. The great majority of the pastors and people favored a presbyterian form of government. Those who desired this form of church government came, in later years, to be known as Presbyterians; and in like manner the people who would have government by bishops and archbishops became known as Episcopalians. In the presbyterian form of church government there were four groups: first was the pastor and the kirk-session of the local congregation; then came the presbytery, made up of a pastor and a lay member of each one of a group of congregations in a given district; then a synod, made up of representatives of a group of presbyteries; and finally the General Assembly, or national body including all Scotland.

In order to retain control of the wealth accumulated by the pre-Reformation Church, the king and his nobles believed that a safer form of ecclesiastical government was that of the episcopacy, with bishops and archbishops under the direct jurisdiction of the government. King James VI looked upon himself as the head of both Kirk and State. In 1572 a convention was called at Leith, soon after the death of John Knox, and in order to retain control of the wealth of the pre-Reformation Church, the king and his followers appointed a number of bishops. These men were not chosen from among the well qualified leaders of the Kirk, but rather from among those looked upon as unworthy. Obscure men, often without either scholarship or decided convictions, were chosen. They were men who craved the office, the purple and the pomp of the prelatic office; and they were given the title of bishop with the understanding that their possessions were to be signed away to their patrons.[2] These men caused endless merriment among the people, who nicknamed them the Tulchan Bishops. The word "tulchan" is derived from the Gaelic *tulachan*, which means "a sham calf."[3] In certain parts of Scotland it was customary to stuff the skin of a calf with straw and set it up within sight of an obstinate cow in order to cause her to yield her milk.[4]

The Prelacy-Presbytery controversy raged from Knox's death in 1572 until 1638. It was a period of turmoil, with two Protestant factions struggling for the control of the Kirk. At times the bishops and the king were in power, again the presbytery gained the ruling power in the Kirk. The king and his bishops were supported by many of the wealthy, land-holding gentry; while the group who favored the presbytery were composed of a large proportion of the local pastors, a minority of the wealthy landed proprietors and most of the common people. It was a period of persecution and of torture and inhuman executions — one of the blackest pages in the history of Protestantism. King James VI was a ruthless tyrant, ready to imprison and execute any man who questioned his right to rule the Kirk, while the worth-

---

[2]. N. L. Walker, *Scottish Church History* (Edinburgh, 1882), p. 41.

[3]. Neil MacAlpine, *A Pronouncing Gaelic-English Dictionary* (Glasgow, ed. 1942). Dr. Malcolm MacLennan's excellent *Pronouncing and Etymological Dictionary of the Gaelic Language* (Edinb., 1925), gives the proper Gaelic spelling as *tulchan*, and the pronunciation as tool-chan, (the "ch" as in the Gaelic *loch* or the German *ach*).

[4]. John Jamieson, *Dictionary of the Scottish Language* (Edinburgh, ed. 1879-87).

less men whom he named as bishops were jealous of their new offices, and too ready to do the king's will. Some of the nobility were sincere men who regretted that eminent clergymen and lay leaders were hanged and beheaded, yet these nobles believed that the episcopal form of government was Scriptural, and must be imposed upon the Kirk even though it meant bloodshed. A few of the nobles were covetous of wealth and power, and were ready enough to support the crown in any policy that would give them the things they craved. Some noblemen of the latter class were eager to add additional lands to their great estates; some of the clerical dabblers in Church and civil politics saw an easy method of rising from obscurity to power at a single leap. The Scottish people had been accustomed for centuries to the old order, and such a democratic method as that of the presbyterian system was looked upon by many as liberalism, and a sudden departure from tradition. A number of learned and pious men, such as Alexander Henderson in his earlier days, were conservative in doctrine and practice, but they had not yet realized that forms of church government are not of divine institution.

In 1584 the notorious Black Acts were passed. They made it mandatory that: 1. No assembly could meet without the king's permission; 2. That no one could say a word, whether in public or private, against the government; 3. To decline the judgment of the Privy Council in any cause, is high treason; 4. All ministers must recognize the bishops as their ecclesiastical superiors.[5]

While King James VI was an eager friend of prelacy, and of a close union of Church and State, yet even here he proved fickle. In 1590, just after his marriage, he attended a meeting of the General Assembly of the Scottish Kirk in order to extend his royal greetings. He praised the presbytery group in florid language, declaring that it was good to live in a day of the pure Gospel, and to be king of the sincerest Kirk in all the world. He sneered at Geneva for retaining the celebration of Christmas and Easter, and he

---

[5]. David Calderwood, *Historie of the Kirk of Scotland* (Edinburgh, 1842-49), vol. 4, p. 63ff.

described the Church of England as "an ill-said mass in English, wanting nothing but the liftings,"[6] that is, the elevation of the host. He urged the Kirk to stand firmly in its convictions, and pledged his ardent support as long as he ruled over Scotland. Two years later the Scottish Parliament repealed the Black Acts, and declared the Kirk, with government by the presbytery, to be the State Church of Scotland. Soon after this was done, the vacillating king was plotting to reinstate the episcopacy, and he succeeded in appointing bishops for Ross, for Aberdeen and for Caithness.

Fortunately for Scotland, and to the sorrow of England, the vain and dictatorial King James VI succeeded to the English throne at the death of Queen Elizabeth in 1603. He went in pomp to London and was crowned King James I of England. He continued to cause Scotland much trouble, yet he was so many miles away that he could not keep closely in touch with the affairs of the Kirk.

John Knox had established Protestantism in Scotland, but when he died the people were not yet unified. It became the lot of an obscure woman, who sold apples in the streets of Edinburgh, to weld the people of Scotland into a unit. Archbishop Laud of England had visited Scotland, and he was surprised at the plainness of the form of worship that he found there. He took it upon himself to provide Scotland with a prayer book and a liturgy. King James died and his son, Charles I, ascended the English throne in 1625. Laud had no difficulty in convincing Charles I that Scotland stood in need of something better than Knox's liturgy. Laud prepared a liturgy for Scotland, based upon the liturgy of the Church of England. The General Assembly and the presbyteries were not consulted. The first that Scotland heard of it was when the new liturgy arrived, together with orders that every clergyman must provide himself with two copies of the new prayer book and see to it that it be adopted at once by every congregation. The clergyman who neglected this order was to be expelled immediately.

On the appointed Sunday, the Scottish kirks were crowded. At St. Giles's, the Dean of Edinburgh, clad in a

---

[6]. *Ibid.*, vol. 4.

white surplice instead of the familiar black robe and bands, arose and started to read an opening prayer from the new prayer book. Jenny Geddes, the apple peddler, had brought her folding stool with her, and had taken her seat as near the chancel as she could. As the Dean started the prayer, she arose and cried: "Villain! Fause loon! Dost thou say Mass at my loog?" (ear). With this, she hurled her stool at the Dean's head.

At once the great congregation was in an uproar. They poured out of the big church, and surged through the streets of Edinburgh, shouting in unison, "Down with the papal Antichrist! The sword of the Lord and of Gideon!" The riots spread to other towns, and the Scottish people took up the cry, and paraded the streets, demanding overthrow of everything remotely resembling Romanism, or interference from the English King or Archbishop.

Matters came to a climax in 1638, in a scene more dramatic than anything else in all the colorful history of Scotland. Edinburgh was a small town in those days, but 60,000 people crowded into it on March 1. Greyfriars Church was filled, and the crowd overflowed into the spacious churchyard, and into all the surrounding streets. The National Covenant, a document pledging its signers to defend the doctrine and practice of the Reformed Kirk of Scotland, which had been drawn up 58 years before, was brought from its half-forgotten hiding place and had been copied on an enormous sheet of parchment. After a prayer by Alexander Henderson, described at the time as "sublime," the National Covenant was read to the great congregation. Then they came forward, nobles and lords, church dignitaries, army officers, professional men, shopkeepers, workingmen and women, peasants, and all, and the Covenant was signed. It was carried out into the churchyard, laid on a flat tomb, and the people who were unable to get into the church crowded up to sign it. When both sides of the huge sheet were filled with names, it was announced that only initials would be permitted, so as to save space. Many opened their arms and signed it with their blood. Hymns of praise were sung, and people in holiday attire paraded the streets, singing and shouting and weeping for joy.

Thus did the folding stool of an uneducated apple woman do more to make permanent the Scottish Reformation than anything else. Covenants had been signed before and soon forgotten. Parliamentary acts had been passed and soon repealed, or else treated as a dead letter. The prelacy group and the episcopacy group had struggled for years, first one triumphant, then the other. It was the cry of Jenny Geddes, and her folding stool, that was the signal for a country-wide uprising. Much blood was soon to be shed on the mountains and in the glens of Scotia, clergymen and lay members of the Kirk were to be executed with shocking barbarism, congregations were soon to meet for worship in remote valleys, with armed guards ready to sound the alarm when the soldiers appeared, but never again did Scotland yield willingly.

It was not merely a feud between two Protestant groups as to the form of their church government. The question of State interference with the internal matters of the Church was involved. The Scottish people were determined that neither their government, nor the English King, should force upon them anything that they did not desire.

The National Assembly was convened in November, 1638, and it sat for a month. It was composed of 140 clergymen, including many of Scotland's most prominent men. It included 98 ruling elders, among whom were 17 noblemen of highest rank, nine knights and 25 landed gentry. Alexander Henderson was chosen moderator, and the king's high commissioner was present at the opening sessions.

After eloquent professions of loyalty to the crown in all civic matters, the Assembly asserted the principle enunciated first by John Knox, namely the right of the Kirk, under the Headship of Jesus Christ, to administer its own spiritual affairs without interference from the crown. The Assembly abolished rule by bishops, it declared the offices of the intruded bishops to be vacant, it rescinded the Five Articles of Perth and it cast out Archbishop Laud's liturgy. It went on record very clearly in matters of Church and State, defining the rights of each, and warning against the encroachment of these rights.

The Westminster Assembly followed. This body met in London in 1643, and it was in session until 1649. Six men were sent from Scotland, and chief among them was Alexander Henderson. This proved to be a noteworthy meeting. The Solemn League and Covenant was adopted in 1643 by the delegates representing not only the Scottish Kirk, but the Church of England, the English Presbyterians and English Independents as well.[7] So great had been the change of opinion that it seemed for a time that the episcopacy would be overthrown in England, and a form of Church government similar to that of Scotland adopted instead. At the same Westminster Assembly the Westminster Confession and the two Catechisms were adopted.

The Scottish pastors and congregations of Covenanter days have been glorified in some quarters and slandered in others. Even Sir Walter Scott describes them as bigoted fanatics, and the men whom he introduces into his novels are caricatures. Sir Walter was the Charles Dickens of Scotland, for he loved grotesque characters. No thoughtful person will declare that Micawber, Fagin and Uriah Heep are representative Englishmen; neither will he accept the absurd characters of Sir Walter Scott as typical Scotsmen. His *Tales of my Landlord* series, and other such writings, are unfortunate, for thoughtless people read them and accept the impossible characters as representative Covenanters. Anglican writers are often supporters of the State-Church idea, and apologists for prelacy as well. To such men, the long years of struggle against State interference, and the determined opposition of the people of Scotland to the introduction of bishops, is narrow sectarianism. Nothing can be more unfair than Dean Stanley's notorious *Lectures on the History of the Church of Scotland.*

On the other hand, Scotsmen have glorified the martyrs of the Covenant as men almost without fault. It cannot be denied that Scotland suffered bitter persecution. Clergymen were imprisoned, burned, hanged, beheaded and assassinated for no other reason than their determination to

---

[7]. See Thos. M'Crie II, *Story of the Scottish Church* (Edinburgh, 1841), pp. 145-147.

preach the Word of God after the king and his bishops had ejected them from their pulpits. Many spent years in foul dungeons, others were sold into slavery, yet others deprived of all their possessions by means of ruinous fines, and for no reason other than their love of religious liberty. It is a wretched story wherein Protestant persecutes Protestant. The tyrants of the House of Stuart asserted the divine right of kings, and this right was thought to include the rule by the king of the Kirk. The bishops whom they forced upon the unwilling Scottish people were too often the willing servants of the crown; and they uttered no protest when some 400 faithful clergymen were driven from their parishes, and unworthy men given their places.

The term "Covenant" had been in use long before what is called the "killing times." In 1557, in the earliest years of the Scottish Reformation, the Scottish nobility prepared and signed the First Covenant. John Knox was living in continental Europe at the time, and the nobles signed a document pledging themselves to defend the principles of the reformed religion even to death. They resolved "to maintain, set forward and establish the most blessed Word of God," and to defend with their "power, substance and very lives" all faithful witnesses of Word and Sacrament.

Other covenants followed. In 1559, when dangers threatened their religious liberty, the nobles drafted and signed the Second Covenant, renewing their determination to defend the cause of the reformed religion. In 1581 the First National Covenant was signed by many, from the king to the humblest subject, and the people pledged loyalty to the crown and urged the king to defend the reformed cause. Several other covenants were drafted and signed.

In 1638 the most famous of all, the National Covenant, was signed by thousands of people in Greyfriars churchyard in Edinburgh. This followed the attempt of Charles I and Archbishop Laud to force an unwelcome prayer book upon the Scottish Kirk. By this time the term Covenanters was in common use, and it was used to describe the clergymen and lay people who accepted the sovereignty of Jesus Christ as Head of the Church, and who rejected the rulership of the crown in spiritual matters. In 1643 the Solemn League and Covenant was sent from Edinburgh to London, and was adopted by the Westminster Assembly by both the Scottish and the English people. By its terms the two countries pledged themselves to exclude popery forever from both England and Scotland.

The signing of the National Covenant in Greyfriars churchyard in 1638 made a lasting impression upon the Scottish people. Not many years ago, on the wall of many a Scottish cottage, whether in the Highlands or the Lowlands, the Western Isles, the Shetlands or the Orkneys, one could often see a steel engraving of the throngs of people in the churchyard, waiting to affix their signatures to the great sheet of parchment that lay upon a flat tomb. In later times, in many homes, two other steel engravings were to be seen: the procession of clergymen in their tile hats moving toward Tanfield Hall, and the picture "The Leaving of the Manse." Even in America, half a century ago, these pictures adorned many a home wherein dwelt people of Scottish background.

Charles I, a son of James VI, reigned over England from 1625 until his execution in 1649. Like his father, he desired to unite England and Scotland, and to bring about church union between the Church of England and the Scottish Kirk. The signing of the Scottish National Covenant in 1638 irritated him. " 'I intend not to yield to the demands of these traitors the Covenanters,' wrote Charles himself, 'and as concerning the explanation of their damnable Covenant, I will only say that so long as this Covenant is in force, whether it be with or without explanation, I have no more power of Scotland than the Duke of Venice would have. I will rather die than suffer it.' "[8]

The reply of Scotland was the National Assembly of November, 1638, with its emphatic declaration of loyalty in civic matters, but its equal determination to accept no dictation from the King in spiritual matters. It overthrew the rule of the bishops, declared their offices vacant,

---

[8]. N. L. Walker, *Scottish Church History*, p. 52.

rescinded the Five Articles of Perth and cast out Laud's liturgy.

In 1639 King Charles raised an army and marched on Scotland, determined to suppress the Scottish people by force. Finding himself outnumbered, he agreed to a truce.

In 1640 he marched on Scotland again with an army, but the Scots went to meet him, crossed the border into England, met the King of England and his army near Newcastle and defeated them with very little loss of life.

The Long Parliament in London followed, sitting from 1640 to 1660. King Charles and his Parliament disagreed, and the people, tired of his tyranny, took up arms, and in 1642 the English Civil War broke out. It ended by the defeat of the Royalists at the hands of the Parliamentarian forces. King Charles I stepped through one of the windows of the Banqueting Hall in Whitehall, near Trafalgar Square, to the scaffold that had been prepared for the occasion, and was beheaded before a great multitude. Opinions concerning him differ sharply to this day. To some he was a tyrant, guilty of great oppression and misrule: to others he is a martyr, and even churches have been named for him.

The people of the Scottish Kirk had no love for him. They had come to value the democracy of their desired form of church government. While it was not entirely congregational, yet the system by which each local congregation was represented by their pastor and a lay member in the presbytery, and then the synod and finally the General Assembly, seemed to them to be the rule by the free voice of the people. The very thought of bishops was distasteful to them, and especially so when the King of a neighboring country sought to establish such a rule by force, as a part of his cherished dream of church union. They looked upon the Church of England as Protestant, but a church body whose Protestantism had not gone far enough. To the Scotsman the episcopal system suggested centralization of spiritual power in the hands of a small group of officials; and an attempt to force upon their Kirk a form of government that was peculiar to another country.

John Welsh (c. 1570-1622)

John Welsh of Ayr, son-in-law of John Knox, was born about the year 1570 at Colliston, in the parish of Dunscore, Dumfriesshire. In his early youth he was a reckless lad, associating with a band of border ruffians. However, he soon gave up his unruly ways, begged his father's forgiveness and promised him to live an upright life if allowed to attend college. He was sent to Edinburgh University, where he became a diligent student and a model Christian. He was graduated with honor in 1588.

In 1590 he was ordained and sent to Selkirk, where his intense zeal in warning the rough inhabitants to abandon their sins and seek divine forgiveness met with opposition. In 1594 he was translated to Kirkcudbright, where he exercised more discretion and met with greater success. In 1596 he preached a sermon in St. Giles' church, Edinburgh, where he dealt in a fearless manner with the King's shortcomings. In 1600 he was translated to Ayr, first as assistant, then as head pastor. There he preached with so great a degree of fervor that in 1603 the town council resolved to build a new church. He preached every day to congregations that filled the church. Street riots broke out in Ayr, and Welsh provided himself with a metal helmet and often rushed among the fighting men and urged them to cease their bloodshed. He was successful after a time, and peace was restored in Ayr.

In 1605 he gave his consent to a meeting of the Assembly which had been forbidden by the King. Although he did not attend the meetings, yet he was brought to trial with the others, found guilty and sentenced to die for treason. The sentence was not carried out, although he was banished from Scotland, and forced to live in France. By intensive study he learned the French language in 14 weeks, and began to preach in Bordeaux. Later he preached in Nerac, Jonsac and St. Jean d'Angely. At the latter place the town was besieged, and Welsh served in the front lines, carrying powder to the gunners. When a shot from the enemy carried away the powder container, he used his hat for the purpose.

John Welsh returned first to London and later to Scotland. His wife appealed in person to King James, begging that her husband might be allowed to return home unmolested. With an oath the King replied that Welsh might return only under condition that he accept the authority of the bishops. Holding up her apron, Mrs. Welsh exclaimed: "Please your Majesty, I'd rather kep his head there."[9]

As Welsh lay on his death bed, King James was finally prevailed upon to remove the inhibition on Welsh's preaching, so that he might die in peace. When the good news was brought to the dying man, he arose from his bed, went to the kirk and preached a sermon. Two hours after his return to his home, he died.

All bear witness to the high order of his preaching. Calderwood describes him as "ane holie man, a painfull and powerfull preachour, and a constant sufferer for the trueth."[10] He was a man of powerful convictions, and this was evident in all his preaching. A volume of his sermons survives to indicate the evangelical fervor of his utterances. They are emotional, expository in form, simple, clear in language, and practical; and there is always a strong appeal, as is the case with so many of the great Scottish preachers. It is entitled *Forty-Eight Select Sermons* (1771). Welsh was also the author of a few controversial essays. An account of his life was written by the Rev. James Young, and is entitled *Life of John Welsh, Minister of Ayr* (1866). Thomas M'Crie includes a short account of him in his biography of John Knox.

David Calderwood (1575-1650)

Although his fame as a church historian causes one to forget that he was an able preacher, yet David Calderwood is worthy of more than passing mention. He was born in Dalkeith in 1575, attended the schools there, and was graduated from Edinburgh University in 1593. In 1604 he was ordained and given the congregation at Crailing. When the

---

9. W. M. Hetherington, *History of the Church of Scotland* (Edinburgh, 1842), p. 128.
10. D. Calderwood, *Historie of the Kirk of Scotland* (Edinburgh, ed. 1842-49), vol. 7, p. 511.

Presbytery-Prelacy controversy stirred the Scottish Kirk, Calderwood became a staunch defender of the presbytery. A remonstrance was drawn up by a group of clergymen and presented to the King, protesting against his attempt to force bishops upon Scotland. Calderwood was appointed, in 1607, to present this protest to the King in person. He was questioned by the King, and threatened with imprisonment or banishment, but nothing could induce him to reveal the names of the pastors who had drawn up the protest. He was imprisoned for a time, and finally banished from Scotland.

In 1619 he went to Holland, returning to Scotland in 1625. In 1640 he was called to Pencaitland, in East Lothian. With David Dickson and Alexander Henderson he was appointed to draw up the Directory for Publish Worship for the Scottish Kirk.

David Calderwood's fame rests largely upon his *Historie of the Kirk of Scotland,* which he was asked to write. First he prepared an enormous work of 3,136 manuscript pages, which was never published because of its size. Some 1,117 pages of this are in the British Museum. Then he prepared a digest of this larger work, which fills eight thick volumes, each containing from 600 to 800 closely printed pages. It was the 1842-1848 edition of this exhaustive work that the writer was permitted to consult. Its spelling is archaic, for in Calderwood's days there was no standardized spelling in Scotland, and each man wrote down his words in whatever local dialect he happened to speak. With all its barbarous spelling, this work is one of the most valuable original sources of Scottish church history available.

Calderwood prepared a brief summary of this eight-volume digest, called *The True History of the Kirk of Scotland from the Beginning of the Reformation to the End of the Reign of King James VI.* This work was not published until 1678. It fills a good sized folio volume. The manuscript in the British Museum is evidently not Calderwood's final draft, for the manuscript for the eight-volume digest is written much more neatly and carefully, and in a beautiful handwriting, with very few corrections.

Much of the early Reformation history of Scotland might have been unknown today, had not David Calderwood taken the pains to write it down at the time, and to preserve for posterity a very detailed life of John Knox, of whom he was almost a contemporary. He is said to have been a good preacher, and it is certain that he was fearless and faithful. Calderwood's *Altar of Damascus* (1621), was considered an important work at the time, and his *The Course of Conformitie* (1622), was often quoted. David Calderwood's biography was written in 1842 by Thomas Thomson.

Alexander Henderson (1583-1646)

This eloquent preacher, whose name is associated with the most significant day in Scotland's history, the signing of the National Covenant, was born in 1583 in Creich, Fifeshire. He was graduated from St. Andrews in 1603, and became regent in the arts faculty and teacher of philosophy and rhetoric.

In 1611 he was licensed to preach, and in 1614 he was ordained and assigned to Leuchars church in Fifeshire. During his early ministry Henderson was a champion of the episcopacy. He was entirely without selfish motives in this respect, and he had not yet studied the two Greek words which were to play so important a part in the controversy.

The people of Leuchars church, aware of Henderson's views, not only protested against Henderson's appointment as their pastor, but on the day of his ordination and installation, they barred all the church doors from within and went to their homes. The men who came to install the new pastor were not to be turned away. Removing one of the windows, the bishop and his associates, together with Henderson, all climbed into the church through the window.

Shortly after this, Robert Bruce of Kinnard preached in the nearby parish of Forgan. Anxious to hear this noted preacher, but unwilling to be seen in the congregation, Henderson went disguised as a farm laborer. It so happened that Bruce used the text, "Verily, verily I say unto you, he that entereth not by the door into the sheepfold, but climbeth up some other way, the same is a thief and a robber." It was purely a coincidence, but Henderson, sitting in a far corner of the church, thought instantly not only of his entry into Leuchars church, but of the fact that the congregation had refused to call him. This, in turn, caused him to give thought to the bishops and their party, and of the methods that they had employed in Scotland. By searching the Scriptures and studying the Greek words, he began to doubt the divine right of the episcopate. In time he went to the other extreme, as had Andrew Melville, and looked upon the presbytery as of divine institution.

In 1618 Alexander Henderson had progressed sufficiently that we find him issuing a spirited remonstrance against the Five Articles of Perth. These enjoined: 1. That the Lord's Supper should be received kneeling; 2. That it might be administered in private; 3. That Baptism might also be private; 4. That children be confirmed; 5. That Christmas, Easter, etc., should be observed as holidays.[11] These things, as one authority shows, would cause little controversy today, but they caused great offense at the time because the King forced them upon the people as a part of his scheme to subordinate the Scottish Kirk to the crown, and to the Church of England.

In 1637 Alexander Henderson took a leading part in the signing of the National Covenant. It was he who read the document in Greyfriars church, and offered the prayer before it was signed. Aberdeen, St. Andrews and Crail hesitated at first, and it was Henderson who was selected to make the document as unanimous as possible. He went to St. Andrews, and so persuasive was his preaching that all the burgesses and townspeople signed. He went with Dickson and Cant to Aberdeen, preached there, and all signed the Covenant except several Doctors. He was moderator of the National Assembly the same year, and showed as much parliamentary wisdom as he had shown pulpit power. After this Assembly had abolished bishops, rescinded the Five Articles of Perth, rejected Laud's ritual and adopted a ringing declaration of spiritual freedom, Henderson dismissed

---

[11]. D. Calderwood, *Historie of the Kirk of Scotland* (Edinburgh, ed. 1842-49), vol. 7, p. 332.

the Assembly, which had sat for a month, with the words, "We have now cast down the walls of Jericho. Let him that rebuildeth them beware of the curse of Hiel the Bethelite."

From that time onward, Alexander Henderson was the recognized leader of the Kirk. In 1639 he was made pastor of Greyfriars church, by this time the most important parish in Edinburgh. Together with this position he was, from 1640 to 1646, rector of Edinburgh University. In 1643 it was he who drafted the Solemn League and Covenant, and he led the delegation of six men who were sent from Scotland to London to the Westminster Assembly, where the Solemn League and Covenant were adopted, as well as the Westminster Confession and the Larger and Shorter Catechisms.

During his lifetime Henderson published but three of his sermons, but in those days the sermons of eminent preachers were often taken down verbatim by reporters. Thus it was that a volume of Henderson's sermons and pulpit prayers was published after his death, and, of course without any editing on his part. Like most of the other Scottish preachers, his sermons are expository. There is a series in which the eleventh chapter of Hebrews is expounded, and another in which the Armour of God is explained in detailed exegesis. He follows the style of his day, with divisions, sub-divisions and numerous sub-divisions of sub-divisions.

Dargan, whose two-volume work is easily without an equal,[12] looks upon Henderson as second only to Knox and Melville, and he adds: "As a preacher he was both popular and powerful, balanced in thought, strong in argument, effective in manner. The published sermons . . . show a masculine intellect, a firm faith, a quiet but determined courage. The tone is noble and modest, the grasp of the subject is clear and firm; there is power of appeal and a secure sense of being right without pride or bitterness."[13] Taylor says that Henderson's sermons are strictly textual, practical,

---

[12]. E. C. Dargan, A History of Preaching, 2 vols. (New York, 1905 and 1912).
[13]. E. C. Dargan, A History of Preaching, vol. 2, p. 175.

80 A HISTORY OF PREACHING

strong in their language, but never bitter; "their style is simple, sometimes almost conversational, and frequently vernacular, but in matter they are always rich in 'that which is good to the use of edifying, that it may minister grace unto the hearers'."[14]

In one of the series of lectures on "The Evangelical Succession," delivered in Free St. George's, Edinburgh, 1881-1883 A. D., one of the speakers, the Rev. G. Webster Thomson, spoke of the life and influence of Alexander Henderson. Among other things he said:

"He also began life as more or less of an apologist for prelacy and the ceremonies, but with deepening seriousness all that was changed. And it is not needful, in order to account for this, to maintain that episcopacy is in itself necessarily unfavourable to vital and evangelical religion. I must not conceal my belief that there are other forms of church order that have proved *more* friendly to it; but many of the best and holiest Christians that the world has seen have been episcopalians. The names that give their titles to the lectures of this course prove that men in the Evangelical Succession are to be found in all the churches. But in Scotland during the seventeenth century nearly all earnest Christians were on the side of presbyterianism, and the whole circumstances of the case made it impossible that it should have been otherwise. No desire for prelacy has ever grown up within the church itself. The church's teachers had not found it in the Scripture. Pious men suspected and feared it, because associated in their minds with the popery from which they had just escaped, and because allied in practice with many things that they judged unlawful and dangerous. Its presence in the church was not in any measure due to the aspirations of its godly ministers and people, but to the intrigues of secular politicians, who sought its introduction for other than pious ends. And the men who lent themselves as tools for carrying out these intrigues were not pious men. It was the more worldly, the more ambitious, the more obsequious of the clergy who were promoted to bishoprics. Even had the king or the regent

---

[14]. W. M. Taylor, *The Scottish Pulpit* (New York, 1887), pp. 83-84.

THE DAYS OF THE COVENANTERS 81

wished it otherwise they had no alternative, and indeed James at one time complained that respectable men could not be got to fill the vacant sees. The piety of the church disliked and opposed the system, and kept aloof from the men who took to do with it; so that in the case of any one who had come to be in earnest about practical godliness there could hardly be hesitation as to the party in the church with which he was to sympathise. . . . Prelacy in Scotland, during the seventeenth century, whatever it may have been in other countries, or in Scotland in later times, was identified in the minds of the people with indifference or actual hostility to the Gospel; and the student of history will utterly fail to comprehend it if he does not recognize the fact that our presbyterian fathers in all their struggles believed themselves to be contending not only for their own views of church order and the church's freedom from secular control, but also for vital and evangelical religion."[15]

In this significant statement, Mr. Thomson uses the words "episcopal" and "presbyterian" as adjectives, and not as the names of particular denominations. While it is true that evangelical truth flourishes more freely under some forms of church government than under others, yet the fact must not be overlooked that no particular form of government is commanded by the Word of God, neither is any form condemned. Each one of us has his own preference, but it is unsafe to say that the episcopacy, prelacy or a congregational form of government is of divine origin. Any form is allowable, so long as it does not interfere with the free and fearless preaching of evangelical truth. If it is to be found that prelacy, or any other system of church administration, interferes with this full and free declaration of the whole Word of God, then it is our duty as faithful Christians to avoid it; but in avoiding it we dare not go so far as to say that such a form of government is condemned by the Lord. We reject one system of administration and we defend another solely because the one appears to restrict the free proclamation of evangelical teachings, whereas the other form seems to us to favor such testimony. Our Lord

---

[15]. *The Evangelical Succession*, 3 vols. (Edinburgh, 1882-1884), vol. II., pp. 95-97.

commands no particular system of organization, but rather does He leave it to our good judgment as Christians to support that form of ecclesiastical order that proves most salutary to a faithful, courageous declaration of the whole revealed Truth.

Alexander Henderson wrote *The Government and Order of the Church of Scotland* (1641). His *Sermons, Prayers and Pulpit Addresses* (1867), edited by R. T. Martin, and *Sermons* (1643-48), contain many examples of his pulpit work. The chief biographies are: R. L. Orr, *Alexander Henderson, Churchman and Statesman* (1919); J. P. Thomson, *Alexander Henderson, the Covenanter* (1912); J. Aiton, *The Life and Times of Alexander Henderson* (1836); and Thomas M'Crie, *Life of Alexander Henderson* (1836).

David Dickson (c. 1583-1663)

David Dickson, a contemporary of Alexander Henderson, and yet another of the evangelical succession, was born in or about the year 1583 at Glasgow, where his father was a wealthy merchant. He attended Glasgow University, graduating M. A. about the year 1610; after which he spent eight years of regency at his alma mater, teaching philosophy. In 1618 he was ordained and given the parish of Irvine, with which his name has even since been associated. In 1622 he protested against the oppressive Five Articles of Perth, and in clear, forceful language he pointed out their thoroughly unevangelical character. For this he was summoned before the high court and deprived of his congregation, but restored again in 1623. In 1639 he became a chaplain to the Covenanters' army and served with bravery and singular faithfulness through those trying times. From 1640 to 1650 he was professor of theology in Glasgow University, going from there to Edinburgh University where he was professor of theology from 1650 to 1660. He was ejected from his professorship in 1660 because of his refusal to take the oath of supremacy.

David Dickson was one of the men who saw immediately that King James, having forced prelacy upon the Kirk, was now determined at any cost to bring the Kirk into conformity with the other churches where the prelatic system was in use.

This extended to all the details of public worship, and even went so far as to make kneeling at Communion a matter of law. Dickson and his contemporaries might have been quite willing to practice kneeling for Communion so long as it remained a matter of Christian liberty, but when the king saw fit to make certain ceremonies compulsory by law, and other customs illegal and subject to fines and imprisonments, he protested that this was a violation of Christian liberty. To enforce one ceremony upon a Christian congregation by law, and to forbid another ceremony by a decree of the government, is an infringement of the sovereign rights of the congregation, and a violation of the individual conscience. Such things are neither commanded nor forbidden by Scripture, and as soon as the State attempts to make them legal or illegal, and regulates their observance under penalty of fines and imprisonments, then the State is guilty of interfering with the spiritual rights of the Church. Dickson's evangelical principles led him to recognize this fact, and he suffered a period of suspension from his pastorate, and later his removal from an important professorship rather than to yield to the tyranny of the king and his bishops.

David Dickson was one of the foremost preachers of his generation. A prominent Englishman visited Scotland, and his words are quoted again and again. He said: "I went to St. Andrews, where I heard a sweet, majestic-looking man (Blair), and he showed me the majesty of God; after him I heard a fair little man (Rutherford), and he showed me the loveliness of Christ; then I went to Irvine, where I heard a well-informed, proper old man, with a long beard (Dickson), and that man showed me all my own heart."[16]

Dickson was a simple, earnest, evangelical preacher. It was customary in his day to preach a series of sermons from a single text. Dickson usually took three or four verses as his text and expounded them; for he said, "God's bairns should get a good blaud (portion) of His own bread."[17] Some of Scotland's popular preachers had formed

---

[16]. Thos. M'Crie II, *Sketches of Scottish Church History* (Edinburgh, 1841), p. 62.

[17]. W. M. Taylor, *The Scottish Pulpit* (New York, 1887), p. 98.

84 A HISTORY OF PREACHING

the bad habit of preaching a lengthy sermon, the first half
of which was devoted to a list of incorrect interpretations of
the text and their answers to these wrong teachings: "God
sent forth His Son; 1. Not an archangel; 2. Not an angel;
3. Not a prophet of old; 4. Not an apostle — but His own
Son." Dickson declared that this was but an affectation, and
a time-consuming parade of the preacher's skill in refuting
arguments. He compared it to a cook who might bring to
the table an attractive dish and say, "This looks like a good
piece of meat, but you must not eat it,"[18] and then another
dish, and another, then finally a dish which the guest was
permitted to eat. Dickson condemned the habit of many
Scottish preachers who liked to announce a text, then read it
in the original Greek and explain each word, supporting their
arguments with Latin quotations which only the university
people could appreciate. He declared that a study of the
Greek text was of greatest importance, but he said that this
must be done in the pastor's study, and not in the pulpit.
The Greek text and quotations from Latin writers are the
preacher's tools. He compared such preachers to a cook
who might bring in his cooking utensils from the kitchen
and show them proudly to the guests seated at the table.
Greek and Latin, he believed, caused only confusion to the
humble cotter and the farm laborer.

When Dickson went back to Irvine after his suspension,
his persuasive preaching of sin and grace caused a great
spiritual awakening there. The tyrannical measures of the
king and the bishops caused a reaction, and seldom has the
preaching of evangelical truth been more powerful in Scotland, nor have the fruits of such preaching been more
apparent. The cruelty of the king and the Kirk's leaders
seemed to drive the clergymen back to their Bibles. They
laid aside some of the more unlovely details of their theological system and began to preach such simple truths as the
inspiration and power of the Word of God, the fall of man
and the sinfulness of all of Adam's descendants, the love of
God and the manner in which He provided a plan of salvation
through His Son, the all-sufficiency of Jesus Christ as Saviour

---

[18]. *Ibid.*, p. 99.

of the world, man's justification by faith through grace, the utter worthlessness of good works as a means of saving man from sin and death, the regenerating power of the Holy Ghost, and the fact that eternal life is the gracious gift to the true believer, while eternal death awaits the unbelieving and the impenitent. The arrogant claims of the king and the bishops caused the preachers of Dickson's time to lay increasing emphasis on Jesus Christ as the Supreme Head of the Kirk — not a king, not the nobles, not the bishops, not the civil government, but the Saviour Himself.

In days of persecution it is just these teachings, which scoffers and liberalists term the "threadbare shibboleths of evangelicalism," which have brought comfort and renewed hope to the men who suffered ejection from their pulpits, fines and imprisonment; and to the faithful people who presently were to be driven from their homes and their homeland, rather than surrender these teachings. Sermons on mental and moral philosophy, such as many parsons loved to preach during the middle of the twentieth century, would have proved poor spiritual food for the oppressed Christians of the seventeenth century.

Some of David Dickson's more important writings are: *An Explanation of the Epistle to the Hebrews* (1635); *Expositio Analytica omnium Epistolarum* (1645); *Exposition of St. Matthew* (1651); *A Brief Explication of the Psalms*, 3 volumes (1653-1655); *Therapeutica Sacra* (1695); *An Exposition of all the Epistles* (1659); and *Truth's Victory over Error* (1772). A life of David Dickson was written in 1772 by Robert Wodrow.

David Forrester (1588-1633)

David Forrester was born in 1588, in or near Stirling. He was graduated from St. Andrews University in 1608, ordained in 1610, and put in charge of Denny church. In 1613 he was translated (as the Scots say) to North Leith. He came into prominence because of his boldness in preaching against the legalistic manner in which the Five Articles of Perth were forced upon the Scottish Kirk. Because of his decided opinions in this matter he narrowly escaped deposition.

In 1620 he was transferred to Rathven, where he preached with equal energy against the papists. King James VI was not pleased with Forrester and his candid views, and he ordered his arrest. Fortunately David Forrester had influential friends who interceded for him, and he was not imprisoned. In 1627 he retired to Leith, and died six years later.[19]

Andrew Cant (c. 1590-1663)

Andrew Cant was born about the year 1590. He came into prominence in 1620, when the people of Edinburgh were anxious to call him to that city. The King objected, and he was not called. In 1633, while pastor at Pitsligo in Aberdeenshire, he supported the Covenanters, and opposed the efforts of the King to establish the episcopacy in Scotland. In 1638 he was sent with Dickson, Henderson and others to Aberdeen to interest the people there in the covenant. He took an active part in the Assembly of 1638, when the prelacy was rejected. Later in the same year he was translated to Newbattle, in Midlothian. In 1640 he became chaplain to the Covenanter army, and was translated to Aberdeen.

Andrew Cant was an ardent Covenanter, and at the same time a staunch royalist. Once, while preaching a sermon in regard to the duty of a loyal subject to the King, several soldiers of Cromwell who were present, arose and advanced on him with drawn swords. Andrew Cant calmly drew back his preaching robe, bared his chest and said: "Here is the breast ready to receive the thrusts, if any will venture to give them, for the truth."[20]

Baillie has described him as "ane super-excellent preacher." Wodrow declares that his congregations in Aberdeen were so great that Cant often had to preach in the great square at the market cross. Once, while preaching in the square, a ruffian threw a dead corby (crow) at him. Cant paused, pointed at the man and declared that as many would gaze upon his death as were present in the

---

[19]. D. Calderwood, *Historie of the Kirk of Scotland* (Edinburgh, ed., 1842-49), vol. I, pp. 379-380.
[20]. R. Wodrow, *Analecta*, vol. 2, p. 162.

congregation that day. Later the ruffian was hanged for robbery.[21]

Robert Blair (1593-1666)

Robert Blair was born in 1593 at Irvine, Ayrshire. After his early education in the parochial school he attended Glasgow University. He taught school for a while, and in 1615 he was made a regent, or teacher, in the university. He was licensed to preach by the Established Church in 1616. About the year 1622 it is said that he resigned because Dr. Cameron, who had become principal of the university, belonged to the prelatic party.

Blair went to Ireland in 1623 and was ordained by the Protestant bishop of Down. His activity in Ireland was noteworthy, and he is one of the men whose labors made the County Ulster a stronghold of Protestantism. He worked among the Scottish people who had gone over to Ireland and settled in the northern counties, and he extended his work to the Irish people as well, many of whom responded to his eloquent preaching.

In 1631 trouble arose and led to his suspension, and a year later to his deposition. The exact nature of the difficulty is not clear. It is said that the charges against him were nonconformity, but it is quite likely that his views in regard to the form of church government by the presbytery, rather than the prelacy, had much to do with it. In 1634 Charles I directed the Kirk to restore him, but it was not long until he was deposed again.

In 1635 he set sail for America with a number of Scots and Irish people who intended to form a colony in the new world, but when within sight of the Newfoundland coast, a series of tempests made further westward progress impossible. The ship turned about and after a rough voyage finally made Ireland. Blair preached in Ayr for a time, and in 1638, by action of the Assembly, he was translated to St. Andrews, where, with the exception of two or three intervals, he spent the next 28 years. In 1640 he marched with the Scots into England. In 1641 he preached for a time in Ire-

---

[21]. *Ibid.*, vol. 2, 155.

land, but returned to St. Andrews. He was elected moderator in 1646, and chaplain-in-ordinary to the King. In 1661, after the Restoration, he was imprisoned briefly on three occasions. Then he became a field preacher, enduring all the hardships and risks of that hazardous calling, until his death in 1666.

Robert Blair was a man of majestic appearance and of great personality in the pulpit. It was he of whom the London merchant said, in characterizing three famous Scottish preachers, that he showed him the majesty of God. He was one of the most highly respected preachers of Scotland, and one of the most gifted. A man of highest integrity, yet he had a certain quaintness of faith, for like William Bray of Baldhu, when strongly inclined to follow some good course, he declared that the Lord had directed him. Among his famous descendents were Robert Blair the poet, Lord Blair the eminent jurist and Dr. Hugh Blair the man of letters. Robert Blair's *Autobiography and Life,* edited by R. B. and W. Row, appeared in 1848. This autobiography is also included in Thos. M'Crie's *Life of Robert Blair* (1848).

Robert Douglas (1594-1674)

Robert Douglas was born in 1594, supposedly in Lochleven. He is said to have been a grandson of Mary Queen of Scots, a thing which he himself never admitted nor denied, although there is no historic evidence for such a supposition. He was graduated in 1614 from St. Andrews. In 1628 he was given the church at Kirkaldy. In 1630 he became one of the chaplains to King Gustavus Adolphus, serving a brigade of Scots who assisted that Swedish leader. In the campaign in Germany, Douglas is said to have committed to memory large portions of the Bible. In 1639 he became one of the pastors of the High Church, Edinburgh, and in 1641 he was given Tolbooth Church, Edinburgh.

Robert Douglas was "a great State preacher, one of the greatest of that age in Scotland — for he feared no man to declare the mind of God to him — yet very accessible, and easy to be conversed with. Unless a man were for God, he had no value for him, let him be never so great and noble."[22]   He was invited to preach before the Scottish Parliament in 1641, 1661 and 1662.

In 1643 he was one of the Scottish commissioners to the Westminster Assembly of Divines in London. In 1651 he was chosen to preach a sermon at the coronation of King Charles II, at Scone. In 1662 he became pastor of Greyfriars Church, Edinburgh, only to be deprived not long thereafter because of his refusal to acknowledge the episcopacy. He was offered the bishopric of Edinburgh on condition that he accept the prelatic rule of the Scottish Kirk, but he refused. In 1669 he was given Pencaitland parish in East Lothian.

While it is evident that Robert Douglas was one of the most eloquent and influential preachers of his day, yet opinions differ in regard to him. The statement that "he feared no man to declare the mind of God to him" may have been true, nevertheless Burnet, who knew him in his old age, says that he was a very prudent man, "for he durst not own the free thoughts he had of some things for fear of offending the people,"[23] and it was also said of him that "he had a singular way of preaching, without doctrines, which some call scumming the text."[24] Dean Stanley, who spoke well of the Moderates, does not hesitate to place Robert Douglas in his list of men (Patrick Forbes, Robert Douglas, Robert Leighton, Lawrence Charteris and William Carstairs), whom he looks upon as the forerunners of Hugh Blair, Principal Robertson, "Jupiter" Carlyle and the other full-fledged Moderates.

Samuel Rutherford (1600-1661)

This famous preacher of the Scottish Covenanters was born in 1600 in Nisbet parish, Roxburghshire. In 1617 he entered Edinburgh University. In 1623 he was made regent of humanities and instructor in Latin at the university. In 1626 he began his theological studies. A year later he was called to Anwoth, Kircudbrightshire. In 1636 he published

[22]. R. Wodrow, Analecta, 3, 82-83.
[23]. A. P. Stanley, Lectures on the History of the Church of Scotland (New York, 1872), p. 118.
[24]. Quoted by Stanley, p. 119.

his *Exercitationes Apologeticae pro Divina Gratia*. Charged
with ultra-Calvinism by the High Commission, he was expelled from his parish and confined within the corporate
limits of Aberdeen, and inhibited from preaching or teaching. In 1638 he was returned to Anwoth by vote of the
Assembly. In 1639 he was elected to the chair of theology
in St. Mary's College, St. Andrews, and was also made
assistant pastor of the parish church. In 1643 he was one
of the eight Scottish commissioners to the Westminster
Assembly. In 1647 he became principal of New College,
St. Andrews, and four years later he was made rector of
St. Andrews. In 1660, after the Restoration, his book *Lex,
Rex* was burned publicly, and he himself was held for high
treason. Before the matter could be settled, he died, in
1661, of natural causes.

Samuel Rutherford has often been called a man of split
personality. The fact is cited that his famous *Letters* (365
in number) are praised in most extravagant terms as among
the most beautiful devotional writings ever published. His
sermons on the Names of Our Saviour are intensely devotional. However, it is also stated that no man of his day,
when thoroughly aroused, could indulge in such bitter
polemical language as one may find in his controversial
writings. However, these apparent contradictions are familiar enough. Luther, for example, was such a man,
urbane, genial, friendly in private life, but capable of scath-
ing language when drawn into an acrimonious doctrinal
debate.

Rutherford has been called arrogant in his attitude
toward men whom he considered errorists, and given to
dogmatic self-assurance. He had no mercy on men whom
he believed to be false teachers, and did not hesitate to heap
bitter scorn upon them. Even Cromwell begged him to consider the possibility that he might be mistaken. Milton
rebuked him sharply in one of his sonnets. Rutherford felt
that he stood on solid theological ground, and whenever his
theology was attacked, he defended it with vehement
language.

His *Letters* have often been compared to the writings
of Thomas à Kempis, and to the curious mysticism of St.

John of the Cross.[25] Although their language sometimes borders on extravagance, yet they reveal the pietistic side of Samuel Rutherford.

As a preacher few men have ever preached Jesus Christ as he did. Some of his sermons went so far as to leave the impression that the Father and the Holy Ghost were of minor importance. When he preached upon the Names of Our Lord, he was at his best. With a high-pitched voice, called in Scotland a pulpit-*skriech,* and trembling with emotion, he would picture the beauties of the Rose of Sharon, the life-giving properties of the Bread of Life, the glory of the Bright and Morning Star, the fruitfulness of the Branch of Righteousness and the Root of Jesse, the invincibleness of the Lord of Hosts and the majesty of the King of Kings and Lord of Lords. Once he said, "Oh! if I might but speak to three or four herd-boys of my worthy Master, I would be satisfied to be the meanest and most obscure of all the pastors of the land."

The familiar story of Samuel Rutherford and the famous Archbishop Ussher is found in many old school readers and books of sermon illustration. It is said that Archbishop Ussher had heard of Rutherford's fame as a preacher, and desired greatly to hear him. Not caring to be seen in a Covenanter meeting house, the noted archbishop visited Anwoth in the rough garb of a wayfarer. Before the church service, Rutherford's wife gathered the servants and strangers for the catechetical hour which she was in the habit of conducting. Noticing the wayfarer, she asked him the number of the Commandments. The wayfarer replied, "Eleven," much to the amusement of the class.

Samuel Rutherford overheard this, and, finding the wayfarer engaged in private devotions, he interrupted him in order to set him right in regard to the Ten Commandments. The poorly-garbed wayfarer insisted that there were eleven. "Then, pray tell me, which is the eleventh?" asked Rutherford. "A new commandment I give unto you, that ye love one another,' That is the eleventh Commandment!" declared Archbishop Ussher significantly, with reference, no doubt,

---

[25]. E. I. Watkin, *The Philosophy of Mysticism.*

to Rutherford's well-known bitterness of language when engaged in theological controversies. Those were stirring days, and standards then differed from those of our day. A certain amount of acrimony was considered entirely proper in religious disputes.

Rutherford's writings include: *Exercitationes Apologeticae pro Divina Gratia* (1636); *A Plea for Paul's Presbytrie in Scotland* (1642); *Lex, Rex* (1644); *Due Rights of Presbytries* (1644); *The Tryal and Triumph of Faith*, 27 sermons (1645); *Divine Right of Church Government* (1646); *Christ's Dying and Drawing Sinners to Himself* (1647), which is a collection of sermons; *Survey of the Spiritual Antichrist* (1648); and *A Free Disputation against Pretended Liberty of Conscience* (1649). Rutherford's letters, said to have been published in 1664, were edited by A. A. Bonar and published in two volumes in 1848. Another collection of letters was published by T. Smith in 1881. Biographies and characterizations of Rutherford include, among others: Alexander Whyte, *Samuel Rutherford and Some of his Correspondents* (1894); R. Gilmour, *Life of Samuel Rutherford* (1904); A. A. Bonar, *Memoir of Samuel Rutherford* (1848); and a biography by Andrew Thomson, (1884).

John Livingstone (1603-1672)

John Livingstone's fame as a preacher rests upon a single sermon which Scotland has never forgotten. He was born in Kilsyth, Stirlingshire, in 1603, and after attending the grammar school in Stirling, he was graduated in 1621 from Glasgow University. Licensed to preach in 1625, he became assistant pastor to Torphichen parish church, and chaplain to the Countess of Wigton.

He became discouraged because he was unable to obtain a parish of his own, and he went to Killinchy, in Ireland, but he was suspended a year later by the Bishop of Down because of his nonconformist views. Later he was reinstated, only to be suspended again. He determined to go to America, and actually set sail, but his ship encountered severe storms and had to put back. Livingstone returned to Scotland, and between 1638 and 1648 he was pastor at Stranraer. In 1648 he was translated to Ancrum, and after the Restoration he was banished to Holland, where he spent the remainder of his life pursuing his Oriental studies and preparing a Hebrew-Latin Bible.

The sermon that made him famous was preached when he was but 27 years of age. A carriage containing some ladies of high rank met with an accident at Shotts, near the parsonage, and the pastor extended the hospitality of the manse until repairs could be made. Noticing that the manse was in a shabby condition, the visitors offered to provide a new manse in a better location. At their suggestion a great Communion service was arranged, and several pastors were asked to take part in it, among them John Livingstone.

Livingstone was invited to preach, but because of his youth and his timidity he was in great distress, pleading "great unworthiness and weakness." Walking alone in the fields, he was on the point of stealing away somewhere so that he would not have to preach. Then he decided to trust in the Lord, and he "got good assistance." The words of Ezekiel 36, 25-26 came to his mind. He preached to an immense gathering of people, and it proved to be a sermon that made history. At its close, some 500 people pressed forward, confessing their sins and renewing their faith in the righteousness and blood of the Saviour. Not only that, but the word spread throughout Clydesdale, and people who had grown careless came back to the churches in such numbers that "many of the most eminent Christians of the country could date either their conversion or some remarkable conformation of their case from that day."[26] This was remarkable, for it was long before the day of what is known now as revivals. It was more than a century before Howel Harris and Daniel Rowland began to preach in Wales, and before the great awakening in America under Jonathan Edwards, and in England under Whitefield and Wesley.

John Livingstone became well versed in Oriental study. He knew Hebrew, Chaldee and Syriac, and even Arabic, to

---

[26]. W. A. Hetherington, *History of the Church of Scotland* (Edinburgh, 1842), vol. I, p. 262.

say nothing of a working knowledge of French and Italian, and a little Spanish. His Hebrew-Latin Bible was the result of a large amount of labor, but for some reason it was never published. After his famous sermon at Shotts, he was in much demand as a preacher, and churches were filled to overflowing wherever he went. Livingstone's writings include *Letters from Leith* (1633); *Lives of Eminent Scottish Divines* (1754); and an *Autobiography* (1754).

Robert Leighton (1611-1684)

Robert Leighton was the son of the Rev. Alexander Leighton, who suffered great physical torture because of his religious views.[27]   The younger Leighton was born in 1611, either in Edinburgh, or perhaps in London where the family lived for a time. He was graduated from Edinburgh University in 1631, after which he spent several years on the Continent, where he studied theology, Latin, Greek, Hebrew and French. While there he came in contact with the Jansenists, and developed an ecumenical spirit that was to influence him for life.

He was licensed in 1641, and ordained later in the same year and assigned to Newbattle parish, where his duties included preaching three sermons each week, and caring for 900 communicant members. In 1653 he was made principal of Edinburgh University, as well as professor of divinity. At the university he preached twice each week, once in English and once in Latin. His Latin sermons were extremely popular with the university people and even with the townsfolk.

In 1661, Episcopalianism was restored in Scotland. Robert Leighton looked upon the form of church government as an external, and a matter of indifference, and he cast his lot with the episcopacy. In 1661 he was appointed bishop of Dunblane. He was very reluctant to accept the office, but was persuaded to do so in the hope that he might, with his ecumenical disposition, heal the bitter feuds that were distressing Scotland. In 1669 he was made archbishop

---

[27]. Thos. M'Crie, *Sketches of Scottish Church History* (Edinburgh, 1841), p. 267.

of Glasgow, but he was never happy in this new office, and in 1674 he resigned and spent the last ten years of his life in retirement.

Robert Leighton published none of his writings, and he left a request that they be destroyed at his death. This was not done, however, and some of his works were printed without the revisions that he would have made, had he cared to have his writings published.

His sermons are devout, evangelical, and wonderfully simple and clear in language. In this respect they are a departure from the prevailing style of his day. It was customary in that age to overload a sermon with classical quotations and allusions, which none but the learned could appreciate. Leighton strove to preach with utmost simplicity, and in language that every hearer could understand, and with similes with which they were thoroughly familiar.

What can be simpler and more beautiful than his description of Messianic prophecy? He describes such prophecy as a number of streams of water, uniting to form a main stream which flowed onward until it "grew greater as it went, till it fell in with the main current of the Gospel in the New Testament, both acted and preached by the great Prophet Himself, Whom they foretold to come, and recorded by His Apostles and Evangelists, and thus united into one river clear as crystal; this doctrine of salvation in the Scriptures hath still refreshed the city of God, His Church under the Gospel, and still shall do so, till it empty itself into the ocean of Eternity."[28]

Robert Leighton was a man of deep piety, described by some as saintly, humble to a degree, and evangelical in his doctrinal position. A lover of peace, he longed to heal the bitter religious differences in his country, but was too mild of manner to do so. His sermons, while beautiful in their simplicity of thought and language, and praised highly by his contemporaries, lack the ruggedness and force that one is accustomed to associate with the better type of Scottish preaching.

---

[28]. W. M. Taylor, *The Scottish Pulpit* (New York, 1887), p. 127.

Leighton's *Commentary on First Peter,* in two volumes (1693), is one of his best known writings. It was praised lavishly by Dr. Doddridge and others. His *Prelectiones Theologicae* (1693), his *Rules and Instructions for a Holy Life* (1708), and a book of sermons (1692), are among his other writings. Several editions of his collected *Works* and his *Whole Works,* in four to six volumes, have been published, of which J. C. Riker's edition (1845), is as good as any.

Biographies have been written by a number of hands: That of Erasmus Middleton (1805), is well known; and others are: T. Murray, *Life of Robert Leighton* (1828); George Jerment, *Life of Leighton* (1806); J. Aikman, *Life of Abp. Leighton* (1839); C. F. Secretan, *The Troubled Times of . . . Abp. Leighton* (1866); Wm. Blair's *Archbishop Leighton* (1883); the same author's *Robert Leighton, Extracts and Introduction* (1907), and *Selections from the Writings of Abp. Leighton* (1883), and D. Butler's *Life and Letters of Robert Leighton* (1903), are all of interest, but perhaps the most complete story of his life is J. N. Pearson's biography, published in 1825. Burnet's *History of His Own Times* (1723-34), contains a careful study of Leighton's characteristics as a man and as a preacher, while John Tulloch's *Archbishop Leighton,* in *Scottish Divines* (1883), will be read with interest. A more recent study is E. A. Knox's *Robert Leighton* (1930).

James Guthrie (c. 1612-1661)

James Guthrie, who suffered death for his religious beliefs, was born about the year 1612 in Forfarshire. He received his education at St. Leonard's College, St. Andrews, and for a time he taught philosophy at St. Andrews. He belonged to the prelatic party at first, but in 1639 Samuel Rutherfurd became professor of divinity at St. Andrews, and through his influence James Guthrie changed his views in regard to church government, and cast his lot with the men who favored government by the presbytery, and not by bishops.

In 1642 Guthrie was ordained and became pastor of Lander parish, in Berwickshire. From 1644 to 1651 he was a member of the General Assembly. In 1646 he was one of the men who attended King Charles at Newcastle. About the year 1649 he went to Stirling, where he remained until the Restoration of 1661. In 1651 an attempt was made to depose him because of his adherence to the cause of the Protesters. This led, in 1661, to charges that he had declined the King's jurisdiction in spiritual affairs. When he was brought into court he astonished friends and foes with his eloquent defense. Although he made it clear that his act of declining the King's authority in spiritual affairs rested on Scriptural ground, yet he was imprisoned in Edinburgh castle, and then at Stirling. The same year he was sentenced to be hanged.

James Guthrie's execution stirred all Scotland. He was allowed to speak to the multitude that had gathered, and for an hour he stood on the ladder and preached just as he might have done had he been in his own church. He concluded by repeating the words of the Nunc Dimittis. After the cloth was placed over his eyes, he raised it for a moment and cried: "The Covenants! The Covenants shall yet be Scotland's reviving!" His head was impaled over the Nether Bow gateway, the estates to which he was heir were confiscated and his family arms destroyed.

James Guthrie was a preacher of unusual power, and a fearless defender of the doctrines that he considered Scriptural. On one occasion he was invited to preach before Parliament, and twice did he preach before the Parliamentary Commission. He might have saved his life had he acknowledged an earthly king as head of the Kirk, but he was convinced that only the spiritual Headship of the Saviour can be recognized; and for this belief he gave his life.

George Gillespie (1613-1648)

George Gillespie was born in 1613 at Kirkcaldy, where his father was a clergyman. He entered St. Andrews University at an early age, and is said to have been graduated at 16 years of age. After serving as tutor and private chaplain to two families of the gentry, he was ordained in 1638 by the presbytery of Kirkcaldy, and appointed to Wemyss,

Fifeshire. In 1642 he was translated to Greyfriars Church, Edinburgh. From 1643 to 1647 he attended the Westminster Assembly in London as commissioner. In 1647 he was called to the High Church, Edinburgh. He was made Moderator in 1648, and died the same year. A tombstone, with a Latin inscription recounting his virtues, was ordered broken at the market cross by the public hangman at the time of the Restoration.

George Gillespie is said by many to have been one of Edinburgh's most distinguished preachers. He is said to have declared the Word of God fearlessly in those days of distress. It is difficult to form an estimate of his preaching, for no authentic sermons have survived. In his day it was a common custom to take down sermons of eminent preachers in shorthand, and when transcribed into English these sermons were often largely in the language of the man or woman who took them down. Gillespie prepared a volume of sermons for publication, but he died at 35, before his book was ready for the publisher. His contemporaries bear witness to the excellency of his preaching, and accept him as one of the great preachers of that time.

Between 1637 and 1648 George Gillespie published a number of separate works. These were collected by William Hetherington, the church historian, and published as *The Theological Works of George Gillespie*, 2 volumes (1844-46). A volume, *Sermons of George Gillespie*, appeared in 1844. A biography, *The Life and Writings of George Gillespie*, by William Hetherington, appeared with the *Theological Works*.

James Sharp (1618-1679)

James Sharp, whose ambition caused him to renounce his early religious convictions and to turn against his friends, is worthy of mention, for in his earlier ministry he gained a certain amount of recognition as a preacher. He was born in Banff castle in 1618. He was graduated from King's College, Aberdeen, in 1637; and in 1640 he was made regent and professor of philosophy in St. Leonard's College, St. Andrews. In 1648, having completed his theological studies, he was ordained and given Crail church, Fifeshire. He was a young man of unusual promise, and was looked upon as a preacher of ability, because he was proposed, in 1650, for one of the churches in Edinburgh. The invasion of Cromwell and his army prevented this, however. In 1651 Sharp was captured by Cromwell, and imprisoned for two years in the Tower.

In 1657 Sharp was looked upon as one of the leaders of the Kirk, and he was selected to go before Cromwell and plead the cause of the Scottish Kirk. In 1660 he was sent to present the cause of the Kirk to Charles II, who was still in Breda at the time. His selection for these most important missions is an indication of the confidence that the Scottish religious leaders placed in him.

Just what happened to cause Sharp, then 42 years of age, to turn against all his associates may never be known. It is supposed that Charles II, or else the influential Earl of Clarendon, discovered that Sharp was not proof against bribery, and that the offer of an archbishopric was made to him, under condition that he would betray his friends. This is the view usually taken by Scottish writers. Anglicans have taken the view that Sharp was not a traitor, but sought to heal the discordant factions in the Kirk of Scotland.

He returned to Scotland, and appeared, at least, to champion the cause of the presbytery, but all the while it appears that he was in secret communication with Charles and the English bishops. In 1661 the rule of bishops was reinstated in Scotland, and Sharp was made archbishop of St. Andrews. His ready acceptance was a shock to all his former friends, and the nonchalance with which he gave up his former religious views and accepted those of the episcopate was a matter of grief and amazement to all Scotland, for he had been looked upon as their trusted leader and spokesman. In 1664 the Court of High Commission was revived, and some who continued to resist were tried and put to death. Sharp's supposed part in this persecution led to an uprising of the Covenanters. In 1679, after one unsuccessful attempt on his life, a group of nine men came upon him on Magus Muir, as he was driving in his carriage with his daughter Isabelle, and Sharp was dragged from his carriage and put to death by means of the swords of his executioners. A merciless period of persecution followed, and a number of Scots were put to death. Hackston, thought to be the leader of Sharp's assailants, was executed with sickening barbarity, and his heart cut out before he was yet dead, and exhibited to the multitude with the words, "Behold the heart of a traitor."

That Sharp, in his parochial days, was a persuasive preacher none can deny. It is most unfortunate that he was an opportunist, and when he observed the way in which things were drifting, he had little difficulty in setting aside his former religious convictions, and forsaking the friends who had looked upon him as a trusted leader. Biographies of James Sharp include David Simson, *A True and Impartial Account of Mr. James Sharp* (1719); *Life of James Sharp, Archbishop of St. Andrews* (1678); Thos Stephen, *Life and Times of Archbishop Sharp* (1839); and references to Sharp in the *Lauderdale Papers,* 1 and 5 (1884-85).

James Durham (1622-1658)

James Durham was born at Easter Powrie, Forfarshire, in 1622. Like two or three other clergymen of his time, he came of a family of landed proprietors. After his education at St. Andrews he lived for a time at the family estate. At the time of the Civil War he became a captain in the forces. On one occasion he went with his wife and her mother to a church service at Queensferry, where the clergyman, Mr. Melvin, expounded 1 Peter 2, 7, "Unto you that believe He is precious." Captain Durham was deeply moved, and he attended Holy Communion that day. On the evening before a battle, he gathered the men of his command and led them in a religious service. It so happened that David Dickson was riding by. He paused and listened, and so impressed was he that he urged Captain Durham to devote his life to the Kirk. Durham entered Glasgow University, and upon completing his studies in 1647, he was licensed to preach, and was given a congregation in Glasgow.

In 1650, at the age of 28, he became professor of theology at Glasgow University, succeeding David Dickson,

2,69 02

who had been called to Edinburgh. About the same time
he became a chaplain to the King. Later he became pastor
of the Inner High Church of Glasgow. Andrew Gray, at that
time, was drawing great congregations at the Outer High
Church in the same city. On one occasion so great was the
congregation at Gray's church that many of them, unable to
find standing room, went to the church of which James Durham was pastor. It so happened that he preached from
St. Matt. 22, 5 that day: "But they made light of it, and
went their ways." It was a memorable sermon for all who
heard it, and its results were apparent for a long time.

Dr. Blaikie tells us that we have ample records of the
preaching of James Durham. Of his sermons Prof. Blaikie
says: "If we were to characterize them in a single sentence,
we should say that the one theme which predominates in
them all is Jesus Christ and Him crucified. His whole
ministry was directed to the object which had been so suc-
cessfully accomplished in his own history by Mr. Melvin of
Queensferry — commending Christ. His sermons for the
most part are long, with little sparkle or play of genius,
yet they were immensely relished, and very useful. They
are constructed on a plan which had now become the ordinary method in Scotland — some observations to begin with,
then a statement and enforcement of the doctrines in the
text, and in connection with each doctrine, a series of uses,
or practical applications. Undoubtedly this method, cum-
brous though it was, conduced materially to fulness and
explicitness in the handling of subjects."[29]

Dr. Blaikie declares that the attractiveness of Durham's
preaching lay not in any remarkable faculty of illustration,
nor in poetic or imaginative touches. He was too serious
a man for that. Blaikie compares the poetic sparkle and the
gushes of emotion of St. Bernard with the plain, conversational style of James Durham, his short sentences, his
intensity and his deep spiritual solemnity.

James Durham died at the age of 36, and as he lay
dying he asked John Carstares, his co-pastor, whether he

---

[29]. W. G. Blaikie, *The Preachers of Scotland* (Edinburgh, 1888),
p. 131.

dare lay all his hope of salvation on a single verse: "Him that cometh to Me I will in no wise cast out." Then he said quietly, "He is come!"

Hugh Binning (1627-1653)

Hugh Binning was born at Dalvenan, Ayrshire, in 1627. His father was a landed proprietor. He entered Glasgow University before the age of 14, and he took his Master's degree before he was 19 years old. In 1645 he began the study of theology. Two years later, upon the urgent request of friends, he allowed his name to be proposed as candidate for professor of theology at Glasgow. Other men, of wider experience, were candidates. A disputation was arranged, and Binning was found so well qualified that the man whom many seemed to think the most eminently qualified, withdrew his name in Hugh Binning's favor. Professor Binning served with distinction for three years. He simplified the method of teaching philosophy, freeing it from the old method of the scholastics, and laid the foundation for the modern method of approach. Meanwhile, having completed his theological course, he was licensed to preach in 1649.

In 1650 he was ordained and given Govan parish, near Glasgow. In 1651, when Cromwell came with his army, he called all the Glasgow clergy before him and was astonished at the learning and wisdom of Binning. Hugh Binning served Govan Church for but three years, for he died in 1653, when not yet 27 years of age. On his deathbed he declared that he "did value more one line of the Word of God than all the human learning in the world."[30]

Binning was an exceptional preacher, and many bear witness to the high character of his sermons. So devoted was he to his calling that he attended a week-day service on his wedding day. The man who was to have preached was detained, and Binning was urged to take his place. He did so, preaching without preparation, but so exceptional was the sermon that people were led to declare that Hugh Bin-

[30]. R. Wodrow, *Analecta*, vol. 3, p. 40.

ning, without preparation, was more excellent than any man of his day with careful preparation.

Binning set aside the traditional homiletics of his day, with its usual method of doctrines, reasons and uses, each one carried out into a multitude of divisions and subdivisions. He preached in clear, practical English, and sometimes did not so much as announce his main divisions. However, as he lay dying, he lamented this fact bitterly, "that his manner of preaching was a matter of greife to him: that his leaving off the ordinary method of doctrine and use, he feared, had made his doctrine useless to the people,"[31] accustomed as they were to the traditional form of sermon construction. His townspeople thought differently, for after his death they erected a monument to him, which contains a Latin inscription with a superlative tribute to his learning and eloquence.

"While he lived, he was highly valued and esteemed, having been a successful instrument of saving himself and them that heard him; of turning sinners unto righteousness, and of perfecting the saints; and died much lamented by all good people who had an opportunity of knowing him. He was a man of singular piety, of an humble, meek, and peaceful disposition, and a judicious and lively preacher. He was justly accounted a prodigy for his natural talents, his great proficiency in human learning, and an extensive knowledge of divinity; but he was too shining a light to shine long, burning so intensely that he was soon extinguished."[32]

Among the published writings of Hugh Binning were: *The Sinner's Sanctuary* (1670), which includes 40 sermons on Roman's 8; *Common Principles of the Christian Religion* (1672), and *Heart Humiliation* (1676). His collected works were first published in 1735, reprinted in 1768 and issued in a three-volume edition in 1839.

Andrew Gray (1633-1656)

Andrew Gray was born in Edinburgh in 1633, the son of Sir William Gray, bart., and a brother of the first Lord

---

[31]. R. Wodrow, *Analecta*, vol. 3, p. 438.
[32]. John Howie, *Scots Worthies* (ed. New York, 1853), p. 378.

Gray. When a boy he was going from Edinburgh to Leith, and a beggar stopped him on the way. Pausing to converse with the beggar, he found that the unfortunate man was a devout Christian who had met with misfortune, but had not lost his faith, and was ready to praise the Saviour for His gift of Redemption to mankind, which neither the loss of family nor of fortune could take away from him. Andrew Gray went on his way deeply moved by the beggar's cheerful faith. He recalled the destitution of this man, who had seen much happier days insofar as his outward lot was concerned, and yet who had expressed such sincere gratitude for the mercies of Jesus Christ, which neither persecution, nor loss of home and earthly goods could take away from him. "Who am I?" Gray asked himself, "well-born, wealthy, and well supplied with every comfort of life, with never a real sorrow to cast its shadow over me; and yet I have never taken the time to pause and acknowledge with thankfulness the spiritual blessings that so far surpass all things. Does this wretched man, in his destitution and misery find cause for thanks, which I have failed to render my Lord?"

Gray entered St. Andrews and was graduated in 1651, and from there he went to Edinburgh University. He was licensed to preach in 1653 and ordained the same year as pastor of Outer High Church in Glasgow. He was but 21 years of age at the time, but his marvellous preaching drew such congregations as the Outer High had never known. His eloquent descriptions of the mercies of God through Jesus Christ, and the joys that He offered the sinner who would turn from his evil ways to the Cross, drew people from Edinburgh, Stirling and many other places, who journeyed to Glasgow to hear the famous young man. Often the church and the churchyard were so densely thronged with people that they were sent in numbers to the Inner High Kirk, and the other churches of Glasgow.

It seems almost impossible that the remarkable career of this young man, whom the Scots considered "an angel come down from Heaven," was confined to three years. He died in 1656 when but 23 years of age, one of the most famous preachers of his day.

Many people, including his wife, formed the habit of taking down his sermons in shorthand — a custom widely popular in those covenanting days. A volume of these ser- mons, as recorded by his wife, was published shortly after his death. His style is somewhat rhetorical, and shows the fire of an exuberant youth. His preaching was not only fervent, reminding one somewhat of the great Summerfield, but he had a gift far beyond most men of appealing in a powerful way to the consciences of his hearers. Few men have excelled him in spiritual earnestness, and the sensa- tion that he created at the time can be compared to that of Summerfield.

Did the preaching of these men prove fruitful? In seeking an answer to this question it is necessary to consider well the authorities whom we may consult. They differ in their answers. James Kirkton's words are often quoted. In his *History of the Church of Scotland from the Restoration to the Year 1678* he goes so far as to declare: "Every parish had a minister, every village had a school, every family almost had a Bible; yea, in most of the country all the chil- dren at school could read the Scriptures, and were provided with Bibles either by their parents or ministers. Every minister was a very full professor of the Reformed religion, according to the large Confession of Faith framed at West- minster. None of them might be scandalous in their con- versation, or negligent in their office, so long as a presbytery stood. I have lived many years in a parish where I never heard an oath; and you might have ridden many miles before you heard any. Also you could not, for a great part of the country, have lodged in a family where the Lord was not worshipped by reading, singing, and public prayer. Nobody complained more of our church-government than our tavern- ers, whose ordinary lamentation was that their trade was broke, people were become so sober." [33]

Other writers, such as Bishop Burnet, can see little good in the preaching of the covenanting period. Dr. W. G. Blaikie, of the theological department of New College, Edin-

---

[33]. John Brown (Whitburn), *Gospel Truth*, p. 3, quoted by W. G. Blaikie.

burgh, calls attention to a "little cloud like a man's hand that next century darkened the horizon." As early as 1645 or 1650 the General Assembly in Scotland spoke of clergymen "who labour not to set forth the excellency of Christ in His person, offices and the unsearchable riches of His grace; the new covenant, and the way of living by faith in Him; not making this the main and chief theme of their preaching, as did the Apostles." Even while the Covenanters were delivering their sturdy evangelical sermons, the devil was not idle. He tempted other men to substitute feeble moralizing for evangelical truth. Such preachers, to quote Dr. Blaikie, "like the dog in the fable, dropped their piece of bread into the water in favour of a shadow." [34] Thus it has been throughout the history of preaching. Evangelical preaching leads to a spiritual awakening, but such is the perversity of man's sinful heart that even before this awakening has reached its full growth, signs begin to appear of the period of decline that is to follow it.

---

[34]. W. G. Blaikie, *The Preachers of Scotland* (Edinburgh, 1888), p. 151.

CHAPTER IV

THE FIELD PREACHERS

THE FREEDOM of the Scottish Kirk from State interference was not to be won without a struggle and without much bloodshed. The small but powerful prelatic faction composed of the king and his followers were eager to force prelacy upon the people. A turn in politics had given Scotland a prelatic Parliament. James Sharp, once a friend of the presbytery group, allowed himself to be appointed archbishop of St. Andrews in 1661 A. D. Episcopacy was once more forced upon a protesting Scotland. In 1662 the infamous Glasgow Act was passed. By its terms all clergymen, under penalty of expulsion, were ordered to secure the presentation of their patron and the collation of their local bishop. This act restored patronage, an abuse by which the king, a noble or a wealthy landlord was given the right to appoint a pastor where a vacancy had occurred, and to settle him even against the protest of the entire congregation. It was a plain violation of the statute which guaranteed to every congregation the right to call the pastor of their own choice. The Glasgow Act restored prelacy, and every pastor was ordered to submit to the rule of his bishop.

A few of the more timid among the clergy accepted the terms of the Act, but some 400 pastors who refused were driven from their congregations, and royal troops were sent to enforce this order. Prelatic curates, brought from afar, were appointed to the vacant congregations; and too often such men were not qualified to fill the positions to which they had been appointed.

Ejected from their own pulpits, the 400 clergymen refused to be silenced. They began to preach in barns, in private homes, and in the open fields when barns and houses became too small to accommodate the growing congregations. The king was resolved to exterminate this sort of nonconformity at any cost, and royal troops were sent to break up any such services. Acts were passed by a packed Parliament declaring that any service not held within the walls of the parish kirk was to be looked upon as a conventicle, and declared illegal. Pastors who conducted such conventicles in churchyards, private homes, barns or open fields, were to be arrested, and people who attended such services were to be fined.

Driven from the barns and open fields, the people had to seek other places in which to hear the Word of God. Fortunately the terrain of Scotland furnishes many admirable places for such services; and in the wild moors, or in a deep glen, or beneath some giant crag of rock, large congregations assembled. In a single day 16,000 people took part in three such outdoor services in Fife alone. The pastors who preached on moor and in lonely glen were arrested and imprisoned, or else forced to flee by night from place to place, hiding in barns or in rocky mountain caves. Indulgences and comfortable livings were offered to all pastors who would submit to the king and his bishops, but very few of the clergy yielded.

There were many eminent field-preachers in those unhappy days. Among the most eminent of them might be mentioned James Guthrie, Hugh McCail, Donald Cargill, Alexander Peden, John Welsh of Irongray, Gabriel Semple, John Blackader, Richard Cameron and James Renwick. In the 28 years of persecution, many of these men were murdered. James Guthrie was executed in 1661 for no cause other than preaching in the open air. The Marquis of Argyle was executed for defending the field-preachers. Hugh McCail, a young pastor, was put to death with torture in 1666. Donald Cargill was beheaded in 1681. John Brown, a layman of Priesthill, was murdered by Claverhouse and his soldiers, while Brown's helpless wife and children looked on. Two women were bound and slowly drowned in the rising tide at Wigtown. Thousands of people who attended the field-services were crowded into the holds of ships and sold into slavery in distant lands. With such outrages as this, one is not surprised that there were uprisings here and there, and that battles were fought for religious freedom at Rullion Green, at Drumclog and at Bothwell Brig.

The tyrant James II fled in 1688, and William of Orange came to take his place. Prelacy was overthrown and government by the presbytery restored in 1690. Only 90 of the 400 ejected clergymen had survived these years of persecution, and these men were allowed to return to their congregations. The prelatic curates were driven out. In view of the cruel persecution suffered by the Scottish people, it is to their credit that these curates who had been forced upon them, were permitted to depart peacefully.

The Covenanters were human beings, and they were not without their faults. After a time a legalistic spirit appeared in a few places, and the acceptance of the principles of the Covenanters was looked upon almost as a test of one's Christianity. These principles at times became "instruments of coercion," and in some cases attempts were made to force the covenants upon others. Such instances were the exceptions, however; and through all these trying years the more thoughtful preachers realized this danger, and voices were raised against such a spirit. There were men, now and then, who indulged in self-pity and looked upon themselves as martyrs to a noble cause, and who insisted that they would count it a privilege to die on the gallows for the sake of their convictions. Such an attitude is common enough in times of persecution, and when we read of the Covenanters and the field-preachers standing upon the scaffold and declaring for the space of an hour to the multitude that it is a great joy to suffer such a death, are we justified in condemning such men as hypocrites? More often than not it is the dying testimony of a courageous hero, and not merely the defiant words of a helpless man.

As one reads the sermons that have come down to us from those field-preachers, one is surprised to observe that there are fewer references to personal sufferings than might be expected. These sermons often show a surprising indifference to the cruelties of the time. Frequently enough these men, who preached with armed sentries standing watch, paid no heed to the dangers that lurked near them, but devoted their sermons to an exposition of sin and grace with a calmness that suggests the peace of some ivy-covered parish kirk on the side of a pleasant brae. There are references at times to the tragic scenes at Ayrsmoss, the Pentlands, Drumclog and Bothwell Bridge, but much more often do we find simple, normal, evangelical sermons in which man's sinful nature and the Saviour's cleansing blood are stressed. Man's lost estate, his complete helplessness, the active obedience of the Saviour, His saving grace, the divine plan of Redemption, the work and witness of the Holy Ghost and the fact that Jesus Christ is the supreme Head of the Church — these were the things that the field-preachers stressed. As one visits the mountains and the remote glens of Scotland today, he realizes that those very crags of rock yonder have echoed the words of evangelical truth, and that these same valleys once formed refuges for great gatherings of people who dared not meet for worship in their own churches.

The sermons of the field-preachers were often from one to two hours in length, and they would be considered tedious today, with their multiplicity of divisions and sub-divisions, but there is always a warmth, a wealth of evangelical teaching, and an urgency of appeal to the consciences of men. The Convenanters and the field-preachers were not satisfied with a mere academic statement of evangelical principles. They sought action on the part of their hearers. The Scots have, in their better eras of preaching, excelled in this respect, and not often have they done it crudely. Their leading preachers, both in Covenanting days and in later years, have had the gift of urging their hearers to action; and they have possessed the skill to do this in a dignified, powerful manner. A field-preacher in the latter part of the seventeenth century was able to make his hearers realize the danger of substituting earthly kings and prelates for Christ the King, and the equally great danger of becoming satisfied with Christ the King, rather than Christ the Saviour.

Did their preaching bear fruit? Those Covenanters and field-preachers built up within the Scottish people a fierce love of religious freedom. The sacrifice that their descendants were willing to make in the year 1843, the readiness with which the Deed of Demission was signed, the appalling hardships of their Moffats and their Livingstones in foreign lands and their MacColls, their Taskers and their Howies in the Wynds of Glasgow and the West Port of Edinburgh, are but evidences of the heroic spirit that was the heritage of the descendants of those people who sang their metrical Psalms on the bleak moors and in the rocky glens.

One cannot endorse the entire theological system of the Covenanters and the field-preachers. There were men among them who preached reprobation as well as justification, and who limited the benefits of our Lord's righteousness and blood to those elected from eternity by a sovereign decree of God. There were men who looked upon divine grace as irresistible, and others who reveal a complete lack of understanding in regard to the Means of Grace. In later years some of these extreme views were modified, and no longer does the average Scotsman declare that the Atonement is limited, and that an arbitrary number of men are lost forever by a sovereign decree of God. While the field-preachers laid great emphasis upon the fact that the conversion and salvation of the sinner is due solely to the grace of God and the righteousness and blood of Christ, yet one wishes that they might have laid equal stress upon the fact that the eternal death of the unbeliever is due solely to his own sin and unbelief.

In the days when Erastianism was the fashion, and rule by a mitered bishop looked upon as the only form of religious government that was pleasing to the Lord, historians used to amuse themselves by reviling the Covenanters. They described them as narrow, bigoted, unreasonable and always ready to attach undue importance to their particular conception of ecclesiastical government. In this respect certain eminent historians have been unfair. The Covenanter believed that an important doctrinal principle was in danger. The men who succeeded one another as rulers of Scotland attempted to make themselves the supreme head of the Church — hence the great emphasis laid by the Covenanters upon the Headship of Jesus Christ. The Covenanters erred when they believed that the Saviour could be made King merely by enacting civil laws recognizing His sovereignty. On the other hand they were quite right in opposing every effort to have an earthly king recognized as the supreme head of the Kirk by the same process of law, for such a kingship is a threat to spiritual liberty. While one must reject certain errors that are inexcusable in the light of

God's inspired Word, yet one must give the old heroes of the covenant credit for their share in establishing the principle of religious freedom, for no king, no Parliament and no house of bishops has the right to deprive the Christian congregation of its spiritual privileges.

Dr. W. M. Taylor, a prominent New York clergyman and author, has made a careful study of the times of the Covenanters and the field-preachers. Those days of persecution and wholesale murder were not favorable to the publication of sermons, yet more material has been preserved than one would suspect, and certainly enough by which to form an estimate of the preaching of what the Scots call the "killing times." Dr. Taylor says of the persecuted preachers: "The great object of all their sermons was the presentation of Jesus Christ and Him crucified. Nothing can exceed the pathos with which they besought their hearers to be reconciled to God and to endure patiently His cause."[1] Again the same writer says: "Then, in the midst of all, was evermore Jesus on the cross. To Him these preachers pointed their hearers; from Him they drew their inspiration; and out of love to Him they carried on the struggle in which they were engaged. 'Ye are bought with a price, be not ye therefore the bond-servants of men'; that was the principle by which they were actuated. They sought independence from men, that they might keep themselves entirely for Christ. This was what they meant by their enforcement of the 'Headship of Christ'; and they contended for Christ's crown because they felt that they had been purchased on Christ's cross. We do not claim for them the highest scholarship, the profoundest thought, the most polished style, or the finest eloquence, but we do claim for them that they preached Christ most effectively, and that they drew for themselves, and exhorted all their hearers to draw, their motives for their daily conduct from the cross of their Redeemer; and to all their detractors they might have said with Paul, 'From henceforth let no man trouble us, for we bear in our bodies the marks of our Lord Jesus'."[2]

---

[1]. W. M. Taylor, The Scottish Pulpit (New York, 1887), p. 140.
[2]. Ibid., pp. 145-146.

In the account of William Guthrie, mention is made of a curious custom that arose about the middle of the seventeenth century. Not only did people come in great numbers to hear the field preachers, but they came prepared to take down their sermons in shorthand. The Scottish people, many of whom were Covenanters, when driven from their kirks, resorted to the glens and the open moors. Even some who had been indifferent to church attendance in peaceful times seemed to long for the kirk, now that its doors were closed against them.

Writers of the time have described the scene. On some wild moor, far from the village, with the purple and the white heather growing almost knee-deep, the great congregation would assemble, often to the number of 10,000 or more. Armed sentries were posted at a distance to watch for the King's dragoons. Sometimes one man preached, more often there were two or three sermons.

A strange mania for studying shorthand took possession of the people, and even in winter many could be seen with their inkhorns and their stubby quill pens, taking down every word of the sermon. This mania had a curious and often a permanent result. Books of sermons by eminent preachers began to appear, and enjoyed a wide circulation. The language was often faulty, for the men who recorded the sermons often transcribed them into inelegant English. The Scottish preachers were forceful, at times quaint, but the printed books of what purported to be their sermons, were often expressed in what Blaikie calls "very flat English."

The libraries of Edinburgh, and other large cities, contain old books of sermons by many of the famous preachers of the covenanting days. Often one wonders at their inferiority both in clearness of doctrine and in well-chosen English. One need only remember that many such books were transcribed by men of varying degrees of talent, from their own shorthand notes, and without the approval of the preacher. These men did it, more often than not, in good faith, eager to preserve the words of their favorite preachers for their children. Thus it was that such eminent men as, for example, William Guthrie, were often obliged in self-defense to publish volumes of authentic sermons, expressed in the careful language in which they had been prepared. In England George Whitefield suffered at the hands of just such well-meaning friends, who recorded his sermons in shorthand, but in their own way.

Writers have mentioned another type of sermon enthusiast who is equally annoying to the Scotsman, namely the "Anglifying editors," as they have been termed, who sought to tone down the vigorous eloquence of the typical Scottish preacher of the covenanting days, and express it in the quiet, polished English so popular south of the River Tweed, in the generations that followed. Thus has the stirring rhetoric of more than one noted Scottish divine become quiet and genteel, and the sturdiness of his doctrine reduced to mere, polite truisms.

Somebody, somewhere, has compared the vigor of the old Scots preaching to an ancient parish church in its "unrestored" condition; with its honest walls of genuine stone, and its ceiling of ancient, hand-hewn oaken timbers. The "edited" sermons of the old Covenanters have been compared to the same ancient kirk, swept and garnished of all things genuine, its side walls covered with stucco without and with white gypsum plaster within, its ceiling timbers of old oak concealed with white plaster, its ancient carved pulpit gone, and one of cheap yellow deal in its place, and a spun brass lectern of the commericial sort, in a conspicuous place. Thus have many of the old churches suffered at the hands of misguided restorers, and the sermons of the men who preached in them toned down in doctrine and in language, to suit the taste of a more elegant generation.

Nevertheless, the popularity of preaching in the covenanting days is remarkable. Somewhat the same thing is to be found a little later in England and Wales, but there the cause was different. In the latter countries the preachers were not inhibited, nor were the people denied the right to worship in their own church. In England and Wales, the polite, non-committal nature of much of the preaching caused people to flock to hear other men who declared the Word of God with great spiritual fervor.

The persecution of the Scottish people at the hands of the tyrannical House of Stuart was a blessing in one way, for it caused many of the lukewarm to appreciate their church, and it deepened the religious fervor of the faithful. Many fine preachers of the time went to the scaffold because of their refusal to conform to the wishes of a renegade Scotsman who had become King, and his unworthy progeny; but as in early days, the blood of these martyrs became the life-blood of the Kirk. Seldom has religious zeal in Scotland burned so brightly as in those unhappy days of persecution and death.

Donald Cargill (1610-1681)

Donald Cargill was born in Rattray in 1610. He was educated at Aberdeen and at St. Andrews University. In 1650 he became pastor of Barony Church, Glasgow, but in 1661 when efforts were being made by King Charles II to compel Scotland to accept the episcopacy, Cargill refused to recognize the authority of the bishops. In 1662 he was ordered banished, but remained as a field-preacher. In 1679 he joined Richard Cameron, Thomas Douglas and their followers, and became one of the leaders of the Cameronians in their struggle against the prelacy.

After the defeat of Bothwell Bridge, he fled to Holland for a time, but returned in 1680, and helped draw up the Sanquhar Declaration, which denounced the despotism of Charles II, and rejected his efforts to rule the Scottish Kirk. When Richard Cameron was slain at Ayrsmoss, in 1680, Cargill was for a short time the leader of the Cameronians. At one of his field services he publicly excommunicated the King and his nobles. For this he was hunted down by the royal troops, captured in 1681, tried at Edinburgh, and beheaded.

Donald Cargill was a courageous preacher, both in his parochial days, and in the times of persecution when he was compelled to meet his congregations in the glens, and remind them that the Lord Jesus is still King of the Church. Deep in those wooded glens, and sometimes in the fields, Cargill, Cameron, Renwick, Peden and other men met the congregations that assembled in secluded places, always fearful lest the King's soldiers might discover them and slay them because of their efforts to keep the Kirk free from royal domination.

Laws were passed requiring all Scottish people to worship in their parish churches. The roll was called at the close of service, and all who were not present were dealt with severely. Soldiers were billeted in their homes, their cattle were taken from them, ruinous fines were imposed upon them, and people were turned out of their homes, to wander throughout the country as displaced persons. The pulpits of the 400 "outed" clergymen were filled with men who were often poorly trained and unfit, lacking in evangelical fervor, and whose only qualification was their readiness to submit to the wishes of the King and his tyrannical efforts to establish church union.

Donald Cargill and many others of his kind endured persecution and often death, rather than yield to the interference of the crown in the spiritual affairs of their Kirk. In those sequestered glens, with sentinels posted to warn them of danger, they preached the Law and they preached Christ crucified; and with such good effect that there are instances where the King's spies, concealed in the congregation, remained to confess their sins and seek forgiveness. Sketches of the life of Donald Cargill are to be found in R. Wodrow's *History of the Sufferings of the Church of Scotland* (1721-22), and in John Howie's *Scots Worthies* (1774).

William Guthrie (1620-1665)

William Guthrie was born in 1620 in Pitfrothy, Forfarshire. His father was a landed proprietor, and of his eight children, four became clergymen. William Guthrie was a kinsman of James Guthrie, the Covenanter, who was hanged because of his religious views. William Guthrie was graduated from St. Andrews University in 1638. He studied theology with Samuel Rutherfurd and James Guthrie, the latter his uncle. He was licensed in 1642, and deeded his estate to a brother so as to give his time exclusively to the Kirk. After serving for a year or so as tutor, he was ordained in 1644 and given the new parish of Fenwick, in Ayrshire.

When he came to Fenwick, Guthrie found the people not only unchurched, but most of them indifferent, and even hostile, to all religion. When many of them would not admit him to their homes, the intrepid young missionary resorted to strategem. Disguising himself as a tourist, and at other times as a country yokel, he would gain admittance to the cottages of the people. He was a very friendly man, and possessed of rare humor. After entertaining the family for an evening with interesting conversation, he would always guide the conversation into serious channels, and end by urging the people to attend church.

Again he would dress informally, and with rod and creel he would come upon a group of fishermen. Before the afternoon was over, he would turn the fishing party into a church service and preach a sermon in which the terrors of the Law and the promises of the Gospel were employed with telling effect. Many a sermon was preached on the banks of a loch or a river. In his 20 years in office, he confirmed thousands of people. His first sermons were preached while the new church was under construction, within the roofless walls of an unfinished building. Within a short time the church could not hold the large congregations that were attracted by his preaching. He visited the curling matches in winter, and often on the ice he would preach to the people. He was a fascinating conversationalist, and skilled at turning the discussion into useful, spiritual directions. Wodrow compares him to Dickson of Irvine, and says that Guthrie equalled, if not excelled him as a preacher.

In 1664, after having built up a large, flourishing congregation, Guthrie was deposed from office by the archbishop of Glasgow, because of adhering to the covenants. His cousin James Guthrie was hanged for the same reason.

In the covenanting days, according to Dr. Blaikie and others,[3] so great was the popular interest in preaching that

---

[3]. W. G. Blaikie, *The Preachers of Scotland* (Edinburgh, 1888), p. 126.

many people learned shorthand in order to be able to take down sermons. At a great outdoor service, with thousands gathered on a heathery moor, many came with inkhorn suspended from their necks, quill pen and parchment. Books of sermons bearing William Guthrie's name appeared, some of them in the language of the man who had recorded them. This led Guthrie to issue a book, *The Christian's Great Interest,* in which were a collection of his sermons as he had preached them. The book was so popular that it was translated into several foreign languages. John Owen, the famous English preacher, declared that this book has more theology in it than all the folios that Owen himself had written. William Guthrie died in 1665, at the age of 45. The Wodrow Society's *Select Biographies* has a memoir.

John Blackader (c. 1623-1686)

John Blackader, a celebrated field-preacher, was born about the year 1623. He was of the ancient house of Blackader of Tulliallan, and was a baron in his own right, although he never made use of the title. After his classical and theological studies, he was ordained in 1653 and became pastor of Troqueer parish, near Dumfries. Here, for nine years, he did a most remarkable work. He found the parish in a deplorable condition. Religious training had been neglected, and the people lived in a rough, ungodly manner. His first work was to indoctrinate the people. By means of Sunday sermons on the fundamental teachings of Christianity, and weekday lectures, he instructed the people. So well were these efforts received that people began to come from neighboring parishes to hear his sermons and attend his instruction periods during the week. Twice a year he conducted catechizations for old and young, and these were attended by large gatherings. He invited John Welsh of Irongray, and Mr. Johnstone of Lochrutton, and these men gave valuable assistance, and he in turn assisted them. A religious awakening was the result. People began to crowd their churches, and the Communion seasons drew multitudes, and lasted for several days. The most conspicuous change was in Mr. Blackader's own parish of Troqueer. At the end of two years the rough, profane, hard-drinking people became devoted church members, and there was hardly a more orderly community in all Scotland.

John Blackader was not permitted to remain in Troqueer, for in 1662 he was ejected by the notorious Glasgow Act. The Dumfries Presbytery protested against the ejection of a number of pastors, but this served no purpose other than to bring 50 troopers to Dumfries. The protesting clergymen were marched to Edinburgh, brought before the courts, but eventually set free. Blackader was allowed to return to his congregation, but was soon deprived of it by the courts.

In 1662 he lived for a time in Glencairn, a more secluded spot. On one occasion he ventured to return to his congregation to preach and catechize. This reached the ears of the King's men, and Blackader and a dozen other clergymen were forced to flee. After hiding in Edinburgh for a time, he made his way to the west of Scotland and became a field-preacher. His sermons drew enormous congregations.

In 1670 he conducted a conventicle at Beith-hill, to which came thousands of people. Fearing the royal troopers, many of the men came armed. When the troopers arrived, they deemed it prudent not to try to overcome so superior a number of armed men, and many of the troopers remained to listen to Blackader's preaching. This is said to be the first conventicle to which the men came prepared to defend their right of religious freedom. However, Blackader was compelled to flee for his life, first to Edinburgh, and then to Merse. He would not be silenced. He went from place to place, preaching on the moors, in the open fields, in the deep valleys, and again in the shadow of towering rocks. Great congregations assembled to hear him. At one place he preached to several thousand people in an open field, while the prelatic curate in the parish church nearby delivered a sermon to 16 people.

John Blackader was declared an outlaw, and a reward offered for his capture, but he went throughout the south and east of Scotland, always eluding his pursuers. In 1680 he visited Holland, where he preached for four months at Rotterdam. Then he returned to Scotland and continued his field preaching. Illness came upon him, making it difficult for him to preach. Some sort of a minor impediment of speech developed, but this did not diminish his fervor, nor did it diminish the number of people who were attracted whenever he preached.

The royal troops finally captured him in 1681. He was tried and found guilty of preaching at conventicles, of celebrating Holy Communion with the people, and with performing pastoral acts after having been deposed by the courts for nonconformity. On one occasion he had baptized 42 children at a single conventicle, and a day or so later, eleven more. He was sentenced to the dreaded prison on Bass Rock, where he spent the last four years of his life. Lying ill in this dungeon, he petitioned for release, but he was refused. He died in prison in the year 1686.

John Blackader was among the greatest of the field-preachers. "A deep sense of religion was ever present on his mind, and pervaded the whole tenor of his life. His trust in the Divine goodness never forsook him." "Though labouring under a defective utterance, his oratory was of such a powerful and impressive kind that there are well vouched instances of the remarkable success by which it was attended. . . . No district in the Lowlands of his native country was left without proofs of his zeal in the itinerating labours of his ministry."[4]

John Welsh (c. 1624-1681)

John Welsh of Irongray was born probably in 1624. His family was a distinguished one, for his father was Josiah Welsh, his grandfather John Welsh of Ayr and his great-grandfather was John Knox. John Welsh of Irongray was graduated from Glasgow University in 1647. In 1653 he became pastor at Irongray, in Dumfriesshire, but in 1666 he was compelled to flee during the times of trouble following the battle of Pentland. Charged with treason, he went from place to place, becoming one of the first of the field-preachers. In 1667 he preached to great gatherings of

---

4. Hew Scott, *Fasti Ecclesiae Scoticanae*, 7 vols. (Edinburgh, 1915-28), vol. I, p. 604.

people in Clydesdale and Fifeshire. Large rewards were offered for information leading to his arrest, but of all the multitudes who gathered in secluded places to hear him preach, none betrayed his identity.

There is a reference to him in 1669. He was in Edinburgh at that time. Hamilton of Kinkell was in prison, but was allowed an occasional period of liberty, and during one of these brief intervals, he is said to have called upon John Welsh.[5]

Welsh went throughout Fifeshire, Perthshire and Lanarkshire, preaching in the fields to congregations that sometimes numbered 8,000 to 10,000 people. In 1671 he preached in Northumberland. He was at Drumclog and Bothwell Bridge, and in 1679 it became necessary for him to go to London, where he died two years later. He is no doubt the man to whom Wodrow refers as follows: "Mr. Welsh's buriall was the greatest that for many years had been seen at London. That most of the Dissenters changed their text that Sabbath he was burryed, that ther congregations were invited to the buriall, at which ther was a vast number of ministers, persons of fashion, and, if my memory fails me not, some hundreds of coaches."[6]

John Welsh of Irongray was in great request at Communion seasons; and in the days of the field-preachers these were held outdoors, and often lasted for several days. Multitudes came from afar. At Skeochhill there are "Communion stones" that are regarded with veneration, and shown to tourists to this day. It was there that Welsh conducted a memorable Communion service in 1667, when a gathering of that character was perilous. On such occasions he stressed the grace and glory of the Saviour, picturing Him as a great nobleman who prepared a feast for all his tenants and debtors, all of whom owed a debt, and had not wherewith to pay. At the feast the Lord of those servants cast all the debts into the fire, forgiving them all, purely out of grace. So it is, he declared, with Holy Communion.

---

[5]. Wodrow, *Analecta*, vol. 4, p. 12.
[6]. Wodrow, *Analecta*, vol. 4, pp. 12-13.

He who receives in true contrition and faith is as a servant whose debt is cancelled.

John Welsh, like Samuel Rutherford, stressed the attributes and the types of the Saviour. He often spoke eloquently of His three-fold office, Prophet, Priest and King. He believed at times that the Scots were suffering because of their unfaithfulness, since some of them permitted a despotic earthly king to exercise his rule over the Kirk of the Living God, thus displacing from His rightful office as Head of the Kirk the Saviour, to whom alone may the Christian pledge his loyalty in all matters of a spiritual nature.

Henry Erskine (1624-1696)

Henry Erskine, the father of Ebenezer and Ralph Erskine, was born at Dryburgh, Berwickshire, in 1624. He is said to have been one of the youngest of 33 children. After his early education in the grammar school, he attended Edinburgh University. He was ordained in 1649, and became pastor of Cornhill parish, in Northumberland. It was a rough town, and the majority of the people were hostile to religion. As he sat in his study, he could hear them curse him as they passed his house. He was faithful in his preaching and his parish duties, and gradually the attitude of the people changed. In 1662, when he was ejected at the time of the Act of Uniformity, many of the people lamented their loss. Several Scottish noblemen, aware of his worth, offered him generous support on condition that he conform to the State Church. He refused, for he deemed it better to cast himself and his family upon the care of Providence than to live in comfortable circumstances, and yet do that which was contrary to his conscience.[7] There were times when his children were hungry, but Erskine would remind them that "the goodness and mercy of the Lord would follow them all the days of their lives, and that it isn't His way to allow even ane of His wee bairns to suffer want." Then he would take his zither from the shelf, and all would sing their Scottish hymns. On one such occasion

---

7. Donald Fraser, *Life and Diary of Ebenezer Erskine* (Edinburgh, 1831), p. 9.

they were interrupted by a countryman who had come to deliver them a cartload of provisions, the gift of a nobleman who had learned of their needy condition.

In 1663, the year following his ejection from the manse, he visited London in order to make a personal appeal to the King. He met with no success. He returned to Scotland by ship, and on the journey it was necessary for the vessel to put into Harwich for six weeks, because of storms on the North Sea. Henry Erskine preached to the people of Harwich. A boy had discovered that Erskine had spent all of his scanty funds, and when the word was passed about in Harwich, the people of the town presented him with a purse, while the master of the ship would accept nothing for his passage.

Upon his return to Scotland, Erskine and his family went to Dryburgh, where they lived in a cottage owned by his brother. For 18 years he preached in Dryburgh, either in his own house or in the fields. Often his field services were attended by large gatherings of people. In 1682 he was arrested on the charge of keeping conventicles. He was sentenced to Bass Rock, a notorious island prison in the mouth of the Forth estuary, but the sentence was changed to exile. He went to Holland for a time, and upon his return he lived at Parkridge, near Carlisle, then at Monilaws, near Cornhill. There he was arrested again because of his preaching, and imprisoned. In 1688 he went to Chirnside, where he seems to have served a church.

Henry Erskine was an evangelical preacher and a man of persuasiveness, Once he came upon a group of 30 peat diggers, who asked him in a spirit of levity to preach to them. He replied that they were "not in a proper frame of mind to hear a sermon." When they urged him, he finally consented, and so effective was his sermon that eleven of the men confessed their sins and their faith in the Saviour. However, a more illustrious man owes his awakening to the preaching of Henry Erskine, namely Thomas Boston.

Boston says that he was taken by his father, in the year 1687, to hear Erskine preach. "There I heard the worthy Mr. Henry Erskine, minister of Cornhill before the Restoration; by whose means it pleased the Lord to awaken me, and bring me under exercise about my soul's state; being then going in the twelfth year of my age. Two of Mr. Erskine's first texts were, John 1, 29, 'Behold the Lamb of God, that taketh away the sin of the world'; and Mat. 3, 7, 'O generation of vipers, who hath warned you to flee from the wrath to come?' By these, I judge, God spoke to me. My lost state by nature, and my absolute need of Christ, being thus discovered to me, I was set to pray in earnest. I also carefully attended, for ordinary, the preaching of the Word at Rivelaw, where Mr. Erskine had his meeting-house, about four miles from Dunse."[8]

Alexander Peden (c. 1626-1686)

One of the field-preachers, whose sermons attracted great congregations to the secluded glens, was Alexander Peden. He was born in Auchincloich, Ayrshire, about the year 1626. After attending Glasgow University he was evidently engaged for a time in teaching. In 1660 he was ordained and given the parish of New Luce, Galloway. In 1663, shortly after the Glasgow Act was passed, ejecting all clergymen who would not recognize the authority of the bishops, he was deprived of his parish. He was given an opportunity to remain, under condition that he make his submission to the bishop, but he refused on the grounds of conscience.

Thereafter he was one of the field-preachers, and toward the end of his life he was forced to live in a cave in a secluded place. As a preacher he attracted many because of the singularly spiritual tone of his sermons, and the firmness of his faith in the promises of the Saviour to protect His followers to the end. Portions of some of his sermons have been preserved. Dr. Taylor gives us the following example:

"Now, sirs, what is it that has carried through the sufferers for Christ these twenty years in Scotland? It is 'the fellowship of His sufferings.' It is the filling up of His sufferings according to the ancient decree of Heaven. For my part, I seek no more if He bids me go. He bade many,

---

[8]. D. Fraser, *Op. cit.*, pp. 23-24.

from 1660 to the year of Pentland, go forth to scaffolds and gibbets for Him, and they sought no more but His commission; they went, and He carried them through.

"Then, in 1666, at Pentland, He bade so many go to the fields and die for Him, and so many to scaffolds and lay down their lives for Him; they sought no more but His commission; they went, and He carried them well through. Again, in 1679, at Bothwell, He bade so many to go to the fields and scaffolds to die for Him; they sought no more but His commission; they went, and He carried them through. He bade so many go to the seas, and be meat for the fishes for Him; they sought no more but His commission; they went, and He carried them well through. And afterward, in 1680, at Airdsmoss, He bade so many go to the fields and scaffolds for Him; they sought no more but His commission and went, and He carried them well through.

"This cup of suffering hath come all the way down from Abel to this year 1682 in Scotland. Our Lord hath held this cup to all the martyrs' heads wherever He had a Church in the world, and it will go to all the lips of all the martyrs that are to suffer for Christ, even to the sounding of the last trumpet. But yet, people of God, it is only the brim that the saints taste of. Be ye patient in believing. . . . Our noble Captain of Salvation hath vanquished these bloody persecutors in Scotland these twenty-two years, more by the patient suffering of the saints than if He had threshed down all in a moment. The patient suffering of the saints, with their blood running, declares His glory much abroad in the world, and especially in these lands. As I came through the country there was a poor widow whose husband fell at Bothwell. The bloody soldiers came to plunder her house, telling her 'they would take all she had; we will leave thee nothing, either to put in thee or on thee.' 'I care not,' said she, 'I shall not want so long as God is in the heavens.' That was a believer indeed."[9] These were the words of a man who had seen many of his fellow preachers slain because of their convictions, and many of their field-congregations per-

---

[9]. W. A. Taylor, *The Scottish Pulpit* (New York, 1887), pp. 142-143.

secuted and banished. The story of his life appears in *Biographia Presbyteriana.*

Thomas Hog (1628-1692)

Thomas Hog, famed throughout the Scottish Highlands as one of the greatest evangelical preachers of his generation, was born in 1628 at Tain, in northeastern Ross-shire. He attended the grammar school at Tain, and then entered Marischal College, Aberdeen, where he received his master's degree in 1650. In 1654 he was licensed to preach and became chaplain to John, Earl of Sutherland. He was a young man of singularly upright deportment, and with none of the shortcomings of youth. While in the home of the Earl of Sutherland, he became aware that his religion was entirely a matter of blameless outward behavior, but without any particular depth of conviction. This caused him great distress, and there were times when he dreaded the ordeal of conducting family devotions. He turned to his Bible and at last found peace in the promise, "I will never leave thee, nor forsake thee."

He was ordained in 1654 and became pastor of Kiltearn Church, not far from Dingwall. He took the side of the Protesters against the Resolutionists, and for this he was deposed in 1661 by the Synod of Ross. He went to Knockgandy, where he preached as circumstances permitted. In 1668 he was cited to appear before the bishop of Moray on the charge of having preached in private houses, thus violating the law against "keeping conventicles." He was found guilty, imprisoned at Forres, but later released upon bail through the efforts of a nobleman. Although strictly forbidden to preach, yet he was arrested again in 1677 at the order of Archbishop Sharp, confined in the Tolbooth and then in the dungeon on the Bass Rock. Sharp declared that Hog "was in a capacity to do more hurt to their interests, sitting in his elbow chair, than twenty others could do by travelling from this land to the other," and under the circumstances he gave orders that Thomas Hog was to be treated with severity, and "if there is any place in the prison worse than another, he should be put there." He was cast into the deepest and darkest part of the prison, far down in the rock. Later he was returned to the Tolbooth through the efforts of influential friends, eventually liberated, but forbidden to preach or to cross the boundaries from Kintyre. However, this did not silence him, and in 1679 he was arrested again and confined in the Tolbooth at Edinburgh. In 1683 he was arrested once more, fined 5,000 merks and banished from Scotland. He went to London, intending to sail for the Carolinas, but he was arrested and confined in prison on the false charge of having plotted against the king. Released in 1685, he went to Holland, where the Prince of Orange made him one of his chaplains. He was not content in Holland, for he could not forget the heather-clad Highlands and the people to whom he had preached. In 1688 he ventured back to Scotland and was cheered when he found that conditions had improved. In 1691 he was appointed one of the king's chaplains and restored to his former parish at Kiltearn after an unwilling absence of 30 years. He died the following year, but at his own request he was buried at the door of the church, and upon its threshold was placed, at his direction, an inscription which read: "This stone shall bear witness against the parishioners of Kiltearn if they bring ane ungodly minister in here."

The Rev. James Hog, of Carnock, of Marrow Controversy fame, said: "I have had the desirable occupation to hear him preach at The Hague, and his sermons were accompanied with the greatest measure of life and power I have ever had the opportunity to observe in my poor life."[10] Numerous testimonies exist as to his fearless and convincing manner of preaching, and of his success in keeping the light of evangelical truth burning in those days of persecution. A biography of Thomas Hog was written by Andrew Stevenson.[11]

John McKilligan (c. 1630-1689)

John McKilligan, a Highland preacher whom no man could silence whether by threats or by imprisonment, first appears in 1656 when he was ordained after receiving a

[10]. David Beaton, *Some Noted Ministers of the Northern Highlands* (Inverness, 1929), pp. 11-12.
[11]. Andrew Stevenson, *Memoirs of the Life of Thomas Hog* (Edinburgh, 1756).

unanimous call to Fodderty Church. In 1661 he took a resolute stand against prelacy, and at a time when very few men dared to express their opinions on this matter. This reached the ears of the bishops, and in 1663 he was ejected from his manse, then cited by the bishop to appear before a diocesan meeting. McKilligan declined to attend. He was deposed from office for his absence from the meeting, for his failure to obey his bishop and for his opposition to prelacy.

In 1675 he moved to Alness, which seems to have been his former home. There he preached to a group of people who shared his views. Sunday after Sunday they came to hear this earnest preacher, and eventually there was a desire on the part of many to receive Holy Communion. Calling upon Hugh Anderson and Alexander Fraser to assist him, Mr. McKilligan conducted at Obsdale the usual Scottish Communion service of three days' duration. There was a preparation sermon on Saturday, two Communion sermons on Sunday and a thanksgiving sermon on Monday. People came from far and wide. A man who attended the three-day service was admonished by a neighbor, who warned him that his presence at the service would mean the confiscation of his property. "I would not only part with my cow and my horse, and these are my only earthly possessions, but with my head likewise, if called upon to do it," he replied. The bishop sent a detachment of soldiers to prevent the service. Through an error they went to Alness, not aware that the Communion service was to be held at Obsdale.

John McKilligan was arrested at Cromarty while baptizing a child of the Rev. Hugh Anderson, another persecuted clergyman. He was imprisoned at Fortrose, then at Nairn, then at the Tolbooth in Edinburgh, and finally in the dungeon on the dreaded Bass Rock in the estuary of the River Forth. There he remained until 1679 when he was released on bail. He returned to the Highlands and preached throughout Ross-shire. For this he was arrested again by the Protestant bishops and in 1683 he was once more cast into prison on the Bass Rock. He became dangerously ill, and in 1686 his enemies relented and sent him home to die. The people

built him a church, and although weakened by his imprisonment, he preached there for two years. In 1688 a group of
faithful people at Inverness urged him to come and preach
for them. He went there, but he was not to preach many
sermons, for he was taken ill and died in 1689.

In describing the remarkable character of the preaching of John McKilligan, the historian Wodrow describes one
of his sermons and says, "the people seemed to be in a
transport, their souls filled with Heaven, and breathing
thither, while their bodies were on earth."[12] It is most
unfortunate that we do not have more of the details of the
lives of such men as John McKilligan. Historians of this
period assure us that there were several preachers of first
rank in Ross-shire alone, while in the same county there
were no less than 30 who may be considered eminent. Like
McKilligan, many of their best sermons were preached at
large outdoor gatherings, when arrest and imprisonment
was too often the lot of the brave men who had the courage
to defy the king and his corrupt State Church. The names
of a few of these noble men have been preserved, and fragmentary records of their lives, but in many cases their
names have been lost, and not even the patient search of
Hew Scott was able to give us, in his seven bulky volumes,[13]
more than the mere mention of the names of some, and
not even the names in other cases.

Gabriel Semple (1632-1706)

Gabriel Semple, another of the field-preachers, was
born in 1632 at Cathcart. He was educated at Hamilton,
then attended Glasgow University, from which he was
graduated in 1653. He was licensed in 1657 and ordained
later in the same year. He became pastor of Kirkpatrick,
in Durham, was deprived in 1662, but restored in 1689.
During the interval he became one of the famous field-
preachers. He was present at the Pentland uprising, and
he preached for a time throughout the north of England,

---

[12]. Robt. Wodrow, *History of the Sufferings of the Church of Scotland,* 2 vols. (Edinburgh, 1721-22).

[13]. Hew Scott, *Fasti Ecclesiae Scoticanae,* 7 vols. (ed. Edinburgh,
1915-28).

as well as in Ireland. He supplied the pulpit for a time at
Ford, in Northumberland, where his Communion gatherings
were attended by multitudes. In 1679 he was declared a
traitor, and a reward of 3,000 merks was offered for his
arrest. In 1681 the King's men seized him and he was confined in the Canongate tolbooth for three months. Upon
his release he went to England, where he remained until
more settled conditions obtained, following the death of
Charles II. In 1690 he was pastor for a time in Jedburgh.

Gabriel Semple was one of the eminent field-preachers
of his day. Thomas Boston once heard him preach, and he
said: "The things he insisted on were common and ordinary,
but delivered in such a manner, and such power accompanied
them, that I was amazed, and they went out through me and
in through me, so that I said in my heart, 'Happy are those
that hear thy wisdom'."[14] This was one of his gifts. Semple
was able to use the familiar truths, so well known to the
people, and present them in a manner that lifted his preaching far above the commonplace.

James Fraser of Brae (1639-1699)

James Fraser of Brae, who is not to be confused with
other James Frasers who won distinction both in Church
and State, came of the nobility. The Clan Fraser, of Norman origin, has produced a number of illustrious men. The
Gaelic name of the Frasers of Lovat is MacShimidh. James
Fraser's father was Sir James Fraser, and his grandfather
was the seventh Lord Fraser of Lovat. The man with whom
we are concerned at the moment was born in 1639 in the
parish of Kirkmichael, in the Ross-shire Highlands. He was
educated in a local grammar school, and later attended
Edinburgh University with the intention of studying law.
His early influences had been strongly religious, and when
17 or 18 years of age he had a spiritual experience which
turned his thoughts to the ministry.

In 1670, when 29 years of age, he was licensed as a
field preacher. He came under the notice of Archbishop

---

[14]. Hew Scott, *Fasti Ecclesiae Scoticanae,* 7 vols. (ed. Edinburgh,
     1915-28), vol. 2, p. 126.

Sharp, of St. Andrews, who had renounced the presbytery for the prelacy. Fraser was accused of having kept conventicles and was imprisoned from 1677 to 1679 on Bass Rock, at the mouth of the River Forth. While in prison he studied Hebrew and Greek, but the lasting monument to his days in prison is his remarkable treatise on Justification by Faith. This was circulated in manuscript form and was not published until long after his death. In the British Museum library is a work bearing the name of James Fraser, and the imposing title: *Some Choice, Select Meditations on: I. The Nature of the Gospel; II. The Necessity and Advantages of Faith; III. The Gospel-Privilege of Justification; and the Difference Between Moral and Saving Grace, Distinctly Handled.* (Edinburgh, 1726.) It is said that there was considerable objection in James Fraser's day to his work on Justification, and he was believed to tend toward universal grace — a teaching not in favor with the Calvinists.

James Fraser's preaching was fearless, and it led to a succession of difficulties. In 1681 we find him in prison again, this time in Blackness Castle; while two years later he was confined in Newgate Prison for refusing to take the Oxford Oath. In 1689 he became pastor of a congregation at Culross, and in 1690 and 1692 his name appears as a member of the Assembly.

Dr. Alexander Whyte, of Free St. George's Church, Edinburgh, delivered a series of 28 lectures on James Fraser of Brae, which were published in the form of a book which deserves to stand, together with John Kennedy's *Days of the Fathers in Ross-shire,* on every clergyman's book shelf.[15] "For an evangelical masterpiece like Fraser of Brae on Justifying Faith," declares Dr. Whyte, "we must go to the Lutherans, or to the Calvinists, or to the Puritans, or to the Presbyterians. The Catholics and the Anglicans have their own masterpieces; but with some noble exceptions, Richard Hooker for one, they are not on the Pauline faith that alone justifies the ungodly. And over and above its evangelical value to its properly prepared readers what

---

[15]. Alexander Whyte, *James Fraser, Laird of Brae* (Edinburgh, 1911).

will always give a truly patriotic interest to this remarkable
little book is the fact that it was written in a Covenanter's
prison cell on the Bass Rock, and with no book beside the
author but his Bible. . . . James Fraser planned and executed
this true masterpiece of apostolical and evangelical and
experimental religion."[16]   Dr. Whyte, in his book, sums up
James Fraser's work on Justification.   However, as another
proof that the reformed type of mind, however acute, has
seldom been able to grasp fully the truth of objective justification, man's salvation is declared to be contingent upon his
arising, like the prodigal son, and returning to his father's
house.[17]   However, Dr. Whyte does declare that our hope
of eternal life does not rest upon what we have in our-
selves — even though we have all the faith of Abraham,
all the meekness of Moses, all the penitence of David and
all the spiritual mindedness of St. Paul; and not even if we
were able to write Augustine's Confessions, Luther's sermons, Rutherford's letters, Bunyan's allegories and the
Olney hymns.[18]   Dr. Whyte quotes a famous saying of Newman on the value of the Church Fathers, but declares that
he himself, like Coleridge, would prefer the writings of
Bunyan, Baxter, Goodwin, Fraser of Brae, Halyburton,
Boston and Chalmers to a whole brigade of Fathers.[19]

James Fraser left a remarkable work, upon which Dr.
Whyte based his 28 lectures. In it he unfolds the "intri-
cacies of my heart and life" in a manner that gives it a place
among the great spiritual biographies.[20] More noteworthy
even than this is his *Treatise Concerning Justifying and
Saving Faith* (1722), written during his imprisonment on
Bass Rock. Due, it would seem, to the objection of his
friends who believed that he had departed from Calvinism,
this significant work was not published until long after his
death. The first part of it appeared in 1722, and the
remainder in 1749. In it he declares that "Christ did, by
His one infinite, indivisible satisfaction and ransom, satisfy

---

[16]. *Ibid.*, p. 241.
[17]. *Ibid.*, p. 247.
[18]. *Ibid.*, p. 243.
[19]. *Ibid.*, p. 8.
[20]. James Fraser, *Memoirs of James Fraser of Brae,* written by himself (Edinburgh, 1738).

Divine justice for the sins of all mankind, though with different intention and ends according to the different objects thereof," (with intention to save the elect), "but not to save the rest, but that they, condemning and rejecting the offer of salvation, might be made fit subjects to show His just Gospel-vengeance and wrath upon them."[21] The words "with intention to save the elect" appear to be an insertion of a later commentator. It is known, however, that Mr. Fraser's friends feared that he was deviating from the old Calvinistic teaching that the grace of God in Christ is limited only to the elect.

The book is significant in the history of doctrine as well as in the history of preaching, for it anticipates a controversy that stirred Scotland for generations, caused disruptions in presbyteries and synods, and led to more than one sensational trial for alleged heresy. James Fraser, in his dungeon, with only the Bible as his text book, was convinced that the offer of grace was given to all men impartially, but, like many other men who followed him, he struggled to reconcile this truth with the Calvinistic principle of a limited Atonement. We are assured that he was a preacher of great forcefulness, and if he declared from the pulpit that "Christ did, by His one infinite, indivisible satisfaction and ransom, satisfy Divine justice *for the sins of all mankind,*" then it is possible that he grasped, even if imperfectly, the truth that *sola gratia* and *universalis gratia* go hand in hand, as the Scriptures teach.

Richard Cameron (c. 1648-1680)

Richard Cameron, a courageous field-preacher, was born in Falkland, Fifeshire, about the year 1648. After he had completed his schooling, he became precentor and schoolmaster in Falkland. He was a member of the prelatic party at first, and attended the services of the clergymen who had yielded to the king's declaration of indulgence. The preaching of the indulged clergy proved unsatisfactory, and he went to hear some of the field-preachers. The evangelical tone of their preaching not only appealed to him, but he

---

[21]. *Op. cit.,* p. 246.

came to a realization of his sinful nature, and of the grace of God in Jesus Christ. He became convinced that no man could, with a good conscience, accept the king's declaration of indulgence, for it meant the recognition of the king as head of the Kirk. King Charles II issued the first declaration of indulgence shortly after he came to the throne, and a second and more formal one in 1672. James II, his successor, issued indulgences in 1687 and again in 1688. While these documents permitted a certain amount of religious freedom, yet the stricter Covenanters refused to accept them, since it meant the recognition of the king's supremacy over the Church.

At the urgent request of the Rev. John Welch and others, Richard Cameron was licensed to preach. His first sermon was preached in a tent at Annandale, and here his great power over a congregation became evident, for many people who had attended merely out of curiosity, were convinced of the correctness of Cameron's position in regard to the declaration of indulgence. In 1677 Cameron, Welch, Semple, Wellwood and others were called before a meeting at Edinburgh to be deposed for preaching against the indulgence and for refusing to have pulpit and altar fellowship with the pastors who had taken the oath of the king's supremacy over the Kirk. Cameron continued his field-preaching; and at Maybole, assisted by several other field-preachers, he conducted what is believed to have been the first outdoor Communion service. Thousands of people attended this great service. So eloquently did Cameron preach against the sinfulness of the indulgence, and the act of fellowship with men who had taken the oath, that he was called upon to attend two more meetings, where efforts were made to exact a promise from him to cease testifying against the king's headship of the Kirk, and to persuade him to practice fellowship with the group who had accepted the indulgence.

In 1678 he went to Holland, where he preached in the Scots' Kirk at Rotterdam. He expounded the text "Come unto Me, all ye that labour, and are heavy laden," declaring that the rest promised to the faithful is not merely a relief from labors and cares of this world, but a true conversion to the Saviour. The leaders in Holland urged him to return to Scotland, declaring that the standard had fallen, and urging him to go back and lift the fallen standard and display it publicly to the people and urge them to rally about it. Cameron realized that this meant death for him, but he did not hesitate. He was ordained by the Scottish and Dutch clergymen, and after the laying on of hands, Mr. MacWard declared solemnly: "Behold, all ye beholders; here is the head of a faithful minister and servant of Jesus Christ, who shall lose this head for his Saviour's interest, and it shall be set up before sun and moon, in view of the world." MacWard spoke of the custom in England and Scotland of displaying upon a pole in the public market place the heads and hands of executed persons.

Richard Cameron returned to Scotland in 1680, and his first task was to call upon the persecuted field-preachers and encourage them to remain faithful. In June of the same year he met with several men and signed the Sanquhar Declaration, so called because they posted it at the public market-cross in Sanquhar. Because of this the men who signed the document were declared outlaws, and large rewards offered for their capture, dead or alive. Cameron went to New Monkland, where he preached to a great gathering of faithful people. He concluded his sermon by predicting that the day was not far away when the Lord should sweep from the throne all who bore the unhappy name of Stuart, that treachery and tyranny would end, and that Jesus Christ should be recognized once more as the sole Head of the Church. In July he preached in the fields near Cumnock, declaring that the death of Charles II would bring to an end the reign of the inglorious House of Stuart; that never another of the family of that name should reign over England or Scotland; that the Lord would give to Scotland a true reformation of religion; that the Lord will raise up friends in foreign lands who shall come to the aid of the oppressed people of Scotland and establish religious liberty throughout the realm.

Cameron's last sermon was preached in Clydesdale. His text was, "Be still, and know that I am God; I will be

exalted among the heathen, I will be exalted on the earth."
Twenty-three horsemen and forty men on foot, all devoted
friends, came to where Cameron was staying in order to
protect him. On the afternoon of July 22, 1680, the king's
soldiers overtook them at a place known as Ayrsmoss.
Cameron begged his friends to leave him, and he cried out,
"Lord, spare the green and take the ripe." His friends
refused to leave him, but surrounded him, after the manner
of the nobles who had defended James IV at Flodden Field,
in 1513. Cameron's defenders were greatly outnumbered
by the king's men, who overcame them without difficulty.
Cameron was cut down; and his severed head and hands
were taken to his aged father, who was in prison because of
his refusal to yield to the king. "I know them!" exclaimed
the aged man. "They are my son's head and hands. Good
is the will of the Lord, who cannot wrong me or mine; but
has made goodness and mercy to follow us all our days."
James Cameron's head and hands were exposed on a pole
at Nether-bow Port, and even one of his most determined
enemies was so moved that he declared, "There are the
hands and the head of a man who lived praying and preaching, and who died praying and fighting." Friends erected
a cairn, or pile of stones, over the grave on Ayrsmoss where
Cameron's headless body was buried; and when Alexander
Peden visited the spot, he cried, "Oh, to be wie Richie!"

Richard Cameron was a fearless and convincing
preacher, and when many of his associates became in-
timidated and yielded to the demands of the king, Cameron
left the safety of his place of exile and returned to Scotland
and to what he knew to be certain death. He did not falter.
His testimony rang clearly, and at the age of 32 the words
spoken at his ordination were fulfilled: "He shall lose this
head for his Saviour's interest, and it shall be set up before
sun and moon, in view of the world."

Short biographies of Richard Cameron appear in R.
Wodrow's *History of the Sufferings of the Church of Scotland* (1721-22), in *Biographia Presbyteriana* (1827), in
John Howie's *Scots Worthies* (1774), and in several other
such works.

William Carstares (1649-1715)

William Carstares, chaplain to King William, was born in Cathcart, near Glasgow, in 1649. His father was an anti-prelatic clergyman, who had suffered because of his convictions. William Carstares received his elementary schooling at Ormison, East Lothian, in which place he lived in the home of a clergyman who made it a rule that Latin must be spoken in his family so that his children might be familiar with it. William was graduated from Edinburgh University in 1667, after which he studied theology in Utrecht.

He returned from Holland in 1672, and got as far as London. In 1674 he was arrested because of a pamphlet which described the sufferings of the Scottish Kirk. Carstares probably had nothing to do with the publication, but he was charged with helping distribute it. Nothing was proven other than that he had carried messages from the Scottish refugees in Holland to those still in Scotland. He was confined for five years in Edinburgh castle. While there he made friends with a lad of 12 years, who came to his barred window daily to hear his tales of his travels in the Low Countries. The boy brought him writing materials, and word from his friends. Carstares did not forget his young friend, and later, when he became a close friend and confidential adviser to King William, he had the boy made Lord Lyon, a title which became hereditary.

In 1683 Carstares was arrested again, charged with knowledge of a plot to assassinate King Charles II. He was put to torture in Edinburgh in an effort to compel him to disclose the names of those suspected. In 1686 or 1687 he went to Leyden and became assistant pastor to a congregation of Scottish refugees who had fled from the persecutions of the prelatic party. While there he was made a chaplain to William of Orange, and when William sailed for England and landed at Torbay, it was Carstares who conducted a service of thanksgiving on the beach, preaching on Psalm 118, and causing all who took part in the landing to repeat the Psalm.

William Carstares remained a close friend and counsellor of William after the latter was made King of England

and Scotland. A staunch champion of the presbytery himself, Carstares induced the King to recognize that party in Scotland, and to put an end to the persecution which they had suffered at the hands of the House of Stuart. With the Revolution Settlement and Claim of Right, William and Mary were proclaimed King and Queen in Edinburgh on April 11, 1689, and the State Church from then onward was the Presbyterian Church.

In 1703 Carstares was made principal of Edinburgh University, where his stirring orations in Latin are said to have "made his hearers fancy themselves transported to the Forum of ancient Rome." [22] Carstares was also pastor of Greyfriars Church, and royal chaplain of all Scotland.

Dean Stanley has nothing but words of highest praise for Carstares, and lists his name with those who paved the way for the Moderates. He describes him as one of the great preachers and leaders of his day, and four times moderator of the Assembly. [23] W. M. Hetherington, the historian, does not speak so well of him, but fears that Carstares was an ardent champion of the presbytery more for political reasons than out of religious convictions. [24] He believes that Carstares saw that the people of Scotland wanted church government by the presbytery, and he was enough of an opportunist to cast his lot with the group now in power. He thinks that Carstares failed to grasp the teaching that Jesus Christ is the Head of the Christian Church, and His teachings the ruling principle of all religion.

It is said that he left nothing in writing, [25] hence it is difficult to judge him on the basis of written evidence. It is certain that he was one of the most influential preachers of his day, and that he, perhaps more than any man of his day, brought about a recognition by the State of the form of church government for which Scotland had been contending throughout a period of 117 years. Biographical information

---

[22]. A. P. Stanley, *Lectures on the History of the Church of Scotland* (New York, 1872), p. 135.
[23]. *Ibid.*, pp. 131-140.
[24]. W. M. Hetherington, *History of the Church of Scotland* (Edinburgh, 1842), p. 300.
[25]. A. P. Stanley, *Op. cit.*, p. 133.

exists in *State Papers and Letters Addressed to William Carstares* (1774), in J. M'Cormick's *Memoir* prefixed to the document just mentioned, and in R. H. Story's *Character and Career of William Carstares* (1874).

Angus Macbean (1656-1688)

Angus Macbean, a courageous young clergyman, died because he considered the power of the Eternal Lord to be greater that that of a tyrannical king. Macbean was born in the Highlands in 1656. He attended King's College, Aberdeen, where he took his degree in 1675. In 1683 we find him in Inverness, the chief city of the Highlands, where he became known for his boldness in denouncing the sins and errors of his day, and for his opposition to the prelatic form of government which the king and his bishops had imposed upon the Scottish Church. After preaching memorable sermons on 2 Cor. 6, 17-18 and on Rev. 18, 4 he announced his withdrawal from the State Church. In 1688 he was arrested and imprisoned because he had declared in a sermon, "I know of no unlimited power but the power of the Eternal Lord God." This was declared to be treason against the majesty of James II. Macbean was confined in the Tolbooth and denied all visitors. His friends, mindful of his frail health, stormed the prison and released him, but they came too late. His privations had so undermined his health that he died two months after his release. He is described as a pale, frail young man, yet absolutely fearless, and a preacher of extraordinary power.[26]

James Renwick (1662-1688)

James Renwick was born in 1662 at Moniaive in Dumfriesshire. He received his education at Edinburgh University. When Donald Cargill was executed in 1681, James Renwick, at that time 19 years of age, stood near the scaffold and heard the last words of that martyr. He left the scene of Cargill's execution determined to cast his lot with the Covenanters. He studied theology at the University of Groningen. He was ordained in Holland in 1683, subscrib-

---

[26]. Murdoch Macdonald, *Covenanters of Moray and Ross* (Nairn, 1875), pp. 169-170.

ing to the Confession and Catechism of the Church of Scotland.

Renwick returned to Scotland very soon after his ordination, only to discover that he was the only living field-preacher. The entire burden of the Covenanting cause rested upon the shoulders of this youth of 21 years of age. He went from place to place, preaching to the congregations that gathered in fields and lonely valleys. It became his duty to issue all public statements, to draft documents, to deal with the churches in Continental Europe and to take over the duties of the men who had paid for their convictions with their blood. For five years he lived as an outlaw, hiding in caves, often without food, tramping long distances in order to keep his preaching appointments.

The king issued two indulgences, offering certain privileges to the clergymen who had been driven from their parishes; but expecting in return an outward recognition of his sovereignty and a tacit recognition of the king as head of the Church. James Renwick refused resolutely to accept these indulgences, and he refrained from practicing pulpit and altar fellowship with the clergymen who took the oath of submission to the king. Because of this, he became unpopular with the clergymen who had yielded to the king. Slanderous reports were raised against him by scoffers, and these rumors were repeated by people of the Kirk. It was said that he had excommunicated all pastors who had accepted the king's declaration of indulgence; that he was a Pharisee, seeking to establish a new sect of his own; that he was a coarse fanatic who went about the land with hatred toward all men, hurling fierce criticism at all orderly Christians. These, of course, were slanderous reports, for Scotland has not often seen a more gentle, courteous, devout young man than James Renwick. He refused to recognize the king as head of the Kirk, it is true, and he merely avoided those clergymen who had submitted to the king. He was a preacher of unusual eloquence, but the sermons that he delivered went no farther than to expound the basic teachings of the New Testament, and to encourage the people to commit their troubles to the Lord

Jesus Christ, in full confidence that He was able to bring about a better state of affairs in Scotland, when all men could worship Him in their own parish churches without molestation.

These slanderous reports reached the ears of the king's council, and they proclaimed James Renwick a traitor and a rebel, because he had declined to take the oath of allegiance to the king, and that he had persisted in his field-preaching after the king and the bishops had declared such preaching unlawful. Other charges were made against him: that he had neglected to pay the king's taxes and that he had declared it lawful for men to carry firearms in order to defend themselves against the soldiers who were sent to disperse the people who gathered to hear his field-preaching. On one occasion, when Renwick was travelling by horseback from one preaching appointment to another, the king's soldiers pursued him, firing upon him repeatedly. Renwick dismounted, fled to a nearby woodlot and concealed himself in a stone pile. The soldiers searched the woodlot, firing their muskets and shouting, but Renwick's hiding place was not discovered. A reward of £100 sterling, a considerable sum in those days, was offered for his person, dead or alive; but Renwick continued to itinerate throughout Scotland, preaching, catechizing, baptizing, encouraging the large number of people who stood firm in their loyalty to the Covenants.

In 1688 Renwick ventured into Edinburgh, which was not a large place in those days, and met in private homes with people who had not yielded to the indulged clergymen. A waiter who chanced to enter the house, recognized Renwick's voice as he preached and prayed. He notified the authorities, and on the following morning the house was surrounded and Renwick was captured, cast into prison and burdened with heavy chains. It must be said in favor of the king's council and the bishops that every opportunity was given Renwick to persuade him to conform. He was offered attractive inducements, religious freedom, comfortable livings, church preferment and positions of importance in Church or State, if only he would agree to recant, and to take an oath recognizing the king as supreme in both Church and State. James Renwick's reply was what might be expected. He declared his willingness to pledge his loyalty to the king in all matters that pertained to the civil government, but he refused again and again to declare the king's authority over the Kirk. Officials of the government were sent to reason with him, bishops and prominent clergymen called on him and sought to persuade him, his mother and his sisters were allowed to visit him repeatedly in his prison. Renwick remained resolute, declaring that it was a matter of conscience with him, and that God's Word speaks plainly. He was willing to suffer death, he declared, rather than accept the crafty king's declaration of indulgence. He restated his readiness to support the king within the prescriptions and limitations of the Word of God, but he declared that the king was required by law to defend the reformed religion, and yet he was plotting to overthrow it. He said that it was the duty of every man to pay taxes to the king, but when taxes were used to suppress the free declaration of the Gospel, such taxes could not be paid with a good conscience. He believed that no man has a right to take up arms to resist the king under ordinary circumstances, but when the king's soldiers are ordered to employ armed force to prevent the peaceful assembly of Christian people to hear the Word of God, then such people may be held blameless, should they arm themselves in order to defend themselves and their families.

James Renwick was found guilty by the council and condemned to die upon the scaffold. The king's men had been assured that Renwick was a huge, blustering, desperate outlaw, and when he was led into court they were astonished to see that the chieftain who had led the Covenanters, single handed and alone, and with such conspicuous ability, was a slight, apple-cheeked young man of 26 years of age. When he spoke in answer to their charges, they found him gentle, courteous and deeply religious. As he was led to the scaffold, drums were beaten furiously lest he might attempt to persuade the multitude with his eloquence. A priest went to the scaffold with him, offering him freedom and religious toleration if only he might agree to yield to the king. James

Renwick's words rang out above the beating of the drums, and those near the scaffold all heard him. "I will discourse no more with you"; he cried, "I am within a little while to appear before the King of Kings and Lord of Lords, who shall pour shame and confusion upon all the kings of the earth who have not ruled according to His will." [27] Then he sang Psalm 103 and repeated the 19th chapter of Revelation. Then he said: "Lord, I die in the faith that Thou wilt not forsake Scotland, but that Thou wilt make the blood of Thy witnesses the seed of Thy Church, and return again and be glorious in Thy land. . . . As to the remnant I leave, I have committed them to God. Tell them for me not to be weary nor be discouraged in maintaining the testimony, and the Lord will provide you teachers and ministers; and when He comes, He will make these despised truths glorious in the earth. Lord, into Thy hands I commend my spirit, for Thou hast redeemed me, Lord God of truth." [28] Three hours before he was executed, Renwick assured his mother and his sisters that his death would mean more for the good of Scotland than any words that he could utter, should he yield to the king. His words were more true than he realized, for James Renwick, at the age of 26, was the last man to die in Scotland on the scaffold for the cause of religious freedom. Among his known writings are *An Informatory Vindication* (of the Covenanters), published in 1744; and *A Choice Collection of Very Valuable Prefaces, Lectures and Sermons Preached upon the Mountains and Muirs of Scotland* (c. 1777). In addition to J. Simpson's biography (1843), accounts of Renwick appear in R. Wodrow's *History of the Sufferings of the Church of Scotland* (1838); A. Smellie's *Men of the Covenant* (1904); and by Alexander Shields in *Biographia Presbyteriana* (1827).

Thomas Halyburton (1674-1712)

Thomas Halyburton was born in Dupplin, Perthshire, in 1674. His father was one of the 300 or so clergymen who were ejected from their congregations in the days of persecution. In 1685 Thomas Halyburton was taken by his

---

[27]. John Howie, *The Scots Worthies* (ed. New York, 1853), p. 605.
[28]. *Ibid.*, p. 605.

mother to Rotterdam, where they sought security from persecution. While there he studied in the school founded by
Erasmus, and in which he mastered the Latin and Dutch
languages. The family returned to Scotland in 1687, and
Halyburton attended St. Andrews University, from which he
was graduated in 1696. During his youth he had a long
period of doubt and spiritual struggle, from which he received an unexpected and joyous deliverance.

He was ordained in 1700 and became pastor of the congregation at Ceres, in Fifeshire. In 1710 he was made professor of theology at St. Leonard's College, St. Andrews, but
his frail body was not equal to the demands made upon it
for a dozen years, and he died two years later, at the age
of 38.

Thomas Halyburton was a preacher of great power, and
with a depth of evangelical zeal beyond the average. His
sermons follow the involved style of his day, with many
divisions and subdivisions. He set forth with great force
the subjects of man's sin and God's displeasure, the utter
ruin wrought by sin, man's helpless and hopeless condition
if left to his own efforts to bring about a rescue from sin,
the free grace of God in Jesus Christ and His power to rescue
man from his lost condition, and the work of the Holy
Ghost in man.

His sermons were often lacking in logical arrangement,
as for example in his description of sin,[29] which he views as
follows: in the glass of God's Law, in the nature of God, in
the threatenings of the Law, in the judgments of God, in
the soul under a sense of sin, in the hideous crimes sin
commits, in the condition of the damned, and in the sufferings of Christ. Here we find a lack of progression which
must have proved confusing to his congregation, yet the
total effect of his preaching, in spite of its defects, seems to
have been powerful upon his hearers. He had the additional defect of viewing sin in the abstract,[30] and his sermons
show a weakness in practical appeal, and in identifying sin

---

[29]. W. G. Blaikie, *The Preachers of Scotland* (Edinburgh, 1888),
p. 250.
[30]. *Op. cit.,* p. 251.

and salvation with the actual needs of his hearers. However, his preaching met with great favor, and he was one of
the foremost preachers of his generation.

His great zeal for immortal souls may be seen in his
deathbed conversations, as given us in great detail by
Middleton.[31] In words of great persuasiveness he urges
upon his physician, his apothecary, several clergymen who
called upon him, and his wife and children, to be mindful
of the awful havoc of sin in the lives of men, and to place
their trust in the Lamb of God, who taketh away the sin
of the world. He lingered for many days, using the time
to admonish the careless and to bear witness of the saving
grace that is in Jesus Christ. Halyburton's most important
writings are: *Natural Religion Insufficient and Revealed
Religion Necessary* (1714); *The Great Concern of Salvation*
(1721); *Ten Sermons Preached Before and After the Lord's
Supper* (1722); *The Unpardonable Sin against the Holy
Ghost* (1784); and his collected *Works* (1835). James
Watson wrote *Memoirs of the Life of Mr. Thomas Halyburton* (1715), basing it upon Halyburton's diary.

What was the reason for the great influence of the
covenanting preachers and the field preachers? Certainly
it was not due to their eloquence, nor to the great crowds
that followed them to the moors and glens. The greatness
of such an organist as the late Lynnwood Farnam is due to
much more than nimble fingers, and the worth of a famous
choir depends upon more than an impressive crescendo. Just
so did the fame of the field-preachers rest upon qualities
much more significant than animated speech and great congregations. It was due to the fact that they preached
evangelical truth in a day when evangelical truth was lacking in most pulpits. True, one may find doctrinal lacunae
in their sermons, and other blemishes, yet they were never
guilty of giving the Lord a mere sentence or two at the
close of the sermon, as is the fashion in some places nowadays. He was present throughout, as the Saviour of poor
sinners, and as the Lord of Consolation of a persecuted
church.

---

[31]. E. Middleton, *Biographia Evangelica* (London, 1810), vol. 4, pp.
188-196.

These men preached enough Law and Gospel that men were brought to a knowledge of their sin, and convinced of the true way of salvation through the grace of God and the merit of Jesus Christ. So zealous were they in laying stress upon the atoning blood of the Lord Jesus that they fell into the error of losing sight of His righteousness. This Active Obedience of our Saviour, namely His perfect keeping of the Law as our Substitute, is much too important an evangelical truth to ignore, and if preached faithfully it closes the door to salvation by works, and leaves no room for synergism. Likewise they preached particular grace so earnestly that they lost sight of universal grace.

Nowhere except in the Scriptures have the truths of saving grace been set forth more fully and more clearly than in the second volume of Dr. Francis Pieper's *Christian Dogmatics*.[32] He declares that the truths of universal grace are revealed so fully in the Scriptures that it seems incredible that *gratia universalis* should ever have been questioned by any Christian.[33] It is most unfortunate that the Scottish field-preachers, with the Word of God before them, should miss the vital truths of our Saviour's Active Obedience, and of His universal offer of grace to all sinners.

---

[32]. Francis Pieper, *Christian Dogmatics*, 3 vols. (St. Louis, 1950-51).
[33]. *Ibid.*, p. 24.

CHAPTER V

THE MARROW CONTROVERSY

THE DISCOVERY of an old book in a low-walled, thatched cottage in Simprin may seem a slight thing, but it brought about a controversy that agitated Scotland for several years, and influenced Scottish preaching for generations. Thomas Boston, a young clergyman, while visiting one of his families in Simprin, Berwickshire, was attracted by two old books lying on the window sill. He was told that they had been found above the window, under the thatch. The father of the family had been a soldier in the Civil War, and he had brought back these books from England. One of the books proved to be of no value. The second bore the title *The Marrow of Modern Divinity*. It had been written by one who called himself "E. F.", and had been printed in England in 1645. Mr. Boston borrowed the book and read it. In it he discovered that God's grace is offered to all men impartially, and not limited to the elect alone, as the Kirk had taught. Holy living is not a condition of salvation, but a result of it. Salvation depends solely upon faith in Jesus Christ, the Saviour of all mankind, and not of a pre-determined few.

The book was written in the form of a religious discussion between four men: an evangelical Christian, a legalist, an Antinomian and a young Christian. Each set forth his views, and in the end the evangelical Christian made clear the errors of the other three, at the same time establishing the fact of universal grace. Luther, Calvin, Beza, Hooker and other authorities were quoted freely.

A few years later Thomas Boston, while attending a meeting of the General Assembly, happened to sit next to a friend, Mr. Drummond of Crieff. He told Drummond of the discovery of the book, and of its teachings. After a search, Drummond located a copy of the volume in an old book shop and read it. He showed it to James Hog, of Carnock, and to others. After several prominent men had read the book, it was decided to reprint it; which was done in 1718, with an introduction by James Hog.

The publication of this book caused a violent controversy in the Scottish Kirk. A number of men, of whom twelve were of some prominence, defended the teachings of the book, and strove to prove that the doctrine of universal grace is not a contradiction of the Calvinistic doctrine of a limited Atonement. In so doing they fell into an error so common in the history of Christian doctrine, namely an attempt to solve by human reason the mystery in the doctrine of Election. These men declared that there had been a gift of the elect to Christ, — "all that the Father giveth Me shall come to Me." At the same time, they insisted, there is a gift of Christ to all mankind, — "For God so loved the world that He gave His only begotten Son," etc. In this manner they sought to reconcile personal election to the fact of universal grace.

These excellent men were sincere evangelicals who accepted the Scriptural teachings of the Fall of man, the complete sinfulness and helplessness of the natural man, the inability of the natural man to find salvation through the Law, and the gracious offer of salvation through the Saviour, who has kept the Law perfectly in man's stead, and died on the Cross for the remission of man's sin. These things they tried to reconcile with the old-time harshness of Calvinism by making a distinction between the gift of the elect to Christ, and the gift of Christ to all mankind.

In the year 1720 the majority of the clergymen who made up the General Assembly were Neonomians, and the liberals who were to develop presently into the rationalistic Moderate party. They were men "who displayed an ominous readiness to accommodate the Gospel to the inclinations of fallen man, and to modify the principles of Church government and discipline so as to meet the views of politicians and men of the world."[1] These unfaithful men, with the spiritual blindness so often found among false teachers, declared themselves to be the champions of sound doctrine in the Scottish Kirk, and they formed a "Committee for Preserving the Purity of Doctrine," with a sub-committee

---

[1]. W. H. Hetherington, *History of the Church of Scotland* (Edinburgh, 1842), p. 344.

headed by the liberal Principal Haddow. They began to publish attacks on the Marrow book and the Marrow Men, as its defenders were termed. These attacks cannot be called fair by any courtesy, for they followed the method so common in doctrinal controversies. By separating statements from their context, and rearranging them to suit their own purpose, they made the Marrow book appear to contain dangerous false doctrine. It cannot be denied that the book contained careless statements here and there, but the Marrow Men insisted that when viewed in their proper context, the teachings of the book were soundly Scriptural, and set forth the plan of salvation through Jesus Christ alone, and man's justification by faith, without the works of the Law.

In 1720 the Committee for Preserving the Purity of Doctrine presented a report to the Assembly, which followed the method used in their previous attacks. Isolated quotations, torn from their context and rearranged to suit the committee, were presented to the Assembly. "By such a sophistical process," says one historian, "Luther may be made the defender of popery, and Calvin of universal redemption; by such a process, Calvin and Beza and Knox, and the Standards of the Church of Scotland, have been made the defenders of patronage and intrusion; and by such a process the Bible itself has been made to give support to heresy. Thus misled by the sophistical report of its committee, the General Assembly was induced to pass an act condemning the *Marrow of Modern Divinity,* on account of the false doctrine which it was said to contain." [2]

The Assembly warned all clergy against the book, and required all of them to warn their congregations against reading it. The 12 most prominent men who had defended it, including Thomas Boston, James Hog and the Erskines, were rebuked publicly before the Assembly. In the years that followed, the liberal party did their utmost to prevent the Marrow Men from receiving calls, and to prevent the calling of young men who were believed to hold Marrow views in regard to universal grace. When it was found that Thomas Boston's health was injured by the severe climate

---

[2]. W. M. Hetherington, *Op. cit.,* p. 345.

of Ettrick, Selkirkshire, the political efforts of the liberal
party prevented his translation to a part of Scotland where
the climate was less severe. All of this apparent zeal is to
be found in the same men who had, but five years before,
dealt leniently with Prof. Simson when he was charged
with teaching Antinomianism, Pelagianism and finally Arianism. It was these men who became the Moderate party who
dragged the Kirk into the morass of doctrinal indifference.

The Marrow Controversy had an important influence on
Scottish preaching. It caused men to make a study of the
doctrine of grace. The Marrow Men and their followers
began to preach universal grace with great fervor. The
Person and work of the Saviour was given a place of greatest
prominence in their preaching. The people were urged to
place their hope of salvation not merely in an outward
assent to the doctrine of salvation, but to place their trust
in an all-sufficient personal Saviour. This idea of a personal
Saviour, and of union with Him, was stressed with intense
earnestness. Thus in an age of spiritual decline, a group
of men appeared whose spiritual zeal kept alive the evangelical spirit. Their doctrinal system was not without imperfections, yet these Marrow Men preached enough of the
truth of Redemptive Christianity that many believers were
brought to the foot of the Cross, and taught to place their
hope of salvation in Jesus Christ alone.

Thomas Boston (1677-1732)

Thomas Boston, one of Scotland's most noted seventeenth century preachers, was born in 1677 at Dunse, Berwickshire. His father had been imprisoned for his nonconformity, and as a young boy, Thomas often spent days in
the prison to keep his father company. The boy was brought
to a knowledge of evangelical truth through the preaching
of Henry Erskine.[3] Two sermons that impressed him greatly
were expositions of the texts "Behold the Lamb of God, that
taketh away the sin of the world," and "O generation of
vipers, who hath warned you to flee from the wrath to
come?" In 1688 when he entered Roxburgh grammar school,
Thomas Boston was found to have a good working knowledge

---

[3]. Thos. Boston, *Memoirs* (Edinburgh, 1776).

of Latin, and by his fourteenth birthday he was reading the standard Latin classics and histories. He attended the University of Edinburgh, and was graduated in 1695. After teaching in a parochial school for a year, he began the study of theology. He was licensed to preach in 1697, and supplied vacant congregations while continuing his theological studies.

In 1699 he was ordained and given the congregation at Simprin, Berwickshire. The parish contained but 90 people of mature years. While at Simprin he discovered the book *The Marrow of Modern Divinity* in a little thatched cottage where he was paying a visit. He was allowed to take this old book with him. He read it, spoke of it to Mr. Drummond of Crieff and to others. The book was reprinted in 1718, as has been mentioned elsewhere, and its publication led to the memorable Marrow Controversy, and brought together a group of evangelical clergymen known as the Marrow Men, who, with Thomas Boston, bore valiant testimony to the truth of the universal offer of grace to all mankind, and of salvation through Jesus Christ alone.

In 1707 Thomas Boston was given the parish of Ettrick, in Selkirkshire, where he spent the remaining 25 years of his life. In 1720 the 12 leaders of the Marrow Men, one of whom was Boston, were brought to trial by a liberal majority who controlled the General Assembly. They were given a public reprimand and allowed to remain in the Scottish Kirk, but the liberal leaders quietly used their influence to prevent the Marrow Men and those who supported them, from receiving calls.

Thomas Boston, in 1720, wrote a book, *Human Nature in its Fourfold State,* which was read widely in Scotland at the time. It discusses Man's Primitive Integrity, his Entire Depravation, his Begun Recovery and his Consummate Happiness or Misery. The book had great influence both in Scotland and England, and many a preacher was awakened by it, and led from a preaching of outward morality to a declaration of evangelical truth.

Boston was a forceful preacher, although not an orator in the popular sense. He bore witness to man's sinful nature and his need of salvation through Jesus Christ alone. William Taylor says of him: "His sermons . . . were cast, withal, in the mould of the times, beginning with a painful opening up of the text and a statement of the doctrine to be insisted upon; then proceeding to an exposition of that through four or five heads, each having under it a series of particulars, and the whole followed by an application in which was a series of uses — as, for example, in one case, taken almost at random — use, first for information; use, second, for trial; use, third, for motive. . . . They are not, therefore, very attractive reading now, and will be resorted to only by those who are impelled to study them for some specific purpose. But they are full of Christ, and they are particularly noteworthy for the fulness and freeness with which they express the offer of Christ and His salvation upon men."[4]

The people of those days welcomed such sermons, involved as their homiletical style may seem to us today; and it was Thomas Boston and like-minded men who kept the light of evangelical Christianity burning, here and there, even in those sad days when the Moderates were coming into power, and their deistic teachings and shallow preaching of natural theology had become the rule.

Davidson of Braintree says of Thomas Boston: "He was indeed one of the most powerful preachers of the Gospel I ever heard open a mouth. It is true he was no Boanerges as to his voice, his delivery being grave and deliberate, yet there was a majestic energy in it, which, together with his venerable and comely aspect, made no small impression to his advantage on the minds of them who had the pleasure of hearing him."[5] Davidson says further that Boston's printed sermons do him an injustice. Boston used a large number of proof texts in his sermons. The printed sermons do not give these proof passages, but only the chapter and verse. In his spoken discourses, Boston quoted these texts in full. So carefully were the proof passages selected that they gave his sermons a striking

---

[4]. W. M. Taylor, *The Scottish Pulpit* (New York, 1887), p. 160.
[5]. E. Middleton, *Biographia Evangelica* (London, 1810), vol. 4, p. 256.

impressiveness. He was accustomed to preach for an hour or more.

Dr. Blaikie of Edinburgh says of Boston: "In regard to the subject of his preaching, the dominant element is grace. Like almost all the great preachers of Scotland, he is of the school of Paul. 'By grace are ye saved through faith' is his watchword as much as it was the apostle's. In opposition to the views that were now predominant in some parts of the Church, mixing up Law and Gospel, and recognizing in man a certain native ability to do right, or to cooperate with God in doing right, he enforced pure grace as the source of salvation. Grace in its sovereignty, 'not of him that willeth, or of him that runneth, but of God that showeth mercy': grace in its freeness, offered to all without money and without price; grace in its fulness, pardoning, adopting, sanctifying, glorifying; grace in its simplicity, without works of Law; grace in its security, ratified by an everlasting covenant; grace in its appointed channels, coming mainly through Word and ordinance; grace in its practical fruit, teaching men that 'denying ungodliness and worldly lusts, they should live soberly, righteously, and godly in this present evil world.' All experience shows that this is the message which most deeply stirs the soul of man, and which furnishes the best foundation for a serious, earnest, holy life." [6]

Dr. Blaikie's last sentence, just quoted, might well be read again and again, and the entire paragraph studied with care. It requires years for many men to grasp these truths: some never grasp them. In our day, when ethical preaching is the rule, and the preaching of the grace of God in Christ the rare exception (albeit all men inadvertently assume that they are preaching it faithfully), no sounder advice can be given a clergyman than to read Dr. Blaikie's tribute to Thomas Boston until its real meaning becomes clear, and its suggestions followed.

The several works of Thomas Boston are included in twelve volumes of his collected writings, edited by S.

---

[6]. W. G. Blaikie, *The Preachers of Scotland* (Edinburgh, 1888), pp. 201-202.

McMillan, and published in 1848-52. His *Crook in the Lot* (1737) was once to be found in almost every Scottish home. His published sermons include: *Sermons and Discourses,* 2 volumes (1753); *A Collection of Sermons* (1772); *Sermons of Thomas Boston,* 3 volumes (1785); and *Sermons on the Nature of Church Communion* (1785). Several biographies exist, such as: J. L. Watson, *Life and Times of Thomas Boston* (1883); *Memoirs, Written by Himself* (1776); *General Account of my Life,* edited by G. L. Low (1908); *Life and Writings of Thomas Boston,* by W. Addison (1936); and *Memoirs of the Life, Time and Writings of Thomas Boston,* by. G. H. Morrison (1899).

James Hog (c. 1658-1734)

James Hog, one of the leaders of the Marrow Men, was born at Larbert, in Stirlingshire, where his father was a clergyman. He was educated at Edinburgh University, where he received his M. A. degree in 1677. He seems to have studied theology in Holland. In 1691 he was ordained and became pastor at Dalserf. In 1693 he declined to take the oath of allegiance, fearing that it implied a recognition of the king as head of the Church. From 1699 until his death in 1734 he was pastor at Carnock, in Fifeshire.

It was in 1718 that Mr. Hog issued a reprint of the *Marrow of Modern Divinity,* with a recommendatory preface. In 1719 Principal Haddow, of St. Andrews, attacked this book in the course of a sermon preached at the opening session of the Synod of Fife. In 1720 the General Assembly denounced the book, warned all clergymen not to recommend it, but rather to warn their congregations against it. It was felt that the book did not tend to encourage holy living, but rather a spirit of Antinomianism. A committee was appointed, and James Hog of Carnock, Alexander Hamilton of Arth, James Brisbane of Stirling and John Warden of Gargunnock were cited to appear before it. Hog insisted that "he had received more light about some important concerns of the glorious Gospel by perusing that book than by any other writings which Providence had brought into his hands." The committee objected to the book on the grounds that it appeared to teach universal atonement and pardon, that it did not regard holiness as necessary to salvation, that fear of punishment and the hope of reward are not accepted as motives of a believer's obedience, and that the believer is not under the Law as a rule of life.

James Hog was a zealous preacher of evangelical truth as he understood it. He seems to have been a man of considerable ability, but his great contribution to the history of preaching lies in the fact that he had the courage to reprint, to recommend and to defend the *Marrow* book. Making due allowance for the defects of the book, doctrinal and otherwise, it did much to free the theology of the eighteenth century from certain legalistic and un-Scriptural teachings. Men came to realize that the gracious God does not offer salvation to a favored few, at the same time passing all others by; nor does He require of the Christian a holy life as a condition of salvation. Divine grace is universal as well as particular; while a holy life is a result and a proof of salvation, not a cause of it.

Mr. Hog wrote *The Controversie Concerning the Marrow of Modern Divinity* (1721-22); *The Scope and Substance of the Marrow of Modern Divinity* (1722); and *Memoirs of the Public Life of James Hog, Written by Himself* (1798).

James Wardlaw (1669-1742)

It is not necessary to give an account of the twelve Marrow Men, nor of those who were influenced by them. They were all conscientious men, struggling to know the truth more clearly and to preach it more effectively. James Wardlaw was such a man. Of his early career not a great deal is told us, but since he was not ordained until the year 1717, when he was 48 years of age, it is possible that his early years were devoted to teaching. At his ordination he became pastor at Cruden, but went a year later to Dunfermline.

In 1721 he came into prominence as one of the twelve men who signed a representation to the General Assembly in which they protested the Assembly's condemnation of the *Marrow of Modern Divinity*. Such an act required courage, for that book was looked upon as thoroughly unsound in doctrine, and the men who upheld it were regarded as heretics, and they risked expulsion from the Kirk.

Mr. Hew Scott tells us that James Wardlaw was "a strenuous opponent of patronage, his conduct in every respect was becoming the character of a gentleman and a faithful minister of Christ."[7] He was one of the minority in the Assembly, and one of those who were given the grace to testify against the unfaithful men and the corruptions that burdened the Church of Scotland during those early decades of the eighteenth century. It was the earnest witness of these Marrow Men that prepared the way for Ebenezer Erskine and the Secession Church. The admonitions of the Marrow Men encouraged the evangelical minority who were to remain within the Kirk and save her from even more serious corruption.

James Bathgate (1684-1724)

James Bathgate spent his early years as a schoolmaster at Inverkeithing. When 31 years of age he felt a call to the ministry, and was licensed in 1715 and ordained in 1716. He became pastor at Orwell, where he served until his death, eight years later. In 1721 he was one of the twelve men who joined in a protest to the General Assembly, following their unfavorable action toward the *Marrow* book.

Mr. Bathgate died at the age of 40, leaving a reputation for "fervent piety and zealous attachment to the doctrines of grace." It was not in the fashionable pulpits of Edinburgh, St. Andrews and the other great centers of culture and influence that men were to be found who proclaimed the doctrines of grace. It was in such relatively obscure places as Ettrick, Maxton, Portmoak and Carnock, and in Orwell, Torphichen, Galashiels and Dunfermline that such men were to be found. It was such faithful men as these who were ready to risk suspension and possible deposition from office, rather than give their silent consent to the Assembly's action in condemning the controversial book. Fortunately there was a delay, caused by the indisposition of the commissioner, and the matter was postponed until

---

[7]. Hew Scott, *Fasti Ecclesiae Scoticanae* (Edinburgh, 1868), vol. II, p. 572.

a later meeting. Such was the state of irritation within the Assembly that, except for this fortunate delay, the twelve Marrow Men might have received severe treatment.

James Haddow (c. 1670-1747)

James Haddow was not a Marrow Man. On the contrary, he was one of their opponents. He was born during or shortly before the year 1670 in the parish of Douglas, Lanarkshire. It is said that he studied in Holland, and some authorities believe that he was acquainted there with James Hog, to whom he took a dislike. Haddow was ordained in 1692 to the second charge at Cupar-Fife, and in 1694 transferred to the first charge. In 1699 he became professor of divinity at St. Mary's College, St. Andrews, and in 1707 he was made principal of St. Andrews.

Whatever his other characteristics may have been, Principal Haddow was a lifelong controversialist. In 1719 he preached the opening sermon at the Synod of Fife, using the opportunity to assail Marshall's treatise on Sanctification, as well as the *Marrow of Modern Divinity*. The sermon was published by order of the Assembly, and a bitter controversy followed. On one side of the controversy were the evangelical and constitutional members of the Assembly, who held firmly to the old teachings of the Scottish Reformation. On the other side were the Neonomians and Moderates, "who displayed an ominous readiness to accommodate the Gospel to the inclinations of fallen man, and to modify the principles of Church government and discipline so as to meet the views of politicians and men of the world."[8] A Committee for Preserving the Purity of Doctrine was formed, and among other activities, Principal Haddow and his associates compiled a list of statements from the writings of the Marrow Men, combining them in such a manner as to make it appear that they had taught false doctrine. Detached expressions were taken here and there from the *Marrow* book, and from the writings of James Hog and others, and combined in such a way as to mislead the members of the Assembly who had not read the book, or the

8. W. M. Hetherington, *History of the Church of Scotland* (Edinburgh, 1842), p. 344.

writings of its defenders. Because of this dishonest act on the part of Principal Haddow and his committee, the liberalists succeeded in persuading the Assembly to condemn the Marrow Men, and the book that they had republished.

This liberal group in the Assembly was composed of the old indulged clergymen, the prelatic clergymen, others who had accepted a modified Arminianism that was then the fashion in England and on the Continent, and the Moderate group. These four groups combined to form a strong faction who supported unsound doctrine and practice, and expressed a vindictive hatred toward the evangelical men.

Robert Wodrow (1679-1734)

Robert Wodrow was born in Glasgow in 1679. In 1691 he entered Glasgow University, and upon finishing the arts course, he took the theological course as well. In 1703 he was licensed and shortly thereafter he was ordained and became pastor of Eastwood Church, near Glasgow. There he enjoyed exceptional popularity as a preacher, and his earnestness and eloquence brought him fame. He had several calls to important congregations in Glasgow, Paisley and elsewhere, but he could not be induced to leave his church in Eastwood, where he remained until his death.

Robert Wodrow is well known as an authoritative writer on Church History. He published a number of writings on this subject, but the one which brought him greatest recognition is his *History of the Sufferings of the Church of Scotland,* published in two large volumes in 1721-22, and later in four volumes. It is an exhaustive work, the result of a vast amount of patient research. Wodrow's fame as a church historian must not cause one to forget that he was a preacher of exceptional gifts. Throughout the history of the Scottish Church, and down to at least the middle of the nineteenth century, it is a fact that most of the eminent theological writers, church leaders and professors were able preachers as well.

Other writings of Robert Wodrow include his *Analecta,* in 4 volumes, in which he sets forth many "remarkable providences" to Christian people; his *Life of Prof. James Wodrow* (1724), his father; *Collections upon the Lives of*

*the Reformers and Most Eminent Ministers of the Church
of Scotland,* 2 volumes (1834-45); *Private Letters* (1829);
and *Correspondence,* 3 volumes (1842-43), edited by Dr.
Thos. M'Crie. A good biography, by Dr. R. Burns, is included
in the second edition of his *History.* The *Analecta,* although
often quoted, is neither as scholarly nor is it as trustworthy
a source material as is his *History,* for in the *Analecta* there
are times when mere sentiment, rather than careful scholarship, is his guide.

John Willison (1680-1750)

John Willison was born in 1680 at Stirling. He entered
Glasgow University in 1695, but there is no evidence of his
graduation. He was licensed in 1701, and in 1703 he was
ordained and became pastor of Brechin parish. In 1716 he
was translated to South Church, Dundee. In 1733 he made
great efforts to prevent the deposition of the Erskines and
their supporters, and the following year he tried equally
hard to reclaim them for the Kirk. During his lifetime he
was drawn into many controversies.

Willison was not the most famous preacher of his time,
but there is one thing for which he won the lasting praise
of many in Scotland, namely his exceptional sacramental
sermons. He laid a well-balanced stress upon the Lord's
Supper. He was grieved at the indifference with which
some people regarded it in his day, and who made every
effort to stress the sermon as the only means of grace. He
was equally sad when he observed the superstitious exter-
nalism in some quarters, as though the mere external
reception of Holy Communion, or even one's presence at a
Communion service as a spectator, could convey some magic
to those who received or attended it.

He held the Sacrament in high esteem, and taught
clergy and congregations to realize its value. His stress
upon the Sacrament was well-balanced, and he avoided
extremes. Through his memorable sermons before, during
and after the Communion seasons, and by means of his
Sacramental Meditations and his *Catechism,* he taught the
clergy and people the great spiritual blessings derived from

a rightful reception of the Lord's Supper, and warned them against a superstitious attitude as well.

Willison's heart-searching sermons caused him to be in great request, especially at times of Communion. He was a man of great sincerity and personal piety, a leader of the Kirk in his day, and a preacher of considerable power. When John Glas and the Sandemanians were spreading their curious, primitive doctrines, Willison was one of the most powerful opponents of this strange new movement, and it was his balanced judgment, his conservative theological position and his positive preaching that did much to keep the people from flocking to the persuasive call of these harmless, yet misguided leaders. John Willison was an evangelical preacher, and his zeal for the salvation of immortal souls made him an acceptable preacher both in Brechin and in Dundee. His testimony against liberalism of all kinds, while often more vehement than persuasive, nevertheless did great good at the time, and kept many a man from falling into the indifferentism of what presently became known as Moderatism.

John Willison's *Example of Plain Catechizing* (1731), and his *Concerning the Sanctification of a Communion Sabbath* (1745), were influential books in their day, while his *Afflicted Man's Companion* (1737) was reprinted again and again during his lifetime and after his death. Other works were *Sacramental Meditations and Advices* (1747); *A Sacramental Catechism* (1734); and *The Christian's Scripture Directory* (1716). His complete *Works* were printed in 1769, with later editions, and his *Practical Works* in 1817. John Willison's books found their way into many hundreds of Scottish homes. During the great Scottish immigration to America in the latter part of the eighteenth and the first part of the nineteenth century, many of Willison's books were brought to America and were read by the family circle in the evening, and they did much to preserve the sturdy Scottish piety for which so many of the early settlers were noted. Willison's *Gospel Hymns* (1791) was a popular book in his time, and his *Balm of Gilead* (1742) was read by many. A memoir, by Dr. W. M. Hetherington, is prefixed to his *Works* and to some editions of his devotional writings.

CHAPTER VI

THE PERIOD OF SECESSION

KING WILLIAM died in 1702, after a reign of 13 years, and he was succeeded by Queen Anne. Proposals of a union between England and Scotland had been discussed from time to time, and after the accession of Queen Anne these conversations were renewed. The queen assured the Scots that their religious liberty would be guaranteed, as well as the government of the Kirk by the presbytery. The Scottish Kirk replied, asserting positively their right of self government in all spiritual matters. Relations between England and Scotland were strained, and war between the two countries seemed probable.

In order to reassure the Scots, an Act of Security was passed in the year 1707. It guaranteed religious liberty to Scotland forever, as well as church government by the presbytery. These things were declared to be conditions of any future treaty between the two countries, and were to form a basis for any possible union of the two. The same year the Scottish Parliament met for the last time. The union of England and Scotland took place.

A period of intrigue followed; and five years after the Act of Security had guaranteed religious liberty to Scotland, the Jacobite party succeeded in restoring patronage in the Scottish Church. This abuse had always been odious to the Scots, and no demand for it had ever come from the people themselves, for it deprived the congregation of the right to nominate and call its own pastors. This right was granted by the king or queen to certain individuals or groups of individuals. They were given the right to "present" or nominate a pastor when a vacancy occurred, and if the congregation objected, the patron, or man who had made the nomination, had the right to force him upon an unwilling congregation. This was known as "settlement by intrusion," and the unwelcome pastor thus "settled" in the congregation became known by the people as an "intruded" pastor. The people of the Scottish congregations insisted, and rightly so, that the authority to call and induct a pastor, in cases where vacancies occurred, belonged only to the Christian congregation, and cannot be delegated to a wealthy landowner, a bishop, a knight or to the king himself.

In 1690 an act was passed that gave the right of naming a pastor of a country congregation to the session and Protestant heritors; and in case of a city congregation the magistrates, town council and session were given the power. The vacant congregation was given the right to accept or reject the candidate, as they saw fit; and in case of an objection, the matter was to be laid before the Church courts, or assemblies of pastors and lay-members, and their decision was to be final. This law was a step in the right direction, for it gave the local congregation full power to accept or reject any candidate who had been nominated to fill their vacancy. It was still a disorderly procedure, for the actual selection of the candidate was made either by the heritors or by the town magistrates and the sessions — not by the congregation itself.

This act caused dissatisfaction, and in 1711 it was rescinded, and the evil old system of full patronage was once more forced upon the oppressed people of Scotland. A number of appeals were received by the General Assembly of the Kirk from congregations who objected to the candidates named by the patrons; but since the Assembly's power was restricted by the new law, they were powerless to act unless it could be shown that the candidate was unsound in doctrine, or had led a life that was a public scandal. A large proportion of the pastors of the Kirk voted and spoke against the forcible intrusion of unwelcome candidates; and they carried out their protest by refusing to be present at the ordination or installation of such intruded candidates. The great majority of the people were opposed to this system of patronage. The Assembly was compelled to obey the hated law of patronage under penalty of suspension or deprivation; and they were forced to resort to an un-Scriptural expedient. They appointed a committee with power to ordain and install an obnoxious candidate, leaving it optional whether the neighboring pastors attended such ordination or installation services, or not.

Cases of forcible intrusion multiplied, and for several successive years, much of the business of the General

Assembly was devoted to the appeals sent up by congregations where unwanted pastors had been imposed upon them. In the year 1730 there were twelve such appeals before the Assembly, each one of which required a lengthy hearing. In certain cases such forcible settlements of candidates were little short of scandalous. At Bathgate, for example, on Sunday, November 17, 1717, the pastors rode through the town escorted by a band of armed dragoons, with drums beating and swords flashing as the soldiers struck right and left in order to keep back the protesting people; "the Sabbath-day being much profaned, not only by the people of the place, but by many coming from other parishes to see a new way of propagating the Gospel by red-coat booted apostles officiating as elders." [1]

As cases of intrusion multiplied, the better men of the Kirk became convinced that such outrageous violations of the rights of the Christian congregation must be checked. It fell to the Rev. Ebenezer Erskine to take the first step in this direction. Mr. Erskine was pastor of a congregation in Stirling, and a man with an excellent reputation as a faithful, successful and talented pastor. He was a man of wide influence, and noted for his evangelical views, and for the fearless, convincing manner in which he presented them. He had been an active defender of the Marrow Men, and had protested vigorously against the heresy of Professor Simson. As moderator, or president, of the Synod of Perth and Stirling, he preached a memorable sermon before his synod, on October 10, 1732. Taking as his text "The Stone which the builders refused is become the head stone of the corner," he described at some length the wickedness of the priests and rulers during the time of our Saviour's ministry on earth; making at the same time some guarded statements in regard to conditions in the Church of Scotland. [2] Although his applications were very general, yet the guilty men took the matter to heart. Several pastors were greatly disturbed, and offered a resolution declaring that the sermon had given great offense, and calling upon Mr. Erskine to arise and

---

[1]. John McKerrow, *History of the Secession Church* (Edinburgh, 1848), p. 35.
[2]. *Ibid.*, pp. 44ff.

admit that he had done wrong in preaching such a sermon. This Mr. Erskine refused emphatically to do.

On the following day a committee that had been asked to consider matters, brought in a lengthy report in which they condemned Mr. Erskine for having described the evils that existed in the Church of our Lord's times, and by implication had made it appear that such evils existed in the Church of Scotland. Mr. Erskine requested a copy of the report, so that he might reply to it, but this was denied him. He spoke at some length, declaring that he knew that there was a large number of faithful pastors in the Church of Scotland; yet it is the duty of every pastor, when preaching the Word of God, to ask his hearers to apply this Word to themselves. If his congregation is composed of his fellow pastors, they are not, in the light of God's Word, exempt from its teachings and its applications. He explained the call of God to a man to enter the ministry, and the call of such a man to a particular congregation; declaring that the latter call dare not be delegated to any set of men, patrons, heritors or whatever they be, the body of Christians having not been allowed to vote in the calling of their pastor. Such a call, he declared, does not come from men who happen to possess titles, or who are rich in this world's goods, but rather from the children of God, who are rich in faith, and heirs of the Kingdom.[3]

The liberal party was in the majority and in that synodical meeting, and by a majority of six votes, it was decided that Mr. Erskine was censurable because of the expressions uttered in his sermon. Thirteen clergymen and two ruling elders immediately protested and declared their intention of appealing to the General Assembly. When the Assembly met it heard the case, and it was decided that Mr. Erskine's sermon contained expressions that gave offense; and that he was to be rebuked publicly and admonished by the new moderator of his own synod. Mr. Erskine protested in writing, and his protest was supported by the signatures of William Wilson, Alexander Moncrieff and James Fisher. The protest caused an uproar in the Assembly, and it was decided

---

[3]. *Ibid.*, pp. 48-49.

that Mr. Erskine and his three co-signers of the protest
appear before the Assembly and retract, under threat of
expulsion from the Kirk. They appeared before a commission and declared that they would not retract. The four men,
all clergymen of prominence in Scotland, were called before
the Assembly and suspended from membership in the
Assembly and from the performance of all ministerial
functions.

This outrageous act on the part of a national church
body in which the liberal group had obtained the majority,
caused excitement throughout Scotland, not only because
of the prominence of the four men, but because of the righteousness of their cause, namely the right of the local congregation, and not the patron, to select their own pastor. Seven
of the synods belonging to the General Assembly sent up
petitions in favor of the suspended men, but these did no
good. Mr. Erskine and his three associates were not only
expelled from the Kirk, but deprived of their congregations
as well.

On December 5, 1733, the four men, together with two
others,[4] Ralph Erskine and Thomas Mair, met at Gairney
Bridge, near Kinross, and founded The Associate Presbytery,
pledging themselves and the new organization to do all in
their power to give relief to the people in every part of
Scotland who were groaning under the yoke of patronage.[5]
Beginning with but four men, the new church body grew
in a short time to 45 congregations.

The new Associate Presbytery drew up a declaration in
which they set forth the errors and abuses of the ruling party
in the Church of Scotland, as well as a statement of the principles of doctrine and practice of the new group. Their
number increased rapidly, and by the year 1744 the growth
of the new church body made it possibly to change to name
to The Associate Synod, with three presbyteries included,
namely Dunfermline, Glasgow and Edinburgh.

In 1745, a dozen years after the beginning of the new
organization, the subject of the Burgess Oath arose. This

---

[4]. Ralph Erskine, brother of Ebenezer, and Thomas Mair, were not
formally received until 1737.
[5]. *Ibid.*, pp. 71ff.

oath included a religious clause that seemed objectionable to some of the clergymen of the Associate Synod. The oath imposed upon the burgesses of Edinburgh, Glasgow and Perth, for example, contained this clause: "Here I protest before God, and your Lordships, that I profess, and allow with my heart, the true religion presently professed within this realm, and authorized by the laws thereof: I shall abide thereat, and defend the same to my life's end; renouncing the Roman religion called papistry." The controversy centered upon the words, "the true religion presently professed within this realm." One group of pastors insisted that this oath constituted a solemn approval of the corruptions that prevailed within the Established Church, and against which the Associate Presbytery, and now the Associate Synod protested. Another group of clergymen declared that those who took the oath gave their assent to the true religion, and not to the manner in which it might be professed, nor the corruptions that might have developed in connection with it. A stormy controversy followed; and in 1747 the Associate Synod suffered a disruption, and the two groups became known commonly as the Burgher Synod and the Antiburgher Synod, or, officially as the Associate Synod and the General Associate Synod.

The secession of the four men who formed the original Associate Presbytery, and the number of pastors and congregations that continued to secede from the State Church and unite with the Secession, failed to bring to repentance the ruling group within the General Assembly. Some the evangelical men who remained in the State Church succeeded in passing a resolution condemning intrusion of candidates upon unwilling congregations, and their settlement by force; but before long this was treated as a dead letter. The better men continued to withdraw from the Kirk and to cast their lot with the Burghers and Antiburghers.

In 1752 a flagrant case of intrusion took place, and a pastor who was not acceptable to a congregation was forced upon them. Six neighboring pastors refused to have any part in the service. One of them, Thomas Gillespie, stated his reasons for refusing, and was deposed from office by the ruling party in the Assembly because of his convictions. Six years later he was joined by Thomas Boston (son of Thomas Boston of Ettrick) and Thomas Collier; and these men became the founders of the Relief Presbytery, so called because it was organized "for the relief of Christians oppressed in their Christian privileges." Their number was augmented from time to time by other men who seceded from the corrupt State Church, and finally it became a synod in its own right, with presbyteries and a theological school. Spiritual pacifists have expressed regret because of these secessions, and the formation of three independent synods. However, the ruling group within the State Church was alone to blame. They not only tolerated, but accepted Erastianism of the most flagrant sort, and went so far as to deprive the local congregations of the right to choose their own pastors; and, as the pastors of the first secession declared, the ruling party in the State Church conferred upon themselves despotic powers, taking action in important matters without submitting the questions to the synods and presbyteries for consideration, much less to the local congregations.

It must not be supposed that sound, evangelical preaching was encouraged in such an atmosphere as that which obtained in the State Church. The history of preaching has shown again and again that corrupt practice seldom exists in a church body where evangelical preaching is the rule. It is hardly necessary to say that the preaching in the National Church fell far short of what it should have been. At the time of the first secession, Ebenezer Erskine and his three associates had protested against "a new and fashionable mode of preaching" that "had found its way into the church," and which satisfied itself in discussing the moral virtues found in man, and rarely if ever giving attention to the fundamental doctrines of the Gospel. This deplorable type of preaching has appeared again and again throughout the ages, and in different lands and in various denominations. Along with such preaching one invariably notes a weakening of doctrinal conviction, a growing willingness to tolerate error, an increase in disorderly practice, a legalistic spirit, and in its later stages a readiness to persecute those faithful men who testify against the evils that have come upon their church organization.

Clergymen who are content to waste the congregation's time on Sunday by delivering colorless essays upon mental and moral philosophy, as the older writers used to call it, and to lay disproportionate stress upon "life" and its implications, may belong to one of several classes. They may be men of uncertain doctrinal convictions, who seek to evade their responsibility by preaching tepid sermons on moral virtues instead of the definite teachings of the Scriptures. They may be men who fear that the truth of God's Word might offend the weaker and more worldly members of their congregations. Again, they may be weak men who are content to preach colorless truisms simply because it happens to be the fashion of the day to do so. The National Church of Scotland had men of these several classes; and when the definite truths of God's Word ceased to be preached in many pulpits, it is but the normal thing that grave abuses made their appearance, and were tolerated and even defended. Courageous men who bore witness against these abuses came to be looked upon as ecclesiastical trouble-makers, and were dealt with so severely that they were forced out of the Kirk.

It must not be assumed that all the pastors of the National Church were unfaithful. A number of men remained within her ranks: men who were faithful to the truth as they understood it, and who continued to preach Law and Gospel to the best of their ability. They remained within the Kirk and testified whenever they could, but their voices did not prevail. The secessions of 1733 and of 1752 were but the prelude to the great disruption of 1843, when a group of 474 clergymen withdrew from the State Church, and for reasons quite similar to those that had caused the first secessions.

Ebenezer Erskine (1680-1754)

Ebenezer Erskine was born at Dryburgh, Berwickshire, in 1680. His father, Henry Erskine, had suffered at the hands of the Stuarts because of his religious convictions. Ebenezer Erskine was educated at Edinburgh University, and was graduated in 1697. For a time he was chaplain to a private family. He was ordained in 1703 and became pastor of the congregation at Portmoak, Kinross-shire, on Loch Leven. In 1731 he was translated to Stirling.

At the outset of his ministry he had no definite religious convictions, but preached a general sort of doctrine that was not greatly superior to natural theology. His wife and his brother Ralph came to an understanding of evangelical truth; and one day as Ebenezer Erskine sat in his study, he overheard through an open window a long conversation between his wife and his younger brother.[6] Not only was he surprised at their grasp of spiritual truth, but their words convinced him that he himself had not yet come to an understanding of Christianity. He studied his Bible, and it was not long until his sermons began to show decided improvement. He began to preach the truths of the New Testament, and especially divine grace.

The effect of this was soon apparent. Not only did the people of his own parish fill the church to overflowing, but others began to come from afar. At Communion seasons his heart-searching confessional addresses and Communion sermons soon drew thousands. After he went to Stirling he was one of the twelve "Marrow men" who defended the doctrine of the grace of God in Christ, in opposition to the Moderate majority in the Assembly. He opposed the Patronage Act of 1732. About that time he was elected moderator of the Assembly, and upon relinquishing his office in 1733, he preached a memorable sermon in which he warned against the evils present in the State Church. For this he was suspended by the Assembly. After a lengthy controversy he, together with three men who supported him, was cast out of the Established Church and deposed from the ministry. These men formed a new organization which they called the Associate Presbytery. By 1747 it numbered 45 congregations.

Ebenezer Erskine and his brother Ralph traveled throughout Scotland after the Secession, preaching and establishing congregations. Ebenezer was a man of intellectual power, an excellent preacher, possessed of a rich voice and a stately, dignified style of preaching. He was a

---

[6]. Donald Fraser, *Life and Diary of Ebenezer Erskine* (Edinburgh, 1831), p. 82.

man of conviction, and when once convinced of a Scriptural truth, he would yield to no man, nor would he soften or suppress a truth for the sake of expediency.

His sermons were lacking at times in carefulness of exegesis, but always centered on the Cross of Calvary, and upon the grace of God offered to the believer through Christ. He did not neglect the preaching of the Law, and he was faithful in his presentation of the prevalence and the awful consequences of sin. Nevertheless, in the witness that he bore to the grace of God in Jesus Christ, there was a joyful ring, more so than in the case of Thomas Boston. The Gospel to him was the glad news of divine grace, and he never failed to impress his hearers with the fact that the power of sin is great, but the power of divine grace infinitely greater.

Erskine preached from the Old Testament more often than from the New, but his sermons were not mere character studies of men. He loved to preach on the Messianic prophecies as contained in the Prophets and in the Psalms. Old Testament incidents and types were used freely, but always with an evangelical purpose, and this he presented in great detail. Although he might begin with an Old Testament text, yet one finds the Cross of Calvary in almost every sentence from beginning to end. He used the old form of homiletic structure, with its observations, doctrines and uses, and every division had a number of sub-divisions; yet there is always a richness of thought and style that made his preaching not only most attractive, but most helpful to all who heard him, and this in a day when Christo-centric preaching was uncommon.

There were times when the homiletic method that he used led him into exegetical recklessness that cannot be defended. For the sake of a wide variety of observations, uses or applications, he did not hesitate to include what a celebrated Edinburgh professor would have called "truths and very important truths, yet not the truths contained in the text."

As an example of Erskine's free exegetical method, one need only cite a sermon, "The Throne of Grace," to be found in his collected writings.[7] Taking the text, "Justice and judgment are the habitation of Thy throne" — Psalm 89, 14, Mr. Erskine begins with three observations as to the nature of the throne: the Royal Person, His badge of royal sovereignty and majesty, and the firm foundation of the throne. Then follows the doctrine, namely, the foundation of the throne of grace is justice satisfied, and judgment executed upon Christ is our surety.

There are five main divisions:

    I. A view of the throne of grace

    II. Its basis or foundation

    III. The pillars surrounding and supporting it

    IV. Why justice and judgment are its foundation

    V. The application of the whole

Each main division has three or more sub-divisions, and these in turn have from three to ten lesser divisions. For example, the first of the five main divisions is disposed as follows:

    I. A view of the throne of grace

      1. What is this throne, and why so called? It is:

        a. A mercy seat

        b. A seat of greatness and majesty

          (1). Majesty in His Name

          (2). Majesty in His looks

          (3). Majesty in His words and voice

          (4). Majesty in His vesture

          (5). Majesty in His sceptre

          (6). Majesty in His acts

          (7). Majesty in His heralds

          (8). Majesty in His tributes and revenues

          (9). Majesty in His gifts and distributions.

      2. How the guilty sinner views the Lord on His throne.

[7]. The Whole Works of the Late Rev. Mr. Ebenezer Erskine (London, 1826), vol. 1, pp. 214-247.

He sees:

a. The Father of our Lord Jesus Christ
b. The God of love
c. The God of peace
d. He sees in Christ the "God with us"
e. A promising God
f. A God wedded to the human family
g. A pardoning God
h. A God of infinite bounty and liberality
i. A prayer-hearing God
j. You see Him as your own God.

3. It is the throne of God and of the Lamb, because:

a. The Father and the Son are equal in this work of grace
b. A river of the water of life flows from this throne
c. The Lamb is in the midst of the throne
d. Seven spirits are before the throne
e. This throne stands on Mount Zion
f. The throne is surrounded by countless worshipers
g. The foundation of the throne is the righteousness of Christ.

It is to be noted that all of this is but the first of the five main divisions. Proof verses are employed copiously, and practically every division, sub-division and sub-subdivision has one or more such verses from the Bible, given in full. The sermon occupies 33 pages of fairly small print. This is not an exceptional sermon, for his discussion of "The Backslider Characterized,"[8] includes seven main divisions, with the usual multiplicity of observations, doctrines, uses and applications. While careless in exegesis and in homiletical exactness, yet Ebenezer Erskine's sermons are always thoroughly centered on divine grace.

Several collections exist of the works of Ebenezer Erskine. His *Works,* in three volumes, appeared in 1799,

---

[8]. *Op. cit.,* vol. 1, p. 32ff.

and *The Whole Works of the Late Rev. Ebenezer Erskine* in 1826. His sermons include: *Discourses on Psalm 2, 6* (1739); *Sermons and Discourses,* 4 volumes (1762); *The Sovereignty of Zion's King* (1739); *Saving Faith* (1843), by Erskine and others; and an excellent work of three volumes, edited by Thomas Bradbury and entitled *Sermons of Ralph and Ebenezer Erskine* (1738). Among the biographies and shorter memoirs of Ebenezer Erskine are John Ker, *The Erskines, Ebenezer and Ralph* (1881); James Fisher, *Memoir of Ebenezer Erskine* (1764); D. Fraser, *Life and Diary of Ebenezer Erskine* (1826).

Ralph Erskine (1685-1752)

Ralph Erskine, younger brother of Ebenezer, was born in Monilaws, Northumberland, in 1685. He was educated in the University of Edinburgh, 1699-1703. In 1704 he began his study of theology, and in 1709 he was licensed and started to preach. He was ordained in 1711, and called to the second congregation in Dunfermline, as well as to Tulliallan, in Perthshire.

His brother Ebenezer seceded from the State Church in 1733, and Ralph followed him in 1740. In 1741 George Whitefield visited Scotland, and Ralph Erskine protested when Whitefield maintained pulpit fellowship with the Established Church.

Ralph Erskine was the more eloquent of the two brothers. He lacked something of Ebenezer's stately style, but he possessed a fervent spirit that gave warmth to his preaching. He set forth Jesus Christ as the Saviour of sinful mankind, and had little use for sermons that were mere displays of rhetoric. William Taylor says of him, "Even Ralph Erskine, whose general scholarship might have enabled him to excel in this department, instead of attempting to conciliate or attract cultivated minds by his attention to literary elegance, accounted it as an evidence of spiritual defection in the community that, as he said, 'a world of people that come under the name of wits, and people of fine taste, are pleased with no sermons but such as are artificially decked with the flowers of gaudy rhetoric and tricky oratory, and this comes to be preferred to plain, powerful, spiritual preaching'."[9] Together with his brother, he preached far and wide throughout Scotland, and did much to keep the light of evangelical Christianity burning in a day when such preaching was not too common.

The preaching of Henry Erskine was the means of awakening Thomas Boston, in 1687. In like manner the preaching of Ralph Erskine, his son, caused John Brown of Haddington to realize more fully the truths of Redemptive Christianity. John Brown declared: "I can never forget those days when I traveled over the hills of Cleish to hear that great man of God, whose sermons I thought were brought home by the Spirit of God to my heart. At those times I thought I met with the God of Israel, and saw Him face to face."[10]

Ralph Erskine was unexcelled in his closing appeals. So many of the sermons in our own day are completely lacking in urgency. Men will build up their theme, step by step, and just where they reach the point that a direct appeal to the conscience is expected, they bring the sermon to a close. Not so with the Erskines. They never dismissed a congregation without urging upon their hearers a personal application of the truth. Herein is one of the reasons for the fruitfulness of their preaching.

The one fault of the preaching of Ralph Erskine, as well as of his older brother, was that he preached sin and grace, and nothing more. One hesitates to call this a fault, for it is a superlative virtue. Nevertheless, one misses such things as a fuller presentation of the Person and work of the Saviour, and stress upon His glory, His mercy, His goodness, and other such attributes. The Erskines laid utmost stress upon man's inborn sinfulness, his complete helplessness, and the riches of the grace of God in Christ. The people who grew up under their preaching were indoctrinated thoroughly in regard to the plan of salvation, but not so fully informed in regard to other teachings of the Bible.

---

[9]. W. M. Taylor, *The Scottish Pulpit* (New York, 1887), p. 177.
[10]. John McKerrow, *History of the Secession Church* (Edinburgh, 1848), p. 856.

This is understood readily enough. The people of Scotland were facing spiritual death because of the unfaithfulness of many of their leaders. The Erskines, and other men who followed in their steps, urged upon the people the truths that they deemed most important under existing conditions. Such men have been criticized because of their neglect of ethical preaching. However, one must consider the critical days in which they lived. Evangelical truth had not been preached in many places for years. When a man is on a sinking ship, our first concern is to guide him to his life-boat station. When he is safely ashore, then it is time enough to teach him the value of the cardinal Christian virtues.

Ralph Erskine followed the involved homiletical structure of his day. In his sermon on Gen. 49, 10, "The sceptre shall not depart from Judah, nor a law-giver from between his feet, until Shiloh come; and unto Him shall the gathering of the people be," Erskine states that in this active gathering at the coming of Shiloh the people act: 1. Spiritually; 2. Knowingly and judicially; 3. Evangelically; 4. Cordially; 5. Humbly and reverentially; 6. Boldly. The approach is made: 1. Penitentially; 2. Obediently; 3. Speedily; 4. Deliberately; 5. Chastely and uprightly; 6. Entirely and undividedly; 7. Exclusively; 8. Progressively. The first head, the Penitential approach, is made: 1. With a tender heart; 2. A tender conscience; 3. A tender eye; 4. A tender ear; 5. A tender lip or tongue; 6. A tender hand. Each head has its subdivisions, and these in turn are divided into a number of heads. He follows the intricate outline of his age, yet through it all he is always forceful, urgent, evangelical, and he employs numerous proof-verses.

Ralph Erskine's collected *Works* appeared in two volumes in 1764-66, and an edition in 10 volumes was published in 1821. His hymns and poems are contained in *Gospel Sonnets or Spiritual Songs* (1726), and *Scripture Songs* (1754). His *Sermons and Other Practical Works*, in two volumes, appeared in 1765, and the standard edition edited by Thomas Bradbury, *Sermons of Ralph and Ebenezer Erskine,* in three volumes, was published in 1738. Biographies include D. Fraser's *Life and Diary of Ralph Erskine* (1834), and John Ker's *The Erskines, Ebenezer and Ralph* (1881).

William Wilson (1690-1741)

William Wilson, one of the founders of the Secession Church, was born at Glasgow in 1690. His father was one of those who had suffered persecution and the loss of his property under Charles II. William Wilson was educated at Glasgow University, taking his degree in 1707. He was licensed in 1713, and for a time he supplied a congregation at Saline. In 1716, having given a good account of himself, he was ordained as pastor of the West Kirk in Perth. It was not long until he became concerned over the abuses in the Church of Scotland, and the misrule of the Moderates. He heard of the Marrow men, made their acquaintance, and decided to cast his lot with them.

In 1732 he was one of the 42 pastors and three elders who drew up a petition to the Assembly, calling upon it to right the wrongs which the Scottish Church had been suffering. This was the same year in which the Assembly passed an act, the object of which was to determine the procedure in cases where vacancies occurred in a congregation. When the patron failed to name a candidate for the pastorate of a vacant church, it was decided that the heritors and elders — not the congregation — should choose a candidate. There were a number of pastors who opposed this action as a disorderly proceeding, and a violation of the Scriptural teachings concerning the Church and the ministerial office. When Ebenezer Erskine, a leader of highest integrity, preached a sermon warning against such a procedure, and when the Synod of Perth and Sterling passed a vote of censure against Mr. Erskine, only four men out of the 45 who had opposed this violation of the local congregation's rights, had the courage to continue to protest. William Wilson was one of them. When committees could not cause them to change their opinions, they were suspended, and dealt with as erring brethren. In 1740 the final sentence of deposition was pronounced against them. William Wilson went to his church and into his pulpit on the following Sunday. A faithful old servant of the family followed him from the manse, and in the presence of the congregation waiting outside the church, with court officers standing near the door ready to serve the legal papers, the old woman cried: "Tak care what ye're about, Mr. William, for I fear if things gang on this way, I'll get your food to carry to the muirs, as I did yer father's before ye!"[11]   Mr. Wilson walked past the officers of the law, and up to the door.   They followed him, and taking him by the arms, ejected him from his own church and locked the doors.   Wilson went at once to the Glover's Yard not far away, followed by his congregation.   Hearing the sound of many footsteps, windows were opened along the street, and by the time the hymns were sung, an enormous congregation had gathered.

Mr. Wilson continued to preach in the open air, but meanwhile a new church, of large seating capacity, had been started, and was hurried to completion.   The facts were known to all the people of Perth, and many came from other congregations to the new church.

Three years after the Associate Presbytery, commonly known as the Secession Synod, had been formed by the four deposed men, William Wilson was chosen as their theological professor.   Theological students began to present themselves, and the whole burden of teaching all the branches of theology fell to one man.   He did his work thoroughly, and his lectures in the more important subjects were delivered in the Latin language, a custom which had not died out in Scotland.

William Wilson was a man of amazing energy.   The strain of prolonged controversy, the establishment of the new Synod, the preparation of all official documents for the new body, the building of a large new church, the pastoral care of a large congregation scattered throughout the city, the enormous burden of teaching a full theological course and the weekly preparation of two sermons proved too great for him.   He broke down in 1741, and died at the age of 51.

---

[11]. Wm. Ferrier, *Memoirs of the Rev. William Wilson* (Edinburgh, 1830), p. 336.

William Wilson was a man of exceptional talents, thoroughly versed in the Scriptures, scholarly, a fine theologian and a preacher of superior ability. People came from all parts of Perth, and the old parish boundaries were ignored. Allowing himself no time whatever for relaxation, he worked long into the night, doing accurately and faithfully everything that fell to his lot. Never was a lecture to his students given except after careful preparation. Hours of labor were devoted to his sermons. His incredible labors never for a moment deprived him of his good nature, and even men who differed sharply with him because of his theological views, admired him because of his perpetual amiability, and respected him because of the high quality of his preaching. No less a man than John Brown of Haddington said of him: "In his preaching he evidenced the greatest concern, heavenliness, mildness, and majesty that I ever heard."[12] Again, the same man said of him, "When sitting on the Brae of Abernethy (at an open air Communion service), I got more insight into the marrow of the Gospel, my God, than I ever got before or since."[13]

Although deposed by the Church of Scotland for his part in the protest against spiritual deadness and unscriptural practice, and dragged from his own church steps by force and ejected from his own church, yet Mr. Wilson, within the short space of one year, became one of the most highly respected of the preachers of Perth. The people flocked to the Glover's Yard, good weather and bad, to hear him preach; and when they buried him from the fine new church in which he had been privileged to preach only a few Sundays, it was one of the largest funerals that the city of Perth had ever seen. The people of Perth loved Mr. Wilson not because of his well-known good nature, nor was it that they pitied him because he had been so unjustly deposed by the Assembly and driven from his own church. It was not even his eloquence that attracted them, for eloquent preachers were to be found in other churches in

---

[12]. John MacKerrow, *History of the Secession Church* (Edinburgh, 1848), p. 824.
[13]. W. G. Blaikie, *The Preachers of Scotland* (Edinburgh, 1888), p. 211.

the city of Perth. They respected him because he was a man of decided religious convictions, with a willingness to suffer deposition and ejection from church and manse for the sake of his principles. Behind his genial smile and his hearty greeting was the old, dogged Scottish spirit that had led his ancestors and theirs to shed their blood at Rullion Green, at Bothwell Brig, at Drumclog, and in the Pentlands for the sake of the things that they considered sound doctrine. This same spirit was found to a degree in William Wilson.

William Wilson wrote: *A Defense of the Reformation Principles of the Church of Scotland* (1739); *The Day of the Sinner's Believing in Christ a Most Remarkable Day* (1742), which was a volume of sermons; other volumes of sermons entitled *The Father's Promise to the Son* (1747); *The Lamb's Retinue* (1747); and a posthumous work, *Sermons of William Wilson* (1748). His collected *Works* have been published, and accounts of his life have been written by Wm. Ferrier, *Memoirs of William Wilson* (1830), and by John Eadie, *Life of William Wilson*, in *United Presbyterian Fathers* (1849).

Alexander Moncrieff (1695-1761)

Alexander Moncrieff was born in the parish of Abernethy, Perthshire, where his father was laird of Culfargie. His grandfather had been a friend of the famous Guthries, James, William and John, who were leaders and noted preachers in the days of the Covenanters. Alexander Moncrieff received his education in the grammar school at Perth, at St. Andrews University and in the divinity hall at St. Andrews, from which he was graduated in 1716. After a year of study in Leyden, he was licensed in 1718 and then ordained in 1720. He became pastor at Abernethy. When the Marrow Controversy arose, he supported Thomas Boston and his associates in their efforts to establish definiteness of doctrine. At the time of the controversy regarding intrusion in 1732, Moncrieff defended Ebenezer Erskine, and with Erskine, Wilson and Fisher was suspended in 1733; and after a lengthy controversy the four were expelled from the Kirk in 1740.

These four men founded the Associate Presbytery, and
in 1742 Moncrieff was made professor of divinity in the
theological hall of the Secession body. Like his associates
he was an able, courageous preacher. His ability lay not
so much in external gifts as in his great earnestness, and
the persuasiveness with which he urged his hearers to
center their faith in the blood and righteousness of the
Saviour. A man of high social standing, he gladly gave up
all thought of wordly honors, or even of a high position in
the State Kirk, and identified himself with the little group
of men who sought to establish a firmer spiritual foundation
than had been the case in the past.

James Fisher (1697-1775)

James Fisher, of the Secession Church, was born in 1697
in Barr, Ayrshire. His father was a clergyman. After his
education at Glasgow University, he was ordained in 1725
and became pastor of Kinclaven, Perthshire. He was in
agreement with his father-in-law, Ebenezer Erskine, in
regard to doctrine and on the subject of patronage. When
Erskine preached at the Synod of Perth in 1732, and was
reprimanded for his sermon, Fisher was one of the three
men who supported him. The four were suspended, and
formed the Associate Presbytery. Most of the congregation at Kinclave remained loyal to Fisher. In 1741 he was
translated to Glasgow, and in 1749 he was made professor
of divinity of the Associate Burgher Synod. He was one
of several men who compiled a catechism, and since much
of the work is his, it was commonly called Fisher's
Catechism. •

James Fisher had many of the gifts of his distinguished
father-in-law, and his preaching proved fruitful both at Kinclaven and at Glasgow. Dr. Fraser, of Kennoway, said of
him that "neither as to sentiment, composition, nor delivery
had he ever heard his superior" in the pulpit.[14]

Adam Gib (1714-1788)

Adam Gib, one of the leaders of the Antiburgher Synod,
was born in 1714 at Castletown, in the parish of Muckhart,

---

[14]. W. G. Blaikie, *The Preachers of Scotland* (Edinburgh, 1888),
p. 210.

where his father was a well-to-do land owner. It was his father's desire that young Gib become a surgeon, and with this purpose in view he was sent to Edinburgh University. While there an incident took place that changed the entire course of the life of the young medical student. Strolling down the West-Bow one day, he rounded a corner and found a crowd collected. Right before his eyes, and almost within reach was a man dangling from a gallows. Young Gib stood there, motionless with horror, as he watched the man die. He was a felon who well deserved this fate, but for days the young medical student could not banish the dying criminal's face from his mind's eye. The great shock of coming face to face with a man dying on the gibbet caused Adam Gib to give serious thought to Eternity. He realized for the first time that he himself was no better in the sight of the Lord than this dying felon, for in the past he had lived a care-free life, dismissing lightly the things that he had learned in the kirk at Muckhart.

For weeks Adam Gib was filled with terror. He could not forget the gallows at Grassmarket, and the question came back to him again and again, "Will this awful sight help prepare me for Eternity?" He became deeply concerned for his soul's welfare. He drew up rules for good conduct and actually signed the National Covenant, but within a few days he found that he could not keep his good resolutions. He borrowed books from the Edinburgh dominies, and read of holy men of old who lived as hermits on desert islands. Upon inquiry he found that there was a barren island off the coast of Scotland, and he packed his belongings and prepared to spend his life there, thinking that the solitude might cause him to live a holy life and merit salvation. One day, in the library of one of the Edinburgh clergymen, he came across a copy of Martin Luther's work on Galatians.[15] He borrowed it and started to read it. In its dedication of seven quarto pages "To all Afflicted Consciences, which Groan for Salvation, and Wrestle under the Cross, for the Kingdom of Christ," and more especially in the Introduction or Preface of twelve pages, Adam Gib

---

[15]. Martin Luther, *A Commentary on St. Paul's Epistle to the Galatians* (London, 1575).

found light. He read the entire book and discovered why his own prayers and self-inflicted penances had brought him no peace of mind.

In 1735, while home on a visit, he found the parish of Muckhart greatly agitated. The congregation was without a pastor, and a man had been forced upon them by intrusion, in the face of an emphatic protest signed by a large majority of the parish. When he returned to Edinburgh, Adam Gib attended the meetings of the General Assembly just then in session, hoping, as Luther did when he visited Rome, to find great holiness there. Instead, he found that cases of intrusion of unwelcome pastors upon unwilling congregations were taken as a matter of course. He became acquainted with the views of the Moderates, and he heard of the disgraceful treatment given sincere men such as the Erskines, Moncrieff, Wilson and Fisher. Gib went to his lodgings, drew up a letter to the Assembly in which he notified them of his withdrawal from the Church of Scotland. This he laid on the Secretary's table during one of the sessions of the convention. Feeling a growing desire to give up the study of medicine for theology, he went two months later to a meeting of the little Associate Presbytery (Secession Church), met its leaders and offered himself as a candidate. He was received into their group, and became their first convert from the State Church. He studied theology, presumably with William Wilson, professor of theology to the Associate Presbytery, and he was licensed to preach in 1740, five years after he seceded from the Established Church. This irritated his father, who had a new will drawn up, disinheriting him entirely. When invited to hear his son preach, the elder Gib refused emphatically, declaring that he would not, by his presence, give silent consent to his son's departure from what he considered the true faith.

In 1741 Adam Gib was ordained as pastor of the Associate Presbytery's congregation in Edinburgh. He proved to be a faithful pastor and a preacher of unquestioned excellency. It was not long until the little Secession Church became agitated over the question as to whether one might, with a good conscience, sanction the burgher's oath. Adam Gib took a leading part in the controversy.

Convinced that no Christian could, with a good conscience, give consent to the burgher's oath as it then stood, he withdrew from the Associate Presbytery. The Antiburgher Synod was organized in his home, and he became one of its foremost leaders.

Meanwhile a reconciliation had taken place between Adam Gib and his father, who had begun to realize the seriousness of the abuses in the Established Church, and the indifference of the party then in power in the Assembly, or general body. Admiring his son Adam's determined stand, and having lost confidence in the good judgment of another son, the elder Gib made out a deed of gift, conveying the entire estate to Adam, the subject of our sketch. When the elder Gib died, the deed was made known by his attorneys. Calling the family together, Adam Gib secured from his brother a solemn promise that he would mend his careless ways. Then lighting a candle, he held the deed in the flame until it was consumed. "The property is all yours," he said, turning to his brother. "See to it that you administer it with wisdom. As for me, my first concern is my church, and I have no further interest in the family estate."

Adam Gib, like his father before him, was a man of determination, and with much of the old-time Scottish doggedness. He was a vigorous preacher. Several individual sermons exists in print, and he left a thick volume of revised sermons and addresses, by which one may judge his official utterances in the Associate Presbytery and later in the Antiburgher Synod. They have a decided polemical tone, and he spared no words in making his religious views clear, or in testifying against the religious opinions of men who differed with him. It is unfortunate that we have so few of the sermons actually preached to his congregation, for when not stirred by the fierce controversies that raged in Assembly and presbytery, he is said to have been a much more gracious man than his synodical sermons and addresses would lead us to believe. His keen mind was quick to detect dangers, and his impulsive nature caused him to rush into print with a dozen or so pamphlets which may be found readily enough today in the reference files of several leading libraries. These, and his last book, would make him seem to be a man of belligerent disposition, only too ready to speak scornfully of men who differed with him, and to put the worst possible construction on whatever they might say.

It is only just to the memory of this able leader and excellent preacher to say that the sermons that he preached to his own congregation were, according to all local traditions, much more temperate than his polemical writings. That type of mind is common enough among the clergy of all denominations: given to sharp invective when on the floor of church conventions or when writing for publication, but friendly and kind when at home among their own congregations. While Adam Gib spared no words when he warned his congregation against sin, yet he was faithful in pointing out to them the one way of rescue from sin, and it is believed that he led many to the foot of the Cross. Adam Gib's principal works are *Present Truth,* 2 volumes (1774), and *Sacred Contemplations* (1786).

John Brown (1722-1787)

John Brown of Haddington, the first of the famous "Brown dynasty" of Scottish preachers, was born in 1722 at Carpow, Perthshire. His early life was colorful. Coming from the family of a poor weaver, and left an orphan at 11, it was necessary for him to interrupt his schooling and become a sheep herder. In order to continue his education, he trudged to the fields each day with his books under his arm, and as the sheep grazed, he studied.

After finishing the more elementary subjects, he began the study of Latin and Greek. He learned the Greek alphabet by comparing Greek proper names with their English equivalents. Too poor to buy a Greek grammar, he compiled an elementary one of his own. As opportunity afforded, he visited Moncrieff of Abernethy and Johnston of Arngask, who assisted him in his studies.

His progress in Greek encouraged him to study New Testament Greek. After he had saved some money, he persuaded another shepherd boy to watch his sheep for a day, and he started at midnight and walked 24 miles to St.

Andrews, arriving just after the shopkeeper had taken down his shutters. The book-seller was surprised that a poorly dressed shepherd boy should be so eager to own a Greek Testament, and he questioned the boy. One or two professors from the university entered the shop and over-heard the conversation. One of them took down a Greek Testament from the shelf, opened it at random and asked the boy to read and translate. John Brown did it so well that all were astonished. According to one version of the account, the professor paid for the book and presented it to the boy; although Mr. William Brown says that the book-seller gave young Brown the book, and refused to take any money for it; and he described a visit of Dr. Brown to the book-seller, many years later, after the shepherd boy had become a famous Bible scholar and writer. His biographer questions some of the details of this story.[16]

John Brown attended Glasgow University, where he studied with Ebenezer Erskine and James Fisher. In 1750 he was licensed to preach, and after his ordination he became pastor at Haddington, near Edinburgh, which he served for 37 years. During December, January and February he preached morning and evening. From the beginning of March to the end of November he preached three times a day: at 10 a.m., in the afternoon and in the evening. He visited every family once a year, and examined them twice a year. The visits were not social calls. It was customary in his day to announce on Sunday the district to be visited, and the time. Then, taking one of the elders with him, it was the custom for the Scottish pastor to visit the families in turn, and catechize first the parents and then the children. Examinations were held at the church on stated evenings. A plan was arranged so that each family appeared twice a year for an examination in the Assembly's Catechism.[17]

John Brown introduced an innovation at Haddington. In 1750 it was customary in Scotland to celebrate Holy Communion but once a year. A celebration of the Lord's Supper required five days, and called for the preaching of

[16]. Wm. Brown, *Memoir of the Rev. John Brown*, pp. 34-35.
[17]. *Ibid.*, pp. 39-47.

at least six sermons, in addition to several Communion addresses. When Mr. Brown attempted to conduct two such services a year, there was considerable opposition at first, but in the end he succeeded. A more detailed account of the old-time Scottish Communion will be found below.

There was more or less superstition among the peasantry in the eighteenth century, and even in his student days, John Brown was regarded with suspicion by those who knew him; for who had ever heard of a shepherd boy who could read Latin and Greek at sight, and with so little schooling? The word was circulated that he had derived his knowledge from the devil. When his old neighbors heard that he had become a successful pastor, and was beginning to write learned books, there was much shaking of heads.

John Brown and his congregation belonged to the Burgher section of the Secession Church. Always a tireless student, he became in time one of the most learned men in Scotland. Although his salary was but 40 pounds a year, yet he managed to support a family and to buy theological books. In 1768 he was made professor of theology to the Burgher Synod, and he filled this position with distinction for 19 years, at the same time carrying on his work at Haddington. In 1769 he published his two-volume *Bible Dictionary*, and in 1778 his famous *Self-Interpreting Bible* appeared. This scholarly work has since been included at the end of many editions of the Holy Bible, and has formed the basis for several other such Bible helps. The New York Public Library has an impressive collection of editions of the Bible, at the end of which are to be found John Brown's Bible helps. He published a two-volume Church history covering the English-speaking countries, as well as two catechisms and various other works.

John Brown of Haddington was a preacher of distinction. Many have paid tribute to him, even David Hume the skeptic, who declared that Brown preached as though Jesus Christ stood at his elbow. Prof. Robert Simpson, of Hoxton College, London, said: "I well remember a searching sermon he preached from these words: 'What went ye forth into the wilderness for to see?' Although at that time

I had no experimental acquaintance with the truth as it is in Jesus, yet his grave appearance in the pulpit, his solemn, weighty, and energetic manner of speaking used to affect me very much. His preaching was close, and his address to the conscience pungent. Like his Lord and Master, he spoke with authority and hallowed pathos, having tasted the sweetness and felt the power of what he delivered."[18]

Two of Dr. Brown's sons became noted preachers, John Brown of Whitburn and Ebenezer Brown of Iverkeithing, the latter a man of unusual power in the pulpit. In the third generation was Dr. John Brown of Broughton Place Church, Edinburgh, and professor of exegesis in the Burgher Synod's theological hall. In the fourth generation we find John Brown, M. D., of Edinburgh, the famous essayist whose delightful story of *Rab and his Friends* was required reading for every American school child of a generation ago.

At one period of his life John Brown of Haddington seems to have believed that while our Saviour fulfilled all righteousness for us, yet He imputed to the individual believer only as much as was necessary to perfect the righteousness of the latter. This, of course, would leave room for synergism. Brown's Introduction to the Haweis *Commentary on the Holy Bible* contains chiliastic teachings.[19]

In addition to the writings mentioned previously, mention may be made of *Select Remains of John Brown* (1789); *Posthumous Works of John Brown* (1798); *A Compend of the Letters of John Brown* (1848); *Explanation of the Westminister Confession* (1758); *Two Short Catechisms* (1764); *An Historical Account of the Rise and Progress of the Secession* (1766); *A General History of the Christian Church,* 2 volumes (1769-71); *A Compendious History of the Church of England,* 2 volumes (1784); *A Concordance of the Holy Scriptures* (1854); *The Psalms of David in Metre* (1775); and *Systematic Divinity* (1782). These learned works are no longer in print and have become rare items in the field of theological literature. The chief

---

[18]. Wm. Brown, *Op. cit.,* p. 71.
[19]. Thos. Haweis, *A Commentary on the Holy Bible* (Glasgow, 1835 ed.), pp. 91, 118, etc.

biographies of Dr. John Brown of Haddington are: J. and
E. Brown, *Memoir of John Brown* (1856) and R. Mackenzie,
Life of John Brown (1918).

John Brown (1754-1832)

John Brown of Whitburn was born in 1754 at Haddington. He was a son of John Brown of Haddington, a brother
of Ebenezer Brown of Iverkeithing and father of John
Brown of Edinburgh. In 1768 he entered Edinburgh
University at the age of 14, the same year that his father
was made professor of theology to the Burgher Synod.
After his theological studies, Brown was licensed in 1776,
and shortly thereafter he was ordained and became pastor
of Whitburn, in Linlithgowshire, where he remained for
56 years.

He was not so famous a preacher as his brother
Ebenezer, but his sermons were thoughtful, clear in language and evangelical. He published some 16 works, several
of them of a biographical character, or discussions of the
works of evangelical preachers and theologians. While his
life and his preaching was less colorful that that of other
members of his family, yet there are some who say that he
was fully their equal in the pulpit.

Among the writings of John Brown of Whitburn are:
Select Remains of John Brown of Haddington (1789); *The
Evangelical Preacher* (1802-06), which contains a collection
of sermons by various men; *Gospel Truth Accurately Stated*
(1817); an account of the Marrow Controversy: *Memoirs
of James Hervey* (1806); *Nonconformist Ministers* (1832);
and biographies of Hugh Binning, Archbishop Leighton,
Thomas Bradbury and others. The best account of the
life, preaching and writings of John Brown of Whitburn is
David Smith's *Memoir of John Brown of Whitburn* (1834).

Ebenezer Brown (1756-1836)

Ebenezer Brown, of the Burgher section of the Secession Church, was born in 1756 at Haddington. His father
was John Brown, the famous Biblical scholar, his brother
was John Brown of Whitburn, his nephew was Dr. John
Brown of Edinburgh, and he was great-uncle of Dr. John

Brown the noted essayist. Ebenezer Brown received his education at the University of Edinburgh, and after his theological course he was ordained about the year 1778 and became pastor of Iverkeithing.

Ebenezer Brown was hardly the equal of his father and his nephew in depth of scholarship, but of all the "Brown dynasty" none could excel him in eloquence. "He was always good and saintly," writes John Brown, M. D., "but he was great once a week. Six days he brooded over his message, was silent, withdrawn, self-involved; on the Sabbath that downcast, almost timid man, who shunned men, the instant he was in the pulpit, stood up a son of thunder. Such a voice! such a piercing eye! such an inevitable fore-finger, held out trembling with the terrors of the Lord; such a power of asking questions and letting them fall deep into the hearts of his hearers, and answering them himself with an 'Ah, sirs!' that thrilled and quavered from him to them!"[20]

Principal Fairbairn includes him among the great preachers of the Secession Church, and calls him "the old man eloquent, Ebenezer of Iverkeithing, who compelled even the heedless people of Edinburgh to listen to him as he summoned the men of faith out of the Old Testament to tell of the faith that justifies; and to start to their feet to see the man of Tarsus, as obedient to his call he seemed to enter at the open door."[21]   Dr. Fairbairn refers to one of a number of legends that have attached themselves to Ebenezer Brown.   Once, when preaching in Edinburgh on Justification, Brown summoned as witnesses a number of Old Testament worthies, after the manner of Ephesians 11. With a vividness of description that might have done credit to George Whitefield or Christmas Evans, he caused them all to pass in review.   Then, pointing to an open door near the pulpit, he exclaimed, "Ah, sirs! And there is the greatest of all the noble witnesses to the truth of Justification by faith alone, the man of Tarsus, St. Paul himself!"   The entire congregation rose to their feet and stood peering in the direction of the preacher's extended forefinger.

---

[20]. John Brown, M.D., *Spare Hours* (Edinburgh, 1859), p. 184.
[21]. *Memorial of the Jubilee Synod,* p. 208.

Many such stories are told of Ebenezer Brown. Once he came upon a group of Highland shearers, and suggested that they hear the Word of God. They replied that they would lose their wages by so doing. Brown offered to give them the equivalent of their pay, and they accepted the offer. During the long prayer before the, sermon the congregation vanished. "Eben, next time ye pay folk to hear ye preach, keep your eyes open during prayer, and then pay them after sairmon," suggested his brother Thomas. On another occasion his horse stumbled and threw him into a snow drift. Several carters rescued him. "Poor auld mon, tak that, it'll hearten ye," they said kindly, offering him a horn of whisky. "Sirs, let us give thanks!" the old man said; and the prayer that he offered moved the rough carriers to tears.

One of the most baffling problems of the history of preaching is the success of some men and the failure of others. Ebenezer Brown was a simple, quiet man. He was pastor of a comparatively small village congregation, he lived quietly and he shunned publicity. His natural gifts were not of the spectacular kind, and he had none of the flashy showmanship of Edward Irving. He preached simple evangelical doctrine, bearing witness courageously against the awfulness of sin, and directing his hearers to the only escape from sin's penalty, namely the saving grace of the Lord Jesus Christ. With singular impressiveness of delivery, and yet without any suggestion of sensationalism or rhetorical bombast, he was able to give to the simple truths of sin and grace a forcefulness that was unique. Other preachers might have said precisely the same thing, and in almost the same words, but when Ebenezer Brown said them, men and women sat in awe, fearing that they might miss a single word. Although simple and quiet when not in the pulpit, yet when he preached, he is said to have been majestic. The evangelical doctrines that he preached were exactly those that his hearers had listened to again and again, but, as in the case of Alexander Whyte, they seemed to be surrounded with a new importance when proclaimed by Ebenezer Brown. There is no doubt that he was a man of exceptional eloquence, but it was an eloquence that was

founded squarely upon deep conviction; and in this all who
have characterized him are in agreement.

John Maclaurin (1693-1754)

John Maclaurin, noted for the excellency of his evangelical preaching, was born in 1693 at Kilmodan, Argyle-
shire. His father, a clergyman, died in 1698, and John and
his brothers were taken under the care of their father's
brother, the Rev. Daniel Maclaurin. John Maclaurin, the
subject of our sketch, took his degree at Glasgow University
in 1712, and after some work at Glasgow Divinity College,
he continued his theological studies at Leyden. His brother
Colin meanwhile remained in Glasgow, devoted his efforts
to mathematics, and eventually became professor of that
subject at Glasgow University.

John Maclaurin was licensed in 1719 and became pastor
of the parish of Luss, Dumbartonshire, on Loch Lomond.
In 1723 he was translated to the Northwest Parish, Glasgow.
Not only did he preach in English, but he gathered a group
of Highlanders who were living in Glasgow, and conducted
a Gaelic service for their benefit. In 1742 he took an active
part in the Great Awakening. He corresponded regularly
with Jonathan Edwards and other leaders, but he proceeded
with caution, convincing himself first of all that the movement was not mere emotionalism. He directed his efforts
towards keeping the movement as far as possible on a solid,
sensible basis, and he discouraged those who had a tendency
toward fanaticism. When Jonathan Edwards was dismissed
by his congregation at Northampton, Mass., and was reduced
to poverty, it was John Maclaurin who became leader of the
group who provided financial support for the famous
American leader.

Dr. Maclaurin's sermons, while of great length, are
nevertheless thoroughly evangelical. The great doctrines of
the Gospel are his theme, especially salvation through the
blood and righteousness of the Saviour, justification by faith
and sanctification by the Holy Ghost. His preaching must
have been of a very high order, because few congregations
today would have the patience to sit through his notable
sermon on "The Necessity of Divine Grace to Make the

Word Effectual," an exposition of Acts 11, 20-21.[22]   It fills
no less than 67 printed pages, and contains some 20,234
words.   Such a sermon would have required several hours
for its delivery.   Six of his printed sermons fill over 200
pages.   They are by no means diffuse.   On the contrary, they
must have required closest attention, for it has been said of
him that every sentence was a sermon in itself.

Dr. Maclaurin's preaching marks an epoch in the history
of the pulpit, because he was one of two or three men who
introduced a new type of sermon structure.   He abandoned
the time-honored method of observations, doctrines and
uses, and became one of the men who laid the foundation
for the modern form of sermon outline.   Previous to his
time the sermon was in the form of a great river with
many tributaries, and the preacher was expected to ascend
this river, stopping on his way to explore to the very end,
each of its tributaries in turn.   Dr. Maclaurin reversed this
process, permitting each branch of the river to contribute
whatever it could to the main stream, which flowed onward
toward a definite goal.

After his death Dr. Maclaurin's works were collected
and published,[23] and in the following century Dr. John
Brown of Edinburgh published a collection of Maclaurin's
theological treatises and six of his most famous sermons.[24]
In his Introduction to this work, Dr. Brown speaks of Maclaurin as a man "whom we have no hesitation in denom-
inating the most profound and eloquent theologian of the
last century."[25]   Speaking of Maclaurin's treatise "On
Prejudices against the Gospel," and the sermons "The Sins
of Men not Chargeable on God" and "On Glorying in the
Cross of Christ," Dr. Brown does not hesitate to say that
these "are compositions, the two first for profundity and
acuteness, the last for impressive eloquence, to which, in the
whole range of theological literature, we will not easily find
anything superior."   He finds in Maclaurin "a mind of

---

[22]. *Works of the Rev. John Maclaurin* (Glasgow, 1830), pp. 526-593.
[23]. *Sermons and Essays of the Rev. John MacLaurin, D.D.* (Glasgow, 1755), 2 vols.
[24]. *Works of the Rev. John MacLaurin* (Glasgow, 1830).
[25]. *Op. cit.*

extraordinary endowments, subjected to the best of all influences, and employing its best energies in the best of causes." [26] Dr. Brown considers the sermon "On Glorying in the Cross of Christ" as "one of the noblest in the language," and that it exhibits "the glories of the Cross of Christ with a depth of spiritual understanding and feeling, and a force of argument and eloquence, seldom equaled, and still more seldom combined."

Since John Maclaurin was one of the first who broke away from the old, artificial form of sermon disposition, it might be well to give an example of his style. In his sermon "The Law Magnified by the Redeemer," [27] he employs five main divisions. We shall give the subdivisions of only the first two of these:

I. The Law is Magnified by the Perfect Obedience that Christ Gave to the Commandments of it. 1. It was a perfect obedience. 2. It was the obedience of the most glorious Person that could be subject to the Law. 3. His obedience was by divine, solemn appointment. 4. His humiliation was the exaltation of the Law. 5. It was an example of universal influence.

II. The Law is Magnified by the Perfect Satisfaction that Jesus Christ gave to the Threatenings of it. 1. The Importance of the Law. a) God is its Author. b) The end of the Law is holiness, the glory of God, and the happiness of man. c) The Kingdom of Christ, governed by the Law, shows the importance of it. 2. The Properties of Christ's Suffering the Penalty of the Law. a) It was a real execution of the Law. b) It was a total execution of the Law. c) It was an execution of the Law upon the most honourable Person that could suffer. d) An execution of the Law upon the nearest relation to the Judge.

Dr. Maclaurin has been described as a man of more than middle height, with a fine countenance, and a man whose cheerfulness was his most noteworthy quality. He was inclined to be talkative, but a man of sincere piety and many genuine excellencies. Gifted with a fine presence, an

---

[26]. *Op. cit.*
[27]. *Op. cit.*, pp. 494-525.

excellent voice and a command of clear, forceful English, he declared evangelical truth in a manner that proved most attractive to his hearers. Dr. John Brown declares without qualification that "the great subjects of his sermons were the peculiar doctrines of Christianity, which were the life of his own soul." *An Essay on the Prophecies Relating to the Messiah* (1773) appeared during his lifetime, *Sermons and Essays*, 2 volumes (1755), was published after his death, and the collected *Works of the Rev. John Maclaurin* (1830) did not appear until long after his death.

John Glas (1695-1773)

John Glas was born in 1695 at Auchtermuchty, in Fifeshire, at which place his father was a clergyman. He was educated in the parochial school at Kinclaven and at Perth grammar school. After his graduation in 1713 from St. Leonard's College, St. Andrews, he attended Edinburgh University.

He was licensed in 1718, ordained in 1719 and became pastor of Tealing, Forfarshire, where he became very popular as a preacher. After a time he began to teach things that were looked upon as peculiar. He succeeded in introducing a weekly celebration of Holy Communion, and he declared that this is the most important act of worship. He preached vigorously against the idea of a State Church, and declared himself in favor of the complete separation of Church and State. He opposed the right of civil courts to exercise jurisdiction in matters pertaining to the congregation. These things were innovations in those days, and they led to his suspension from office in 1728, and later to his deposition from the ministry. In 1739 the sentence of deposition was rescinded, but Glas was not received as a pastor of the Church of Scotland. He became an Independent Presbyterian.

About the year 1730 he went to Dundee, where he formed an independent congregation. He refused to recognize the King as temporal head of the Church. He insisted upon certain customs of early Apostolic days, such as the agape, the kiss of peace and foot-washing. To a limited extent the common ownership of goods was practiced. He favored a form of church government by bishops, elders and teachers. Games of chance, and decision by lot, were forbidden.

In 1733 John Glas went to Perth and built a chapel. Robert Sandeman (1718-1771), his son-in-law, joined him there. While Glas was not a man of deep scholarship nor of exceptional eloquence, yet his quiet persuasiveness as a preacher brought him much popularity in his earlier years. After his deposition in 1728, this popularity waned somewhat, although he was always able to win followers to his sect. In theology he held firmly to the fundamental principles of strict Calvinism, and deviated very little from it except on minor points of practice. He was a quiet man, deeply spiritual except for his mild fanaticism, and he was entirely sincere in his belief that the church life of his day should be conformed as much as possible to that of the Apostolic Church. The idea of a weekly Communion, which he defended so earnestly from the pulpit, caused consternation in his day, but in later years it became somewhat common in England, and not altogether unknown even in the Scottish Kirk. His principle of the complete separation of Church and State, of the independent jurisdiction of the congregation in its internal affairs, and his denial of the right of the civil courts to intrude in spiritual matters, brought upon him great opposition at the time, but these are well-recognized principles today. His opposition to games of chance will find many supporters today. Some of his primitive Christian customs would brand him as a mild fanatic nowadays. His son-in-law emigrated to America, and died in Danbury, Conn. Many of his day were drawn into the "Sandemanian heresy," or the "Glassite movement," as it was called. Even the great Christmas Evans was all but won by it for a brief time.

John Glas wrote *The Testimony of the King of Martyrs* in 1729. His collected *Works,* in four volumes, appeared in 1762, and a five volume edition in 1782.

John Porteous (1704-1775)

John Porteous, when a young man, was stoned and driven out of his first parish, yet he lived to become one of the noted preachers of the Scottish Highlands. He was born in 1704 at Inverness, and took his degree at King's College, Aberdeen, in 1720. After his theological studies he was licensed to preach in 1727. In 1729 he was presented to the livings at Daviot and Dunlichity. There was a protest against his settlement, and when he came to preach his first sermon the people stoned him and drove him out of the parish.

In 1734 he was called to Kilmuir, but again there was objection to his settlement. The leader of this opposition seems to have been the influential Earl of Cromarty, who sent for the young pastor, whom he treated with great rudeness of speech, and finally ordered him out of his mansion. As Mr. Porteous took leave of the earl, he said to him, "You may treat me with harshness of speech, and you may command me to leave your home, but as the Lord liveth, the day will come when I can enter the door of your castle without opposition, and remain in it as long as I choose." These words proved true, but in a manner that neither John Porteous nor the Earl of Cromarty suspected. At the Rebellion of 1745, the Earl was captured and imprisoned for life. His beautiful castle, without its inhabitants, soon fell into a ruinous condition. The doors swung on rusty hinges, and boys broke all the windows and scattered the furnishings. The day came when John Porteous walked without opposition through the doorway, and made his way from room to room, unmolested.

John Porteous was a man of commanding appearance. He was exceptionally tall and strongly built, and he always dressed well. He preached with considerable animation He was skilled in the use of apt illustrations, but these tended at times to become too detailed. As one reads his sermons today, he will find illustrations that fill an entire printed page. However, sermons were lengthy in the eighteenth century, and if John Porteous indulged in an illustration, or in an allegory, that consumed five or ten minutes, he could be depended upon to devote an hour to expository preaching of a more substantial kind.

Duncan Macpherson (c. 1711-1757)

Duncan Macpherson, known throughout the Scottish Highlands as *Ministeir Mór*,[28] was born about the year 1711. He attended the University and King's College, Aberdeen, where he received his degree in 1731. He was licensed to preach in 1742 and a year later he was ordained as missionary to Glenroy. He was transferred to Mull in 1744 and called to Laggan, Abernethy, in 1747.

Tales are told throughout the Highlands that recall the legends of Paul Bunyan. Most of these have their origin in the fact that *Ministeir Mór* was famous for his great size, his physical strength and endurance and his vehement eloquence. The members of his congregation lived on both sides of the River Spey, which was crossed by means of a ford. Mr. Macpherson had no trouble in crossing the stream at times when it overflowed its banks, and rushed like a torrent toward the sea. There were times when the Spey was in full spate when no man other than the pastor dared cross the stream. On such occasions Mr. Macpherson would preach at the river's edge, part of the congregation gathered on one bank and part on the other, but so powerful was his voice that all could hear distinctly above the roar of the flood. Under no circumstances would he omit a service, morning, evening or week night; but when drenching rains fell, or blizzards howled, he was at the kirk. If part of his congregation could not reach their place of worship, the service was held at the river's edge.

On one occasion banns were to be read. Mr. Macpherson shouted the words of the liturgy to the prospective bride and groom on the far bank of the river, and since he was required by law to ask for a fee, he shouted: *"Ma chuireas tusa nall an t-airgiod, cuiridh mise null am focal."*[29] The fee was wrapped in a cloth together with a stone, and thrown across the river. On another occasion a child was to be baptized. The parents and sponsors stood on one side of the river, and Mr. Macpherson, in a stentorian voice which even a gale could not drown out, read the baptismal service

---

[28]. *The Gigantic Pastor.*
[29]. *"If you will send the money over here, I shall send the Word over there."*

on the opposite shore. Then, scooping up a handful of water
three times, he flung it across the river and succeeded in
sprinkling not only the child, but the parents and sponsors
as well.[30]

Duncan Macpherson was a man "distinguished for his
herculean strength and his no less vigorous powers of mind."
The legends of his amazing strength and physical endurance
are not his only claim to fame, for we are interested in him
especially as a preacher. He was a conservative of the old
school, and always ready to defend the teachings of God's
Word with a zeal that men learned to fear, and unfortunate
was the person, either in pastoral conferences or in private
conversation, who dared question the literal truth of anything taught in the Bible, or assumed to be found therein.
The keen mind, the quick answer and the booming voice of
Ministeir Mór convinced his opponent that silence was a
matter of prudence. Macpherson was not a conservative of
the disagreeable type, but rather was he a plumed knight
of orthodoxy, always eager to match wits with any adversary
and to silence him. It appears that he was in office but 14
years, yet in that brief period he established a reputation
that is lasting.

------

[30]. *Transactions of the Gaelic Society of Inverness*, 1888-89, pp.
226-227.

CHAPTER VII

THE MODERATES

THE MORIBUND condition of religion, so widespread in Europe, in the British Isles and in America during the closing years of the seventeenth century and the early part of the eighteenth, was felt in Scotland as well. One of its products was the appearance of a strong party in the Scottish Church who called themselves the Moderates. They were liberalists, and their method was an insidious one. They did not proclaim false doctrine nor did they attack the vital teachings of the Gospel. They merely avoided these things. They cultivated a fine literary style of preaching, and they used enough of the old phraseology to deceive the simple-minded. However, the all-important truths of Law and Gospel, of sin and grace, were avoided with great care. Under the colorless preaching of these unfaithful men, sinners were not brought to repentance, nor were men assured of the grace of God in Christ. Their sermons were devoted to polished essays on the cultivation of some useful moral virtue.

It is difficult to find a date for the beginning of Moderatism, for its growth was gradual. In 1685, according to Hetherington, three parties existed within the Kirk.[1] One group included about sixty clergymen who had survived the days of persecution. A second group was composed of some 130 men who had yielded to the king in his prelatic efforts, and who were indifferentists in doctrine and practice. A third group was made up of but three men, the remnant of the Covenanters who had followed Cameron and Cargill.

The Scottish Church had made a grave mistake. They had accepted into their General Assembly many of the prelatic clergy who not only were willing to yield to the king's dictation, but who had been guilty of the inhuman persecution of those clergymen who had opposed the rule of the State and the bishops. The acceptance of these men into the Kirk "infused a baneful poison into her very heart,

---

[1]. W. M. Hetherington, *History of the Church of Scotland* (Edinburgh, 1842), pp. 305-06.

whence, ere long, flowed forth a lethal stream, corrupting and paralyzing her whole frame. It sowed the noxious seed which gradually sprang up and expanded into the deadly upas tree of Moderatism, shedding a mortal blight over the whole of her once fair and fruitful vineyard, till it withered into a lifeless wilderness."[2]

In the year 1711, in addition to the large group of lax clergymen, another party appeared, composed of a number of younger men who accepted a modified Arminianism, then popular in England and on the Continent. In years to come this Arminianism followed the familiar course. Pelagianism, then a modified form of Socinianism followed.

Moderatism was in evidence as early as the year 1720, although 1750 is the time when it became a ruling power. "There would be no difficulty in giving a still more appalling exposure of the principles and the practice of that party, then and still known by the designation of the Moderate party, who, after a long struggle, had succeeded in usurping the government of the Church of Scotland, and under whose baleful domination truth was stifled, faithfulness punished, piety expelled, conscience outraged, heresy protected, immorality permitted to prevail almost uncensured, and the Christian community injured and despised."[3] This deplorable condition continued to flourish unchecked until it reached its climax in the 17 years that Principal William Robertson ruled the Scottish State Church, or from 1763 to 1780.

The Moderates laid stress upon good literary style and fine rhetoric, two things that had been neglected in the previous generations of uncertainty and bitter persecution. However, the Moderates did not employ their improved literary style to set forth the truths of God's Word. Toward vital Scriptural doctrines they showed a marked indifference. In their sermons they discussed only such things as are common to natural theology. They dwelt upon self-improvement and the development of moral virtues and civic righteousness. Such basic things as the fall of man,

---

[2]. *Ibid.*, p. 306.
[3]. *Ibid.*, p. 368.

their efforts could do comparatively little toward counter-acting the unwholesome influence of the majority.

"In the dissenting churches the state of things was un-doubtedly greatly better, for in them no toleration was given to unsound doctrine, and the tone of religious sentiment and feeling was much higher than in the Establishment. Still there was but little of energetic piety even among them; little of aggressive activity in the propagation of the Gospel; little of what Shaftesbury derisively and yet most truly called 'the heroic passion of saving souls'; and along with this there was a much too prevalent disposition to set the mere apparatus of ecclesiastical order above the great ends for which such alone is valuable. And as religion shared in the general apathy amid which the eighteenth century was advancing to its close, so it shared, also, in that sudden awakening which the startling events in the neighbouring country (i. e. France) had produced. Men roused out of their long repose became painfully aware of necessities which craved immediate relief. They felt that hunger of soul for suitable spiritual food which naturally follows a long period of spiritual destitution or inadequate supply. And as the existing ecclesiastical bodies were not sufficiently elastic — did not quickly enough expand — to meet the new and enlarged capacities and wants of the people, the latter impetuously rushed forth to find elsewhere what was denied them at home. Hence the crowds that followed Messrs. Haldane and Aikman on their first tours of preach-ing through Scotland. Hence the thousands upon thousands that covered the slopes of Calton Hill to listen to the preachers from England; and hence the almost instantaneous rise into considerable strength of a new religious body hitherto nearly unknown in Scotland, and for which, as subsequent events proved, the Scottish mind was not in reality cordially prepared. The new wine could not be stayed in the old bottles, and so when it burst forth it was caught and kept by those who alone at the time were prepared to receive it."[6]

---

[6]. W. L. Alexander, *Memoir of Ralph Wardlaw,* pp. 43-44.

The Scottish pulpit was sadly decadent during the reign of Moderatism. Hugh Blair's sermons, extremely popular among the elite, were but a fad, and had nothing to commend them other than their literary style. Principal Robertson's eloquent preaching and his stirring utterances during the long years that he ruled the Assembly, may have made many converts to liberalism in his day, but his religious writings carry no weight for later generations, because, as in the sermons of Blair, the fire of Gospel truth is missing. "Jupiter" Carlyle's sermons were so lacking in evangelical vitality that even his deistic friends were able to jeer at his worldliness.

The Moderates were but a part of that decadent spirit which was present throughout Europe and America, under different forms. Whether one call it Rationalism, Deism or Moderatism, the spirit was basically the same. Men had substituted human wisdom for the everlasting Gospel, as has been the case from time to time throughout the Christian era; and in all such times, spiritual deadness is the certain fruit of the type of preaching that is indifferent toward sin and grace.

Early in the nineteenth century the Moderate movement began to wane. The influence of such men as Andrew Thompson, the Erskine brothers, Thomas Boston and Thomas Chalmers was beginning to bear fruit. It had been a long period of darkness, but at last the brightness of a new day had dawned on Scotland.

Hugh Blair (1718-1800)

During the second half of the eighteenth century, no Scottish preacher was more popular than Hugh Blair. He was born in 1718 in Edinburgh, and he received his education in the University of Edinburgh. He was licensed to preach in 1741. In 1742 he was pastor at Colessie, in Fifeshire. A year later he became second minister at Canongate church, Edinburgh. In 1754 he was minister of Lady Yester's, and in 1758 he became minister of the High Church, which he served the remainder of his life.

When the rhetoric and belles-letters lectureship was established at Edinburgh University, Blair became lecturer

in 1759, professor in 1760 and royal professor from 1762 to
1783. His published lectures, entitled *Lectures on Composition* was looked upon for generations as the most significant book of its kind. In 1777 he published the first
volume of his sermons.

Hugh Blair was extremely popular in his day. Far
and wide he was looked upon as an example of everything
that a preacher should be. His printed sermons were as
popular as his spoken discourses. Even today they are considered examples of literary excellence, concise, clear and
beautiful. Their chief fault is that they often lack spiritual
depth. In striving for (and attaining) high literary quality,
they. sometimes become mere essays, delightful from a
rhetorical standpoint, but not always possessed of religious
fervor.

Not all of his sermons share this fault, for some of them
are evangelical. Nevertheless, too often the great doctrines
of the Scriptures are overlooked. His sermon on St. John
17, 1: "Father! the hour is come," is one of his best. It
presents the Atonement with admirable attention to the
passive obedience of our Lord, but Blair, like so many other
famous preachers, misses entirely the significance of the
active obedience of our Saviour. He mentions the fulfilment
of the Law, it is true; yet he finds in this only a setting
aside of a preparatory dispensation. He fails to grasp the
fact that the Law demands obedience, as well as perfection.
Jesus Christ became man's Substitute not only in suffering
the penality of the Law, but in keeping it perfectly as well.
He fulfilled all the Law's demands in so perfect a manner
that His righteousness was accepted by the Father as a substitute for the righteousness that man was unable to attain.

Where this truth is not understood, — and Blair seems
to see it but vaguely, — the preacher is never clear in his
own mind as to the true relation of faith and good works.
If all the demands of the Law were met for us by our
Saviour, then the keeping of the Law is no longer a condition
of our salvation. His perfect obedience is accepted by the
Father as though it were ours. From the hour that He
finished the work of Redemption, good works became a fruit
of man's faith, not a condition of salvation.

Although many of the preachers of Hugh Blair's day declared that they preached justification by faith, yet not many of them grasped the significance of our Lord's active obedience. Rather did they, like many in our own day, lay all the stress upon His passive obedience. In addition to several volumes on English literature and rhetoric, Blair published five volumes of colorless sermons (1771-1801). Three biographies exist.[7]

William Robertson (1721-1793)

William Robertson, leader of the Moderate party, was born in 1721 in Borthwick, near Edinburgh. His education was received in Edinburgh University, from which he was graduated in 1742. He was licensed in 1743 and given Gladsmuir parish. In 1756 he was translated to Lady Yester's Church, Edinburgh. In 1761 he was called to Old Greyfriars' Church, as colleague of Dr. John Erskine.

While yet a young man, and while pastor of a country congregation, Robertson appeared before the Assembly and "led them captive by his eloquence."[8] This address is said to have led to the deposition of Mr. Gillespie of Carnock, and to the formation of the Relief Church.[9] For almost thirty years, and until his resignation in 1780, William Robertson ruled the Assembly and led the liberal Moderate party. He was Moderator from 1763 to 1780. From 1762 to 1792 he was principal of Edinburgh University. He published a history of Scotland, a history of the American colonies and a history of Charles V.

Dean Stanley, who speaks in high terms of Principal Robertson, calls him "as thorough a Latitudinarian as Leighton."[10] Robertson was an eloquent preacher, but his sermons, as was the case with those of other Moderates, had little comfort for the poor sinner, nor did they point him to the way of salvation. Robertson was on most cordial terms with David Hume the Deist, with Gibbon the historian

---

[7]. Jas. Finlayson, Life of Hugh Blair (1801); John Hill, Life of Hugh Blair (1807); J. Hill, Life and Writings of Hugh Blair (1807).
[8]. A. P. Stanley, Lectures on the History of the Church of Scotland (New York, 1872), p. 145.
[9]. N. L. Walker, Scottish Church History (Edinburgh, 1882), p. 113.
[10]. A. P. Stanley, Lectures, p. 145.

and with Mrs. Siddons the actress. William Wilberforce speaks of men of that period who "have discovered such lukewarmness in the cause of Christ as to treat with especial goodwill and attention and respect those men who, by their avowed publications, were openly assailing or insidiously undermining the very foundations of the Christian hope — considering themselves as more closely united to them by literature than severed from them by the widest religious differences," and he adds in a note, "It is with pain that the author finds himself compelled to place so great a writer as Dr. Robertson in this (second) class. But to say nothing of his phlegmatic account of the Reformation . . . his letters to Mr. Gibbon, lately published, cannot but excite emotions of regret and shame in every sincere Christian." [11]

W. M. Hetherington calls attention to the fact that the Moderate party, under Principal Robertson's administration, not only showed a curious spirit of indifference toward any preaching of the vital doctrines of the Gospel, but that they permitted matters to go from bad to worse. Heresies were tolerated without a protest. Arminianism developed naturally into Pelagianism, then into views not far removed from Socinianism. Should any one come forth with charges of heresy, not only was he discouraged, but he was admonished to act with greater charity toward others, and to cease his heresy hunting. [12]

Principal Robertson may have been a preacher of rare eloquence and great learning, as his fellow Moderates declare, but under his years of complete absence of doctrinal discipline, Scottish preaching degenerated into rhetorical harangues on good outward deportment. The vital fire of the Gospel was all but extinguished. Robertson's *History of Scotland,* 2 volumes (1758-59), was reprinted in 14 editions within 34 years. His *History of the Reign of the Emperor Charles the Fifth,* in 3 volumes (1769), and his *History of America,* 2 volumes (1777), are good as histories go, as is his *Historical Disquisition Concerning . . . India*

---

[11]. N. L. Walker, *Scottish Church History* (Edinburgh, 1882), p. 113.
[12]. W. M. Hetherington, *History of the Church of Scotland* (Edinburgh, 1842), p. 367.

(1791). His biographer says that only one of Robertson's sermons appeared in print during his lifetime, namely "The Situation of the World at the Time of Christ's Appearance" (1755), preached before the S.P.C.A. Stewart considers it among the best models of pulpit eloquence in the English language, and it was reprinted five times and translated into German. It may be eloquent in language, but as a declaration of sin and salvation it falls far short of what such a sermon might be. The chief biography of Principal Robertson is Dugald Stewart's *Account of the Life and Writings of William Robertson* (1801). Lord Brougham's *Life of Robertson* (18145-46) adds but little to Stewart's account. The *Works of William Robertson,* in 11 volumes, edited by Dugald Stewart, first appeared in 1801-02, and a number of additional printings have appeared from time to time.

Alexander Carlyle (1722-1805)

Alexander Carlyle, of the Moderate or rationalistic party, was born in Prestonpans, Haddingshire, in 1722. His father was a clergyman in the Scottish Church. Alexander Carlyle entered Edinburgh in 1835, and then attended Glasgow and Leyden. He had no inclination toward the ministry, but decided to enter it merely to please his father. He was licensed in 1846, and in 1848 he was assigned to Inveresk, which he served after his manner for 57 years.

Alexander Carlyle, known as "Jupiter" by his worldly friends, was a man of good moral character, and was religious in a professional way, but he lacked evangelical zeal. He was one of the leaders of the Moderate party, which was responsible for so much spiritual lukewarmness in Scotland. He was a friend of Adam Smith and the Deist, David Hume. After hearing him preach as guest speaker at a neighboring church, Hume said, "I did not think such heathen morality could have passed in East Lothian." [13]

Carlyle caused great offense to his fellow clergymen by his attendance at the theatre in Edinburgh and London, in a day when it was considered very improper for clergymen

---

[13]. W. M. Taylor, *The Scottish Pulpit* (New York, 1887), p. 159.

to do such a thing. He was brought to trial by his conference, and escaped public rebuke by but a few votes. Carlyle
was a good speaker, and enjoyed quite a reputation among
Moderates and Deists. His gifts were employed only to set
forth the religion of the natural man, and he showed much
more zeal in placing liberal young men in desirable congregations than in bearing witness to the message of Redemption.

Carlyle's *Autobiography*, in two volumes (1860),
reveals only too plainly the worldliness of its author. In
addition to this work, a few printed sermons remain. They
are significant only in the fact that they demonstrate that
Christless preaching was a characteristic of the Moderates.

John Logan (1748-1788)

Somewhat better than his fellow Moderates was John
Logan, who was born in 1748 at Soutra, Midlothian. He
attended an elementary school at Musselburgh, and in 1762
he entered Edinburgh University. After serving as tutor to
a prominent family, he was licensed to preach in 1770 and
ordained in 1773, becoming pastor at South Leith. In 1775
he served as a member of the committee appointed to revise
the hymnal. From 1779 to 1781 he lectured on the philosophy of history at Edinburgh University. In 1786 difficulties
arose in his congregation because of Logan's interest in the
theatre, and these led to his resignation.

John Logan was a popular preacher in his day. He had
somewhat more earnestness than Blair, Robertson and
Carlyle; and his sermons seem to contain more spiritual
warmth, and a stronger appeal to the conscience. The great
defect of his sermons is the lack of the doctrine of saving
grace. He mentions the Lord Jesus and His work, but seldom in a manner that would make clear to his hearers the
fact that they stand in need of salvation, nor does he lay
stress upon the fact that Jesus Christ alone can give it. He
could descant with glowing eloquence upon the Christian's
robe of righteousness, but he reveals a shocking ignorance
in regard to its true meaning: rather does he give the impression that this righteousness is a quality that is within
the reach of all, not easily attained, but possible neverthe-

less. That this robe of righteousness is the spotless garment of the Saviour's own righteousness, with which He covers the filthy rags of man's spiritual garments, Logan never seemed to realize.

Logan published some poems that were well received. His "Ode to the Cuckoo" is well-known and is said to be of considerable merit. He produced a play which was not successful. It is said that he took to drink, laid down his office at 38, and died in London at the age of 40. In 1790 and 1791 two volumes of his poems were published. He is mentioned now and then among the lesser poets of the eighteenth century, but his sermons will never gain for him a place in the evangelical succession. Logan's writings include the two volumes of sermons (1790-91), of which there are various editions. His biography was written by Dr. Robert Anderson.

Chapter VIII

THE EVANGELICAL AWAKENING

It must not be supposed that the light of evangelical truth had been extinguished entirely in Scotland. Even in the darkest days there were faithful men, here and there, who preached Christ crucified with great zeal. During the early decades of the eighteenth century conditions were deplorable. Not only had sad conditions appeared in the General Assembly itself, when faithful men of true evangelical spirit were disciplined because they felt it their duty to protest against the abuses in the Kirk; but, what is even worse, it was one of those recurring periods familiar enough to every student of Church history. It was an era in which, to quote Ebenezer Erskine, "sapless and lifeless descanting upon the moral virtues" was the fashionable mode of preaching, while "the peculiar doctrines of the Gospel were seldom if ever alluded to." We find identical conditions in Scotland, England, Wales, America and in continental Europe.

The evangelical awakening appeared in America in 1734, with the preaching of the Tennents and Jonathan Edwards. Strangely enough, it was at precisely the same time that Howel Harris and Daniel Rowland began to preach in Wales. Five years later the evangelical awakening appeared in England when George Whitefield began to preach on Kingswood Common, near Bristol. A year later John Wesley joined him. Two years later the Cambuslang Awakening gave notice to the people of Scotland that the evangelical movement had reached their country as well. The awakening began almost simultaneously at Cambuslang, a village of 900 souls, located six miles south of Glasgow, and at the village of Kilsyth, in Stirlingshire.

Mr. James Robe, pastor of the parish of 1100 souls at Kilsyth, has left us an extended account of the awakening. "I observed that the far greater part of every public audience were secure, unconcerned and fearless; and therefore I preached the terrors of the Law in the strongest terms I could, that is to say, in express Scripture terms. I feared to daub or deal slightly with them, but told great and small that they were the children of the devil while they were in the state of unbelief, and that if they continued so to the end, in our Lord's plain terms they would be damned. I resolved that I would cry aloud and not spare, and preach with that seriousness and fervour that became me as knowing that my hearers must either be prevailed with or be damned; and that they might discern I was in good earnest with them, and really meant as I spoke. . . . I can instance and show sermons containing the terrors of the Law that I have preached many years ago without known success, but which I have again preached now, in weaker terms, with great success; so that all might see that it is not from man, but the Spirit of the Lord, that there is so great a difference as to efficacy." [1]

Meanwhile Mr. William McCulloch, of Cambuslang, had been preaching Law and Gospel to his congregation. In both villages great interest was aroused. Congregations overflowed the churches, and outdoor preaching became necessary. Two or three Sunday services, a mid-week service, and finally daily sermonic lectures on Christian doctrine and living were demanded by the people of both villages.

Mr. McCulloch and Mr. Robe suffered much at the hands of the Moderates, for these men ridiculed and condemned their preaching. Greatly exaggerated reports were circulated, and like all rumors, these grew with the telling and the retelling. The enemies of the two evangelical preachers stopped at nothing. They went so far as to say that the outdoor congregations at Cambuslang and at Kilsyth were fanatical, that they screamed and shouted, that they threw themselves on the ground in frenzy. Some of these slanders appeared in print, and they are repeated now and then even today.

The truth of the matter seems to be that George Whitefield, who had just returned from America, was invited to

---

[1]. James Robe, *Narrative of the Extraordinary Work of the Spirit of God at Cambuslang, Kilsyth, and Other Places* (Glasgow, 1790, 1840), p. 59.

visit Cambuslang. He arrived on July 6, 1743, and preached from two o'clock in the afternoon, with two brief intermissions, until 11 at night. More than 20,000 people attended, remaining until Mr. Whitefield had finished, and then crying out, begging him to continue. Even Mr. Whitefield was weary after his nine hour sermon, and he called upon Mr. McCulloch to continue. McCulloch preached from 11 P. M. until one in the morning. Many of the people remained all night, devoting the time to the singing of hymns, and hoping that Mr. Whitefield would preach again on the following day.

This remarkable preaching mission ended on July 11, with an outdoor congregation of 20,000 people. Many neighboring pastors had come to Cambuslang, and the preaching mission ended with a Communion service. It was not an indiscriminate service, for tokens were distributed to those entitled to receive the Sacrament. 1700 people received Holy Communion at a great outdoor service. On August 15 there was another outdoor Communion service, with 30,000 people present, many of them from the surrounding towns and country. The preaching mission continued for five months, and only a severe winter halted it. Four hundred new members were gained by the local congregation, and Mr. McCulloch's successor declared that the influence of the Cambuslang "work" was still evident thirty years later, not only in the singularly upright lives of the people as far as outward deportment is concerned, but in their evangelical spirit as well.

Dr. Blaikie, who treats the subject impartially, says that when a conviction of sin fell upon the people that they "sometimes manifested their emotion in convulsive sobbings and protestations most difficult to subdue."[2] However, McCulloch, Robe and the other pastors did their utmost to discourage such emotionalism, and to urge their hearers to direct their thoughts to the Cross of Calvary. "When they apprehended the grace of God in Christ," says Dr. Blaikie, "their distress was followed by a peace and joy in believing of almost rapturous intensity, and a marvellous relish for

---

[2]. W. G. Blaikie, *The Preachers of Scotland* (Edinburgh, 1888), p. 257.

the Word and ordinances of God. And according to the testimony of those most cognisant of the movement, the change effected on the subjects of the awakening was highly beneficial, not only in its religious but in its moral and social aspects. Where vice had prevailed, it was abandoned, injuries were forgiven, estranged families reconciled, restoration made of property that had been unjustly appropriated, and a new conscientiousness manifested in matters where before there had been much remissness. The movement reached its climax when Whitefield came to the Communion at Cambuslang. His power not only of arresting the multitude but impressing the individual was marvellously manifested, and the results were like those of the day of Pentecost at Jerusalem. The direct presentation and free offer of all the blessings of Redemption through the blood of Christ fell like the bread of Heaven on many a heart that had been made sore and hungry under the searching and soul-emptying preaching of the ministers on the nature and need of Regeneration." [3]

The spiritual awakening was felt throughout Scotland. Cambuslang, Kilsyth, Irvine and many other communities were involved. Sermons were preached daily, and often twice daily, to great congregations who gathered in the open fields because no church in Scotland was large enough to hold them. There was a genuine hunger for evangelical preaching. The Moderates, who preached only natural theology, and rejected the idea of a spiritual awakening, ridiculed the movement and spread distorted reports concerning it. The pastors of the Secession synods could see no good in it, and they warned their people against it; for they looked upon the National Church as spiritually dead, and they doubted that any genuine manifestation of spiritual fervor could be possible within such an organization.

The evangelical awakening was not a revival in the modern sense of the term. It was one of those unusual eras, such as one may find from time to time in the history of the Christian Church, when people who have long been deprived of evangelical preaching, discover some clergyman,

3. *Ibid.*, pp. 258-259.

or a group of clergymen, willing to preach Law and Gospel. The evangelical awakening in Scotland was but part of a movement that was present in America, England, Wales and Cornwall.   After a long period of spiritual hunger, new voices began to be heard: Jonathan Edwards, George White-field, John Wesley, Howell Harris, Daniel Rowland, William McCulloch, James Robe and others.

These men had certain things in common.   They were noted for their preaching of the Law, which they declared with terrible force.   Jonathan Edward's famous sermon on "Sinners in the Hand of an Angry God" is an example of the kind of preaching that brought terror to the multitudes. The same men also preached the Gospel, which is the gracious offer of salvation through Jesus Christ alone. Other clergymen had preached their churches empty by means of ethical sermons.   A sermon should have a certain ethical element, but this must be used with discretion, like sugar in one's tea.   At recurring intervals it has been the fashion of the day to preach sermons that are entirely ethical, and when little or nothing is said in regard to sin and salvation.   Many an eminent preacher has confessed that there was a period in his life when he preached sermons of the self-improvement type, and with no results other than the sight of a dwindling congregation.   Then he has had an awakening himself, and has turned to the preaching of Law and Gospel.   Where this was done correctly, people have turned from their complacency and their worldliness, and have been filled with genuine concern for their spiritual welfare.   In some cases neighboring pastors have done like-wise, and churches and chapels were crowded once more. Often there was a genuine thirst for the Gospel, and in a number of cases the people themselves demanded more than a single weekly sermon.   They flocked to their churches night after night, and where the preacher was able to proclaim with conviction the truths of sin and grace, there was an awakening of fresh life among what had seemed to be but dry bones.

It does not require a deep understanding of the spiritual psychology of Law and Gospel to account for such periodic awakenings.   Periods of spiritual decline have been followed by times of spiritual awakening and refreshment.   Such things are impossible in an age of Rationalism, or of Deism, or of Modernism; neither have the destructive Biblical critics and their spiritual progeny the liberalists ever brought about such an awakening.

The Scottish Moderates were quite correct when they said that the evangelical preachers had but one stock outline that they fitted to every text: I. The fall of Adam and the depravity of the natural man; II. The way of recovery through the righteousness and blood of the Lord Jesus Christ; III. The practical application of these things by the Holy Ghost to the individual sinner.   This, said in derision, was a sincerer compliment than the Moderates realized. Evangelical preachers have not always confined themselves to the exact wording of this three-fold outline, but they have kept closely to the truths that are set forth by it.   Many of them have erred in matters of detail, but where these fundamental truths are declared, there has always been a marked improvement in the faith and life of the individual.

The Scottish Communion Service

A Scottish Communion service, in the eighteenth century, was an important event.   In our day, when the popular demand is for a service not longer than one hour and fifteen minutes, it is difficult to realize that the people of Scotland devoted five days to the celebration of Holy Communion.

The service started with a day of fasting and preparation.   This was the Thursday or Friday previous to Communion Sunday.   The day was observed with characteristic strictness.   On Friday the people went to the kirk for what was called an Exercise.   On Saturday there were two sermons in the afternoon and at least one more in the evening. On Sunday morning the Action Sermon was preached by the pastor of the church, followed by the Debarring.   I Cor. 11, 23-32 was read, and the people were carefully instructed in regard to worthy and unworthy reception of the Sacrament.   A prayer of consecration followed.   Then a group of communicants came forward to the "table seats," and the

pastor delivered another address to these people. After
they had received Holy Communion, they returned to their
seats, and another group came forward, and there was
another address. This continued until all had received.
Such a service required from eight to nine hours, and sometimes longer, the people remaining in the church until the
close of the service. On Monday there was a service of
Thanksgiving, with at least two sermons.

This is the type of service found at Haddington about
the year 1750, when John Brown had just become pastor.
Even more lengthy were the services of a previous generation, for we have an account of the customary Communion
service in James Fisher's church in Glasgow, in the latter
part of the seventeenth century. At that time Thursday was
observed as a day of strict fasting, and there were two
sermons at the kirk, one in the morning and one in the
afternoon. On Friday there was a sermon in the evening.
On Saturday there were four sermons during the day, two
within the church, and two in a tent erected for the purpose
in the churchyard. On Saturday evening there was the
service known as the Exercise. On Sunday the Action
Sermon was preached by the pastor of the church, and this
was followed by no less than 18 "table services," at which
visiting pastors addressed the communicants. This Sunday
service lasted without interruption from 9.30 a. m. until
9.30 p. m. This was not all, for meanwhile nine more
sermons were preached by seven different pastors, in the
tent in the churchyard. On Monday the thanksgiving
services were held, and two sermons were preached in the
church and two in the tent. In all, 24 different sermons
had been preached within five days.

It was the custom at that time to conduct but one
Communion service a year, but it must not be supposed that
the people received Communion but once a year. Churches
"gave way" to one another. On the Sunday that Holy
Communion was celebrated in James Fisher's congregation,
many of the nearby congregations closed their doors, and
their members attended the various services, and received
Communion at the church in question. Two, three, and
sometimes as many as seven or eight pastors took part in

such a service. The sermons were rarely less than an hour in length, although the addresses at the "table services" were shorter, where large numbers of communicants presented themselves.

People came from the neighboring congregations, and from surrounding towns. Often in reading the biographies of the celebrated preachers of those days, one comes across the words, "he was especially noted for the impressiveness of his sermons at Communion seasons, and his services were always in great demand upon such occasions." Preachers prepared for weeks, and even months, for these Communion sermons, studying, writing, revising, rewriting, and then rehearsing their discourses. Every now and again one comes upon the statement that some clergyman locked himself in his room, and preached his sermon again and again, with all the vigor that he employed on Sunday.

It must not be assumed that these customs led to indiscriminate practice. Denominational lines were drawn sharply in those days. The Burghers would have little fellowship with the Anti-burghers, and neither Burgher nor Anti-burgher cared to mingle with the State Kirk. It was in relatively recent times that unionism crept in, and this was met with vehement opposition by many.

When men such as John Brown of Haddington suggested two Communion services a year, in the same congregation, they met with much opposition, but after a time two services a year became common, then three, then four, and finally six. When this came about, needless to say the old-time Sunday service of eight to ten or more hours in length became a thing of the past, neither were there from 12 to 24 sermons preached at a single five-day Communion season.

William McCulloch (1691-1771)

William McCulloch was born in 1691 in Whithorn, where his father was master of the parish school. He attended Edinburgh University, going from there to Glasgow University where he received his degree in 1712. After his theological studies he was licensed in 1722, and became chaplain to the laird of Aikenhead. He was ordained in

1731 and became pastor in the town of Cambuslang, near
Glasgow. His life among the weavers, who made up a large
part of the population of Cambuslang, was not particularly
eventful until the year 1742. Like James Robe of Kilsyth,
Mr. McCulloch preached a series of sermons on Christian
doctrine, explaining these teachings and applying them to
the needs of his congregation. In the eighteenth century
such a thing as this was not common in Scotland, and the
preaching of Law and Gospel was the exception rather than
the rule. Great interest was aroused; there were many
requests for Bibles; and a number of people asked Mr. Mc-
Culloch to start a Bible class so that the people of the village,
with its population of 900, might receive instruction.

During the months that followed, the people came in
increasing numbers and studied such things as the Fall of
man, the sinful nature of the human race, the need of
regeneration, justification by grace through faith and the
sanctifying work of the Holy Ghost. The church was not in
good repair, and when spring came the pastor began to
preach in a nearby glen. The congregation increased, and
the place of worship was moved to a hillside. People came
from the surrounding countryside, and from Glasgow six
miles away to what came to be known as "the preaching
brae," and it was not long until "the Cam'slang wark"
became known in more distant places. Pastors from other
towns came, either to see and hear for themselves, or to
take part in the services. Congregations of 20,000 people
were not unusual, and at times there was a sermon every
evening. On certain occasions there were three sermons on
Thursday, Saturday and Monday, with no less than six sermons on Sunday, preached by Mr. McCulloch and the
visiting pastors.

Mr. McCulloch insisted upon thorough instruction, and
the results of the preaching mission, which continued for
six months, were permanent. In 1757, fifteen years after
this remarkable spiritual awakening, Mr. McCulloch published a detailed report of the results, and the permanent
changes in the lives of the people of Cambuslang.[4] In all,

---

[4]. Wm. McCulloch, *Attestation* (Glasgow, 1757), with a document of
verification by the Kirk-session of Cambuslang.

some 400 people had been gained by the churches of the vicinity, of whom 70 united with Mr. McCulloch's congregation. He declared in his report that the cursing and swearing for which the village had been notorious, was a thing of the past; men who formerly spent their evenings in the taverns, drinking and gambling, now remained at home with their families, and daily Bible study and family prayer was general; drunkards who had once slept until 8 or 9 a. m., now rose at daylight in order to engage in the systematic Bible study that had been one of the results of the preaching mission; violent family quarrels became a rarity; covetous and worldly-minded people were not only induced to give liberally to missions and charity, but Mr. McCulloch was obliged at times to discourage people who sought to give really more than they could afford; there was unusual zeal for the Word, and the Thursday evening Bible hour was attended by the people of the village, by farm laborers and by servants; the voluntary attendance at Holy Communion increased greatly, and there was a request for two Communion services a year, in a day when but one annual Communion was the rule in Scotland.[5]   These were the conditions fifteen years after the close of the preaching mission.

Perhaps the most remarkable change was that of Mr. McCulloch himself. During his first ten years in Cambuslang, he was called "the ale-house meenister," not because he frequented the taverns, which was not the case, but because of the fact that when he mounted the pulpit there was a general departure of the men of the congregation to the nearby ale-houses. He had not been considered a good preacher because of his unusual slowness of delivery. During and after the preaching mission, Mr. McCulloch seemed to be filled with new zeal, and his sermons became very acceptable to all.

Mr. McCulloch was a man of exceptional ability, well acquainted with several languages, and an authority on mathematics and astronomy. He helped prepare a number of young men for college. "As a Christian," says one

---

[5]. Jas. Robe, *Narrative of the Extraordinary Work of the Spirit of God at Cambuslang, Kilsyth, and Other Places* (Glasgow, 1790, 1840), pp. 246-271.

writer, "he was modest and humble, spiritual and resigned, watchful and circumspect in conversation and conduct. Few ever exemplified the character of a Christian with more success, yet with less show. As a minister he was an earnest and affectionate preacher of the Gospel, and a laborious workman in the Church; careful, studious and exact in his preparation for the pulpit. Though often obliged to preach on short notice, he always brought forward well-digested Scriptural discourses."[6] He was a devoted friend of the missionary cause and other worthy objects. Although his salary was never at any time large, yet during his lifetime he saved £200, which he contributed in 1769, two years before his death, to the work of the Society for the Propagation of Christian Knowledge. The cause of foreign missions lay close to the hearts of a few men, here and there. Mr. McCulloch was one of these; and his frequent presentation of this cause, established within his congregation an interest for missions that was notable years after his death. In addition to the *Attestation* (1757), William McCulloch's *Sermon's* (1793), exist in print.

James Robe (1688-1753)

James Robe was born at Cumbernauld, where his father was pastor of the parish church of that place. He received his education at Glasgow University, was licensed to preach in 1709 and ordained in 1713. His first and only congregation was that of Kilsyth, in the shire of Stirling, which he served from 1713 until his death in 1753. Mr. Robe found much spiritual indifference in his parish. Church attendance was poor and the people were worldly in their habits. Many of them frequented the ale-houses and drank to excess. Cursing and swearing were common, and lying and cheating were taken for granted.

Mr. Robe sought to bring about an improvement in the lives of the people by preaching sermons on good conduct. His sermons were not identical to those of the Moderate party, who purposely avoided evangelical truth, and preached only upon the cultivation of moral virtues. James

---

[6]. Hew Scott, *Fasti Ecclesiae Scoticanae* (Edinburgh, 1868), vol. II, p. 273.

Robe was a sincere young clergyman, but he had not yet learned that it is folly to attempt to reap a harvest before the seed has been sown. Like Chalmers at Kilmany a century later, Mr. Robe preached earnestly, urging his people to reform, but without any visible fruits of his labors to be seen.

In the winter of 1732-33, a terrible epidemic visited Kilsyth, carrying away many of the people of the village. So severely did the congregation suffer that within three weeks, sixty people were buried in the churchyard, and among them some of the most faithful members of the congregation. In the spring of the same year there was a tempest more frightful than any that had ever been known in that part of Scotland, with much property damage due to lightning, wind and hail. The same year internal difficulties arose, and some of the families withdrew from the congregation. These things caused much perplexity, and it was the general feeling throughout the community that these things were certain indications of the Lord's displeasure. Aware of the imperfect religious understanding of the people, Mr. Robe resolved to preach for one year on the important truths of Christian doctrine.

Among his early sermons in the series were several discussions of Regeneration, its nature and its necessity. Much interest was evident, and the people petitioned Mr. Robe to conduct a mid-week service. Later a number of the people requested a preaching mission, with services every evening. Mr. Robe discussed the fundamental doctrines of the Bible, but in such a way that the sinfulness of mankind, and God's plan of salvation through Jesus Christ, were kept as the great central truths. As at Cambuslang so also at Kilsyth. First the people of the village, then from the surrounding country, then people from more distant places came to attend these daily preaching services. Mr. Robe does not attempt to deny the fact that there were some demonstrations at the outset.[7] When the people realized their sinful condition, there was audible weeping. Penitent sinners remained in the church at the close of the service,

---

[7]. Jas Robe, *Op. cit.*, pp. 5, 38-39.

weeping, and begging Mr. Robe to explain in yet greater detail the way of the Cross. He instructed such people in his home, and when the group grew too large for the manse, the church had to be used.

It was not a time of temporary emotional excitement, for Mr. Robe gives us some of the fruits of this preaching of Law and Gospel. They were quite like those at Cambuslang. Cursing and swearing became the exception rather than the daily rule; the groups that spent their evenings drinking and gambling in the ale-houses dwindled; persons who had wronged their neighbors hastened to settle their difficulties; restitution was made of money and property wrongfully gained; family Bibles were brought out and family devotions inaugurated; a great love for the Scriptures became evident, and many people came to the pastor for religious instruction. The life of the entire parish showed lasting indications of improvement.

James Robe was an active defender of evangelical principles against the corrupt innovations of the Moderate party in the Kirk. He belonged to the faithful minority in the Church of Scotland who had no sympathy for the ruling party in the General Assembly, nor had he any part in the abuses which they defended. He was not one of the Marrow Men who signed the declaration of 1721, nor does he seem to have been involved in any way in the Marrow Controversy. He did not withdraw at the Secession of 1733; but remained in the State Church, testifying in his own community against error, and striving to develop the religious knowledge and the spiritual life of his congregation. He published several religious works, one of which was a careful and detailed account of the religious awakening in his village of Kilsyth, and in Cambuslang. This well-known book has been reprinted several times. His collected works were published after his death.

The leaders of the Secession were displeased when Mr. Robe, Mr. McCulloch and a number of other leaders of the Evangelical Awakening decided to remain within the National Church. They could not understand how such men could be content to remain and have fellowship with the corrupt ruling party in the Establishment. However, as one authority declares,[8] it was a good thing in the end that these faithful men remained in the old Kirk, for it was their spiritual sons who formed the great evangelical party of the nineteenth century, and who withdrew in 1843 at the time of the Disruption and founded the Free Church of Scotland.

James Robe's *Narrative of the Extraordinary Work of the Spirit of God at Cambuslang, Kilsyth, etc.* (1742), usually known as *Robe's Narrative,* was long a favorite among Scottish evangelicals. Other works are: *Letters to the Rev. J. Fisher* (1742), *Counsels and Comforts* (1749), and *Sermons at the Lord's Supper* (1750).

Alexander Webster (1707-1784)

During the time of the evangelical awakening in Scotland, the pulpit of Tolbooth Church, Edinburgh, was occupied by the baffling figure of Dr. Alexander Webster. No one will for a moment question the fact that he was a powerful leader and an exceptional preacher of evangelical truth, nevertheless it has always been a question whether he belongs to the Moderates or to the Evangelicals.

This puzzling leader was born in Edinburgh in 1707. His father was pastor of Tolbooth Church, and had suffered imprisonment because of his religious fidelity. The younger Webster received a thorough education at Edinburgh, and in 1733 he became assistant pastor at Culross, and then the sole incumbent. In 1737, at the age of 30, he was called to his father's old congregation in Edinburgh, which he served for 47 years. In 1748 he was made chaplain to the Prince of Wales, and in 1753 the Assembly conferred upon him the highest honor at her command by making him moderator. In 1771 he was made dean of the Chapel Royal.

Dr. Webster was a public spirited man. His calculations for clergymen's insurance proved so accurate that they are said to form the basis for tables of modern insurance. In 1755 Webster was in charge of the first census of Scotland. It was he who developed and carried out the project

---

[8]. W. G. Blaikie, *The Preachers of Scotland* (Edinburgh, 1888), pp. 258-260.

for the magnificent New Town of Edinburgh, which has given that city the reputation of the most beautiful metropolis in the world. He was one of the founders of the Society for the Promotion of Christian Knowledge.

Alexander Webster was a man of agreeable appearance, forceful personality, nation-wide popularity and with unexcelled gifts of leadership. He was a man of the hale-fellow-well-met sort. Many tales were told of the convivial drinking bouts in which he was accustomed to take part. These rumors did not seem to lessen his popularity, for people crowded Tolbooth Church, drawn by his fame as a pulpit orator. Dr. Webster was the unquestioned leader of the evangelical party within the State Church, yet so thoroughly was he imbued with church unionism that he lived on most cordial terms with the Moderates.

When the evangelical awakening appeared at Cambuslang, Kilsyth, and then in many other places, the Moderates condemned it; and even men of evangelical views were disposed to look upon it as mere emotional excitement. Dr. Webster studied the Cambuslang work carefully and became convinced of its sincerity. His hearty endorsement of this awakening did much to give it influence throughout Scotland.

Perhaps Dr. Webster's reputation for hard drinking and worldliness is due to the published assertions of his intimate friend Dr. "Jupiter" Carlyle, who describes Dr. Webster as a man who could outdrink all his rollicking companions; a man pliable in his convictions, and a hypocrite whose evangelical preaching was but a mask to hide a shameless life. There are men who do not take Dr. Carlyle too seriously. They prefer to accept Dr. Webster as a man whose early life was worldly, but who mended his objectionable ways because of the influence of the evangelical awakening. One can only regret that this preacher of surpassing eloquence neglected to leave the world written evidence of his reformation.

Robert Walker (1716-1783)

Robert Walker was born at Canongate, Scotland, in 1716. He was educated at the University of Edinburgh, and ordained in 1738, and assigned to Straiton church. In 1746 he was called to South Leith, and in 1754 he became one of the pastors of High Church, Edinburgh, where he was associated with Hugh Blair.

Walker was a man of deep piety and sound judgment. His sermons were evangelical, practical, clear, and they contain many Scripture verses. His literary style, as observed in his printed sermons, is excellent. Of his sermon on the text "Come unto Me, all ye that labour, and are heavy laden, and I will give you rest," Fish says: "The sweet invitings of the compassionate Saviour have seldom been set forth in a more charming, yet faithful manner, and in a more winning and affectionate spirit."[9] This sermon is deeply spiritual in tone, yet much is said in regard to the blood of the Saviour, but little if anything in regard to His righteousness. Fish says that Robert Walker "may perhaps be regarded as among the safest models for the study of young ministers."

It is interesting to observe that Hugh Blair, with his celebrated rhetorical style but his lack of evangelical warmth, and Robert Walker, with his fervent evangelical preaching, were associates at one of the most prominent churches in Edinburgh, and at one and the same time. This situation was even more marked a few years ago in Germany, for returning tourists have declared that they have heard the Saviour confessed by one preacher at the 10 o'clock service, and denied by a second preacher at 11 o'clock, and in the same prominent church.

Robert Walker's *Sermons on Practical Subjects*, in two volumes, were printed in 1764-65, and a number of later editions appeared from time to time, in two, three and four volumes. Prefixed to some of these are accounts of his life by Hugh Blair and by G. B. Cheever.

Hector Macphail (1716-1774)

Hector Macphail was born in 1716 in Inverness. After his elementary and college education he was licensed in

---

[9]. H. C. Fish, *Masterpieces of Pulpit Eloquence* (New York, 1869), vol. 2, p. 271.

1746, ordained the same year, and assigned to the congregation at Resolis, in the North of Scotland. Brought up under the teachings of the Moderates, he preached only outward good conduct, and not sin and grace. He married a young woman of Christian character, who had received great benefit from the evangelical preaching of John Porteous, a faithful Highland pastor of a nearby parish. Shortly after their marriage, Mrs. Macphail told her husband one Sunday morning that she intended going that day to Kilmuir, to hear John Porteous once more; that "her soul was starving for the Gospel," and she was "compelled to go for the bread of life to Kilmuir."

John Porteous was surprised to see her in his church, and assured her that "the Lord will soon give you the very finest of wheat, and from the hand of your own husband." Hector Macphail was deeply grieved, not at the words of his wife, but at the sudden realization of his own unfaithfulness. Months of untold spiritual distress followed, and so great was his sense of unfitness that he resolved to lay down his office. He invited his friend, the Rev. James Fraser of Alness, to preach for him, and to announce to his congregation this decision. Fraser came, and he preached Jesus Christ the Saviour of sinners. Macphail could not hide his tears. "Give me another chance, O Lord, and help me to become a faithful witness!" he said in a whisper.

He went to the same source of light that has helped Chalmers and so many others, and by his diligent study of the Scriptures he learned to preach evangelical truth so effectively that James Calder was able to say of him that he was "the most eminently pious, zealous, active, laborious minister of Christ that I ever saw, and the most lovely, living image of his adorable Lord and Master that I ever was acquainted with." [10]

Macphail's sermons, in the Gaelic language, are entirely unknown to the average English reader. They are said to be deficient in orderly arrangement and in this respect not models of correct homiletics. Nevertheless all who have read them bear witness to the fact that they are full of the

---

[10]. James Calder, *Diary,* quoted by David Beaton.

saving grace of Jesus Christ. He did not have the fiery eloquence of John Macdonald and John Kennedy, but the deeply spiritual nature of his preaching, throughout almost three decades, was extremely fruitful. He died at the comparatively early age of 58, and was mourned far and wide by the Gaelic-speaking parts of Scotland.

George Campbell (1719-1796)

George Campbell was born in 1719 in Aberdeen. After attending Marischal College, Aberdeen, he studied law at Edinburgh University, but in the end he decided to study for the ministry. He was ordained in 1748 and became pastor of Banchory Ternan Church, near Aberdeen. In 1757 he became pastor of a congregation in Aberdeen, and two years later he was made principal of Marischal College. In 1771 he became professor of theology in the same institution. Principal Campbell was an influential preacher in his day, and he secured for himself a place among the noted Scottish preachers of the eighteenth century. He was a lifelong student, and at the age of 70 we find him applying himself diligently to the study of German, so that he might read the works of Luther in the original. He published a number of works that were useful in their time. Among them were A Dissertation on Miracles, (1762), which was reprinted a number of times and translated into French, Dutch and German. It was an able defense of miracles against the claims of the Rationalists. Other works by the same author were: The Four Gospels Translated from the Greek, 2 volumes (1789); Lectures on Ecclesiastical History, 2 volumes (1800), a work often reprinted; Lectures on Systematic Theology (1807), a two-volume work on The Philosophy of Rhetoric (1776), and several sermons. Principal Campbell's more important writings are contained in his collected Theological Works, 6 volumes (1840).

John Erskine (1721-1803)

John Erskine, leader of the evangelical party in the Church of Scotland, champion of missions and friend of the American colonies, was born in Edinburgh in 1721. His father was a noted attorney, whose Institutes of the Law of

Scotland have caused him to be known as the "Scottish Blackstone." In order to gratify the wishes of his father, John Erskine read law for a time, but finally gave it up and studied for the ministry. He was educated in Edinburgh University, licensed to preach in 1743, ordained in 1744, and called to a small rural parish at Kirkintilloch, near Glasgow.

In 1753 he was called to Culross, and in 1758 to New Greyfriars church. In 1767 he went to Old Greyfriars church, where he was associate to Dr. Wm. Robertson.

John Erskine carried on an extensive correspondence with religious leaders in other countries, including Jonathan Edwards. He was friendly toward Whitefield, invited him to Scotland, and asked him to preach in his church. He was acquainted with the Wesleys. Erskine preached strong missionary sermons in a day when few people recognized any missionary obligation, and when many opposed it. He led the minority group who supported the missionary cause at the celebrated debate, in 1796, at the convention of the Church of Scotland. Erskine preached vigorous sermons against engaging in war with the American colonies, and he published a pamphlet, "Shall I go to War with my American Brethren?" He published 25 different works, including two volumes of sermons.

The parents of Sir Walter Scott were members of Erskine's congregation. Sir Walter himself seems to have favored the Moderates, rather than the evangelical party, nevertheless he has words of praise for John Erskine, who appears as one of the characters in his *Guy Mannering.*[11]

Scott describes Mr. Erskine as a man with a remarkably fair complexion, a black wig, with a narrow chest, stooping shoulders, his hands placed like props on either side of the pulpit. He preached with but a small scrap of paper before him, which contained the main heads of his sermon. He appeared embarrassed at first, but soon became eloquent, so that seldom was "so much learning, metaphysical acuteness and energy of argument brought into the service of

[11]. Sir Walter Scott, *Guy Mannering,* chapter 37.

Christianity. 'Such' said he . . . 'must have been the preachers to whose unfearing minds and acute though sometimes rudely exercised talents we owe the Reformation'."

John Erskine's chief writings are: *Theological Dissertations* (1765); *Considerations on the Spirit of Popery* (1778); *Sketches of Church History and Theological Controversy*, 2 volumes (1790-97); and *Discourses on Several Occasions*, 2 volumes (1798-1804). H. M. Wellwood's *Life and Writings of John Erskine* was published in 1818.

John Witherspoon (1723-1794)

It is hard to know whether to classify John Witherspoon as a Scottish preacher or as an American college president, for he devoted a quarter of a century to each calling. He signed the American Declaration of Independence, and the citizens of Philadelphia erected a statue of him, of heroic size, in Fairmount Park.

Witherspoon was born at Gifford, in the parish of Yester, near Edinburgh. His father was a clergyman, and his mother was a descendant of John Knox. After attending Haddington grammar school, he studied at Edinburgh University, and continued his theological work at the same university.

He was licensed to preach in 1743, and in 1745 he became pastor of a congregation in Beith, Ayrshire. In 1757 he was called to Paisley, Renfrewshire, where he won an excellent reputation as a preacher. He declined calls from important churches in Dublin, Dundee, Rotterdam and elsewhere.

In 1768 he was called as president of Princeton, then a small college in a little village in America. In addition to his collegiate work, he was pastor of a congregation in Princeton. Witherspoon did excellent work at Princeton, building it up from a country-town college of virtually one building, to an institution of recognized rank. He was a member of the Continental Congress for six and one-half years, and was the only clergyman who signed the Declaration of Independence. He published a number of works, one of which is an attack on the Moderates, or liberals, in the Scottish church. Another is a treatise on justification by faith. His work at Princeton has been compared to that of Thomas Arnold, of Rugby.

President Witherspoon's *Ecclesiastical Characteristics* (1753), was an important work, and there were five editions of it within ten years. Other important writings were: *A Serious Apology for the Characteristics* (1763); *Essays on Important Subjects*, 2 volumes (1764); *A Treatise on Regeneration* (1764); and *Connection Between Justification and Imputed Righteousness* (1756). His pulpit discourses include *Seven Single Sermons* (1758); nine sermons entitled *Discourses on Practical Subjects* (1768); fourteen sermons called *Practical Discourses* (1768); and *Sermons on Various Subjects* (1798). His *Collected Works*, in 4 volumes, were published in 1795, soon after his death, and reprinted from time to time. *Miscellaneous Works* appeared in 1803, *Select Works*, 2 volumes, in 1822 and *Essays, Lectures and Sermons*, in 6 volumes, in 1822. Samuel S. Smith's memoir is prefixed to several editions of Witherspoon's *Works*, and among other accounts of his life is a biography by John Rogers, published in 1795.

Charles Calder (1748-1812)

Charles Calder, of Ferintosh, was one of a family of Scottish clergymen. His father, James Calder, his grandfather and several relatives, are listed in the Rev. Hew Scott's monumental *Fasti*. Charles Calder was born in 1748 at Croy. He attended grammar school and King's College, Aberdeen, where his degree was received in 1767. In 1773 he was licensed to preach, and a year later he was ordained and became pastor at Urquhart, or Ferintosh as it is more often called. There he spent the remaining 38 years of an eventful life.

At a time when earnest evangelical preaching was by no means the rule, Mr. Calder preached sin and grace unceasingly. So fully did he dwell upon the grace and love of Jesus Christ that he was known far and wide as *piobaire an aon phuirt*, that is, "the piper of one tune." Dr. John Kennedy describes a Communion service at which Mr.

Calder preached.   So great was the atmosphere of solemnity that the people left the place in profound silence, not one of them, not even the catechist, remaining to greet Mr. Calder. The pastor was greatly distressed, fearing that he had offended the congregation, until his catechist told him a few days later that not one of the people dared break the spirit of solemnity that his sermon had created.

Dr. Kennedy tells us that Charles Calder was possessed of a vigorous mind, and his sermons were prepared with extreme care and thoroughness.   "All was subordinated by him to the great end of setting only Christ before the eyes of sinners.   His great theme was the love of Jesus.   His own soul kept lying at the feet of Jesus; he was wont to give forth, with all the freshness of a present experience, his utterances regarding the Person, life, death, and salvation of the blessed Redeemer.   There never was a more affecting preacher when discoursing on his favourite theme.   Often have his whole congregation been in tears, as in his own tender, solemn way, he commended Jesus as a Saviour to the lost; and when, with a tremendous voice, but with the authority of one who knew he was conveying a message from Jehovah, he warned the unbeliever of his danger, the most indifferent were compelled to tremble."

Charles Calder's biographer says: "His expositions and sermons were composed with such studied chasteness of thought and classical beauty and accuracy of language that they contributed in no small degree to improve the taste, as well as impart a high tone to the Scriptural piety and experience of an extensive religious community; and also of a few young men who became preachers themselves, and whose labours have been highly countenanced in other portions of the vineyard."[12]

It is interesting to recall the fact that Charles Calder's successor at Ferintosh was the famous John Macdonald, known as the Apostle to the North.   The people of that congregation enjoyed for 74 years the ministry of these two noted evangelical pastors.   From the year 1774 to the year

---

[12]. John Kennedy, *The Days of the Fathers in Ross-shire* (Edinburgh, 1861), p. 53.   R. Findlater, *Memoir*, pp. 35-36.

1849 the congregation was an evangelical center of influence, and the tradition lived long afterward. A little book entitled *Three Sermons by the Rev. Charles Calder, Ferintosh* was published in 1877 in Edinburgh.

George Lawson (1749-1820)

George Lawson, of the Burgher Secession Synod, was born at Boghouse farm, in the parish of West Linton, Peeblesshire, in 1749. After attending the University of Edinburgh, he studied theology with John Swanston, and with John Brown of Haddington. Licensed in 1771, he became pastor of the Burgher congregation at Selkirk, where he spent his entire life. At the death of John Brown of Haddington in 1787, George Lawson was made professor of theology in the Burgher Synod, and he held this position for 33 years in addition to his congregational work.

Dr. Lawson's reputation as a preacher does not rest merely upon his eloquence nor upon his literary style, but rather upon his exceptional ability as an expositor of the Scriptures. It is said that his memory was so remarkable that he could quote correctly any portion of Scripture required of him. He memorized large portions of the Scriptures, not only in English, but in the original Hebrew and Greek. It was his custom to expound the Scriptures in an orderly manner at his morning service. His method was to read a portion of the Bible, then close the Book and expound what he had read, verse by verse, quoting with perfect accuracy.[13] During his 49 years at Selkirk, he preached through the entire Bible. As a rule he used a simple sermon plan, with a few main divisions, but without the multitude of subdivisions that were still popular in his day. His immense exegetical knowledge was never paraded before his congregation. Although fluent of speech, and with extraordinary gifts as an extemporaneous speaker, he subordinated eloquence to simplicity and clearness. He used to tell his theological students that the chief object of preaching is not to make a congregation weep and rejoice in turn, but rather to bring out in simple language the meaning of the text, make clear to the humblest people its doctrines, and

---

[13]. John Macfarlane, *Life and Times of George Lawson* (1862).

press home its applications. In all preaching the cross of the Crucified Saviour must be given a prominent place. In his morning Bible expositions, and his evening sermons, Dr. Lawson put into practice these principles, and so effectively that few men in Scotland have been held in veneration more highly than he. He is commonly called "the Scottish Socrates," and Carlyle speaks of him as one of the grand and rugged figures of his day. Among the clergymen of the Burgher Synod, Lawson stands second only to Dr. John Brown of Haddington. When he died, in addition to his theological writings, he left 80 volumes of manuscript, forming a connected expository study of the entire Bible.

George Lawson's writings include: *Discourses on the Whole Book of Esther* (1804); *Lectures on the Whole Book of Ruth* (1805); *Lectures on the History of Joseph,* 2 volumes (1807); *Exposition of the Book of Proverbs,* 2 volumes (1821); *Discourses on the History of David* (1833); and *Sermons of George Lawson* (1810). His biography was written by John Macfarlane, and is entitled *Life and Times of George Lawson* (1862). A sketch appears in Dr. Robert Jamieson's *Cyclopedia of Modern Religious Biography* (1853).

Sir Henry Moncreiff (1750-1827)

Sir Henry Moncreiff was born in Blackford, Perthshire, in 1750. His father and his grandfather had both been pastors of the church in Blackford. He was educated in the parish school and in 1763, at the age of 13, he entered Glasgow University. In 1767 he went to Edinburgh for his degree.

In 1771 he became pastor at Blackford, succeeding his father and his grandfather. The congregation had waited for three years, after the death of his father, in order that Henry Moncreiff might finish his schooling. However, four years later he left Blackford and became pastor of St. Cuthbert's in Edinburgh, where he soon became one of the most prominent clergymen in the Scottish metropolis. He was famed for his vigorous eloquence and for his great influence, as leader of the evangelical party, in the affairs of the Scottish Church. Four volumes of his sermons have been published.

Sir Henry came of a titled family, and he inherited the baronage and the family estate. His principal writings are: *Sermons*, 4 volumes (1805-31); *Discourses on the Evidence of the Jewish and Christian Revelations* (1815); *An Account of the Life and Writings of John Erskine* (1818); and *Life of Dr. Henry* (1793).

Lachlan Mackenzie (1754-1819)

Lachlan Mackenzie, a Highland preacher famed for his eloquence, was born in 1754 at Kilmuir-Wester, Ross-shire. He was educated in the parochial school at Pettie, and was graduated from Marischal College, Aberdeen, in 1776. He was schoolmaster for a time at Lochcarron. Grieved at the spiritual thirst of the people, due to the absence of sin and salvation in the preaching of the Moderates, Mackenzie began to conduct Bible hours for the people. The deeply spiritual tone of his teaching was discovered quickly by the people of Lochcarron, who flocked to his Bible hours and his prayer services, much to the displeasure of the Moderate clergy of the district, who did their utmost to silence the schoolmaster.

Urged by the people, and encouraged at the success of his Bible hours, Mackenzie was licensed to preach in 1782, but in the face of a vigorous protest from the local clergy. Urged by influential families, he was appointed pastor of the parish church, and ordained by the presbytery.

Mackenzie's great success at Lochcarron is a tradition throughout the Highlands to this day. In his day there was much hard drinking, even among church people. A christening, a funeral, and even the occasional Communion seasons were looked upon by many as an excuse for drunken celebrations in the very churchyard. Years before such a thing as a temperance movement had suggested itself, Mackenzie began to preach moderation. He drew up a pledge with seven items, and asked his congregation to join him in resolving to practice strict moderation in the use of hard liquor, and to refrain from drinking after christenings, funerals and Communion services. So successful was he that Lochcarron, once notorious for its drunkenness, became a community of well-behaved Christian people.

His testimony against Moderatism was equally fearless. He insisted that the Christian pulpit dare not declare anything, however praiseworthy in itself, that tends to obscure or crowd out the full declaration of man's sinful nature, his utter inability to save himself, and the offer of salvation through the imputed righteousness and atoning death of Jesus Christ, and the believer's justification by faith without the works of the Law.

The story of an evil woman known as Ceit Mhor is still told in many a Highland cot-house.   Ceit Mhor, a woman more than 80 years of age, had been known for her wickedness throughout her long life.   Never could she be induced to enter church nor chapel.   She loved music, however, and never missed one of the *ceilidhs,* with their songs and pipe music, where the bards met in an outdoor congress, usually for three days.   Lachlan Mackenzie composed a poem in the Gaelic language, and in bardic style, in which he denounced in language of great vigor the various sins of the evil woman Ceit Mhor. He set the poem to music, and asked the younger bards to sing it.   Before they had finished, Ceit Mhor uttered a wild scream, and began to weep hysterically. Nothing could quiet her.   She wept for days, and finally blindness came upon her.   Mackenzie and many others tried in vain to quiet her.   When the next Communion season came, Ceit Mhor, now totally blind, asked to be led to the service.   For the first time in many days she had ceased weeping.   She came to the Communion table, confessed her many sins and confessed her faith in her Saviour. Mackenzie instructed her in the fundamental teachings of the Christian faith, and for the few remaining years of her life she was an exemplary member of the kirk at Lochcarron.

Lachlan Mackenzie, commonly called "Mr. Lachlan" by his friends, was a man of picturesque personality, of intense zeal, of deep piety, somewhat eccentric at times, but always widely popular as a preacher.   Dr. John Kennedy of Dingwall said: "Owing to his genius, his peculiar Christian experience, and his great acceptance as a preacher, he retained a firmer hold of the memories of the people than any other besides."[14]   On another occasion Dr. Kennedy said that Mackenzie's preaching was remarkable, of great originality of thought, striking in the manner of his illustrations, clear and emphatic in utterance, unction and authority, with a powerful appeal to the conscience of his hearers, and with frequent outbursts of feeling.[15]   Mackenzie may correctly be included among the most eminent of the group of famous preachers of the Scottish Highlands.

James Hall (1755-1826)

James Hall was born at Cathcart, near Glasgow, in 1755. He received his education at Glasgow University, after which he studied theology with John Brown of Haddington. He was licensed by the Associate Presbytery at Glasgow in 1776, and was offered a good congregation of the Established Church, but refused it.   In 1777 he was ordained by the Associate Presbytery and became pastor of their congregation at Cumnock.   He was translated in 1786 to the Rose Street Church in Edinburgh, where the excellency of his preaching attracted many people, and the church was soon filled to overflowing.   In 1820 a larger church building was erected in Broughton Place.

Dr. Hall was one of Edinburgh's noted preachers for forty years.   A man of polished manners, and with a fine reputation as a preacher, his influence extended far beyond his own congregation.   He was widely known throughout Edinburgh and respected by all, and during his ministry Broughton Place Church enjoyed a distinction that was perpetuated by Dr. John Brown III, his successor both at Rose Street and at Broughton Place.   Dr. Hall is buried in the New Calton Cemetery in Regent Road, and upon his monument is a significant inscription which expresses admirably the character of his preaching.   It reads in part: "By him the violated Law spoke forth its thunders, and by him, in strains as sweet as angels use, the Gospel whispered peace."   The wording of the inscription is somewhat

---

[14]. Hew Scott, *Fasti Ecclesiae Scoticanae* (Edinburgh, 1915-28 ed.), vol. 7, p. 160.
[15]. J. Kennedy, *Days of the Fathers in Ross-shire* (Edinburgh, 1861), p. 62.

flowery, but the facts that it declares form one of the highest tributes that may be paid to a preacher.

John Robertson (1758-1825)

John Robertson was born in 1758 in Auchenhalrig, Bellie, Banffshire. After his elementary education, he became a schoolmaster. He was not a "man of the North" by birth, and hence he spoke no Gaelic, but living among the Highlanders, he was anxious to learn their language. By diligent study he mastered it after a time. This led him to a study of Latin and Greek. He attended King's College, Aberdeen, and then the theological hall. He was ordained in 1789, at the age of 31, and was given charge of Achrenie. In 1794 he assumed charge of Eriboll Mission, and in 1799 the Chapel of Ease at Rothesay. In 1810 he became pastor of Kingussie, where his most effective work was to be done.

John Robertson was a preacher of exceptional talent. There were certain misgivings at first, since he was from the South, and not born to the Gaelic tongue; but so diligently did he apply himself that his preaching in that language was flawless. His sermons were remarkable for their clearness of understanding, their solid exegetical and doctrinal character, their richness and variety of illustration and their direct and telling appeals to the heart. He had the happy gift of making difficult doctrinal truths seem wonderfully simple and clear. "With a full heart he poured out the spiritual, weighty message, as if standing beside the Cross, praising and exalting the Lamb." [16] He was in great demand as a speaker at Communion services, which were always occasions of great importance in Scotland. Dr. John Macdonald, the Gaelic poet, dedicated one of his most noted elegies to Robertson, *A Mhaighstir Robinson na h-àill'*. It is unfortunate that his richly spiritual sermons have not been translated into English.

John Jamieson (1759-1838)

John Jamieson, of the Antiburgher section of the Secession Church, was born in Glasgow in 1759. He received

---

[16]. David Beaton, *Some Noted Ministers of the Northern Highlands* (Inverness, 1929), p. 52.

his education at Glasgow University and at Edinburgh. He was licensed in 1789, and after his ordination he became pastor of the Antiburgher congregation at Forfar. In 1797 he was called to the Nicholson Street Antiburgher congregation in Edinburgh, where he remained for many years. In 1820 he took an active part in the union of the Burgher and Antiburgher synods of the Secession Church. His *Etymological Dictionary*, in six large quarto volumes brought him fame throughout the world, and is a standard reference work to this day.

Mr. Jamieson was a solid, evangelical preacher. He attached but little importance to rhetorical adornment. Although a philologist, historian, poet and story writer, yet he subordinated all these gifts entirely, and preached a simple, evangelical Gospel of sin and grace, according to the interpretations of Calvinism. He left two volumes of sermons, and among them are his well-known discourses on the human heart: its deceitfulness by nature, its inborn enmity against God, the evil fruits that proceed out of it, the fact that it is powerless to bring about its own cleansing — but the marvellous effects that are wrought within the human heart when touched by the grace of God in Jesus Christ. His writings include: *An Etymological Dictionary of the Scottish Language* (1808), and with later revised and enlarged editions, *Use of Sacred History*, 2 volumes (1802); *A Vindication of the Doctrine of Scripture and of the Primitive Faith*, 2 volumes (1794); *Historical Account of the Ancient Culdees of Iona* (1811); three long poems, published 1789-98; and *Sermons on the Heart*, 2 volumes (1789-90), the last a work of unique interest, and one that might well be more widely known nowadays. An account of his life was published in 1879-82 by J. Longmuir and D. Donaldson.

Angus Mackintosh (1763-1831)

Angus Mackintosh, a Highland preacher of great excellency, was born in 1763 at Strathdearn. He was educated at Fortrose Academy and at King's College, Aberdeen, from which he was graduated in 1784. After tutoring and teaching school for five years, he was licensed to preach in 1789, and ordained as pastor of the Gaelic Chapel of Ease, Glasgow, in 1792. In 1797 he was translated to Tain, where his greatest work was done.

Dr. Mackintosh may rightfully be numbered among the large group of Highland preachers whose names are household words to this day wherever Celto-Scottish people are to be found. Hugh Mackenzie says: "The great Ross-shire ministers now gone had each his own characteristic excellency. Mr. M'Phail's preaching was experimental, Mr. Fraser was a systematic divine, and Mr. Porteous was the expounder of Scripture, and my belief is that Mr. Mackintosh combines the excellencies of the three." [17]

His Communion sermons were notable. "By telling sinners of their danger, he spoke as one who saw it vividly; his fine eye was frequently filled with tears, and his voice and manner made us feel as if thunder were rolling over our head. This was followed up by holding forth Christ as the living, present, all-gracious Saviour, and by the most melting appeals to the worst and vilest to come to Him even now, with all their sins, that they might even now be saved. He seemed unwilling to part with them till they fled for refuge to Christ, and, with a thorough knowledge of their own language and phrases, he plied them with illustrations and arguments." [18]

"Seemed unwilling to part with them!" It must be remembered that Scottish Communion services of a century or more ago were not as frequent as today. One such service lasted for several days, and three of four pastors took part in it. The tables were in the open air, because of the great number of people who came from miles around. It is said that Dr. Mackintosh's Communion seasons drew 10,000 or more people. After the "fencing of the tables," and the address so full of solemn warning to the impenitent, and so full of tender encouragement to the genuinely penitent, the Communion took place. Even after all had received, Dr. Mackintosh seemed reluctant to let them go.

---

[17]. Angus Macgillivray, *Sketches of Religion in the Northern Highlands* (1904), p. 35.

[18]. *Ibid.*, p. 38.

It required little persuasion to cause them to stay, while he pleaded with great eloquence, urging those who had not participated to amend their lives and to strengthen their faith by means of the living Word of God, which alone is able to cause the feeble flame of faith to burn brightly. With equal urgency he would plead with the faithful to keep their lamps filled with the oil of God's Word, so that their spiritual life might not languish.

With a deep, melodious voice of great carrying power, Dr. Mackintosh could make himself heard to the most distant row of people in the vast, outdoor congregation. With a beautiful command of rich Gaelic, the richness of idiom and the fiery zeal of the Celt, he was a preacher of exceptional excellency. Although he did not see as clearly as one might wish the true nature of the Lord's Supper, yet in his attitude toward the Gospel as a life-giving means of grace, he came close to an understanding of the truth. Certainly he is one of the most eminent of the large group of Gaelic preachers of the northern Highlands.

Samuel Gilfillan (1762-1826)

Samuel Gilfillan, of the Secession Church, was born in 1762 in Bucklyvie, Stirlingshire. He entered Glasgow University in 1782, and after his graduation he studied theology with Prof. Wm. Moncrieff and Prof. Archibald Bruce, of the Antiburgher Synod. He was licensed in 1789 and sent to Comrie, in Perthshire. In 1791 he was ordained. Samuel Gilfillan was the father of two noted sons: George, the literary man, and James, a preacher of some reputation. The elder Gilfillan was a strict Calvinist in theology, and a forceful preacher, using the Gaelic and the English languages with equal ease.

Alexander Stewart (1764-1821)

Alexander Stewart was born in 1764 in the Scottish Highlands. He was ordained in 1786 to Moulin parish. After having been there for ten years, Mr. Stewart heard another pastor describe a death-bed scene. This caused him to realize that there was something lacking in his own preaching. He studied his Bible with renewed diligence,

242 A HISTORY OF PREACHING

and became convinced that his was but an outward, speculative belief, but without real spiritual warmth. About this time Charles Simeon visited him, and found him to be "very defective in his views of the Gospel." Simeon gave his friend much sound advice, urging him to enter the pulpit determined to know nothing but Jesus Christ and Him Crucified.

The people at Moulin noted a change in Stewart's preaching. He began to declare that "all men are by nature enemies to God, disobedient to His Law, and on that account exposed to His just indignation and curse." However, there was no improvement in the spiritual life of his congregation. Then Mr. Stewart made the acquaintance of a pious invalid, to whose home two devout young people used to come. From this little group Mr. Stewart learned many spiritual truths of utmost value. He began to see, dimly at first, the proper uses of Law and Gospel, and he attempted to direct his uncertain footsteps toward the light. During this period there was a sharp decline in attendance at Holy Communion. People realized their sins, but feared themselves unworthy. Then a gradual awakening of spiritual life became evident, and as Alexander Stewart's understanding of sin and grace became clearer, his preaching became more fruitful. In 1799 Alexander Stewart preached a series of sermons on Regeneration. The results were remarkable. Stewart had no confidence in emotional excesses and mere excitement, and he was able to keep the awakening religious life of his community from becoming a superficial thing.

In 1805 Alexander Stewart went to Dingwall, where he spent the next fifteen years of his life. In 1820, because of his exceptional gifts, he was translated to Canongate, Edinburgh, but he died less than a year later at the age of 57. Among his published works one may mention a Gaelic translation of the Shorter Catechism and a widely-known Gaelic grammar. He assisted in translating the Psalms into Gaelic. After his death a volume of sermons appeared, as well as a book *Hints on Faith and Hope.* The latter is said to exhibit traces of Sandemanianism. Alexander Stewart was a preacher of eminent ability, thoroughly at home both in the

English language and in Gaelic. An excellent account of his life is to be found in David Beaton's *Some Noted Ministers of the Northern Highlands* (1929).

James A. Haldane (1768-1851)

James Haldane was a lay preacher of rare eloquence, who stirred Scotland by his evangelical fervor, at a time when religious life was at a low ebb. He was born in Dundee, Scotland, in 1768, and was a son of Captain James Haldane, and a brother of Robert. He was educated in the grammar schools of Dundee, the Edinburgh High school and Edinburgh University. In 1785 he went to sea as midshipman, and made four voyages to India and China.

In 1794 he gave up the sea and lived for a time in Edinburgh, where he began to preach. Lay preaching met with considerable opposition in his day in Edinburgh, but Haldane was not to be discouraged. In 1797 he made preaching tours throughout Scotland, where his powerful sermons attracted great gatherings of people. In 1799 he withdrew from the Church of Scotland and became a Congregationalist, organizing the first Congregational church in Edinburgh and becoming its pastor.

In 1801 his brother Robert built him a tabernacle seating 3,000 people, where he became one of Edinburgh's most noted preachers, filling the great tabernacle for fifty years until his death. Although condemned by the Church of Scotland, yet he was very successful wherever he went to preach. His brother Robert educated three hundred young men for the ministry. At Geneva, Switzerland, he delivered lectures on the Book of Romans at the University, and among his pupils were Monod and d'Aubigné. Haldane wrote *Social Worship of the First Christians* (1805); *Forbearance* (1811); *Baptism; The Association of Believers; Revelation*, 2 volumes; *Self-Examination* (1806); *Man's Responsibility* (1842); *The Inspiration of the Scriptures* (1845); and *An Exposition of Galatians* (1848). The story of his life is to be found in Alexander Haldane's *Memoirs of Robert and James A. Haldane* (1852).

James Struthers (1770-1807)

This accomplished and eloquent Scottish preacher was born in 1770 at Glassford. After his education at Glasgow University he was ordained in 1791 and became pastor of the Relief Chapel in College Street, Edinburgh. Here his splendid talents as a preacher soon attracted wide notice. He was made moderator of his denomination when but 30 years of age. His brilliant career was cut short in 1807, when he died at the age of 36.

His monument in Greyfriars Churchyard, near the east wall and not far from the Martyrs' Monument, reads in part: "A tribute of admiration, affection, and regret to the memory of the late Reverend James Struthers, a man of superior understanding and worth, whose talents and success as a pulpit orator were not excelled and scarcely equalled in the place and period which were honoured by his short but distinguished mortal existence." A son, Dr. James Struthers, was pastor for many years at St. Andrew's Church, Demerara. His *History of the Relief Church* (1843) is his most important work.

Thomas M'Crie (1772-1835)

Thomas M'Crie, who occupies a high place as a historian and biographer, was also a preacher of superior ability. He was born in 1772 at Dunse, Berwickshire. After a thorough preliminary training in the parochial school, he entered Edinburgh University in 1788. In 1791 he opened an Anti-Burgher school at Brechlin, Forfarshire. He studied theology at Whitburn under the General Associate, or Anti-burgher teachers. He was licensed to preach in 1795 by the General Associate Synod, ordained a year later and became pastor of Potterow Church, Edinburgh. In 1806 he left the Antiburgher Synod and with three others founded the Constitutional Associate Presbytery. This step was the result of a long controversy in their Synod in regard to the interference of the civil magistrates in Church affairs. The Constitutional Associate Presbytery existed for 21 years, and then united with the Synod of the Original Seceders.

Mr. M'Crie's congregation became involved in litigation and lost their property in 1809, but another church was built in West Richmond Street, where Dr. M'Crie served until his death in 1835. From 1816 to 1818, in addition to his parish duties, he was his denomination's professor of theology.

In 1812 he published the two-volume work that was to bring him lasting fame.[19] The religious world was surprised that such a important biography should come from the pen of a relatively obscure man, and from a small and unpopular synod. The reviews were highly favorable, and Edinburgh University, which he had left two decades previously without receiving his diploma, awarded him an honorary Doctor's degree — a thing reserved in those days only for men of eminent scholarship. Dr. M'Crie's biography of John Knox (1811) was history-making, for it made a hero of a man who had been looked upon by many as a leader of inferior quality. In 1819 Dr. M'Crie added further to his reputation by publishing a biography of Melville.[20] These two biographies rank highly to this day. Dr. M'Crie's conservatism, and his keen, logical mind quickly discovered the insincerity of most doctrinal declarations where church union is involved. He was convinced that such mergers usually involve compromise, and lead to a weakening of definite testimony. In 1821 he published a work[21] which he declared was "to point out the fallacious and unscriptural character of modern plans of union, particularly that adopted by the United Secession." His general principles might well be reprinted and serve as a warning to those who would enter into a union that involves ambiguity of doctrinal statements. Other works by Dr. M'Crie include an account of the Reformation in Italy[22] and in Spain,[23] and a life of Calvin which he left unfinished when he died of a stroke of apoplexy in 1835. As a scholar and a historian he is a man of whom Scotland is justly proud.

Dr. M'Crie was an admirable preacher, although his sermons appealed to the more thoughtful people of his day

[19]. Thos. M'Crie, *Life of John Knox*, 2 vols. (Edinburgh, 1811).
[20]. Thos. M'Crie, *Life of Andrew Melville*, 2 vols. (Edinburgh, 1819).
[21]. *Two Discourses on the Unity of the Church* (Edinburgh, 1821).
[22]. *History of the Progress and Suppression of the Reformation in Italy* (Edinburgh, 1827).
[23]. *History of the Progress and Suppression of the Reformation in Spain* (Edinburgh, 1829).

rather than to the popular crowd. He was too serious a man to resort to flashy sermon topics and popular lectures merely to attract large congregations. Dr. Taylor describes his sermons as "weighty and solid, somewhat heavy in style, but always luminous, and invariably Jesus is in the midst." [24] His sermon "The Prayer of the Thief on the Cross" is remarkable, but in most printed versions of it there seems to be a condensation which is unfortunate. [25] He makes a careful analysis of every word spoken by the Saviour and by those standing at the foot of the cross, and even an exposition of the inscription over the cross. This he does in order to prove that the dying thief's faith was not something within him by nature, but was due to the means of grace. By some unfortunate omission he makes it appear that the Gospel can produce repentance. The solemn warning to the Jewish nation, St. Luke 23, 27-31, is not mentioned.

In a published sermon on the Crucifixion [26] Dr. M'Crie mentions the fact that "Christ hath redeemed us from the curse of the Law, being made a curse for us." He brings out well the fulfillment of the words of the prophets. He warns against the mistake of pondering over merely the tragic historic details of our Lord's physical suffering and overlooking the benefits to the believer of His suffering and death. In his conclusion he errs in speaking of the Sacrament as merely a memorial of the Saviour's Passion. Were it not for this serious flaw, Dr. M'Crie might make an admirable Lenten preacher.

John G. Lockhart, the essayist, says: "I went to hear Dr. M'Crie preach, and was not disappointed in the expectation I had formed from a perusal of his book. He is a tall, slender man, with a pale face, full of shrewdness, and a pair of black piercing eyes, a shade of deep secluded melancholy passing ever and anon across their surface and dimming their brilliancy. His voice, too, has a wild but very expressive shrillness in it at times. He prays and preaches very much in the usual style of the Presbyterian divines; but

---

[24]. W. M. Taylor, *The Scottish Pulpit* (New York, 1887), p. 234.
[25]. H. C. Fish, *History and Repository of Pulpit Eloquence* (New York, 1856), vol II, pp. 302-318.
[26]. *The Scottish Pulpit* (periodical), April 28, 1832, pp. 55-60.

about all he says there is a certain unction of sincere, old-fashioned, haughty Puritanism, peculiar, so far as I have seen, to himself, and by no means displeasing in the historian of Knox. He speaks, too, with an air of authority, which his high talents render excusable, nay proper — but which few could venture upon with equal success." [27]

Dr. M'Crie was a preacher whose merits have been too often overlooked. He was a preacher for the educated, and would hardly have been appreciated at the West Port Church, had he lived another decade. He never chose to bring his thoughts down to the popular level, nor to indulge in the luxuriant rhetoric and story-telling so admired by the class of people found in every large city, who flock to the services of whatever preacher they happen to like. He considered the Gospel a serious thing, and any attempt to adapt it to a popular style seemed to him to detract from the graveness of the doctrines that he stressed. Thomas M'Crie's sermons, recast into the style of the popular orator, are as unthinkable as an old Scottish kirk whose severe lines might be defaced by the insertion of gaudy windows of the pictorial kind, and lurid wall decorations. Dr. M'Crie never descended to the level of the popular crowd, but rather did he seek to lift his congregation to a higher standard of appreciation. He is buried in Greyfriars churchyard, where his ancestors signed the National Covenant. On his monument is a long inscription which reads in part: "He contended with unfaltering firmness for the principles of the Reformation, the memory of whose champions he has vindicated and embalmed in the pages of imperishable history."

One of his great services to his country, too often overlooked, was his valiant answer to the sneers of Sir Walter Scott,[28] whose malicious caricature of the Covenanters has caused these defenders of religious freedom to appear in the light of cranks and fanatics. It is an unfortunate fact that one school of historians and at least one school of religious thought have seen fit to look upon Sir Walter's grotesque

[27]. J. G. Lockhart, *Peter's Letters to his Kinfolk* (Edinburgh, 1819).
[28]. Scott, *Old Mortality*, 1816.

characters as authentic.   It cannot be denied that the Covenanters, like all religious groups, had their radical minority, who, had they been given the power to do so, might have set up a despotic rule as intolerant as that of the King and the bishops whom they opposed.   This imprudent minority was small, and cannot possibly be looked upon as representative of the true spirit of the Covenanters, whose better men sought nothing more than to secure freedom of worship, and freedom from interference on the part of a domineering King and despotic bishops.   Thomas M'Crie's able defense of the Covenanters not only put an end to many of the old slanders, but established his own reputation as one whose thorough knowledge of religious history made him a man with whom none cared to engage in a controversy. In addition to the important biographies and histories already mentioned, Dr. M'Crie published a book of sermons (1836).   His collected *Works,* in 4 volumes, and *Miscellaneous Writings* (1841) contain his other writings.   A good biography was written by his son.

Henry Belfrage (1774-1835)

A number of notable preachers were to be found in some of the smaller independent synods of Scotland, such as the Associate (Burgher) Synod, the General Associate (Antiburgher) Synod, the Relief Synod and others.   Some of these men are remembered to this day, but others who were well known at the time have become but a memory today. One of these was Dr. Henry Belfrage.   He was born in 1774 at Falkirk, where his father was pastor of a Burgher congregation.   The Falkirk manse was a place where the old-fashioned type of Scottish piety prevailed, and the young lad Henry was set apart for the ministry, and trained carefully with that object in view.   He was educated in the parish school at Falkirk, and trained at home by his devout parents.   At the age of 13 he was able to enter Edinburgh University.   After completing his university work, he was trained in theology by the Rev. George Lawson, of Selkirk, at that time the professor of theology of the little Burgher Synod.

Licensed in 1793, he received three calls. At the advice of the Associate Synod, who were mindful of his youth, he served for a time as his father's assistant. The Falkirk congregation numbered 2,000 souls and 900 communicants, and these were scattered widely over a large territory. The parish was divided into several districts in which catechizations were held from time to time, with an annual public examination. Mr. Belfrage made it a rule to visit every family once a year, a task which required two full days out of each week, and over a period of eight months. Beginning as assistant to his father, he became his father's associate pastor, and eventually his successor. In 1814 Henry Belfrage began to publish a series of books that became very popular in his day. Among his many publications were a catechism, a manual for communicants, and a series of sermons on the Ten Virgins, entitled *The Visible Church in the Last Days*. This book of sermons enjoyed a wide circulation. Other works of Dr. Belfrage include: *Practical Discourses for the Young* (1817); *A Practical Exposition of the Assembly's Shorter Catechism,* 2 vols. (1834); *A Monitor for Families* (1823); *Discourses to the Aged* (1826); and *Sacramental Addresses and Exhortations,* 2 vols. The story of his life is told in McKerrow's *Life and Correspondence of Henry Belfrage.*

Dr. Belfrage was an excellent preacher. He was a man of fine personal appearance, his bearing was dignified and his delivery unusually impressive. His command of the English language was exceptional, his sermons rich in imagery and strongly doctrinal. In addition to the well-known book of sermons already mentioned, he wrote a life of John the Baptist, biographies of Dr. Waugh and Dr. Lawson, an exposition of the Shorter Catechism, various devotional books, sermons and catechetical addresses. So highly esteemed was he as a forceful preacher that he was selected by the London Missionary Society to deliver the sermon before their 1825 convention, one of whose founders, 30 years previously, had been another noted Scotsman of evangelical views, the Rev. John Love.

Andrew M. Thomson (1779-1831)

One of Scotland's most attractive preachers was Dr. Andrew M. Thomson, of St. George's, Edinburgh. He was born at Sanquhar, Dumfries-shire, and his father, Dr. John Thomson was at one time a prominent Edinburgh clergyman. The younger Thomson attended the parish school at Markinch, Fifeshire, and Edinburgh University. After teaching school for two years he was licensed to preach in 1802 by the presbytery of Kelso, and ordained later in the same year as pastor of a congregation in Spronston, Roxburghshire. While there he published a catechism on the Lord's Supper that was used quite generally in other parishes in addition to his own. In 1808 he became pastor of East Church, Perth.

It was in Edinburgh that he achieved his great fame as a preacher. In 1810 he received the presentation to New Greyfriars. This was unusual, for the congregations of that city were usually given by the magistrates to men of mature years, and often to old men. His lucid expositions of the Scriptures and his eloquent appeals for benevolent and charitable causes brought him into general notice. He began to publish the *Christian Instructor,* writing most of the articles himself. He contributed several important articles to Dr. Brewster's *Edinburgh Encyclopaedia.*

In 1814 the new St. George's Church was opened, and Andrew Thomson was called as its pastor. Its great dome, marking the end of George Street, is familiar to every one who has visited Edinburgh. The new church stood in what was then the edge of the city, and the people who lived nearby were cultured and well-educated, but without any particular regard for the teachings and obligations of evangelical truth. Mr. Thomson was informed from the outset that his success in this select neighborhood depended upon his willingness to make certain concessions to the wishes of the people. Thomson refused to compromise, or to soften his testimony. He was aware of the havoc of Moderatism, and he believed that the people of his new parish needed the Law and the Gospel no less than the humblest cotter. By his fearless public testimony, and by much private persuasion he gradually won the hearts of the people, and the great church was filled to capacity.

Mr. Thomson's preparation for the pulpit was thorough. He arose at an early hour, he studied his texts with great care, and he wrote out fully two sermons every week. He felt the need of a Christian day school, and he raised the funds for its erection. For some time he taught the school himself, until his people had become convinced of its value, and allowed teachers to be called. He conducted catechetical instruction between the morning and the afternoon church services, and many young people beyond day-school age attended. Finding the text books available for parish schools to be inadequate, due to the influence of Moderatism, he wrote and published a new series of school books, in which evangelical truth received due attention.

These activities did not interfere with Andrew Thomson's excellency as a preacher. He found time in the early morning hours for thorough preparation. Fortunately he had an acute mind and an excellent memory, and the people of Edinburgh found in him a singularly able and powerful preacher. Not only was he definitely evangelical in his preaching, but he became a leader and spokesman for the evangelical group, and a foe of Moderatism. By means of his emphatic preaching and through the columns of the magazine that he edited he wielded a great influence in Scotland. He was a popular platform speaker, and able to hold the close attention of his hearers for three hours. Few men have been so gifted in fluency of speech and in convincing, logical argument, and Andrew Thomson was a man whom the Moderates learned to fear. He bore fearless witness against the abuses of patronage, against pluralism and against slavery in the colonies. When the British and Foreign Bible Society included the Apocrypha in their Bibles, Thomson led the crusade which, after long and bitter argument on both sides, finally ended in the removal of the books against which he testified. In a celebrated debate in Edinburgh, in 1830, it was the arguments of Andrew Thomson that turned the tide. It had been proposed that after December 31, 1831, all children born in slavery should be considered free. Thomson demanded immediate abolition of all slavery in the British colonies. It was one of the most famous speeches of his career, and there are many persons who look upon it as the turning point in the debate. In 1833 complete freedom was given to all slaves, wherever found in any of the colonies. Thomson has been called the Abraham Lincoln of the British Empire; and the example of England was followed by other nations until finally slavery was wiped out in other lands.

Andrew Thomson was interested in church music, and deeply interested in the improvement of Psalmody. He raised the musical standards of his own congregation to a high degree of excellence; and by his writings and his lectures he established that excellency of musical taste that is characteristic of the Scottish Church to this day.

Dr. Thomson was noted for his sound judgment, and his wise advice was sought by the leaders of the Kirk. Few men have had so thorough a knowledge of human nature. Dr. Thomas M'Crie, the great Scottish church historian says of him, "In particular, he bore no inconsiderable resemblance to Luther, both in excellencies and defects — his leonine nobleness and potency, his maculine eloquence, his facetious-ness and pleasantry, the fondness which he showed for the fascinating charms of music, and the irratibility and vehemence which he occasionally exhibited." [29] Dr. Thomson was quick to forgive. Once a vigorous piece of writing was published anonymously. It gave great offense to some men, and it was generally attributed to Dr. Thomson, who in reality had not written a word of it, nor did he know anything about it. Discovering that it was the work of a close personal friend, who apologized to Thomson for the trouble it had caused, Dr. Thomson not only forgave him, but he bore the cost of a lawsuit, rather than disclose the name of the man who had written the objectionable article.

As a preacher Dr. Thomson had few peers. While his careful sermons were read from a manuscript, yet so skilfully did he do it that very few of his congregation were aware that he "made use of the paper." He made apt use

---

[29]. *Sermons and Sacramental Exhortations by the Late Andrew Thomson,* D.D. (Edinburgh and Boston, 1831), p. liv.

of illustrations, and used to say that an illustration, if good, could be depended upon to arouse even a dull congregation for twenty minutes. He was always careful in the pulpit, but when engaged in public debate during the Apocrypha Controversy and the Anti-Slavery Debate, his strong convictions led him, in a few instances, to lose his temper for the moment and to say things that he regretted afterward. However, in private life he was a friendly man, and on good terms even with his most outspoken opponents in debate.

People who came to his church as visitors expected to find a fighting crusader. They were surprised to find a man of youthful appearance, with a wealth of curly hair, a ruddy countenance and an expression of good nature. Dr. William Taylor says of him, "He had a fine, manly presence, a wonderful ear for music, in which he was greatly proficient, a voice of surpassing power and flexibility, and an exquisite sense of rhythmic harmony in the selection of words. He had a commanding intellect, a thorough knowledge of the world, unwavering faith in the great principles of the Gospel, and unflinching boldness combined with a wonderful tact in the advocacy of unpopular truth. As Lord Moncrief said lately, 'he was one of those orators who made your heart palpitate to hear'."[30]

"Dr. Thomson was decidedly evangelical in his doctrinal sentiments," said Dr. Thomas M'Crie, "which he did not disguise or hold back in his public discourses; but he was a practical preacher, and instead of indulging in abstruse speculations or philosophical disquisitions, made it his grand aim to impress the truths of the Gospel on the hearts of his hearers. . . . It is well known that Dr. Thomson belonged to that party in the Church of Scotland which has defended the rights of the people in opposition to the rigorous enforcement of the law of patronage; and in advocating this cause in the Church courts he has for many years displayed his unrivalled talents as a public speaker, sustained by an intrepidity which was unawed by power, and a fortitude which was proof against overwhelming majorities. . . . His exertions in behalf of the doctrines and standards of the church,

---

[30]. W. M. Taylor, *The Scottish Pulpit* (New York, 1887), p. 180.

against some recent heresies and delusions, afford an additional proof, not only of his unwearied zeal in behalf of that sacred cause to which he has devoted all his energies, but of his readiness at all times to 'contend earnestly for the faith which was once delivered to the saints'."[31]   Again Dr. M'Crie says, "To a manner of great animation and fire, yet restrained and dignified, he added a style of uncommon simplicity and spirit, which nature enabled him to set off to advantage by the tones of a voice remarkable for compass and harmony."[32]

Among a number of writings must be mentioned a book of select sermons,[33] which appeared just after his death. The opening sentence of his sermon on Ephesians 2, 8 might be called a summary of his theology. It reads: "If there be one truth more distinctly stated than another in the Bible, it is the truth contained in our text — that salvation flows entirely from divine grace, without any merit on the part of the sinner to deserve it, and without any ability on his part to accomplish it." Dr. Thomson was a man of prodigious energy, and he died at the relatively early age of 52, suffering a heart attack on his own doorstep, as he returned from a meeting of church leaders.

John Macdonald (1779-1849)

Dr. John Macdonald the famous "Apostle of the North" was born in 1779 at Balbein, in the parish of Reay, Caithness, near the northeastern tip of Scotland. His father was the parish catechist. Shortly after his birth, his parents took him to a neighboring clergyman for baptism. The clergyman was absent on a shooting trip, and the catechist and his wife started to return across the moors. They met the clergyman returning from his hunting trip, and explained their errand. It was in the month of December, and the pastor, a Moderate, merely broke the film of ice on a nearby

---

[31]. Quoted in a Memoir prefixed to *Sermons and Sacramental Exhortations by the Late Andrew M. Thomson, D.D.* (Edinburgh and Boston, 1831), pp. liv-lvii.

[32]. *Ibid.,* p. xix.

[33]. *Ibid.* Also *Sermons on Various Subjects* (1829); *Lectures Expository and Practical,* 2 vols. (1816); *Lovers of Pleasure more than Lovers of God* (1818); *Sermons on Infidelity* (1821), etc.

pool, recited a part of the baptismal service, and sprinkled a few drops of the icy water on the face of the infant.

John Macdonald attended the parish school at Reay, and in 1797 he entered Aberdeen University, where he was noted both for his fine scholarship and for his skill at playing the pipes. While at the university he read the writings of Jonathan Edwards, and this turned his thoughts toward the ministry. He was licensed in 1805 and served a mission congregation for a time at Berriedale, but gave no indication of his coming powers as a preacher. He was translated in 1807, a year after his ordination, to the Gaelic Church in Edinburgh, on the presentation of the S.P.C.K. Here his preaching was in Gaelic at first, although it was not long after his coming that a controversy broke out in the congregation regarding the language question. There were children who understood English more readily than Gaelic. Some of the grown people, upon moving to Edinburgh, had ceased to speak Gaelic, and chose to speak only English. Still other were Lowlanders who understood no Gaelic, but who had begun to attend the Gaelic Church through the influence of relatives or friends. Although there was vigorous opposition upon the part of the people from the Highlands and Islands, yet Mr. Macdonald began to preach in both languages.

While in Edinburgh the young pastor passed through some sort of a spiritual awakening, the exact details of which even his biographer is unable to explain. His sermons became rich in evangelical truth, and people were attracted to his bi-lingual church in growing numbers. In 1813 he was translated to Urquhart, also called Ferintosh, where he spent the remaining 36 years of his life. His predecessor had been a worthy man named Charles Calder, whose faithfulness to evangelical principles was in welcome contrast to the surrounding Moderate clergy. John Macdonald not only found the spiritual life in the parish in a satisfactory state, but the people of Ferintosh showed but little opposition when their pastor began to receive urgent invitations to preach in other places. Moderatism had held sway for many years, and a genuine "Gospel thirst" as the Scottish people termed it, was evident in many surrounding parishes.

John Macdonald began to make preaching tours into the surrounding country, and it was not long until his exceptional ability as an evangelical preacher was known everywhere. In a parish not far distant the pastor, a Moderate, was a cattle-trader during the week, the best dancer at social gatherings, and a man who could sit at a table after a wedding and drink whiskey after all the other guests were thoroughly drunk.   This man had a borrowed sermon which he preached without alteration on every important occasion.

With such men as this in too many parishes, it is not surprising that John Macdonald's ringing evangelical sermons were received as a welcome shower after a long drought.   There were a few evangelical pastors here and there, and the people took their infants to these men in the middle of the night for baptism, so that their own pastors might not know of it.   Throughout the Highlands, men such as Hector Macphail, Lachlan Mackenzie, John Robertson, Donald Sage, John Macrae and the great John Kennedy of Dingwall were as bright lights in the darkness, while in later days Thomas Chalmers and Thomas Guthrie came up from the South now and then and preached to multitudes.

The people of Dornoch urged John Macdonald to preach for them.   The Moderate pastors passed a resolution making it illegal for him to preach within the bounds of their presbytery.   Not to be defeated, John Macdonald came to the boundary line and preached to a gathering that numbered thousands, taking care not to cross the boundary.   So energetic was he that it is said his feet wore a depression in the turf, which was shown proudly by the local people to visitors for several years.   He was invited to Strathbogie, where seven of the ten clergy were Moderates.   He went without fear and preached to great outdoor gatherings. Determined efforts were made in the Assembly to silence Macdonald.   It is significant that the leaders of this movement were the same men who refused to exercise discipline in the case of a Moderate clergyman who was charged by his congregation with having preached but once in seven months.

Far out in the Atlantic, more than 40 miles from the nearest land, is the little Isle of St. Kilda.   It is but two

pression was singularly great; his illustrations, always apt, were often striking; his practical counsels to Christians, suggested by his own experience, were always wise and sensible; and his appeals to sinners were most solemn and powerful." [35] Dr. Macdonald pictured sin in its hideousness and pointed to the one and only source of salvation: the grace of God in Christ Jesus. His biographer says elsewhere: "for clearness and skill in unfolding the doctrines of grace, and in fervent appeals to the Christless, Fraser and Macdonald excelled them all." [36] Dr. Macdonald is also known for his beautiful Gaelic elegies. Wherever Highlanders have emigrated, his reputation as a peerless preacher has been taken, and among Scottish Gaels his name is even yet a household word.

Dr. Robert Buchanan says of John Macdonald: "It is enough to say that he was the Whitefield of the Highlands of Scotland. The proudest and most powerful chieftains of the Celtic race never possessed such a mastery over the clans, which the fiery cross or the wild pibroch summoned into the field in the fierce days of feudal strife, as belonged, in these more peaceful modern times, to this humble minister of Christ. From Tarbatness to the outer Hebrides, — from the Spey to the Pentland firth, — the fact needed but to be known that John Macdonald had come and was about to preach the Word, in order that the country for twenty miles around should gather at his call. Ten thousand people have often been swayed as one man, stirred into enthusiasm, or melted into sadness, by this mighty and faithful preacher's voice." [37] Among the greatest of Scotland's preachers will ever be Dr. John Macdonald, known everywhere as "the Apostle to the North."

Ralph Wardlaw (1779-1853)

Ralph Wardlaw, a noted Scottish Congregational preacher, was born in 1779 in Dalkeith, Midlothian. On his mother's side of the family he was a direct descendent of

[35]. John Kennedy, *The Apostle of the North* (London, 1867), p. 331.
[36]. John Kennedy, *The Days of the Fathers in Ross-shire* (Edinburgh, 1861), p. 24.
[37]. Robt. Buchanan, *The Ten Years' Conflict,* 2 vols. (Glasgow, 1849).

260 A HISTORY OF PREACHING

King James V of Scotland. He was educated in the grammar schools of Glasgow, and in 1791 he entered Glasgow University. From 1795 to 1800 he studied in the theological seminary of the Burgher Secession Kirk. While there he became influenced by James and Robert Haldane, the lay preachers, and in 1800 he united with the Congregational denomination. He accompanied the Haldanes to Edinburgh, Perth, Dundee and other places, and was found to have coming pulpit power.

In 1803 he became pastor of the North Albion Street Congregational church in Glasgow, which he served for fifty years. In 1819 it was necessary to build a large church in West George street, to accommodate the increasing congregation, and to provide room for visitors of various other denominations who were attracted by Wardlaw's preaching. In 1811 he was made professor in the Congregational theological school in Glasgow, where he taught, in addition to his parish duties. He was active in the London Missionary Society and in the British and Foreign Bible Society. He was known throughout Scotland and in many parts of England as a preacher of exceptional gifts, and was often invited to preach on important occasions in places far removed from Glasgow.

Wardlaw's sermons show a marked vigor of thought, a solidity of doctrinal content, an evangelical spirit and a spiritual tone. In theology he was a liberal Calvinist. He published several theological books but his best known work is his book entitled *On Miracles,* first published in 1852. W. L. Alexander published his *Memoirs of the Life and Writings of Ralph Wardlaw* in 1856.

CHAPTER IX

THE DISRUPTION OF 1843

FOR ALMOST three centuries the people of Scotland had declared from time to time their determination to protect their religious liberty. It was this struggle for spiritual freedom that led no less that 474 clergyman to withdraw from the State Church and to found the Free Church. The abuses which led to this incident, known as the Disruption, were eight in number, and are summed up in the protest read to the General Assembly on May 18, 1843.

First, there was the matter of intrusion. The evil system of patronage still existed. Privileged men, by virtue of wealth or position, were given the right not only to choose the candidates when a congregation became vacant, but to employ the arm of the civil law to compel an unwilling congregation to accept such a man. In 1834 the congregation at Auchterrarder became vacant. The patron presented a candidate so distasteful to the congregation that only two people voted to accept him. 287 heads of families out of 330 drew up a protest. The civil courts decided that the obnoxious candidate must be installed. The case was appealed in 1839, and the House of Lords sustained the decision of the civil courts.

Other cases of the same kind followed. The Scottish Kirk declared that there must be a call from the congregation before a candidate could be ordained or installed. The civil courts decided that the very nature of a State Church implies civil control of its actions. Lord Campbell declared in the House of Lords that so long as a congregation was content to remain within a State Church, it must be willing to perform the duties imposed upon it by the civil authorities; whereas a Free Church may be governed entirely by its own decisions in spiritual matters. Sir Robert Peel declared later: "I think it of the greatest importance that the spiritual authority of the Church should be restrained and made subordinate to Parliament."

A second evil was the interdict. The civil courts declared the right to prohibit the preaching of the Gospel and the administration of the Sacraments, under certain conditions. Thus when seven pastors in Strathbogie were suspended, they applied to the civil courts. The courts not only claimed the right to exercise the Office of the Keys and restore these men, but they placed the Strathbogie area under an interdict, and prohibited any outside pastor, under penalty of imprisonment, to preach in that community. Great excitement was caused throughout Scotland, for it had always been recognized that any pastor in good standing, regardless of his denomination, had the right to preach wherever there were people who wished to hear him.

Dr. Guthrie was invited to preach at Strathbogie. Just before service, papers were served, forbidding him to preach in any church, school or churchyard, which the Court of Sessions declared to be the property of the State. Guthrie declared: "When the Lords of Sessions forbade me to preach my Saviour's blessed Gospel and offer salvation to sinners anywhere in that district under the arch of Heaven, I put the interdict under my feet and I preached the Gospel." [1]   He preached night after night in the open air to great gatherings of people.

A third evil was the power claimed by the civil courts to suspend spiritual censures pronounced by the Kirk against clergymen and probationers, and by interdict prevent such spiritual censures from being carried out. Still other evils against which the evangelical party protested were: That the civil courts claimed for themselves the right to set aside the action of the Kirk, in cases where a clergyman had been deposed, or a probationer deprived of his license to preach; that the civil courts claimed the right to determine who may or may not have voice and vote in church conventions; that the civil courts insisted upon the privilege of depriving a majority of their spiritual functions, and to give the minority party the right to exercise these functions; that the civil courts assumed the right to reverse the decision of the church authorities in cases of church discipline; and that the civil courts believed that no pastor has a right to exercise spiritual privileges in any church assembly, superior or inferior, without the coercion of the civil court.

---

[1]. *Autobiography of Thomas Guthrie, and Memoir by His Sons* (London, 1874), vol. 2, p. 18.

The evangelical group admitted that where a State Church exists, the government may claim certain rights in regard to things that are purely temporal. However, as Thomas Guthrie expresses it, "we maintained that Christ had, in His Church, a kingdom in this world separate and distinct from all earthly ones, whether monarchies or republics; that it was by the Acts of the Apostles, and not by Acts of Parliament, that the Church was to guide herself in all strictly spiritual matters. We held, therefore, that the State could not hinder us from restoring to the people their rights in the election of a minister; nor from depriving a minister of his status, when, in our judgment, he had committed an offense for which he ought to be deposed." [2]

In 1842 a special convocation was called in Edinburgh and was attended by 474 clergymen. For eight days they discussed the evils that had come upon them because of State interference in spiritual matters. They drew up a petition to the Government asking that these wrongs be remedied, and they pledged one another that they would withdraw from the State Church in case their petition was refused. A few weeks later the Crown rejected their petition. An appeal was made to Parliament, but this body refused to hear it. Finally the men who had drafted the petition decided to withdraw from the State Church, even though it meant the surrender of their congregations, their manses and their livings.

Throughout the winter, delegations of clergymen were sent to every part of Scotland. The country was thoroughly aroused, and large gatherings of people assembled everywhere. In some places the visiting clergymen were not allowed to speak in the church or the school house, and great mass meetings were held in the open air. In many a parish church sermons were preached dealing with the relation of Church and State. Everywhere the fact was stressed that every Christian must be loyal to his Government in all temporal matters, but equally determined to preserve the liberties of the Church in matters that are purely spiritual. An intensive campaign of indoctrination, such as Scotland had not seen in generations, took place that winter. Even

---

[2]. *Op. cit.*, vol. I, pp. 228-229.

the farm laborers, on market day, gathered in groups and discussed the relation of Church and State, reviewing the arguments of the clergymen, and the proof texts that they were accustomed to use. The Moderate party, generally, were hostile to the entire matter; and they predicted freely that very few pastors would have the courage to sacrifice their congregations, their comfortable homes and their assured incomes for the sake of their convictions. There was a mediating group, including such excellent men as the Macleods, who were opposed to State interference in spiritual matters, and yet who urged one another to remain in the Established Church and reform it from within.

On the 18th day of May, 1843, the General Assembly met in Edinburgh. People came from all parts of Scotland, and Edinburgh was crowded as it had not been since the signing of the National Covenant. Dr. David Welsh preached the opening sermon, using the text: "Let every man be fully persuaded in his own mind." Then the pastors and elders filed out of the church where the opening service had been held, and moved through crowded streets to St. Andrew's Church, where the first business session was to be held. The crowds were so dense that it was with great difficulty that a way was cleared for the delegates. Many had come hours before the opening of the Assembly, and it had been necessary to place padlocks on the doors to prevent the use of duplicate keys.

Dr. Welsh, the retiring moderator, called the Assembly to order, and announced that because of certain proceedings which threatened the rights and privileges of the Church, it was impossible to proceed with the business of the day. Then he read the protest, in which the eight claims of the civil courts were mentioned. Dr. Welsh bowed to the Queen's Commissioner, who was present, and then he laid the protest on the table.

The scene that followed is without parallel in Church history. Dr. Welsh moved toward the door, accompanied by Dr. Thomas Chalmers, who had stood beside him when the protest was read. Candlish, Cunningham, Gordon, Guthrie and other influential leaders arose and followed. Then row after row of benches were vacated, as the men rose from their seats and followed the procession that moved slowly through the church doors. The astonished Moderates and the mediating group who remained behind gazed in silence at the seats left vacant by the men who had departed. No less than 474 pastors, including most of the great leaders of the Kirk, had walked out that day.

In the streets an enormous crowd awaited them. Places of business had been closed. Hundreds of policemen were required to keep the way open for the pastors and their elders, who marched slowly, four abreast, clad in the black coats and tall silk hats which were the fashion in those days. Every roof was crowded, and people leaned from every window. Cheers broke forth at times, but, generally speaking, an air of utmost seriousness was evident, and many a fervent wish for the best was spoken to the men as they passed by. Now and then there was a scream or a sob, as a wife or a child recognized a husband or father in the procession. Everybody realized that these 474 pastors had given up congregations, friends of long standing, homes and salaries, and were facing an uncertain future, and all for the sake of conscience. Some of the largest and wealthiest congregations in Scotland were given up that day. The people realized all this fully, for sermons had been preached all winter and spring, mass meetings held in the remotest Highlands and Islands, and the whole country had been flooded again and again with pamphlets, through a systematic campaign of education directed by the administrative genius of Dr. Chalmers and a staff of able assistants. The procession that emerged from the doorway of St. Andrew's Church moved down the long street to Canonmills, and to a future that might well mean lives of privation for many.

The men made their way to a large building known as Tanfield Hall, which was seated for 3,000 people. Here they were called to order, they signed the Deed of Demission in which they surrendered all their previous rights, and then they proceeded, according to a carefully pre-arranged plan, to organize the Free Church of Scotland, independent of State control, and in which the sovereign rights of every congregation were safeguarded. Dr. Thomas Chalmers was chosen moderator of the new organization, and there were none who questioned the wisdom of this choice. It was his remarkable talent for leadership that had directed the work for months. It was he and his thoroughly capable associates who had organized all Scotland, who had arranged the preaching services and mass meetings in every city, village and hamlet both in English-speaking and in Gaelic-speaking parts of Scotland. Printed literature had been sent out, wave upon wave of it, often as many as 150,000 copies of a single pamphlet. Everything had been planned with such skill that the convention of the new Free Church moved forward smoothly, with nothing left to guess-work.

The tremendous task that faced them had been anticipated to its smallest detail. While 474 pastors had withdrawn for the corrupt old State Church, the seceding congregations numbered 500 or more. Every one of these had to be provided with a new place of worship, for their former churches had been surrendered to the State. In addition to the 500 churches, even a larger number of parish schools had to be built. The pastors who had withdrawn must be provided with homes, for their former manses were State property. Colleges and theological halls must be built. Every foreign missionary, to the last man, had "come out with the Free," and the entire home and foreign missionary organization had to be reconstructed afresh. Theological and college faculties had to be elected, and a multitude of boards and standing committees constituted. The publication of books and literature was a huge task in itself, for the congregations that seceded were left without so much as a pulpit Bible or a single hymn book. Weekly and monthly church periodicals had to be established, and publishing houses created. Dr. Chalmers and his staff had anticipated all these things, and long before a man walked out of St. Andrew's Church that historic May 18th, options had been obtained on building materials, church equipment of every description, and even upon printing presses and tons of type.

The State Church had reported about 1,000 parish schools that year. The new Free Church organized 712 new parish schools, and with 62,660 children enrolled. In a single year $250,000 was raised for the support of these schools. Meanwhile new churches were under construction everywhere. Fortunately Scotland had a beautiful spring and summer that year, and many congregations met in the open air while their churches were under construction. In some cases the buildings were not ready when winter set in, and cases of real hardship could be mentioned; nevertheless the resolute people assembled from Sunday to Sunday, sometimes in drifting snow.

The pastors had vacated their manses, and there is a large steel engraving well known to many a Scottish home. It shows a clergyman and his family leaving the door of the house that had been their home for so many years, their goods piled in wagons, and the family facing an unknown future, but confident that the Lord would neither leave them nor forsake them. It fell to the lot of Thomas Guthrie to raise the $500,000 manse fund, which he did during the year 1845. His famed eloquence and his peculiar gift of persuasiveness were used to good effect, but the year of exertion undermined his health, and he was never the same thereafter.

This Disruption of 1843 attracted attention throughout the world, and the 474 clergymen and their congregations were the heroes of the hour. It loosed the springs of Christian giving in a way that astonished the world, for the average Scotsman of those days was a poor man, living in his little but-and-ben, with but little income. Men and women of means were among those who left the State Church, and had it not been for their generous giving, New College in Edinburgh, and its Divinity Hall, might not have been built on the imposing scale that they were, nor would the colleges and divinity schools in other cities have been possible. The lay people of the Disruption deserve their full share of credit.

A great literature grew up about the Disruption. Generally speaking the heroism of the movement was applauded throughout the world. There were some, especially among the Moderates, who ridiculed the movement, declaring it cheap exhibitionism on the part of a group of men who made sure in advance that they were on the popular side, and who laid great stress upon the sovereign rights of the common people in order to win their support. It was said more than once that many an unworthy man withdrew from the State Church not because of his religious convictions, but because it seemed the popular thing to do.

One cannot praise the 474 pastors and their congregations too highly. On the other hand, one is not justified in saying that the men who remained in the old State Church were all unworthy men. Some of them were definitely opposed to the evils which had fastened themselves upon the Establishment, but they did not think that a split in the ranks was the best solution. They fought the abuses of their day from within. There were courageous men among them, for it was no easy task to remain in the State Church and to face the problem of rebuilding. They were left with over 500 church buildings that were all but empty, with parish schools without teachers or pupils, with colleges and seminaries with depleted faculties and decimated student bodies, with foreign mission stations but not a single missionary, and with empty mission treasuries. Many of the Gaelic-speaking pastors had withdrawn, and the task of raising up a new generation of men to serve the Gaelic Highlands and the Western Isles, was a severe one. While Moderatism was a curse that is wholly indefensible and unpardonable, yet one must not be too sweeping in his condemnation of the men who remained behind. Their mistakes were often grievous, and too often they were compelled to place poorly qualified men in important congregations and professors' chairs simply because better men could not be found. They had worthy men among them in the members of the mediating group, known as "The Forty," and had it not been for these, the State Church might have suffered a blow from which she never would have recovered. Many of The Forty were foes of Moderatism and liberalism of every kind, yet because of family ties, or a sentimental attachment to the old Kirk, or for some other reason they were not ready to sever their connection. They remained behind and became an evangelical leaven, such as it was, in the corrupt old Establishment.

The Disruption had a far-reaching influence upon preaching. Scotland has always been famed for her preachers, and has given the world more such men than any other country of her size, and far out of proportion to her small size. There has never been a time when faithful witnesses were lacking. Even in times when it seemed that the evangelical lights had gone out all over the world, a few faithful men remained. They formed an "evangelical succession" and bore valiant witness to the great truths of the utter helplessness of man by nature, and his salvation through the blood of Jesus Christ, without the works of the Law. They erred in limiting this salvation to a chosen minority whom God had elected by divine decree, at the same time passing all others by. Defective as their evangelical preaching was in this respect, yet they never fell into the spiritual sloth of many men, who were content to preach a shallow morality in which the Cross was too often entirely absent.

There were men scattered throughout Scotland, even in the darkest days of spiritual decline, who cried aloud to the sinner to repent, and to trust solely in the redemptive work of Jesus Christ. There were not many of them, and often they were not men of conspicuous gifts. The mother of Thomas Guthrie was a woman of great force of character. In Guthrie's childhood days, she decided that the Christless sermons to which she was compelled to listen were poor pabulum, as she termed it, for her soul. In the little Burgher chapel of Brechin was a humble clergyman who preached sin and grace with great diligence, and there Mrs. Guthrie directed her steps, taking her children with her, while her husband continued to attend the State Church. Such humble chapels existed here and there, and it was these that preserved, perhaps in a partial way, the elements of evangelical truth.

Even before the Disruption there were evidences of a spiritual awakening, and influential men, here and there, began to give more attention to the great doctrines of Redemption. No longer did truth-seekers have to discover some homely little chapel in a forgotten street, and find in it the Bethel that he desired. The powerful sermons of Dr. Chalmers drew multitudes during his Glasgow ministry and later in Edinburgh. Long before the doors were opened,

crowds milled about at Old Greyfriars and later at St. John's
to hear Thomas Guthrie set forth the plan of Redemption in
his pictorial manner.   John Macdonald, Roderick Macleod,
and others stirred great congregations in the Gaelic Highlands and Islands.

A strange phenomenon, often to be observed in the
history of preaching, was taking place.   For no apparent
reason men who had not been especially noted for their
evangelical preaching, began to bear witness to Redemptive
Christianity.   "I was led," writes George Innes, "by the
blessing of God to a more evangelical style of preaching and
to greater seriousness than at the earlier period of my
ministry."[3]   Robert Jeffrey, of Girthon, stated "that from
the first he had preached the Gospel to the light he had
received, but that a great change had taken place fifteen
years before, when his views of religion became much more
earnest and deeply evangelical."[4]   Dr. David Landsborough
had been a Moderate, but was brought to an understanding
of the plan of salvation.   Contrasting his preaching in the
days when he belonged to the liberal party and with that
of later days, he says, "How great was then my darkness,
how unfit my spirit for the solemn work on which I was about
to be engaged. . . . What changes in the world since my life
began! How many changes in my own life! Thou hast
borne with me . . . Thou hast enlightened me. I have
reason to hope that I am renewed, and on the way to
Heaven."[5]   Roderick Macleod is even more definite. "During the first three years of my ministry I was an entire
stranger to the Gospel scheme of salvation," he declared,
"and no wonder, for the staple theology of Skye preaching
in those days was nothing better than scraps of Blair's sermons or of some other equally meagre stuff, so that I have
often thought that I scarcely ever heard the Gospel till I
began to preach it myself, with the exception of going two
or three times to the Gaelic Chapel in Aberdeen."[6]   Mr.
Macleod read Bellamy's *Christian Religion Delineated,* and

---

[3]. *Disruption Manuscripts,* xv, p. 1.   See Thos. Brown, *Annals of the Disruption* (Edinburgh, 1893), p. 7.
[4]. *Parker Manuscripts, Presbytery of Kirkcudbright.*
[5]. *Memoir,* p. 163.
[6]. *Parker Manuscript, Presbytery of Skye.*

Dr. Chalmers' *Lectures on Romans*. These books led him to study his Bible and to preach its teachings to his congregation, and he became a great evangelical leader in the Western Isles.

Walter Wood describes a preaching tour, about the year 1838, in and around Cairnie. Not satisfied with two or three services on Sunday, so great was the Gospel hunger of the people that they asked for "diets of catechizing" on weekday evenings. Mr. Wood preached in a large barn on Monday night and it was crowded to capacity. As he rode to his next appointment on the following day, some 40 or 50 people accompanied him, closing round his horse to converse with him, then falling back in order to allow another group of people to gather about him. Now and then they would stop and say, "Eh, sir, there's an auld man lying bedrid in yon cothouse, and naebody gaes near to speak wie him about his soul. Would you no just go in and see him for a minute or twa?" Mr. Wood conducted catechizations each day, and by Saturday night there were 100 present. He was in that district for two weeks, and every effort was made by the Moderates to learn his name in order that they might serve legal papers forbidding him to preach. So loyal were the people to him that nobody asked him his name, lest the word might reach the ears of the wrong people. He conducted a three-day Communion service in the open air, with the preparation sermon on Saturday, the celebration of Holy Communion on Sunday and a thanksgiving service on Monday. There was a large gathering of people, and the Moderates looked on, but since they could not learn his name their court papers were worthless.

In the year 1839 the people of Kilsyth, from July to the end of October, flocked to their churches as they had not done for generations. The same thing was taking place at Strathbogie, Lawers, Collace, Lochtayside, Tain and in many other places. At Rosskeen the interest was so great that David Carment had to preach weekday evenings as well as on Sunday. At a single Communion service more people received the Sacrament than the entire total for the previous 18 years of Mr. Carment's pastorate there.

At Kilsyth "their thirst for hearing became so intense
. . . that for nearly four months it was found desirable to
have public worship almost every night"[7] in a densely
crowded church.   Dr. Thomas Brown, in his *Annals of the
Disruption,* devotes a number of pages to examples such as
these.   Churches which had been empty were filled to
capacity, the people demanded weekday preaching services,
and everywhere this thirst for the Gospel was evident.   The
explanation is simple enough.   The people had been starved
for generations by the Moderates.   Men here and there, by
the grace of God, were beginning to read their Bibles, and
to preach the elements of Redemptive Christianity to a
nation of spiritual hungry people.   Christianity had suffered,
but had not died out during the long years of evangelical
decline.   In many a household a "chapter" was read
morning and evening and prayers were said.   Even in the
darkest days the old Scottish Sabbath was observed, a relic
of earlier days.   After listening to a sermon, which too
often was entirely devoid of evangelical truth, or more than
likely remaining away from the parish kirk entirely, Sunday
afternoon was spent indoors.   No work of any kind was
allowed.   The reading of secular books and the singing of
secular songs was prohibited.   In the corner of every cottage, however poor the people, was a little book shelf, and
on this was the family Bible, the Larger and the Shorter
Catechisms, and several books whose brown leather binding
had become smooth with age.   One may pick up some of
these very books today in the second-hand book shops of
Edinburgh or Glasgow.   They are the devotional writings
of eighteenth and early nineteenth century clergymen.
These, and a book or two of "divinity" or theology, were to
be found in every Scottish home, and Sunday afternoon was
devoted to their reading.   After the children had been
examined in the Shorter Catechism, and had recited one or
more metrical Psalms, the old leather-bound religious books
were taken from the shelf.   In some homes this was done
because a genuine spirit of piety prevailed: in other homes,
doubtless, it was merely an old custom.   Whatever may have
been the motive, these Scottish Sundays, devoted to Bible

---

[7]. Thos. Brown, *Op. cit.,* pp. 11-12.

reading, the Catechism and religious writings, preserved a certain degree of evangelical awareness in many a Scottish home, and a race of people who devoted one day out of every seven to religious study and instruction in the home, was certain to make its influence felt. Not only did this become evident at the time of the Disruption, but long before that the tens of thousands of Scots who had emigrated to America, and had settled in Pennsylvania, Western New York, Virginia, Ohio and then in the country east of the Mississippi, left an influence upon American life that has never been fully appreciated.

After the Disruption of 1843, the rising tide of evangelical interest received a great impetus. All over Scotland new church buildings, new parish schools, new manses and homes for the teachers were being built. In several of the larger cities imposing college buildings and theological schools were under construction. Almost overnight the people learned a lesson in Christian giving that might well put to shame our own generation. Within three years 700 new churches and 712 new parish schools were either completed or else under construction. They were, as a rule, good sturdy buildings, and as one visits Scotland today he is surprised to find that they were often of considerable size. Even in our own prosperous country, where people live in what a Scotsman would consider luxury, our religious denominations, often numbering 5,000 or more congregations, think in terms of cheap little mission chapels for their new congregations. The Scottish people of 1843, most of them living in small cottages or crowded city tenements, built spacious churches, often severely plain, but so substantial in their construction that they are still in use, in many cases, after more than a century. As these church buildings were completed, the congregations that gathered twice each Sunday filled every seat on the main floor and in the galleries which so often ran along both side walls and across the back of the building.

This remarkable interest in church attendance was not due merely to novelty. The pastors of the new Free Church preached evangelical sermons, and it was this that attracted the people. They were not evangelical in the sense that the term is often applied to the preaching of the American revivalist, neither was their evangelical preaching all that might be desired. Men who had been trained in theological halls where Moderatism held sway did not become thoroughly orthodox overnight, even though they had the light of God's Word as their guide. Too often we find evidence in their sermons of the error of a limited Atonement — a limiting of the offer of salvation to a minority, selected from eternity by an arbitrary decree of a sovereign God. Again we find many a man who lays utmost stress upon what he considers a divine obligation to keep the Sabbath. We find clergymen, even in the Free Kirk, thundering away against Sunday railway trains when they might well have been warning against the false doctrine of materialistic evolution and against German higher criticism, which was beginning to reach Scotland. We find them preaching vehement sermons against such innovations as church organs and against all hymns other than metrical Psalmody. While one cannot endorse such extreme views today, yet it must be admitted that the preaching of the Disruption period was a great improvement over that of the days of Moderatism. Once more the people were reminded in no uncertain terms of their sins, and of the suffering and death of Jesus Christ for the redemption of mankind. There was a great revival of interest in mission work. Although the people had given to the utmost in order to build new churches, parish schools, colleges and seminaries, yet they responded nobly when asked to provide places of worship in the slums, which had been neglected for so long. They gave liberally to the cause of missions in heathen lands, and among the Jews. They even gave to assist congregations of their own denomination in the United States and Canada.

For a considerable time the preaching of the Free Church was evangelical, and the method was textual and expository. Sermons were not often devoted to mere civic righteousness. It was a revolt against the time of Moderatism, when the Lord Jesus was banished from the average sermon; and once more their preaching was centered about the Saviour, His person and work. Men were proud to call themselves orthodox — an orthodoxy of the reformed type, and based upon the Westminster standards. This type of preaching continued for a number of years, until the unfortunate days when it became quite the fashion for theological students, having finished their work in the Scottish theological halls, to go to Germany for a year or so of post-graduate work. There they became tainted with the prevailing textual criticism, and came back to Scotland only, in many cases, to bring back with them the very blight that had destroyed German religious thought.

The Free Church was fortunate in having a group of exceptional preachers. What other country or what religious denomination could boast of such undying names as those of Thomas Chalmers, Robert Candlish, Robert Buchanan, Thomas Guthrie, William Cunningham, James Gibson, James Begg, the Bonar brothers, John Macdonald, Robert Gordon, Roderick Macleod, Alexander Macleod, Alexander Stewart, John Kennedy, John Macrae and others? These men were preachers of exceptional gifts, and there was a Spurgeon in many a Scottish pulpit. Edinburgh alone had an impressive group of such men.

While the State Church was left with few great leaders after the 474 seceded, yet she was not without good preachers. Not all the gifted men withdrew. Men of evangelical convictions remained in the old Kirk and saved her from decay. The United Presbyterians, the Congregationalists, the Baptists and other minority groups had men who were eminent preachers and who did not cease to preach Christ crucified. The same awakening of an evangelical spirit which had brought the Free Church of Scotland into being was felt in these other denominations, for it was a wide-spread reaction against the spiritual deadness of the previous generation. Moderatism began to lose its influence in the State Church; and in the minority groups just mentioned the example of the Free Church proved wholesome. Not for many years had the preaching of the Cross been heard in so many of Scotland's pulpits. This spiritual awakening was not to endure for long, and materialistic science, higher criticism, liberalism and modernism were, before many years, to destroy much of what Dr. Chalmers and his associates had accomplished.

Preaching to the Outcasts

Few things are more stirring than an account of the mission work in Scotland's underworld, where so many modern miracles of grace are to be found. Courageous preachers have penetrated those jungles of infamy, where human life was never safe. Armed only with the Word of God they have transformed those "thieves' kitchens" into areas which in turn have become famous centers of missionary effort. Debauched men and women have been transformed into devout Christians and have been organized into large congregations, and these have become spiritual centers from which missionary effort has radiated far and wide, and daughter congregations established in other abandoned areas. It is a question whether such a story of missionary triumph can be found anywhere, although the remarkable work in London's underworld may be considered second only to that of Glasgow and Edinburgh.

Dr. Thomas Chalmers was among the pioneers. As early as 1815 he became interested in the neglected masses of Glasgow, and in 1819 his zeal had become so great that he resigned the large and important Tron Church and took part in the creation of a new parish called St. John's. Beginning with nothing, he put in five years of hard labor, tramping the narrow, filthy streets every day, climbing dilapidated wooden stairways of tenements five and six stories high and even higher. He was a remarkable organizer, and in a short time he had a staff of volunteer workers to assist him. Two parochial schools were started, and 50 branch Sunday-schools.

When called to Edinburgh in 1828, Dr. Chalmers was not content merely to teach at the University. It was not long until he found the West Port, a district second only in depravity to the scene of his remarkable success in Glasgow. His professorship left him a certain amount of leisure time, and no man of his tremendous energy and evangelical zeal could be idle. Laying aside his academic robe, he would hurry from the quiet campus to the filthy West Port, and begin once more the task of climbing the rickety stairways of the tall tenements.

Standing at the bedside of some human derelict dying of cholera or typhus, he would read a chapter of God's Word, expound it briefly, utter words of admonition and of comfort, and then depart after a brief prayer. Sitting down on the stone steps where some drink-sodden man or woman was just awakening from an alcoholic slumber, Chalmers would read the Scriptures, expound and admonish. Going down some dismal passageway, he would interrupt the shrill curses of grimy children, gather them about him and tell them the story of the Christ Child. To the people of the West Port, he was, at the outset, "just one of the old professors from the college." The dying derelicts at whose bedsides he expounded the Scriptures may never have known that Chalmers was one of the most famous expositors of his day, and one of the most eminent preachers of modern times.

Chalmers spared neither time nor his own personal funds. About the year 1844 he opened a mission in a room over a tanner's shop. In the immediate vicinity were 2,000 people, 1,500 of whom never entered a church. There were 450 children of school age, 290 of whom had never set foot within day school or Sunday-school. In 1844, the year after the Disruption, Dr. Chalmers divided the West Port into 20 districts, and gathered and trained a staff of Christian people. These workers went from house to house, reading the Scriptures to the people, teaching their children, and telling old and young of the proposed church in the tanner's loft.

After six months of intensive work on the part of Dr. Chalmers and his faithful workers, the first service was held in January, 1845. A dozen old women were the net result of months of hard work. Any man less resolute than Dr. Chalmers would have given up the experiment, declaring that the people of the district were not the kind who can be interested in religion. Dr. Chalmers encouraged his disappointed staff of helpers, and their effort continued. Gradually the attendance increased. Dr. Chalmers had resigned his professorship at Edinburgh University at the time of the Disruption and had become principal of the Free Church's New College and professor of theology in

Divinity Hall. These activities, together with his office of moderator of the Free Church's General Assembly, and his task of directing the work of the newly formed Free Church, left him but little time for detailed work in the West Port. Thus he decided to place a full-time man in the field, working under his immediate direction. This man was William Tasker, of whom we shall speak presently.

In 1847, just a month before his death, Dr. Chalmers dedicated the first permanent church in the West Port, a building seating 520 people. He had charge of the first Communion service. The work prospered beyond expectation, and within a short time branch missions were being opened and branch schools established. Others took up the work where Dr. Chalmers had laid it down at his death, and before many years Edinburgh had an imposing chain of flourishing congregations in the parts of the city that had been neglected areas.

The story has an interesting sequal, for both in Edinburgh and in Glasgow, as men and women were reclaimed from the underworld and made devout Christians and law-abiding citizens, they felt out of place in their old haunts. They moved to better parts of the city and became faithful members of other congregations. A large majority of them remained loyal Christians until death. The removal of many such families and individuals, who had been rescued from their old life, left vacant places in the church, but these were soon filled by other recruits from the underworld. The West Port Church and its daughter congregations became storehouses of missionary energy, and former drunkards and thieves became energetic workers among their former associates.

The methods of missionary work in the West Port were not spectacular. Devoted men preached the message of the Cross, employing the Law to bring sinners to repentance, and the Gospel to give them the assurance of salvation. Bands of trained workers went from house to house every week. The district was organized in such a way that every home was visited. These workers were trained to read passages of Scripture selected at first by Dr. Chalmers, and later by Mr. Tasker.

Work was started in Edinburgh by Dr. Chalmers, and then in Glasgow by Dr. Buchanan, of Tron Church. Mr. Dugald MacColl, who was the first man who gave his full time to the Wynd Mission in Glasgow, met with notable success. Within four years his church was filled to overflowing, and branch congregations were started one by one until there were sixteen of them in addition to the original Wynd Church. The mission field was, if anything, worse than Edinburgh's West Port. The area known as the Wynds covered 12 acres, and no less than 12,000 people were crowded into the grimy tenements of the district. It was not merely a slum: it was Glasgow's underworld, where the lowest grade of pickpockets, sneakthieves and even cut-throats had their hiding places. Many of the inhabitants of the Wynds lived by begging or stealing, haunting the stale-beer shops, which were dark and filthy beyond words, and staggering out at night in quest of money for more beer or cider.

Here and there Mr. MacColl and his helpers found exceptions to this general rule, for in a remarkable book published years ago,[8] and still to be found frequently in the Scottish second-hand book shops, Mr. MacColl gives us a detailed account of his experiences. Now and then he would find a family, or some old man or woman, who had managed to lead an honest life and to keep alive the flame of faith even in those appalling surroundings. One of these was an old blind woman who had buried her husband and all her children, and who was ending her days in miserable poverty. She lived in an unlighted room in a tumbled-down tenement, but she managed to live happily by remembering that there was one Friend who had never forsaken her. An aged man, lying on a bundle of rags and dying of cancer in a room into which no ray of sunshine ever penetrated, comforted himself by singing aloud the old hymns of the Scottish Psalter and reciting chapters of the Bible which he had memorized years before in the Christian day school.

In our own day, when some of our conferences have nothing more important to discuss than ecclesiastical millinery, it might be a useful thing to send to Scotland for a

---

[8]. Dugald MacColl, *Work in the Wynds* (London, 1867).

copy of Mr. MacColl's book, and to read and discuss selections from it in conference, inquiring at the same time whether we are doing our full duty today if we neglect these blighted areas of our cities. What was done in Edinburgh in 1847 and in Glasgow in 1853 can be done in America, assuming that the same missionary spirit is there. The Word of God has not lost its power to transform even the most unpromising lives. The ragged drunkard with the blotched face, lying in a stupor on the very church steps, might, by some miracle of grace, be transformed into a faithful Christian, able to arise before others and speak to them of the power of God's Law to reveal sin in all its hideousness, and to lead the repentant sinner by the power of the promises of the Gospel to the foot of the Cross. Just this was done in Scotland: it can be done in America.

At the end of four years, Bridge Gate ("Briggit"), Church was founded, and 448 communicants and six elders, mostly reclaimed people, were given a peaceful dismissal to establish it. In 1860 Robert Howie was called to Wynd Church, for Mr. MacColl had taken over the new Bridge Gate Kirk. Howie found 250 communicants, but the number increased quickly to 1,100, with 200 applicants under instruction. In 1864 Trinity Church was started in Charlotte street with 400 communicant members. Within three years it had grown to 1,100 communicants. The old Wynd Church started yet another mission, this time in the Barony parish. A fine church building was erected through the generosity of two wealthy merchants named Burns, the son and grandson of Dr. Burns, for 60 years pastor of Barony Church.

All the while the work in Edinburgh was growing. In the West Port, where a series of shocking murders had been committed, William Tasker had the satisfaction of seeing the very house in which one of the most notorious murderers had lived, transformed into an institute for Christian instruction in the Scriptures. Some of Mr. Tasker's experiences are recorded by Mr. Joseph Jolly, his assistant and successor.[9] On one occasion Mr. Tasker visited a home, only to find a mother huddled in a corner trying to hide two blackened eyes and a face that was terribly bruised and

9. Jos. Jolly, *The Story of the West Port Church* (Edinburgh, 1882).

swollen. Her drunken husband, after spending his wages at a nearby public house, had beaten her when she asked for money to buy bread for the children that were crying because of hunger. Placing a kettle of water over the fire, Mr. Tasker hurried downstairs to a grocer, bought half a stone of oatmeal, and made a great kettle of porridge for the hungry family. He succeeded in persuading the family to attend church and to attend his instruction classes. The father of the family, who could hardly read or write, was enrolled in an evening class with his own boys, and taught the elementary school subjects. In time the family became well-behaved Christians and loyal members of the con-gregation.

In visiting a filthy tenement one day, Mr. Tasker found a drunken mother lying on the floor, unaware of the fact that her children were crying with hunger. Going to the bake-shop at the head of the street, Tasker bought several large loaves of bread and took them to the home of the drunken woman. An hour later, in passing a public bar, Tasker saw the same woman attempting to exchange the loaves of bread for a drink of whiskey. Entering the public house, Mr. Tasker seized the bread, carried it to the home where the hungry children were still crying, broke the bread into small pieces so that the woman could not trade them for drink, and then took his departure. This drunken woman, through the power of Law and Gospel, became a sober, well-behaved member of his congregation.

In visiting a squalid tenement one day, Mr. Tasker found several drunken people, and in a corner an old woman lying ill on a filthy cot. Mr. Tasker brought her food, and called on her during her illness. She was an old washerwoman, who was rarely sober. After her recovery she began attending church, gave up her drinking, and insisted upon contributing a shilling a month from her meagre earnings to the church. Months afterward Mr. Tasker visited a dying man, and learned that the same old washerwoman, having learned of his great poverty, was buying food and bringing it to him regularly.

Mr. Tasker, upon hearing of the death of a man in one of the most filthy closes in the West Port, called at the home, only to find the family and their neighbors so drunk that there was no one who was able to carry out the coffin. It was necessary for him to go out and find strangers to perform this last service to the dead man.

The "territorial scheme," as Dr. Chalmers called it, bore rich fruit, and it might well serve as a model of such work in our own day. A territory is selected, a group of forty workers are trained, and the district is divided into twenty subdivisions, each containing about twenty families. Each subdivision is placed in charge of two workers, who are pledged to visit every family once a week. A printed paper, drawn up by Dr. Chalmers, is left at each home. The workers are trained carefully, and are given instructions to read selected Scripture passages in each home, and to admonish the people according to their needs. Where this method was employed, the results for the first few weeks were most discouraging. Usually but a dozen old women appeared for church service. The workers were urged to continue their work, and after a few weeks the results of their efforts became apparent in a growing number of people at the church service. The parochial school was an important part of the territorial plan, and Dr. Chalmers and the men who succeeded him made every effort to establish strong schools, and persuade the people to enroll their children. Sunday-schools were maintained, and evening classes for the religious instruction of young and old. People were found in the slum areas who could barely read or write, and classes were formed for them, meeting in the evening, and they were taught the common school subjects. Perhaps at no time in history have the results proved more fruitful, not only in the establishment of a succession of strong congregations, but, better still, in the thousands of cases where drunkards and criminals were transformed, by Law and Gospel, into upright Christians.

Scottish Eloquence

Somebody has said that Scottish preaching is noteworthy for its tremendous earnestness and its depth of thought, rather than for its eloquence. This is but a partial truth. Intense earnestness is there, and so is depth of thought, but it is incorrect to say that the Scottish preachers are not eloquent. In the days of the Moderates this was true, and even the famous evangelical preacher, Thomas Boston, was noted for his majestic gravity and intensity of feeling, rather than for what usually is termed oratory.

However, in the eighteenth century, and even before, Scotland was fortunate in having more than her share of preachers of exceptional eloquence. In the parts of Scotland where the Gaelic language was used, there had always been preachers of great eloquence. They drew congregations of 10,000 or more people when they announced a day of preaching in the open air. The famous Lachlan Mackenzie reached the height of his powers during the last decade of the eighteenth and the first two decades of the nineteenth century. John Robertson was another man who used the Gaelic language with marvellous effect. James Haldane, of Edinburgh, preached for fifty years to congregations that overflowed a tabernacle seating 3,000. Andrew Thomson was another Edinburgh preacher of great power. John Macdonald, John Macrae (Mac-Rath Mor), Donald Sage and the matchless John Kennedy of Dingwall are other men of rare eloquence.

Then, of course, we have Thomas Chalmers and Thomas Guthrie, to say nothing of the tragic career of Edward Irving. In the same period belong such eminent pulpit orators as Archibald Bennie, Robert Candlish, Lindsay Alexander, James Hamilton, Thomas M'Crie and a score of others. Chalmers, of course, is the greatest of them all, and the most baffling. A. K. H. Boyd records the fact that Chalmers was asked to deliver a sermon in London. Canning and Wilberforce, keen judges of good preaching, went to hear him. After the service Canning declared that he had heard many great preachers, but "the tartan beats us; we have no preaching like that in England." [10] Mr. Boyd declares further that "Preaching in Scotland is a totally different thing from what it is in England. In the former country it is generally characterized by an amount of excitement in delivery and matter, which in England is found only among the most

[10]. A. K. H. Boyd, *Concerning the Pulpit in Scotland* in his *Recreations of a Country Parson* (Edinburgh, 1859), p. 364.

fanatical Dissenters, and is practically unknown in the pulpits of the national church."[11] He tells us that Scottish sermons were seldom less than 40 minutes to an hour in length. There is an introduction, two or three main divisions clearly announced, a practical conclusion, and then a summary of the entire Calvinistic system of theology.

"While English sermons are generally read with quiet dignity, in Scotland they are very commonly repeated from memory, and given with great vehemence and oratorical effect, and abundant gesticulation."[12]

Lockhart says of Thomas Chalmers, "I have heard many men deliver sermons far better arranged in point of argument; and I have heard very many deliver sermons far more uniform in elegance, both of conception and of style; but most unquestionably, I have never heard, either in England or Scotland, or in any other country, a preacher whose eloquence is capable of producing an effect so strong and irresistible as his."[13]

However, this is judging Scottish preaching merely by externals. John Kennedy, himself a preacher second only to Chalmers, declares that the worth of a Scottish preacher, especially in the Highlands, depends not upon his oratory, his learning or his talents, but upon "a profound experience of the power of godliness, a clear view of the doctrines of grace, peculiar nearness to God, a holy life, and a blessed ministry."[14] He asserts that John Caird's famous sermon, "Religion in Common Life," which Dean Stanley called the greatest sermon of the century, and Thomas Guthrie's sermons in his *Gospel in Ezekiel* would have been deemed "worthless, because Christless."[15] John Kennedy, in this observation, understands the secret of effective preaching much more fully than does A. K. H. Boyd, the brilliant essayist. Kennedy says, "Calder and Macphail preached in clear, unctuous words filled full of Christ crucified, while from their manner and language all was carefully excluded

---

[11]. *Ibid.*, p. 365.
[12]. *Ibid.*, p. 365.
[13]. J. G. Lockhart, *Peter's Letters to his Kinfolk*, vol. 3, p. 267.
[14]. John Kennedy, *The Days of the Fathers in Ross-shire* (Edinburgh, 1861), p. 19.
[15]. *Ibid.*, p. 20.

that might withdraw the minds of their hearers from the spiritual import of the message which they carried."[16] He says again, "Their preaching was remarkable for its completeness. It combined careful exposition, fulness and exactness of doctrinal statement, a searching description of experimental godliness, and close application of truth to the conscience. The admixture of these elements, in wisely-adjusted proportions, constitutes the true excellence of preaching."[17]

The relationship of the *manner* of preaching to the *message* that is preached finds its parallel in the case of a printed book. While it is a delight to read a Bible that is beautifully printed in clear type, on excellent paper, and enhanced by means of a costly binding, yet the promises of that Bible are equally precious when read from the pages of a cheap Testament, purchased at the dime-store. So it is with preaching. The delivery of Jonathan Edwards was poor, Robert Candlish had several bad mannerisms, Chalmers floundered pathetically for the first five minutes, and in our own day W. A. Sunday's preaching was marred because of his husky voice, his street slang and his violent gestures; yet these men made an emphatic impression upon tens of thousands because they pictured the horrors of sin and the gracious gift of salvation in Jesus Christ. John Kennedy of Dingwall was correct when he said that "words filled full of Christ crucified" are more powerful than mere oratory.

The intense earnestness of Scottish preaching has been noted by many writers. In describing a typical sermon of Chalmers, his biographer says: "It was transcendently grand, a glorious burst. The energy of his action corresponded. Intense emotion beamed from his countenance. I cannot describe the appearance of his face better than by saying it was lighted up almost into a glare. The congregation was intensely excited, leaning forward in the pews like a forest bending under the power of the hurricane, — looking steadfastly at the preacher, and listening in breathless wonderment. So soon as it was concluded, there was (as invariably was the case at the close of the Doctor's

---

[16]. *Ibid.*, p. 23.
[17]. *Ibid.*, p. 24.

bursts) a deep sigh, or rather gasp for breath, accompanied by a movement throughout the whole audience."[18]

Thomas Chalmers (1780-1847)

Thomas Chalmers was one of the greatest religious leaders of the century, and like Spurgeon and Moody he seems to belong to all Christendom. He was born in 1780 in Anstruther, near St. Andrews, Fifeshire. Educated in the parish school, he entered St. Andrews University at the age of 12. Here he distinguished himself, especially in mathematics. While in school he read Jonathan Edwards' *Freedom of the Will*, which made so deep an impression upon him that he declared long afterward, "I spent a twelve-month in a sort of mental elysium." At the University the boys were called upon to conduct morning prayer after the manner of the Church of Scotland, and so eloquent were the efforts of young Chalmers that his name became known among the townspeople, who attended chapel on the days that he officiated. Although a lad of exceptional promise, and thoroughly convinced of the truths of Christianity in an intellectual manner, yet he declared later that his religion was thoroughly deistic, without the slightest understanding of the meaning of sin nor of the riches of the grace of God in Christ.

The regulations of the Established Kirk did not permit a young man to preach until he had reached the age of 21, but since Chalmers was so exceptional, and "a lad of pregnant pairts," an exception was made in his case and he was licensed in 1799, when but 19 years of age. In 1803 he became pastor of Kilmany Church. He had grown up among the Moderates and knew nothing but Moderatism. He preached eloquent, but thoroughly futile sermons, urging his hearers to mend their ways, to follow Christ and to imitate Christ. This outward reformation which he urged upon his congregation was based solely upon their own efforts and good works, and as he admitted to them a few years later, "I never heard of any such reformation having been effected among them." He spent a dozen years in this

---

[18]. Wm. Hanna, *Life and Writings of Thomas Chalmers* (Edinburgh, 1849-52), vol. I, pp. 467-8.

little Fifeshire town, lying as it does in a fertile valley just across the Firth of Tay from the city of Dundee. Like all Moderates, his duties were taken lightly. He performed them in so perfunctory a manner that even when he met his parishioners in the highway he was in too much of a hurry to do more than bid them the time of day.

Chalmers did not grasp the spiritual meaning of Christianity until he was 33 years of age. He had been asked to contribute an article on Christianity to the work that was known later as the *Encyclopaedia Britannica,* but which was called at the outset the *Edinburgh Encyclopaedia.* While he was working on this article, a serious illness, as well as deaths in his own family, caused him to turn to William Wilberforce's *Practical View of Christianity.* This book led him to read his Bible, which had been more or less neglected hitherto. Alone in his room, recovering from his illness, he read chapter after chapter. From the Law he came to a realization of his sin, and a period of great distress and fear followed. He had days of despair, fearing that he might be cast off eternally. In each case he took up his Bible again and read, and at last he found and rejoiced in the hope of salvation through the merit of Jesus Christ the Saviour.

From that time onward his preaching was entirely different. He was no longer the self-satisfied intellectual, seeking by his gift of oratory to prevail upon his people to reform their ways of living. He now preached as a poor sinner to other poor sinners. The new evangelical tone of his sermons impressed the people, and the half-empty parish church began to fill. It soon became crowded, and people from the surrounding countryside, spiritually starved in those days of Moderatism, began to be seen in Kilmany Church at its Sunday services.

Of his former manner of preaching he himself writes: "But the interesting fact is, that during the whole of that period, in which I made no attempt against the natural enmity of mind to God; while I was inattentive to the way in which this enmity is dissolved, even by the free offer on the one hand, and the believing acceptance on the other, of Gospel salvation; while Christ, through whose blood the sinner, who by nature stands afar off, is brought near to the heavenly Law-giver whom he has offended, was scarcely ever spoken of, or spoken of in such a way as stripped Him of all the importance of His character and His offices, even at this time I certainly did press the reformations of honour and truth and integrity among my people; but I never once heard of any such reformations having been effected among them. If there was anything at all brought about in this way, it was more than ever I got any account of." [19]

A severe tempest swept the coasts of Scotland, and a ship was breaking up off shore. A young candidate for ordination, John Honey, rescued seven men from the sinking ship, but he died in October, 1814, from the effects of exposure. Thomas Chalmers was asked to preach at the funeral service. Hardly had he left his home when a delegation of five men from Glasgow knocked at his door. The historic Tron Church, in Glasgow, had lost their pastor, and having heard of the fiery eloquence and fearless preaching of sin and salvation on the part of the young pastor of Kilmany Church, they had come to interview him. Finding him absent, they made inquiry, and were directed to the church where the funeral was to take place. When they got there they beheld a strange sight. The church was crowded, the churchyard was filled with people, and horses and carriages lined the roadways. Several men had just finished taking out one of the windows, and extending several planks through the opening. A stand for the Bible and a chair were placed upon it, and a young man emerged from the church window and took his seat. The men from Glasgow were disappointed, for the young man had a full face and a listless eye. He sat there for a few moments, his face of an ashen color, and he gazed helplessly at the multitude. He arose, gave out the Psalm and read the Lesson. The he began to preach. His opening sentences were spoken with hesitation, and in a muffled voice. The he seemed to take fire, and never had the Glasgow men heard such a torrent of eloquence, as he described the visit of the

[19]. William Hanna, *Memoirs of the Life and Writings of Thomas Chalmers* (Edinburgh, 1849-52), vol. I, pp. 408-409.

angel of death, and the coming of the mighty Prince of Life, who robbed death and the grave of its terrors.

Dr. T. S. Jones wrote to the people in Glasgow, and after paying a glowing tribute to Chalmers he said of this sermon, "In the pulpit his language is provincial and his manner unpolished; but there is a novelty and loftiness of thought, a sublimity of sentiment, a brilliance of imagination, a strength and point of expression, a power of eloquence, that not merely arrests, but lifts up and bears away the attention wheresoever he wills." [20]

Chalmers received the call to Tron Church and he accepted it.   In his farewell sermon to the congregation at Kilmany, he said: "You have at least taught me that to preach Christ is the only effective way of preaching morality in all its branches, and out of your humble cottages I have gathered a lesson which I pray God I may be enabled to carry with all its simplicity into a wider theatre, and to bring with all the power of its subduing efficacy upon the vices of a more crowded population." [21]

It was in 1815 that Thomas Chalmers became pastor of Tron Church in Glasgow, and the next ten years were busy and eminently successful ones.   In 1819 a new parish was created for him, and St. John's church was built. Many things are told by his biographer, both of his work at Tron and at St. John's.   At one time the crowds were so great in the streets that their surging broke down the heavy doors of the church, and a struggling stream of people rushed into the church, climbing over the backs of the benches in order to find seats near the pulpit.   At St. John's, Thomas Chalmers built up what Dr. Taylor calls "perhaps the greatest and most effective parochial organization which the Christian Church has ever seen in operation." [22]   The parish numbered 10,000 people, many of whom lived in tall, crowded tenements that faced dark, narrow, ill-smelling little wynds, or passageways, into which the sun rarely was able to shine.

Thomas Chalmers, from the outset, had shown great concern for the neglected poor and the unchurched.   He

---

[20]. *Ibid.*, p. 440.
[21]. *Ibid.*, p. 443.
[22]. W. M. Taylor, *The Scottish Pulpit* (New York, 1887), p. 210

went from tenement to tenement, climbing long flights of
dark stairways, visiting family after family in their dark
little apartments. Often he found poverty and suffering
almost beyond belief. Two parochial schools were established for the tenement children. Finding that one man
could not possibly reach all these tenement dwellers,
Chalmers organized a large group of people, had frequent
meetings with them and trained them carefully for their
work. He divided the parish into a number of districts,
with trained leaders in charge of each, and a group of
workers to assist each leader. At the head of this elaborate
organization was Chalmers himself, directing every detail.
He held regular meetings with his workers, drilling them
carefully, teaching them how to approach others, what to
say, how to answer objections, and he even selected the Bible
verses that they were to use. He taught them how to read
the Scriptures and pray with the people, and how to act
when cases of distress were encountered. No detail was
overlooked. He established a fund that could be drawn
upon where actual need existed, and in case of death, there
was a burial fund, so that no person within the parish need
be buried as a pauper. In cases of dire necessity, rents
were paid, and food and fuel provided. His methods of
reaching every family in the parish, church people as well
as the unchurched, have never been improved upon, and
have formed the basis for all sound work of this character
from his day to this.

Meanwhile Thomas Chalmers was preaching his remarkable sermons to congregations that filled his church to overflowing three times a week. He organized no less than
fifty branch Sunday-schools in various parts of his parish,
and provided each one with a staff of trained teachers. Since
his own church was taxed to capacity, he conducted Thursday afternoon services for the merchants of Glasgow, who
crowded the place of worship an hour ahead of time, and
were thankful to find standing room, and to hear what John
Foster has called "the brilliant glow of a blazing eloquence."
It was at these services for men that he delivered his famous
Astronomical Discourses. It was at a time when scientific
thought was beginning to question certain Bible truths.

Chalmers had always shown a great interest both in science and mathematics, and in his early days he had taught the latter subject for a short period.

As a result of this activity, his rugged health suffered, and in 1824, when an offer came to become professor of moral philosophy at St. Andrews University, he accepted it solely because no man could endure for long the enormous burden of work that he had assumed at St. John's Church. He had hoped to gain rest by a change of work, but four years later he was urged to accept the chair of theology at Edinburgh University, one of the highest honors that the Scottish Kirk could offer him. He accepted the appointment, and served with distinction, not only teaching theology, but preaching at the same time to the people in the poorer parts of the city. His popularity as a preacher was, if anything, exceeded by his popularity as a professor. Even the townspeople crowded into his lecture room, and Dr. William Knight tells of other professors who were obliged to complain because of the bursts of applause that eminated from the Chalmers lecture room whenever he indulged in a brilliant burst of eloquence.

Dr. Chalmers might have spent the remaining two decades of his life as professor of dogmatics at Edinburgh University, had it not been for the Disruption of 1843. For those especially interested in this stirring incident in Church History, there are a number of books, including the *Ten Years' Conflict*,[23] the *Annals of the Disruption*[24] and various other writings. Dr. Chalmers, as leader of the evangelical group in the General Assembly, was only too well aware of the shocking abuses that were tolerated in the State Church, especially the manner in which pastors were "settled" wherever a vacancy occurred. Not only were influential patrons permitted to name the candidates, but where the congregation objected, as was too often the case, the patron or the presbytery resorted to a court order, and the unwelcome pastor was forced upon a protesting congregation. It became evident that a disruption could not be avoided. Dr.

[23]. R. Buchanan, *Ten Years' Conflict; History of the Disruption of the Church of Scotland,* 2 vols. (Glasgow, 1849).
[24]. Thos. Brown, *Annals of the Disruption* (Edinburgh, 1893).

Chalmers, with an able staff of associates, planned everything with care. Speakers were sent throughout Scotland, the country was flooded with printed literature, details of the meeting were planned. The greater task of rebuilding was not overlooked, for it involved building 500 churches and over 700 parish schools. It meant building manses, to say nothing of supporting the 474 pastors who had agreed to withdraw from the State Church. All this was carried out with remarkable efficiency. The same administrative talent that had been so evident in St. John's parish became apparent on a greater scale. Dr. Chalmers was surrounded by men of unusual ability, but the general oversight of the entire project, and its multitude of details, show only too well his leadership. The 474 evangelical pastors left the assembly and they organized the Free Church, with Dr. Chalmers as the first moderator.

As soon as possible after the new organization had come into being, Dr. Chalmers turned his attention once more to his mission project in the West Port. He had given up his professorship at Edinburgh, but had at once become head of New College, the institution established by the Free Church. Nevertheless, Sunday always found him among the poor of the West Port. He rented a large loft over a tannery, and there he conducted his church. He secured the help of a younger man, William Tasker, who relieved him of part of the burden at the start, and eventually took over the mission. Many things might be said of his West Port mission. For example, an old woman from the tenements was asked by a neighbor whether she still attended St. Andrew's congregation. "I naught can go doon there the noo," she said. "I'm going to kirk at a tanner's loft ower, where ane Tammy Chalmers preaches. I think we ought to encourage him, poor body." She was not aware that this same "Tammy Chalmers" had been asked to preach in London, and he was unable to get near the church because of the enormous crowds that surged about its doors. Finally he was taken down another street by the police, through a house and into the back garden. A plank was thrown from the garden wall to the sacristy window, and thus Dr. Chalmers got into the church where he was to preach. "All the world is wild about Doctor Chalmers," once wrote Wilberforce. Lord Jeffrey, a great orator himself, declared that Chalmers reminded him "of what one reads as the effect of the eloquence of Demosthenes." Chalmers was asked to preach before the London Missionary Society. He began, as usual, in a weak, hesitating manner, and with a broad Fifeshire accent. Rowland Hill, the great London preacher, stood beneath the pulpit with cold sweat on his brow, feeling that the day was ruined. However, Chalmers quickly shook off his initial nervousness and launched into his subject with such a blaze of oratory that when he finished, the aged Rowland Hill, beside himself with excitement, exclaimed aloud, "Well done, Thomas Chalmers!" [25]

Dr. Chalmers was of stocky build and almost rustic in appearance. When in repose his face looked dull, and his greyish eyes were misty. He often hesitated and stammered at the beginning of a sermon, but soon he was ablaze with personality — the dull face brightened, his eyes gleamed and his eloquence roused his congregation to such an extent that we have more than one report of a great gathering, on some important occasion, when all rose to their feet during the concluding sentences of his sermon. However, he was content to teach at New College and in the Divinity Hall of the Free Church, and to preach ordinarily at his tanner's loft in the West Port. He finally saw a permanent church built in that part of the city of Edinburgh. It was dedicated in 1847 and Chalmers officiated at the Communion service. In a letter to Mr. Lennox, a New York friend, he describes the joy of the occasion, and the realization of his ambition; but he was not to preach very often in his new church. A month later he was found dead in his bed. On a table beside him were the writing materials that he had laid out, expecting to use them in the morning. He had died peacefully in his sleep, almost as Whitefield had done half a century before. Dr. Chalmers was 67 at the time of his death.

The sermons of Thomas Chalmers have a structural peculiarity. Where other clergymen take a theme and find

[25]. J. B. Waterbury, *Sketches of Eloquent Preachers* (New York, 1864), p. 107.

two or three main divisions, which they proceed to develop step by step, Chalmers took a single idea and constructed his sermon in the form of a circle around it, exhibiting it from every angle. He stated it over and over, causing the sermon to revolve around that central truth, and emphasizing it in a manner that few could forget. Dr. W. M. Taylor compares his preaching to the hunter who whirls his sling around and around and finally sends the stone whizzing with certain aim directly at the mark. He compares it to an eagle circling around its prey and finally swooping upon it. Chalmers's sentences are often of considerable length, and now and then one comes upon one that contains 400 words. These he uttered with a rush, and with a face ablaze with earnestness.

John Brown, M. D., the great Edinburgh essayist, in his *Quiet Hours,* gives us the following description of a sermon by Chalmers:

"We remember well our first hearing Dr. Chalmers. We were in a moorland district in Tweedale, rejoicing in the country after nine months of the High School. We heard that the famous preacher was to be at a neighbouring parish church, and off we set, a cartful of irrepressible youngsters . . . the moor was stretching away in the pale sunlight — vast, dim, melancholy, like a sea; everywhere were to be seen the gathering people, 'sprinklings of blythe company'; the country-side seemed moved to one center.

"As we entered the kirk, we saw a notorious character, a drover, who had much of the brutal look of what he worked in, with the knowing eye of a man of the city. . . . He was our terror, and we not only wondered but were afraid when we saw *him* going in. The kirk was as full as it could hold. How different it looks to a brisk town congregation! . . . The minister comes in, homely in his dress and gait, but having a great look about him, 'like a mountain among hills.' He looks vaguely around upon his audience, as if he saw *one great object, not many.* We shall never forget his smile — its general benignity; how he let the light of his countenance fall on us! He read a few verses quietly, then prayed briefly, solemnly, with his eyes wide open all the time, but not seeing. Then he gave out his text; we forget it, but the subject was, 'Death Reigns.'

"He started slowly, calmly, the simple meaning of the words: what death was, and how and why it reigned; then suddenly he started and looked like a man who had seen some great sight, and was breathless to declare it. He told us how death reigned — everywhere, at all times, in all places; how we all knew it, how we would yet know more of it. The drover, who had set down in the table-seat (square pew) opposite, was gazing up in a state of stupid excitement; he seemed restless, but never kept his eye from the speaker. The tide set in; everything added to its power; deep called to deep, imagery and illustration poured in, and every now and then the theme — the simple, terrible statement — was repeated in some lucid interval.

"After overwhelming us with the proofs of the reign of death, and transferring to us his intense urgency and emotion, and after shrieking, as if in despair, these words, *Death is a tremendous necessity!* he suddenly looked beyond, as if into some distant region, and cried out, 'Behold! a mightier! Who is this that cometh from Edom, with dyed garments from Bozrah? This that is glorious in His apparel, traveling in the greatness of His strength? I that speak in righteousness, mighty to save.'

"Then in a few plain sentences he stated the truth as to sin entering, and death by sin, and death passing upon all. Then he took fire once more, and enforced with redoubled energy the richness, the freeness, the simplicity, the security, the sufficiency of the great method of justification. How astonished and impressed we all were! He was at the full thunder of his power; the whole man was in an agony of earnestness. The drover was weeping like a child, the tears running down his ruddy, coarse cheeks, his face opened out and smoothed like an infant's, his whole body stirred with emotion. We had all insensibly been drawn out of our seats, and were converging toward the wonderful speaker; and when he sat down, after warning each one of us to remember who it was and what it was that followed Death on the pale horse, and how alone we could escape, we all sunk back into our seats. How beautiful to our eyes did the thunderer look! — how exhausted, but sweet and pure. How he poured out his soul before his God in giving thanks for sending the Abolisher of Death! Then a short Psalm, and all was ended.

"We went home quieter than we came. We did not recount the foals, with their long legs and roguish eyes, and their sedate mothers; we did not speculate upon whose dog *that* was, and whether that was a crow or a man in the dim moor. We thought of other things — that voice, that face, those great, simple, living thoughts, those floods of resistless eloquence, that piercing, shattering voice, that 'tremendous necessity'." [26]

Dr. Chalmers published a number of important writings. They include his *Institutes of Theology,* 2 volumes (1852); several exegetical works, among which are his *Lectures on Romans,* in four volumes; as well as works on political economy, mental and moral philosophy and several volumes of sermons. These writings have been reprinted in 25 uniform volumes entitled *The Complete Works of Thomas Chalmers* and nine volumes known as *Posthumous Works of Thomas Chalmers* (1847-49). A number of biographies have been written, but the standard work of this class is Dr. William Hanna's *Memoirs of Thomas Chalmers,* 4 volumes (1849-52). From a list of Chalmers biographies those of D. Fraser (1881), E. B. Ramsay (1865), A. Philip (1929), W. G. Blaikie (1896), Mrs. Oliphant (1893), James Moffat (1853), J. L. Watson (1881), W. J. Symington (1878), and J. Dodds (1892), each will prove of interest to the admirers of one of the greatest of all Scotsmen.

Norman Macleod, Sr. (1783-1862)

It is not always an advantage to have an illustrious son. Norman Macleod the Elder, as he is known in Scotland, was an eminent man in his own right, and a preacher of admirable gifts. One would hear much more of him except for the fact that the mention of his name always brings forth the reply, "he was the father of the great Norman Macleod." Norman Macleod the Elder was a son of Norman Macleod of Morven, an influential Scottish clergyman. The numerous

---

[26]. John Brown, M.D., *Spare Hours* (Edinburgh, 1859), pp. 379-382.

Macleod family (the name is pronounced as though spelled MacCloud), are of ancient and illustrious Highland stock. The brilliant orange, grey and black tartans of the Macleods of Lewis, and the more subdued green, grey and lavender of the Macleods of Macleod, are familiar sights at every coronation and royal marriage. The current British *Who's Who* includes some 31 of them, of whom many have become distinguished Church leaders.

After his student years Norman Macleod the Elder was licensed in 1806, served the kirk at Kilbrandon in Argyle, was ordained in 1807 and received from the duke of Argyle the presentation of the parish of Campbelltown, in Argyle. In 1825 he was presented with Campsie, in Stirlingshire, and ten years later he became pastor of the Gaelic chapel-of-ease in Glasgow. He was made moderator of the General Assembly of the State Church of Scotland in 1836, and in 1841 he was appointed chaplain in ordinary to her majesty the Queen. At the time of the disruption he followed a mediating course, and in the end remained with the Church of Scotland together with his son. We find no less than five clergymen bearing the Macleod name, however, who "went out with the Free" at the time of the Disruption.

Norman Macleod the Elder was a man of striking appearance. His snow-white hair, his patriarchal bearing and his commanding personality insured immediate attention whenever he arose to speak, whether in church or in the Assembly. He was at his best in Scottish Gaelic, which he was able to use so effectively as to leave no doubt in the minds of the older Scots who liked to say that the English language is a poor medium in which to express Christian truth, in comparison with Scots Gaelic. Not only did Norman the Elder engage in preaching tours throughout Scotland, but he mastered Irish Gaelic, and went on frequent preaching tours throughout Ireland, where he was always heard by great gatherings of people. He was the "old man eloquent" of the Macleod clan, although in the Free Church Roderick Macleod, of Snizort, was considered his equal in this respect. Norman Macleod the Elder had an intense interest in the promotion of popular education in the Highlands and Islands, and on many of his preaching tours he

defended the cause of the parish school. Many people who
are hardly aware of his reputation as a preacher, know him
well as the author of the *Dictionary of the Gaelic Language,*
which he compiled in 1831 together with Dr. Dewar. Of a
number of well-known Gaelic dictionaries, his holds a high
place, although in recent years it has found rivals in the
Maclennan and other such dictionaries. However, the
Macleod dictionary will continue to be popular among
Scottish people, and its author holds the same place with
them as does Noah Webster in America.

Dr. Macleod published a metrical Psalter for the
Church of Ireland in 1836. It was known as *Psalma Daibi.*
He started a monthly paper in 1830 which bore the title
Teachdaire Gaelach, or the Gaelic Messenger. In 1840 he
founded another paper, *Cuairtear nan Gleann,* meaning The
Traveller of the Glens. His best writings, including a number of his Gaelic sermons were published at Glasgow in
1868, bearing the title *Caraid nan Gaidheal,* or The Friend
of the Gael. It contains an account of his life by his son
Norman. Dr. Macleod the Elder has left a written account
of a Communion service at Campbelltown. Some 4,000
people heard the action-sermon and 1,100 received Holy
Communion. He describes the church officers walking in
procession, bearing the Communion vessels, singing the
24th Psalm as they walked, and timing it carefully so as to
sing the seventh verse as they entered the door of the tent
which had been erected because of the great gathering of
people. At the time of the potato famine, the Highlands
suffered as well as Ireland. There were two famines in
the Highlands, one in 1836-37 and the other ten years later.
Dr. Macleod toured England, preaching in the interest of
famine relief, and obtaining much assistance for the sufferers. He did not cease his work in behalf of parish schools,
of which there were eventually 233 schools, with 22,000
pupils enrolled. He visited the Roman Catholic Bishop
Macdonald and secured his support with the understanding
that these schools should be open to Roman Catholic children
as well as Protestants, and that the former would be excused
from the study of the Westminister Catechism.

John Brown (1784-1858)

John Brown of Edinburgh was born in Whitburn in 1784. He was the son of John Brown of Whitburn and the grandson of John Brown of Haddington. He attended Edinburgh University from 1797 to 1800, and then the theological hall of the Burgher Synod at Selkirk. He was licensed in 1805, and ordained in 1806 to the Burgher congregation at Biggar, Lanarkshire, which he served for 16 years.

In 1822 he was called to Rose Street Church, Edinburgh, and in 1829 to Broughton Place Church, in the same city. After going to Edinburgh he started a class in New Testament Greek for young men who had the ministry in view. One of his pupils was David Brown, one of the authors of the Jamieson, Fausett and Brown *Commentary*. In 1834 he became professor of exegesis in the United Associate Synod's theological hall.

Dr. Brown was a man of fine appearance, and possessed of a clear, pleasant voice. He was an exceptionally good expository preacher. He studied his texts in the original with scholarly thoroughness and then gave his congregation the benefit of his labors in language that all could understand. His sermons were written in minute script with almost the exactness of a steel engraving, and then read to the congregation.

In his earlier years his preaching was joyous and rhetorical. "It's maist o't tinsel wark," one of his older members remarked. About the year 1820 his wife died. After one terrible, momentary cry of anguish, Mr. Brown regained his self-composure immediately, and after his aged father had conducted the service at the grave, the bereaved man went back to his church and preached to his congregation. From that day onward his flowery style changed. "He became concentrated, urgent, moving (being himself moved), keen, searching, unswerving, authoritative to fierceness, full of the terrors of the Lord, if he could but persuade men." [27]

---

[27]. John Brown, M.D., *My Father's Memoir in Spare Hours* (Edinburgh, 1859), p. 136.

W. M. Taylor declares that the name of Dr. John Brown of Edinburgh marks a new era in Scottish preaching. Previous to his day the sermons of the men were solid and substantial, systematic in form, but usually with but little beauty of style, felicity of illustration or exegetical exactness. Dr. Taylor calls Brown "the regenerator, if not the father, of exact Scriptural exegesis. . . . His expository discourses were perhaps a little too learned for the pulpit, and a little too popular for the professor's chair — a thing almost inevitable from the fact that they had to pay a double debt by doing duty in both; but they were always clear, honest, independent, and for the most part satisfactory. He never needed anyone to interpret his meaning, and he shrank with his whole soul from handling the Word of God deceitfully. A very common formula with him was this: 'That is truth, and a very important truth, but it is not the truth taught in this passage'."[28]

In 1845 Dr. Brown was charged with heresy. His opponents accused him of teaching that Jesus Christ died for all mankind, and not for the elect only, and that divine grace is universal. This was a departure from the rigid Calvinism of his day. After a sensational trial he was acquitted on the ground that he believed that Jesus Christ died for the elect only, yet His death laid the foundation for the offer of the Gospel to all mankind.[29]

Dr. Brown was a diligent writer, and some of his more important works are: *Discourses Suited to the Lord's Supper* (1816); *Analytical Expositions of St. Paul to the Romans* (1857); *Expository Discourses on First Peter,* 3 volumes (1848); *An Exposition of Our Lord's Intercessory Prayer* (1850); *The Resurrection of Life* (1852), an exposition of I Cor. 15; *The Suffering and Glories of the Messiah* (1853); *Expository Discourses on the Sayings of Our Lord,* 3 volumes (1850); *Expository Discourses on Galatians* (1853); *Exposition of the Epistle to the Hebrews,* 2 volumes (1862); and *Life of John Bunyan* (1887). John Cairns's *Memoirs of John Brown of Edinburgh* (1860), includes a tribute by

[28]. W. M. Taylor, *The Scottish Pulpit* (New York, 1887), pp. 236-239.
[29]. J. R. Fleming, *A History of the Church in Scotland* (Edinburgh, 1927-1933), vol. I, pp. 45-47.

John Brown, M. D., one of the most exquisite biographical gems ever written. Young men who would learn the art of expository preaching will find it worth their while to collect from the catalogues of Edinburgh book sellers the writings of John Brown of Edinburgh. Allowance must be made, of course, for his "reformed" viewpoint. It is his method that will prove helpful, and not necessarily his exegetical conclusions. One volume by Brown of Edinburgh is better than a dozen books of the theological superficialities of our own day. His valuable test: "This is true and it is important, but is it the truth taught in this text?" will teach the young clergyman exegetical accuracy.

Robert Gordon (1786-1853)

Had a visitor to Edinburgh a century ago inquired of any pedestrian whom he chanced to meet on Sunday morning the names of the two greatest preachers of that Athens of the North, the reply would have been, without hesitation: "Dr. Thomas Chalmers and Dr. Robert Gordon." Today one is reasonably safe in saying that Chalmers is one of the most eminent preachers of the last thousand years of history. Gordon, for all his former fame, is hardly remembered by the average person.

Robert Gordon was born in 1786 at Glencairn, Dumfries, where his father was a parochial school teacher. Having completed his education in the parish school, the lad, when but 15 years of age, was elected as his father's successor. After teaching for a few years, the young man entered Marischal College, Aberdeen, and Edinburgh University. For a time he was master of Perth Academy.

He was licensed in 1814 and ordained two years later, becoming pastor of Kinfauns parish. In 1821 he became pastor of St. Cuthbert's, a chapel-of-ease in Edinburgh. So well did he give an account of himself that in 1824 Hope Park Chapel was built for him in Edinburgh. The congregation learned soon enough that they could never hope to keep so able a preacher, and in 1825 he became pastor of New North Collegiate congregation, going from there to the High Church in 1830.

In 1843, at the Disruption, he seceded from the State Church, and nearly all of his congregation followed him. Almost at once Free High Church was organized and an imposing building erected, where Dr. Gordon preached to great congregations for the remaining ten years of his life, gaining a reputation equal to that of Candlish and Guthrie, and excelled only by Dr. Chalmers.

Dr. Gordon had a homiletical style that seemed to fascinate the people. According to Dr. John Duncan, a man of shrewd judgment, Dr. Gordon's method was to keep his congregation in suspense. Duncan contrasted the preaching of Chalmers and of Gordon.[30] He compared Chalmers to a man on a stage who might exhibit a box to his audience, showing them the top of it, the bottom of it, then each side of it in turn, then the inside of the box. Thus did Dr. Chalmers reveal his text to his congregations. Dr. Gordon, however, chose to adopt the method of the huntsman, and he treated his text as though it were a fox. He pursued it from this woodlot to that, and from this covert to another, beating the bushes everywhere, with a great cry, then pursuing his text through thicket and over the moors until finally he caught up with it. Just a second or two before he captured it, and when the interest of his congregation was intense, he would close his Bible and bring the sermon to a sudden close, allowing the congregation to draw their own conclusion.

However, it must not be assumed from this keen observation of good old "Rabbi" Duncan that Dr. Gordon was a mere sensationalist. Few men in Scotland were more serious than he. Eminent as a preacher, sincerely pious, possessed of deep learning, and with his full share of the urgency for which the Scots preachers are noted, it is quite wrong to think of him as a mere seeker of popularity. His method of preaching was a thing all his own, and it is a question whether the more conventional styles of preaching would have proved natural to him. As Dr. Gordon employed it, his style was as baffling as it was unusual in the Edinburgh of a century ago.

---

[30]. Wm. Knight, *Colloquia Peripatetica* (Edinburgh, 1870), pp. lxxix-lxxx.

Just why Dr. Gordon is so completely forgotten that modern writers, in discussing the Scottish Church, hardly so much as mention his name, is hard to say. The congregations that flocked to Old Greyfriars to hear Thomas Guthrie, and who followed him to St. John's and then to Free St. John's, were equally large. Today Guthrie is known the world over. Both men were extremely popular in their day. Guthrie's publishers were enterprising men, and they preserved his perfervid eloquence, printed large editions of his many books, and distributed them throughout the world, wherever the English language is spoken. It seems to have been otherwise with Dr. Gordon. His sermons at times have more evangelical truth in them than those of Guthrie, but as is often the case they lack the fire of the original utterances. As for Dr. Chalmers, his fame would endure even though his printed sermons might cease to exist. There have been few men such as Chalmers.

When Dr. Gordon's *Twenty-two Evangelical Sermons* appeared in 1825, a writer in the London Eclectic Review declared: "These are orations, these are arguments, worthy of a high and permanent place in our theological literature. They display a vigour and originality of thought which it is truly refreshing to meet with in printed sermons, and are at the same time boldly explicit in the enunciation of the Gospel system." Gordon's *Christ as Made Known in the Ancient Church,* a four-volume work, is a study of the revelations of divine grace in Old Testament times. It is too bad that this excellent work is not more widely studied today.

Alexander Macleod (1786-1869)

Alexander Macleod, the great missionary to the Isle of Lewis, was born in 1786 at Balachladich, Stoer. He was licensed to preach in 1818, when 32 years of age, and a year later he was ordained as pastor of the Gaelic Chapel in Dundee. In 1821 he was translated to Cromarty, and in 1824 he went to Uig, in the Isle of Lewis. This island, about thirty miles wide and sixty long, lies thirty-five miles off the Northwestern coast of Scotland.

The Isle of Lewis had suffered great spiritual neglect. It faces the fierce gales of the Atlantic, and many wrecks

occur on its rugged coasts.   While there is no evidence that
deliberate wrecking was practiced by the islanders, yet it is
said that even the church people were known to pray,
"Forbid, Lord, that there shall be a wreck on this stormy
nicht, but if a wreck *does* occur, grant, O Lord, that it may
be on our coast."   The salvaging of such wrecks was looked
upon as a legitimate enterprise.   Not only was this the case,
but Alexander Macleod found that even the most pious
church people looked upon the death of the Saviour as a
great misfortune, and our Lord Himself a mere martyr to a
noble cause.   A succession of Moderate pastors had preached
their rationalistic doctrines, and spiritual life among the
islanders was at low ebb.

At his first catechization Macleod discovered that many
of the older people of his parish were unable to give the
names of Adam and Eve, and had never heard of Noah.
When asked concerning the way of salvation, they replied
that it depends upon living as good a life as possible.   Indiscriminate Communion was the rule, and people were
expected to attend, whether they were able to examine
themselves or not.   It is but natural that such lax practice
had led to great indifference.   Preaching services were
attended poorly, and at the first Communion service conducted by Alexander Macleod, but twenty people were
present, and of these, only six presented themselves at the
Communion table.

The laborious work of indoctrination carried on by
Alexander Macleod forms one of the bright pages in missionary history.   He was an eloquent preacher, and thoroughly at home in the Gaelic tongue.   It was not long until
his empty church was crowded, and he was urged to preach
in many places nearby.   His catechizations were attended
by large numbers, from the oldest patriarchs of the island
to young children.   Not only did the people crowd the
churches wherever he went, but four years after his coming
to Uig, his Communion service, held in the open air, was
attended by 9,000 people.   A great spiritual awakening was
felt at Uig and throughout the surrounding country.
Macleod expounded the Scriptures with care, first explaining
the text, then making clear its doctrinal content, and finally

applying it forcefully to the practical needs of the people. Before many years the people of Uig and vicinity were well indoctrinated, they attended church with great regularity, family prayer was the rule, morning and evening, and the conduct of the people throughout the week was beyond reproach. His success in transforming the lives of the rugged islanders by means of God's Word may be compared to that of Baxter of Kidderminster.

In 1843 Alexander Macleod withdrew from the Kirk of Scotland and united with the Free Kirk. A year later he was translated to Lochalsh, and in 1846 to Rogart, where he remained for 23 years. He died in 1869 at the ripe age of 83, respected throughout the Highlands.

Alexander Macleod's life was remarkable, and the rich spiritual blessings that accompanied his preaching for over half a century deserve to be more widely known. The secret of his great success lies in the fact that he depended solely upon the Word of God to transform the lives of sinful men. He loved that Word, he studied it diligently, and on Sunday the fruits of his labors were shared with his hearers. By the old-time Scottish method of "opening up the text" by means of exposition, then making clear its doctrinal teachings, and finally applying these to the particular needs of his people, he was able to see a bountiful harvest in the form of spiritual growth. He employed the Gaelic language, which, with its warmth lends itself so well to persuasive preaching. It is most unfortunate that the colorful lives of so many of these splendid Gaelic-speaking preachers are so little known among people who are unable to read and speak that ancient language. Even some of the foremost writers in the field of the history of preaching dismiss the great Highland preachers with but a paragraph or two.

James Henderson (1787-1858)

James Henderson of Galashiels, a prominent pastor of the United Presbyterian Church, and one of Scotland's most eloquent preachers, was born in 1787. He was ordained in 1810 and became pastor of a United Presbyterian congregation in Galashiels. In 1844 an imposing new place of worship known as the East United Presbyterian Church, was built for him in Galashiels. John Brown, M. D., the noted essayist,

and one of the most discriminating judges of pulpit worth
of his generation, does not hesitate to name James Henderson as one of the greatest Scottish preachers of his time. He
describes him as "a remarkable man and exquisite preacher,
whose intellect and worth had for nearly fifty years glowed
with a pure, steady, and ever-growing warmth and lustre."[31]
Dr. Brown questions whether anywhere in all the British
domains there was a man who could produce two new sermons each week, for fifty years, and these so careful in
thought and faultless in language that they might be compared to Cicero or Addison in composition, yet excelling
these masters in spiritual warmth. Shortly after the turn
of the century there were people of Scottish birth in
Western Pennsylvania, who could remember the preaching
of James Henderson. He had a sermon "The Bright and
Morning Star," which he was called upon to preach again
and again, in churches throughout Scotland. When he
accepted such an invitation, the United Presbyterian church,
whether in a great city or a country town, was crowded
with people long before the hour of service. However,
James Henderson was not a man whose wide reputation
depended upon one sermon. His preaching was always of a
high order of excellence.

James Henderson was a man of leonine appearance, and
at a post mortem examination after his death, his brain was
found to be the largest ever measured by his physicians.
He had attended the funeral of Dr. John Brown, pastor of
Broughton Place U. P. Church, Edinburgh. He preached a
sermon on the text "For me to live is Christ, and to die is
gain." A few days later he himself succumbed to a heart
ailment from which he had suffered for years, dying, like
Chalmers, in his sleep. During his later years he would
often say, in recalling his heart condition, "I carry my coffin
beside me."

Dr. Henderson disliked books of sermons, and for years
he refused the requests of his admirers, for he was well
aware that printed sermons are often cold and stilted in
comparison with the spoken word. Finally he yielded, and
allowed a volume to be printed in a limited edition. The

[31]. John Brown, M.D., *Spare Hours* (Edinburgh, 1859), p. 194.

supply was exhausted quickly, and no amount of persuasion would make him consider another edition. After his death a new volume appeared, entitled *Sermons of James Henderson, Galashiels* (1859). It contained a memoir written by John Cairns. Treasured copies of this book existed many years ago in the homes of Scottish people who had come to America, but it is listed as a rare book today, and even the largest city libraries seldom possess a copy. Even the greatest preachers are often forgotten with the passing of the generation that knew them, unless they publish their sermons. It was not so with Dr. Henderson, for there are still many people who remember the descriptions given by their grandparents of the great preacher of Galashiels. He was described as a man who had a rich, melodious voice, powerful, resonant, yet without giving the impression of undue loudness. Often he spoke quietly, but with a resonant tone that people have described as a majestic organ heard at a little distance. His exquisite command of language, his clear exposition, and above all, his Christ-centered preaching produced, it is said, an impression that his hearers carried with them to the end of their days. In many a home in America, when people from Scotland gathered at evening to sing the songs of their homeland, the conversation often drifted to the great preachers of former days. On such occasions, many years ago, there were old men and old women who were sure to tell of some memorable sermon, perhaps "The Bright and Morning Star," preached by Dr. Henderson of Galashiels. His preaching was described by Dr. Brown as like "a spring of pure water I once saw near the top of Cairngorm; always the same, cool in summer, keeping its few plants alive and happy with its warm breath in winter, floods and droughts never making its pulse change; and all this because it came from the interior heights, and was distilled by nature's own cunning, and had taken its time — was indeed a well of living water." [32]

Donald Sage (1789-1869)

Donald Sage, famed throughout the Scottish Highlands as an expository preacher, was born in 1789 in Kildonan.

---

[32]. *Op. cit.,* p. 198.

His father and grandfather were clergymen. He was educated at Aberdeen University, and after his graduation he was tutor for a time. He was licensed in 1815, and upon his ordination he was given Achness, a mission of the Royal Bounty. In 1819 he became pastor of the Gaelic chapel at Aberdeen, and in 1822 of Resolis. In 1843 he cast his lot with the seceding clergymen who formed the Free Kirk.

Donald Sage's first attempts at preaching in Gaelic were most discouraging, and more than once he found himself unequal to the task, and had to resort to his manuscript. However, his determination led to success, and in time he became one of the most noted preachers in the Highlands. He was excelled by few as an expository preacher. "Always careful to trace from its starting point the train of thought throughout the preceding paragraph on to his text, he usually gave, in the introduction of his sermon, a most instructive exposition. When the text was reached, it was opened up with marvellous skill, and its several parts were logically arranged. . . . Each sermon he delivered left abundant materials for future meditation in the minds of all earnest hearers; and never could they, in course of reading, meet a text on which they heard him preach but the light of his sermon still hovered over it, and made them fain to linger on it."[33]

Edward Irving (1792-1834)

Had one walked down Grey's Inn Road, in London, about the year 1824, he might have noticed a striking looking young man coming along. He stood a head taller than any other man in sight. His hair was black, and he wore it down almost to his shoulders. He was a handsome man, and might well have been mistaken for some famous Shakespearean actor. This man was Edward Irving, London's most famous preacher of the day.

Edward Irving was born in 1792 in Annan, Scotland. One of his boyhood friends in the same village was Thomas Carlyle. Irving attended the University of Edinburgh, entering it at the age of 13, and graduating at 17. For a time he taught school, first at Haddington and then at Kirk-

---

[33]. J. Kennedy, *Disruption Worthies of the Highlands*, p. 52.

caldy. In 1815 he was licensed to preach, but his early efforts were not successful, and he was considering either going to America, or else going as a missionary to Persia, when the famous Thomas Chalmers, of Glasgow, heard him preach. Chalmers was convinced that the young man of 30 was no ordinary man, and he asked him to come to Glasgow as his assistant. Chalmers at this time was at St. John's. Irving went to Glasgow, but he proved to be unpopular with many of the congregation. For a few years he assisted Chalmers, as he went through the slums of Glasgow, climbing the endless stairs of the rickety tall tenements. Work among the people of slumland did not appeal to him, much as Chalmers loved it. In 1822 a call came from a small group in London, and Irving accepted it.

He found a handful of fellow Scots, and a small, shabby chapel in a side street. They wanted him to preach in their native Gaelic, but Irving knew no Gaelic, since he was a south-countryman himself. He did preach in English, however. His striking appearance, his rich, resonant bass voice, his dramatic manner of delivery soon became known outside the little circle of nonconformist Highlanders who had called him to London. Within a year the elite of London were crowding their way into his little chapel. His old friend Thomas Carlyle was among them. Members of Parliament, lords and ladies, and many of the most fashionable people of London society drove up in their grand carriages. Admission even for standing room, was by ticket, and footmen were sent a week or two in advance for these tickets.

Then they built Edward Irving a stately church in Regent Square, off Grey's Inn Road, and once more the intellectuals and the noted people of London society packed his church.

At the height of his fame, when all London was flocking to hear him, Irving fell a victim to fanaticism. Henry Drummond, a London banker (not to be confused with the Rev. Henry Drummond), had taken up the study of chiliasm. Through his influence, Irving began to read chiliastic works, and it was not long until he began to preach strange new things to his fashionable congregation. He went so far as to predict the Second Coming, which was to take place in the year 1864.

The General Assembly of his church met in Scotland, and Irving attended. Because of his great fame, it was arranged that he should preach every morning at 6 o'clock. Half an hour before the time of service the large hall was packed, day after day.

Then his mind seemed to totter. In his church in London he began to say strange things in regard to apostolic times, and to take an interest in what he called the "gift of tongues." One Sunday somebody arose in his church and began to utter something in a strange language. Irving was convinced that it was genuine.

In 1832 he was deposed by his presbytery. Disruption arose in the congregation, and many of the noted people who once crowded so eagerly into his church, became alienated.

Irving resigned under fire, and for a time preached in a nearby hall. Later an upstairs chapel was fitted out in Newman street. His fame was gone, however, and Irving was discredited. He died at the age of 40, repeating the Twenty-third Psalm in Hebrew. He is buried in Glasgow Cathedral.

There are some who have called Irving the most eloquent preacher of the century, and who have compared him to Demosthenes. Had he been possessed of a solid theological foundation, he would not have been turned aside so easily by the wave of chiliasm of his day, and the story of his life might have been different.

Some of his followers founded a new chiliastic sect known as the Catholic Apostolic church. It had its origin in Scotland even before Irving became interested in it, but his connection with it has caused it to be known popularly as the Irvingite Church.

Irving's writings include: *The Oracles of God* (1824); *Babylon and Infidelity Foredoomed*, 2 volumes (1826); *Sermons, Lectures and Occasional Discourses*, 3 volumes (1828); *Homilies on the Sacraments* (1828); *Selections*, edited by E. G. Craig (1830); *Expositions of the Book of Revelation*, 4 volumes (1831); *The Last Days* (1828); and

his *Collected Writings,* edited by E. G. Carlyle, 5 volumes
(1864-65). Biographies of Edward Irving were written by
H. Bonar (1850); Mrs. Olyphant, 2 volumes (1862); W.
Jones, 2 volumes; Washington Wilkes (1855); and others.
Carlyle wrote an essay on Irving. In spite of Irving's erratic
theological opinions, a number of famous men were impressed by his preaching. "He was unquestionably, by many
degrees, the greatest orator of our times. Of him indeed,
more than any man whom I have seen throughout my whole
experience, it might be said with truth and emphasis, that
he was a Boanerges, a son of thunder," declared De Quincy,
in his *Literary Remains.* Sir Walter Scott, while admiring
Irving's impassioned oratory, said, "He put me in mind of the
devil disguised as an angel of light." [34] As one of the
greatest pulpit orators of the nineteenth century, Irving
cannot be ignored, although his writings will prove of
interest only to the student of abnormal theological thought.

David Welsh (1793-1845)

David Welsh was born at Braefoot, Moffat, Dumfriesshire, in 1793. He was educated in the parochial school at
Moffat, and in the high school at Edinburgh. He was
licensed in 1816, ordained in 1821, and given Crossmichael
parish, Kirkcudbrightshire. In 1827 he became pastor of
St. David's Church, Glasgow. From 1831 to 1843 he was
professor of church history in Edinburgh University, in addition to parish duties. In 1842 Dr. Welsh became moderator of
the Assembly, and it was he who made the opening statement on the memorable day when the 474 clergymen arose
and left the convention, and proceeded to Tanfield Hall
where the Free Church was organized.

In 1844 and 1845, Dr. Welsh, who had been one of the
seceders, was named as one of the first faculty members in
New College, Edinburgh. In 1844 he became the first editor
of the *North British Review.* He undertook to raise £21,000
for buildings for New College, and his efforts met with complete success.

Dr. Welsh, like so many Scottish leaders and professors,
was an excellent preacher. Two volumes of his sermons

---

[34]. J. G. Lockhart, *Life of Scott,* 7 vols. (1837-38).

exist in print, and some of his writings and lectures on church history appeared in print after his death. His visit to the leading German universities in 1834 is said to mark the first contact between the Scottish leaders of his day and the German seats of learning. David Welsh was not aware that his visits to the German universities, his meeting with leading German theologians of that day, and his description of conditions in the German educational field, were to have a decisive effect on Scottish preaching. It was not long until it became the fashion to go to Germany for post-graduate theological study. The young Scottish preachers, in the years that followed, began to be influenced by the rationalism that still existed in Halle and elsewhere, and in the destructive Biblical criticism that presently became the fashion in Germany. This did not take place to any extent during Dr. Welsh's lifetime, but in the years that followed, the men who went to the German universities to study became unsound, in many cases, in the matter of Biblical criticism.

David Welsh's published works include: *An Account of the Life and Writings of John T. Brown, M.D.* (1825); *Sermons on Practical Subjects* (1834); *Elements of Church History* (1844); and a posthumous book, *Sermons of David Welsh* (1846). He edited Thomas Brown's *Lectures on the Philosophy of the Human Mind* (1834), and contributed articles to the *Encyclopaedia Britannica*.

Roderick Macleod (1794-1868)

Roderick Macleod, known in the Islands as *Maighstir Ruaraidh,* or Master Roderick, was a native born Islander. The place of his birth was the manse at Glen Haltin, in the parish of Snizort, of Eilean Sgianach, that is, of the Isle of Skye. This island is separated from the mainland by a very narrow channel. The father of Roderick Macleod was Malcolm Macleod, an Island clergyman who was generally respected throughout Scotland, and especially in Gaelic Scotland. Ruaraidh Macleod, as he was called when a boy — the first name is pronounced "Roary" — was a bright, intelligent lad, always at the head of all his classes both in the parish school and in King's College, Aberdeen, where a relative of his father's was Principal. After taking his arts degree in 1815, he studied theology, for his immediate family and his clan had given a number of men to the ministry, the educational world and the State. He was licensed in 1818 and appointed to the mission of Lyndale, which lay within his father's parish.

Ruaraidh was an excellent young man, with admirable intellectual gifts, but his theology had been but another interesting study. He came to his first congregation without any deep religious zeal, and like other young men of his kind (for Moderatism was not yet dead), he was more interested in hunting and sailing than in his parish work. In the parish lived an old catechist, who was entirely blind, a man named Donald Munro. He was a man of deep religious zeal, and the people had built a chapel for him, where he preached and catechized, affording much spiritual comfort to the more devout members of the community. As they observed the huntsmen in their crimson jackets, with the dashing young Master Roderick among them, they muttered uncomplimentary things about the fox-hunting parson. They were accustomed to call him *Ruaraidh Dubh.* or "Black Roderick." When this reached the ears of Donald Munro, the blind catechist, he said to a group at the chapel door one day, "Call him not *Ruaraidh Dubh,* for I predict that the day will come when you shall be proud to call him your *Ruaraidh Geal,*" which means "White Roderick." [34]

This day came sooner than the devout old catechist suspected. Roderick Macleod went one day to call upon the Rev. John Shaw, of Bracadale, and just as many a young clergyman has done, he walked about the room examining Mr. Shaw's books. Seeing a copy of Bellamy's *Christian Religion Delineated* on the shelf, he pulled it down and paged through it. "This is a book I should like to read," he said. He took the book with him and read and re-read it. As in several parallel cases, the reading of the book, and Dr. Chalmers' Lectures on Romans led him to study his Bible. His congregation soon became aware of a change in the young pastor, for his sermons had a new ring of con-

---

[34]. There is a play upon words here, since *ar Ruaraidh Geal* may also mean "our beloved Roderick."

viction and a deeper spiritual note; while he began to give faithful attention to the sick and the neglected of the parish. He gave up his hunting and boating, and his mornings were spent in study and his afternoons in parish and missionary activity. He became a great friend of the old blind catechist, whose little cottage he had avoided hitherto, and about whom he had spoken jestingly. When asked how so brilliant a young man as he could find so much in common with an old blind man of limited education, he replied, "I expect to spend Eternity with him."

In 1823 John Shaw of Bracadale died, and Tormoid, Chief of Macleod of Macleod, presented Bracadale to Roderick Macleod. He did not disappoint his eminent kinsman, for he remained at Bracadale for 15 noteworthy years. John Shaw had been an honorable man, but in some manner much laxity had arisen within the parish, due to the influence of Moderatism, with which the older pastor had been unable to contend. Mr. Macleod determined to put an end to this laxity. He aroused the antagonism of several influential people by a more conservative practice in regard to the administration of Holy Baptism. They filed a complaint which caused much heated discussion in the presbytery and in the synod, where the Moderates were influential. The Macleod Case was taken before the Assembly on appeal in 1827, and the libel which had been found against Mr. Macleod was finally dismissed, but only after more than three years of stormy debate in the Assembly. Roderick Macleod had the valuable assistance of Mr. (later Lord) Cockburn, who acted as his counsel.

This trouble in Mr. Macleod's parish did not injure his standing with the great majority of the members of the congregation. The church was crowded from Sunday to Sunday, people walked as far as 20 miles to attend his services, and even mothers came from great distances with babies in their arms. To this day the name of Roderick Macleod is revered in the Isle of Skye, and almost within living memory there were eminent Christians who attributed their religious awakening to the Word of God as preached by Mr. Macleod.

At the time of the Disruption no man worked harder than he. The Isle of Skye was dominated by Moderates, and for a time Roderick Macleod stood alone in his efforts to win the people to the cause of the evangelicals. He met with bitter opposition from the Moderate clergy of the Island. When the memorable May 18, 1843 came, he was one of the 474 men in the long procession to Tanfield Hall in the Canonmills. He returned to Skye to find himself virtually alone, and his duties now required oversight of eight congregations and a population of 20,000. A part of Long Island was added to his duties, with a population of 16,000. One other man assisted him for a short time, but was soon called elsewhere. Roderick Macleod's labors are almost beyond belief. There were times when he was compelled to stand on a hill-side, in a howling blizzard, and preach to some congregation that had been deprived of its place of worship. The winter of 1843-44 was mild on the mainland, but any who have visited the Western Islands will know the fury of the winds as they beat in from the Atlantic. Mr. Macleod remained faithful to his duties, and eventually he saw every congregation under the care of a competent pastor. He had been called to Snizort in 1838, and he remained there until his death in 1868. He was faithful to the last, for when almost 74 years of age he insisted upon going in an open boat to a distant preaching station, although the weather was stormy. He contracted an illness which left him in a weakened condition. He returned to his pulpit in Snizort against the advice of friends, for he was determined not to disappoint his congregation. He gave out his text in Gaelic, St. Luke 2, 14, first clause. He got no farther. With the words "Glory to God in the highest . . . ." on his lips he collapsed in the pulpit. He was assisted to the manse, but he never preached again. His burial took place at Bracadale churchyard, nine miles from Snizort. Although the hearse stood ready before the church, yet his church members took up the casket, placed it on their shoulders and insisted upon carrying it the entire distance to Bracadale, with hundreds of people from throughout the Island following on foot.[35]

---

[35]. See Mackintosh Mackay, *Life, Character and Ministry of the Rev. Roderick Macleod.*

Roderick Macleod was handsome in his youth and handsome in his old age. He had a pleasant face, snow white hair, and just a suggestion of a white beard that surrounded a face that was otherwise smoothly shaven. He had a voice characterized by resonance and warmth, but he rarely indulged in the flights of vehement eloquence so characteristic of the old-time Gaelic preachers. He spoke with animation, with fluency, with a moderate degree of deliberation, and his language was always of the choicest, whether he preached in Gaelic or in English. His fine voice, always under perfect control, his freshness of thought and earnestness of manner proved so impressive that old men and women, at the end of the nineteenth century, were accustomed to speak of him with utmost affection. He preached sermons that were evangelical, and never failed to remind the sinner of his lost condition, and to conduct him straightway to the foot of the Cross, bearing witness to Jesus Christ as the only Saviour of mankind. Throughout the Western Islands few men have left so lasting an impression as he.

John Macrae (Mac-Rath Mor) (1794-1876)

John Macrae, known as Mac-Rath Mor, was born at Achadh-nan-gart, Kintail, in 1794. In his youth he was deeply moved by a sermon preached by Dr. Macdonald, and was in great distress for a time. Finally, at a Communion service, the promises of the Gospel stressed by the preacher on that occasion, brought him assurance of salvation. After his elementary schooling he attended Edinburgh University. He was licensed to preach in 1830, and became assistant to James Russel, at Gairloch. In 1833 he was ordained and became pastor at Ness, Lewis, in the Hebrides. He soon became famed for his fiery eloquence, and his powerful presentation of sin and salvation. "Mr. Macrae was at the zenith of his power about this date, and under his rugged and powerful eloquence, his hearers were held spell-bound as they listened to the dreadful threatenings of Sinai, followed by the gracious tidings poured forth from a deeply taught heart and from lips that had been touched with a live coal from off the altar." [36]

---

[36]. David Beaton, *Noted Ministers of the Northern Highlands* (Inverness, 1929), p. 226.

John Macrae was a giant in stature, and the Gaelic people called him Mac-Rath Mor. Congregations numbered by the thousands gathered on the Highland hillsides to hear him, and his fiery preaching, so dear to the Celt, moved them deeply. In 1839 has was tranlated to Knockbain. When the days of the Disruption drew near, Dr. Chalmers selected him to present the cause throughout the Highlands and the Northern and Western Islands. Not only did his great eloquence convince many, but his quick Celtic wit often silenced the Moderates who came to interrupt him with embarrassing remarks.[37] On one occasion a Moderate preacher said audibly, "I remember this man when he was a lad, hunting foxes." To which Mac-Rath Mor replied instantly, "It would seem that there is one fox that I didn't catch."

In 1849 he was translated to the Gaelic church in Greenock, and in 1857 to Lochs, Lewis. In 1866 he became pastor at Carloway, but four years later, at the age of 77, failing strength caused him to retire. This huge Highlander, with his powerful voice, his deeply spiritual manner of preaching and his sharp wit in debate at gatherings of clergymen, was one of the most picturesque preachers of his day. Living in a remote part of Scotland, he is not so widely known as some of the famous preachers of Edinburgh, but he is one of the few who may be classed with John Kennedy, "prince of the Highland preachers."

Alexander Stewart (1794-1847)

The name of Stewart of Cromarty is known throughout the Scottish Highlands, and is associated with such illustrious names as those of John Macdonald of Ferintosh, John Macrae (Mac-Rath Mor) and John Kennedy of Dingwall. It was such intrepid missionary preachers as these who carried the message of the Cross throughout the mountains of the North.

Alexander Stewart, the son of a clergyman, was born in 1794 at Moulin in Perthshire. He was educated in the parochial school at Moulin, at Tain Academy and at Aberdeen University. He spent some time in a commercial office, and then attended Glasgow University and the divinity

---

[37]. *Ibid.*

school at Glasgow. While in Glasgow he used to attend St. John's Church, while Thomas Chalmers was pastor there. Chalmers took a great interest in the promising young man, and when he left Glasgow, Chalmers urged Stewart to become his successor at St. John's. Pleading youth and inexperience, Alexander Stewart declined so responsible a position. Licensed to preach in 1823, he supplied the Chapel of Ease at Rothesay for about a year, and in 1824 he was called to Cromarty, where he was to spend the remainder of his eventful life.

Stewart of Cromarty, as he is familiarly known, was not a man of pleasing appearance. His thick sandy hair sprang from an inch or so above his eyebrows, and was combed pompadour style, giving him a strange, ape-like appearance. When in repose he might have been mistaken for a moron, but the moment he ascended the pulpit his stolid face took on an expressive look that commanded instant attention. He had the emotional fire of the true Celt, but this was combined with an effort to conceal any appearance of emotion, such as one finds commonly enough among Lowlanders. However, Stewart, when in the pulpit, seemed at all times on the verge of some outburst of feeling. His face would flush blood-red with pent up enthusiasm and his eyes would kindle, yet he would remain calm. Again he would seem to be on the verge of tears, but he would never permit them to flow. All the while he would preach, not with the expected oratorical fire of the Celtic Highlander, but in a tone of great animation that was, nevertheless, always under complete control. Unconsciously he had learned by sitting under the ministry of Thomas Chalmers, to face his congration with the expression of a man who had something momentous to disclose, and yet with the appearance of a man who is doing his utmost to tell it without excitement.

Alexander Stewart was celebrated because of his vivid descriptions and illustrations. These were almost invariably drawn from the Scriptures, but he had an unusual way of telling them that aroused eager attention and led up to a striking climax. For example, he might tell his congregation that he was reminded of a man who went from place to place, bearing witness to the marvellous grace of

God, and the salvation which is to be found not in right living but only in God-given faith in the Saviour, conveyed to mankind by the Holy Ghost. This man was treated harshly on many occasions, even cast into prison, or perhaps beaten until almost dead. He suffered untold hardships, but never for a moment did he soften his message, or try to win the applause of the people. At length, after a life of hardships, this courageous missionary of the Cross summed it all up by declaring: "For I am persuaded, that neither death, nor life, nor angels, nor principalities, nor powers, nor things present, nor things to come, nor height, nor depth, nor any other creature, shall be able to separate us from the love of God, which is in Christ Jesus our Lord." Stewart knew his Bible as thoroughly as he knew his Highland Gaelic, and his sermons are not only rich in thought, but equally rich in Scriptural illustrations. Where preachers of later days drew upon green fields, dark forests, blue skies and the sea thundering against the rocky headlands for their illustrations, the old Highland princes of the pulpit employed countless Biblical incidents with rare effect — incidents too often unknown to the congregations in later times.

Together with many of the Highlanders, Alexander Stewart went with those of the Free Kirk in 1843. He died four year later, at the age of 53. A good memoir of Stewart of Cromarty is included in David Beaton's *Some Noted Ministers of the Northern Highlands* (1929).

William Symington (1795-1862)

William Symington was born in Paisley in 1795. He entered Glasgow University at the age of 15, and after completing the four year arts course, he entered the theological hall of the Reformed Presbyterian Church in 1814, and completed his course in 1818. He was licensed to preach in 1818 and ordained in 1819. His first congregation was Stranraer church, where his preaching attracted attention far beyond his own denomination. People from other church groups came to hear him, and in 1824 it was necessary to build a new and larger church to accommodate the congregations that gathered regularly. In 1839 he was called to the Great Hamilton Street Reformed Presbyterian church, where his preaching attracted large congregations. His Sunday evening lectures were equally popular. In 1853 he was made professor of theology in the Reformed Presbyterian theological school. William Symington was one of the most widely known and most powerful preachers of the Reformed Presbyterian church of his day. He wrote *The Atonement and Intercession of Jesus Christ* (c. 1860); *Messiah the Prince* (c. 1838); and published a volume of sermons.

John Duncan (1796-1870)

The history of preaching includes not only the men who were learned and popular, but many a man of great learning who failed to gain popularity because of some unfortunate external handicap. Such a man was John Duncan, a man of exceptional gifts, but so notoriously absent minded that his actual parochial work was limited to but a dozen years.

John Duncan was born at Gilcomston, in the parish of Old Machar, Aberdeen. His father, a shoe maker, was a devout member of the Original Secession Synod. The boy was sent to Aberdeen Grammar School, and in 1810 to Marischal College. In 1813 he became a divinity student in the Constitutional Associate Presbytery (Antiburgher Secession) organization, only to change in 1816 to the Established Kirk, and to enter their theological hall the following year.

He completed his studies in 1821, but did not seek to be licensed at first because he was unable to accept the entire Westminster Confession. In 1825 he was finally licensed, and a year later, when Dr. Caesar Malan, of Geneva, preached in Aberdeen, young Duncan's theological position was strengthened considerably. In 1830, not yet ordained, he preached for a time at Persie Chapel, Perthshire, and his exceptional ability attracted favorable attention. In 1831 he became assistant to Robert Clark at the Gaelic Chapel in Duke street, Glasgow, where his Sunday afternoon lectures in the English language attracted the deeply spiritual people of the city. So great was the impression he made that he preached for a time to large congregations in a school house in West Nile street.

Mr. Duncan was ordained in 1836, at the age of 40, and became pastor of Milton congregation. Always unmethodical and absent minded, his work at that place can hardly be called successful. His exceptional sermons brought him invitations to preach at important gatherings, but so absent minded was he that his misadventures are related in Scotland to this day. More than once he became so absorbed in a book that he sat in a railway station and allowed the train to leave without him. Again, his interest in the study of Hebrew would cause him to forget his waiting congregation in the church next door.

A brilliant student of Hebrew, he was sent to Pesth, Hungary, in 1840, partly as chaplain to a group of Scottish engineers engaged in building a bridge, and partly as missionary to the Jews of the two cities, at that time known as Buda and Pesth. There he became acquainted with a young Jew of rare intellectual gifts, named Alfred Edersheim. In 1843, Duncan was one of the men who withdrew from the Established Kirk, and when New College was founded the same year, Dr. Duncan was brought back to Edinburgh as the logical man to teach Hebrew and Oriental Languages in the divinity hall. Alfred Edersheim accompanied him to Edinburgh, having accepted Christianity meanwhile. Edersheim's books are known to clergymen of all denominations, and his work at Oxford is known to many.

Dr. Duncan taught Hebrew at New College for 27 years. Although but 47 years of age when he began teaching, he was patriarchal in appearance, with his flowing white beard, his somber countenance, his aquiline nose and his billowing academic robes. From the start his students called him "Rabbi" Duncan, and thus is he known to this day in any part of the world where Scots have emigrated.

While the poor old "Rabbi" was subject of many a jest among the students, who invented the most fabulous stories concerning his complete lack of methodical discipline and his absent mindedness, yet no man, not even Dr. Chalmers himself, was more respected because of his great learning. Measured by today's standards, Dr. Duncan was not a highly efficient Hebrew teacher, but his genuine piety and his zeal for expository preaching made a great impression upon every student. It may be true that he opened every teaching session with a free prayer, and at times consumed half of the lesson period in this manner, yet the fact must not be overlooked that his positive attitude did much to upset the influence of the destructive Biblical critics who were beginning to return from Halle with their new theological views.   .

Dr. Duncan was not idle on Sunday. He preached frequently in the most prominent Free Church congregations, and he was especially welcome at Communion services, where his preparatory and his post-Communion addresses never failed to make a deep impression upon his hearers. It is quite true that many have said: "Dr. Duncan appealed greatly to the intellectual people, but he was never popular with the common people." This is the usual saying of the group in the Scottish Kirk who had become tainted by negative Biblical criticism, but there are numerous words of testimony to the contrary.

No less a man than Dr. Kennedy, of Dingwall, tells of going to Milton Church to hear John Duncan, long before he had become a professor. "The building was fairly large," said Kennedy, "but the congregation was small and scattered. The light was not very good, but the brilliance of the sermon in close reasoning and soul-stirring power, I shall never forget."[38] Years later, when Dr. Duncan preached at Free St. Luke's, Dr. Kennedy went to hear him. He says: "I stole quietly into the church, and heard a sermon that did not seem to have been prepared on earth, but felt as if one of the old Prophets had come from within the veil to tell us what was going on there. Nothing more heavenly did I ever hear from human lips."[39]

Alexander Ross said of Duncan: "Eminently gifted by, and taught of God, he was one of the most tender, gracious, loving and lovely expositors of His most blessed and holy Word, and many have regretted that he himself wrote so little for publication."[40] Alexander M. Stuart pays highest

---

[38]. J. S. Sinclair, *Rich Gleanings after the Vintage*, p. 7.
[39]. *Ibid.*, pp. 7-8.
[40]. *Ibid.*, p. 7.

tribute to Dr. Duncan's preaching, but says that it was unequal. At his best he was a preacher of rare quality, but even at his poorest he was capable of great depth of thought.[41]

Two books of sermons and Communion addresses, two biographies of Dr. Duncan and several shorter accounts of his life appeared in print after his death. One of the most remarkable is a book by Dr. William Knight, who took down Dr. Duncan's "table talk," and published it with the title *Colloquia peripatetica*.[42] It is a book that might well be in every clerical library. An example or two of Dr. Duncan's informal remarks will indicate that he was not the somber man that some declare him to have been.

"Hyper-Calvinism," said Dr. Duncan, "is all house and no door: Arminianism is all door and no house."

"There is no such thing as Calvinism," he said at another time. "The teachings of Augustine, Remigius, Anselm and Luther were just pieced together by one remarkable man, and the result baptized with his name. Augustine taught and developed the doctrine of salvation by grace and the divine election; Remigius, particular redemption; Anselm, the doctrine of the vicarious atonement; and Luther, that of justification by faith."[43]

Dr. Knight's fine memoir of "Rabbi" Duncan, and his collection of the old Doctor's brilliant comments on a variety of subjects is a classic, while the two books of Duncan's sermons and Communion addresses[44] give evidence (if a printed page really can) of the richness of his spiritual thoughts. Dr. Duncan's edition of Robinson's *Lexicon* (1838), is known to every seminarian. It is most unfortunate that the learned Doctor's peculiarities of dress and manner have made men hesitate to give him the high place in the history of the Scottish pulpit that he so well deserves. To be a great preacher involves more than building up a

---

[41]. A. M. Stuart, *Disruption Worthies* (Edinburgh, 1876), p. 48.
[42]. Edinburgh, 1907.
[43]. Wm. Knight, *Op. cit.*, p. 9.
[44]. *In the Pulpit and at the Communion Table* (1874), and *Sermons and Communion Addresses of John Duncan*, edited by David Brown (1874). See also Jas. A. Sinclair, *Rich Gleanings after the Vintage from "Rabbi" Duncan,*

large congregation or attaining personal popularity. In the
days of bitter controversy men of the liberalistic school did
their utmost to discredit the great Scottish scholar and
preacher; for his uncompromising loyalty to a verbally inspired Bible aroused their antagonism, and they replied with
sharp ridicule, and invented fictitious tales of class-room
prayers one hour in length. Despite all their ridicule, Dr.
John Duncan is remembered as a Hebrew scholar of majestic
learning, and a preacher of surpassing eloquence. David
Brown's *Life of the Late John Duncan* (1872), kept by
libraries in a locked bookcase, is well worth reprinting.
There are good memoirs by Moody Stuart and by William
Knight.

Archibald Bennie (1797-1846)

Among the group of brilliant preachers who added
lustre to the name of Edinburgh in the third and fourth
decade of the nineteenth century was Dr. Bennie, of Lady
Yester's Church. Archibald Bennie was a west-coast Scotsman, having been born in Glasgow in 1797. His father
was a well-known merchant in that city. Archibald Bennie
was educated in Glasgow University, licensed in 1820 and
ordained in 1823 as pastor of the Albion Street Chapel in
Glasgow. In 1824 he was translated to the third church in
Stirling, in 1825 to the second and in 1829 to the first.

In 1835 he became pastor of Lady Yester's Church in
Edinburgh, where his fame as an eloquent preacher became
known throughout Scotland. This was the golden age of
the Edinburgh pulpit. Dr. Thomas Chalmers, Robert
Candlish, Thomas Guthrie, Thomas McCrie, Lindsay Alexander, James Hamilton and Andrew Thompson were but a
few of more than a score of preachers of first rank, who
graced the pulpits of Edinburgh in the thirties of the nineteenth century.

In 1841 Dr. Bennie was made dean of the Chapel Royal.
He was also one of His Majesty's Chaplains in Ordinary.
His preaching was characterized by vigor of thought and
language, brief and striking illustrations and an evangelical
appeal. In theology he was a moderate Calvinist.

James Gilfillan (1797-1874)

James Gilfillan was born in 1797 in Comrie, Perthshire. His father, Samuel Gilfillan, was a preacher of considerable ability, and his mother was known throughout the north of Scotland as "the Star of the North," because of her exceptional beauty and the excellency of her accomplishments. James Gilfillan was a brother of George, who was also a clergyman, and who won fame as a literary man.

James Gilfillan was educated in the grammar school at Comrie, and in 1808 he entered Glasgow University before he had reached the age of 12. He studied theology in the school of the Antiburghers. In 1821 he was licensed by the United Secession Church, ordained in 1822, and called as pastor of the Secession congregation in Stirling. He was a preacher of much more than ordinary ability, and a representative of the old school of Scottish preaching. He came into prominence in the early eighteen forties because of his active part in the Sunday Question. The new railway between Edinburgh and Glasgow had been opened, and the traditional sanctity of the Scottish Sabbath was threatened. Gilfillan not only preached vehemently on the Sunday Question, but he published a book, *The Sabbath*, which aroused public opinion to a high pitch. Gilfillan was an excellent preacher, although not one of the greatest of his day, but he deserves the place that he holds because of his part in the violent controversy as to whether or not the Old Testament Sabbath had been set aside in New Testament days.

James Gilfillan wrote *The Sabbath in the Light of Reason, Revelation and History* (1861); *The Philosophy of the Sabbath* (1863); and a volume entitled *Discourses* (1865).

James Gibson (1799-1871)

James Gibson, a noted conservative leader in the Free Church, was born in 1799 in Crieff, Perthshire. He entered Glasgow University when but 12 years old. In 1820 he was licensed to preach, but acted as tutor for a time. In 1825 he visited the Continent. Upon his return he was assistant pastor at West Church, Greenock, and later he served as assistant at the College Church, Glasgow. He was also professor of theology in Glasgow College.

In 1839 a church was built for him in Kingston by wealthy friends. In 1843, at the Disruption, he lost this church, but another was built for him. In 1856 he was made professor of systematic theology and Church history in the Free Church theological school in Glasgow. In 1859 he became involved in a case of discipline. Seven students were charged with heresy because of their views regarding the unity of God, and the Scriptural doctrine of human depravity. The case came before the college, and then before the General Assembly. Gibson insisted that their views were unsound, but the Assembly found no heresy, and the students were merely admonished.

James Gibson was a vigorous preacher, very conservative in his doctrine and practice, but he was not popular. His learning and his strength as a preacher were admitted by all, but the latter part of his life was spent in a period of time when the old, rigid Calvinism of the Kirk was disintegrating. Younger men with liberal views had come upon the scene. Gibson felt called upon to defend the old doctrine and practice of his denomination, in his preaching, in his writings and in the meetings of the Assembly. His public utterances took on a polemical tone that did not prove popular in those days of transition. He was a firm believer in doctrinal discipline, and when heresy cases came up from time to time, he urged adherence to the old conservatism of the Kirk. He spoke vigorously against the acceptance of women as voting members. He protested against fraternal relations with the Evangelical Alliance, which he declared to be a unionistic body that encouraged fraternizing with Arminians and Erastians. When the subject of church union came up in 1856 and the years that followed, Gibson was a tireless opponent of union with the United Presbyterians and other such bodies on any basis other than a definite and full agreement in doctrine. In the suggested doctrinal declarations of those days he found only evasive language which left opportunity for divergent doctrinal views. In addresses often an hour or more in length, he urged the Free Kirk to hold firmly to its early doctrinal position.

The more liberal younger men of his day were reluctant to give James Gibson a place as one of the great preachers of that period, for his tireless defense of an uncompromising conservatism in doctrine and practice came in time to weary the younger men, who looked upon church union, the franchise for women in church gatherings, and the new German theories of Biblical criticism as desirable progress. Professor Gibson was aware of his growing unpopularity, yet in his preaching and in his debates in the Assembly he defended the cause of conservatism to his dying day.   Dr. Gibson's chief works are: *The Inability of Man to Receive the Testimony of God* (1846); *The Marriage Affinity Question* (1854), an authoritative work on the forbidden degrees; *The Principles of the Bible Temperance* (1855); *Present Truths in Theology,* 2 volumes (1863); *Connection between the Decalogue and New Testament Morality* (1865); *The Public Worship of God* (1869); and *The Church in Relation to the State* (1872).

William Anderson (1799-1873)

William Anderson, once a popular Glasgow preacher, was born in 1799 at Kilsyth, where his father was pastor of the local Relief congregation.   After his academic and theological training he was ordained in 1822 and became pastor of the John Street Relief Church in Glasgow.

Dr. Anderson was a man of powerful oratory, and he was noted for views that were considered liberal in his day. This did not apply to theology, but rather to such innovations as church organs and the reading of sermons.   In a day when a church organ was looked upon as a "kist o' whussles," and a relic of popery that dare not be brought into a church lest the congregation fall into the sin of "worshiping the Lord by machinery," Anderson used his persuasive eloquence in behalf of the despised organ.   As early as 1829 he began to urge the use of organs, and a pamphlet which he published on the subject dealt with the usual objections in a way that few could answer.   In his day the mention of politics in the pulpit was abhorrent to every devout Scot, but Anderson did not hesitate to preach with all his might on the separation of Church and State. He was an out-spoken opponent of popery, and of anything suggesting the Latin Church.

Dr. Anderson was vehement and old-fashioned in his manner of preaching, but in one respect he was a crusader for new ways of declaring the Word of God. It had always been traditional in the United Presbyterian Church to pre-pare a sermon with great care, to memorize it thoroughly and then to preach without "paper." Dr. Anderson began to read his sermons, and when the subject became a matter of controversy, he defended the right of every pastor to fol-low the custom most suited to him. A resolution against the reading of sermons was passed, yet it contained a pro-vision allowing those men who were already accustomed to the manuscript, to use their best judgment in the matter.

As an example of his old-fashioned manner of preach-ing, Dr. Nicoll cites the following from one of his sermons: "Ho, miscreants! Death, inevitable death, is on your track. How the thought of it comforts me about you! It is the Lord's consolation, and I will not shut my heart against it. 'Fret not thyself because of evil-doers, neither be thou envious against the workers of iniquity. For they shall soon be cut down like the grass, and wither as the green herb'." [45] Dr. Anderson was a popular platform speaker, and much in demand at great gatherings on national and civic occasions, when his stirring orations brought him great fame. In theology he was a moderate Calvinist, and a Chiliast as well. In 1850 he published a notable book on Regeneration.

John McLeod Campbell (1800-1872)

One of the unfortunate men of the Scottish Church was Dr. John McLeod Campbell. This noted preacher and theologian was born in 1800 at Kilninver, Argyllshire, where his father was a clergyman. He attended the Universities of Glasgow and Edinburgh, completing his theological studies in 1821. He was ordained in 1825 and became pastor of a congregation at Row, Dumbartonshire. He found the con-

---

[45]. British Weekly, Jan. 8, 1920, p. 343.

gregation in a state of spiritual apathy, and although he preached with the zeal of a prophet he was unable to see the improvement that he desired.   Thinking that the rigidness of the old-time Calvinistic theology might be responsible for the conditions in his parish, he began to study the Scriptures, and to examine the Calvinistic system as it existed at that time, comparing it with the New Testament. He began to preach an unlimited Atonement, and an assurance of faith.   From the strict standpoint of the old Calvinism this was heresy, and he was cited to appear before the Dumbarton Presbytery in 1830, and then before the Glasgow Assembly.[46]

McLeod Campbell was but 30 years of age when the charges were first made against him, while his accusers were older men, "skilled in every subtlety of Calvinism." His defense was that of a young man whose views are not yet clear, and the impression that he made was not satisfactory.   He admitted that he had preached to his congregation that the Atonement is not limited to the elect only, but is offered to all.   It does not actually save every man, but it makes it possible for all men to be saved, and if a man is lost, it is not because God so desires it.   He declared that pardon is universal in the sense that the barriers between man and God have been removed in the case of all men. He admitted that he had preached assurance of faith, but not in the sense that every Christian enjoys this blessing in an unbroken manner.   Rather did he believe that where there is a saving trust in the Saviour, this conveys to the Christian a firm confidence that his sins have been forgiven and that reconciliation exists between the Saviour and the believer. There may be times when this assurance is not strong, and it may seem to disappear completely at times, but this is not an indication that it does not exist.

McLeod Campbell's heresy trial stirred Scotland.   He was found guilty and expelled from the Church of Scotland. He returned to the Highlands for two years, but in 1833 he

---

[46]. Donald Campbell, *Memorials of John McLeod Campbell*, 2 vols. (London, 1877); also see *Whole Proceedings in the Case of John McLeod Campbell* (Greenock, 1831); J. M. Campbell, *Reminiscenses and Reflections* (London, 1873); *The Row Heresy* (Glasgow, 1831).

became pastor of an independent congregation in Glasgow. It was a small chapel in Blackfriars Street, and Mr. Campbell looked upon himself as an independent State Churchman. He labored in Glasgow with moderate success for some 26 years. In 1856 he published a notable book on the Atonement.[47] In his later years he won the respect of men who had begun to preach a less rigid form of Calvinism, and in 1868 Glasgow went so far as to confer a degree upon him.

Dr. Campbell was a devout man, and his difficulties were those of a man who was struggling toward the truth. The doctrines that concerned him have caused controversies for ages, and more gifted theologians than he have grappled with them. The Word of God is clear enough, but it is the exceptional man who has been able to cause his human reason to bow completely to the inspired truth. Dr. Campbell was a devout man and a thoughtful theologian, but he was not a theologian of the type of Dr. Francis Pieper. Campbell, in his younger days especially, was not clear. He used terms in a sense that lacked precision, and it is doubtful whether he ever learned the art of self-defense. When attacked, his thinking became confused. Even his book on the Atonement, written a full quarter of a century after his heresy trial, is not a book of exact language. It would not be looked upon today as a correct presentation of the doctrines in question, yet it had its influence upon theological thought in Great Britain. He caught sight of partial truths which he never understood fully.

As a preacher Dr. Campbell made a deep impression upon many of his day, including Dr. Norman Macleod, who looked upon him as one of the most devout men of his generation. He was a man of exceptional character, deeply religious, and with many of the qualifications of a truly great preacher. However, he never seemed to grasp the facts of objective and subjective reconciliation, and their distinction. Where these are lacking, even a forceful enunciation of what one believes to be the truth, is of little value, nor can spiritual warmth in itself atone for a failure to distinguish clearly between Law and Gospel.

----

[47]. *The Nature of the Atonement* (Cambridge, 1856).

Dr. J. M. Campbell's writings include: *The Nature of the Atonement* (1856); *Sermons and Lectures* (1832); *Christ the Bread of Life* (1851); and *Thoughts on Revelation* (1862). Students of the history of doctrine will find it well worth their while to study *The Whole Proceedings . . . in the Case of the Rev. J. McL. Campbell* (1831), because the well-known Campbell Case marks one of the early stages in the breaking down of strict Calvinistic orthodoxy. A two-volume work, *Reminiscences and Reflections* (1873), was begun by Dr. J. M. Campbell and completed by his son, Donald Campbell.

Robert Buchanan (1802-1875)

Robert Buchanan was born in 1802 in St. Ninan's, near Stirling. After his education in Glasgow University he was ordained in 1826 and became pastor of Gargunnock church. In 1829 he was translated to Salton, East Lothian, and in 1833 he became pastor of Tron Church, Glasgow, where Thomas Chalmers had been pastor from 1805 to 1819. Like Chalmers, he had a great interest in the tenement dwellers, and his remarkable work in the Wynds district is second only to the work of Chalmers among the neglected classes. He established churches and schools, and by his earnest preaching and his missionary activity he won the confidence of thousands.

Robert Buchanan was one of the leaders in the Assembly, and in 1838 he formulated a resolution which established the principle that the Kirk stood ready to yield to the civil courts in all purely civil matters, but is was equally determined to assert its own rights in spiritual matters, without interference from the State.

In 1843 Dr. Buchanan was one of the men closely associated with Thomas Chalmers in the Disruption. He withdrew with the other seceders, and with Chalmers, Candlish, Cunningham and Guthrie became a leader of the Free Church. In 1860 he was elected moderator.

Dr. Buchanan was an earnest preacher of Calvinistic orthodoxy, a wise, influential leader of the Assembly and a man of solid learning. Toward the end of his life he sought to bring about a better understanding between the

Free Church and the United Presbyterians, for he believed
that doctrinal unity existed. His *History of the Ten Years'
Conflict* is the best known of his several writings.[48] He was
given the oversight of the Sustentation Fund, and labored
from 1847 to 1875 in behalf of it. In 1875, while on a visit
to Rome, he died in his sleep. Dr. Buchanan was one of
the great leaders of Disruption days, and he stood on the
platform of Tanfield Hall at the right hand of Dr. Chalmers
when the Free Church was formally founded. He was a
man of lasting influence, and after the death of Chalmers he
was one of a small group who directed the multitude of
activities of the new organization.

In addition to his *History of the Ten Years' Conflict*
(1849), which is a very careful, two-volume work, well
documented, Dr. Buchanan published a commentary on the
Book of Ecclesiastes and a work entitled *A Clerical Furlough,*
which is an account of a trip that he made through the Holy
Land. His biography was written by N. L. Walker, and bears
the title, *Robert Buchanan: An Ecclesiastical Biography*
(1877). An account of his life is also included in *Disruption Worthies* (1876), and was contributed by Principal
Robert Rainy.

James Wright † 1879

About the middle of the nineteenth century, James
Wright, of the Antiburgher Synod, was one of the famous
preachers of Edinburgh. He was pastor of the Lauritson
Street Church, and both he and his congregation declined
to enter the union with the Burgher Synod in 1842. They
were still of the opinion that no Christian could, with a
good conscience, take the oath required of all burgesses.

James Wright was a preacher of marked ability, and
his sermons on prophecy drew great congregations during
the middle decades of the nineteenth century. The church,
which seats 800, was filled to overflowing every Sunday
evening. In 1874 Mr. Wright ordained Walter McLeod, a
former missionary in the Free Church, as his successor. Mr.
McLeod was pastor until his death in 1912. The Lauritson

---

[48]. 2 vols., Glasgow, 1849.

Street Church still exists, and is said to be the sole survivor of the Antiburgher Church.

Thomas Guthrie (1803-1873)

One of the greatest pulpit orators of the Scottish Free Church was Thomas Guthrie. He was born in 1803 at Brechin, Forfarshire, on the east coast of Scotland. His father was one of the leading merchants of the town, and for years the provost, or chief magistrate. He was a man in comfortable circumstances, and able to give his family of thirteen the advantages of an excellent education. In the Guthrie household the strictest standards of piety prevailed. Morning and evening the family gathered for their devotions. On Sunday they attended the kirk both morning and evening, and the remainder of the day was spent in reading the Bible, studying the Shorter Catechism and reading religious books. Whistling and levity were not tolerated on that day.

Thomas Guthrie's first school was kept by a pious weaver. His large front room was used for this purpose, and there was a hand loom in one corner where the schoolmaster sat and followed his trade during the study periods. Guthrie's next school was the parochial school of the local Antiburgher congregation, and in this school Thomas McCrie had taught when but 14 or 15 years of age. On Sunday the Guthrie children attended the Burgher, or Secession congregation. In his first school Thomas Guthrie was taught to read, and the Book of Proverbs was his textbook. This was customary in those days in Scotland. "That book is without a rival for beginners," declared Dr. Guthrie, "containing quite a repertory of monosyllables and pure Saxon — English undefiled. Take this passage, for example, where, with one exception, every word is formed of a single syllable, and belongs to the Saxon tongue, — 'Train up a child in the way he should go: and when he is old, he will not depart from it.' What a contrast to the silly trash of modern schoolbooks for beginners, with such sentences as, 'Tom has a dog'; 'The Cat is good'; 'The Cow has a calf.' While learning the art of reading by the Book of Proverbs, we had our minds stored with the highest moral truths;

and, by sage advices applicable to all ages and departments of life, the branch, while it was supple, received a bent in a direction highly favourable to future well-doing and success in life. The patience, prudence, foresight and economy which used to characterize Scotsmen — giving occasion to the saying, 'a canny Scot' — and by which they were so often able to rise in the world and distance all competitors in the race of life, was to a large extent due to their being thus engrained in youth and childhood with the practical wisdom enshrined in the Book of Proverbs." [49]

Thomas Guthrie entered Edinburgh University at the age of twelve. While he was an excellent student, yet there were times when he was disciplined because of his readiness to engage in a fight. At the age of 15 he stood six feet three inches in height, and older boys learned to their sorrow that it was unsafe to ridicule him because of his broad Forfarshire "Doric" accent. He received his theological training in the Divinity Hall of Edinburgh University. After having spent four years in the University and four additional years in his theological studies, he was graduated at the age of 20, but was not granted a license to preach because of his youthfulness. He was licensed in 1825, and was offered a large, affluent congregation. It was made clear to him that before accepting the call, he must go to St. Andrews and pay his respects to Dr. Nicol, a leader of the Moderate party. Guthrie refused emphatically to do this, for he had learned to distrust the Moderates. He declined the call rather than pledge himself to one of their leaders. This action on his part caused the Moderates to enter his name, figuratively speaking, in the Black Book; and for the next five years they made it impossible for him to receive a call. He took some further work at the University and spent 1826 and 1827 studying at the famous Sorbonne, in Paris. Returning to Scotland he was still unable to secure a call, since his decidedly evangelical views were known to the dominant Moderate party. Some of his family were bankers, and he worked as bank manager for two years.

---

[49]. *Autobiography of Thomas Guthrie* (London, 1874), vol. 1, pp. 28-29.

Finally, in 1830, through the efforts of an influential friend, he was given a small country congregation at Arbirlot, Forfarshire. He was required to pay sixty pounds, half of which went to the Crown and the other half to the local presbytery, who used it for a dinner where wine flowed freely. The church building at Arbirlot was in bad repair, and its floor was nothing more than hard clay. The manse was hardly fit for human habitation. Guthrie, 27 years of age at the time, entered upon his work with great zeal, and the languishing congregation took on new life. He started catechetical instruction, which had suffered during the long infirmity of his predecessor, a man of 87 years at his death. He opened a lending library in the front room of the manse, and when the farm laborers and the villagers came for their books, he engaged them in conversation in regard to their spiritual problems, and imparted wholesome advice and instruction.

Guthrie's sermons were remarkable from the start. Although he had bought the best critical and devotional commentaries, he relied almost entirely upon Cruden's *Concordance* and Dr. Chalmers' *Scripture References,* with the Bible his chief text book. During his years in Edinburgh he had heard many eminent preachers, and observed that many indifferent sermons were made impressive by a vigorous delivery, while many a fine sermon was reduced to feebleness by a delivery that lacked animation. He spent his evenings, while a student, studying public speaking; walking almost entirely across Edinburgh, late at night, year after year, until all his bad mannerisms were corrected and he became an exceptional speaker. At Arbirlot he studied hard, wrote out his sermons with care, speaking them aloud as he wrote them. Opposite each page of his manuscript he left a blank page. He revised his sermons again and again, striving to express them in simple, pithy Anglo-Saxon. He made a careful study of the style of the Old Testament prophets, of the Lord and of His disciples, seeking to imitate the simplicity and clearness of their style. On Sunday he preached without his manuscript. Dr. James McCosh, later the illustrious president of Princeton University, was his nearest neighbor, and he pays highest tribute to Guthrie's power in the pulpit, even in his earliest years. Sir William Hamilton, the metaphysician, was another who spoke in highest terms of Guthrie. Not only was he a preacher of exceptional external gifts, but he was a pronounced evan gelical from the outset. It is most unfortunate that his first published volume, *The Gospel in Ezekiel*, which appeared some years after his Arbirlot days, gained such wide popularity. Of all his published writings this is the least representative of the real Guthrie. His sermons on *The Parables* are decidedly more evangelical.

At Arbirlot he conducted a two-hour service at noon, with a lengthy sermon. Between its two main divisions a Psalm was sung. At six in the evening he had a service for young people between 15 and 25 years of age. After Psalm-singing, Scripture reading and prayer, he expounded one or two paragraphs of the Larger Catechism, questioning the young people carefully. After the singing of another metrical Psalm, he conducted a catechization based upon the morning sermon, taking it up point by point, not only questioning the young people, but illustrating his morning sermon by means of vivid illustrations drawn from their own countryside scenes and their daily lives. These evening catechizations became so popular that the older people of his congregation crowded the church, aisles and all. People from Dr. McCosh's church, three miles away, walked to Arbirlot to hear Guthrie's catechizations. Soon his name was known throughout Forfarshire. Of the thousand people who lived within the boundaries of his parish, all attended his church but three, and during the seven years of his ministry there, but one crime was committed in Arbirlot and vicinity.

Guthrie took an active part in the controversy on Voluntaryism, and it was soon learned that the tall, genial young Presbyterian clergyman was a fighter. Once, when the chairman of a meeting refused to recognize him, and when the crowds in the church aisles would not make way for him, Guthrie made his way to the platform by walking on the backs of the benches, followed by several friends. There he delivered his address in spite of another speaker who insisted upon talking at the same time. Guthrie continued to speak with great vehemence until his opponent finally gave up the unequal contest and sat down.

His activity in the controversy on Voluntaryism brought him to the attention of the town council of Edinburgh when a vacancy occurred at Old Greyfriars, one of the most important churches in that city. Eleven candidates were placed upon the slate, and although Guthrie anticipated an American presidential candidate by almost a century in declaring that if placed on the slate he would decline, and if called he would not accept, yet it was he who was called. Older clergymen urged him to accept, reminding him that a man of his pronounced evangelical views, and his power in the pulpit, would mean much to the conservative cause in Edinburgh. He finally yielded to their persuasion, declaring, however, that if their hopes were not realized, he intended to emigrate to America.

Mr. Guthrie served Old Greyfriars together with a worthy associate pastor. When the associate preached, the large church was but comfortably filled. When Guthrie preached, every aisle and every gallery was packed, and long queues stood outside, hoping that somebody would leave the church so that the ushers would admit them. Affiliated with Old Greyfriars was Magdalene Chapel, where Mr. Guthrie preached each Sunday afternoon. The poor people of the district were not required to pay pew-rents. Sittings were free to them, and the well-to-do were obliged to wait outside in two long queues until all the poor were seated.

Guthrie spent the first two or three years of his Edinburgh pastorate in visiting the squalid wynds and closes in his parish — or as we might say in America, the alleys and narrow passage-ways. We have nothing in America remotely like them. In Edinburgh, Glasgow, London, Dublin and scores of other cities in the British Isles and on the Continent, narrow lanes used to open out of the wider streets, and from these there ran very narrow passage-ways. Squalid tenements, often as much as eight and ten stories high, lined them. The poverty and misery in those wynds and closes defies description. In some of Dr. Guthrie's books he describes, with a vividness of language of which he was

a master, the conditions in those frightful slums, beside
which the slums of New York and Boston are almost a
luxury. Families composed of a father, mother and a dozen
or more children were crowded into one dark room into
which no ray of sunshine ever entered. A candle thrust
into an empty beer bottle was the only source of light.
Often an old, blind grandfather or grandmother shared the
wretched room. The children were compelled to beg in
the streets, and the money they obtained was, more often
than not, spent by their parents for cheap liquor. Cholera
and typhus were common.

During the regime of the Moderates, these frightful
slums were neglected. One very prominent Edinburgh
clergyman used to make an annual visitation of these awful
districts. Standing in the main thoroughfare, at a safe
distance from all this misery, and looking down one of the
appalling passageways, he would lift his kid-gloved hand to
Heaven, raise his eyes sanctimoniously and "bless" the
wynd and all who dwelt therein, calling upon the Lord to
watch over them in their misery. Never was he known to
penetrate any of these abodes of wretchedness.

Not so with Dr. Guthrie. Like Chalmers and Tasker,
like McColl and Ross, and like a number of other faithful
men, he spent his afternoons among just such people. He
arose every day at five in the morning, devoted his forenoons to diligent preparation of his Sunday sermon, and
every afternoon found him seeking out the poorest people
in the parish. He went from house to house and from room
to room, never asking whether they were members of his
congregation or not. The district was a neglected one, and
he considered them all under his care, since others showed
no interest in them.

It was not long until he became convinced that the only
method of dealing with such congested slums is the territorial system, a form of which had been used with great
success by Dr. Chalmers, in Glasgow. In one of his sermons
he speaks of a prominent Edinburgh congregation where
two pastors were expected to serve no less than 50,000
people. Guthrie declared that no pastor can serve more
than 1,000 people and do justice to the task. By means of

the territorial system, which he favored, the parish was divided into districts, and trained elders and deacons placed over each district. Each elder and deacon had from ten to twenty families under his immediate care, and he was expected to visit these once a week. Men blessed with dominating personalities — men such as Guthrie and Chalmers — were able to put such a plan into operation, and by dogged Scottish determination to insist that every elder and deacon do his duty faithfully. It is a far cry from the gloved and perfumed type of clergyman who spends his summers at the seaside resorts and the remainder of the year attending meetings, delivering addresses and drinking wine with the lairds and lords — and men such as these determined evangelicals who spent six afternoons each week visiting the poorest parts of the city, and directing a large staff of elders and deacons in the same work. Dr. Guthrie declared that no one man, not even a city missionary, can more than scratch the surface. He compared it to a great ocean liner putting out to sea with only a captain on the bridge, and no crew.

Dr. Guthrie was not particularly unionistic. However, he suggested a plan by which the leading denominations of Edinburgh, at that time the Church of Scotland (Presbyterian), the Baptist, the Independent, the United Presbyterian, the Episcopal, and later the Free Church, should agree in a friendly manner to divide a slum area into several districts, and each one be assigned a district. Each congregation was to be held responsible for 500 souls who were not otherwise reached by organized religion. Their task was not only to win the unchurched, but to provide adequate Christian day schools for the children.

Guthrie's tireless labor was not in vain. In 1839 the foundation stone of a new church and parish school were laid. These buildings were in the Nether Bow, later known as Victoria Street. The church was called St. John's, and unlike most Old World churches, it included a basement, as did the parish school. As soon as the basements of the two buildings were completed, Dr. Guthrie began to preach in the one, and to maintain a day school in the other, while the masons and carpenters were still busy overhead. Late in the year 1840, the new St. John's Church was completed, and Dr. Guthrie became its pastor. The 650 sittings on the main floor were free, and were reserved for the poor. A gallery, running around three sides of the church, contained 350 additional sittings, and these were rented to the well-to-do. From the start, every aisle was filled, and Dr. Guthrie's sons tell us that people laid planking around the ventilator openings in the church attic, and sat there, summer and winter, so crowded was the church below.

Dr. Guthrie's evenings, which he had planned to spend with his large family, soon had to be devoted to a new task. He was a leader of the Anti-Patronage group, small at first, but growing year by year, and a man with his extraordinary gifts as a persuasive speaker was not allowed much time to himself. He was called upon to deliver addresses in the surrounding country. When the time of the Disruption drew near, few men worked harder than he, preaching in churches where this was permitted, or in town halls, barns or in the open fields where the Moderates refused the use of a local church. His stirring eloquence won many a pastor and many an entire congregation to the cause of those men who insisted that every congregation should have the right to choose its own pastor, and that the Lord Jesus Christ, not the king and the civil courts, is the Head of the Church.

Dr. Guthrie has often been called the Apostle of the Ragged School Movement. However, he was not its originator. That honor goes the Sheriff Watson, who opened the first ragged school in Aberdeen, in 1841. While preaching one Sunday in Anstruther, on the Firth of Forth, Dr. Guthrie was told of a cobbler who was conducting a ragged school. He called upon him the next day, found him sitting at his work bench, and all about him a group of ragged children whom he taught as he pegged his shoes. In visiting a city prison, he saw many homeless children who had come there to spend the night. The sight of the old cobbler "humbled and shamed" Guthrie, and the experience in the prison spurred him to action. He discovered that scores of children, whose parents were usually drunkards, roamed the streets of the large cities, often without food or shelter. At once Dr. Guthrie devoted all of his matchless eloquence to the cause, and some of the most moving sections of his sermons are his word pictures of the misery of these abandoned children. The Ragged School Movement, by which such children are not only gathered into Christian day schools, but given food and clothing as well, owes much to the determined efforts of Thomas Guthrie, and his stirring sermons, lectures and books.

During his Edinburgh days, Dr. Guthrie was a preacher of world-wide reputation. Summer visitors in that city, certainly the most beautiful in the world, were drawn to St. John's Church in numbers. Americans, colonials, people from the Continent, stood in long lines waiting for the doors to open, mingling with many of Edinburgh's most eminent citizens who found their way to slumland in order to hear Guthrie. He was six feet three inches tall, broad shouldered, with a dark complexion and an abundance of black hair which became iron-gray as he grew older. He had deep-set gray eyes and a prominent nose. His features expressed his determination, and yet his expression was always that of friendliness. He had a magnificent voice, deep, powerful, clear and beautifully modulated, and a dramatic ability that he was not always able to hold within bounds, especially when delivering a ringing appeal for missionary work among the poor, or for his beloved Ragged Schools. A magnificent black collie followed him wherever he went, and in his days as a country pastor this dog was allowed to lie at his feet inside the pulpit. Guthrie's accent was Scottish and his gestures were easy and graceful. He was not a profound scholar nor was he a great theologian. He was a pronounced evangelical of the "reformed" type.

His sermons, while beautifully simple in thought and language, might be looked upon as ornate today. However, he lived in an age when ornate language in the pulpit was the fashion. His style was highly pictorial. Today a pastor would hardly say: "How has it wrung our heart to see a ragged, famished boy looking greedily in at a window on the food he has no one to give him, and dare not touch, — to watch him, as he alternately lifted his naked feet, lest they should freeze to the icy pavement. He starves in the midst of abundance. Neglected among a people who would take more pity on an ill-used horse or a dying dog, he is a cast-away upon the land. Of the throngs that pass heedlessly by him to homes of comfort, intent on business or on pleasure, there is no one who cares for him. Poor wretch!" [50] Such language might be considered sentimental today, but it served its purpose at the time.

Thomas Guthrie was noted for his pictorial style. By means of word-pictures he made Bible scenes live before his hearers. Sometimes he seems to overload his sermons with illustrations. One sermon begins with a lengthy description of a submerged forest off the coast of Scotland, where the sea has inundated many acres of woodland. At once Guthrie proceeds to describe streets in Edinburgh, where beautiful homes, once occupied by the wealthiest citizens, had become the wretched haunts of poverty and misery.

Guthrie is one of the few great preachers whose printed words move one profoundly. The tall, powerful man, in his black preaching robe and white bands, his Scottish accent and his rich, vibrant voice, is gone. His dramatic gifts and his powerful personality are but a memory, but his printed sermons (barring that unfortunate *Gospel in Ezekiel* and one or two others) still reflect something of his strange power of persuasive oratory. We can overlook his lush illustrations and regret that there is not greater doctrinal solidity in his sermons. He had but little interest in theology as a systematized science, and fortunately the writings of the Higher Critics were unknown to him. The plan of salvation that he proclaimed was a very simple one, and he did not attempt to explain the relation between subjective and objective justification; neither did he attempt to explain why two men might hear the same Gospel, and yet one be saved and the other lost.

At the age of 70, Thomas Guthrie, a worn-out old man, lay dying. One of his sons attempted to raise the head of the dying man from the pillow. "Heave awa', lad," he said cheerfully, "Heave awa', I'm no dead yet!" Then he said to his sons, "Just give me a bairn's hymn." When they had sung his favorite hymn, he said "Pray that I may have a

---

[50]. *The City, its Sins and Sorrows* (London, 1857).

speedy entrance into Heaven, where we shall no longer have to proclaim Christ — but where we shall enjoy Him forever."

His *Autobiography,* to which is added a *Memoir* by two of his sons, is a two-volume work that deserves a much better fate than to stand on the shelf of a second-hand book shop. It contains much source material, written in vivid language, of the days of spiritual darkness that prevailed in many lands in the early nineteenth century, and of the period of reaction that followed it. In his lively manner he gives us pen-pictures of the men who strove to bring about a spiritual awakening, and of the events in which they had a part. More than a dozen or Dr. Guthrie's books exist, some of which contain sermons, others including articles contributed to *The Sunday Magazine* of which he was editor.

Dr. Guthrie's unfortunate *Gospel in Ezekiel* (1856) has not yet ceased to be popular. Men read it for its style and its fresh illustrations. His *Seed Time and Harvest for Ragged Schools* (1860), is an eloquent plea for religious work in the slums, and especially for the Christian education of slum children in parochial schools. His *Christ and the Inheritance of the Saints* (1858) is a series of studies in Colossians. *Parables of Our Lord* (1866) has been reprinted again and again. *The City, its Sins and Sorrows* (1857) might well be read by congregations of today who feel tempted to desert their old, downtown location and move to the more fashionable suburbs. Guthrie, Ross and many other Scotsmen proved that strong congregations may be built up in the most unpromising parts of a great city, and that the Word of God has power to make devout Christians out of the very drunkards that sprawl in the doorways. Many other writings of Guthrie are well known to this day. Some of them are: *Bear ye One Another's Burdens* (1863); *The Way to Life* (1862); *Speaking to the Heart* (1862); *The Angel's Song* (1865); *Early Piety* (1867); *Out of Harness* (1867); *Our Father's Business* (1867); and *Studies of Character* (1868).

John J. Bonar (1803-1891)

John J. Bonar was not as famous as his two younger brothers, Horatius and Andrew, yet all of them were exceptionally good preachers, however they may have differed in style. Like his brothers, he was born in Edinburgh, attended high school there, and then Edinburgh University. He was licensed to preach in 1827. In 1835 he became pastor of St. Andrew's Church at Greenock. During the Ten Years' Conflict previous to the Disruption of 1843, he was a non-intrusionist. His evangelical preaching proved most acceptable to those who had no sympathy for Moderatism, and his congregation grew steadily in numbers and spiritual strength. At the time of the Disruption he became a member of the Free Church. He preached a sermon at Torwood upon the occasion of Donald Cargill's anniversary. It was a masterpiece of persuasive eloquence, and so impressed were his hearers that much of the Larbert district was won for the Free Church.

On the floor of the General Assembly John Bonar was not as influential as his brothers Horatius and Andrew, and he did not speak frequently, although when he did, his words carried weight. It is said that his preaching caused a separation wherever he went, for he distinguished so clearly between right and wrong that his hearers could not remain neutral. Christians who were strongly evangelical gathered around him, while the indifferentists heard him a few times and then went their way.

David Brown (1803-1897)

David Brown was born in 1803 at Aberdeen. Having taken his degree at Aberdeen University in 1821, he studied theology and was licensed in 1826. From 1830 to 1832 he was assistant to Edward Irving in London. He was ordained in 1836 and became pastor of a country congregation near Banff, in Scotland. In 1843 he was one of the men who withdrew from the State Church and formed the Free Church, and during the same year he became pastor of St. James' congregation, Glasgow. In 1857 he became professor of New Testament exegisis, apologetics and Church history at Free Church College, Aberdeen, and from 1876 to 1887 he was principal of this institution. He was moderator of the Free Church in 1885. He served as a director of the National Bible Society of Scotland, and was one of the founders of the Evangelical Alliance.

Dr. Brown published a number of exegetical works, but he is best known because of his connection with the Jamieson, Fausset and Brown Commentary, (six volumes), which appeared 1864-1870. As a member of the New Testament Revision Committee he took a very conservative position. He published a biography of Dr. John Duncan, the noted Hebrew scholar.

Dr. Brown was an able exegetical preacher. During the thirty years of his congregational experience he became known as a Biblical expositor of unusual ability; and during the thirty years spent in teaching, he preached frequently, maintaining his high reputation for his reverent attitude toward the Scriptures. When Robertson Smith, professor of Hebrew, was disciplined by the Free Kirk because of his critical attitude toward Biblical inspiration, David Brown was one of the men who opposed Dr. Smith and his modernism. Like a certain type of fundamentalists, David Brown at times was not able to distinguish between conservatism and literalism. This drove him, more than once, into the chiliasm which appears both in his exegetical writings and in his sermons. He died in 1897 at the age of 94 years.

Principal Brown delighted in revivals. He often sat among the congregation, singing with fervor the Gospel hymns that he loved, and listening with an eager expression to the urgent words of the evangelist. He regarded the central truths of evangelical Christianity as things of utmost importance. He was convinced that our Lord came to seek and save lost sinners, and not to offer a cure for the social and economic ills of the world. He liked to say that the great truths that form the center of Christianity are the ones that must be preached, and not the lesser things that lie on the periphery of religion.

Dr. Brown's most important work was *Christ's Second Coming: Will it be Premillennial?* (1843), and a number of editions were published. *The Apocalypse: its Structure and Primary Predictions* (1891), and *The Restoration of the Jews* (1861), found a place in theological literature. Principal Brown's *Life of the Late John Duncan* (1872), and *The Rev. John Duncan in the Pulpit and at the Communion Table* (1874), preserve for posterity an account of one of

Scotland's most learned and colorful clergymen and professors. Dr. Brown's biography, *David Brown, a Memoir,* was published in 1898 by Dr. W. G. Blaikie.

Robert Lee (1804-1867)

Robert Lee was born in 1804 in Tweedmouth. He attended grammar school at Berwick-on-Tweed, and was graduated with great distinction from St. Andrews University in 1832. He was licensed the same year, ordained in 1833, and became pastor of Iverbrothock. In 1836 he was translated to Campsie and Autermony. In 1843 he was called to Old Greyfriar's, Edinburgh, where he soon won for himself a reputation as an exceptional preacher. In 1847 he became professor of Biblical Criticism in Edinburgh University, at the same time continuing his parochial work.

Robert Lee's reputation as a preacher was considerable, but it became somewhat obscured because of his stormy career as leader in the Innovations Controversy. He was a man of restless spirit, a born reformer, a lover of innovations, and possessed at the same time of great courage, persistence, sharpness of speech and ability in debate. Believing that the form of worship in the Church of Scotland was dull and uninteresting, he set about to reform it. He declared that the Psalms were sung lifelessly, the lengthy free prayers uttered in a way that was tiresome, and the Scriptures read in an unsystematic manner.

Some of his earliest attempts at Old Greyfriar's went no farther than to read the Lessons in some sort of a systematic manner, and to introduce shorter prayers, often prepared in advance. In 1857 he had brought his congregation to the stage where they accepted a very simple liturgical service in which certain prayers were read from printed forms, with an occasional brief response from the congregation. They were encouraged to rise at certain parts of the service, and to kneel for prayer. These innovations caused unrest among the other pastors of Edinburgh, and charges of ritualism were heard. It was feared that the "Puseyism" of England had reached Scotland.

In 1858 the matter was brought before the Assembly, and an effort made to restrain Robert Lee in his attempts at liturgical reform. He defended his position with great vigor, and although the Assembly decided against him, yet his eloquence began to make converts among the younger men.

The Innovations Controversy began about the year 1856, and reached its height in 1859. It was in that year that Lee added to his unpopularity among his fellow clergymen by introducing stained glass windows in his church. This gave grave offense to many of the pastors of the city, for stained glass windows, paintings and carvings had always been looked upon as "graven images," and expressly forbidden by the Scriptures.

In 1865 three young clergymen formed a society for the study of liturgics, and with the intention of preparing fixed forms for public worship and for occasional ministerial acts. Lee was not one of the founders, but he became one of the society's vice-presidents. He had attempted to introduce an "American organ," or harmonium, but protests from his fellow pastors only led to the installation of a pipe organ in 1865. Lee was not a pioneer in this respect, for unsuccessful attempts had been made in 1807 at St. Andrew's in Glasgow, and in 1829 at Roxburgh Place Relief Chapel.[51] Claremont United Presbyterian Church, in Glasgow, had been more successful in 1856. Among the nonconforming bodies, Dr. Lindsay Alexander's Independent congregation in Edinburgh had purchased an organ in 1845.[52]

Robert Lee's pipe organ caused a great commotion, and it led the Assembly to place all innovations in the hands of the presbyteries, forbidding any independent action on the part of any pastor or kirk session. Any change in the form of worship in one congregation was looked upon as a matter of concern to all the other congregations of the community. The Kirk had always treasured her traditions of utmost simplicity in worship. The singing of uninspired hymns, the use of musical instruments of any kind, the reading of a prayer from a printed page, responses by the congregation, specified pericopes such as those of the Anglican Church

[51]. J. R. Fleming, A History of the Church of Scotland (Edinburgh, 1927-33), vol. 1, p. 117.
[52]. Ibid.

and the Lutherans of Germany and the Scandinavian countries, were all looked upon as ritualism, and the middle ground between Protestantism and Romanism.

Robert Lee did not live to see the final triumph of his long battle for worship reform, for in 1866 he suffered a paralytic stroke while riding his horse. He lingered for some months, but finally died in 1867 in Torquay, where he had been taken in the hope that the milder climate would improve his health.

Lee was an able preacher and a determined man in debate. However, his contribution to Scottish preaching was to be more far-reaching than he himself suspected. The *Book of Common Order* was published in 1867 by the new Church Service Society. There was much unfavorable comment, but it was tolerated so long as no presbytery objected. This new attitude of toleration was harmless enough in so far as it was confined to adiaphora. Toleration is an excellent thing so long as it is confined to those things neither commanded nor forbidden by the Word of God; but Church history has shown, more than once, that men often fail to distinguish between matters of indifference on the one hand, and fundamental doctrinal teachings on the other. When religious conventions learn to practice toleration toward unimportant things, there is always the danger that this toleration may be extended to deviations from orthodoxy.

Although Robert Lee cannot be blamed for it, yet the kirk sessions, the presbyteries, the synods and the Assembly learned quickly enough to pass resolutions which seemed on the surface to forbid the use of church organs and liturgies and uninspired hymns, but at the same time left a way of escape somewhere. Deliberative bodies gradually fell into the habit of passing resolutions that appeared to be extremely conservative, and yet left room for freedom of action on the part of the liberals. The day finally came when both the State Church and the Free were willing to tolerate men whose attitude toward Biblical criticism might have caused gravest concern to their forefathers.

This gradual decline in the matter of doctrinal discipline, for which especially the Free Church was noted in its earlier days, was in time to open the doors to liberalism. It led to a breakdown of the old type of Calvinistic orthodoxy, and a gradual substitution of ethical preaching for the old expository kind for which Scotland had so long been noted — with the exception, of course, of the Moderates.

Dr. Lee wrote *The Family and its Duties* (1863); *The Reform of the Church in Worship, Government and Doctrine* (1864); and *Prayers for Public Worship* (1857). A volume of his sermons appeared in 1874. *The Life and Remains of Dr. Robert Lee,* by R. H. Story, was published in 1870.

William Cunningham (1805-1861)

One of the most majestic preachers of Disruption days was Dr. William Cunningham. He was born in 1805 at Hamilton, near Glasgow. While attending Edinburgh University he was influenced by the evangelical preaching of Dr. Robert Gordon, whose remarkable sermons were stirring both the University and the townspeople. In 1828 young Cunningham was licensed to preach, and two years later he was ordained, becoming assistant pastor of Greenock Church. In 1834 he was called to Trinity College Church, Edinburgh. The people were not slow to discover his exceptional gifts, and the young man of 30 years became one of Edinburgh's foremost preachers. In 1833, the General Assembly was astonished when this young clergyman arose and delivered an address, two hours in length, on the doctrine of the call. This led one of the older leaders to declare that they had among them a theological mind with which the Scottish Church would have to reckon. In 1842 Cunningham's fame as a preacher and a theologian had reached America, and Princeton conferred upon him a Doctor's degree.

During the days of controversy that preceded the Disruption of 1843, Dr. Cunningham was not silent, and together with Robert Candlish he became one of the close associates of Dr. Thomas Chalmers. A less resolute young man might have hesitated to give up Trinity College Church and the great congregations that had been gathering each Sunday, but on the memorable 18th of May, his tall figure was one of the first to emerge from St. Andrew's church. When the new Free Church established their New College at Edinburgh, Cunningham was made a member of the faculty and was associated with Dr. Chalmers, David Welsh and John Duncan. Toward the end of 1843, he was sent to America, together with Mr. Henry Ferguson of Dundee. He addressed gatherings in some 40 large cities, setting forth the principles of the Free Church of Scotland. With Thomas Guthrie and Henry Grey he went to London and addressed meetings that overflowed Exeter Hall and other large places of Assembly. Meanwhile he was lecturing on Church History and Apologetics at New College, then in temporary quarters in a building in George street. It was not until 1850 that the new buildings on the Mound were ready for occupancy. In 1847, at the death of Dr. Chalmers, Cunningham was made principal of New College.

The death of Thomas Chalmers was a blow to the new Free Church, coming as it did but four years after the Disruption. However, new and powerful leaders appeared at once, and among these the most influential were Robert Candlish and William Cunningham. These two men were not always in full agreement. They differed in the matter of the establishment of colleges in Glasgow and Aberdeen, yet in most instances they worked side by side, and Candlish's leadership and Cunningham's remarkable skill in debate guided the Free Church through two difficult decades. Time and again did the theological acumen and the massive scholarship of William Cunningham silence some zealous opponent.

Cunningham was a man of solid learning, one of the ablest theologians of his generation, a debater with almost no equals, and an exceptional preacher. His sermons were scholarly, yet clear, expository in their method, and decidedly evangelical. He had no sympathy with the new theological ideas which had begun to invade Scotland from Halle and other German centers shortly after the Disruption. He accepted a verbally inspired Bible as the one rule of Christian doctrine and living, and Jesus Christ as the only Saviour of a sin-cursed race. Unfortunately he defended the old-time Calvinistic views in regard to Election and to the Lord's Supper. In his preaching and in his debates on the floor of the Assembly he never failed to defend thoroughly

conservative doctrine and practice, as these things are understood by Calvinists of the old school.   However, in 1861, he
astonished his conservative friends by opposing James Gibson, another defender of Old School Calvinism, in a debate
regarding the United Presbyterian Church.   Principal Cunningham had become convinced that doctrinal differences no
longer existed between these two leading Free Church
bodies.   This declaration was recalled in later years by a
liberal group, when the church union controversy was
agitating Scotland, and Cunningham's words were quoted in
an unwarranted manner in order to further their arguments.

Principal Cunningham was made Moderator of the Free
Church General Assembly, and in his address to that body
in 1859 he called attention to a remarkable awakening of
religious life which had appeared in Scotland and in parts
of Ireland during the previous year.   Preaching missions had
become very popular, and laymen as well as pastors were
conducting them.   Some of the laymen were University men,
and in some cases they were men of wealth and social position.   Other popular missioners were men who had been
weavers, stone-cutters, colliers, and in some cases even fish-
curers and prize-fighters.   While Dr. Cunningham rejoiced
in the widespread demand for evangelical preaching, yet the
Assembly was faced with the problem of lay preaching.
There were many of the old Scottish school of thought who
declared that no man should preach without a call. A specific
case was that of Brownlow North, a grandson of a bishop
and grand-nephew of Lord North.   His early life had been
worldly, but he had given up his careless manner of living
and had become a successful lay preacher.   Men such as Dr.
John ("Rabbi") Duncan opposed North because of his lack
of a formal theological education.   It was due largely to the
sound judgment of Principal Cunningham that such cases
were put into the hands of a committee that included the
Free Church theological faculty and three other clergymen
of unquestioned theological learning, who were to examine
all such men and determine whether or not they were eligible
to preach.

The State Church was faced with the same problem,
but they settled it in a less direct manner.   One of the pop-

ular lay preachers was Reginald Radcliffe, Esq., a well-known attorney, who had preached with enormous success to gatherings of University students. An attempt was made in the State Church, in 1859, to close the pulpits of their denomination against such men. After a long debate they passed a resolution which prohibited laymen from preaching at the Sunday services — but with the tacit agreement that there could be no objection to the duly called pastor who might invite qualified laymen to address gatherings on other occasions.

Dr. Cunningham was a man of noble personality. Dr. J. W. Alexander, of New York, gives his impressions as follows: "He is the most satisfactory foreigner I have seen. By the Scottish papers I perceive he ranks among the first four or five of the Free Church. Height about six feet, and large in proportion — a stout but finely formed man, very handsomely dressed, and in an eminent degree the gentleman in everything. . . . Powerful reasoning and sound judgment seemed to be his characteristics, and he is a walking treasury of facts, dates and ecclesiastical law. I heard him for an hour on Friday in a speech to the students. Indescribable Scottish intonation, but little idiom and convulsion of body, but flowing elegant language, and amazing power in presenting an argument. . . . He is a powerful fellow, and a noble instance of what may be done without any pathos or any decoration." [53]

Principal Cunningham died in 1861. His principal writings, all of which were published after his death, include *Historical Theology*, 2 vols. (1862); *Discussion of Church Principles* (1863); *The Reformers and the Theology of the Reformation* (1863); *Sermons from 1828-1860* (1872); and *Lectures on Subjects Connected with Natural Theology* (1878). With the exception of the collection of sermons, these works are based upon his classroom lectures. A good biography, *Life of Principal William Cunningham,* was written by Robert Rainy and J. Mackintosh (1867). The well-known Cunningham Lectures were established at Edinburgh in 1864 in memory of Principal Cunningham. These, at

[53]. Rainy and Mackintosh, *Life of Principal Cunningham* (Edinburgh, 1867), p. 203.

least six in number, are delivered annually on some subject connected with the Bible and with Christian doctrine.

Alexander J. Scott (1805-1866)

Alexander J. Scott was born in 1805 at Greenock, where his father was a clergyman. Both parents were people of high culture. The boy was educated at the grammar school in Greenock, and at the age of 14 he entered Glasgow University, where he took his degree in 1826. He was licensed the same year and became a tutor at Edinburgh. There he met Thomas Erskine and Macleod Campbell, and came under their influence. He became interested in Campbell's views in regard to the universal love of God and the unlimited Atonement. This led him to discard the rigid Calvinism of the Church of Scotland, which he did only after a severe inward struggle.

In 1828 Edward Irving invited him to go to London and become his assistant at the Scottish Church in Regent Square. Scott became interested in the gift of tongues mentioned in the New Testament, and while on a visit to his native Scotland he preached a sermon on this subject. As a result of his sermon, several people professed to have received this gift. When Edward Irving heard of this incident, he became greatly interested and finally fell a victim to this fanaticism. Scott, on the contrary, soon lost confidence in it. This led to a less cordial feeling between himself and Edward Irving.

In 1830 Alexander Scott was called to the Scottish congregation at Woolwich, a London suburb. He declined to subscribe to the doctrines of particular election and a limited Atonement, declaring his belief in universal grace and his rejection of the divine obligation to observe the Sabbath. He addressed a letter to the moderator of the London presbytery, in which he made these things clear. The case came before the General Assembly in 1831 — the same Assembly that had just deposed Macleod Campbell. Not a voice was raised in defense of Scott except that of his own father. He was given a severe reprimand, deprived of his license to preach, and all pastors were warned not to permit him to preach in their parishes. Young Scott returned to Woolwich where he gathered a small congregation, built a small church and continued to serve there as an independent pastor. In 1848 he was elected professor of the English language and literature at the University of London. He lectured in London and throughout England. In 1851 he was made principal of Owens College, Manchester, where he taught several subjects in addition to his administrative duties.

Alexander Scott was a splendid speaker, and had all the qualities of a good preacher, but his congregation was always small. Like his friend Baldwin Brown he detested publicity and he made no effort to attract large congregations. He preached to a small, but very select group of people. Among his personal friends he numbered Carlyle, Thomas Erskine and Maurice. He had been called a Unitarian, but this is unfair, for he accepted the doctrine of the Incarnation, which he believed is the central teaching of Christianity. He fell into the error in laying more stress upon the Incarnation than upon the Passion, Death and Resurrection of our Saviour. Calvinism in its old-time harsher forms was the dominant note in the Assembly of 1831. Today the very things that were thought to be heresy are preached without apology by men who are looked upon as thoroughly conservative.

William Tasker (c. 1805-1879)

One of Scotland's most remarkable preachers was William Tasker, who was born at Perth in the early years of the nineteenth century. His father died before the boy was 14, making it necessary for the lad to lay aside his school books and support the family. After working for a merchant, he taught school at Blathayock, Tealing and Falkland. Next he became a lay missionary at Port Glasgow.

It was not until 1844 that he was able to enter New College, Edinburgh. Thomas Chalmers at once realized his worth. Calling him in one day he asked Tasker, "Will you take the West Port Mission for £80 per year? I have started a new congregation in a tanner's loft, and I need a man to assist me." William Tasker pleaded with Dr. Chalmers, declaring that he was but poorly qualified. "Let me be the judge of that, sir," was the reply.

In April, 1845, William Tasker began his work in the West Port, as assistant to Dr. Chalmers. When the latter died in 1847, Tasker was ordained and assumed full charge of the congregation. The work was discouraging and the progress slow at first. When Dr. Chalmers preached in the morning, the tan-loft was filled to overflowing. At the afternoon service Tasker preached to seven or eight grown people and a few children. The mission was a result of the "territorial scheme" of Thomas Chalmers, and it was located in a neighborhood noted for the lawless character of its inhabitants.

On a certain rainy Sunday evening the congregation numbered but a scant dozen people. Telling them to wait a few minutes, Tasker hurried to the head of the narrow street, borrowed a chair which he mounted, and began to sing a metrical Psalm in a loud voice. Doors and windows were opened, and it was not long until a great crowd collected to see what madman was conducting a religious service in the downpour of rain. Tasker read a Scripture lesson, sang another hymn and then gave out his text. Then he said, "The sermon will follow, but because of the inclement weather, it will be preached in yon tanner's loft. I want you all to come with me." He returned the chair to the astonished owner, and hurried to the tan-loft, followed by several hundred people.

During his lifetime, Dr. Chalmers either preached himself, or else attended the service when William Tasker preached. One Sunday evening Tasker was but poorly prepared, and to his great relief he found that Dr. Chalmers was absent. He had not preached five minutes when he looked back and saw the dreaded figure of Dr. Chalmers in the rear of the building. For a moment Tasker was speechless. As the two walked home together after the service, the rare tact of Chalmers became evident. He said to his assistant, "Your discourse was full of excellent material, and fitted to prove very useful; but to me the most effective was your solemn pause. Cultivate the pause, sir. Cultivate the pause."

William Tasker was taken ill, and his physician ordered a complete rest for six months, telling him to go to Gibraltar, where the climate was less rigorous. At Gibraltar Mr. Tasker found a colony of convicts from the British Isles, whose spiritual welfare had been neglected by the post chaplain, an archdeacon. Tasker secured permission from the keeper of the prison to preach to the convicts. The archdeacon, who had little love for Nonconformists, informed Tasker rather curtly that these men were under his own spiritual care. Tasker protested, and finally the archdeacon agreed to allow Tasker to preach to the convicts, with the understanding that only those men who were affiliated with the Free Church of Scotland would be allowed to attend. The matter was explained to the convicts, and cards were distributed upon which each man was to name his church connection. When the cards were collected, practically every man claimed membership in the Free Church of Scotland. The archdeacon saw the humor of the situation, and Tasker was allowed to preach to congregations that filled the chapel.

William Tasker's rare ability to deliver a rebuke without giving offense is still proverbial in Edinburgh. One of his most regular members was a woman who lived directly opposite the place of worship, but who always came in when the sermon was half over. "When are you going to flit farther away from us?" Mr. Tasker inquired of her one day. "If you lived a bit farther away, you might manage to get to church on time." On another occasion he met an old woman who had not been attending church very regularly. "Oh, Mr. Tasker," she said with a note of insincerity, "I'm no' that verra strong, and I whiles gang into St. Cuthbert's Kirk." "Have ye no heard the old Scottish saying, Mary, that 'it's an ill dog tha' has twa hames?'" asked Tasker. Meeting a man on the street one day, Mr. Tasker asked him why he had been neglecting his church. "If ye were compelled to choose between a good thing and one that is not so good, which would ye do?" asked the man evasively. "Well, I certainly should not neglect them both, as you do," replied Tasker. A woman once told Tasker that she could not join his church because she owned a little shop which she kept open on Sunday. "I've got to live," she said. "I see no necessity for that," replied Tasker. The woman was aghast.

"Can you name anybody in the West Port who would thank God for your existence — that you ever did them any real good for time or for Eternity?" asked the pastor.

William Tasker conducted three services on Sunday, and he insisted that only Law and Gospel be preached. As the work grew gradually, James Jolly was called as his assistant, some years after the death of Dr. Chalmers. The assistant suggested that the evening service be devoted to a popular lecture on some famous Bible character. Mr. Tasker rejected the suggestion emphatically. "Three Sunday services are little enough to set forth all the riches of the Gospel," was his reply.

Mr. Tasker was a preacher of exceptional gifts, with great powers of persuasiveness. No man in Edinburgh could excel him in his ability to bring comfort and strength to the sorrowing. His sermon on "Elijah's Translation," following the death of Dr. Chalmers, was considered by many as one of the greatest memorial sermons of the century. The text was, "My father, my father, the chariot of Israel, and the horsemen thereof." [54] The sermon was printed and for a long time it enjoyed a large circulation. [55]

"His preaching was always the delight of the people of God, and, by the divine blessing, reached the consciences of the ungodly, containing as it did such a fulness of Gospel truth declared with courageous faithfulness and delivered with the most intense and sometimes vehement earnestness of manner." [56]   After one of his sermons preached on the Sunday following the funeral of one of his members, a man and his wife came into the vestry. "Mr. Tasker," said the woman, "my husband here is a member of the State Church o' Sco'land, and I'm a United Presbyterian. We couldna agree what church to join, so we joined nowheres. But efter the service this morning I said to my husband, 'Oh John, wasna yon a la-men-table sermon?' so we decided then and there to join your church."

William Tasker received a number of calls from important congregations, and among them an urgent call from

---

[54]. II Kings, 2, 12.
[55]. Wm. Tasker, *Elijah's Translation* (Edinburgh, 1847).
[56]. Jas. Jolly, *The Story of the West Port Church* (Edinburgh, 1882), p. 34.

the wealthiest and most influential congregation in the Free Church, but he declined them all. His work was in the West Port, and nothing could induce him to leave it. Chalmers, before he died, declared that Tasker was a man with "distinguished abilities as a preacher" and praised him publicly for having declined calls to important pulpits. Mr. Tasker served the West Port Church for 34 years, and before he died he had built up a congregation of almost a thousand communicants, and had the joy of seeing the West Port underworld transformed into a community of well-behaved, church-going Christians, with literally every child enrolled in his parochial schools. Some men are remembered long after they die because of their eloquence, but William Tasker had more than eloquence. He was able, by the power of Law and Gospel, to transform the terrible wynds of the West Port into a community of exemplary Christian people. "And they that be wise shall shine as the brightness of the firmament; and they that turn many to righteousness as the stars for ever and ever." [57]

Robert S. Candlish (1806-1873)

Robert S. Candlish, for years one of the most influential leaders of the Free Church of Scotland, as well as one of its most eloquent preachers, was born in 1806 at Edinburgh, where his father was a medical professor. The family name was MacCandlish, but it had been shortened to Candlish. After his elementary school training, Robert Candlish entered Glasgow University at the age of twelve, and was graduated in 1823. During these college days, Thomas Chalmers was pastor of St. John's Church, and Edward Irving was his assistant. For some reason Irving was not popular, but the young Candlish was one of his admirers.

In 1823 Candlish entered the Divinity Hall and completed the three sessions' work in less than a single session, but because of his youth he attended the full course. Dr. Stephen Gill, a professor of divinity at Glasgow, was a man of decided evangelical views, and it was largely through his influence that Robert Candlish became a pronounced evangecial. He was licensed in 1828 and became assistant pastor

---

[57]. Daniel 12, 3.

at St. Andrew's, Glasgow, and then at Bonhill, Dumbarton-shire. Although not yet ordained, he preached twice each Sunday both at Glasgow and later at Bonhill. In those places he prepared and delivered some of the sermons that were to bring him national fame a few years later at Edinburgh. While at Bonhill he began to attract attention because of his fervent evangelical preaching.

In 1831 Dr. Andrew Thompson, one of Edinburgh's most distinguished preachers, died. A successor was called, but his health soon failed. Among those asked to supply this important pulpit was Robert Candlish, and so great was the impression that he made that many were eager to call the youthful Bonhill clergyman as pastor of St. George's. During the summer of 1833, not long after the dismissal of the unfortunate Edward Irving, Candlish was asked to supply for four Sundays at the Scottish National Church in London. There the people were determined to call him, but mean-while an urgent call had come from St. George's, Edinburgh, which he accepted. He was ordained in 1834 and began his work at St. George's. There the young Candlish soon took his place among the brilliant group of men who filled the pulpits of Edinburgh's most prominent churches.

In 1839, when but 33 years of age, he delivered an address at the General Assembly that made a decided im-pression upon the older men, who saw readily enough that here was one of the Kirk's coming leaders. In 1843 he withdrew from the Established Church with the 474 founders of the Free Church, and became pastor of Free St. George's, where he remained until his death thirty years later. He was urged in 1847 to become the successor of Dr. Chalmers, as professor of divinity at New College. Alexander Stewart, of Cromarty, who had been selected as his successor at St. George's, died before he could be inducted, and thus it was that Candlish remained with his congregation the remainder of his days. In 1862 he was elected principal of New College. He accepted the honor, but with the understanding that he would be permitted to remain as pastor of St. George's. In 1870, when the burden of his double duties became too great, Alexander Whyte was called as his colleague.

From the death of Dr. Chalmers onward, much of the burden of establishing the new Free Church fell upon Dr. Candlish. He proved himself a leader of rare talents, a Church statesman of the first rank, and a man noted for his sound judgment and his solid conservatism. Among a multitude of other labors, he was tireless in his efforts to establish parochial schools throughout the Free Church, and in this he was successful to a degree. In 1845 he became one of the founders of the Evangelical Alliance.

Dr. Candlish was a man of peculiar appearance. He was small in stature, but with an exceptionally large head, crowned with a great shock of unruly hair. His pulpit mannerisms were abrupt. Before the close of the second hymn he would rise suddenly from his chair, walk rapidly to the pulpit and announce his text in a tone that was almost defiant. His gestures were not graceful. He might clutch at his black robe with both hands, or pound the pulpit with his fist, or brandish the open Bible at arm's length, all the while uttering a vehement stream of eloquence. All of these mannerisms were forgotten quickly by his hearers, because of his tremendous earnestness, his fervid oratory and his amazing spiritual and intellectual power. He was a man of emphatic personality. Many a young pastor attempted to imitate him, even to his unkempt hair and his habit of springing suddenly from his chair and hurrying to the pulpit. They imitated his peculiarities, but none could imitate his power as an evangelical preacher, nor his expository gifts, nor his exceptional personality.

"Here was an instance," says one who knew him personally and often heard him preach, "of a man pushing his way into the very front of pulpit orators, in spite of many positive blemishes, by the pure force of his intellectual pre-eminence, spiritual insight, and impassioned fervor, and there were not wanting many imitators who thought that they had clothed themselves in the strength of their model when they succeeded only in putting on one of his weaknesses." [58]

---

[58]. W. M. Taylor, *The Scottish Pulpit* (New York, 1887), p. 268.

Dr. Candlish published a three-volume exposition of the Book of Genesis, a number of books of sermons and other writings. His sermons read well today. They are logical in arrangement as a rule, clear in language, forceful and often original in thought, and of a definite evangelical tone. Thought follows thought in rapid succession, leading up to a climax. Here, for example, is the climax and the conclusion of his sermon on Isaiah 55, 6, "Seek ye the Lord while He may be found." Imagine the following, delivered in a veritable torrent of rushing oratory:

"Thus to win Christ and be found in Him, how blessed! 'To be found in Him' — when? Now, O my brother! most emphatically now! Not an hour, not a moment to be lost! Now is the accepted time; now, and only now.

"When? does one ask again? When but always, in all circumstances, evermore? When enemies reproach you, when your heart misgives you, when doubts arise within, and dark questionings invade your peace; when difficulties are started which you cannot solve, and the ground seems giving way under your feet: Oh, to be found in Christ then, as little children nestling in His bosom, not careful to deal with every foe, or with any fear, content to look up into His loving face and say, 'Thou shalt answer, Lord, for me!' To be found in Christ, when hell threatens and all its pains take hold on you; in Christ, who Himself descended thither and spoiled all its principalities on His cross: to be found in Christ when Heaven opens, that you may sit with Him in the heavenly places; to be found in Christ when earth vexes, and all on earth is felt to be vanity, still able to say, 'If I have nothing else worth living for, to me to live is Christ'; to be found in Christ, when duty calls, in Him who said: 'I must be about My Father's business'; to be found in Christ, when sin besets, in Him who said, 'Get thee behind Me Satan'; to be found in Christ when sorrow comes, in Him who wept at Bethany, and as He went on His way to Calvary, could still say, 'The cup which My Father giveth Me, shall I not drink it?' to be found in Christ in the hour of death, in Him who cried, 'Father, into Thy hands I commend My spirit!' to be found in Christ in the day of doom, in Him to

Whom, at His own bar, you may lift the living, trusting voice,
'Thou hast answered, Lord, for me.'

"To be found in Christ! When? does one ask? When,
but through endless ages, in those realms of unfading beauty
and bliss, where all the family of God, angels and men together, are gathered into one in Christ? Then shall ye be
found in Christ, associated forever with all the holy ones;
found in Christ, sharing His glory and His joy, to the praise
of God the Father, world without end. Amen.

"And what of you, who in death, on the judgment day,
throughout eternity, are not found in Christ? What is to
become of you, when, too late, the discovery flashes upon
you that you have not won Christ, and are not to be found
in Him? Where are you to be found? In whom? Lying in
the wicked one, doomed to everlasting fire prepared for the
devil and his angels; none to answer for you then; hell opening its wide jaws to receive you.

"Oh! ye Christless, Godless men! Is it not high time for
you to awake out of sleep! You may have some sort of
goodness, in which you think you may perhaps wrap yourselves in the trying hour. You may lean on a name, a profession, a creed, a form; or some amiable qualities you seem
to possess, some decent virtues you cultivate, some pious
deeds you do. But will these be gain to you in the day when
the secrets of all hearts are revealed, and your deep aliena-
tion from God, amid them all, is relentlessly laid bare? What
a discovery to make then, that they are loss, that they are
all dung! to discover that then; when there is no Christ to
be won, and all hope of your being found in Him is gone
forever! Oh! rather let the discovery be made to you now
by the Holy Ghost, and acquiesced in by you, in your
quickened conscience and broken heart: 'Seek ye the Lord
while He may be found'." [59]

During his last illness, Dr. Candlish often asked Alexander Whyte, his assistant, to read certain Psalms to him.
Again and again he exclaimed, "O man! I wish I had committed all the Psalms to memory!" When the end drew
near he sent for Robert Rainy, and as Rainy knelt at his

[59]. *Sermons by Robert S. Candlish, D.D.* (New York, 1874), pp.
217-219.

bedside, Dr. Candlish laid a withered hand upon him and committed the college and the General Assembly to him, and his congregation to Alexander Whyte. Dr. Thomas Guthrie preached the funeral sermon, ending with the well-known words: "Friend and brother, comrade in the fight, companion in tribulation! Farewell, but not forever! May my soul, when the hour comes, be with thine!"

Dr. Candlish was the author of more than a dozen books. Among these mention should be made of *Lectures on Genesis*, 3 volumes (1842); *The Atonement* (1845); *Life in a Risen Saviour* (1858); *Reason and Revelation* (1859); *The Two Great Commandments* (1860), a series of sermons on Romans 12; *The Fatherland of God* (1864); and *The First Epistle of John*, 2 volumes (1866). A book of sermons, *The Gospel of Forgiveness* (1873), his *Expository Discourses on I John* and a posthumous work, *Sermons of Dr. R. S. Candlish* (1874), are among his homiletical works. Biographies include William Williams', *Memorials of R. S. Candlish* (1880); J. L. Watson's *Life of R. S. Candlish* (1882), and a memoir by his son, James S. Candlish.

Alexander Duff (1806-1878)

Alexander Duff, the first of the Church of Scotland's missionaries to India, was a preacher of remarkable power. He was born on a farm known as Auchnahyle, near Moulin, Perthshire, in 1806. After a good elementary training, he entered the University of St. Andrews, where he was influenced greatly by Thomas Chalmers.

He was ordained in 1829 and set sail for India. He was shipwrecked twice on the journey, and lost all his books and other belongings. In 1830 he founded an English school in Calcutta, in which the Bible was given an important place. The school prospered beyond expectation, and it was not long until 600 to 700 pupils were enrolled.

In 1834 he returned to Scotland, and went throughout the country speaking on missions, and winning friends for the cause wherever he went. He returned to India in 1840. In 1843 the Secession took place, and every missionary joined Dr. Chalmers and the founders of the Free Church.

They lost their property, including the school at Calcutta, but a new school was founded without delay.

In 1849 Alexander Duff visited England and appeared before Parliament in the interest of a vast system of education for India, which was to include schools of every kind, from primary schools to universities and technical schools. His great zeal and his eloquence won the support of the first Lord Halifax and many other influential people.

In 1854 Dr. Duff visited America, and made a triumphal tour of a number of cities. His visit here attracted wide attention, and it was declared at the time that no visitor since the days of George Whitefield had been so well received. In 1856 he returned to India, and helped found the University of Calcutta. In 1864 he returned to Scotland, and became professor of missions at New College, Edinburgh. He died in 1878, at the age of 72.

As a preacher, Dr. Duff was remarkable. He was six feet tall, ruddy of countenance, and spoke with a decided Scottish accent. He was an energetic man, and when presenting a cause to an assembly of people, his earnestness has been described as "apoplectic." His sermons and addresses were lengthy, but so full of thought and delivered with such a degree of fervor that he could hold the close attention of his hearers for two to three hours. At a great farewell gathering in Free High Church, Edinburgh, just before he sailed for India, he spoke for two hours. In 1834, when but 28 years of age, he appeared before the General Assembly of the Church of Scotland and held the attention of the great gathering for three hours.

Dr. Duff's 35 years in India were interrupted by two trips to Scotland and one to America, and during those trips he delivered many sermons and addresses, and by his eloquent presentation of the cause, he aroused wide interest in missions in Scotland, England and America. Not only was he a famous missionary, but he was one of the most convincing pulpit orators of the middle decades of the nineteenth century. While Dr. Duff's five or six books are not particularly significant, yet they are worthy of a place in the section of one's library devoted to missions. Among them are: *Missions the Chief End of the Christian Church*

(1839); *India and Indian Missions* (1839); *Missionary Addresses* (1850); and *Addresses to the Assembly* (1851). The standard biography is G. Smith's *Life of Alexander Duff*, 2 volumes (1879). W. Paton's *A Pioneer of Missionary Education* is worthy of study.

David King (1806-1883)

David King, a forceful preacher of the United Presbyterian Church, was born in 1806 in Montrose, where his father was a clergyman. He entered Aberdeen University in 1820, but a year later he enrolled in Edinburgh University. He studied theology in Glasgow with John Dick, of the Secession Church. In 1830 he became pastor of the First United Secession Church of Dalkeith. From 1833 to 1855 he was pastor of Greyfriars' Secession Church in Glasgow. Here his preaching proved to have a wide appeal to young men, and many of them from various denominations formed the habit of attending his church. Many students came to hear him.

In 1847 he took an active part in the formation of the United Presbyterian Church. He was also a leader in the Evangelical Alliance. In 1848 he visited the United States and Jamaica. In 1860 he founded a congregation in Bayswater, London, which he served for nine years. In 1869 he was called to Morningside, near Edinburgh, but four years later he resigned because of failing health. The last ten years of his life were spent in retirement, but he preached as his physical condition permitted. David King was a clear thinker and an earnest preacher, and there were times when he almost seemed to depart from the old Calvinistic teaching that salvation is offered to the elect only, and to teach that there is an offer of salvation through the Gospel to all mankind. At the famous John Brown heresy trial in 1845, it was Dr. King who offered a resolution that left room for the teaching that salvation is offered to all mankind, and not merely to the elect, the others being passed by.

David King's writings include: *Ruling Eldership in the Christian Church* (1844); *On the Lord's Supper* (1846); *Principles of Geology in Relation to Religion* (1850), written at a time when men were disturbed by the claims of science;

A Concordance on the Basis of Cruden; Exposition and Defense of the Presbyterian Form of Church Government (1853); and *The Power of Zeal* (1867).

The United Presbyterians, considering their relatively small numerical strength, have produced their full share of exceptional preachers such as David King. The books that these men published, and the biographies written after their death, seem to have been issued in comparatively small editions. Thus it is that the famous United Presbyterian preachers are not always known as widely as are those of the Established (Presbyterian) Church and the Free Church. John McKerrow, an eloquent preacher, published his *History of the Secession Church* (1839), a bulky volume, and in its closing chapters he includes short biographies of the founding fathers and the most famous preachers of his denomination. Among them he mentions a certain Clarkson of Ayr, known as the Scottish Whitefield, whose power in the pulpit was so great that large crowds followed him from town to town. Certainly such men deserve to be more widely known. In the case of David King, there is a short memoir by his wife, published in 1885, together with a few of his sermons.

Charles Calder Mackintosh (1806-1868)

One of the Free Church pastors, highly esteemed throughout the Scottish Highlands, was Calder Mackintosh, of Tain. He was born in 1806 at Tain, where his father, Dr. Angus Mackintosh, was pastor. After attending Tain Academy he entered Aberdeen University at the unusual age of eleven. His divinity studies were pursued at Glasgow University. Having come across the writings of Thomas Halyburton, he was deeply impressed. In his youth he was overcome by a lingering sense of unworthiness that led him to doubt that the mercies of the Lord, however richly bestowed upon others, were really meant for him. After months of suffering he went to his father who gave him great help by assuring him that it delights the Saviour's heart to pardon iniquity, transgression and sin; and where sin hath abounded, there will grace abound much more.[60]

---

[60]. See Wm. Taylor, *Memorials of the Life and Ministry of Charles Calder Mackintosh,*

Calder Mackintosh was licensed to preach in 1827, and in 1828 he was ordained as assistant to his father. In 1831 when the elder Mackintosh died, his son became his successor. In 1840 the remarkable awakening of spiritual zeal that had been felt at Kilsyth, Dundee and elsewhere, was felt at Tain as well. As a result of the preaching of Law and Gospel there was a remarkable increase in spiritual zeal in the congregation, and a marked improvement in the daily lives of the people of Tain.

The Disruption followed three years later, and Mr. Mackintosh and his congregation united with the Free Church. It was his custom to preach three times every Sunday. His strength, never too great, gave way gradually, and not long before his death he resigned and went to Dunoon, where the duties were lighter.

Dr. Mackintosh was a man of spiritual fervor, and an unusual preacher. Dr. John Kennedy paid highest tribute to his ability in the pulpit, saying that "his clear views of truth welled through a sanctified intellect from the depths of a broken heart, in words so fitly chosen that there was never one superfluous nor obscure. I never could listen to him without an impression that he had asked and received his very words from God. . . . To commend Christ as all in all was his absorbing ambition in the pulpit." [61]

Alexander D. Davidson (1807-1872)

Alexander D. Davidson was born in Aberdeen in 1807. He was educated in Aberdeen University. In 1832 he was ordained and given South Church, Aberdeen. In 1836 he was translated to West Church. Davidson was extremely popular as a preacher, and students and the cultured people of Aberdeen flocked to his services. He had an important part in the overthrow of Moderatism, and in influencing not only his own large congregation, but the other churches of Aberdeen as well, to return to evangelical Christianity. In 1843, when the Disruption took place, Davidson and his congregation seceded and became members of the new Free Church of Scotland.

---

[61]. David Beaton, *Some Noted Ministers of the Northern Highlands* (Inverness, 1929), p. 231.

When Alexander Davidson died, he left 2,000 or more complete sermons, carefully prepared. A number of these were published after his death. Davidson was not only a man of decided evangelical convictions himself, but he was able, through his preaching, to persuade others to a decision. It was largely his influence that caused Aberdeen to be an evangelical stronghold for years.

John McFarlane (1807-1874)

John McFarlane, who was a popular preacher for 31 years in Scotland and then for 13 years in London, was born in 1807 in Dunfermline, where his father was a clergyman. He entered Edinburgh University at the age of 13, and in 1823 he entered Glasgow University. In 1825 he went to the divinity hall of the United Secession Church. He was licensed to preach in 1830, and ordained in 1831, becoming pastor of Kincardine-on-Forth. In 1840 he became pastor of the Nicholson Street United Presbyterian church in Glasgow. His ability and popularity as a preacher attracted attention, and in 1861 he was persuaded to go to London, to become pastor of a congregation in Clapham. It was a small group of 36 people, but John McFarlane's ability as a preacher caused the little congregation to grow from 36 to 800 communicants in a little over a decade. John McFarlane published a number of books of sermons and devotional writings, which were well received in their day.

William Hanna (1808-1882)

William Hanna was born of Scottish parents at Belfast in 1808. His father was a prominent clergyman of the Presbyterian Church. Young Hanna attended Glasgow and Edinburgh Universities, was ordained in 1835 and became pastor of a Presbyterian congregation in East Kilbride, not far from Glasgow. In 1837 he was given a congregation in Skirling, Peebleshire, and at the time of the disruption of 1843, Hanna and his entire congregation united with the Free Church. In 1847 he became editor of *The North British Review,* and in 1850 he was called to Free St. John's Church, Edinburgh, as colleague to Dr. Thomas Guthrie.

William Hanna's great gift to the Christian world was his excellent four-volume biography of his father-in-law, Dr. Thomas Chalmers, published 1849-52, and reprinted several times. He edited and published the *Posthumous Works of Thomas Chalmers*, 9 volumes (1847-49), and *A Selection from the Correspondence of Thomas Chalmers* (1853). Other works are: *Our Lord's Life on Earth*, 6 volumes (1869); *The Last Days of Our Lord's Passion* (1862); *On Religion* (1857); *Wycliffe and the Huguenots* (1860); *The Ministry in Galilee* (1868); *The Forty Days after Our Lord's Resurrection* (1863); *The Earlier Years of Our Lord's Life on Earth* (1864); *Letters of Thomas Erskine of Linlathen* (1877); *The Close of the Ministry* (1869); and the important work, *Essays by Ministers of the Free Church of Scotland* (1858), which he edited. He published a book of Lenten sermons entitled *The Passion Week* (1866).

James Begg (1808-1883)

James Begg, one of the staunch defenders of conservatism in the Scottish Free Kirk, was born in 1808 in New Monkland, near Glasgow. His father was a clergyman of the Scottish Kirk. James Begg was educated in the parochial school in his native village, and in Glasgow University. After his theological studies he was licensed in 1829, ordained in 1830 and given the parish of Maxwelltown, Dumfriesshire. Shortly afterward he was colleague at Lady Glenorchy's Chapel, Edinburgh. In 1831 he was called to Middle Parish Church, Paisley, and in 1835 to Liberton, near Edinburgh. In 1843, at the time of the Disruption, he went to Newington, Edinburgh, where he served for 40 years.

In his earlier years, James Begg's eloquent pleas for work among the slums and the tenements of the larger cities, stirred the Assembly. What he had observed in Edinburgh, Glasgow and elsewhere horrified him. Begg was a fine preacher. Possessed of an excellent appearance, a commanding voice, magnetic personality, a cheerful way of presenting even an unpopular subject, and an endless store of good nature, Begg was able to command a ready hearing, and at times to impress even his opponents. In church conventions, in the pulpit and on the lecture platform, Begg

became a volunteer crusader for the forgotten tenement
dwellers, and in urging not only what is now called city
mission work, but better housing as well. He succeeded, in
1858, in getting a survey made of the shocking conditions
among the poor. In Edinburgh alone, the Athens of
Northern Europe, it was shown that 13,209 families, numbering 50,000 people, each lived in a single room with one
window. In the same city, 121 families lived in a single
room with no windows. Of the 666,786 houses in Scotland
as a whole, 226,723 were houses of but one room each, and
of these, 7964 were windowless. James Begg's eloquent
pleas for the forgotten and neglected poorer classes
awakened all Scotland. Federal and local agencies undertook to remedy evil housing conditions, and the Free
Church, and other denominations as well, had their attention called forcefully to their neglect of spiritual care of the
slum dwellers in the past. In 1865 Begg's popularity led
to his choice as Moderator of the Assembly.

During the next 18 years of his life, Dr. Begg's great
popularity waned. As a preacher he had few equals. In
theology he was a pronounced evangelical, and extremely
conservative. He felt himself called upon to oppose everything that suggested the slightest change in doctrine or in
practice. Not only did he employ his matchless eloquence
and his gifts of persuasion in trying to keep the Kirk exactly
as Chalmers and Candlish had moulded it, but he went even
farther. His convincing arguments, his commanding voice
and personality, and his good nature won the hearts of the
men from the North of Scotland, and Begg succeeded in
defeating attempts at church union.

Dr. Begg was a crusader in many directions. He edited
The Bulwark, which was an anti-Roman Catholic publication;
The Signal, which was opposed to church organs and *The
Watchword,* which was anti-Church union. He opposed lay
patronage, he opposed voluntarism, he denounced anything
remotely unionistic, and his conservatism even went so far
as to condemn in most vigorous language such things as a
simple liturgy, stained glass windows, the use of hymns in
public worship (rather than the Psalms of David), and the
opening of city parks and museums on Sunday afternoon.

Dr. Begg was an eloquent preacher, popular in the pulpit and on the platform, but conservatism became such an obsession with him that he became legalistic even in adiaphora. He traveled in many lands, preaching to eager congregations everywhere. On one occasion he preached by invitation before the United States Congress.

Dr. Begg was certainly one of the Scottish Free Church's most noted preachers, but his own generation, and those that followed, gave him but grudging credit. During the last 25 years of his life, the old-time, strict, Calvinistic type of conservatism was on the decline. Even the hearty good nature of Dr. Begg could only retard for a time its waning influence. As he saw his cherished doctrines and practice slowly losing ground, his rousing appeals began to weary his friends. Finally, when he went so far as to condemn the idea of allowing the Scottish people to walk through the public parks, or visit the museums on Sunday afternoon, lest they might violate the traditional quiet of the Scottish Sabbath, his friends began to lose patience with him. Writers of today overlook Dr. Begg's many excellencies, and are too ready to call attention to what they term the "unlovely" aspects of his later preaching and writing. His powerful sermons and public lectures did vast good in correcting the shocking evils of his day insofar as the neglect of the poor, spiritual and physical, is concerned. His testimony on unionism prevented what might have been a hasty outward union without inner unity. In many ways he was a useful man, in a day when such men were needed.

Some of Dr. Begg's books are: *A Handbook of Popery* (1853); *The Use of Organs Indefensible* (1866); *Happy Homes for Workingmen* (1866); *A Treatise on Free Church Principles* (1869); *The Causes and Probable Remedies of Pauperism in Scotland* (1870); *Principles, Position and Prospects of the Free Church of Scotland* (1875); and *A Treatise on Worship*. The story of his energetic life is told in Thomas Smith's *Memoirs of the Rev. James Begg,* 2 volumes (1885).

W. *Lindsay Alexander (1808-1884)*

W. Lindsay Alexander, the noted Scottish Congregational pulpit orator and Biblical scholar, was born in Leith in 1808. After attending the elementary schools at Leith and East Linton, he entered Edinburgh University at the age of 14, spending three years there. In 1825 he went to St. Andrews University where he came under the powerful influence of Dr. Thomas Chalmers. Further training was received at the Congregational Theological Seminary at Glasgow. In 1834 Dr. David Welsh paid a visit to Germany and while there he visited some of the leading universities. Lindsay Alexander, who had been a classical tutor at the Independent, or Congregational, College at Blackburn, went to Halle for further studies, and he was one of the first of the Scottish young men to study in that seat of rationalistic thought. Others followed his example, and for almost three generations it became quite the fashion among the young clergymen of Scotland. Whatever else one may say of the old-fashioned, uncompromising Scottish Calvinists of the first half of the nineteenth century, they deserve credit for their positive belief in a verbally inspired Bible. When Lindsay Alexander and others began flocking to the German universities, they brought back to Scotland the first indications of a coming liberalism.

In 1832 Lindsay Alexander became pastor of Newington Chapel in Liverpool, and two years later he was called to Argyle Square Chapel, North College street, Edinburgh, beginning what was to become a powerful ministry in that city. In 1861 a new church, called Augustine Church, George IV Bridge, was built, and here Dr. Alexander served for the remaining 23 years of his life. In addition to his pastoral work, Dr. Alexander became professor of theology, in 1854, at the Congregational Theological College, Edinburgh. From 1877 to 1881 he was principal of that institution. In 1861 he was made examiner in mental philosophy at St. Andrews University. In 1870 he became an influential member of the Old Testament Revision Company. From 1835 to 1840 and again from 1847 to 1851 he edited the *Scottish Congregational Magazine.*

During the middle years of the nineteenth century a group of unusually able men occupied the pulpits of some of Edinburgh's churches, and among these men Dr. Alexander was one of the most brilliant. "His sermons were generally on great subjects," says a prominent New York clergyman who often heard him. "One, I remember with a vivid distinctness, was on the Eternity of God; another from the text, "Be sure your sins will find you out,' burned indelibly into me the difference between the expressions 'your sins will be found out' and 'your sins will find you out.' They were all remarkable for the weight of their thought, the clearness of their style and the earnestness of their appeal. His pathos was a power. It never unmanned him, but it always affected you. And sometimes when he was roused, his indignant scorn of wrong-doing, or his withering sarcasm in the exposure of some specious infidel objection was positively tremendous. In his later days some of these qualities were absent, and the mellowness of experience came in their stead to give a new charm to his addresses. I never heard him in a regular series of expositions through any one book, but indeed the groundwork of every sermon he preached was exposition; for the first thing he always did was to show the meaning of his text, and lift his subject naturally out of it. . . . In the brilliant galaxy of preachers who made Edinburgh famous during the fifth and sixth decades of this century he had a place distinctively his own, and they who heard his discourses wondered no less at their excellence than at the number and ability of his published works." [62]

Although some of his contemporaries considered him mildly liberal in his theology, yet Dr. Alexander took a decided stand in 1866 against James Cranbrook, a fellow Congregationalist, who was suspected of crypto-Unitarian leanings. Dr. Alexander and several others refused to engage in pulpit and altar fellowship with him.

Dr. Alexander published many books. His three-volume edition of Kitto's *Biblical Cyclopaedia* (1861-70), is well known among clergymen of all denominations. Several standard German theological works were translated and

---

[62]. W. M. Taylor, *The Scottish Pulpit* (New York, 1887), p. 257ff.

published by Dr. Alexander. His *System of Biblical Theology*, 2 volumes (1888), is one of his most important
writings. Other works of merit are: *The Connection and
Harmony of the Old and New Testament* (1841); *Christ
and Christianity* (1854); *Christian Thought and Work*
(1862); *St. Paul at Athens* (1865); *Zechariah, his Visions
and Warnings* (1885); and a collection of 16 sermons published in 1875. He published a work on Switzerland and
its churches, and works on early British Christianity and on
the Isle of Iona. Modern research contradicts some of his
theories in regard to the origin of Christianity in the British
Isles, while his theological writings, while giving evidence
of great scholarship, are tainted here and there with German
Rationalism. An interesting biography of this great Scottish
Hebrew and Greek scholar, entitled *W. Lindsay Alexander:
his Life and Work*, was written by James Ross and published
in 1886.

William Arnot (1808-1875)

William Arnot, of the Scottish Free Church, was born
in 1808 in Scone, Perthshire. He attended the elementary
schools at Forgen and the parish school at Abergaldie. The
religious training at the Abergaldie school made a deep impression on the boy, and he became a diligent reader of the
Bible, of Watts' hymns and Baxter's *Saints' Rest.*

Unable to continue his schooling, he worked for several
years as a gardener. One of his tasks was to spade large
areas of land. Three or four men worked together, each
one spading a furrow the width of the field. It was a rule
that each man had three or four minutes rest at the end of
each furrow. William Arnot carried a Latin or a Greek book
with him, and at the end of each furrow he would open the
book, read over a rule of grammar, or a few words of
vocabulary, and then repeat what he had read until he
reached the other end of the furrow. Then he would open
his book again, and verify what he had memorized. In this
manner, after a few years, he had learned enough Latin and
Greek to satisfy the master of a preparatory school at Perth.
He had saved 20 pounds, and in due time he entered this
school. In 1829 he was able to enter the University of
Glasgow, where he proved to be a diligent student.

He was licensed in 1837 and became assistant pastor of a church at Larbert, and of an affiliated congregation at Dunipace. In 1839 he was given St. Peter's Church, in Glasgow. Four years later the Secession took place, and Arnot and his congregation withdrew from the State Church and decided to go with the new Free Church. In 1845 he secured a leave of absence for a short time to serve the new Free Church in Montreal, Canada. He returned to his old congregation in Scotland, but in 1849 they lost their property to the Established Church. A year later, under Mr. Arnot's leadership, a new church was built by the congregation. In 1863 he was called to the Free High Church in Edinburgh.

Dr. Arnot was an exceptional preacher, and his congregations always included an abnormally large proportion of young men. In spite of a few mild peculiarities, he was always held in highest esteem. One of his contemporaries said of him: "He was a real genius; a rough diamond, but still a diamond. A clear head, a warm heart, an awkward, yet strangely expressive manner, a fine fancy, strong common sense, and pawky humor were his outstanding peculiarities. He was the most Scotch of Scotsmen, but of him, too, it was true that he was best on the platform. The raciness and appropriateness of his anecdotes were equal to those of Guthrie. The one was all nature, the other's art had become natural." [63]

Among a number of books of which he was the author, Dr. Arnot's *Race for Riches* (1851) proved extremely popular and had a wide circulation for years. Of more permanent value are his *Parables of Our Lord* (1864), and his *Lesser Parables of Our Lord* (1883). His *Proverbs: Laws from Heaven for Life on Earth*, 2 volumes (1857-58), found many readers during Dr. Arnot's lifetime. Among his other works are *The Roots and Fruits of the Christian Life* (1859); *The Anchor of the Soul and other Sermons* (1876); and his *Life of James Hamilton* (1870). Dr. Arnot's *Autobiography*, with a memoir by his daughter, Mrs. A. Fleming, was published in 1877.

---

[63]. W. M. Taylor, *Op. cit.*, p. 273.

James Veitch (1808-1879)

James Veitch was born in 1808 in Inchbonny, Jedburgh. After his education at Edinburgh University he was ordained in 1834 and became pastor of Galashiels parish. In 1840 he was translated to Newbattle, and in 1843 he became one of the pastors of St. Cuthbert's, Edinburgh, commonly called the West Kirk. James Veitch had a fine reputation as a preacher. Hew Scott says of him, "He was an earnest and polished preacher, and had the reputation of being deeply read in theological literature." [64] This tribute is unusual, for Scott, in his monumental work, rarely took the trouble to express an opinion in regard to the thousands whose biographies he prepared. James Veitch was a determined opponent of all innovations in the field of theology, as well as in the forms of worship of the Kirk. His best known writings are *A Statement Concerning Innovations* (1866), and a posthumous book of sermons (1880), to which is prefixed a good memoir.

William Wilson (1808-1888)

William Wilson was born in 1808 at Blawearie, Bassendean, Berwickshire. After finishing the parochial school, he entered Edinburgh University in 1825, where Thomas Chalmers, David Welsh and Alexander Brunton were among his teachers. He was licensed in 1830 and became a parochial missionary in Glasgow. From 1835 to 1837 he edited the *Scottish Guardian*. He was ordained in 1837 and became pastor of Carmyllie, Forfarshire. In 1843 he was one of the men who went out with the Disruption and took part in the formation of the Free Church. Deprived of his former church building, the congregation and Wilson worshipped for five years in a makeshift wooden chapel. In 1848 he was called to Mariner's Church in Dundee, where he served as pastor for almost 30 years. He was made moderator in 1866, and secretary of the sustentation fund in 1877. He was at one time Chalmers lecturer at the university.

In his earlier years in office, Wilson was recognized as a preacher of considerable power, and he maintained this

---

[64]. Hew Scott, *Fasti ecclesiae Scoticanae* (Edinburgh, 1915-1928 ed.), vol. 1, p. 103.

reputation throughout life. It is strange that men of his reputation have been forgotten by so many of our day, and their names so seldom included among the noted preachers of the past.

Horatius Bonar 1808-1889)

Horatius Bonar, the noted hymn writer, was born in Edinburgh in 1808, and was the second of the three well-known Bonar brothers. Like his brothers he attended elementary and high schools in Edinburgh, as well as Edinburgh University, where one of his professors was Dr. Thomas Chalmers. He was licensed to preach, and after some experience in mission work at Leith, he was ordained in 1837 and became pastor of New North Church in Kelso, one of the new congregations organized through the influence of Dr. Chalmers. At Kelso Mr. Bonar became famous as a preacher and became known throughout Scotland. He was decidedly evangelical, and often conducted a series of eight or more services of preaching and prayer on the same number of consecutive days. He was a tireless worker, and numbers of evangelical books and tracts were the product of his efforts.

In 1843 he seceded with the Free Church's founders; and in 1866 he became pastor of Chalmers Memorial Church in Edinburgh. In 1883 he was moderator of the Assembly. Dr. Bonar was a prolific hymn writer. Among his most familiar hymns are, "I lay my sins on Jesus," "I heard the voice of Jesus say," and "What a Friend we have in Jesus." Julian and Duffield each devote two pages to him. However, it is as a preacher that Horatius Bonar especially claims our attention. He preached with a simple warmth and urgency but without any attempt at fine rhetoric or oratory. Like his two brothers, he believed that the great object of preaching is to save immortal souls, and to this object he directed his efforts. His style was direct, gripping and benevolent. In private life he was a quiet, humble man, and he preached with a simple earnestness that proved most effective. It is said that many children were attracted by his preaching, for he had the rare gift of gaining and holding their closest attention. His preaching, like his hymns, tends to be rather subjective at times. His position is generally pre-millennial.

The writings of Dr. Horatius Bonar include: *The Night of Weeping* (1846); *Prophetical Landmarks* (1847), in which his pre-millennial theories are evident; *Hymns of Faith and Hope,* three series (1857-66); *God's Way of Peace* (1862); *The Song of the New Creation* (1872); *Hymns of the Nativity* (1878); *The Story of Mr. McColl's Mission* (1879); *Songs of Love and Joy* (1888); and *Until the Daybreak* (1890). His biography is entitled *Horatius Bonar, a Memorial* (1889). Short biographies are to be found in Julian and in Duffield.

John Eadie (1810-1876)

John Eadie, the noted Biblical scholar of the United Secession Church, was born in 1810 at Alva, Stirlingshire. As a boy he was noted for his remarkable memory. He is said to have memorized all of Milton's *Paradise Lost.* After his elementary schooling, he attended Glasgow University, where he distinguished himself. His theological work was taken at the United Secession seminary.

In 1835 he was ordained and given the Cambridge Street Church in Glasgow, and in 1863 he became pastor of the new Lansdowne Church, a daughter congregation of his old parish. From 1838 onward he added teaching to his parish duties. He was professor of Hebrew in Anderson's College for two years, and from 1843 onward he was professor of Biblical Literature. His duties required him to teach from five to six months each winter.

Dr. Eadie was a member of the New Testament revision committee. In addition to all these duties, he published commentaries on the Greek text of Ephesians, Colossians, Philippians, Galatians and I Thessalonians. He published an abridged edition of *Cruden's Concordance,* a *Biblical Encyclopaedia* (1849); a *Bible Dictionary,* an *Analytical Concordance,* an *Ecclesiastical Encyclopaedia* (1861); and a two-volume work called *The English Bible* (1876), with an account of its several translations.

As a preacher, Dr. Eadie's strength lay in his expository gifts rather than in his eloquence. He spoke with a rather thick Scottish accent, and made no attempt at fine rhetorical effects. His effort was to make clear some Bible passage that had seemed obscure before, so that his congregation might go away feeling that they had learned something about the teachings of God's Word. His skill at expository preaching drew many thoughtful people to his church. Many of them came out of curiosity at first, but felt themselves moved to attend again and again, their admiration increasing Sunday by Sunday, until they could not be induced to go elsewhere. A man who attended his church regularly in his student days says, "I never heard him without having something added to my stock of knowledge, or some difficulty removed out of my mind, or some new interest given to some particular portion of the Word of God." [65] Some of the great preachers of the past are famous because they stated familiar truths in beautiful language, or with great fervor. Dr. Eadie's reputation lies in the fact that he sought out difficult Bible passages, and after careful exegetical research, presented them in the simplest possible language to his congregation. His purpose was to increase their knowledge of Biblical truth, rather than to awaken their admiration.

Dr. W. Robertson Nicoll, the great exegetical scholar, described Eadie as "a man of splendid physical frame, with a wealth of beautiful hair," but he did not consider Eadie an exact and finished Greek scholar. In addition to the works on the English Bible Dr. Eadie published a commentary on the Greek text of Thessalonians (1877), and commentaries on Ephesians (1853), Colossians (1856), Philippians (1859), and Galatians (1869). He wrote a life of John Kitto (1857), and on St. Paul's characteristics as a preacher (1859).

Andrew A. Bonar (1810-1892)

The youngest of the three noted Bonar brothers was Andrew, who was born in 1810 in Edinburgh. He attended the high school of his native city, as well as Edinburgh University. He was licensed to preach in 1835, and after supplying pulpits in and around Jedburgh and Edinburgh,

---

[65]. W. M. Taylor, *The Scottish Pulpit* (New York, 1887), p. 242.

he was ordained in 1838 and became pastor at Collace, in Perthshire, where he remained until 1856. In 1843 he cast his lot with the Disruption and became a member of the Free Church, serving Finnieston, Glasgow, until his death in 1892. In 1878 he was chosen moderator of the General Assembly of the Free Church. Andrew Bonar, like his brothers, was an earnest evangelical preacher of more than ordinary gifts. He was a premillennialist.

"His preaching was full of urgency. Earnestness about the truth is not the same thing as earnestness about souls. Perhaps there is as much desire to know and speak the truth as there ever was; but that which chiefly concerned Dr. Bonar was its effect on the people. He knew that the work of the Christian Church makes for the great ends of conversion and sanctification, and all his preaching was ruled by a desire for results. He mourned when he could see none. What really gladdened him was the news of souls awakened and confirmed, and when such things grew rare his heart was heavy."[66] Many have regretted the pronounced millennialism of Dr. Bonar. It is said by some that on this account he was buried for 18 years in the little village of Collace, and then assigned to the most unpromising mission congregation in Glasgow, where he remained for almost 50 years, and which grew to a congregation of 1,100 communicants. Many of his members did not agree with his chiliastic views, but all admitted that he was a gifted preacher.

Andrew Bonar is well known because of several books of which he was the author. Some of these were: *Christ and His Church in the Book of Psalms* (1859); *Divine Compassion* (1864); *Samuel Rutherford's Letters* (1864); *Commentary on Leviticus* (1846); *Biography of R. M. M'Cheyne* (1844); and his chiliastic *Redemption Drawing Nigh* (1847). Together with M'Cheyne he published a *Narrative of a Mission of Inquiry to the Jews* (1842), today listed by libraries as a rare book. His *Diary and Letters,* edited by his daughter, appeared in 1893, and *Reminiscenses of Andrew A. Bonar,* by M. Bonar in 1897. A biography of Bonar was written by Prof. F. Ferguson.

---

[66]. *British Weekly,* Dec. 7, 1893.

James McCosh (1811-1894)

James McCosh spent 34 years of his career in Scotland and 20 in America. He was born in 1811 at Carskeoch farm, in the parish of Straiton, in Ayrshire. He came of a family of Covenanter background. After studying with Quentin Smith he entered Glasgow University in 1824, and from there he went to Edinburgh University, taking his degree in 1834. Thomas Chalmers was his professor of theology. He was licensed in 1834, and in 1835 he became pastor at Arbroath, where his congregation was composed of seafaring men and artisans. From 1838 to 1850 he was pastor of Brechin, Forfarshire. While at that place the Disruption occurred, and Mr. McCosh was one of the men who helped form the Free Church. His teaching career began in 1850, when he became professor of logic and metaphysics at Queen's College, Belfast. However, he did not give up congregational work, for he founded a church in Smithfield, and took an active part in the organization of schools.

In 1866 he visited America in order to study the educational system of that country. In 1868 he became president of Princeton University, a position which he held for twenty years. He introduced the elective system, and in addition to many other activities he taught philosophy in the seminary. He published a number of works, mainly on philosophical and psychological subjects.

When the controversy arose in regard to evolution, Dr. McCosh made a study of the subject, attempting to reconcile the theories of the scientists with the teachings of Scripture. He won distinction as a preacher, a lecturer, a philosopher and as an educator. His chief fame lies in the field of philosophy, although he has been included among the thoughtful preachers of his day. His printed sermons are lengthy, closely reasoned, and they reveal his interest in science and philosophy. While not without references to evangelical truth, yet their compact, scholarly tone would hardly appeal today to the popular audience.

Among his more important works are *Methods of the Divine Government* (1850), and *Intuitions of the Mind Inductively Investigated* (1860). Other writings include: *The Supernatural in Relation to the Natural* (1862); *Laws of Discursive Thought* (1870); *The Typical Forms and Special Ends in Creation* (1855), this written in collaboration with George Dickie; *An Examination of J. S. Mill's Philosophy* (1866); *The Scottish Philosophy* (1874); *Psychology* (1886-87); *Religion in a College* (1886); *The Religious Aspects of Evolution* (1888); and *Gospel Sermons* (1888).

Norman Macleod (1812-1872)

Few Scottish clergymen have been held in higher esteem than Norman Macleod. He was one of a noted family of clergymen. His father was Norman Macleod of St. Columba, Glasgow, and dean of the Chapel Royal. His grandfather, a brother and several cousins and uncles were clergymen of more or less prominence in the Church of Scotland. Norman Macleod was born in 1812 at Campbeltown, in Kintyre, that remarkable peninsula that reaches out from the west coast of Scotland and comes within a dozen miles of the Irish coast. The Macleods were Islanders, and traced their lineage to Olaf, the thirteenth century King of Man. Norman spent his early boyhood in Campbeltown, as well as in Morven, where his grandfather was pastor. Some of his most delightful writings are descriptions of these places. He attended the Burgh school at Campbeltown, and when his father was translated to Campsie in 1825, he attended the parish school at that place.

In 1827 he entered Glasgow University. His record there gave little indication of his coming greatness, although he was active in various student organizations, and showed certain talent for leadership. He was a friendly lad, but not taken seriously because of what his father termed his "buffoonery" and his "acting the fool." So given was he to mimicry that he seldom spoke in his natural voice. It was the death of a brother, to whom he was greatly attached, that brought him to his senses. He walked to the bedside of his dying brother and astonished the family by offering a free prayer in a manner that would have done credit to an experienced clergyman. In 1831 he went to Edinburgh University, where he came under the powerful influence of Dr. Thomas Chalmers. Another man whom he respected was Dr. Welsh, who at that time taught Church History at Edinburgh. For three years Macleod was tutor to the family of Henry Preston, Esq., of Moreby Hall, Yorkshire; and part of this time he spent with his pupils in Weimar and other German cities. While there was much in Germany that proved most attractive to him, yet in his letters to his family he expressed horror at the rationalistic views of many of the German clergy, some of whom he declared to be little better than unbelievers.[67] In 1835 he returned to Scotland and completed his theological studies.

Mr. Macleod was licensed to preach in 1837, and a year later he was ordained and became pastor of Loudoun parish, in Ayrshire. The parish extended for six miles along Irvine Water, and included the villages of Newmilns and Darvel. Its population was 4,000, and the people were hand-loom weavers and farmers. The farmers were of Covenanter stock, and they still spoke proudly of Drumclog and Bothwell Brig. The weavers, locally called "websters," were radicals, ready at all times to protest bitterly against the age of machinery which threatened their craft. The weaver, with his hand-loom in the large front room of his cottage, and with living quarters in a lean-to, or but, in the rear, had seen his industry ruined by the industrial revolution, and the quiet villages and beautiful valleys of Scotland spoiled by tall, smoking factory chimneys and heaps of coal slag. He had seen the development of hideous slums in the wynds and closes (alleys) of the growing industrial towns. When Norman Macleod went to Loudoun, he found the hand-loom weavers disposed to condemn the churches of Scotland for their alleged failure to take a positive stand against these evils.

Norman Macleod's first task was to make a house-to-house canvass of the parish, and to invite all the inhabitants to his church. When the weavers declared that they had no good clothing, Macleod started evening services for men in working clothes. At first the rougher members of the community came to the church for the purpose of creating a disturbance. On one occasion Mr. Macleod paused in the

67. Donald Macleod, *Memoir of the Rev. Norman Macleod* (London, 1876), vol. I, pp. 49-50.

midst of his sermon and asked the orderly portion of the congregation to eject the trouble-makers from the church. This was accomplished, and there was no disturbance thereafter. Many of the weavers received the new pastor with genuine friendliness. When his opponents found that the pastor was a big-hearted man who had a friendly greeting for everybody, they soon ceased their criticism, and in some cases became loyal friends.

He found drunkenness, profanity and a contempt for Sunday to be common. Not only did he preach eloquently against those things, but during his first year he excluded fourteen people from Communion, either for habitual drunkenness or for living in open enmity with one another and refusing reconciliation. Although he had a friendly greeting for all, yet church discipline was enforced, and the community soon learned that their pastor could take a firm position in spiritual matters. Attracted by his friendliness and his eloquent preaching, the people soon crowded his church to capacity at both services, and the fame of Norman Macleod as a preacher reached every part of Ayrshire.

During the six years spent by Norman Macleod in Loudoun, the Ten Years' Conflict was at its height. Although he was a great admirer of Dr. Chalmers, leader of the Evangelical party, yet Macleod decided to take a middle course. He had nothing in common with the Moderates, but at the same time he was opposed to any withdrawal from the State Church. He published a pamphlet, *A Wee Crack aboot the Kirk, for Kintra Folk,* written in "braid Scots," and which had a wide circulation. This was followed by other pamphlets, and Macleod became one of a group called The Forty, who advised all pastors and lay people to remain loyal to the Kirk and reform its evils from within. When the notable May 18 came, in 1843, Mr. Macleod kept his seat in the Assembly, but in his journal and by means of letters to his friends, he expressed his amazement and dejection when he saw the vacant seats of such men as Chalmers, Welsh and Gordon, Candlish, Cunningham and Guthrie.[68] He complained for months, declaring that the Kirk had been left without leaders. Now and then his

---

[68]. *Op. cit.,* pp. 130-138.

words are bitter. He admitted that many fine, heroic men
gave up their congregations, their manses and their livings
for the sake of their religious convictions, but he declared
that some of the 474 who withdrew were mere exhibitionists
who cast their lot with the popular side. He declared from
the pulpit and in his writings that it required courage to
leave the State Church. However, it required just as much
courage to refuse to withdraw, he said, for those who remained behind were faced with the task of finding men for
some 400 or 500 vacant pulpits, and with the entire recon-
struction of all their missionary agencies, because every
missionary had united with the new Free Church.

In 1843 Mr. Macleod became pastor of Dalkeith Church,
near Edinburgh. The population at that time was 5,000, and
there was a fine old kirk, but crowded within by tier upon
tier of galleries, with texts and painted arms of craftsmen's
guilds everywhere. The town had its narrow wynds and its
closes where the poverty and misery of the people were
appalling. Mr. Macleod visited the people from house to
house, not overlooking the darkest and filthiest of the
closes, or alleys. He opened three mission stations, expanded the parish school system, organized branch Sunday-
schools, and evening classes for the instruction of young
and old. His eight years at Dalkeith bore rich fruit, and as
at Loudoun, his church soon became too small for the great
congregations that assembled there.

In 1845 he was appointed by the General Assembly to
visit America, in company with two others, and conduct a
visitation of the Scottish churches there. Although his
preaching had been largely in English, yet Gaelic was his
mother tongue, and he could use it with great effect in the
pulpit. His tour of the Gaelic-speaking communities of
Eastern Canada brought great joy to the Highlanders and
Islanders who had emigrated to the New World. To this
day there are places in the Maritime Provinces where Gaelic
is still spoken, and where the name of Norman Macleod is
remembered in church circles.

In 1847 he was one of the founders of the Evangelical
Alliance, an organization which, while unionistic, did much
to combat Moderatism and Rationalism. In 1849 Macleod

became editor of the *Christian Instructor*, a household magazine that became popular throughout Scotland. This experience in editorial work was followed in 1860 by the publication of his *Good Words,* a household journal that actually achieved world-wide fame in its day.

In 1851 Norman Macleod became pastor of Barony Church in Glasgow, where his greatest work was done. Here he had a parish that included a population of 87,000 souls. The church is a plain, unpretentious building that is often passed by because of the great cathedral across the street. However, from 1851 to 1872 it was the Barony, rather than Glasgow Cathedral, that attracted the visitor. Dr. Macleod was then at the zenith of his powers as a preacher, and his missionary and philanthropic work in Glasgow would make a long chapter in itself. He formed a kirk session composed not only of the pastor and elders, but of deacons as well. The office of deacon had become all but extinct in Scotland, and Dr. Macleod was among the first to revive it.[69] At the Barony the diaconate was more than an honorary position. Macleod divided the parish into twelve districts, with elders and deacons placed over each district. Under their immediate oversight intensive missionary work was done throughout the great parish, and at frequent intervals there were meetings at which each deacon was required to give a complete account of his labors. During the first decade of his ministry several new parish schools were organized in addition to those existing when Dr. Macleod came to the Barony. These schools provided instruction for 2,000 children. Several evening schools for grown people were organized, and in one of these the enrollment numbered 220. From seven to twelve Sunday-schools were conducted in various parts of the parish during his pastorate, and in one or two of these the enrollment reached 1,400. During his pastorate of 21 years, Dr. Macleod organized six mission congregations and helped provide each with its own place of worship. His work at the Barony compares favorably with the remarkable missionary work of Chalmers in Glasgow and Edinburgh, and with that of such men as William Tasker,

---

[69]. *Ibid.,* p. 216.

Dugald MacColl, William Ross of Cowcaddens and John Macleod of Govan, a cousin of Dr. Norman Macleod.

Dr. Macleod's greatest popularity suffered a temporary blow in 1865 when he delivered an address of two and one-half hours at the Glasgow Synod. In this address he declared that there is no divine obligation, under the liberty of the New Testament, to keep the Sabbath. Had a man of less popularity said such a thing, his deposition from office would have been certain, for the Scottish people were rigid Sabbatarians. To attack the Sabbath as a divine institution was to reject the Westminster Standards, and this no Presbyterian Synod of those days would have tolerated. In one afternoon Dr. Macleod became the most hated man in Scotland. Old friends refused to greet him in the streets, one clergyman hissed him as he passed, and a man of great prominence wrote some ribald verses which became known to every Scotsman: "Have you heard of valiant Norman, Norman of the ample vest? How he fought the Ten Commandments, in the Synod of the West? . . . Still from out the monster's stomach, in the choicest Glasgow brogue, he is heard to curse the Sabbath, and to ban the Decalogue." Efforts were made to bring charges of heresy against Dr. Macleod, but he escaped with a sharp admonition, and with resolutions which, without actually mentioning his name, condemned his views on the Sunday question. His opponents did not hesitate to say that this was but an indication that doctrinal discipline had broken down in the Kirk. The incident was forgotten, and in 1867 Dr. Macleod was sent to visit the mission stations in India, and in 1869 he was made moderator of the General Assembly.

As a preacher Dr. Macleod had many qualifications: an impressive appearance in the pulpit, a fine voice, an exceptional command of clear, vigorous English, a fine command of the Gaelic language, a winning persuasiveness and great evangelical fervor. As a hearty, whole-souled man, he loved his fellow men and in turn was loved by them. He was enormously popular as a preacher. The people of his parish idolized him. At a time when there was an outbreak of typhus, the people of his parish had an understanding among themselves that he was too valuable a man to call to the bedside of a victim of this disease. Other pastors were called, and when questioned his members said, "Oh yes, we belong to the Barony; but, ye see, this is an unco' smittal fever, and it wad never do to risk Norman."[70] While it is true that Dr. Macleod believed firmly in Jesus Christ as the only Saviour of sinful man, and even though he preached Christ crucified with all his Celtic fervor, yet in theology he sometimes lacked definition. He was a man of great energy, and his ceaseless work among the poor and the neglected of Glasgow left him insufficient time for careful study. He was inclined at times to resort to generalities. He could describe the scene on Calvary with marvellous effect, and exhort his hearers to come to the foot of the Cross and lay their sins at the feet of the crucified Saviour, yet if he understood clearly the difference between objective and subjective grace, it is not made clear in his printed sermons; neither does he seem to lay stress upon the value of the Gospel and Sacraments as means of grace, nor upon the manner in which the Holy Ghost employs these means, in a practical way, to apply the benefits of our Lord's Redemption to the believer. Men who have heard him preach have said that he was inclined at times, when preaching an expository sermon, to skip from verse to verse, causing an attentive hearer to regret that certain truths had not been developed more fully.

While Dr. Macleod was an evangelical, in the reformed sense of the term, yet, from the standpoint of the strict Calvinism of his generation he was a Broad Churchman. He was inclined to accept the view of his cousin, John Macleod Campbell, who was expelled from the Church of Scotland in 1831 "for preaching the unlimited Atonement of Christ as the only warrant for bidding men to be assured of God's love to them."[71] In this respect, and in his attitude toward the abrogation of the Sabbath, Norman Macleod was more orthodox than those who sought to bring charges of heresy against him. Through the influence of Thomas Arnold, Macleod is said to have favored a unionistic State Church

---

[70]. T. R. Barnett, *The Makers of the Kirk* (Edinburgh, 1915).
[71]. Geo. P. Fisher, *History of Christian Doctrine* (New York, 1913), p. 477.

"so comprehensive as to include in it the body of the people, and thus to become literally national."[72] This is to be regretted, for any church union on so nebulous a basis can lead only to doctrinal decline and decay, as history has so amply proved, even in Scotland.

Dr. Norman Macleod's writings include his famous pamphlets *A Wee Crack aboot the Kirk, for Kintra Folk; A Second Crack aboot the Kirk* and *A Third Crack aboot the Kirk,* none of which are dated. He wrote an excellent biography of John Mackintosh, entitled *The Earnest Student* (1854); *Life and Travels of St. Paul* (1861); *The Lord's Day* (1866); *Simple Truths Spoken to Working People* (1866); a splendid work entitled *Reminiscences of a Highland Parish* (1867); and other writings. His *Works* were published in 1892 and his *Selected Writings,* in 2 volumes, in 1899. The standard biography, which is well known throughout the world, is his brother Donald Macleod's two volume memoir, published in 1876 and reprinted from time to time.

Robert M. McCheyne (1813-1843)

Although he died at the age of 30, Robert McCheyne was one of the best-known Scottish preachers of his day. He was born in 1813 in Edinburgh. He learned the Greek alphabet at the age of four, and he was able to write it correctly on his slate. At the age of eight he entered the high school, and when but fourteen he entered Edinburgh University. In 1831 be began his theological studies in the Divinity Hall, where Dr. Chalmers and Dr. Welsh were among his professors. During the same year an older brother died, and this cast a shadow over the life of Robert McCheyne that remained with him until his own death a dozen years later. He observed the anniversary of his brother's death as a day of fasting, and recorded his sorrowful memories in his journal. He read *The Sum of Saving Knowledge,* the works of Jonathan Edwards and the *Letters* of Samuel Rutherfurd. Although a youth of singularly blameless life, yet he recorded in his journal words of sorrowful self-reproach, looking upon himself as chief of

---

[72]. Donald Macleod, *Op. cit.,* p. 451.

sinners. A lapse or two into worldliness, such as once when
he was persuaded to play a game of cards, or when he
attended a social gathering with his friends, was followed by
days of bitter self-examination, all of which he recorded
in his diary.

He was licensed in 1835, and four months later he
became assistant to the Rev. John Bonar at Larbert and
Dunipace, Sterlingshire, a parish of about 6,000 souls. He
became famous for his preaching even before his ordination,
and his sermons at Larbert attracted attention far beyond
his parish. In his collected writings, published shortly after
his death, are most touching letters written to young people
of his congregation who had been guilty of some slight
transgression. In gentle language he pleads with them, all
the while confessing his own great unworthiness. In 1836
he was ordained pastor of St. Peter's, Dundee, a newly
organized *quoad sacra* congregation. This new district included 1,100 communicant members and between 3,000 and
4,000 souls. In 1838 he was appointed, because of his
remarkable gifts, to make a tour of Forfarshire with Dr.
Guthrie in the interest of church extension work. In 1839
he was sent with Andrew Bonar and others on a tour of
Palestine in the interest of the General Assembly's Jewish
missionary project. In 1842 he engaged in a preaching tour
throughout the northern part of England, followed by preaching missions in London and Aberdeenshire. In March, 1843,
he was taken ill rather suddenly and died at the age of 30.

Robert McCheyne, in his short career of less than seven
years, had become famous throughout Scotland. His singularly upright character and the deep spirituality of his
sermons and writings led men to call him "the saintly
McCheyne," and they said this in utmost sincerity. He had
a fine, clear voice, a good face and a most attractive manner.
His power of analysis was unusual. His sermons are expressed in clear, simple language. His printed sermons
rarely exceed three or four pages, and are often without
introductions, conclusions or applications. His spoken sermons were often lengthy. It was his custom to write out
the body of his sermon with great care, striving for utmost
simplicity of language. With this as a foundation, it was his

custom to add an appropriate introduction, amplifications, searching applications and appeals and a fitting conclusion at the time that he preached the sermon. His sermons were strongly doctrinal and expository, but those who knew him well, such as his friend Andrew Bonar, regret the fact that his matchless applications and direct appeals to his hearers were all delivered impromptu.

In his spoken sermons he first announced his text, then explained its relation to its context, and then announced and expounded the chief doctrine that he wished to emphasize. He was noted for his skilful divisions and sub-divisions. These were never arbitrary, never artificial, never an attempt at cleverness. He derived them from the text itself, and usually in the very words of the text, so that it might be impressed upon his hearers. As one pages through his printed sermons, these divisions and subdivisions are often so simple as to seem almost childish, yet one cannot deny that they are completely Scriptural. He used to tell his friends that every sermon must be constructed upon the basis of two grand principles: Ruin by the Fall and Recovery by the Mediator. His preaching was doctrinal, but no matter what might be the doctrine that he was expounding, Jesus Christ always occupied a central place. He was thoroughly evangelical, and he declared that Moderatism was a weed that had not been planted by the Lord, but which the Lord Himself would soon uproot. He favored strongly a Scottish Church that should be independent of the civil powers in spiritual matters. He records with joy in his journal every settlement of a faithful pastor in a Scottish congregation. He belonged to a small conference which included Andrew Bonar and one or two others. They wasted no time in reading the minutes of the last meeting, nor in discussing business matters or questions of casuistry. Their entire day was spent in Bible study, and in confession of those shortcomings which are peculiar to the clergyman. Mr. McCheyne was an admirable Hebrew scholar as well as a hymn-writer. Two of his best-known hymns are "Chosen not for good in me" and "When this passing world is done," to be found in the standard Scottish hymnals. Duffield devotes two pages to Robert McCheyne.[73]   He mentions an incident first related by Andrew Bonar.   When McCheyne returned from his trip to Palestine he reached Dundee on Thursday afternoon.   He hurried at once to St. Peter's Church, where he found a great assembly of clergymen and townspeople awaiting him.   He gave out the sixty-sixth Psalm, and then read I Cor. 2, 1-4, "And I, brethren, when I came to you, came not with excellency of speech or of wisdom, declaring unto you the testimony of God.   For I determined not to know any thing among you, save Jesus Christ, and Him crucified," etc.   Then he preached an admirable Gospel sermon, making no reference whatever to his trip to the Holy Land.   People crowded about him after the service, and he continued to speak to them in regard to Christ crucified.   It had grown quite dark outside, and on his way home people thronged about him, shaking hands, and asking about his journey, but he continued to expound his text, bringing out thoughts that he had not touched upon in the church.   This continued until he reached his home, now completely exhausted.   Several of Robert McCheyne's works have been published, including a work on Jewish missions, also his *Exposition of the Epistles to the Seven Churches,* and a posthumous collection of sermons. His biography, by Andrew Bonar,[74] has seen several reprintings.

"McCheyne brought into the pulpit," says Dr. Blaikie, "all the reverence for Scripture of the Reformation period; all the honour for the headship of Christ of the Covenanter struggle; all the freeness of the Gospel offer of the Marrow theology; all the bright imagery of Samuel Rutherfurd; all the delight of the Erskines in the fulness of Christ.   In McCheyne the effect of a cultured taste was apparent in the chastened beauty and simplicity of his style, if you can call it a style — in a sense he has no style, or rather it was the perfection of style, for it was transparent as glass.   The new element he brought to the pulpit, or rather which he revived and used so much that it appeared new, was *win-*

---

[73]. S. W. Duffield, *English Hymns* (New York, 1886), pp. 82-84.

[74]. Andrew Bonar, *Memoir and Remains of the Rev. Robert M. McCheyne* (Dundee, 1844).

someness. It was an almost feminine quality. A pity that turned many of his sermons into elegiac poems, thrilled his heart, and by the power of the Spirit imparted the thrill to many souls. How precious his example and memory have been to Scotland is shown by the continued demand for his *Life and Letters.* And how invaluable the evangelistic labours begun by him and his brethren, and still continued and often blessed throughout our country, no Scotch audience needs to be told."

In addition to the works mentioned, several works appeared after McCheyne's death. They include: *Additional Remains of Robert M. McCheyne* (1846); *The Works of R. M. McCheyne,* 2 volumes (1847); *Select Pieces* (1847); and *Familiar Letters of Robert M. McCheyne* (1848). In addition to A. A. Bonar's famous biography, other biographies have been written by J. C. Smith, in 1910, and by A. Smellie, in 1913.

David Livingstone (1813-1873)

David Livingstone was one of the greatest missionaries of all time, and one of the world's great explorers. It is unfortunate that more is not known of his preaching. He returned from Africa to England for a period of a year, and at that time his personality and his earnest pleas for the country he loved convinced many that he was a preacher of much more than ordinary ability. He was born at Blantyre, Lanarkshire, near Glasgow, in the year 1813. The original name of the family was Livingston. At the age of 10, David Livingstone was obliged to leave school and work in a cotton mill. Anxious for an education, he saved his money, bought a Latin grammar and other books and studied until long into the night. About the year 1836 he entered Anderson's College, Glasgow, where he studied Greek, theology and medicine, working during the summer months in order to pay his college expenses during the school term.

Having become acquainted with the work of Gutzlaff, he turned his thoughts to the foreign field. His first thought was to go to China. He offered his services to the London Missionary Society and secured support for his further education, but the outbreak of the Opium War prevented it.

He studied medicine in London and had some hospital experience. He met Robert Moffat and became interested in his work in Africa. Livingstone was ordained in 1840 and left for Africa late in the same year. He went to Moffat's station at Kuruman, and from there to Mabosta, Bakwena and Kolobeng, where he established mission stations. On one of his long journeys he discovered Lake Ngami, and later he discovered Victoria Falls on the Zambezi River. The falls are more than a mile in width and 354 feet high, as compared to Niagara's 167 feet. Livingstone's discoveries of Lake Shirwa, Lake Nyasa, Lake Moeru, his Zambezi expedition and his attempt to reach the sources of the Nile all form a brilliant chapter in the history of exploration, but have slight bearing on his reputation as a preacher.

He spent a year in England in 1856, but much of his time was occupied by writing. He spoke on several occasions, and from his ability to present the cause of his missionary work there is little doubt that his gifts must have been considerable. Since much of his preaching was done in Africa, and in places remote from white occupation, not much is known of the actual character of his preaching. During his journeys he is said to have covered one-third of the African continent; and it is known that he conducted Sunday services to the last. His long absence in the interior of Africa, Stanley's search for him and his final death among his African friends, are incidents in his life that are known to all. He is buried in Westminster Abbey, where a conspicuous slab in the pavement, in the center of the nave, marks his resting place.

Livingstone's writings include *Missionary Travels and Researches in South Africa* (1857); *Narrative of an Expedition to the Zambesi and its Tributaries* (1865); and *The Last Journals of David Livingstone,* 2 volumes (1874). A number of spurious works were published, purporting to be journals of Livingstone and even autobiographies of Livingstone. This led him to write a letter of warning and protest to the *London Athenaeum,* which appeared in print March 21, 1857. A number of biographies were written. They include: H. M. Stanley, *How I Found Livingstone* (1872); Jabez Marrat, *David Livingstone, Missionary and Discoverer*

(1877); Wm. G. Blaikie, *Life of Livingstone* (1880); H. H. Johnson, *Life of Livingstone* (1891); and C. J. Finger, *David Livingstone, Explorer and Prophet* (1928).

Gustavus Aird (1813-1898)

One of the last survivors of the golden days of Highland preaching was Dr. Gustavus Aird, of Creich. He was born in 1813 at Heathfield, Kilmuir-Easter, in Ross-shire, and he lived almost to the beginning of the present century. Educated at King's College, Aberdeen, taking his degree in 1830, he was licensed to preach in 1841 and ordained to Croick, at the head of Strathcarron, later in the same year. Two years later he united with the Free Kirk, taking with him all the families of his congregation but two. That year he was called from Croick to Creich, where his first task was to build a church and parish schools. In 1888 the Assembly recognized his ability by electing him moderator, at Inverness. In 1897 he secured a co-pastor and went south to Manchester, hoping to improve his health, but he died in 1898, at the age of 85.

Dr. Aird was one of the great preachers of the Highland country. He was one of several men who were much in request on those solemn Communion occasions which drew multitudes. People came from throughout the Highlands when it was learned that he was to preach. With a thorough acquaintance with the Scriptures, a fine command of the expressive Gaelic language, a voice of great range and power and a forceful personality, Dr. Aird was one of the influential Free Church pastors of the nineteenth century. He was positive in his theology, making no concessions to Arminianism nor to such innovations as the results of German Biblical criticism, and he was one of the staunch defenders of the old days of Scottish orthodoxy. When the several phases of the innovations controversy swept through the Scottish churches, the defenders of the old order could always depend upon Dr. Aird for active support.

In his preaching he had no sympathy for the passing homiletical fads that arose from time to time. He insisted that every true sermon must rest upon the three R's, namely,

Ruin, Redemption and Regeneration. A number of his sermons exist, both in Gaelic and in English, and they all run true to his principles: Mankind is not merely weakened spiritually, but utterly ruined because of sin; Redemption is the one thing of paramount importance, and this is possible only through the mediation of Jesus Christ the Saviour; Regeneration is possible only through the work of the Holy Ghost, Whose office it is to convey to mankind the benefits of the atoning death of Jesus Christ.

In the days when ethical preaching threatened to crowd out the message of sin and grace, a Scottish dominie met an old lady in the street and asked her to define the word "Trinity." "Aye, sir," replied Janet. " 'Tis the God in two Persons, the Father and the Son." "But Janet, are there not three Persons in the Trinity?" "Aye, the Apostles' Creed do say so, sir; but after sitting under your preaching these forty years, I have heard the Father mentioned often, the Son occasionally, and the Holy Ghost never."

Such a rebuke could never have been spoken to Dr. Aird, for his sermons were a summary of Calvinistic doctrine, whatever the occasion. Man's election is sure because the Father so decreed it from Eternity; Jesus Christ was made incarnate not to become a great Teacher, but rather a Saviour; and the benefits of His Atonement can come only through the work of Regeneration in the Holy Ghost. Dr. Aird did not always seem to realize that the Holy Ghost chooses to use a vehicle, the means of grace, by which to enter the heart of man, neither does he seem inclined to accept universal grace. His theology contains several of the flaws of his particular school, but on the other hand it must be said to his credit that he did not surrender to popular theological opinion in an age in which men feared the rationalistic higher critics more than they respected the witness of the Word of God.

James Hamilton (1814-1867)

James Hamilton was born near Paisley, in 1814. His father was a clergyman. He was graduated from Glasgow University in 1829, and then attended Edinburgh. In 1838 he became assistant to Robert Candlish, at St. George's, Edinburgh. A year later he was given the parish of Abernyte, and in 1841 he became pastor of Roxburgh Church, Edinburgh. In 1841 the National Scottish Church in Regent Square, London, was seeking a pastor, and Hamilton was called, and served with distinction until his death. In 1843, the year of the Disruption, Hamilton seceded from the State Kirk with Chalmers, Candlish and their followers.

James Hamilton was a preacher of exceptional gifts, evangelical in his doctrinal position, a master of the English language, possessed of imagination and a convincing speaker. His method of preaching was expository. "He possessed a vivid imagination, a brilliant fancy and a sparkling phraseology. His sentences are strings of pearls, and whatever subjects he touches, he invariably adorns. His affluence of imagery is surprising. To illustrate some particular Scripture, he will lay science, art, and natural history under contribution. But plenteous as are the flowers of eloquence, their sweetness does not cloy. And withal, a spirit of earnest piety pervades the discourse. There is only one drawback — the broad Scotch accent in which it is delivered." [75]

Although he lived a century ago, Hamilton's style, like that of Christmas Evans, is strangely of our own day. In his sermon on St. Matt. 28, 20, he says: "This is what the Gospel does. It just offers you a Friend, who can both save and satisfy your soul. Jesus, the Son of God, God manifest in the flesh, Immanuel, the Gospel offers this Friend to you — not more tender than He is holy, not more divine than He is human. Instead of clutching to props which cannot elevate you, or if they do bear you up for a moment, must soon be withdrawn again — the Gospel bids you grow against the Tree of Life, and just as you grow up in Christ, you will grow up into holiness and into happiness." [76]

This particular sermon, like those of many of the Scottish preachers of that day, has a lengthy introduction,

---

[75]. H. C. Fish, *Pulpit Eloquence of the Nineteenth Century* (New York, 1871), p. 725.
[76]. *Ibid.*, pp. 726-735.

three main divisions, three "inferences" of about the same
length as the main divisions, and a conclusion.

In addition to several religious books of a devotional
character, James Hamilton was editor of two or more
religious periodicals. His writings include: *The Harp on
the Willows* (1843); *The Church in the House* (1846);
Life in Earnest (1852); *The Mount of Olives* (1853); *The
Lamp and the Lantern* (1853); *Lives of Bunyan, Henry
and Hall* (1853); *The Royal Preacher, Ecclesiastes* (1854);
Emblems from Eden (1855); and *Christian Classics.* His
collected *Works,* in 6 volumes, were published in 1869, and
W. Arnot's *Life of James Hamilton* in 1870.

William C. Burns (1815-1868)

William Chalmers Burns was born in 1815 in Duns,
Forfarshire. After attending Marischal College in Aberdeen,
he studied law for a time. His theological training was
received at Glasgow. He was licensed in 1839, and preached
for a time in Dundee. He gained a reputation as an eloquent
evangelical preacher because of a preaching tour that took
him through the British Isles and Canada.

In 1847 he was sent to China as the first missionary of
the English Presbyterian Missionary Society. He adapted
himself to the customs and dress of China as much as possible, and he travelled far inland on his preaching tours, at
a time when missionary activity was centered mainly in the
coastal cities. His lively, evangelical manner of presenting
the fundamentals of Christianity made a deep impression
upon the people, and he did much to open up China to later
missionary effort. Among his writings perhaps the best
known is his Chinese translation of Bunyan's *The Pilgrim's
Progress.* The biography of William C. Burns, entitled
A Memoir of W. C. Burns (1870), was written by Islay
Burns.

James Morison (1816-1893)

James Morison, founder of the Evangelical Union, and
a preacher of great fervor, was born in Bathgate, Linlithgowshire, where his father was a pastor of a United Secession congregation. He was educated in the parochial school
and in the academy in Bathgate. He was graduated from

Edinburgh University in 1834, and then entered the United Secession's Divinity Hall, where Dr. John Brown was his teacher.

Morison was licensed to preach in 1839, and his sermons at Cabrach and in the surrounding towns, attracted widest attention. A great revival took place, not in the sense of modern revivals, but rather was it a great awakening of evangelical zeal. During the year or so that he was thus engaged, he published a tract entitled, *The Question: What must I do to be Saved?* In this tract he declared that salvation is offered freely to all men, and not to the elect few. In 1840 he was called as pastor of the United Secession Synod's congregation at Clerks Lane, Kilmarnock, but his presbytery refused to ordain him unless he suppressed the tract, and declared his belief in limited election. Morison appealed his case to the Assembly, thus gaining time. He served the congregation at Clerks Lane while the case was pending, and by his remarkable preaching he gained 578 new members in two years. In the end he was excommunicated, for he insisted that God the Father loves all men without distinction or exception, and that it is not His will that any be lost; that Jesus Christ died for all men without distinction or exception, and will not cast out those who come to Him; and that the Holy Ghost strives to apply the benefits of Christ's righteousness and blood to all men without distinction or exception, and man's own unbelief is alone the cause of his damnation.

James Morison's trial was the occasion for a national sensation. He was but 25 years old at the time, already a preacher of great power, and many were inclined to take his part. His own father defended him, and was excommunicated for it, as were two other pastors. After Morison was found guilty of heresy and expelled from the United Secession Synod, he, with his father and two others, founded the Evangelical Union, which flourished for 33 years, grew to 81 congregations, and finally merged with the Congregational Union.

"Morisonianism," as the teachings of the Evangelical Union were called, caused greatest bitterness of feeling at the time. Morison was a preacher of great ability, and his racy polemics attracted attention throughout Scotland. He did not hesitate to indulge in invective, and he is said to have declared: "Calvinism is the teaching that God blew out man's candle from Eternity, and then cast men into hell because they were found to be in the dark."

In 1851, the North Dundas Street Church in Glasgow was built for him, and people from all denominations flocked to hear him.   Strangely enough, the bitterness died out, and a general acceptance of his views on the Atonement began to develop.   Morison was Scriptural in teaching that salvation is offered freely to all men, but he erred in teaching the freedom of the will.   He never saw clearly the fact that man may refuse salvation, but of his unaided reason or strength he cannot choose salvation.   He seems unclear in regard to the fact that man's conversion and salvation is wholly through the grace of God and merit of Christ, while the rejection of this grace lies wholly in man's own sinful unbelief.

In his later years, Morison's fiery polemical preaching was greatly mellowed, and he became one of the gentlest of men.   He was looked upon as an exceptional Greek scholar, and his commentaries on St. Matthew and St. Mark, and upon Romans ix (Pauline Election), carried his fame throughout the world at the time.

John R. MacDuff (1818-1895)

J. R. MacDuff, as he is commonly known, was a man who was able to express his thoughts as vividly on the printed page as in the pulpit.   He was born in Bonhard, in the parish of Scone, Perthshire.   After finishing the common schools and the high school at Edinburgh, he attended Edinburgh University, where one of his professors was Dr. Thomas Chalmers.   It was Chalmers who influenced the young man to become an evangelical preacher.

He was ordained in 1843, and became pastor of Kettins, Forfarshire.   In 1849 he was called to St. Madoes, Perthshire, and in 1855 to Sandyford Church, in Glasgow, where he had a large, handsome church building and a large, intelligent congregation.   In 1870 he retired to Chiselhurst and devoted the next 25 years to writing the remarkable series of books which have made him known throughout the world.

As a preacher he was a man who loved to describe the incidents in the life of our Lord in language so effective that these scenes seemed to live once more before the very eyes of his hearers. He was equally skilled as a writer, and he undertook the task of giving to the world a life of the Lord Jesus Christ in a series of books, with such titles as *Memories of Gennesaret, Memories of Olivet, Memories of Bethany,* etc., as well as works on the Miracles and the Parables. He published other books on the life of St. Paul and on Old Testament incidents.

These books are written in simple, vivid English, they are devotional in tone, and they have been read by Christians throughout the world. Their language is simple and clear, the analysis of the subjects is careful, and the word-pictures almost without an equal. As an example of his treatment of the incidents in the life of our Lord, one might mention his chapter on "The Storm on the Lake." [77] He describes the ship setting sail at twilight, and on it the Infant Church. It is freighted with the world's salvation. Then he describes the humanity of the Saviour, for He was tired after a day of unremitting labor, and found deep sleep, wrapped in a rough coat of a fisherman, His head on a pillow at the ship's stern-post. "The Lord of Glory — Immanuel, God with us — out on the bleak sea; — the dusk of approaching night for His curtains, the sky for His canopy — stretched like a helpless babe in the arms of sleep — lulled to rest by the music of oars and the ripple of waters." Then the sudden storm is described, the roaring of the wind and the waves, and the ship filling with water. He stresses that humanity of the Lord, Who grew weary on the long, dusty road through Samaria, and thirsty when He sank down on the rim of the well, and Who suffered pain when scourged, crowned with thorns and crucified.

Then His divinity is described, and a graphic account of the stilling of the tempest follows. At the word of His command, "Every wave rocked itself to rest. The winds

---

[77]. J. R. MacDuff, *Memories of Gennesaret* (New York, 1869), pp. 151-167.

returned to their chambers. The lights on the shore were once more reflected in the waveless sea: — 'Immediately there was a great calm.' Well might the disciples, as they beheld the power of that marvellous mandate, exclaim, in the words of their Psalmist King, as they crouched adoring at their Master's feet, 'The sea is His, and He made it; and His hands formed the dry land. Oh, come let us worship and bow down, let us kneel before the Lord our Maker!' "

Perhaps such language might be termed "flowery" today, but the simple, picturesque, yet devotional style of his many books have made them favorites for almost a century after the original sermons were first preached. The merit of Dr. MacDuff's 76 or more books lies not in their ornate style, but rather in the fact that he has the rare gift of making one feel that he has stood in the very presence of the Saviour, and has seen with his own eyes the incidents that have been mentioned.

It is hardly possible to mention all of J. R. MacDuff's books. A few representative examples are: *The Mind and Words of Jesus* (1855); *Memories of Gennesaret* (1858); *Footsteps of Jesus* (1856); *Memories of Bethany* (1857); *Noonday at Sychar* (1868); *The Shepherd and His Flock* (1865); *Memories of Olivet* (1867); and one or two others, form almost a complete account of our Lord's earthly life and work. *Sunsets on the Hebrew Mountains* (1861), a series of biographies of Bible characters, is one of MacDuff's best works, although suited for the Bible class rather than for the pulpit. Alexander Whyte was entirely correct when he said that biographies of Old Testament worthies are lectures and not sermons, and have no place in the pulpit, since they consume the time that might have been devoted to the exposition of evangelical truth. J. R. MacDuff wrote several excellent biographies of St. Paul, St. Peter and other Bible characters. The pastor who has patience to collect the 76 or more books written by MacDuff will find himself richly repaid for the trouble. They are still available at many second-hand book shops, for there are thousands of them as a result of their enormous popularity in the latter nineteenth century. The younger clergyman will find them rich in suggestion, even though the style may be rather ornate. Their fine devotional tone is their chief merit. Generally speaking they are conservative in their theology, they are expository, and their simplicity of language often causes one to forget that they really contain considerable depth of thought.

John Cairns (1818-1892)

John Cairns, noted United Presbyterian preacher and leader, was born in 1818 at Ayton Hill, near Berwick-on-Tweed. He attended the University of Edinburgh, and was graduated in 1840. His theological studies were pursued at Secession Hall, from 1840 to 1843. During the next year or so he studied in Germany. He was ordained in 1845 and became pastor of Golden Square United Presbyterian Church, Berwick-on-Tweed. A year later John Brown, M.D., the noted writer, said of him, "he is Augustine, Calvin, Jonathan Edwards and himself, all in one." After serving his congregation for 31 years, he was made professor of apologetics in the United Presbyterian Theological Hall, Edinburgh, and he filled that position for nine years. Then he was elected professor of systematic theology and apologetics, and in 1879 he became principal. In 1872 he was elected moderator of the Assembly. In 1880 he paid a visit to America.

John Cairns was one of the foremost leaders of the United Presbyterians, and greatly interested in the Evangelical Alliance. He possessed "a nature as simple as that of Guthrie," and he was able to preach doctrinal sermons in a way that the simplest people could understand him. He spoke with great conviction. His favorite subjects were the separation of Church and State, home and foreign missions, temperance, and disestablishment of the State Church. He became interested in the efforts to bring about a reunion of the State Church, the Free Church and the United Presbyterians. He had visions of world-wide Presbyterianism, for his biographer says that he spoke of "a great Presbyterian Church as wide as the English language and as comprehensive as Episcopacy — a Church which, while separately organized in different countries, should be one in basis and spirit, taking the Reformed Faith as its creed, simplicity as its guide to worship, and the Bible as its supreme standard, but which both in formation and administration must be independent and free from constraint by civil powers." [78] Among his writings, one of the best known is his life of Dr. John Brown of Edinburgh, the third of a dynasty of four men bearing that name. His Cunningham lectures were published in 1881 under the title *Unbelief in the Eighteenth Century*. A book of sermons, *Christ the Morning Star* (1892), may be mentioned; as well as his *Romanism and Rationalism* (1863); *Outlines of Apologetical Theology* (1867); *The Doctrine of the Presbyterian Church* (1876); *Doctrinal Principles of the United Presbyterian Church* (1888); *The Scottish Philosophy* (1856); and *Oxford Rationalism and English Christianity* (1861), the last a reply to the liberal *Essays and Reviews*. In addition to the biography by Dr. A. R. MacEwen, an account of the life of Principal Cairns is included in the *Famous Scots Series*.

John Kennedy (1819-1884)

Scotland has given the world so large a number of remarkable preachers that it is strange that a comprehensive history of Scottish preaching has not yet been written. Dr. Blaikie's Cunningham Lectures appeared years ago in book form, as well as Dr. Taylor's Yale Lectures. Valuable as these two books are, yet they were prepared for the lecture room, hence the material was kept within a relatively small compass. A few great names required presentation, while others, almost equally great, had to be passed by with regret. Certainly Dr. John Kennedy of Dingwall deserves a place in Scotland's hall of fame, as does Dr. Alexander Whyte and other comparatively recent preachers. If John Macdonald of Ferintosh was the Apostle to the North, John Kennedy was his worthy successor.

Mr. Kennedy was born in 1819 in Killearnan, where his father was pastor. He grew up in that parish, attended the parochial school, and as a boy he spoke the Gaelic language as fluently as English. The schoolboys of those days were not ashamed of their mother-tongue, which is one of the oldest and most highly expressive of all languages. John

---

[78]. J. S. MacEwen, *Life of John Cairns* (London, 1898), pp. 501-502.

Kennedy employed it with great skill throughout his life. At the age of 17 he entered Aberdeen University, receiving his master's degree from King's College in 1840. Later in the same year he entered the Theological Hall, and when he finished his studies in 1843 he was licensed to preach by the Established Church of Scotland. He was ordained a year later, and became pastor at Dingwall. The Disruption had just taken place, and the congregation to which he was called had just been established by the Free Church of Scotland. For the next 41 years Mr. Kennedy served Dingwall. Not only was he pastor of that important congregation, but he became one of the foremost leaders of what was called the "Hieland host," the great champions of old-fashioned Presbyterian orthodoxy. So rigidly conservative were Dr. Kennedy and his Highland associates that they looked upon hymns of human composition as abject sectarianism. They would permit only the Psalms of David in their rhythmic form; and anything that went beyond that was opposed with firmness and finality. Dr. Kennedy and his associates were alarmed when some of the more liberal congregations in the Lowlands began to look with toleration upon such things as church organs. We may call these men fanatics today, but they were of the firm opinion that a church organ, while not in itself sinful, is but the entering wedge for other things, such as hired singers, processions, secular music during the hour of worship and the gradual introduction of a spirit of liberalism. The church service would cease to be an hour or more of solemn worship and instruction, and would become a popular Sunday gathering, with ear-tickling anthems and solos in the choir loft and book reviews and sprightly discussions of current events and personality problems in the pulpit.

Dr. John Kennedy was certainly one of the great preachers of the nineteenth century. David Beaton calls him the "prince of Highland preachers." Had he spent his ministry of 41 years in Edinburgh instead of among the crags of Ross-shire, some enterprising publisher would have issued printed volumes of his remarkable sermons, and the world today would not hesitate to give him his rightful place together with such men as Alexander Maclaren, Alexander Whyte and Campbell Morgan.

Unfortunately Dr. Kennedy's printed sermons, like those of George Whitefield and John Summerfield, fall short of his spoken utterances. These sermons were written under adverse conditions — either "in the cool retirement of his study" with no congregation before him to awaken the oratorical fire that was in him, or else, in some cases, while he was lying ill in bed. The preaching of the real John Kennedy has been lost forever, except in the memories of very old men and women who heard him, and who describe him in superlatives. He visited America in 1873, preached in important churches, and not many years ago there were old professors and clergymen who were ready to tell of his great power in the pulpit.

He was a man of dignified appearance in the pulpit, gifted with a superb intellect, a remarkable memory, a fine command of the English language and a devotion to "the old doctrines of Redemption" that had become almost an obsession. His biography of John Macdonald is not remarkable as biographies are judged today,[79] but it should be on the "required list" of all young clergymen, if only for the striking things that Mr. Kennedy has to say in regard to evangelical preaching. The same may be said of his history of the famous preachers of his own Ross-shire.[80]   As a critical historical document it has certain shortcomings, but as a defense of Christ-centered preaching it deserves to be reprinted in a beautiful little volume and given to every young pastor on the day of his ordination. There are paragraphs in it and pages in it that none who have read it will ever forget. What can be more stirring than the contrast that Dr. Kennedy draws between the preaching of the great Gaelic Scotsmen and that of the over-rated author of the sermon "Religion in Common Life," and of Dr. Guthrie's *Gospel in Ezekiel*, both of which he declares to be "worthless because they are Christless."

---

[79]. John Kennedy, *John Macdonald, the Apostle to the North* (London, 1867).

[80]. John Kennedy, *The Days of the Fathers in Ross-shire* (Edinburgh 1861).

Perhaps there has never been a finer Gaelic preacher than Dr. Kennedy, although his command of the English language was almost equally faultless. During his ministry of 41 years, he was called upon to preach as often as ten times in a single week; and it was not uncommon for him to deliver a masterpiece in the Gaelic language, and after the singing of a hymn, to arise and deliver an equally impressive English sermon. He received calls to congregations continually. Large city congregations in Scotland, England, the United States, Canada and Australia tried repeatedly to induce him to leave his beloved Highlands. After his American visit he is said to have received calls from New York and other large cities, with the assurance that any salary that he might name would be most readily provided. It still remains for some qualified biographer to write a memoir of Dr. Kennedy that is truly representative of his greatness. The biographies by Auld[81] and by Wylie[82] are good, yet hardly adequate; and as one of the great Scotsmen of the nineteenth century a more detailed account of his remarkable career might well be given.

When John Kennedy was ordained, Alexander Stewart of Cromarty said to him, "John, I think I know you now. Take one advice from me: don't write your sermons. Spend your time in thinking, for, be assured, if you do not express clearly it will be because you have not thought sufficiently." Mr. Kennedy heeded the advice of the older pastor, and for thirty-eight years he prepared only outlines. At the age of 62 his friends realized that his health was failing, and they persuaded him to allow a reporter to take down his sermons in shorthand, and to publish one sermon each week. The first sermon of the series, in the form of a twelve-page pamphlet, appeared in November, 1882. Dr. Kennedy preached but five sermons of the series, for a month after the publication of the first one he was confined to his bed. However, he had promised his friends a sermon every week, and for a year he lay in bed, writing a sermon each week, often writing out from memory some sermon

---

[81]. Alex Auld, *Life of John Kennedy* (London, 1887).
[82]. Wylie, *In Memoriam, the Rev. John Kennedy* (Inverness, 1884).

previously preached at Dingwall or elsewhere. Shortly before his death a collection of fifty-four of these sermons appeared in book form.[83] It would be difficult, in reformed Protestant circles, to find a book of sermons as rich in evangelical substance as these.

Toward the end of his life Dr. Kennedy, in a letter to the readers of his sermons,[84] described himself as one of the last defenders of the old doctrines of grace. In his letter he admonished the new generation of Scottish preachers who had departed far from the ways of Balfour and Love, of Rutherfurd and Halyburton, and of Lachlan Mackenzie, Porteous, Mackintosh and Macdonald of Ferintosh. He urged men to return to the old ways of their forefathers, "who knew the doctrines of the Gospel, and who preached them with precision and power." He reminded them that: "The cowards are always the most advanced when the army is in retreat. And fast retreating before the enemy that attacks the foundations of true faith, and of true morality, is the generation in the midst of which we live. In that retreat those who most lack Christian firmness and fortitude are they who will be the readiest to assume the lead." [85]

Dr. Kennedy preached not only the passive obedience of the Lord Jesus, but His active obedience as well. In a noteworthy sermon on "The Preaching of Christ Crucified," he said:

"We preach Christ crucified, and in doing so we preach peace to sinners through 'the blood of His cross.' We do so because He, in the work finished on the cross, laid the one foundation on which divine mercy, to the praise of all the divine name, may bestow the blessing of peace upon a sinner. O what a blessing is peace with God to a sinner condemned to die! He has been convicted of being a death-deserving sinner, the sentence of eternal death lies upon him, the face of 'God the Judge of all' is set against him, and for him, apart from the sovereign exercise of divine mercy, there is no way of escape from everlasting woe. But that mercy cannot be extended to him except in a way that

---

[83]. *Sermons by the Rev. John Kennedy, Dingwall* (Inverness, 1883).
[84]. *To the Readers of the Sermons* (Inverness, 1883).
[85]. *Ibid.,* p. 3.

will secure honour to the Law, satisfaction to the justice, and glory to the name of God. And how can all this be secured? The sinner himself can do nothing to meet the Law's claims, for he hath no strength, but power only to transgress; and the demands of divine justice he himself can only meet by yielding up his whole person in order to an experience of eternal dying. But Christ crucified hath done and suffered all that is required in order to a free and full exercise of divine mercy such as shall be to the praise of the divine glory. He, as representing all who shall be saved, gave to the Law an obedience by which it was magnified, and to justice an atonement for sin which was infinitely precious, and an opportunity to God of so dealing with Him, and through Him with sinners, as admits of an infinite display of the glory of all His name. In preaching Christ crucified there is presented to the sinner this one ground on which he is called to take his stand before the mercy, free and infinite, of God, to receive 'without money and without price' the blessing of everlasting peace with God. . . . It is Christ crucified that is preached when peace through His blood is preached, and not apart from himself can the peace which He procured by possibility be found. Him 'God hath set forth to be a propitiation, through faith in His blood,' and only as you reach Him in faith, and trust in His blood, as the one ground of your acceptance before God, can peace be yours." [86]

The sermon from which this quotation was taken ends with a solemn warning. Dr. Kennedy says:

"Pauline preaching is becoming, in the estimation of many, an antiquated kind of thing, which, in an age such as ours, should be quite laid as a fossil on the shelf. And what do they propose to substitute? Some would have a more unsystematic mode of presenting the truth. They would cast the federal theology aside, and must have a fresh cast of thought and an altogether new phraseology. And what is this new thing which they have introduced? It is not easy to describe it, for it is neither Law nor Gospel, and it is a rare eye that can discern it to be common sense. It is suited neither to saint nor to sinner, and where to find an audience

---

[86]. *Sermons by the Rev. John Kennedy* (Inverness, 1883), pp. 544-545.

for such preaching, in which neither of these shall be, it is utterly impossible to conjecture. Others would have *intellectual* preaching from which the old story of the Cross would be excluded, and nothing supplied either for the heart or for the conscience. Others still desire what they regard as *advanced* teaching. Of course in their view this crave is a desire for progress, but what really is the thing which they seek? It is to go back from all the positions reached during the religious conflicts of the past, to abandon the whole sphere of vital godliness, to treat with disrespect the divine authority of the Word of God, and to decry as superstition all effort to walk in the fear of the Lord. Besides all these there are some who are enamoured of what they call *practical* preaching, by which they mean preaching which is not doctrinal, for they dislike to be made to feel how ignorant they are of the divine scheme of grace, preaching which, taking it for granted that all are Christians, deals out its counsels to all indiscriminately; and which, coming down to the everyday cares and anxieties of life, tends to cheer men in their daily toil by comforts which are furnished by reason rather than by Scripture, and which never flowed from 'the fountain of living waters' through Christ crucified. These are the new styles of preaching, and if recent progress is maintained, Pauline preaching will soon cease to be heard from Scottish pulpits." [87]

In his own preaching Dr. Kennedy did not fall into the error which he mentions. He was never guilty of yielding to the fads of the day. He made it his rule to consider four classes of hearers,[88] and for each one of these classes he had some helpful truth. These classes included: 1. The experienced, well indoctrinated Christian, known in the Scottish Highlands as "the men." They knew their Bibles, they studied them daily and they read and expounded them every evening with their families. They were firmly opposed to liberalism in all its forms and they rejoiced in the preaching of conservative men who proclaimed the great truths of Redemption. 2. Willing Christians, who were devout church-goers, but were not as well indoctrinated as "the

---

[87]. *Ibid.*, p. 550.
[88]. Alexander Auld, *Life of John Kennedy* (London, 1887), pp. 93-95.

men." They were God-fearing people, but their lack of thorough indoctrination caused them to have periods of weakness and uncertainty. In his preaching Dr. Kennedy sought to instruct these people and give them a more thorough understanding of the truths of God's Word. Many a willing, but poorly instructed Christian was strengthened by Dr. Kennedy's preaching, and not many years ago there were people in Scotland, in the United States and in Canada who spoke with gratitude of the help that he had given them in their youth. 3. People who heard Law and Gospel willingly, but realized that mere intellectual assent to the teachings of the Bible is not enough. Dr. Kennedy sought to build up in such people a living faith in the Lord Jesus Christ. 4. There were many who flocked to hear him merely because he was a preacher of exceptional ability, yet they went out of curiosity, indifferent as to their own spiritual welfare. They spoke highly of his superb gifts as a preacher, but went to hear him as they might go to hear a great musician or a famous statesman. Dr. Kennedy was given the rare skill of reaching the hearts of such people and making them feel that he was speaking to each person individually. His biographer devotes pages to the written testimony of such persons whose lives were changed permanently. In one case a man walked 15 miles to hear John Kennedy, and so greatly impressed was he that he walked 15 miles every Sunday for the next 10 years, regardless of the weather, to hear this great Highland preacher.

The method used by Dr. Kennedy is interesting. After a careful exposition of his text he applied it adroitly to these four classes of people, often saying, "There is one listening to me today who . . ." then proceeding to describe a spiritual condition with such startling accuracy that the hearer was positive that a part of the sermon was written for his individual benefit. Strange to say, such people rarely were offended. Dr. Kennedy was not a revivalist, and his methods were not those of revivalism, yet hundreds of people were awakened by his Christ-centered preaching. He was one of Scotland's greatest preachers, and one of the best types of preacher that reformed Protestantism has produced. He was the Spurgeon of the Highlands, and had he preached in Edinburgh rather than in Dingwall, his weekly congregations would have been equal to those of Spurgeon. His one great mistake lies in the fact that he published none of his sermons until virtually upon his death bed. His writings include: *Days of the Fathers in Ross-shire* (1861); *The Apostle of the North* (1867); *Man's Relation to God* (1869); *Introduction of Instrumental Music into the Worship of the Free Church* (1883); and *Sermons by Rev. Dr. John Kennedy, Dingwall* (1883). In addition to Alexander Auld's biography, *In Memoriam, John Kennedy* (1884), presents the story of his life.

John Ker (1819-1886)

John Ker, (pronounced Car), was born on Bield farm, Tweedsmuir parish, Peeblesshire, in 1819. In early life he was influenced by the preaching of John Brown of Edinburgh. He was educated in Edinburgh High School, and in 1835 he entered Edinburgh University, where he became distinguished for his good scholarship. In 1838 he entered the theological school of the United Secession Church. During his school vacations he studied French, German, Hebrew and Aramaic. After finishing his theological studies, he went to Halle, where he studied with Tholuck, and to Berlin, where Neander was one of his teachers.

He was ordained in 1845 and became pastor of a church in Alnwick, Northumberlandshire. In 1849 he went to Barrhead, and in 1851 to the East Campbell Street Church, Glasgow. This church soon became so crowded that a new and much larger one was built in 1857 in Sydney Place. In 1876 he became a professor in the theological seminary of the United Free Church.

His published sermons have gone through a number of editions. Fleming[89] declares that he was a preacher of rare quality. His sermons are solid, full of information, with a warmth, a spontaneity and an appeal that has caused them to be held in high esteem. He did not escape entirely the spirit that prevailed in Halle, although Tholuck, while not orthodox in all things, did much to modify the rationalistic spirit which had prevailed in Halle.

---

[89]. J. R. Fleming, *The Church in Scotland* (Edinburgh, 1927-33), vol. I, p. 255.

John Ker's several books of sermons, while cast in a style that is hardly popular today, will prove of more than passing interest to the thoughtful preacher. The homiletical structure, while somewhat old-fashioned, nevertheless reveals the painstaking care of a generation when men took time to do such things well. John Ker lived in an age when a highly complicated form of parochial activity did not keep a pastor in a church office by day, and at a meeting every night. Men such as John Ker considered the preparation of a sermon a serious task. They planned their sermons with care, they developed them logically, and they paid much attention to the art of careful exposition of their text. To announce a text, and then make no further reference to it, was to such men a betrayal of a solemn obligation to their people. Such men lived simple lives and devoted much time to their books and to thoughful, methodical preparation. The superficial psychological studies, heard in too many pulpits in recent years, would have aroused only severe condemnation from the sturdy old Scottish parsons of John Ker's day.

Professor Ker's best collection of sermons is a two-volume work entitled *The Day-Dawn and the Rain, and Other Sermons* (1869), evidently preached in his Glasgow days. Other volumes followed: *Sermons, Second Series* (1886); *The Psalms in History and Biography* (1886); and *Thoughts for Heart and Life* (1887). However, the book by which John Ker is known the world over is a single volume entitled *Lectures on the History of Preaching* (1888). These were delivered to his students as a part of their course in Homiletics. After Prof. Ker's death, only 21 of these brilliant lectures could be found among his papers. There are seven lectures on pre-Reformation preaching and 14 lectures on the great preachers of Germany in Reformation and post-Reformation days. His students recalled many other lectures, but apparently they were delivered from notes. The subject was a new one in Prof. Ker's day, and it required laborious research. The book, while not a small one, is a classic in its way, although one closes it with disappointment as he recalls the wealth of material pertaining to other countries that has never been brought to light. A number of eminent German preachers are characterized in an able manner, and the book, fragmentary as it is, will prove a valuable addition to the library of all who would understand the spiritual awakenings and declines in Germany. Dr. Dargan has covered much of the same ground, and in greater detail, in his classic of two volumes,[90] covering as it does, chiefly continental Europe; but John Ker's lectures will long remain a valuable work for those fortunate enough in finding a copy in the rare book shops.

Prof. Ker wrote an interesting work on *Scottish Nationality* (1887); and with J. L. Watson he wrote *The Erskines: Ebenezer and Ralph* (1881). Ker's collected *Letters* have been published, as well as several short memoirs.

John Cunningham (1819-1893)

John Cunningham was born in Paisley in 1819. His early education was received in the Paisley grammar school. He entered Glasgow University in 1836 and Edinburgh in 1840. In 1845 he was licensed to preach, and shortly after he was ordained and given the church at Crieff, Perthshire, of which he was pastor for 41 years.

In 1867 the "Crieff Organ Case" caused a controversy in Scotland. As early as 1807, St. Andrew's, Glasgow, had attempted to introduce a church organ. In 1829, Roxburgh Place Relief Chapel had attempted the same thing. Public opinion was strongly against it, and neither attempt was successful. In 1856, Claremont United Presbyterian Church, Glasgow, set up an organ, and petitioned their Synod to permit its use. They were refused, and the organ remained unused until 1872, when the U. P. Synod passed a slightly less rigid resolution, yet warning against giving offense by such an innovation as an organ. When Ira D. Sankey came to Scotland in 1874, his small American organ paved the way, and the more daring congregations began to introduce organs. The Crieff Case, of 1867, was one of several of these contests, and John Cunningham favored the group

---

90. E. C. Dargan, *A History of Preaching*, 2 vols. (New York, 1905-1912).

within his congregation who asked for instrumental musical accompaniment.

The agitation did not do the congregation harm, for so effective was John Cunningham as a preacher that a large new church — with an organ — had to be built. In 1886 Cunningham was made principal of St. Mary's College, St. Andrews. His best known work is his *Church History of Scotland,* two volumes, an authoritative work that covers the period down to the Disruption of 1843. However, Dr. Cunningham's sympathies at times seem to favor the Moderates rather than the Evangelicals.

As a preacher, Dr. John Cunningham is said to have been a man gifted with considerable freshness and vigor of expression, and his sermons are described as having had a pronounced individuality of their own. However, in his day, Scottish preaching was giving indications of a loss of evangelical vigor. In softening down the rigidity of the old-time Calvinism, and in adopting declarations for church union that were not always in definite language, many went too far, and succeeded only in modifying the emphatic stress on sin and grace that had been characteristic of a number of their famous preachers in the past.

In addition to his *Church History of Scotland,* two volumes (1859), John Cunningham wrote *The Quakers from their Origin till the Present Time* (1868); *A New Theory of Knowing and Being* (1874); *Episcopacy, Presbytery and Puritanism in Scotland* (1881); and *The Growth of the Church in its Organization and Institutions* (1886).

A. Campbell Fraser (1819-1914)

Alexander Campbell Fraser was born in 1819 at Ardchattan manse, Argyll. His father, Hugh Fraser, was a clergyman in the Scottish Kirk. After his education in Edinburgh University, Campbell Fraser was ordained in 1842 and became pastor of Cramond parish. Although in parish work but four years, yet he won for himself a reputation for effective preaching. In 1846 he was made professor of logic at New College, of the Free Kirk. In 1850 he became editor of the *North British Review*. This noted magazine flourished under his able leadership, but an article by a contributor caused offense, and he resigned his editorship. In 1856 he became professor of logic and methaphysics in Edinburgh University. It was a contest between Fraser, an evangelical, and Ferrier, whose views in regard to philosophy were looked upon by many as liberal. Fraser's election to the chair was looked upon as a victory for the conservative party. He held the position until 1891, when he was made professor emeritus. In 1894-1896 he was Gifford lecturer in natural theology at Edinburgh. He was author of a number of writings.

Dr. Fraser is so well known as a philosophical writer that his ability in the pulpit is often overlooked. Like a number of other Scottish professors and writers, he preached from time to time in the important churches of Edinburgh and elsewhere. His *Philosophy of Theism* (1895) is well known. Earlier works were *Essays in Philosophy* (1856), and *Rational Philosophy in History and in System* (1858). He edited the four-volume edition of the works of George Berkeley (1871), and published an autobiography.

John Caird (1820-1898)

In the year 1855, John Caird, a Scottish preacher, gained fame throughout the English speaking world because of a sermon preached before Queen Victoria and her husband. John Caird was born in Greenock, Scotland, in 1820. After attending the elementary schools in Greenock, he entered the office of his father, an engineer, with the intention of following that profession. In 1837 he entered Glasgow University where he studied mathematics and logic. Changing his mind, he began the study of theology in the same university, and was graduated in 1845.

He was ordained and assigned to the parish of Newton-on-Ayr. Two years later he became pastor, at the age of 27, of the important Lady Yester's church in Edinburgh. He resigned two years later, because of poor health, and accepted the less exacting duties of Errol, Perthshire, and then, in 1857, of Park Church, Glasgow. In 1862 he became professor of theology in Glasgow University, and in 1873 he was made principal of that institution.

His famous sermon, "Religion in Common Life," based on Rom. 12, 11, was preached before the Queen and her husband in 1855. So impressed were they that they asked for a copy of it. After reading it carefully, the Queen commanded that it be printed. Very few sermons have attained so widespread a circulation. Dean Stanley pronounced it the greatest sermon of the century. Reading it today, it is difficult to account for its surprising popularity. Beginning with a questionable exegesis of the word "business," it is a forceful appeal to apply the principles of Christianity to the affairs of one's daily business or professional life. It is a masterpiece in its way, but it cannot be said to be remarkable from an evangelical point of view. It speaks frequently of the Lord Jesus, but there is hardly a mention of sin and grace. Perhaps John Caird was like the preacher who was asked why he never mentioned the truths of redemptive Christianity. He replied, "I don't preach such things any more. We all take them for granted."

John Caird was a man who combined great depth of thought with all the gifts of an orator. In his earlier years he was an evangelical preacher of rare power, but his philosophical studies, and particularly his admiration for Hegel, seemed to diminish his ardent testimony in his later years. His *Introduction to the Philosophy of Religion* (1880), is Hegelian throughout, and seeks to present Hegelianism in its most favorable light. His *Fundamental Ideas of Christianity,* in two volumes (1899), contains his Gifford lectures. *Sermons of John Caird* appeared in 1858, while his *University Sermons* (1898), and *University Addresses* (1898), appeared soon after his death. Two biographies have appeared: Edward Caird's *Memoir of Dr. John Caird* (1899), and C. L. Warr's *Life of Principal Caird* (1926).

William G. Blaikie (1820-1899)

William G. Blaikie, of Scotland's Free Church, who won national fame as a preacher and teacher and world-wide fame as an author, church historian and biographer, was born in 1820 in Aberdeen. He entered Marischal College in 1833, and completed his studies at Aberdeen and Edinburgh

Universities. He was licensed to preach in 1841 and ordained in 1842 as pastor of Drumblade, Aberdeenshire, then
a congregation of the State Church. At the time of the
Disruption of 1843, Blaikie and most of his congregation
withdrew from the Established Church and united with the
Free Church. From 1844 to 1868 he was pastor of Pilrig,
Edinburgh. He took a deep interest in the poorer people
of Edinburgh, and drew large numbers of them into his
congregation.

In 1868 Dr. Blaikie was made professor of Apologetics
and Pastoral Theology in the Free Church's New College,
Edinburgh, and he filled this position with distinction for
almost 30 years. In 1870, together with William Arnot, he
visited America, attending the convention of the Presbyterian
Church in Philadelphia, and preaching in several leading
pulpits. From 1849 to 1853 he edited the *Free Church
Magazine,* and from 1860 to 1863 he was editor of the
North British Review.

W. G. Blaikie was an excellent preacher, and during his
24 years of parish work in Edinburgh, his evangelical sermons and his moving pleas for the people in the neglected
areas of the great city, kept his name prominently before
the entire country. His lengthy and eloquent address before
the Free Church Assembly of 1864 was easily the most important event of that convention, yet the meeting adjourned
without taking definite action in regard to the people of the
tenements, among whom Dr. Blaikie urged his associates to
carry on missionary work. The fruits of his years of labor
were to come later.

Dr. Blaikie was the author of a number of books,
several of which have become theological classics. His
Bible History (1859) was used for generations as a standard
text-book in theological seminaries in Britain, the colonies
and America. His *The Preachers of Scotland from the
Sixth to the Nineteenth Century* (1888) is by far the best
work ever written on Scottish preaching, and its admirable
style has given it a place in every thoughful clergyman's
library. With its publication Dr. Blaikie proved that church
history may be written dramatically, and yet in a scholarly

way. It lacks the critical documentation that one expects today, but in Blaikie's day, few writers gave much attention to this detail. His *For the Work of the Ministry* (1873) was long considered a valuable work on homiletics and pastoral theology. *The Public Ministry and Pastoral Methods of Our Lord* (1883) is a worthy companion volume. In his *Better Days for Working People* (1861) he pleads for a class so often forgotten in his generation. Other notable books were: *Glimpses of the Inner Life of Our Lord* (1876); *Life of David Livingstone* (1880); *Life of Thomas Chalmers* (1896); *Robert Rollock* (1884); and *David Brown, a Memoir* (1898). While his biographies are somewhat brief and of the old school, yet they are unique in their own way. The story of Dr. Blaikie's own life is told in his *After Fifty Years* (1893), and *Recollections of a Busy Life* (1901).

Dr. Blaikie belonged to the conservative school of Scottish Presbyterian thought, and in his preaching the evangelical spirit was always present. He was an ardent admirer of the Covenanters and he had no good word for those who sought to introduce prelacy into Scotland. He was a staunch Free Churchman, always ready to defend from the pulpit and in print the distinctive beliefs that were associated with the founding fathers of that body. He was a typical example of old-fashioned Free Church conservatism, and well worthy of a place among the great preachers of his native country whom he brought to life on the printed page.

William B. Robertson (1820-1886)

William B. Robertson, the famous "Robertson of Irvine," was born in Greenhill, Stirlingshire, in 1820. After attending the village school in Greenhill, he entered Glasgow University in 1832, and from 1837 to 1841 he studied at the Secession Theological Hall, Edinburgh. In 1841 he entered Halle, where Tholuck was one of his professors. He was one of the first of many Scottish students who studied in Germany, and brought back with them theological ideas and other innovations that were fairly conservative at first, but in years to come which were to introduce destructive Biblical criticism into Scotland.

Robertson was licensed in 1843 and became pastor of the Secession Church, later known as the United Presbyterian Church, at Irvine, Ayrshire.   In 1868 he arranged a Christmas Eve service that caused great commotion in Scotland. For many generations any suggestion of the Church Year had been looked upon in Scotland as rankest Romanism, and Christmas, Easter and other such festivals were disregarded. The Christmas Eve service at Irvine was of the simplest sort.   "O come, all ye faithful," and other Christmas hymns were sung.   The Apostles' Creed and the Lord's Prayer were recited in unison, after which the choir responded with a simple Amen.   The excitement caused at the time is hard to understand nowadays. *The United Presbyterian Magazine* led the attack, but in the end, Robertson's Presbytery upheld his Christian liberty in the matter, and nothing further was done about it.   A parallel case is that of the Rev. H. C. Schwan, who conducted a Christmas service, about the year 1840, with a Christmas tree, in a Lutheran church in America, and was criticized severely by the Protestants of his community for introducing what was considered a Roman Catholic innovation.   In the case of Robertson of Irvine, he recalled Christmas services that he had attended while a student at Halle, and he attempted in a very simple manner to introduce a custom that had already existed in continental Europe.

Dr. Robertson was a famous preacher, magnetic, forceful, evangelical, and able by his wonderful sermons to produce so marked an effect upon the community that the rough miners of Ayrshire were made devout Christians, and his biographer goes so far as to declare that the women grew up to look like Madonnas, and both men and women learned to sing like angels.   Unfortunately Dr. Robertson published none of his sermons, and what we have today are sermons that have been reconstructed from notes taken at the time by the people of his village.   Dr. Robertson is one of several men who have given us their translation of *Dies Irae*.   His is not so widely used as those of William Irons, Dean Stanley, Capt. John Newton and others, but it is worthy of mention.

Dr. Robertson visited Glasgow at the laying of the foundation stone of the new university. One of the sermons on that occasion was notable for its ornate rhetoric rather than for its depth of evangelical thought. Upon being asked how he liked the sermon, Dr. Robertson pointed with his cane to a new wooden bridge across the Kelvin, which had been painted to imitate blocks of granite. "Man," he said, "I like a wooden brig, — but I hate the *pent.*"[91]

In addition to the book of sermons, reconstructed from notes taken by the villagers, a small book containing Dr. Robertson's lecture on Martin Luther, and two other lectures, was published in 1892. Dr. James Brown's *Robertson of Irvine,* (1888), is the standard biography, and Arthur Guthrie's biography, bearing a similar title, is well known to all the admirers of this eminent United Presbyterian pulpit orator.

William Milligan (1821-1893)

William Milligan, the son of a clergyman, was born in Edinburgh in 1821. He attended Kilconquhar School, Edinburgh High School and St. Andrews University, from which he was graduated in 1839. He continued his studies at Edinburgh University. He was licensed in 1843, and the following year he became assistant at Abercrombie. He was ordained in 1844 and became pastor of a church in Cameron. In 1845 he spent a year studying in Halle. He was translated to Kilconquhar in 1850, and ten years later he was made professor of Biblical criticism in King's College, Aberdeen. In 1870 he became a member of the New Testament revision committee. He visited America in 1872, where he was in much demand as a preacher and lecturer. In 1876 he was moderator of the Assembly of the State Church.

Dr. Milligan was one of a number of professors who were at the same time gifted preachers. He was often asked to preach in the important churches in Edinburgh, Aberdeen, Glasgow and elsewhere, and was looked upon as among the seven or eight most eloquent preachers of the

---

[91]. Jas. Brown, *Life of William B. Robertson* (1888).

Scottish Church. He was a pioneer in the Scoto-Catholic movement, and interested in the Scottish Church Society. This organization, in 1892, declared that it laid stress on fundamentalism, upon more regard for the Sacraments, and it set forth the doctrine of the continuity of the Church.

Dr. Milligan's chief works are: *The Decalogue and the Lord's Day* (1866); *The Revelation of St. John* (1866); *Elijah, his Life and Times* (1887); *The Resurrection of Our Lord* (1881); and, with A. Roberts, *Words of the New Testament as Altered by Transmission and Ascertained by Modern Criticism* (1873) — the last containing considerable nonsense.

John Tulloch (1823-1886)

John Tulloch was born in 1823 at Dron, near Perth, where his father was a clergyman of the State Church. After attending the grammar school at Perth, he entered St. Andrews in 1837, and later he attended Edinburgh University. He was licensed in 1844, and a year later he became pastor of St. Paul's Church in Dundee, going from there to Kettins, in Forfarshire, in 1849. In 1854 he was made principal of St. Mary's College, St. Andrews, and professor primarius of divinity. He was but 31 years of age at the time.

Tulloch's inaugural address on "Theological Tendencies of the Age" caused surprise, and even adverse comment. It was believed that Principal Tulloch tended toward the theory of doctrinal development. In 1854 any such teaching was regarded with disapproval in the State Church as well as in the Free Church. If theology is truly a statement of the truths taught in the Word of God, how can such truths change or undergo development? The *Church of Scotland Magazine,* in 1855, expressed disagreement with Tulloch's views, while publications of the Free Church found in the controversy additional proof of the breakdown of orthodoxy in the older Kirk from which they had separated a decade or so before. While Tulloch declared his firm belief in the Bible as the final authority in all matters of doctrine, yet he quoted Schleiermacher with seeming approval, and seemed to be on familiar terms with German Biblical criticism.

In 1858 Prof. Tulloch opened the Scottish Presbyterian Church in Paris and preached there during the summer. In 1860 he was made senior principal of his school, and about the same time he was appointed chaplain to Queen Victoria. When the fierce controversy on the Sunday question agitated all Scotland, from the halls of the great universities to the most remote shieling on the moors, Tulloch defended Dr. Norman Macleod, of the Barony, who had delivered a fiery address three and one-half hours in length, declaring that there is no divine command to keep the Sabbath. So bitter was the feeling at the time that even boys on the streets jeered at Dr. Macleod and his allies, Tulloch, Lee and Burns.

In 1874 Principal Tulloch visited America, and in an address he admitted that liberal theories existed within the Church of Scotland. This, he attributed to a wider critical study of the New Testament, to an acquaintance with certain trends of English thought, and to a wider acquaintance with the writings of the German theologians of the time. He was made moderator of the General Assembly in 1878 and dean of the Chapel Royal in 1882. In 1884 he opened the Scottish Church in Pont street, London.

Throughout his life Principal Tulloch was a preacher of distinction. He had a stately presence, a resonant voice and eloquence of language. Lord Sands declared him to be the third on a list of the eight leading preachers of his day. In theology he was a Broad Churchman, although he himself preferred the term "broad evangelical." Although he often defended orthodox theology, yet he was not opposed to widest liberty of theological opinion in the State Church. He favored a Kirk that would bring together on terms of toleration divergent shades of theological opinion. In addition to several articles in the *Encyclopaedia Britannica* he published a dozen or more religious works. His earlier writings, *Theism* (1855), *Leaders of the Reformation* (1859), and *English Puritanism and its Leaders* (1861), can hardly be said to give evidence of depth of scholarship, while his *The Christ of the Gospels and the Christ of Modern Criticism* (1864) is inadequate. More careful in workmanship is his two-volume study of *Rational Theology and Christian Philosophy in England in the Seventeenth Century* (1872). This was followed by *The Christian Doctrine of Sin* (1877) and *National Religion in Theory and Fact* (1886). Tulloch left two volumes of sermons, *Some Facts of Religion and Life* (1877) and *Sundays at Balmoral* (1887). An account of his life and work is set forth in Mrs. M. O. Oliphant's *Memoir of the Life of John Tulloch* (Edinburgh, 1888).

Chapter X

HIGHER CRITICISM, MODERNISM, CHURCH UNION,
AND FUNDAMENTALISM

FROM the time of the Reformation until the latter part of
the nineteenth century, Scotland's confidence in the
Holy Scriptures had remained undisturbed. Conflicts had
shaken the Scottish Kirk, and there had been times when
men suffered imprisonment, banishment and death for their
convictions, but rarely if ever was God's Word assailed. To
every Scotsman the Bible was an impregnable Rock, God-
given, verbally inspired, and the one infallible rule of faith
and conduct. When troubles arose, men all appealed to the
Bible. When the distressing Prelacy-Presbytery Conflict
raged, the king and his bishops cited the Scriptures no less
than the men who defended the presbytery. When the
several Covenants were signed, determined men died for
these declarations because they believed that they were
based upon Scriptural truths. The men who persecuted the
signers of the Covenants quoted the Scriptures and felt that
they had done the Lord a service in checking what they
imagined to be heresy. The valiant men who defended the
right of the local congregation to choose its own pastor,
quoted the Scriptures in support of their contention; while
the Erastian party, strange as it may sound, had Scripture
verses and their own peculiar exegesis to defend their
claims. The evangelical party preached the more important
doctrines of the Bible with great fervor, while the Moderates
attempted to hide their lukewarm doctrines behind plausible
Bible terminology. When Thomas Chalmers and his determined four or five hundred passed through the streets of
Edinburgh to Tanfield Hall on that memorable May morning
in 1843, they opened the new Free Church with a declaration
of loyalty to God's Word.

However these men, in the several serious controversies
that arose, differed in their views, there was one thing upon
which they all agreed: the Bible was God's Word from cover
to cover, and verbally inspired. A Bible lay on the pulpit
of every Scottish kirk, no matter how remote its location

in the Highlands or in the Islands; and Scottish expository preaching became famous the world over. Scottish Bible scholarship was respected and considered second to none throughout the countries where English or Gaelic were understood. A Bible was to be found in every Christian home, and in former years that included almost every home in the land. Every evening the devout father of the family "had a chapter" with all who dwelt within the house.

In the early years of the nineteenth century, educated Scotsmen began to hear persistent rumors that German Biblical scholarship was beginning to challenge Scotland's leadership in that field. They had utmost respect for Germany, for to the Scottish mind it was the land of Luther, and to the true Scotsman Luther was a spiritual authority scarcely less than Calvin and Knox. In the year 1834 David Welsh, an orthodox Scottish clergyman, visited Germany and became acquainted with some of the great universities and the famous theologians of the day. Like all educated Scots, Welsh had a working knowledge of German, but hardly enough to realize at first what was going on in that land. Learned professors of more than national reputation spoke with glowing enthusiasm of the Scriptures, and told Mr. Welsh of the great interest that had been shown in Biblical research. Welsh understood the older language of theology, but he had yet to learn the new interpretations of the old terminology. He returned to Scotland and gave an account of what he had learned and seen, and of the learned Biblical scholars that he had met.

Lindsay Alexander, then a young man, decided to study in Germany, and he attended Halle and Leipsic. He was followed in the early forties by William Robertson of Irvine, John Cairns, John Ker and other young men. From the middle of the century until early in the twentieth century it became the ambition of many a young Scotsman to finish his education, or at least to take post-graduate courses, in the German universities. The writings of Hengstenberg and Olshausen appeared in English, and then a famous publishing house began a comprehensive series of English editions of the books of German commentators and theologians. The titles alone fill several pages of print. The critical

theories of John Eichhorn, of Jena and Göttingen, became
known in Scotland; as well as the works of De Wette, Vatke
and Leopold George. Men read Hupfeld, Reuss, Graf,
Kuenen and Wellhausen. They began to speak with growing familiarity of Baur, Zeller and Schwegler, and to quote
Hilgenfeld, Volkmar, Köstlin and Ritschl. A flurry was
caused in Scotland when Prof. Samuel Davidson's work on
the Old Testament led to the expulsion from his professorship at Manchester, and when Bishop Colenso was deposed
because of his attack on the Pentateuch. Scotsmen were
interested, but they declared that such heresies could never
take root in Scotland, the great stronghold of Calvinistic
conservatism. They believed that their young men were so
well indoctrinated that no amount of German Biblical
criticism could shake their confidence in the Scriptures. If
anything, it was their duty to become acquainted with the
claims of the German negative critics so that they might be
able to defend the integrity of the Scriptures. Dean Stanley's rationalistic *History of the Jewish Church* appeared in
England, but it left the people north of the Tweed undisturbed.

In the year 1875 the first volumes of the ninth edition
of the *Encyclopaedia Britannica* appeared. All educated
Scotsmen awaited it with impatience, for this great reference work was their very own, having been founded in
Edinburgh in the year 1778. When the ninth edition appeared, all Scotland was agitated. One of their noted professors, Robertson Smith, who occupied the chair of Hebrew
at the Free Church's Aberdeen College, had been asked to
write the article on the Bible. Scottish Christians were
grieved when they discovered that Mr. Smith's article
showed that he had been influenced by negative Biblical
criticism. Several years of agitated controversy followed,
and in 1881 Professor Smith was expelled from his position
in the college. Professors A. B. Bruce, T. M. Lindsay and
the younger Candlish defended Smith, and a group of young
pastors and theological students became his followers.
Marcus Dods and Walter C. Smith were mentioned openly
·s men who held liberal views, as well as Professor A. B.
·avidson. Even Alexander Whyte was suspected, when he

spoke in favor of free investigation. Years of controversy followed, there were several sensational investigations, and the Church of Scotland, the Free Church, the United Presbyterians and the Independent bodies became involved. All the while the new theories were spreading. Conservative leaders opposed the new teachings with utmost vigor, but at last the day came when it was the proud boast of the liberal group that there was not a university, college or theological school in Scotland where the new theories in regard to the Bible were not taught. This may be an exaggerated statement, for there were cases where university and seminary faculties were divided, some of them teaching the rationalistic views in regard to the inspiration and authorship of the Bible, while others defended the orthodox position. As in England and in America, there were many men who attempted to cling to the teachings of the Scriptures, and yet maintain what they termed an open mind in regard to the degree of inspiration, and the authorship of the various Books of the Bible. Such men declared that it is not important whether Moses wrote the Pentateuch or not, so long as the truths contained in it are accepted; that the authorship of Isaiah and Daniel are matters of indifference so long as the truths of these writings are received.

It is not surprising that such conditions led to Modernism. At first it was known as the New Theology, and there were many faithful men who condemned it. Modernism was concerned with such things as the origin of the world and of man, the deity of our Lord, the Virgin Birth, the Resurrection, the Atonement, the matter of a literal devil and a literal hell, the Second Coming and other such teachings. With the authority of God's Word under serious question, one need not wonder that many men accepted the theory of evolution, that they began to question the Virgin Birth and the deity of the Saviour, and finally to doubt the entire plan of salvation as revealed in God's Word. The Foundation had been undermined, and it was but natural that the structure that had been built upon it toppled.

The news of Scotland's growing theological liberalism shocked the world. Although they differed widely in certain doctrines, yet Scottish Presbyterianism and the rapidl growing Synodical Conference Lutheranism in America were looked upon as the very foundation walls of uncompromising conservatism in theological matters. Whatever else the Scottish preacher might declare from his pulpit, the non-Scottish world could depend upon him to defend vehemently the doctrines of Verbal Inspiration, the Virgin Birth, the Deity of Our Lord, the fact of man's sinfulness by nature and the way of salvation solely through the crucified, risen and ascended Saviour. Almost in a single generation these great truths had come to be treated as matters of opinion. In spite of bitter controversies in the kirk sessions, the presbyteries, the synods and in the General Assembly, liberal theologians were given places on the faculties of the theological halls and the great Scottish universities. In the face of ringing protests, liberal books were published, circulated widely, reviewed in favorable language and quoted with approval.

Modernism did not appear at once in the pulpit, nor can it be said that it is preached openly even today. The sermons still had a conservative tone, for there were many liberal clergymen who were careful of their words when facing their congregations. Some men expressed themselves rather freely, but the method of many others was more insidious. They merely ignored evangelical truth, after the manner of the old-time Moderates, and preached sermons on good, moral living. They used much of the old terminology, but they no longer confined their preaching to the great doctrines associated with man's sin and his redemption. The older books of published sermons contained discourses on the Fall of Man, Original Sin, the Messianic Promises, the Virgin Birth, Justification by Faith, Salvation through Jesus Christ Alone, Saving Faith, the Work of the Holy Ghost and allied subjects. Even today, when men assure us that there is a decided trend toward the old-time doctrinal truths, the collections of sermons by one of the most popular preachers of Scotland, are likely to contain such subjects as these: On Being Disciplined by Life; Living Adventurously; Facing Life Unafraid; Overcoming Frustration; Opening the Door to Commitment. In the entire volume one will probably find no mention of the Bible as the inspired, infallible Word of God; and when the Lord Jesus is mentioned, it is not to confess Him as the Lamb of God that taketh away the sin of the world. On the contrary, He is described as One whose chief work seems to be to help us solve the perplexities of this life.

A famous American radio preacher, in a sermon that he prepared but never lived to preach, declared that the great majority of the churches of half a century ago stood squarely upon the Bible as the infallible Word of God. The great majority of preachers of those days believed that Jesus Christ had shed His cleansing blood to rescue mankind from eternal ruin. "Today all this is changed," he continued. "Within fifty short years entire denominations, the great majority of their leaders, and in some cases most of their preachers, refuse to receive the Bible as the Almighty's inspired, errorless Word and to exalt the divine Christ as their Redeemer. We have divinity schools in the United States in which not one teacher believes Scripture's inerrancy or the Saviour's atonement."[1] It cannot be denied that there are many such clergymen in Scotland today, and in England, as well as in America. The theological liberalism that brought spiritual ruin to continental Europe has been only too evident in the countries where English is the spoken language.

Modernism did not go unchallenged. In Scotland, as well as in England, Wales and America, there were many men who came to be known as Fundamentalists. This term seems to have originated in America and it is used to describe those who not only reject liberal theology, but who defend that which some call the old-time religion. They accept the Bible as inspired and as infallible, and they do not hesitate to declare that man is by nature dead in trespasses and sins. They declare that the sinner's only salvation is through the grace of God in Jesus Christ. The orthodoxy of such men is often of the "reformed" type, and many of them lay utmost stress upon the Second Coming of our Lord, which they believe is imminent.

The prominent men whose names are mentioned in the following pages were not all liberal theologians. A number

---

[1]. *The Walter A. Maier Memorial Booklet* (1950), p. 22.

of them were Fundamentalists. They held valiantly to the old teachings of the days of conservatism, and they did not hesitate to bear witness against all who had rejected the infallibility of the Bible and who no longer preached Christ crucified. Many Fundamentalists were not clear in regard to certain truths, for some of them confused the purposes of Law and Gospel, and their preaching often contains indications of legalism. Their preaching was centered upon the Cross, however, and if one can detect errors in it, yet they preached enough evangelical truth that many of their hearers were brought to a knowledge of salvation in Jesus Christ.

The church union controversy agitated Scotland for decades. As early as the year 1820, the General Associate Synod (Antiburgher) and the Associate Synod (Burgher) settled their differences and united. In 1845 the Evangelical Alliance was formed. It was a federation of men who accepted nine fundamental teachings, namely: the inspiration and authority of the Bible; the right of private judgment; the doctrine of the Trinity; the utter corruption of man's nature through the Fall; the deity of the Lord Jesus, and His work of Redemption; justification by faith alone; the work of the Holy Ghost in converting and sanctifying man; the immortality of the soul, the resurrection of the body, the Judgment, eternal salvation and eternal punishment; the divine institution of the Christian ministry and the recognition of Holy Baptism and the Lord's Supper as "perpetual ordinances." In 1847 the Secession Church with 400 and the Relief Church with 118 congregations united and formed the United Presbyterian Church.

Through the efforts of Mr. John Henderson of Park, a layman of the Secession Church, a volume of essays was published in 1845. Its title was *Christian Union,* and a number of prominent men contributed essays. Some of the essays were cautious, but Dr. Gavin Struthers of Glasgow wrote an essay on "Party Spirit: its Prevalence and Insidiousness," in which he made some statements that anticipated the arguments of the church unionists of today. In 1856 Sir George Sinclair, a layman of the Free Church, by means of letters to the press and the publication of a pamphlet, urged a union of certain Presbyterian groups. Dr. Gibson, always a champion of conservatism, led the opposition, nevertheless the subject of church union became a major issue. A union of the Presbyterian groups in Australia, in 1859, caused some men to ask: Are the Free Church and the United Presbyterians justified in remaining apart?

In his two-volume work *A History of the Church in Scotland* (1927-33), Dr. J. R. Fleming traces at great length the various stages of the church union controversy. Committees were appointed, joint meetings of these committees were called, doctrinal differences discussed, declarations issued, and the matter was debated with vigor in the conventions of the several Presbyterian groups. Conservative leaders warned against union without true unity. The liberal group, by means of declarations, printed pamphlets, letters to the church periodicals and speeches in the church conventions, presented the familiar arguments for church union that have been repeated again and again to the present day. In 1900 the Free Church and the United Presbyterian Church merged, forming the United Free Church.

This victory did not cause the men who had brought it about to consider their task finished. Almost at once the suggestion was was made that the United Free Church and the old Established Church consider a plan of union. There was much opposition, for there were men who remained loyal to the principles of the Disruption. Dr. Chalmers and his associates had separated from the State Church as a matter of principle. Why destroy the very thing that these 474 men had built up at so enormous a cost? Once more the familiar answer was heard: Moderatism (Rationalism) was practically dead and the Established Church had been growing year by year in conservatism. The usual statements were made that the divided state of their denomination was a sin and a scandal, and that its lamentable divisions brought untold sorrow to the Lord Himself. After years of negotiation and debate, the United Free Church and the Church of Scotland united in October, 1929. At the time of the union, 106 congregations, numbering 13,791 com-

municants, declined to unite with the Established Church.
They became known as the United Free Church Continuing.
Other nonconforming groups include the Reformed Presby-
terian Church, the Original Secession Church and the Free
Church of Scotland which is a group that declined to take
part in the union of 1900.

The inroads of Higher Criticism caused many Scottish
preachers to lay less stress upon the Bible as the supreme
authority for both doctrine and daily living. Modernism
caused some to question, at least within themselves, certain
basic teachings of the Scriptures. Fundamentalism encouraged others to hold firmly to the old, reformed type of conservatism. Another influence whose importance cannot be
overlooked was the growth of the revival system in Scotland.
Mention has been made of Mr. Moody's early visits. When
Moody and Sankey first came to Scotland in 1873, they were
unknown Americans, and it was predicted everywhere that
the conservative Presbyterians of Scotland would never be
misled by "American showmanship." One must not overlook the fact that many Scottish congregations would not so
much as tolerate a musical instrument, even as recently as
1873. Hymns of the popular sort shocked the old-time
Scotsman. Church services were of a type of dignity that
was not altogether lacking in stiffness. Preaching was
usually of the traditional Scottish kind — careful sermons
that were textual and expository, and expressed in churchly
language.

Mr. Moody was a blunt, plain man, a layman and not
an ordained clergyman. His sermons were practical talks
on the great subjects of sin and salvation, and his language,
while dignified, was the language of the common man and
not of the universities. The Scottish people discovered at
once that Moody was utterly serious and wholly sincere. If
he indulged in crude grammar, (such as "he done it" and
"when I first come to Edinburgh,") the people forgave him
readily enough, and soon the largest places of assembly
in Edinburgh were crowded.

Mr. Sankey was a man of almost frightening personality.
Some of us who can recall him in his old age, sitting at his
little American organ, singing in a powerful staccato, "The

Ninety and Nine," or "Hold the Fort," can well imagine the way in which he took all Scotland captive. He had a splendid voice, and while his hymns lacked literary and musical merit, yet they always spoke in their crude manner of the Cross, and of the Lord whose cleansing blood is the only cure for the blackness of man's sins.

The three visits of Moody and Sankey to Scotland broke down the traditional dignity of both Scottish worship and Scottish preaching. The prejudice against organs and against popular hymns vanished in a matter of months. There had been revivals long before Moody's day, but even the revivals at Cambuslang, Kilsyth and elsewhere were far from the American type. At the outset, many people condemned Moody and Sankey and declared their methods unchurchly, and even sensational; but in a short time many of the most eminent clergymen and professors were drawn into the movement. The formal, literary style of preaching gave way to a more free and practical manner of expression. One must not conclude that all Scotland adopted the methods of American evangelism, but the waves of revivals that spread over the country after the visits of Moody and Sankey, from 1873 to 1892, have left their influence upon Scottish preaching. One may visit many prominent churches in Scotland today and hear nothing of the favorite expressions of Moody and a number of American revivalists who followed him, yet the pulpit style of most Scottish clergyman is more free and more practical than before the days of the evangelistic campaigns.

At the turn of the century a certain British theologian had much to say in regard to the discovery of the Christ of history. This theory influenced theological thought both in England and in Scotland. Then came a reaction. German Form Criticism, or *Formgeschichte,* as set forth by Rudolf Bultmann and Martin Dibelius, engaged the attention of clergymen in England and Scotland. The Crisis Theology of Karl Barth and Emil Brunner attracted wide notice, and their books were read, both in the original German and in English translations. These men disguised the old-time Modernism with the language of orthodoxy, and there were many who hailed this new restatement of liberal thought as

a return toward orthodoxy. However, it rested upon a
foundation of negative Higher Criticism, and their Jesus
Christ was but an idealized man. All of this is set forth
with ability by Dr. Cornelius Van Til, of Westminister
Theological Seminary, in his book *The New Modernism*,
which is a detailed answer to Barthianism.

Walter C. Smith (1824-1908)

Walter C. Smith was born in 1824 in Aberdeen. He
attended Marischal College, Aberdeen, where he took his
degree in 1841. From there he went to Edinburgh University. When 19 years of age he stood with the great
crowd at George and Hanover streets and watched the 474
men file out of the church where the General Assembly of
the Established Church had just convened, and he watched
the long procession as it made its way down to Tanfield Hall,
where the Free Church was founded. Fifty years later,
when moderator of the General Assembly, he described this
scene — the crowded streets and balconies, the crowded
roof-tops, people perched on poles and in trees, the cheers
and the sobs, and the procession of men who had given up
congregations, manses and livings as a matter of conscience.

After his ordination in 1846, Walter C. Smith served
a congregation in London, going from there to a Free Church
in Orwell, Kinross-shire, Scotland. In 1862 he was called
to Glasgow, and finally to the Free High Kirk in Edinburgh.

Smith's liberal tendencies appeared as early as 1860,
when he published a poem "The Bishop's Walk," under the
pseudonym of Orwell. Its author was recognized quickly
enough, and there was much unpleasant comment. The
conservative Free Kirk was grieved that one of their number,
and a man who bore their founder's name — his full name
was Walter Chalmers Smith — should so far forget himself
as to write a poetic eulogy of a man so infirm of purpose as
Robert Leighton, who exchanged his convictions for the
bishop's mitre, and eight years later the archbishop's office.
It had been traditional among all orthodox Scots to regard
the Covenanters as the fearless heroes of post-Reformation
days, and to look upon the turncoat Leighton as a traitor
to his people.

Seven years later, in 1867, Smith published a volume of sermons entitled *The Sermon on the Mount,* in which he declared that "the New Testament is the one supreme, authoritative document for declaring God's purpose, and it holds the place of high and exclusive power just because it has fulfilled, and in fulfilling has abrogated, the whole Old Testament dispensation." To a Lutheran such a sentence, if rightly understood, would not have proved objectionable, but not so to a Scottish Presbyterian of 1867. Their regard for the sanctity of the Sabbath was so great that when an effort was made to run excursion trains on Sunday, and to throw open the public parks to pleasure-seekers, there was a lively protest from Scotsmen of both major faiths. The "Smith Case" was the occasion for heated debates in Presbytery and Synod, and it came before the Assembly in 1867. Smith, in his defense, declared:

"1. I hold most firmly the immutability of all Divine Moral Law, and that the Decalogue contains a divinely authorized summary of that Law which is everlastingly binding: only that the New Testament contains a fuller and clearer statement of that Law. 2. That the Scriptures of the Old and New Testament are the Word of God and the only rule of faith and manners; and, further, that their organic relation is of such a nature that the Old Testament does not derive its authority from the New, but both have the same kind of authority, and that both taken together are the complete revelation of the divine will. I therefore now as always unhesitatingly disclaim any opinion at variance with these truths which has been ascribed to me or supposed to be taught in my sermons." The Smith Case led to a memorable controversy. The Presbytery was not satisfied with his explanation, and found Smith's sermons in disagreement with the Word of God and the Westminster Confession. The Smith Case came before the General Assembly. Smith received a sharp public reprimand, and was warned to avoid statements such as those that had given great offense.

The Smith Case is noteworthy, for it gave evidence of a new spirit in the Free Church. He was found guilty of rash statements, if not of opinions in conflict with the teachings of the Confession, yet he was merely admonished and no further disciplinary action taken. Years later, Dr. F. Pieper said, in an entirely different connection: "If it were shown us that even but one pastor were preaching false doctrine, and that even but one periodical were in the service of false doctrine, and we would not put a stop to this false doctrine, we would thereby have then ceased to be an orthodox Synod, and would have become a unionistic fellowship. In short, it is the earmark of an orthodox fellowship that throughout it only the pure doctrine is not only officially recognized, but actually prevails."[2]   Walter C. Smith was correct in believing that the Old Testament Sabbath, in its original sense, has been set aside by the teachings of the New Testament; nevertheless the action of the Free Church indicates that doctrinal discipline had begun to break down, and a man whom they considered guilty of false teaching, was given nothing beyond a public admonition. While one cannot endorse the opinions of Dr. Begg and his associates on the Sunday question, yet they must be given credit for their effort to maintain doctrinal discipline. They predicted that the Smith Case had established a precedent, and marked the day of a spirit of toleration. When these champions of Calvinism died, a different spirit prevailed, and eventually Walter C. Smith was made Moderator of the General Assembly, and he presided over its jubilee convention in 1893. Smith's writings include his *Lectures on the Sermon on the Mount* (1867); books of verse; a number of hymns; and a book of sermons published in 1909, the year following his death.

Alfred Edersheim (1825-1889)

Although he was not a preacher of the first rank, yet Alfred Edersheim deserves at least passing mention. He was born in Vienna of Jewish parentage, attended the gymnasium and a synagogue school in his native city, and then Vienna University. He went to Pesth to teach, and there he met the Rev. John Duncan, the great Scottish Hebrew scholar, who was in Pesth acting as chaplain to a group of Scottish engineers engaged in building a bridge across the Danube.

---

[2]. L. & W., XXXVI, pp. 261ff.

438 A HISTORY OF PREACHING

Young Edersheim embraced Christianity, and in 1843 when
Duncan was called back to Scotland to teach Greek and
Hebrew in the newly founded New College, Edersheim
accompanied him. He studied at New College, and then at
Berlin University. In 1846 he was ordained by the Presby-
terian Free Church and became missionary to the Jews at
Jassy, Roumania. He returned to Scotland and in 1849
became pastor of the Free Church in Old Aberdeen. In
1861 he went to Torquay and became pastor of St. Andrew's
Presbyterian Church, and in 1872 he was sent to Bournmouth
to rest. Toward the end of his life he took orders in the
Anglican Church, holding a curacy at Christchurch, Hants.,
and later the office of vicar at Loders, Dorset. He was
Warburton lecturer at Lincoln's Inn, 1880-84, select preacher
to Oxford University 1884-85 and Grinfield lecturer on the
Septuagint in 1886-89. Among his writings *The Life and
Times of Jesus the Messiah*, 2 volumes (1883), will long
remain a monument to his learning. His *Bible History*,
7 volumes (1876-87), covers the Old Testament period.
Among a number of other books are *History of the Jewish
Nation* (1856), *The Temple, its Ministry and Services*
(1874), and *The World before the Flood* (1875). His
biography was written by Ella Edersheim (1890).

Andrew K. H. Boyd (1825-1899)

A. K. H. Boyd, of the Church of Scotland, was born in
1825 at Auchinleck, Ayrshire. His father was at one time
the pastor of Tron Church, Glasgow. Young Boyd was
educated at Ayr Academy, at King's College, London, and at
the University of Glasgow, where he took his degree in 1846.
He studied law, and was a member of the Middle Temple
in 1842.

In 1850, having decided to become a clergyman, he was
licensed and became assistant pastor of St. George's, Edinburgh. He was ordained in 1851 and became pastor of New-
ton-upon-Ayr. In 1854 he was translated to Kirkpatrick-
Irongray, and in 1859 he came back to Edinburgh, becoming
pastor first of St. Bernard's, and then, in 1865, at St.
Andrews. He was made moderator in 1890.

Although known chiefly as an essayist, yet Boyd was a preacher of unquestioned gifts. In 1850-51, when assistant at St. George's, he attracted city-wide attention because of his lively, evangelistic preaching, and it was assumed by many that another great pulpit orator had arisen. Then he went to the country for eight years. Upon returning to Edinburgh, it was soon evident that his style of preaching had changed. His sermons were still admirable. and he was compared by many with such men as Norman Macleod, John Caird, John Tulloch, Robert Flint, James Macgregor and William Milligan. Excellent as he was, yet there were no longer the great crowds waiting outside for the church doors to open. Rumor had it that his former evangelical fervor had diminished somewhat.

Dr. Boyd was known throughout Britain and America as a clever essayist. He wrote a number of books that were popular in his own generation. Few of his "Country Parson" series, once so popular, are read today, although his characterization of Scottish preaching in *The Recreations of a Country Parson* (1859) is of lasting interest as a record of the preaching of that period. His *Twenty-five Years of St. Andrews,* 2 volumes (1892), while not especially scholarly, will be read with interest by students of Scottish religious history. The account is continued in *St. Andrews and Elsewhere* (1894), and *The Last Years of St. Andrews* (1896). Boyd's manner of preaching is revealed in *Sermons and Stray Papers* (1907). A score of titles might be mentioned readily enough, but Boyd's writings, while clever enough, might be classed as popular theology, and such things hardly fall within the realm of the History of Preaching, admirable as they might be if printed in a religious magazine intended for the family circle.

Donald Fraser (1826-1892)

It is difficult to know whether to include Donald Fraser under the heading of Scotland, England or Canada, because he was active in all these places. He was born in 1826 at Inverness and received his education at King's College and the University of Aberdeen, receiving his degree in 1842. He engaged in business for a short time in Canada, studied theology at John Knox College, Toronto, completing his work there in 1848, and then going to New College, Edinburgh. He was licensed to preach in 1851 and ordained some months later, going to Montreal, where he served a congregation of the Free Church for eight years.

In 1859 he was called to the Free Church's congregation at Inverness, his native city, and he remained there for a number of years. He went to London in 1870 as pastor of the Presbyterian congregation in Marylebone, where he served until his death 22 years later. He was a popular preacher and held a conspicuous place among the Free Church pastors of London. He was a clear, forceful preacher, and whether in Canada, Scotland or London his sermons were heard by people who admired his excellent style, his precision of statement and his ability to present spiritual truth in a simple, practical manner. His most important work is *Synoptical Lectures on the Books of Holy Scripture,* 3 volumes (1871-76). Other writings are: *Leaves from a Minister's Portfolio* (1858); *The Church of God and the Apostasy* (1872); *Thomas Chalmers* (1881); *The Speeches of the Holy Apostles* (1882); and *Metaphors in the Gospels* (1885).

Robert Rainy (1826-1906)

Robert Rainy, of the United Free Church, was born in Glasgow, in 1826. His father was professor of medicine in Glasgow University. He attended the high school in Glasgow, and was graduated from the University in 1844. In 1847, at the funeral of Thomas Chalmers, John Mackintosh pointed to Rainy and declared that he was one of the future leaders of the Kirk. Rainy was but 21 years of age at the time. He attended New College, Edinburgh, from 1844 to 1848, where his professors were Chalmers, Welsh, Wm. Cunningham, A. C. Fraser and "Rabbi" John Duncan.

In 1849 he was licensed to preach, and for a short time served Inchinnan mission. In 1851 he was given the Free Church at Huntley, Aberdeenshire, and in 1854 he was transferred to Free High Church, Edinburgh, where his power as a preacher brought him into prominence. In 1859 he made a deep impression upon the Assembly because of an address in connection with a case of discipline involving seven Glasgow students suspected of liberal views.

In 1862 he became professor of church history in New College, and occupied this chair for 38 years. In 1867, in a memorable address before the Assembly in regard to church union, he made so great an impression that thereafter he was one of the unquestioned leaders of the Assembly. From 1874 onward he was principal of New College. Possessed of a quiet, authoritative personality, he was regarded with veneration both in New College and in the Assembly. His look of quiet consciousness of power set apart Principal Rainy from all others in an academic procession on commencement day, and there was no need for a stranger to inquire which was he. His simple dignity caused a hush to fall upon the lines of spectators as he passed by in the black-robed procession on such state occasions.

In 1872, Arthur Penrhyn Stanly, Dean of Westminster, published his lectures on the Scottish Kirk,[3] and caused grave offense in Scotland.   Stanley was a champion of Erastianism, and in his lectures he spoke rather kindly of the Moderates of the eighteenth century.   Principal Rainy answered him in a series of three lectures,[4] which have become authoritative on those particular questions.

Although inclined to be an Evangelical himself, yet Principal Rainy felt called upon to defend any men who were suspected of liberal views.   The seven Glasgow students have been mentioned. He defended Marcus Dods and A. B. Bruce in 1890, when their views on verbal inspiration were questioned.   In 1900 he opposed the heresy charges against Sir George Adam Smith, who was somewhat influenced by German Biblical criticism.

Robert Rainy was a man of marked ability in the pulpit, forceful, earnest, generally evangelical, with an excellent command of simple, well-chosen English, and with a quiet but powerful personality. He understood how to be dignified, and at the same time humble.   Among his pub-

---

[3]. A. P. Stanley, *Lectures on the History of the Church of Scotland* (London, 1872).

[4]. R. Rainy, *Three Lectures on the Church of Scotland* (Edinb., 1872).

lished works are his lectures in reply to Dean Stanley and a
life of William Cunningham. It is hardly fair to call him a
liberal. He lived in a transition period, when the grim
orthodoxy of such men as James Gibson gave way to a spirit
of toleration, which was to open the door to theological
decline. Rainy professed belief in verbal inspiration himself, but it is to be regretted that he was ready to deal
leniently with men who had begun to question it.

Principal Rainy was somewhat of an enigma. His friend
Mr. A. Taylor Innes goes so far as to call him a "great
opportunist." He describes Rainy as a man who was tra-
ditionally conservative himself, yet as a sense of duty he felt
called upon at times to yield to the opinions of his friends.
Men under attack could often rely upon him to defend them,
from the days of the seven Glasgow students to the Marcus
Dods, A. B. Bruce and George Adam Smith investigations,
yet it was Rainy who delivered the sharp public rebuke to
Walter C. Smith. Principal Rainy was a leader almost
without equal, after Candlish's day, but he never was the
doctrinal disciplinarian that we find in the case of James
Gibson. An excellent biography of Principal Rainy was
written by Dr. P. Carnegie Simpson.[5] It was a popular work
in its day, and often mentioned as one of the three or four
best biographical writings of its time, but as interest in
Rainy has gradually declined, the biography is not as
popular as in former days. Another biography was written
by R. Mackintosh.[6]

Principal Rainy's most important works are: *Life of
William Cunningham* (1867), in which he collaborated with
James Mackenzie; *Three Lectures on the Church of Scot-
land* (1872), a telling answer to Stanley's unkind lectures;
Delivery and Development of Christian Doctrine (1874);
The Bible and Criticism (1878); *The Epistle to the
Philippians* (1893); *Presbyterianism* (1894); *The Ancient
Catholic Church* (1902); and a book of sermons, *Sojourning
with God* (1902).

---

[5]. P. Carnegie Simpson, *Life of Principal Rainy*, 2 vols. (London,
1909).
[6]. R. Mackintosh, *Principal Rainy, a Biographical Study* (London,
1907).

Alexander Maclaren (1826-1910)

One of the most famous Scottish preachers of the nineteenth century was Alexander Maclaren, but since his long ministry was spent in Southampton and Manchester, an extended account of his distinguished career is included in our volume on English preaching.

Dugald MacColl (1827-1882)

Now and then a man appears who is able to use the Word of God in such a way that the most wretched people are persuaded to live decent Christian lives. Dugald MacColl was such a man. Popular opinion may not rate him as highly as Robert Hall or H. W. Beecher, but when one recalls the fact that "they that be wise shall shine as the brightness of the firmament; and they that turn many to righteousness as the stars for ever and ever," then Dugald MacColl deserves a place among the great. After his university course, and while yet a student in the Free Church's college, he was sent in the year 1853 to assist in the Wynds of Glasgow, where Dr. Buchanan, of Tron Church, had decided to start a mission.

"The Wynds of Glasgow," writes Mr. MacColl, "are in the heart of the city, long, narrow, filthy, airless lanes, with every available inch of ground on each side occupied with buildings, many of them far gone, yet packed from cellar to garret with human life." [7] These Wynds were not always the haunts of wretchedness. Many years ago the nobles and the lairds of Glasgow dwelt here in fine mansions. The streets were attractive, and between the great mansions were built narrow lanes, leading from the Trongate into the Bridgegate. These lanes ran between gardens where beautiful flowers bloomed in profusion, and where green lawns were the pride of the yard-men of the wealthy. St. Mary's Church, commonly known as Tron Kirk, stood nearby, and here was the old Wynd Church. As the city grew, the wealthy people moved to suburban areas, and the Wynds became built up with tenements, covering completely what were once the beautiful flower gardens and fair lawns of the lairds and nobles. Narrow passageways, called "closes,"

---

[7]. Dugald MacColl, *Work in the Wynds* (London, 1867), p. 23.

were built between the tenements, and into these the sun never cast its beams.

In 1810 the old church was demolished after 120 years of service, and the Kail Market took its place. In 1815 Dr. Chalmers became pastor of Tron Church nearby, and his labors among the unchurched population of Glasgow have been mentioned. In 1853 Dr. Robert Buchanan and the Free Church Presbytery revived the old Wynd Church, and Dugald MacColl, who was completing his theological studies, was asked to assume charge of the work. The old site was purchased and a church was built. A parochial school was opened in an old candle factory, and not long thereafter a second school was started in a hayloft. This was the beginning of the remarkable work in the Glasgow Wynds. The parish covered but twelve acres, and its population was 12,000. In addition to Dugald MacColl, such men as Robert Howie, James Wells, John Riddell and George Reith were among the early workers in the Wynds.

Within four years the church was filled to overflowing, and many of the most faithful members were people who had never entered a church until the Wynd mission was started. A neatly dressed verger within the church door had been a drunkard four years before, sleeping in doorways. An organist and choirmaster had once frequented the filthiest cider bars of the slums. Mr. MacColl and his helpers went unharmed through winding passageways into which policemen never ventured except in pairs. They climbed the rickety stairways of tenements six and seven stories high, whose grimy windows looked out upon endless rows of broad chimneys, each of which terminated in eight or ten terra-cotta chimney pots. In summer the air in those tenements was stifling within, and the squalor and the reeking odors would have repelled any but the most resolute. Whiskey-sodden men and women, with blotched faces, sprawled in the doors of these wretched "rows." Scrawny children, clad in rags, swarmed the narrow streets, screaming curses and obscene epithets at any stranger who ventured into the district. The ale shops were of the filthiest description, where stale beer and cheap whisky were served to the more prosperous and hard cider to the less fortunate.

The people lived by robbing strangers, by picking pockets, and by begging in other parts of the city.   One of Mr. Mac-Coll's faithful workers said: "Ah, sir, it's awfu' wark this. The folks here are like rotten wood.   They winna haud the nail!"[8] Typhus and cholera were prevalent, and wretches lay dying on piles of filthy rags spread over even filthier mattresses.   Rats and vermin swarmed everywhere and flies came literally in clouds to torment the dying. Many people lived in unlighted basements, with a candle thrust into an empty bottle when they could afford it, and in total darkness when there was no money for candles.

"I often visited in these times thirty or forty houses a day," writes Mr. MacColl, "now standing beside a woman busy at her wash tub, speaking about the things of her peace till she would wipe the soap-suds from her arms and then the tears from her eyes: again, sitting beside the shoemaker or the tailor, urging them to arise and seek the Lord, and getting perhaps the usual promise, 'I'll may be give you a call.'" [9]

The methods used by Mr. MacColl were based upon those of Dr. Chalmers.   He organized a group of about forty Christian people and trained them to go from house to house, reading a portion of Scripture, leaving tracts, and inviting the people to attend church.   Mr. MacColl and his workers visited tirelessly, regardless of the wild orgies of Saturday night, and the roaring drunkenness and open vice that accompanied the Glasgow Fair.   When people excused themselves on the pretext that they lacked suitable clothes, Mr. MacColl started a Sunday evening service for just such people and encouraged them to come in shabby clothes. His band of workers were instructed to attend in the poorest garments that they could find, so that others would have no excuse.   A Night Brigade was organized, and men went out in small groups, each provided with a bull's-eye lantern, penetrating the darkest alleys and passageways, and bringing back with them all who could be persuaded to come. At the first evening service but 30 people could be induced to attend.   A week later the attendance was increased to

[8]. Dugald MacColl, *Work in the Wynds* (London, 1867), p. 28.
[9]. *Ibid.*, p. 34.

90, then to 150, and by the end of the month the church was half filled. In a few months the building could no longer hold the large congregations that attended these evening services.

Mention has already been made of the remarkable expansion of the work. Again and again the Wynd Church was filled to overflowing, and daughter congregations were established again and again. Sixteen congregations were direct off-shoots of the Wynd Church.

When we boast today of our missionary prowess, the reading of such a book as Mr. MacColl's *Work in the Wynds* is sufficient to humble us. We park our motor cars before our comfortable churches nowadays, paying but scant heed to the riff-raff population close by; and when these people encroach upon us, we sell our church property and move to the outskirts of the city, so as to follow the "better people" who have moved from the old neighborhood to avoid the foreigners. This is hardly an evidence of a missionary spirit. When Dugald MacColl began his work in Glasgow's Wynds, there were 12,000 people in his parish. Of these, 800 claimed some church connection, while 11,400 were unchurched. Of the 12,000, approximately 4,000 were Scotsmen, while 8,000 were foreigners, whose religious background was neither Free Church, Church of Scotland nor any of the independent religious groups. Mr. MacColl did not pass them by with the excuse that they were foreigners, or of a different religious background; neither did the nucleus of lifelong church people who united with the Wynd Church protest, saying that people from the alley slums would make their congregation the dumping ground of all manner of undesirable people. Such arguments have been heard again and again in our own day. There are streets in New York and other cities where ragged men and women lie in a drunken stupor in the doorways on Sunday morning. People making their way toward their churches pass them with but a glance of disgust, and many an outcast could say with the Psalmist, "No man careth for my soul." Dugald MacColl and his associates proved that such people may be reached, and that the Law and the Gospel, when rightly used, are able to make well-behaved Christian citizens of them, and devoted members of the church.

It is an easy matter to say that the young missionary in Glasgow's Wynds, who preached with his broad Scottish brogue, declaring in language that laid no claim to literary polish the simple truths of repentance and faith in Jesus Christ, was not a man whom we are justified in calling a great preacher.   However, any man who is able to use God's Word in such a way that a strong congregation and sixteen flourishing daughter congregations were recruited from one of Glasgow's most wretched slums, deserves to be included among the great preachers of his generation.

Andrew B. Davidson (1831-1902)

Andrew B. Davidson, who was a world-famous Old Testament scholar as well as a persuasive preacher, was born on Kirkhall farm, in the parish of Ellon, Aberdeenshire.   He was graduated from Marischal College, Aberdeen, in 1849.   His education was made possible because of the great sacrifice of his parents.   His mother used to walk 20 miles every two weeks in order to bring him supplies.

From 1849 to 1852 he taught in the Free Church school in Ellon.   In 1856 he was graduated from the theological school of New College, Edinburgh, a Free Church institution.   He was licensed to preach the same year, and for two years he supplied pulpits in the vicinity.   He had excelled in Hebrew when a student, and in 1858 he was made assistant professor of Hebrew at New College, in 1863 he became professor of Oriental languages, and in 1870 he was made a full professor of Hebrew.

Andrew Davidson was not idle on Sundays.   He was a preacher of unusual ability, but from the start he insisted upon supplying the pulpits of the smaller and more humble rural kirks, rather then the well-known city congregations.   He became famous for his expository sermons on great Bible characters, both in the Old and in the New Testament.   After a very careful study of his subject, on the basis of his rich scholarship, he wrote out his sermon in a manner that could be grasped by the simple people in the little congregations where he loved to preach.

Davidson gave the world his famous *Introductory Hebrew Grammar* in 1874.   This work has gone through many editions, and has been used probably more than any other Hebrew Introduction by theological schools throughout the world. His *Hebrew Syntax* is almost equally famous. He edited the *Cambridge Bible for Schools,* and published works on Old Testament prophecy, as well as a book of sermons on great Bible characters. His unfinished *Commentary on Job* is one of the most scholarly works on that particular subject, but it must be studied with caution.

Unfortunately Dr. Davidson did not escape the Biblical criticism that found its way into Scotland in his younger days. In 1865 he wrote a letter to a friend [10] in which he spoke of the transition period in the Scottish Kirk. He had not yet made up his mind whether this new spirit was good, or whether it was Antichrist. He spoke of himself as a sick man, waiting at the side of the pool for the angel to come and trouble the waters, so that he might be healed.

While Dr. Davidson was more conservative in his critical views than many who were to follow him, yet Fleming [11] looks upon him as one of the men whose Biblical criticism marked the dawn of a new day in Scottish theology, when the old-time rigid orthodoxy of the Calvinistic type began to give way to modern thought.

As a general rule the Scottish churches chose their professors from among the men who had established a reputation as excellent preachers and successful pastors. Dr. Davidson was one of the exceptions, for he became a professor almost from the outset. He won his reputation as a preacher after he had gained recognition as a professor. Since he was not faced with the necessity of preparing two new sermons each week, as is usually the case in Scotland, he made it a rule not to write a sermon unless he felt that he had something important to say. There were times when he prepared but three or four new sermons in the course of a year, and he used these at various small and obscure congregations where he preferred to preach. But few of his sermons give evidence of his somewhat liberal position in

---

[10]. Jas. Strahan, *Life of Andrew B. Davidson,* pp. 102-104.

[11]. J. R. Fleming, *The Church in Scotland* (Edinb., 1927-33), vol. 1, p. 162. However, Dr. Davidson rejected the Creation and the Flood narratives as mere folk lore. (*Biblical and Literary Essays,* London, 1902.)

matters of textual criticism. Although he spoke with a decided Aberdonian accent, yet there were many who considered him one of the best of the Scottish preachers of the latter nineteenth century. In his private conversations and to a certain extent in his teaching he considered parts of the Old Testament to be mere tradition. He did not take seriously the inspired account of the Creation, and he questioned certain miracles of the Bible. The people who crowded the little country churches where he so often preached, would have been surprised had they been told that their beloved Dr. Davidson rejected a single statement in the Bible. Like many a preacher in the early stages of Modernism, he thought it best not to disturb the simple faith of the people. His references to the Garden of Eden, the flood, the plagues of Egypt and the crossing of the Red Sea, were without comment, and his hearers assumed that he accepted these truths. A modern historian of the Scottish Church describes Davidson as a silent, almost sinister figure, "the real father of the Higher Criticism in Scotland," saying little, but exerting a powerful influence over other men who were more outspoken in their liberalistic views. Davidson's *Hebrew Grammar* (1874), and *Hebrew Syntax* (1894), were daily companions to many of us, and one can but regret that the famous Silent Scotsman was deluded by the idle speculations of the German school of destructive criticism. Davidson never finished his *Commentary on Job* (1862), but years later he compiled a popular commentary on Job for the Cambridge Bible series. Among a number of other works were *The Theology of the Old Testament* (1904), in which his attitude toward textual criticism is not absent; *Old Testament Prophecy* (1903); *The Epistle to the Hebrews* (1882), another of the Cambridge Bible series; and several books of sermons and essays, such as *The Called of God,* two volumes (1903); *Bible Characters* (c. 1904); *Waiting Upon God* (1904); *Biblical and Literary Essays* (1902); and part of *Book by Book* (1892). A biography of Dr. Davidson was written in 1917 by James Strahan.

When one reads of Davidson's mother, and many other devout Scottish mothers of a century ago, facing the savage winds that sweep across the bleak Scottish moorlands in winter, bending under the weight of a heavy bag of rolled oats, oat cakes and butter from the little shieling on the few acres of farmstead, where parents, brothers and sisters hoarded every sixpence so that some laddie of the family might complete his education, such tales of labor and privation recall the grim heroism of a vanished generation. Those pious old fathers and mothers loved their Bibles. The family gathered at evening to "read their chapter," as Burns so well describes it in his Cotter's Saturday Night. Were one to question the accuracy of a single word of the Inspired Record, they would have been indignant and horrified. It is a merciful thing that such people did not live to see the withering blight of Rationalism and Higher Criticism shake the faith of those very boys whom they educated at the cost of cruel sacrifice.

Alexander B. Bruce (1831-1899)

Alexander B. Bruce was born in Aberargie, parish of Abernethy, Perthshire, in 1831. He was educated in Edinburgh University, having been graduated in 1849. He entered the Free Church divinity hall in 1849. He was settled at Cardross in 1859, he became pastor of the fashionable East Free Church, Broughty Ferry, Forfarshire, in 1868, and in 1875 he was made professor of apologetics and New Testament exegesis in the Free Church Theological Hall, Glasgow. Suspected of liberal views, he was cited to appear before the Assembly in 1890, but was acquitted. He was Cunningham lecturer in 1874, Ely lecturer in New York City in 1886 and Gifford lecturer at Glasgow in 1896-1897.

Cardross, his first congregation, was a small group of about 80 communicants, mostly farmers who had been brought up on the strong meat offered by the older school of Scottish Calvinistic preachers. Bruce met with considerable disfavor at first, because he sought to avoid such terms as "regeneration," "sanctification," "prevenient grace" and "concreated righteousness." He termed "justification" the "spiritual adjustment of man." This aroused the suspicion of his congregation, familiar as they were in those days with the older theological terms. They suspected that their young pastor, in avoiding the older terminology, was avoiding the doctrines as well. After a time they became accustomed to his new mode of expression and accepted it somewhat grudgingly.

Bruce met with better response when he went to the important congregation at Broughty Ferry. His series of sermons, later to become his famous book *The Training of the Twelve,* established his reputation as a noted preacher. These sermons were delivered extempore, after careful preparation. While Alexander Bruce was a popular preacher and highly esteemed as a professor, he caused much sorrow to the conservative men of the Free Church. More than once he was charged with holding liberal views. On one occasion he is said to have declared that he disliked St. Paul, because he befogged the simplicity of the Gospel teachings. On another occasion he was charged with having said that he was in sympathy with modern religious thought while retaining all the best in the theology of the past, and that he believed in freedom of inquiry on the basis of evangelical faith. Shortly after his death an article appeared in the *Encyclopedia Biblica* on the Saviour. It caused a commotion, for he was thought to have taken a purely naturalistic view of Jesus Christ, with all divine elements excluded. These accusations did not seem to diminish his reputation as a forceful preacher, for during his lifetime his services were in constant demand. He lived at a time when the importation of liberal German theological theories, and the translation of many Germany theological and exegetical writings into English, were causing a gradual breakdown of the old type of Calvinism.

Dr. Bruce was the author of a number of important theological and Biblical works. His *The Training of the Twelve* (1871) has long been a classic. His *The Humiliation of Christ* (1876) sets forth very fully the unsound Kenotic theory. Other writings followed: *The Chief End of Revelation* (1881); *The Parabolic Teaching of Christ* (1882); *The Galilean Gospel* (1882); *The Miraculous Element in the Gospel* (1886); *The Kingdom of God* (1889); and his great work entitled *Apologetics* (1892). Other writings are: *With Open Face* (1893); *St. Paul's Conception*

of *Christianity* (1894); *The Providential and Moral Order
of the World* (1897); and *The Epistle to the Hebrews*
(1899). Together with T. K. Cheyne he issued the *Theological Translation Library* (1894), and he contributed a
commentary on the Synoptic Gospels to *The Expositor's
Greek Testament* (1897). His theological tendencies are
apparent in his *F. C. Baur and his Theory of the Origin of
Christianity and of the New Testament* (1885). His ability
in biographical writing is revealed in his *Life of William
Denny* (1888). His writings are of a massive, scholarly
character, and it is unfortunate that his tendency toward
Rationalism appears from time to time. Books such as his
The Kingdom of God caused Free Churchmen of the old
school to classify him with the Higher Critics, and it cannot
be denied that he dealt with the inspired records in a spirit
of rashness that might well arouse the ire of the opponents
of liberalism.

James Stewart (1831-1905)

James Stewart was born in 1831 at Edinburgh. After
attending the high school at Edinburgh he continued his
studies at Edinburgh University and at the Free Church
Divinity Hall. As early as the age of 15 it was his desire to
become a foreign missionary, and with this in view he
studied medicine, taking his degree in 1866. He met David
Livingstone in 1857 when the great missionary returned to
Scotland to seek men for Africa. James Stewart offered to
go, and was accepted as a probationer in 1860. A year later
he went to Africa as an assistant to Livingstone, and was
stationed in Central Africa. In 1867 he became associated
with the Rev. William Govan, founder of Lovedale Missionary
Institute, and in 1870 he became Govan's successor.

James Stewart attracted attention throughout the world
by declaring that the Negro and the white man were of one
blood, and were entitled to equal educational opportunities.
If given such opportunities, he was assured that the Negro
would compare favorably with the white race. He preached
these things with conviction and gained many friends who
provided the means for training young Negroes for the professions. In 1873 he started another school at Blythewood.

In 1874 he toured Scotland, where his preaching in behalf of foreign missions attracted widest attention. He established the New East African Mission in 1891, and a year later he returned to Scotland. In 1899 he was made moderator of the Free Church, and in 1902 he delivered the Duff Missionary Lectures at Edinburgh. Returning to Africa in 1904, he died the following year at the age of 73.

James Macgregor (1832-1910)

During the latter part of the nineteenth century one of Edinburgh's most eloquent preachers was James Macgregor, of the Church of Scotland. He was born in 1832 at Brownhill, Scone. Finishing the parochial school at Scone, he attended Perth Academy and St. Andrews University. He was licensed in 1855 and became assistant at Newton-on-Ayr. Later in the same year he was ordained and became pastor of the High Parish, Paisley. In 1862 he was translated to Monimail, and in 1864 he went to Tron Church in Glasgow. From 1873 to 1910 he served St. Cuthbert's, or West Kirk, Edinburgh. He was chaplain-in-ordinary to Queen Victoria and to Edward VII. In 1891 he was made moderator of the General Assembly.

Dr. Macgregor was looked upon as one of the most fervent of Scotland's preachers. He had a manner that was unusually convincing, and this was apparent both in the pulpit and elsewhere. Once, according to the *British Weekly*, he was asked to address a gathering of people, presumably in a lecture hall. He began by saying, "There was a day on which an ancestor of mine was sentenced to be hanged." Loud applause greeted this statement. "I have no doubt that it was for stealing," he continued. The audience cheered. "Allowed to select the tree upon which he was to be hanged, he selected a goose-berry bush. When told that it was too small for the purpose, he said, 'Let it grow. I am in no hurry'." The audience was frantic with delight. What he said was not important at all, and if said by the average speaker it might have brought forth nothing more than a polite ripple of laughter; but Dr. Macgregor had a manner, whether in the pulpit or on the platform, that an audience found irresistible. In the pulpit he was serious, and he used his peculiar gift of utterance in a way that was singularly impressive. Even the most commonplace statements, when they fell from his lips, seemed significant. He had, to a lesser degree, that quality that is so difficult to define, that was found in George Whitefield, who could thrill his hearers, or cause them to burst into tears merely by the way in which he uttered the word "Mesopotamia." This gift is to be found occasionally in some of the most famous public speakers, and it is doubtful whether anybody has ever been able to explain satisfactorily its characteristics. Although slight of body, almost frail, yet he had the fiery eloquence of the Celt. His voice was of surprising strength, resonant, and of great range and flexibility. Within a minute's walk of one another were the churches in which such men preached as Alexander Whyte, John Kelman, Archibald Scott, Wallace Williamson and James Macgregor, all men of singularly rare gifts.

Dr. Macgregor loved his follow men, and took the keenest interest in their welfare. So deferential was he to their opinions that those who knew him but slightly doubted his sincerity. However, Macgregor was genuine, and his kindly interest extended to all men, from the earl to the collier and the cotter. It was a part of his warm-hearted Celtic culture, for were an acquaintance in need, Dr. Macgregor would go to endless inconvenience to help him. If he visited a poor family, and found their need genuine, he did not hesitate to empty his pockets to the last halfpence, even though it meant a walk of several miles to his home.

Many tales are told of Dr. Macgregor's pawky humor. On one occasion Dr. Whyte came to him and asked him with some concern whether it might not be wise to call a colleague to assist him at Free St. George's. "A splendid idea!" declared Macgregor. "With a colleague you'll be sure never to find yourself in purgatory. It's either Heaven or hell, — and generally it's not Heaven."

Macgregor was more often serious than witty. One day, in 1909, when his neighbor Dr. Archibald Scott lay ill, Lord Sands came upon Macgregor, standing forlornly in Melville street, gazing at the lofty dome of St. George's Kirk. "What troubles you, Doctor?" asked his lordship. "It's Scott!

Wae's me for Scott! For thirty years we've been neighbors." When Scott died a few days later, Macgregor was in tears. "What ever shall we do without Scott?" he moaned. "Why am I left here, a mere cumberer of the ground?"

Dr. Macgregor had a famous sermon, "The Fulness of Time," which he had preached on a number of occasions. Many a congregation was delighted with it, and years later it was usual for some "auld body" to say to him: "O Doctor, I hear ye are to preach in our kirk once more. Do ye ken that fine sermon ye preached in 1872, on 'The Fulness o' Time?' Maist of the auld folk would have ye preach it again if ye only will." Macgregor usually granted such requests, although that particular sermon, in view of the changing demands of forty years, had been reduced from sixty to twenty-five minutes in length, often to the disappointment of the older people, who declared that they would sit most willingly for two hours, were only Dr. Macgregor in the pulpit. A biography, *The Life and Letters of James Macgregor* (1912), was written by Lady E. Balfour.

Marcus Dods (1834-1909)

Marcus Dods, of the United Free Church, was born in Belford in 1834. After his graduation from Edinburgh in 1854, he attended the Free Kirk's New College, Edinburgh, from 1854 to 1858. He was ordained in 1864 and served Renfield Free Church, Glasgow, from 1864 to 1889. In 1889 he became professor of New Testament theology in New College, and from 1907 to the time of his death he was principal. In 1890, Marcus Dods and Prof. A. B. Bruce, of Glasgow, were charged with holding advanced views in matters of Biblical criticism. After a hearing before the Assembly, they were admonished, but not removed from their offices. Marcus Dods is author of a number of widely known writings, including several commentaries.

Dods was a preacher of ability. His sermons were learned, thoughtful, usually expository in method, but at times they seem to depart somewhat from the old orthodox position of the Free Kirk. For some reason his ability in the pulpit was not recognized for a quarter of a century. On one occasion he was invited to deliver a sermon before the University on Revelation and Inspiration. The comment at the time was not favorable. His gifts as a preacher were admitted readily enough, but it was believed by some that Dods, by implication at least, gave the impression that there were "errors and imperfections" in the Bible. His attitude toward the doctrine of Inspiration was questioned, as well as his attitude toward German Biblical criticism, which at that time was a burning question in the Kirk.

Professor Dods is sometimes confused with Marcus Dods (1786-1838), the Scottish theologian, who was also a preacher worthy at least of a word of mention.

Of the thirty or more writings of Marcus Dods, some of the more important are: *Epistles of Our Lord to the Seven Churches* (1866); *The Bible, its Origin and Nature* (1905); *The Prayer that Teaches to Pray* (1863); *Mohammed, Buddha and Christ* (1877); *Israel's Iron Age* (1874); *The Parables of Our Lord,* 2 volumes (1881-84); *Haggai, Zechariah and Malachi* (1879); *The Gospel According to St. John* (1897), in *the Expositor's Greek Testament.* Dods edited the English edition of Lange's *Life of Christ,* 6 volumes (1864), and *Augustine's Works,* 15 volumes (1872-76). In many respects the numerous writings of Principal Dods, of which we have listed but a few representative works, are scholarly and useful, and it is to be regretted that his attitude toward textual criticism compels one to include him among the liberal Bible scholars, whose writings must be read with extreme caution. His published sermons, such as *Christ and Man* (1909), are less objectionable than his *Introduction to the New Testament* (1889), *Handbook on Genesis* (1882), and other such writings. Principal Dods lived in a period when the fierce attacks of infidels, sceptical scientists and German Rationalism were echoed widely in many a theological lecture room. It was quite the fashion for professors of the so-called Progressive School to make concessions especially to the claims of science and to the enemies of verbal inspiration. Principal Dods did not live through this period unscathed, and his advanced views led to bitter criticism on the part of the vehement defenders of old-time Calvinistic orthodoxy.

Robert Flint (1834-1910)

Robert Flint, of the Church of Scotland, was born in a shepherd's cottage at Greenburn, Sibbaldbie, Dumfriesshire. He was educated at Evan Water and Moffat schools, and later at Glasgow University. He was licensed in 1858, and for a year he served as assistant to Norman Macleod at the Barony Church, Glasgow. He was ordained in 1859 and given the East Parish in Aberdeen. Here his exceptional ability in the pulpit brought him favorable notice. In 1862 he was translated to Kilconquhar. In 1864 he was called to St. Andrews University as professor of moral philosophy and political economy, and in 1876 he was given the coveted chair of divinity at Edinburgh University. In 1895 he became moderator of the Assembly, a position reserved in Scotland for only the most eminent men.

Dr. Flint was a profound scholar, a theologian and a preacher whose fame reached far beyond his native land. He has been termed by some as one of the two or three most prominent men in the State Church of his generation. Several great universities offered him professorships, all of which he declined. He died at the age of 76, having made the long journey from a shepherd's but-and-ben to the highest positions in the educational world and in the counsels of his denomination that could be offered to him; and famed for his pulpit eloquence no less that for his scholarship.

Dr. Flint's writings include: *Theism* (1877), which reflects the modern trend in philosophy; *Philosophy of History in France and Germany* (1874); *Socialism* (1894); *Antitheistic Theories* (1879), his Baird lectures; *Agnosticism* (1903); *Theological and Biblical Subjects* (1905); and *Philosophy as Scientia Scientarium* (1904). His best sermons are to be found in a rather rare book, *Christ's Kingdom upon Earth* (1865), and *Sermons and Addresses* (1885). Two biographies have appeared, namely D. Macmillan's *Life of Robert Flint* (1914), and R. Howie's *Life of Professor Flint*.

J. Oswald Dykes (1835-1912)

J. Oswald Dykes was born at Port Glasgow, Renfrewshire, in 1835. After attending Dumfries Academy, he entered Edinburgh University, taking his degree in 1854. His theological training was received at New College, Edinburgh, and in 1856 he attended Heidelberg and from there he went to Erlangen in 1857. He was ordained by the Free Church in 1859 and became pastor of East Kilbride, Lanarkshire. In 1861 he was called as Dr. Candlish's assistant at Free St. George's, Edinburgh. In 1865 he went to Melbourne where he lectured for three years. In 1869 he became pastor of Regent Square congregation in London, in which place he remained for 19 years; going from there to Cambridge to become principal and professor of theology at Westminster Presbyterian College.

In his preaching Dr. Dykes was noted for his purity of style, his telling illustrations and his earnestness. He looked upon sin as the cause of every ill that mankind suffers, and that all remedies for such ills are vain, for sin can only be removed by the gracious merit of the Lord Jesus Christ. The sermons of Oswald Dykes are textual and expository, and their literary style is of a high order.

The people of Edinburgh were puzzled in 1861 when Dr. Candlish brought a young country boy, with hardly two years of experience in the ministry, to become his assistant at Free St. George's, one of Scotland's most famous pulpits. Many came out of curiosity when young Dykes preached his first sermon. He preached on the text "Your life is hid with Christ in God." The people went away that Sunday declaring that the young man deserved a place among the great preachers of Scotland, and his fame in the pulpit was secure from the very outset. When he went to Melbourne four years later, his fame became almost world wide. During his nineteen years in London, the Regent Square church was crowded with visitors from all countries, even in a generation when London was fortunate in having many famous preachers. His great fame in Scotland, in Australia and in England was not due solely to his eloquence and the rare beauty of his style. He preached sin and grace with utmost earnestness. While his point of view is certainly "reformed," and while his early days at Heidelberg and Erlangen sometimes arose to mock him, yet it cannot be said that Dykes failed to preach Christ-centered sermons;

and any man who preaches Christ crucified with a ring of conviction, as did Dr. Walter A. Maier half a century later, will be known far beyond his own continent, whatever his minor faults may be.

Almost a score of the books of Dr. Dykes were popular long after his death in 1912. Among them one might select as representative of his manner of preaching: *The Written Word* (1868); *From Jerusalem to Antioch* (1874); *The Beatitudes of the Kingdom* (1872); *The Laws of the Kingdom* (1873); *Abraham, Friend of God* (1877); *The Manifesto of the King,* 3 volumes (1881); *The Law of the Ten Words* (1884); *The Gospel According to St. Paul* (1888); and *The Relations of the Kingdom to the World* (1874).

Archibald H. Charteris (1835-1908)

A. H. Charteris, of the Church of Scotland, was born in Wamphray, Dumfriesshire, in 1835. After his elementary education in the parish school he entered Edinburgh University, from which he was graduated in 1852. He attended Tuebingen in 1870 and Bonn in 1871. In 1858 he was ordained and became pastor of the parish of St. Quivox, Ayrshire. In 1859 he was called to New Abbey, Dumfriesshire, and in 1863 he became John Caird's successor at the Park Church, Glasgow. From 1868 to 1898 he was professor of Biblical criticism in Edinburgh University. In 1869 he was appointed chaplain to the Queen. When Moody and Sankey visited Scotland in 1874, Charteris was much impressed, and wrote an appreciative article for the Church of Scotland *Record.* In 1892 he was chosen moderator of the Kirk, and from 1901 to 1908 he was chaplain-in-ordinary to the King.

During his five years of work at Park Church, Glasgow, his able preaching attracted many, and made Park Church as famous as it had been during the five years of John Caird's pastorate. However, his chief fame as a preacher lies in the work that he did beyond the bounds of his parishes. His ardent efforts in behalf of deaconess work did much to introduce the female diaconate into the Church of Scotland, and to establish deaconess training schools and hospitals. He was in much demand as a speaker at gatherings of young people, and in connection with the Christian Life and Work Movement. In theology he considered himself a conservative. Among the works of Charteris are: *Life of Prof. James Robertson* (1863); *Canonicity: Early Testimonies to the Canonical Books of the New Testament* (1880); *The New Testament Scriptures* (1882), his Croall lectures; *The Church of Christ* (1905); and *The Church of Scotland and Spiritual Independence* (1874). His biography was written by A. Gordon.

William Ross (1836-1904)

During the latter half of the nineteenth century one of Glasgow's most prominent clergymen was William Ross, of Cowcaddens Free Church. Mr. Ross was born in 1836 at Allt-a-Chliabhan Mill, Caithness, in the extreme northern part of Scotland. His father, a miller, was one of a group known as "the Men." They were unordained religious leaders who conducted church service in the absence of an ordained pastor, visited the sick, and in some cases kept alive the evangelical faith in the days of the rationalistic Moderates. The miller of Allt-a-Chliabhan conducted church services on two Sundays out of three, between the visits of a clergyman. Instead of a sermon he usually read a Gaelic translation selected from the writings of such men as Thomas Boston and John Bunyan.

William Ross, the miller's son, attended the elementary schools at Rangog, Latheron, Wick and Newlands. In 1857 he won the Queen's Scholarship which entitled him to attend Moray House, Edinburgh, the teachers' college of the Free Church. He finished his studies and was given a certificate permitting him to teach school, and the certificate mentioned his special proficiency in the Gaelic language. Ross, however, decided to enter the ministry, and he went to Edinburgh where he received four years of college work and four years of training in the theological department of New College. While yet in college his exceptional maturity of mind led to his election to membership in the Society of Antiquaries of Scotland, to the office of secretary of the Highland Committee of the Free Church and to the post of inspector of the Gaelic schools.

When he finished his seminary work, William Ross received three calls. His interest in the Gaelic work of the Free Church led him to accept the call to Chapelhill Gaelic Church at Rothesay. The church, seating 600 people, was built on the edge of an old stone quarry on the outskirts of the city. During June, July and August Rothesay was crowded with holiday-makers from all parts of Scotland and England. They soon heard of the eloquent preacher at Chapelhill Church, and they came in numbers to hear him. Many of these visitors could not understand Gaelic, and they urged him to start an English service. An assistant was called, and a second congregation was formed in the center of the town, and work was carried on in both languages. During his 16 years in Rothesay he reached not only the townspeople, but thousands of people from every part of the British Isles. These summer visitors went back to their homes with nothing but praise for William Ross, and he received many invitations to preach at the three-day Communion services which were the rule in Scotland. He was also in demand for special Gaelic preaching missions. An illness caused by overwork forced him to spend some time in Ireland, but even there he was not idle. His exceptional knowledge of the Gaelic language enabled him to speak to the Irish people. In 1878 he paid his first visit to America. In spite of his outside activities he built up a strong congregation at Rothesay.

One fine spring day William Ross sat in his study looking out over Rothesay Bay, famous for its beauty. His thoughts were on the great need of home missionary work in the larger centers of population. He thought to himself: "What right have you, an active man of 47, to spend your life in this pleasant spot, enjoying the comparative ease of an established congregation, while there is a critical need of men in the home mission field?" He resolved that if a call were to come, that he would not shirk his duty. He had not long to wait. In the autumn of the same year, 1883, a call came from Cowcaddens Church, Glasgow, and Mr. Ross accepted it.

His parish lay to the northwest of the Buchanan Street railway station. It was a congested district of the poorest

class of tenements   Dark "closes" or passageways led from
the side streets, and in a single close dwelt as many as 120
families in utmost misery.   Public houses and pawnbrokers'
shops lined the streets.   There was a large church building,
seating 1,150 people, but the congregation numbered but
200.   Mr. Ross's predecessor had worked hard, but with
scant success, and there were many pastors in the Free
Church who were in favor of giving up the unpromising field
and relocating in the suburbs.

William Ross made it clear from the start that he proposed to lay utmost stress upon spiritual methods.   He
declared that it is the task of a Christian congregation to
supply the people with the Bread of Life, and not to lay
stress upon free meals and clothing distribution.   He declared that the church itself, and not the social hall, must
become the chief center of interest.   No sooner had he
established himself in Glasgow than his study was besieged
by a swarm of beggars who lived on the bounty of the
churches.   He refused from the start to pay the fines of
wrong-doers, and he exercised greatest caution in giving
money to those who came with stories of distress.   He
learned quickly that such money was spent in the ale shops
nearby.   He refused in all cases to assist men and women
who were known drunkards, and only in exceptional cases
would he redeem a pawn ticket.   He found that the great
majority of the people of his parish were deeply in debt to
pawnbrokers, who charged a shilling a week for the loan
of a pound note.   Men and women came to him who had
paid their money-lender as much as 50 shillings for a 20
shilling loan.   He went out on the streets at night and saw
hundreds of men and women lying drunk in their doorways.
Bands of teen-age boys and girls roamed the streets in all
stages of intoxication, roaring lewd and profane songs at the
tops of their voices.   Theft was taken for granted, and every
kind of vice made the Cowcaddens district notorious throughout the West of Scotland.

Considering the bad character of the neighborhood, Mr.
Ross decided to abandon the traditional methods of church
work.   He was dealing with a crowded tenement district,
made up largely of unchurched people who lacked any sug-

gestion of religious instruction. They were people who did not hesitate to pawn the household furniture and the very carpet from their floors in order to buy drink. When nothing was left to pawn, they went from church to church with fictitious stories of hardship, and when the clergy and church workers finally cut them off, they begged on the streets in spite of the watchful police. Mr. Ross conducted three church services each Sunday, and the evening service was of a conservative rescue mission type. An adult class for religious instruction was conducted every Tuesday night, twelve months in the year. Young peoples' societies were Bible study hours, and social features were given a minor place. Mr. Ross was too busy a man to play games of any kind, and he looked upon such things as of slight value in church work. To those who told him that "we must provide games and social events for the young people in order to keep them interested," he replied, "the work of the Christian Church is to save the immortal souls of sinful men and women, and not to teach them to play games." Even some of his close friends predicted that his policy would soon close the doors of Cowcaddens Church, but to their surprise the big church was soon crowded three times every Sunday. It was not at all unusual to find 1,500 people crowded into a building seated for 1,150. The adult class was always a large one, and there were meetings for instruction, for Bible study and for the training of workers every night in the week, and it was Ross's rule to let no evening go by without proclaiming Christ crucified to some group. Like Chalmers, Tasker and MacColl, William Ross was successful in training bands of volunteer workers who went into the dark and grimy closes not to distribute charity, but to read the Bible and pray with the people.

Ross believed thoroughly in preaching missions. Two of these were conducted every year. Prominent speakers were brought in from a distance, and the preaching missions were given widest publicity. Often the church was crowded long before the hour of service, with long lines of people waiting outside. Mr. Ross became acquainted with Dwight L. Moody, and he caused misgivings among many of the more conservative Presbyterians of both Free Church and

State Church by permitting what was known in those days
as an inquiry room, where people with spiritual problems
were granted a personal interview after the preaching
service.   These preaching missions drew thousands not only
from the Cowcaddens district, but from all over Glasgow.

In spite of an extremely busy life, William Ross found
time to pursue his hobby, which was the study of languages.
He mastered a language quickly and thoroughly, although
Greek and Latin had been his weakest subjects in college.
This was due to the fact that he devoted so much time,
during college days, to the study of Gaelic.   In his Rothesay
and Glasgow days he mastered a number of languages.
Danish interested him greatly, and during a brief visit to the
Scandinavian countries, he was able to preach to the people
fluently and eloquently in their own language.

William Ross was one of the foremost philologists and
Gaelicists of his generation.   He had an important part in
the work of the Gaelic Revision Committee, a joint committee
appointed to issue a new edition of the Gaelic Bible.   Prior
to the year 1807 Gaelic Bibles were available, but they were
costly, and some of the poorer Gaelic pastors could not afford
a complete Bible.   In 1807 a five-shilling Gaelic Bible was
printed, but the work was not done with sufficient care, and
there was need for a new edition in better and more accurate
Gaelic.   In this work Mr. Ross gave valuable assistance.

On those rare occasions when he had a free evening,
Mr. Ross was almost sure to be found in some distant part
of Scotland delivering a lecture before some philological
society on the great antiquity of the Gaelic language, and of
the debt that other languages owe to it.   He made it clear
that many place-names and family names throughout
Europe are derived from the Gaelic, and that its influence
on many other languages is apparent enough to the expert.

In his earlier years Mr. Ross became an inspector of
the Gaelic schools, and although this made necessary many
flying trips, and the preparation of sermons in railway trains
and in hotel rooms, he kept it up for many years.   Gaelic is
the mother tongue of many Highlanders and Islanders, and
Mr. Ross could see no merit in a policy which at one time
prohibited the wearing of the Highland dress, and compelled

children to learn English through the medium of English. He found after many tests that thousands of children and grown people had been compelled to memorize sounds without any clear knowledge of what they meant. He found men and women in the Highlands and in the Islands who could read an entire chapter from the Bible in faultless English, but when asked to explain what they read, they had not the slightest notion of its meaning. After much effort he succeeded in convincing the authorities that English should be taught to Highlanders through the medium of the Gaelic language. He was a tireless worker in a society which provided for the education of native Gaelic teachers for the Gaelic schools, and native Gaelic-speaking young men for the Gaelic congregations of the Highlands and Islands. He himself taught the Gaelic class in the Free Church college and seminary at Glasgow. He taught Gaelic for a short time at two of the other colleges, but the great burden of his other work made it impossible to continue. At one time he was nominated as head of the Gaelic department at Edinburgh University, but his friends declared that his work at Cowcaddens was more important, and another man was given the position by a majority of one vote.

William Ross might well have become the greatest philologist of his time, but he chose to devote the greater part of his energies to his congregational work, and to give attention to his Gaelic studies only when this would prove of practical benefit to the training of Gaelic-speaking young men for the pulpit or the teaching profession.

Mr. Ross was a great preacher, but even with a fine staff of helpers, the burden of his congregational work was so great that he had insufficient time for study. His sermons, while delivered with the well-known fire and fervor of the Celt, were often lacking in careful preparation. He had a fine intellect, a trained homiletical sense, his doctrinal position was thoroughly evangelical, he had a gift of persuasiveness that others envied, an excellent delivery and a fine command of faultless English and Gaelic. However, as his biographer admits, there were times when his sermons indicated plainly enough that unusual demands had been made upon his time during the week. He was what our day

would term a thorough Fundamentalist, although he believed
that most men of that school devote too much attention to
the Second Coming of our Lord, and to chiliastic speculation.
During the time that the Higher Criticism controversy was
raging throughout Scotland, he took the conservative position, although he admitted that his multitude of duties at
Cowcaddens left him little time to make a careful study of
the subject.   His biographer tells us that "the center of all
his preaching and teaching was Jesus Christ, and especially
Christ crucified."

Although the inequality of William Ross's preaching
does not justify one in giving him a place among the greatest
of Scotland's preachers, yet is proved most effective in
accomplishing the task to which he had been called.
Literally thousands of the people of the Cowcaddens district
were reclaimed, and became useful Christians.   When he
came to Glasgow in 1883, Ross found a congregation of 200.
When he died in 1904, Cowcaddens was one of the largest
congregations in Glasgow.   The population is a shifting one,
yet during the last seven years of his ministry, Mr. Ross
received 1,025 new members, most of whom were missionary
material.   The story of his life was told in detail by his son,
J. M. E. Ross, in his book *William Ross of Cowcaddens*
(1905).

Robert Howie (1836-1918)

Robert Howie was born at Kilwinning in 1836.   He received his education at Irvine Academy, Glasgow University,
Glasgow Free Church College and Edinburgh Free Church
College.   In 1858 Prof. James Gibson, of Glasgow College,
charged Howie and six others with unsound views, because
of essays or utterances in regard to the unity of God, and
the doctrine of human depravity.   The matter came before
the Assembly in 1859, but the Assembly decided against
Prof. Gibson, and the seven young men received only a mild
admonition.   The incident was looked upon by Gibson, Begg
and other conservatives as the beginning of a breakdown in
doctrinal discipline.

In 1860 Robert Howie was called to the Wynd Free
Church in Glasgow, which served a slum area of 12,000

people in the central part of the city. It was an area of evil repute, where a mission had been opened in 1853 under the leadership of Dugald McColl, a theological student. The mission flourished, and a church was built at the end of a year. Within four years this church was filled to overflowing, and larger quarters had to be found in the city hall. Then a second church was built. About the time that Howie came to the Wynd mission, it reported 1,100 communicants and 200 applicants for membership. A third congregation was started, and then a series of services, often in the open air, were conducted. This was one of the early stages of an extensive home mission and city mission program carried on with great success by the Free Kirk.

In 1864 Robert Howie assumed charge of Trinity Free Church, in Glasgow, and in 1872 of St. Mary's Free Church at Govan. For years he was a leader in mission work, interested especially in the neglected areas of the large cities: a work in which Thomas Chalmers was interested. During his lifetime Howie had a part in the building of 44 churches, at an expenditure of 300,000 pounds.

Robert Howie had a quality that was found in many of the older Scottish preachers, namely persuasiveness. In direct appeal to the consciences of his hearers, not many men could excell him. Whether in the pulpit of a slum church, whether addressing a great open air meeting amid the tall tenements, or arousing to immediate action a national convention of church people, Howie seldom failed in his purpose. Chalmers had made it clear to all that ethical preaching and missionary appeal must rest upon a solid foundation of evangelical truth. Howie had learned this lesson, and while his teachings were less rigid than the strict Calvinism of Gibson and Begg, yet he realized that the Cross of Calvary must have a central place in any effective preaching, whether it be an evangelistic effort in the squalid streets of Glasgow's depressed areas, or a sermon before a missionary gathering in a fashionable church.

William A. Knight (1836-1916)

William A Knight, of the Church of Scotland, was born in 1836 in Mordington. His father was a clergyman. He was educated in the Free Church's college in Edinburgh, after which he served as assistant at Free St. John's. He was ordained in 1866, and became pastor of St. Enoch's Free Church in Dundee.

Mr. Knight was recognized as an able preacher, and was called upon to preach frequently in other churches. In 1872 he was invited to preach in the Unitarian Chapel in Little Portland street, London. This caused a grave scandal in the Free Church, and he was placed under censure by his presbytery. He admitted his fault, but he refused to admit that Unitarianism is not a part of the Christian Church. Two sermons, and certain articles in *The Contemporary Review* were called in question. The presbytery was dissatisfied with his vagueness, yet they dismissed the case. In 1874 Knight withdrew from the Free Church and sought membership in the State Church. A minority objected to his reception, but by a vote of 152 to 53 he was accepted. Two years later he was made professor of moral philosophy in St. Andrews University. He edited a volume called *Scotch Sermons,* which appeared in 1888, and caused much unfavorable comment because of the lack of evangelical spirit in some of the sermons, which are by various clergymen. Among other things he published a book of sketches of eminent men,[12] but his most valuable work by far is his collection of the priceless sayings of Dr. John ("Rabbi") Duncan.[13] It is a small volume, but it preserves the clever definitions and the shrewd observations of that famous professor and eloquent preacher, whose real worth has so often been overlooked by men who could see nothing beyond his harmless peculiarities of dress and manner of speech.

Other works of Prof. Knight are: *Studies in Philosophy and Literature* (1879); *Aspects of Theism* (1894); *Christian Ethic* (1894); *Rectorial Addresses at St. Andrews* (1894); *Hume* (1886); and *Life of William Wordsworth,* 3 volumes (1889). Knight published various works on English literature, on biography and on aesthetics which need not concern us here. His *Philosophy of the Beautiful* (1891), was once a popular text book in aesthetics.

---

[12]. *Some Nineteenth Century Scotsmen* (Edinburgh, 1903).
[13]. *Colloquia Peripatetica* (Edinburgh, 1870).

Alexander Whyte (1836-1921)

For half a century one of the brightest lights of the Edinburgh pulpit was Dr. Alexander Whyte, of Free St. George's. There are people who declare without qualification that he was the greatest preacher of his generation. Alexander Whyte's origin was obscure, and his early life was one of poverty. He was born at Kirriemuir, Fifeshire, and his mother was a harvest hand. Of his father very little is known. His schooling was limited, and at an early age he was apprenticed to a cobbler. Out of his scanty earnings he paid another lad to read to him. The Disruption took place when he was but seven years old, and his mother became a determined adherent of the Free Church. He attended a congregation of that denomination on Sunday morning, but in the afternoon his grandmother took him with her to the Auld Licht Kirk, whose pastor was James Paxton. This is the little kirk that has been immortalized by J. M. Barrie in his *The Little Minister, Sentimental Tommy,* and other books.

Despite his limited opportunities, Alexander Whyte was a diligent student, and in this he was encouraged by two pastors of the village. For a while he taught in the Free Church school at Airlie. The Rev. David White, a fine scholar, prepared him for King's College, Aberdeen, which he entered at the age of 22, supporting himself by teaching at night. After his graduation in 1862, he studied theology at New College, Edinburgh, and was ordained in 1866. After acting as assistant at St. Luke's and St. John's, Glasgow, he became assistant in 1870 to Dr. Robert Candlish, at Free St. George's, Edinburgh. As Dr. Candlish lay dying, in 1873, he called in Robert Rainy and Alexander Whyte. To Rainy he delegated his work at New College, and to Whyte the work at Free St. George's, and thus did the career of these two prominent men begin. Alexander Whyte proved a worthy successor to Dr. Candlish, and Principal Rainy won equal fame as an educator.

Alexander Whyte was a man of many excellencies, but the Rev. Hunter Smith declared that the secret of his power lay in the fact that he told men the awful truth about themselves, probing to the very depths of the human heart where sin has its roots. Dr. Whyte tells us how this came about. Once, while on holiday in the Scottish Highlands, he was walking alone, brooding over his work. A thought came to him that he verily believed to be the voice of the Lord. "What seemed to me to be a Divine Voice spoke with all-commanding power in my conscience, and said to me as clear as clear could be: 'No! Go on, and flinch not! Go back and boldly finish the work that has been given you to do. Speak out and fear not. Make them, at any cost, to see themselves in God's Holy Law as in a glass. Do you that, for no one else will do it. No one else will so risk his life and his reputation as to do it; and you have not much of either left to risk. Go home and spend what is left of your life in your appointed task of showing My people their sin and their need of My salvation.' . . . I know quite well that some of you think me little short of a monomaniac about sin, but I am not the first that has been so thought of and so spoken about. I am in good company, and I am content to be in it."[14]

It was not an easy task to carry out this vocation when one remembers that it was not fashionable to preach about sin in the eighteen seventies. No less a man than Sir George Adam Smith declared that any preaching of sin in those days was either done in an abstract manner, or else elegantly let alone. Alexander Whyte went home and began to preach against sin in a manner that caused men to tremble. He became convinced that no man can declare the grace of God in Jesus Christ unless he likewise convinces men of the awfulness of sin.

Dr. J. H. Jowett, at one time Dr. Whyte's assistant, tells of a sermon that Whyte preached, using the text, "Deliver me from bloodguiltiness, O God, Thou God of my salvation: and my tongue shall sing aloud of Thy righteousness." A large number of medical students were in the church, and these young men and the assistant pastor sat in awe as Dr. Whyte lit up the crooked pathways of sin, as, Dr. Jowett says, the blinding flashes of lightning light up the dark alleys.[15] He showed them the terrible nature of sin, and its effects, and straightway led them from the black night into

---

[14]. *British Weekly,* Jan. 13, 1921, p. 322.
[15]. J. H. Jowett in *The British Weekly,* Jan. 13, 1921, p. 321.

the sunshine of the grace of God in Jesus Christ.   Jowett
says that Dr. Whyte loved to dwell upon the seventh chapter
of Romans, but in every case he led them from that chapter
to the eighth chapter, declaring with the victorious ring of
faith, "For I am persuaded, that neither death, nor life, nor
angels, nor principalities, nor powers, nor things present,
nor things to come, nor height, nor depth, nor any other
creature, shall be able to separate us from the love of God,
which is in Christ Jesus our Lord," for "where sin abounded,
grace did much more abound: that as sin hath reigned unto
death, even so might grace reign through righteousness unto
eternal life by Jesus Christ our Lord."

Dr. John Kelman, another of Dr. Whyte's assistants,
tells of a sermon that Whyte preached on the Rich Young
Ruler. He "made his congregation see him wheeling
blindly down into the black depths of the inferno, circle
after circle, until just as he disappeared on his way down
into its bottomless abyss, he, who had been bending over the
pulpit, watching him with blazing eye, shouted: 'I hear it!
It's the mocking laughter of the universe, and it's shouting
at him over the edge, Ha, ha! Kept the commandments!' " [16]

One evening two young miners from Lanarkshire, after
a Sunday spent in seeing the sights of Edinburgh, found
their way to Free St. George's, to hear the famous Dr.
Whyte.   Throughout the long sermon they sat in speechless
awe, as he painted sin in its blackest colors.   As they came
out of the church, one of them was heard to say: "Aye, yon
man must have been one deevil when he was a laddie!"

Dr. Whyte, like Thomas Guthrie, made use of illustrations in a striking manner.   He tells of walking one day on
a hillside.   "Now as God would have it," he said, "there
had been a whole night of the densest sea-fog from the
Atlantic, and the wet spray stood in millions of shining gems
all over the broom and the bracken, and the bushes of whin,
and the bushes of heather.   Had I not seen the scene with
my own eyes I could not have believed it.   The whole hill-
side was absolutely covered from top to bottom with spider's
webs past all counting up."   Then he reminded his hearers

[16]. E. H. Jeffs, *Princes of the Modern Pulpit* (Nashville, 1931), p. 102.

that in every one of those thousands of shining webs lurked a blood-thirsty spider, with diabolical cunning. "So it is with thousands of Satan's death-spreading snares in the case of every human soul!" he cried.[17]

Once Dr. Whyte preached on Jezebel. After giving an account of her life, he said: "Now! If Jezebel had been chastened and evangelized, evangelized and chastened, she might have repented; but you, my brethren, have been chastened and evangelized, evangelized and chastened, yet you have not repented. Therefore it shall be more tolerable for Jezebel in the Day of Judgment than for you." [18]

In those days more than one Edinburgh church could boast of long lines of people waiting outside for the doors to open, but at no church were the queues longer than at Free St. George's. However, Dr. Whyte cared little that crowds of people waited, even in the rain, for the church to open. He declared: "It is the rankest superstition to think that such going to church — unconvicted and unconverted — has anything to do with true religion," and again, "Come to church twice a day as long as you are able; but twice a day put away some wickedness out of your heart and out of your life before you go home. Twice every Sabbath day become more sensible of the danger and the evil of sin." [19]

One Sunday, when the church was crowded as usual to the very pulpit steps, he described a scene in which a sick man, upon hearing the truth, turned his face to the wall and would say nothing. At the close of the service a man, evidently unaware of Dr. Whyte's commanding personality, came into the sacristy. He informed Whyte that the man whom he had described needed fresh air and sunshine, and not an admonition to repent of his sins. "Sir!" thundered Whyte, "it is only too evident that you are unaware of the appalling blackness that lurks in the depths of the average human heart."

One day the door bell rang, and the visitor to Dr. Whyte's home proved to be a pastor from a poor Highland congregation. He explained his difficulties, and Dr. Whyte

[17]. W. R. Nicoll, *Princes of the Church* (London, 1921), pp. 320-321.
[18]. *British Weekly*, Jan. 27, 1921, p. 362.
[19]. Alfred Fawkes in *The Expositor* (London), March, 1921, p. 191.

gave him a letter to several of his well-to-do church members. When the Highland pastor returned, he mentioned the fact that he had received a curt refusal from a very prominent man. "What did you tell him?" asked Whyte. "I said to him, 'Sir, dinna ye speak tae me that way. Man, dinna forget ye're no' but a puir, hell-deserving sinner like me'sel'.'" "Did you really tell that to Sir George?" mused Dr. Whyte. "Man, man, many's the time I've wanted to say that to him myself. Here, let me give you five pounds for your church."

Dr. Whyte's Sunday night and mid-week lectures became as famous as his morning and evening sermons. After the evening service he delivered lectures to a group of 400 to 500 young men. On Wednesday afternoon he lectured to an equally large group of young women. These lectures, that continued year after year, are surprising in their scope, and would have done credit to Edinburgh University. The young people who attended them were not allowed to sit in idleness, for Dr. Whyte gave them outside work to do, and few university professors have given out heavier assignments. One had to be a hard worker if he wanted to become a member of Dr. Whyte's classes. Not only the Bible, but the lives of great men and women of Bible times, and throughout the history of Christianity, and all manner of other subjects related to religion, were discussed. Dr. Whyte's biographer gives pages, merely of the titles of these many series of lectures.[20]

Dr. Whyte took a great personal interest in the succession of young men who acted as his assistants, and a number of them became men of prominence. Whyte was a tireless worker himself, and he insisted that his assistants work hard. He looked upon the claims of the pulpit as by far the most important work of the clergyman, and the young pastor who had not yet learned to busy himself with his books, and make every sermon a serious piece of craftsmanship, learned quickly enough under the forceful, yet kindly guidance of Alexander Whyte. He had a magnificient library, and he used to tell his assistants, and later his

---

[20]. Geo. F. Barbour, *The Life of Alexander Whyte, D.D.* (London, 1923), p. 647ff.

students after he had become a professor, "Young men, buy books. Buy many books. Sell your bed, if need be, to buy books — but buy books of the right kind." He gave away books by the score. If an assistant, or a visiting pastor, preached a good sermon in his church, he was sure to receive a good book, or even a set of books, from Dr. Whyte, in addition to his financial reimbursement. On one occasion he sent one of his assistants a fine copy of Goodwin's works, and a day later, not yet satisfied, he presented him with a set of Jeremy Taylor, in 12 volumes. With every such gift, a beautiful note of appreciation, in Dr. Whyte's own hand, was received. Many an old pastor of later years included among his most cherished possessions, certain books with the familiar "A. W." on the fly-leaf.

Although Alexander Whyte was a man of almost regal dignity, yet there was always a pathetic humility combined with it. Were he to withhold unintentionally a word of appreciation for some favor shown him, he would hurry after the man, and with tears in his eyes apologize for his oversight. He detested sham as much as he detested shoddy scholarship, and were an assistant pastor to appear without adequate preparation in the pulpit, Dr. Whyte was capable of rebuking him severely, but always in a manner that caused the unhappy victim of his admonition to respect him. He advised young men not to waste their time trying to write articles or books, but to concentrate upon hard study for the pulpit. He believed that the only sure foundation consisted in laborious attention to the claims of the pulpit, and he had little confidence in the clergyman whose popularity rested upon any other basis. He was a firm believer in the summer holiday, or "vacation," so long as it was not merely a time of recreation. He set an example by taking such vacations himself, and wherever he went, heavy packing cases of books accompanied him, and each day he was up at daylight and at his studies, storing up useful material for his preaching.

In his earliest days he had read *Pilgrim's Progress,* and this was one of a number of books that were his favorites throughout his life. Were he to discover that some young pastor had not read this book, he was sure to send him a fine copy of it by the next post, with a note of appreciation of the book's value. Goodwin was another of his favorites, and perhaps it was his admiration for Goodwin more than anything else that won for him the title "the last of the Puritans."

In theology Dr. Whyte was a Calvinist, although at one time in his life he was looked upon as mildly liberal. This was at the time of the Robertson Smith case of 1877-1880. Dr. Whyte defended Smith, although he made it clear that he himself detested "the unbelieving, disintegrating and unremorseful criticism of the great foreign schools," namely the movement that came to be known as the higher criticism. Nevertheless, he believed that the proper course was an investigation of such problems, and not an arbitrary suppression of the difficulty.

Toward the end of his life Dr. Whyte said: "If I am to have some spare time to prepare myself finally before I die, I know the great masterpieces of salvation that I shall have set on the shelf nearest my bed. Shall I tell you some of them? My New Testament; my 'Paradise'; my 'Bunyan,' and especially the Jordan scenes at the end; my 'Saint's Rest'; and it is my old classfellow, William Young's beautiful and fit edition; my lifelong 'Goodwin'; my 'Rutherford'; my 'Catechism on the benefits of being a believer'; my 'Gerontius' and Olney and Wesley and kindred hymns. . . . Since I may any day die in a moment, let me have my hand on that heavenly shelf for a few minutes every day, and especially every night, lest the cock crow in my case suddenly." [21] Alexander Whyte died in his sleep, like Chalmers, and it was in January, 1921. The lad who had started as a cobbler's apprentice and then a hand-loom helper, had become the greatest Scottish preacher of his generation, moderator of the General Assembly and principal of New College.

"He began life as a hand-loom weaver," declared Alfred Fawkes, "his indomitable energy and a natural love of letters enabled him to use to the full the advantages of the admirable Scottish parish school system; his schoolmaster and his minister lent him the helping hand which

---

[21]. W. R. Nicoll in *The British Weekly*, Jan. 13, 1921, p. 322.

in Scotland is never wanting to 'worth by poverty depressed'; and before he was twenty he found himself a student at the University of Aberdeen."[22]   Not only that, but for half a century no man was more admired and none more highly respected than Alexander Whyte. He made his mistakes, as do all men. In his preaching too often he gave the wrongful impression that he himself had once lived an evil life. Once, in preaching to a group of people in a part of the city not noted for its righteousness, he declared, "I have just discovered the name of the wickedest man in Edinburgh. It is Alexander Whyte." His error in defending Robertson Smith lay perhaps in an exaggerated respect for the right of private judgment. He lived long enough to see that same spirit of toleration bring about sad havoc in his beloved Free Church. Such things are but a proof that perfection cannot be found even in the most illustrious men.

Dr. Whyte wrote a number of things. Some of them are: *Bunyan Characters* (1893); *William Law: Character and Characteristics* (1893); *Jacob Behmen* (1894); *Samuel Rutherford and his Correspondents* (1894); *Launcelot Andrewes and his Private Devotions* (1895); *Santa Teresa* (1897); *Father John* (1898); *Bible Characters,* 6 volumes (1897); *J. H. Newman* (1901); *The Apostle Paul* (1903); *Bishop Butler* (1903); and *The Walk, Conversation and Character of Jesus* (1905). He published a *Commentary on the Shorter Catechism* (1882), a book of sermons entitled *With Mercy and Judgment,* and other works. He edited the valuable three-volume set of biographies entitled *The Evangelical Succession* (1882-84).

Archibald Scott (1837-1909)

Archibald Scott, of the Church of Scotland, was born in 1837 at Bogton farm, in the parish of Cadder, Lanarkshire, not far from Glasgow. He attended the parish school and Glasgow High School. After receiving his degree at Glasgow University in 1856, he took the four year theological course at the same institution. Licensed in 1859, he became assistant first to Dr. Watson, of St. Matthew's, Glasgow, and then to Peter Balfour, of Clackmannan. He was ordained

---

[22]. Alfred Fawkes in *The Expositor* (London) March, 1921, p. 190.

in 1860 and received the presentation of the East Church, Perth. In 1863 he was presented with the curacy of Abernethy, Perthshire, and in 1865 he became pastor of Maxwell Church, Glasgow, a new congregation numbering 214 communicants, and worshipping in a temporary wooden chapel while a permanent church was being built. Here Scott introduced one of the first church organs in the Church of Scotland, for instrumental music had been looked upon with much disfavor. He remained at Maxwell Church for four years, and his record there was remarkable. The little group of people grew to a congregation of 806 communicants, with a Sunday-school of 600 children, taught by 60 teachers. He founded a territorial mission, with a parochial school of 370 pupils, and a Sunday-school numbering 370 children and 30 teachers.

Scott's next congregation was St. Michael's, Linlithgow, to which he received the presentation in 1869. Here he found an ancient stone church, one of Scotland's well-known architectural monuments. In 1871 he became pastor of Greenside Church, Edinburgh, where he made known his ability at raising funds, for in a single year $24,000 was raised for local and outside purposes. In 1890 he became pastor of St. George's, Edinburgh, perhaps the most influential congregation in the Church of Scotland. Every visitor to Edinburgh recalls the beautiful George Street, guarded at one end by the Melville Monument, and at the other by the imposing dome of St. George's Church. It was here that Archibald Scott remained for the next nineteen years.

In 1887, three years before coming to Edinburgh, Dr. Scott had become the unquestioned leader of the State Church. His ability was so well recognized that there was a saying in Scotland that wherever Archibald Scott happened to sit, there was the head of the council table. His powerful leadership remained unquestioned for more than twenty years. In 1896 he was made moderator of the General Assembly. He was Croall lecturer in 1889 and Baird lecturer in 1892-93.

Just around the corner from St. George's were such men as Alexander Whyte, John Kelman, James Macgregor and A. Wallace Williamson. Dr. Scott may not have enjoyed the world-wide reputation of Dr. Whyte, nor had he the gift of racy eloquence of Dr. Macgregor, nevertheless he was looked upon as a worthy member of this group of five famous preachers. His greatest fame as a preacher was gained in his earlier days, when he gave his sermons a practical turn in an age when most sermons were theological essays. If he was less popular in Edinburgh it was not because his preaching was beneath his usual standard. It was due to the fact that tastes had changed. Congregations had developed a taste for illustrations, and for personal experiences. Dr. Scott abhorred such things. He believed that the preacher who became popular because of the interesting anecdotes and personal references that he wove into a sermon, was guilty of poor craftsmanship. Dr. Scott's sermons are good illustrations of certain rules that he laid down. He declared that a sermon must never be: 1. Merely a literary or ethical essay; 2. Never a political discussion; 3. Not a theological exposition; 4. Not an apologetic argument. Rather must a sermon be a recognition of the preacher's duty to proclaim the Gospel, and to seek to apply its teachings to the mind and conscience, the life and conduct of his hearers.[23] Dr. Scott refused resolutely to preach an old sermon. Even when asked to preach far from his own congregation, he always wrote a new sermon. In this respect he was at a disadvantage when compared to certain very famous Scottish preachers, who might preach a favorite sermon a number of times.

Dr. Scott prepared his sermons with extreme care. Every word was written out, for he declared that he could think better on paper. Then he preached without manuscript or notes. Often enough, after writing a sermon in full, he read it to himself, tore it up, and started anew. In 1860, while at Perth, his sermons numbered about 5000 words, and filled nineteen written pages. At St. George's he reduced the length to 1600 words, or eight written pages. He was particularly successful in preaching to children,[24] and these sermons were prepared with particular care. Professor Blackie once said of Dr. Scott: "He is a very remark-

[23]. The Hon. Lord Sands, Dr. Archibald Scott, of St. George's, Edinburgh (Edinburgh, 1919), p. 58.
[24]. Ibid., pp. 63-66.

able minister; for when I address him in Greek, he knows it isn't Gaelic."

Dr. Scott's hobby was books. He had little time for recreation, but few things delighted him more than to visit the secondhand book shops of Edinburgh, or to sit late at night absorbed in a catalogue of second hand books. Men who knew him used to say: "Dr. Archibald Scott is too methodical a man to forget an appointment, but should such a thing ever happen, he will be found quickly enough at his favorite book seller's." He had an exceptionally fine library of useful theological reference works, and he was a painstaking student throughout his life.

Dr. Scott's chief works are: *Endowed Territorial Work* (1873); *Buddhism and Christianity* (1890); *Sacrifice: its Prophecy and Fulfilment* (1894); and *Our Opportunities and Responsibilities* (1896).

Andrew M. Fairbairn (1838-1912)

Andrew M. Fairbairn, a noted Congregationalist of Scotland, was born in 1838 at Inverkeithing, Fifeshire. He was a student at Edinburgh University in 1857-60, and his theological studies were pursued at the Evangelical Union's Theological Academy in Glasgow. He studied at Berlin University for a year or two. His first congregation was at Bathgate, West Lothian. In 1872 he became pastor of the St. Paul Street Church, Aberdeen. In 1877 he was made principal of Airdale College, Bradford, and from 1886 to 1909 he was principal of Mansfield College, Oxford. In 1883 he was chairman of the Congregational Union. He was Muir lecturer at the University of Edinburgh 1878-1882, Lyman Beecher lecturer at Yale 1891-1892, Gifford lecturer at Aberdeen 1892-1894, Haskell lecturer in India 1898-1899 and Deems lecturer at New York University in 1906. He published a number of theological works, and a Life of Christ.

Principal Fairbairn was a noted preacher, but the late G. Campbell Morgan once said of him: "I consider . . . Dr. Fairbairn to be one of the greatest hindrances to the cause of true religion in Great Britain, inasmuch as he is giving to the present generation of ministers an intellectual, as

---

[25]. *Hom. Review,* 1920, p. 278.

distinguished from a spiritual conception of religion."[25] To this statement Dr. James M. Campbell took exception. He cited a sermon delivered by Dr. Fairbairn in Boston, on one of his American visits. His text was, "I am not ashamed of the Gospel of Christ, for it is the power of God unto salvation to every one that believeth." Dr. Campbell said, "It was one of the most powerful apologetics for evangelical Christianity to which I ever listened; and afforded abundant evidence that the highest intellectually and deepest spiritually may be blended together."[26]

Dr. Fairbairn had the ability to present extremely dry philosophical theories and difficult theological problems in a lucid, popular manner. It was said of him that he "made Hegelianism sound like a novel." He was one of those unfortunate Scotsmen who had studied in Germany in the days when negative Biblical criticism was the fashion. While pastor of the Evangelical Union congregation in Bathgate, he struggled to reconcile the old truths with the new theology. Some of these men, such as Fairbairn and Denney, held to the old evangelical truths, but at the same time sought to rest them upon a foundation of destructive German Biblical criticism. Some of them actually appeared successful, as for example the man who said: "I shall hold fast to the divinity of my Saviour and to His saving grace, even though modern scholarship disproved the authenticity of every book in the Bible." If it is true that these older men dabbled approvingly in negative Biblical criticism and yet retained their evangelical faith, it is equally true that they have left few, if any, spiritual progeny.

Dr. Fairbairn's sermons were lengthy, learned and philosophical. They proved a severe tax upon the attention of the average congregation. He had fine powers of description, but his sermons were too intellectual for the average man. Fairbairn was as great of heart as Norman Macleod or James Macgregor, yet his intellectual strength stood as a barrier between himself and his hearers. He had two forms of preaching. The most usual one was an appeal to man's reason. The other, used less commonly, was an appeal to the heart. Dr. Garvie, one of his former pupils, recalls two

<hr>

[26]. *Ibid.*, p. 278.

sermons preached by Dr. Fairbairn on the same Sunday. In the morning he used the text, "The love of Christ constraineth us." It was an appeal to the heart, and it left a lasting impression upon the congregation. In the evening his text was, "What think ye of Christ?" It was a thoughtful sermon, and closely reasoned, but beyond the intelligence of most of his hearers. The congregation praised the morning sermon, but said nothing in regard to the other one; Dr. Fairbairn himself was proud of the evening sermon.[27]

Among his published works are: *Studies in the Philosophy of Religion and History* (1876); *Studies in the Life of Christ* (1881); *The City of God* (1882); *Religion in History and in Modern Life* (1884); *The Place of Christ in Modern Theology* (1893); *Christ in the Centuries* (1893); *Catholicism: Roman and Anglican* (1899); *Philosophy of the Christian Religion* (1902); and *Studies in Religion and Theology* (1910).

James Iverach (1839-1922)

Principal Iverach was born in 1839 at Halkirk, Caithness. He attended Edinburgh University from 1859 to 1863, and New College, Edinburgh, from 1863 to 1867. He was ordained in 1869, and served as pastor of West Calder, Edinburgh, from 1869 to 1874, making a name for himself in that mining village as a man of emphatic, outspoken convictions. In 1874 he became pastor of Ferryhill, Aberdeen, which he served for 13 years. From 1887 to 1907 he was professor of dogmatics and apologetics at the United Free Church's college at Aberdeen. From 1905 to 1907 he was principal of this college, and from 1907 onward he was professor of New Testament language and literature. In 1913 he was made moderator of the Assembly. In 1920 he resigned his professorship but continued as principal of the college.

Principal Iverach was a large, loosely built man, with dark hair and beard, and an imperial personality. Men spoke with awe for years of a speech that he made in the church courts about the year 1890. Professors Marcus Dods

---

[27]. A. E. Garvie, *Life of Andrew Martin Fairbairn* (London, 1914), pp. 267-268.

and A. B. Bruce were accused of denying verbal inspiration
and tampering with the truths of Scripture. The pastors in
the Gaelic Highlands were greatly disturbed, and demanded
the exercise of doctrinal discipline, predicting that the
toleration of such teachings would throw open the doors for
unrestrained liberalism. Dr. Iverach addressed the Assembly
in defense of the accused men, and with devastating sarcasm
and a flood of thunderous oratory he silenced the opponents
of Dods and Bruce. Principal Iverach's last appearance
before the Assembly was almost equally dramatic. A lengthy
address had been made by one of the leaders. It was one
of the kind familiar enough to men of all denominations,
wherein the printed statements of certain leaders of
previous years were compared with their statements in the
year 1921. It was Principal Iverach's turn to reply. The
Assembly expected a lengthy, impassioned address. Iverach
arose impressively, and after a pause he said quietly: "The
address to which we have just listened reminds me of the
old farmer up in Argyll. There had been heavy rains that
spring, and the burns were all running at full spate. In
trying to ford one of these streams, his donkey was almost
drowned. He came to the same ford a few months later,
in dry weather, when the burn was reduced to a mere
trickle. The donkey balked, and refused to cross. 'Toot
beastie!' cried the farmer. 'I doot yer memory is better
than yer guid jidgment.'" Dr. Iverach sat down amid
prolonged roars of laughter. Perhaps he recalled the
dramatic moment in Parliament, when, after a lengthy and
vehement speech by the opposition, Lord Titmouse replied
by arising solemnly, waving his arms and crowing like a
rooster.[28]

Principal Iverach was a preacher of unusual forcefulness. He had a powerful voice, somewhat marred by a reedy
quality, but he was a man whose great learning made a lasting impression upon his hearers. Too many such men value
too highly the conclusions of human reason, and Principal
Iverach, unfortunately, was such a man. He was ready to
make concessions to science, wherein it conflicted with

---

[28]. See Samuel Warren's inimitable *Ten Thousand a Year* (London),
1839, etc.).

revelation. His well-known *Theism in the Light of Present Science and Philosophy*[29] is a case in point.

Among the other writings of Principal Iverach were *The Life of Moses* (1881); *Is God Knowable?* (1884); *St. Paul, his Life and Times* (1890); *Christianity and Evolution* (1894); *The Truth of Christianity* (1895); *Descartes, Spinoza and the New Philosophy* (1904); *The Other Side of Greatness* (1906); and *The Christian Message* (1920).

John Macleod (1840-1898)

John Macleod was born at Morven in 1840. His father was a well-known Highland preacher. He was graduated from Glasgow University in 1858, and was licensed to preach in 1861. In 1862 he became pastor at Duns, and in 1875 he was called to Govan Church, in Glasgow. It was a great industrial area, in what had been the outskirts of the city. The parish was an old one, and was served at one time by Andrew Melville.

At Govan, John Macleod established a reputation as a fervid evangelical preacher. In 1884 he built one of the finest churches in Scotland, where he conducted preaching services every day, and with a monthly Communion service. The congregation grew to 3,000 communicants.

Like his distinguished cousin Norman, John Macleod was interested in the welfare of the working people, and under his direction a vast church extension program was carried out. A number of new congregations, Govanhill, Hillhead, Kinning Park, Queen's Park, and others, were opened nearby. Because of his eloquent, evangelical preaching, and his tireless activity among the people of the densely populated industrial districts of Glasgow, John Macleod became one of the best known preachers of the State Church in Glasgow. He was one of the founders of the Scottish Church Society.

In his younger days Macleod was interested for a time in worship reform, and in 1871 he urged daily services, monthly Communion and the observance of Lent. He admired the ritual and the teachings of the Catholic Apostolic Church.

---

[29]. (New York, 1899).

George Matheson (1842-1906)

George Matheson, the famous blind preacher of the Scottish State Church, was born in Glasgow in 1842, the son of a prosperous merchant. During his elementary school days, his eyesight was poor, and only by the use of thick spectacles was he able to study. Despite his handicap, he was an exceptional student. When he entered Glasgow University in 1861, his eysight was almost gone. He had an older sister who was exceptionally kind to him, and who read all his lessons to him, and wrote out all his school papers as he dictated them. In his early ministry she wrote out his sermons at his dictation.

Glasgow University, in the year 1861, still occupied its old buildings. It had been founded in mediaeval days, and later, Andrew Melville was its distinguished principal. The university stood where the grimy railway station now stands, and it is hard to picture its ancient buildings and its shady quadrangles in the forbidding part of the city now occupied by railway yards. In those days the students ranged in age from 12 years to 40 or more, and the son of a Highland shepherd sat next to the son of an earl or viscount.

His first sermon was preached at an evening service in the College Church in High street. It was the custom in the theological course to preach a sermon before the professors and students. This was a part of their training, and if the sermon was a good one, the student was given an opportunity to preach it in one of the city churches. Young Matheson, after his sermon criticism, was asked to preach in the College Church. Instead of preaching his class-room sermon, he prepared a new one, using the text, "Precious in the sight of the Lord is the death of His saints." The professors and students who had come to hear him were astonished at his freshness and vigor of thought, and his ability to present familiar truths in a new and striking manner. It was predicted at the time he would take his place among Scotland's most eminent preachers.

Matheson was licensed in 1866, and a year later he was called to his home congregation, Sandyford Church, Glasgow, to become the assistant to the famous J. R. Macduff. During a trip to the Holy Land, Dr. Macduff left young Matheson in full charge of the congregation. His work in the pulpit, and his pastoral ministrations were exceptionally good, and in 1868 his name was suggested as pastor of Innellan Church. The people there had heard enough in regard to his unusual pulpit power to be fully convinced, but grave fears were expressed lest his blindness might prove an obstacle to his parish work. However, he remained there for 18 years, and at all times he performed all his parochial duties as efficiently as a man with perfect eyesight. In his early days his sister read to him, and wrote as he dictated, but later he was able to hire a full-time secretary to do this for him.

In 1886 he was called to St. Bernard's church, one of the largest and most important congregations in Edinburgh, where he served with great success for 13 years. His appearance in the pulpit was impressive. He was sturdily built, he wore a full beard, and his ruddy, kindly face and his constant cheerful nature made an impression upon everybody. Although blind, yet his eyes appeared normal, and had a sparkle to them that led those who did not know him to insist that his eyesight was entirely normal. He had a quick memory, and his Scripture lessons and the Psalmody were memorized, and recited in such a manner that none would suspect that he could not see. An open Bible lay before him, and unconsciously he would glance at it from time to time as he recited the Lessons, or during his sermon. His sermons were gems. They were brief, yet noteworthy because of their perfection of thought, their excellent form, their fascinating diction, freshness of thought and cheerfulness of delivery. His introductions were brief, his divisions almost always three, and each division led up to a spirited climax. Men competent to judge, declared that his preaching was equal to that of Guthrie, Macleod, Caird, Macduff and Tulloch.

While at the University of Glasgow, George Matheson was perhaps the most popular student of his time. Not only did he excel in scholarship, but his unusual cheerfulness, his hearty nature, his irenic spirit, and his warm friendliness to all, caused him to be admired by professors and students alike. These qualities went with him through life. His irenic spirit went so far that he was led in time to such a degree of broad toleration that he all but disregarded denominational distinctions.

Matheson wrote a number of books on theology and philosophy, including discussions of some of the current German theologians. He was Baird lecturer in 1881. He preached by command before the Queen at Balmoral. He composed several hymns, one of which is, "O love that will not let me go." Although blind, he was able to write letters to his friends in longhand, and in his earlier years his handwriting was unusually good. From 1899 onward he gave most of his time to his writings. Of his thirty or more published books, his two-volume *Studies in the Portrait of Christ* (1899) enjoyed an exceptionally wide circulation. Other works that continue to be read long after their author's death are his *Representative Men of the Bible,* 2 volumes (1902); *Representative Men of the New Testament* (1905); and *Representative Women of the Bible* (1906). In some of his earlier works he expresses uncertainty in regard to the theory of evolution, but in later life he came to the conclusion that its claims are baseless. Matheson's biography, *The Life of Dr. George Matheson,* by D. MacMillan, was published in 1907.

George Reith (1842-1919)

One of Glasgow's prominent clergymen, noted for the freshness and vigor of his preaching, was Dr. George Reith. He was a native of Aberdeen, having been born there in 1842. His father was a railway official, at one time manager of a Scottish railway, and later manager of the Grand Trunk Railway of Canada. He was a strong and resourceful man, honest, proverbially, and a devout Christian. George, his fifth child, was educated at the famous Aberdeen Grammar School and at Marischal College. He took his degree at King's College in 1861. At the age of 17 his father took him on a trip that included many of the most prominent cities in America. At 19 he entered the Free Church Theological College at Edinburgh, where his professors, among others, were Dr. A. B. Davidson and Dr. Robert Rainy. Among his friends and classmates were Whyte, Dods, G. W. Thomson, Simeon MacPhail, G. D. Low and

Taylor Innes. In 1864 he spent six months in Germany, where he made the acquaintance of Delitzsch and others.

George Reith's father was a remarkable man, and his letters to his son are worthy of publication. He warned him against the type of clergyman who becomes little more than a popular social leader of his congregation, who softens his testimony in order not to offend, and whose chief ambition seems to be to make a good numerical record rather than to preach repentance and faith.

In 1866 George Reith was licensed, and he became an assistant to the pastor of the Wynd Mission. The work in this slum area had been revived in 1857 by Dr. Robert Buchanan, and was carried on with conspicuous success by Dugald McColl, Robert Howie, James Wells and John Riddell. Mr. Reith became assistant to James Wells. Not only did he preach in the Wynd Church, but his duties included outdoor preaching, sometimes in Jail Square, and at times under the shelter of a bridge when the weather was bad.

Dr. Robert Buchanan, who had general oversight of the work in the Wynds, was not slow to discover the worth of Mr. Reith, and he persuaded him to come to the College Church not as his assistant, but as his colleague. The College Church was one of the most famous in Glasgow. With a history extending back to the year 1293, it had been known first as St. Mary's Collegiate Church, then Tron Church and finally the College Church. It had been moved in 1857 to the West End, and near to the Free Church Theological College.

When Mr. Moody visited Glasgow in 1873, there were men who held aloof from his evangelistic campaign, but George Reith was one of several who entered whole-heartedly into the effort, and won the warm commendation of Mr. Moody. Dr. Buchanan died in 1875 and Mr. Reith became his successor. Few men have been privileged to serve so notable a church. Among the office-bearers were such men as Fairbairn, Douglas, Bruce, Denney and other noted principals and professors. It was a common saying in Glasgow that so many of the city's leading professional and business men were members of the College Church that a meeting of its voting members might be adjourned and immediately reconvened as a legal meeting of the Glasgow Chamber of Commerce.

The missionary spirit of the congregation was known throughout Scotland. Not only did they contribute at all times more for missionary and charitable purposes than for local purposes, but they assisted less prosperous Glasgow congregations. One of their most important projects was the support of a mission congregation that became known as Stevenson Memorial Church. The College Church provided this new congregation with a beautiful $250,000 place of worship.

In 1903 College Church was overtaken by a calamity, when their own fine building was destroyed by fire. After making use of two temporary places of worship, Kelvingrove Church, not far away, offered to change their hours of worship in order to allow College Church to use their beautiful French Gothic place of worship. So harmonious was the arrangement that it led, in 1908, to a consolidation of the two congregations. By a strange coincidence this church was destroyed by fire in 1925.

Dr. Reith's preaching was always of a high order. He had a high conception of the dignity of the pulpit and the importance of the hour of worship. He felt that a preacher stands in the very presence of the Lord, hence any effort to provide enjoyment to the congregation by means of flashy rhetoric, bursts of oratory or the discussion of current events is entirely out of place. He used few illustrations from literature or art, few quotations from secular writers, and no anecdotes or personal references. To him the clergyman who began a sentence with the words, "One day as I stood before the Temple of Diana the thought came to me . . ." was not only guilty of bad taste, but of wasting the precious time that might be spent to greater advantage in the exposition of spiritual truth. He confined his preaching to the great themes of the Christian faith. On one occasion he preached an entire series of sermons on the Transfiguration, a subject that finds far too little a place in the preaching of most clergymen. Among his writings one of the most important is an exposition of the Gospel of St. John.

Dr. Reith was made moderator of the General Assembly in 1914. One of his sons, Sir John C. W. Reith, has been director-general of the British Broadcasting System since 1927, besides filling several high cabinet offices. Among Dr. George Reith's works mention may be made of *Reminiscences of the United Free Church General Assembly, 1900-1929*. The story of his life is told in W. M. Clow's *A Scottish Ministry* (1928).

William Hastie (1842-1903)

William Hastie, of the Church of Scotland, was born in 1842 in Wanlockhead. After his classical education he taught school for a time. He attended Edinburgh University, and was graduated in 1867. Then he studied for a time at Glasgow, and from 1870 to 1878 he studied at universities in Germany, Holland and Switzerland. In 1875, at the age of 33, he was licensed to preach. In 1876 he served the Ford-Lochawe mission, and the following year Haddam, *locum tenens,* and assisted at Galashiels. He was ordained in 1878, and made principal of the Church of Scotland's college at Calcutta. Five years later difficulties arose in regard to matters of discipline, and he was relieved of his position. Principal Hastie was a man of great learning, a proficient linguist and an eloquent preacher. He delivered the Croall lectures in 1892, and in 1895 he was made professor of divinity at Glasgow University. In addition to the many German theological and philosophical works that he translated into English he wrote *Theology as Science* (1899), and the important *Theology of the Reformed Church* (1904). His biography was published by D. Macmillan in 1926.

John Smith (1844-1905)

John Smith, a prominent United Presbyterian clergyman of Edinburgh, was born in 1844 at Forres, Morayshire. He received his education at Forres Academy, the grammar school at Aberdeen and the University of Aberdeen. His theological studies, at the United Presbyterian theological hall were followed by his ordination in 1873, and pastoral activity at Burghead and at Fraserburgh. In 1878 he became pastor of Wallace Green Church, Berwick-on-Tweed, and his reputation as a preacher led to a call to Edinburgh, where he became colleague and then pastor of Broughton Place Church.

Dr. Smith took a conservative attitude toward higher criticism and the tendency toward theological liberalism. He was an evangelical preacher who produced a deep impression upon his hearers because of his fervent earnestness and his conservative attitude toward the disturbing theological innovations of the latter nineteenth century. His *Integrity of Scripture: Plain Reasons for Rejecting the Critical Hypothesis,* is a manly answer to the Higher Critics.

James Orr (1844-1913)

James Orr was born in 1844 at Glasgow. He took his degree at Glasgow University in 1870, and at the United Presbyterian Divinity Hall in 1872. He was ordained in 1874 and became pastor of East Bank United Presbyterian Church, Hawick, where he remained for 17 years. During this period, and until 1901, he was professor of Church history in the United Presbyterian Theological College. From 1901 to 1913 he was professor of apologetics and systematic theology at Glasgow College of the United Free Church.

Professor Orr was a forceful preacher and lecturer, and he was well known in the United States because of his lectures at Allegheny, Auburn, Princeton, Chicago, Toronto and other colleges and seminaries. He has preached in a number of prominent American pulpits. Professor Orr was thoroughly acquainted with the claims of the higher critics and rejected many of their more radical assertions. He accepted the Mosaic authorship of the Pentateuch, but with reservations, declaring that he was not ready to conclude "that Moses himself wrote the Pentateuch in the precise shape or extent in which we now possess it; for the work, we think, shows very evident signs of different pens and styles, of editorial redaction, of stages of compilation. . . . In the collation and preparation of the materials for this work — some of them, perhaps, reaching back into pre-Mosaic times — and the laying of the foundations of the existing narratives, to which Moses by his own compositions, according to constant tradition, lent the initial impulse, many hands and minds may have co-operated, and may have continued to co-operate, after the master-mind was removed; but unity of purpose and will gave a corresponding unity to the product of their labours." [30] He believed that David wrote most of the Psalms. He based his belief upon the fact that Psalm 18 bears every internal evidence of Davidic authorship. Taking this Psalm as his beginning, he compares the language, literary style, constructions and peculiarities of other Psalms to the 18th Psalm, thus by a process of reasoning, concludes that most of the other Psalms were written by David.

Professor Orr was a positive Rationalist. He employed the processes of human reason to prove that the Bible is trustworthy, and written, in most cases, by those authors to whom the various Books are ascribed. Like most men of his generation he did not consider it intellectually honest to reject speculation entirely, in favor of faith alone. While it is gratifying to know that men such as James Orr made a painstaking examination of the internal evidence regarding the genuineness of the Scriptures, yet one cannot overlook the fact that these men, perhaps without realizing it, placed human opinion on a higher plane than divine revelation. Such men lacked the spiritual courage of Dr. John Smith of Edinburgh, who wrote *The Integrity of Scripture; Plain Reasons for Rejecting the Critical Hypothesis.*[31]

James Orr published many books. Among these are: *The Christian View of God and the World* (1893); *The Supernatural in Christianity* (1894); *The Early Church* (1901); *The Progress of Dogma* (1901); *The Early Church; its History and Literature* (1901); *God's Image in Man* (1905); *The Problem of the Old Testament* (1906); *The Bible Under Trial* (1907); *The Virgin Birth of Christ* (1907); *The Resurrection of Jesus* (1908); and *Sidelights on Christian Doctrine* (1909).

Dr. Orr's last and perhaps his greatest work was his *International Standard Bible Encyclopaedia,* in five large volumes (1915). In this work, conservative scholarship and a simple, easy literary style are combined. Dr. Orr was assisted by other conservative scholars. Valuable as

[30]. Jas. Orr, *The Problem of the Old Testament* (New York, 1906), p. 369.
[31]. (New York, 1902).

the work is, yet it cannot be accepted without reservation. While conservative up to a point, yet concessions are made from time to time to the views of the more moderate critics. The doctrinal articles are not always in full harmony with the teachings of God's Word, and in some cases authorities holding conflicting opinions have been placed side by side, giving the impression to the casual reader that many doctrines are merely matters of human opinion. This is an obvious error. Either a doctrine is set forth in the Bible or else it is not. Nothing is proved by presenting the right and the wrong of it. A revised edition, edited by Dr. Melvin G. Kyle, appeared in 1930, and was reprinted in 1949, and sought to attain a more even presentation where there were conflicting views.

Dr. Orr was one of the men who checked the spread of radical criticism; and he called Bible scholars back to a more conservative position. If there is a tendency today toward orthodoxy, as many authorities assure us is the case, then Dr. Orr is among the noted scholars responsible for the change. Thoroughly conservative men of evangelical views will not be ready to endorse many statements in Dr. Orr's works, yet they will rejoice in the fact that he did much toward turning the tide at a time when speculation was unrestrained. However, he did not have the uncompromising conservatism of Dr. W. H. T. Dau, one of the contributors to the *International Standard Bible Encyclopaedia.*

James Stalker (1848-1928)

A Free Church clergyman who attained fame as a preacher, theological lecturer, professor and author was Dr. James Stalker of Aberdeen. He was born in 1848 at Crieff, in Perthshire. After receiving his degree at Edinburgh University in 1872, he attended Berlin and Halle. He studied theology in New College, Edinburgh, was ordained in 1874 and became pastor of St. Brycedale's, Kirkcaldy, where he served for 13 years. In 1887 he became pastor of St. Matthew's Church, Glasgow, where he remained for 15 years, and established a reputation as an able preacher. In 1902 he was called to the chair of Church History in the United Free Church College at Aberdeen.

James Stalker was known throughout Britain and America. He was much esteemed as a preacher and as a special lecturer at universities and theological schools. In 1891 he delivered the Lyman Beecher Lectures on preaching at Yale University, which appeared later in book form, and retained popularity for many years. In 1899 he was Cunningham Lecturer at New College, Edinburgh, in 1901 he delivered the Gay Lectures at the Baptist Theological Seminary in Louisville, Ky., and lectured at the Presbyterian Seminary in Richmond. While in America he preached in a number of prominent pulpits and was well received wherever he went.

At the time of his ordination at Kirkcaldy in 1874, Stalker became interested in the Moody and Sankey evangelistic campaigns, which were stirring Scotland at the time. He entered into the work with energy, and although but 26 years of age at the time, his gifts were recognized by Mr. Moody, together with those of three other young men who were to become famous: Henry Drummond, John Watson (Ian Maclaren), and George Adam Smith.

Professor Stalker was the author of a number of books which became famous throughout the world. His *Life of Jesus Christ* (1879), although comparatively brief, became widely known. Other works followed: *The New Song* (1883), which is a collection of sermons for children; *The Life of St. Paul* (1884); *Imago Christi* (1889); *The Preacher and his Models* (1891); *The Four Men* (1892); *The Trial and Death of Jesus* (1894); *The Two Saint Johns of the New Testament* (1895); *The Christology of Jesus* (1899); *The Seven Deadly Sins* (1901); *The Seven Cardinal Virtues* (1902); *The Life of John Knox* (1904); *The Atonement* (1908); *The Ethic of Jesus* (1909); *Christian Psychology* (1914); *The Beauty of the Bible* (1918); and several other works.

John Watson (1850-1907)

John Watson ("Ian Maclaren") was born in Manningtree, Essex, in 1850. His Scottish parents were living temporarily in England, but when John Watson was four years old, they returned to Perth, Scotland. The boy attended the Perth grammar school and Stirling high school.

He was graduated from Edinburgh in 1870. From 1870 to 1874 he studied theology at New College, Edinburgh, where two of his teachers were Robert Rainy and A. B. Bruce. Following his seminary studies, he attended Tuebingen for a semester.

In 1874 he became assistant pastor of Barclay Church, Edinburgh. In 1875 he became pastor of Logiealmond Free Church, Perthshire, and in 1877 he went to St. Matthew's Free Church, Glasgow, first as associate pastor and later as pastor. In 1880 he assumed charge of Sefton Park Church, Liverpool, a new congregation, where he remained for 25 years. His work in Liverpool was remarkable, for the congregation became noted for its great wealth and culture. During Watson's pastorate, they built a church costing £150,000, which was one of the most imposing Presbyterian churches in the British Isles. In 1903-1906 Dr. Watson was one of the leaders in the founding of Liverpool University.

Dr. Watson made three lecture tours in the United States, during which he delivered series of addresses at several leading universities. He published a number of books which attained great popularity both in the British Isles and in America. He died in Mount Pleasant, Iowa, during his third lecture tour.

Dr. Watson was somewhat liberal in his theology, although he considered himself an evangelical. He was an unusually popular preacher and lecturer. His sermons and his books were somewhat of a departure from traditional theology, and caused him to be suspected of liberalism. Dr. Watson was able to express himself in a pleasant, popular manner, and he used evangelical terminology in such a way that his liberal views in matters of Biblical criticism were not always evident. He declared his firm belief in the deity of the Saviour, and in the Atonement, and he insisted that salvation is by faith in the merits of Jesus Christ alone. Moreover, he believed that a limited election to salvation is not consistent with the love of Jesus Christ. He belonged to the new school of thought whose adherents insisted that the deity of Jesus Christ and the fact of salvation by grace do not depend upon the authenticity of the sacred writings of Holy Scripture.

John Watson, under the name of Ian Maclaren wrote a number of books of a popular nature, usually with a religious background. Of his religious writings, the best known are: *The Mind of the Master* (1896); *The Cure of Souls* (1896); *Companions of the Sorrowful Way* (1898); *The Doctrines of Grace* (1900); *The Life of the Master* (1902); *Respectable Sins* (1909); and *Inspiration of our Faith* (1905). An excellent biography of Dr. Watson was published in 1908 by Sir W. Robertson Nicoll.

Sir W. Robertson Nicoll (1851-1923)

William Robertson Nicoll was born in 1851 at Lumsden, Aberdeenshire. He came of pure Celtic ancestry. His father was a clergyman of the Free Church who had succeeded in accumulating a working library of 17,000 books, although his salary had ranged from £100 to £200 per year.[32].

Robertson Nicoll received his early education in the parochial school at Auchindoir. This school contained a single large room seating 130 children, all these taught by one schoolmaster. Boys began the study of Latin at the age of eight. After completing his work at this parochial school, Robertson Nicoll attended Aberdeen Grammar School and then Aberdeen University, where he took his degree in 1870. He studied at Free Church Divinity Hall from 1870 to 1874. In 1872 he was licensed to preach.

In 1874 he was ordained and became pastor of the Free Church at Dufftown, Banffshire. "Dufftown survivors recall how the boyish-looking Free Church minister brought into our secluded life fresh thoughts and new emotions which, without ingratitude to the old, we were thirsty to drink of. Who that heard and saw can forget the eager face and pleading voice as he would lean forward over the clasped hands laid on the pulpit? How keenly the preacher felt, how livingly he believed!" [33] Village gossip the world over has a habit of finding flaws in others, whether they exist or not, but in the case of Robertson Nicoll this gossip took an un-

---

[32]. T. H. Darlow, *William Robertson Nicoll* (London, 1925), p. 7.
[33]. *Ibid.*, p. 31.

expected form.   There was some quality in the young man that caused idle tongues to invent strange tales — but always to the decided credit of their pastor.   There were whispered tales of his great literary ability, and of flattering offers from publishers in Edinburgh and London.

Robertson Nicoll's unusual preaching brought him invitations to speak in various places, and in 1877 he was called to the Free Church at Kelso, where Horatius Bonar had been pastor from 1837 to 1853.   Nicoll remained in this famous border town for eight years.   In 1886 he published a book of sermons, *Calls to Christ,* which received high praise from C. H. Spurgeon, Joseph Parker, Henry Drummond and others. His fame as a preacher brought him invitations to preach at such noted places as Free St. George's in Edinburgh, City Temple in London and at *la Salle Évangélique,* at the Paris Exposition.   He received a call to Chalmers Presbyterian Church at Adelaide, but declined it.   When the great Central Hall, Tolcross, Edinburgh, was dedicated, many of the most famous clergymen of Scotland took part, but it was W. Robertson Nicoll who was selected to preach the chief sermon.

He was taken ill in 1885, and since his mother, a brother and a sister had died of tuberculosis, his physicians insisted that he go south to the mild climate of the South Devon coast.   He went to Dawlish for a time, and upon recovering his health he went to Hamstead, in London.   He had already begun writing for the *Expositor,* and after going to London he founded the *British Weekly,* a journal for the Nonconformist churches of England and for the Scottish churches. It was a magazine of high literary standard, and among its contributors were James Denny, Marcus Dods, Ian Maclaren, Alexander Whyte, George Morrison and James Moffatt. Robertson Nicoll is said to have discovered J. M. Barrie and introduced him to the public through the *British Weekly.* Robertson Nicoll's skill as a writer and editor brought him international fame, and in 1909 he was knighted by the King.

Sir William's reputation as a preacher did not rest upon mere external gifts nor upon a commanding presence, for he was slight of build, and except for an intense earnestness and an arresting pulpit personality he had few of the qualities of the popular orator. His biographer says, "his vigorous thought and lucid arrangement, together with a wealth of felicitous and fluent language, made up for any defects of voice or delivery in a preacher who was so unmistakably sincere." [34] His busy editorial life did not cause him to neglect preaching. He was in great request at important gatherings, and he delivered two or three sermons a month upon such occasions. The mere mention of his name was sufficient to insure a large congregation of people of the more thoughtful kind. His arduous editorial work did not diminish his lifelong interest in theology, neither did his long residence in England cause him to lose his Scottish characteristics or his accent. His capacity for work was enormous, and few men of our time have written as much as he. In addition to the distinguished editorials that appeared weekly in his *British Weekly* over a long term of years, he gave the world such valuable works as *The Expositor's Bible,* 49 volumes (1891ff); *The Expositor's Greek Testament,* 5 volumes (1897); *The Expositor's Dictionary of Texts,* 2 volumes (1910); and *The Expositor's Treasury of Children's Sermons* (1912); all of which he produced with the assistance of a staff of authoritative writers. His *The Incarnate Saviour* (1881), *The Lamb of God* (1883), *A Life of Christ* (1881), and *The Return to the Cross* (1897) are remarkable books when one considers the fact that they were written at a time when the great majority of his associates were questioning the fundamentals of our faith. *The Church's One Foundation* (1901) is his reply to the negative Higher Critics of his day. *Princes of the Church* (1921) is a collection of biographical gems, reprinted from *The British Weekly.* With the titles of two score of his books and larger works before me, it is difficult to select a few of the more important titles, for all that Dr. Nicoll wrote was important. No mention has been made of several books of excellent sermons, nor of biographies that set a high standard in that field.

Sir W. Robertson Nicoll is usually considered a conservative evangelical. His writings cause one to rejoice that he came so close to the truth in a generation when the

[34]. *Op. cit.,* p. 37.

truth was so often questioned and even attacked. A careful reader will observe that he was not clear on such things as the Sacraments, in regard to which he took the reformed position; and there were other doctrines where his reformed training is in evidence. It is most unfortunate that such men as Robertson Nicoll, who strove so valiantly for an understanding of the truth, were not assisted by men to whom the Lord has given a fuller understanding of such things. Had the writings of the clearest and most conservative of our theologians been available to him, the results might have been different. There are church bodies who have had the priceless advantage of great teachers whose clear thinking and great theological knowledge has left a lasting mark upon their teachings. It is a pity that such denominations have not attempted to train more men with the ability to speak to the whole Christian world, both by word of mouth and by the printed page. By means of the radio, by conducting great preaching missions in a way that there is no compromise with error, and by a world-wide circulation of books, it ought to be easy enough to make known to such sincere men as Dr. Nicoll such things as the distinction between objective and subjective justification, and to make it plain that an acceptance of the Real Presence in no wise involves consubstantiation. Any man who can write so excellent a book as Dr. Nicoll's *The Incarnate Saviour*, which comes so close to the truth, would no doubt welcome additional light on such things as objective justification. The two standard biographies are T. H. Darlow, *Life and Letters of Sir W. Robertson Nicoll* (1925), and J. F. Stoddard, *W. Robertson Nicoll, Editor and Preacher* (1903).

Henry Drummond (1851-1897)

During the closing years of the nineteenth century the name of Professor Henry Drummond was known to college and university boys throughout the world. Few men have been so idolized. From 1884 to 1894 he devoted much of his time to what was known at that time as the Student Movement. He addressed hundreds of great student gatherings, his books gained a world-wide popularity that is hard to understand today, and young men of several countries crowded about him seeking personal interviews in regard to their spiritual problems.

Henry Drummond was born in 1851 in Park Place, Stirling. His father and grandfather were well-known seedsmen. The Drummond home was of the old-fashioned, evangelical Scottish Presbyterian kind, with Sunday devoted to church going and study of the Bible and the Shorter Catechism. Young Drummond attended the high school in Stirling, and Morison's Academy at Crieff. While yet a small boy he went with the other lads of his school to hear James Robertson, a famous preacher of the time. Because he answered a question correctly, Mr. Robertson asked him to stand in the pulpit and read the text, which Drummond did without hesitation. In 1866 he entered Edinburgh University, but he did not complete the full course. In 1870 he went to New College, Edinburgh, of the Free Church, for his theological studies. There he had such professors as Dr. Blaikie, Dr. Duff the famous missionary, and Dr. Davidson the Hebrew scholar. About the year 1870 or 1871 Dr. Davidson began his series of lectures on the Higher Criticism of the Pentateuch that were to prove so controversial in the Scottish churches, and which did their full share toward undermining the doctrine of verbal inspiration. German scholarship was held in high esteem, and the boys from the Scottish universities and theological halls were flocking to Halle and Berlin, to Erlangen, Goettingen and Tuebingen. At the last of these Drummond went for a semester, in the year 1873.

In 1873-75, when Moody and Sankey visited the British Isles, Henry Drummond became associated with them, first as a personal worker and then as an organizer of work among young men. He was but 22 years old, but so greatly was Mr. Moody impressed that he sent Drummond to such places as Sunderland, New Castle and South Shields, and then to Dublin, Manchester, Sheffield, Birmingham and Liverpool to carry on work among young men. Drummond's meetings attracted thousands. Young men everywhere were agitated because of the new claims of natural science, and all day long and until far into the night came an endless procession of young Scotsmen and Englishmen seeking personal interviews with Henry Drummond and a friend or two who assisted him. When Mr. Moody returned to America he urged Drummond to go with him. Although Drummond could not do this at the time, yet in later years he lectured at Mr. Moody's Northfield school. In 1875 Mr. Drummond returned to New College to complete his theological studies, and in 1877 he was made lecturer in natural science at the Free Church College in Glasgow. His lectures were delivered during a five-month Winter term, leaving seven months for other activities. In connection with this teaching, Mr. Drummond served a mission congregation in Possilpark, a suburb of Glasgow. In 1879 he visited America for the first time, not as a lecturer but as a member of a geological expedition to the Rocky Mountains; and in 1883 he took part in a geological expedition in East Central Africa. His lectureship in natural science had become a full professorship, for it was at a period when the conflict of science and theology was acute, and such a lectureship in a theological school was considered important. Drummond was ordained at the age of 33, and became a theological professor of the Free Church.

Henry Drummond's most important work was his leadership of the Student Movement, to which he gave much of his time between 1884 and 1894. He began a series of services at Edinburgh, and he delivered what he called lectures or addresses, rather than sermons. This became a permanent institution in Edinburgh, and from there it spread to the other Scottish universities, to England, America, Germany and Australia. Professor Drummond visited scores of universities during that busy decade, he became a lecturer at Moody's school in Northfield, at the original Chautauqua in western New York State, and at various other Summer assemblies then so popular. His influence over students reached fantastic proportions, and his biographer declares that it is literally true that Protestant young men, here and there, prayed to him after his death. The number of young men who sought personal interviews with him, and who wrote him letters, is almost beyond belief; and Professor Drummond, always humble and easily accessible, actually wore himself out and died at the early age of 45 because of the burden of this work among students.

Henry Drummond was a man of culture and fine personality, and perhaps no man has ever attained the same popularity as a lecturer and preacher to university students. We wish that we might say that this man, with his many gifts, was orthodox in his theology, but Henry Drummond was a peculiar man. While he insisted emphatically, especially during the question-box period that often followed his addresses, that he believed firmly in every teaching of evangelical Christianity, at the same time he made important concessions to scientific thought, and especially to the theory of evolution. Like certain other men of his generation he seemed to think that there is a dualism of thought. He was able to deliver a lecture on evolution, and in the next breath declare his implicit belief in all the teachings of orthodox Christianity. He was unable to see the conflict between the outspoken claims of the scientists of his day and the teachings of the Scriptures. Men of the orthodox schools attacked his teachings, both in Scotland and in America. One prominent British religious journal refused to make mention of his work, and at Northfield, Mass., Mr. Moody was urged to drop his name from the list of lecturers. Even his emphatic profession of evangelical belief was challenged, for men declared that he had an insufficient understanding of the Law and its uses, and that he stressed the love of God much more frequently than the suffering and death of the Saviour. His *Natural Law in the Spiritual World* (1883), with its many apparent defects, was read in every country, as was his *Ascent of Man* (1894), and his other writings. An exceptional biography was written by Sir George Adam Smith.[35] Henry Drummond is not to be confused with Henry Drummond (1786-1860), an associate of Edward Irving and a leader of the Catholic Apostolic Church.

While the name of Henry Drummond is often included among the great preachers of the nineteenth century, and his sermons often found among the collections of great sermons of the ages, yet his fame began to decline with the passing of the generation that knew him personally. He is significant in the history of preaching because he is a representative of the strange dualism that men attempted

---

[35]. G. A. Smith, *The Life of Henry Drummond* (London, 1898).

to uphold. In an age when the claims of science were especially vocal, some clergymen believed that natural science and divine revelation could follow two parallel paths, even though their teachings might often be in flat contradiction. Others, such as Professor Drummond, attempted to reconcile the two, and by a juggling of words make it appear that there is no real contradiction. Drummond's friend Sir W. Robertson Nicoll says that Drummond soothed and strengthened his hearers, but did not seem to arouse them to a sense of sin and a need of a Saviour.[36]

One thing is worthy of notice: it is seldom that a man who accepts rationalistic science or Negative Criticism is to be heard proclaiming sin and grace with the assurance that Moody and Spurgeon preached those things. Drummond's *Greatest Thing in the World* (1894), his *Natural Law in the Spiritual World* (1883), and his *Ascent of Man* (1894) are too well known to need mention, and in spite of a certain superficiality, they have had an enormous circulation. His other books are all but forgotten today. The story of his great popularity among young men is told in George Adam Smith's *Life of Henry Drummond* (1889), a particularly good example of the older type of biography, and in C. Lenox's *Henry Drummond* (1900).

J. P. Struthers (1855-1915)

One of the most noted preachers of the Reformed Presbyterian Church was J. P. Struthers of Greenock. After attending the high school in Glasgow, he studied at Glasgow University, taking his degree in 1875. After his theological studies he was ordained in 1878, becoming pastor at Whithorn. In 1882 he was called to Mount Park, Greenock, where he remained for 33 years until his death.

Mr. Struthers was a preacher of unusual talents, and he was known throughout Scotland because of his publication *Morning Watch,* intended for children and young people, but read widely by both young and old. It was due partly to the whimsical humor of this popular paper that the Scotsman's reputation for thrift became so widely known. Who will forget his story of the schoolboy who finished his studies and

---

[36]. W. R. Nicoll, *Princes of the Church* (London, 1921), p. 95.

went away and left the gas burning; or the story of the lad who was given "tuppence," but put only a penny and three farthings in his missionary envelope; or the man who diluted his ink so that he might give an additional three-pence to the missionary cause?

In 1895 the University of Glasgow offered the degree of Doctor of Divinity to Mr. Struthers, but with his characteristic modesty he declined it.   Over his pulpit at Greenock was a clock bearing the inscription ΕΡΧΕΤΑΙ ΝΎΞ: "The Night Cometh."   On the afternoon of Jan. 17, 1915, Mr. Struthers was stricken while preaching in this same pulpit, and he died a few hours later.

The Reformed Presbyterian Church, to which J. P. Struthers belonged, produced such men as J. G. Paton, the famous missionary, as well as James Denney, John Laidlaw and J. E. McFayden, all of whom began their careers as Reformed Presbyterians, or Covenanters. This small denomination is a direct descendent of the Cameronians or old Covenanters.   It still lays stress upon the old Covenants, upon the Kingship of Jesus Christ in Church and State, and upon the Westminster Confession and Catechisms.   In the days of J. P. Struthers it insisted upon a high standard of conduct as a qualification for church membership, it was strongly anti-Roman, and it opposed secret societies.

Sir George Adam Smith (1856-1942)

George Adam Smith was born in Calcutta during the time that his father, Dr. George Smith, was president of Doveton College in that place. His Scottish parents returned to their native land, and the boy was sent to the Royal High School in Edinburgh and then to Edinburgh University. From 1875 to 1878 he attended New College of the Free Church.   In 1876 he went to Tuebingen and in 1877 to Leipsic, where he came in contact with liberal German theological thought.   This was followed by a period of travel in Egypt and Syria, where he continued his studies.

He was ordained in 1880 and became assistant pastor of the West Free Church in Brechin.   From 1880 to 1882, in addition to his pastoral duties, he was a tutor in Hebrew in the Free Church College in Aberdeen.   From 1882 to

1892 he was pastor of Queen's Cross Free Church, Aberdeen. In 1892 he became professor of Old Testament languages and literature in the United Free Church College in Glasgow, and in 1909 he was made principal of Aberdeen University.

Principal Smith's scholarship was recognized far beyond Scotland. He was Turnbull Lecturer at Johns Hopkins in 1896, Lyman Beecher Lecturer at Yale in 1899 and Jowett Lecturer in London University in 1900. In 1916 he was knighted by King George. In 1922 he was Baird Lecturer at Glasgow.

Sir George was one of the prominent preachers of his day. Dr. Dargan says that his sermons are notable for their "great spiritual force, poetic quality and a vivid and popular style of address," [37] and they are admired by those who like exposition of the clever sort. Sir George was a man of brilliant scholarship, and his style is fresh and ingenious, but unfortunately he is not free from the type of Biblical criticism that was common in his earlier years, and is by no means dead today. Tuebingen and Leipsic left their marks upon him. While he is without doubt one of the most famous of the later United Free Church scholars and preachers, and while he is often described as a conservative Bible critic, yet his position is a departure from the stern Calvinistic orthodoxy of the early Free Church leaders. These Disruption fathers erred in regard to the doctrine of election, they held false views in relation to the Sacraments and they believed in a divine obligation to observe the Old Testament Sabbath, yet they accepted without question the truth of verbal inspiration, and the complete inerrancy of the Bible. Later Free Churchmen, such as Smith, made light of verbal inspiration.

Sir George's *Historical Geography of the Holy Land* (1894), was reprinted some 30 times. His *Modern Criticism and Preaching of the Old Testament* (1901), shows only too clearly his liberal leaning. Other works are *The Preaching of the Old Testament to the Age* (1893); *The Book of Isaiah*, 2 volumes (1888-90); *The Twelve Prophets*, 2 volumes (1896-97); and perhaps his most famous work, *Jeru-*

---

[37]. E. C. Dargan, *A History of Preaching* (New York, 1905-12), vol. 2, p. 571.

salem, in two large volumes (1907). Other writings include *Our Common Conscience* (1918); *The Kirk in Scotland, 1560-1929,* which was the work of John Buchan, assisted by Smith. *Life of Henry Drummond* (1898) by Smith, is a distinguished piece of literary craftsmanship, but marred by unwarranted jeers at the truth of verbal inspiration. *Forgiveness of Sins* (1904) will give the reader an idea of Sir George's manner of preaching, while the story of his life will be found in Mrs. G. A. Smith's biography of her husband, published in 1943.

James Denney (1856-1917)

James Denney was born in Paisley in 1856, of Cameronian, or Reformed Presbyterian stock. He was brought up in Greenock, attended the Highlanders' Academy, and then worked for two years in an office. In 1874 he entered the University of Glasgow, where he was noted for exceptional scholarship, especially in the classics. His theological work was taken at Free Church College, in Glasgow. While still a student, he had charge of East Hill Street mission of Free St. John's Church.

In 1886 he was called to East Free Church, Broughty Ferry, where he became successor to Alexander B. Bruce. There he preached Christ crucified with ever increasing power.[38] Discarding all gesture and declamation, he depended wholly upon telling phrase and pulpit lucidity.[39] A theologian himself, he learned from the example of his predecessor to explain theological truths in non-technical language.

In 1897 he was called to the chair of systematic theology at the Free Church College, Glasgow, where he was successor to Dr. David Candlish. So highly esteemed was he in Broughty Ferry that the Rev. Frank Cairns, his successor, declared that "Dr. Denney was minister of the East Church from 1886 until his death." When he left Broughty Ferry, he burned all his sermons. However, he continued to preach as long as he lived.

---

[38]. T. H. Walker, *Principal Denney, a Memoir and a Tribute* (London, 1918), p. 42.
[39]. *Ibid.,* p. 43.

He visited America in 1894, where his theological
lectures caused astonishment and considerable confusion,
for Dr. Denney proved a puzzle to all. In theology he
appeared to be thoroughly conservative, except in regard
to verbal inspiration. In that field he caused much sorrow
to the conservatives, while the liberals were confused at his
strangely conservative views on Christology and soteriology.
James M. Campbell declared him to be like Nebuchadnezzar's
image, with its head of gold, its breast and arms of silver,
its body and thighs of brass, and its feet a mixture of iron
and clay.[40]

However, Dr. Denney was representative of the new
school of thought that had grown up in Scotland after it
became the fashion to study in the German universities, and
come back influenced by Germany's negative higher criticism.
Such men could see nothing inconsistent in accepting the
orthodox theological views of their fathers, yet upon a
foundation of advanced Biblical criticism. Dr. Denney, for
example, rejected the Davidic authorship of Psalm 110, but
in 1904, when taken to task for this, he declared that this
had not shaken his belief in Jesus Christ and His Atonement.
However, his wife insisted that he read Spurgeon faithfully,
and this led him to become more conservative. He was a
profound admirer of Chalmers and Spurgeon, whom he
regarded as two of the greatest preachers of all time. At
the same time he was a great admirer of German theology,
and in 1913, when war was threatening, he urged that peace
be sought with Germany, declaring that country to be close
of kin to Scotland.[41]

In 1900, at the merger of the Free Kirk and the United
Presbyterians, he became professor of New Testament language, literature and theology in Free Church College, Glasgow, succeeding Dr. A. B. Bruce. He was also principal of
that institution.

Dr. Denney was always a popular preacher. He studied
hard, spoke without notes, and was a marvellous impromptu
speaker. His mind was so well stored that he was able,
upon short notice, to deliver a sermon that had every

---

[40]. *Homiletical Review,* Oct. 1920, p. 279.
[41]. J. R. Fleming, *A History of the Church in Scotland* (Edinburgh,
1927-33), vol. 2, p. 95.

characteristic of careful preparation. He never tired of assuring his hearers that he had little use for the man who forever sought to "negotiate with Christ," and to make the strait gate wide and the narrow way broad for man's particular benefit. In many ways Dr. Denney was puzzling, for he could lay utmost stress upon salvation through Jesus Christ alone, and at the same time declare that denominational creeds are of little importance. Of his many writings, but one book of sermons seems to have been published under his name. His commentaries in the *Expositor's Bible* series are known to all.

In a magazine article Dr. Denney declared that Psalm 110 was not written by David nor about David. He looked upon it as the work of an unknown poet of much later date. The fact that the Lord Jesus recognized David as the author of this Psalm is disposed of by Dr. Denney in the statement, "it was part of His true humanity that He should think on such questions as others in His situation naturally thought." [42] With these words Dr. Denney not only rejects the teaching of Scripture concerning our Lord's omniscience, but he follows the false teaching of that school of theology which refuses to accept the fact of the communication of attributes of our Saviour. This false school of theology declares that unless all divine attributes may be predicated of the human nature of Jesus Christ, none are to be ascribed to it. The Scriptures, on the contrary, ascribe to our Saviour's *human nature* the attributes of divine omnipotence, omniscience and omnipresence, but not eternity, infinity or immensity. Dr. Denney also rejected the first three chapters of Genesis in favor of the scientific theory of Creation.[43]

Dr. Denney's chief writings are: *Studies in Theology* (1895); *Gospel Questions and Answers* (1896); *The Death of Christ* (1902); *The Atonement and the Modern Mind* (1903); *Questions of Faith* (1904), an exposition of the Apostles' Creed; *Jesus and the Gospel* (1908); *The Way Everlasting* (1911), a collection of sermons; *War and the Fear of God* (1916); *The Christian Doctrine of Reconciliation* (1918); and *Letters to W. Robertson Nicoll* (1920).

---

[42]. *The Expositor* (London), Fifth Series, vol. 3, p. 448.
[43]. *Studies in Theology* (London, 1895), pp. 78-79.

The book of studies in the Creed was written jointly with
Dr. Orr. Denney was one of the contributors to *The Expositor's Bible* and *The Expositor's Greek Testament*.

Andrew W. Williamson (1856-1926)

Andrew W. Williamson was born in 1856 at Thornhill,
Dumfriesshire, of Saxon stock. He was educated at Morton
School and at Wallace Hall Academy, going from there to
the University of Edinburgh, where he was graduated in
1878. His theological work was taken at the same institution. He was licensed in 1881, and became assistant at
North Leith. A year later he was ordained and became
pastor at North Leith. This was exceptional, for the congregation was one of the most important in Scotland,
numbering 2000 communicants. Williamson was but 25
years of age, and his two assistants were 23 and 21 years old
respectively. Much comment was caused throughout Scotland by the "three boy preachers" in charge of so influential
a congregation as that of North Leith, and it was considered
at the time as a questionable violation of Scottish tradition.
However, it was soon evident that young Wallace Williamson,
as he was known to his friends, was a man of noteworthy
gifts. His sermons were so exceptional that even the
important church at North Leith could not hold him, and in
1883, at the age of 27, he was translated to St. Cuthbert's,
one of Edinburgh's most important pulpits. Here he became
not assistant, but colleague, to no less a man than James
Macgregor, whose racy eloquence was known throughout
Scotland. Thus in ten years young Wallace Williamson had
risen from an unknown school boy to the position of
co-pastor of one of the Church of Scotland's most noted
churches. The congregation worshipped in a huge, barn-
like building, with its two tiers of galleries, and its unsightly
box pews. In 1894 this ungainly church was rebuilt, and
its interior was declared to be one of the most beautiful in
Scotland, with a chancel that would do credit to one of the
liturgical denominations.

In 1907 and 1908 Mr. Williamson was university
lecturer in pastoral theology, and in 1907 he was Croall
lecturer. In 1910 he was translated to St. Giles's Church,
formerly the cathedral. The success of Mr. Williamson can

be appreciated when one recalls the fact that within a radius of 150 yards of his former congregation were such men as Scott of St. George's, Whyte and Kelman of Free St. George's and several others almost equally famous. In coming to St. Giles's, Williamson became dean of the Order of the Thistle and Chapel Royal in Scotland. The Chapel of the Thistle, added to the old cathedral by Sir Robert Lorimer, is one of the most magnificent places of worship in the British Isles. Here Mr. Williamson, since 1906 Chaplain-in-Ordinary to the King in Scotland, was free to carry out certain ideas that were looked upon as distinctly of the High Church type, and the great Gothic church and its gorgeous Chapel of the Thistle furnished him a background for his innovations.

However, it is Dr. Williamson as a preacher, rather than as a liturgical reformer, that must concern us. In his old days at North Leith, he is said to have been superb. There were old people not long since who declared that every sermon of his youthful days was notable, and was discussed for days by the people of his community. One of his sermons is still remembered at North Leith, even today. Mr. Williamson compared the flying roll of Zechariah 5, 1 with the flying angel with the everlasting Gospel, of Revelation 14, 6. There is a tradition at North Leith that the whole community discussed this sermon with bated breath for months. An example of Williamson's youthful preaching is given by his biographer. It is florid and rhetorical, and yet it points in every sentence to Jesus Christ the King of Glory, — an example and a warning to those preachers of today who mention the Saviour only in the closing paragraph of their sermons.

It is to be regretted that Dr. Willamson's brilliant preaching lost some of its radiance as he grew older. His sermons were doctrinal and philosophical, but their style was somewhat monotonous, due to the fact that he maintained a tone of uniform earnestness from beginning to end. This proved tiresome to many of his hearers, who would have welcomed an occasional sentence delivered in a less solemn tone of voice. His preaching is said to have suffered due to the fact that he repeated sermons that had already appeared in print. Dr. Williamson was considered a great preacher until his retirement in 1925, but there were people in Scotland who declared that his finest work was done at North Leith, rather than at his two Edinburgh churches. He was not entirely untouched by the higher criticism. Perhaps his more exacting duties at Edinburgh left him less time for the preparation of sermons, yet it is entirely possible that his dazzling success in his first congregation led people to expect too much of him. His writings include *Ideals of Ministry* (1901); *The Person of Christ* (1920); and *The Glorious Gospel* (1928). *Life of A. Wallace Wiliamson* (1929), was written by Lord Sands (C. N. Johnson).

J. T. Forbes (1857-1936)

John T. Forbes, one of the leading pastors and educators of Glasgow, was born in Nottingham in 1857. After attending Peoples College, Nottingham, he studied at Glasgow and at Edinburgh Universities. He read law until 22 years of age. In 1886 he was ordained and became pastor of a Baptist congregation at Cupar, Fife. This was followed in 1888 by a pastorate at Westgate Road Church, Newcastle, and in 1895 of the Dublin Street Church in Edinburgh, where he was successor to Dr. Landels. In 1901 he was called to Hillhead Baptist Church, Glasgow, where he served for 27 years. He was president of the Baptist Union of Scotland in 1904-05, and of Great Britain and Ireland in 1915-16. In 1919 he became professor and in 1922 principal of the Baptist Theological College.

Dr. J. T. Forbes was one of the bright lights of the Baptist Church in Scotland, and he held a high place as a scholar, a theologian and a magnetic preacher. His sermons are notable because of their sincerity, their background of scholarship and their spirit of human sympathy. He was a forceful thinker and a vigorous preacher during his long parochial experience, and when he became a theological professor he impressed upon the young men of his college the importance of exact scholarship and of master craftsmanship in their pulpit work. He looked upon the preparation of a sermon as a serious matter, and never a hasty assemblage of half-considered and poorly arranged thoughts. His own sermons were object lessons of this teaching.   Dr. Forbes contributed *Socrates* to *The World's Epoch Makers* (1904).   A collection of sermons, *God's Measure,* was printed in 1898.

William M. Macgregor (1861-1944)

William M. Macgregor, of Edinburgh, came from a family of Highland preachers, for his father, his brother, and several uncles and cousins were clergymen.   He was educated at Glasgow University and ordained in 1886.   He became pastor at Troon, and served until 1900, when he succeeded Marcus Dods as pastor of Renfield Church, Glasgow.   In 1908 Dr. Macgregor was called to St. Andrew's, Edinburgh.   He was elected moderator in 1919, and at the same time he was called to the chair of New Testament language, literature and theology at Glasgow.   Having gained a reputation as a preacher of marked ability, a friend expressed surprise that he should accept a professorship.   Dr. Macgregor replied, "I have learned a few things from Dr. Bruce, and I would fain pass them on to others before I die."   In 1928 he was made principal of Trinity College, Glasgow.   In 1942, at the age of 80, he delivered the Warrack lectures, traveling across Scotland daily in order to do so.   In 1944, having written an article on Dr. Moffatt, he died as he was posting the article to the publishers.

Dr. Macgregor was a stately man, scholarly in appearance, and with a face that one would not forget.   His profile has been compared to that of Dante.   His preaching lacked the fire and the flowing eloquence that his Highland background might suggest.   He spoke in a slow, measured, yet incisive manner, often pausing for some seconds in order to utter the precise word that he required.   It has been said that his one Celtic characteristic was his tendency to prolong the "a" in nouns ending in —"ation."   Despite his deliberate speech and his slight suggestion of a mournful tone of voice, yet he was looked upon as an admirable preacher.   His morning service was always crowded, while the evening service, if somewhat smaller in its attendance, included many of the most thoughtful people of Edinburgh.   This was not due to personal popularity, for Dr. Macgregor's ascetic appearance and the fact that he had "a distinction, even a majesty, about him that cleared a space around him, and made others in his vicinity look dull and commonplace and drably ordinary," [44] acted as a subtle barrier. He was neither haughty nor aloof, but was modest and even shy. After becoming a professor he liked to attend the churches where his students preached, but because of his shyness, he seldom offered suggestions. He had a phenomenal memory for faces and names, and he could meet a countryman in the street and inquire concerning his whole family, calling all the children by name. If the countryman expressed amazement, the Doctor would reply with a smile, "You forget that I enjoyed the hospitality of your home one night, years ago, when I preached nearby."

Principal Macgregor's sermons are gems of polished, precise English, and one can only regret that the evangelical note is not sounded more fully. He suggests it admirably at times, as for example in the Warrack lectures, where he declares that Christ must be central in all preaching; yet one misses the next logical truth, namely that it must be a preaching of Jesus Christ, God's Son, who redeemed sinful mankind from sin, death and the power of the devil. We have had enough preaching of Christ the Example, who came to teach men how to face the problems of life. More needs to be said in regard to the life in the world to come.

Foremost among Dr. MacGregor's books are: *Jesus Christ, the Son of God* (1907); *Some of God's Ministries* (1910); *Christian Freedom* (1914), which is not only a series of studies in Galatians, but a discussion of the great principles set forth by St. Paul; *Repentance unto Life* (1918); *Christ and the Church* (1938); *Persons and Ideals* (1939); and *The Making of a Preacher* (1945). The book on Galatians is considered one of Dr. MacGregor's best efforts, but like most liberal evangelicals, he conveys the impression without realizing it that St. Paul declares great principles that are the product of his own reasoning. While he accepts the fact that the Epistles of St. Paul are inspired, yet he does not seem to lay sufficient stress upon the fact that the truths set forth by the great Apostle were not

---

[44]. A. J. Gossip's Foreword to *The Making of a Preacher* (London, 1945), p. 7.

merely his own teachings. They are the revealed truths of the Triune God.

John Kelman (1864-1929)

John Kelman was born in Leith, where his father was pastor of the Free Church congregation. He was educated in the Royal High School in Edinburgh, and in Edinburgh University. He began his theological work in New College, Edinburgh, but interrupted it to spend three years in Australia, where he tutored, and continued his studies at Ormond College, Melbourne. He retured to Scotland, and in 1890 he became assistant to George Adam Smith at Queen's Cross Free Kirk, Aberdeen.

In 1891 he was ordained and given the Free Kirk at Petercutler, Aberdeenshire. In 1897 he was called to New North Free Church, Edinburgh, where he found a large, unsightly building in a run-down neighborhood of rooming houses. He set about with great energy to reach the young men and women in this neighborhood, many of whom where students. He organized a Sunday evening Bible class for them, which became so popular that it had to be held in the large church, at the close of the evening service. Kelman often drew lessons from the lives of Stevenson, Browning, Arnold and other literary men; and on one occasion his fellow pastors presented him with a copy of the Bible, and in a half humorous manner suggested that this is the traditional material to be used in Bible classes.

His church services soon became so popular that long queues waited outside the church before the doors were opened, and were admitted in the order in which they stood in line. In the evening the congregation was dismissed after the evening service in order to make room for the lines that were waiting outside to gain admittance for the Bible class.

In 1907 he received an urgent call from St. George's Free Church to become assistant to Alexander Whyte, who was in declining health. Here the same scenes took place, with long lines of people waiting outside for the doors of the church to open. He served this congregation for 12 years, except for a time spent in YMCA work in France, during the first World War. He visited American cities in

1918, and while here delivered the Lyman Beecher lectures at Yale, as well as preaching in many important places.

In 1919 he was urged to accept a call to become successor to Dr. J. H. Jowett, at Fifth Avenue Presbyterian Church, New York. However, he came to that congregation a worn-out man, prematurely old at the age of 55. In 1924 failing health caused him to resign. He attempted for a year to serve Frognal Presbyterian Congregation at Hamstead, but his health was so poor that he was unable to continue. He died in 1929, when 65 years of age.

Of a high-strung, intensely active temperament, Dr. Kelman wore himself out with his many activities. It was said of him at the time of his death that John Kelman had little interest in people who were cultivating their own spiritual life, nor did he show concern for those who were firmly grounded in the Christian faith. He devoted his energies to those who had not yet been reached. At New North Church and at Free St. George's in Edinburgh, he devoted much time to missionary and pastoral calls, and was especially successful with those in trouble.

As one reads his printed sermons, one cannot help wondering what it was that made him so famous a preacher. The sermons are very brief, rather tense in style, and almost entirely in the form of application. Exposition of the text has a minor place in his printed sermons. Here again is a case of a man whose spoken works must have possessed a vividness and a much fuller exposition of the text than the rather sketchy printed discourses would seem to indicate.

John Kelman wrote a number of books, and among these the following are representative of his style and thought: *Honour toward God* (1904); *The Light that Saves* (1907); *From Damascus to Palmyra* (1908); *Ephemera Eternitatis* (1911); *The Road: A Study of Bunyan's Pilgrim's Progress,* 2 volumes (1912); *Salted with Fire* (1915); *The Foundations of Faith* (1921); and *Prophets of Yesterday* (1924).

George Jackson (1864-1945)

In the latter part of April, 1945, the daily papers contained a brief statement that Dr. George Jackson, a Methodist clergyman, had died at Dhalling Mhor, Kirn, on the Firth of Clyde, at the age of 81. To those who knew George Jackson's remarkable work in Edinburgh, the brief announcement recalled many things.

George Jackson was born in 1864 at Grimsby. After attending the Collegiate School at Grimsby he studied theology at the Wesleyan Methodist College in Richmond, Surrey, near London. The success of Hugh Price Hughes of the West London Mission, and of Samuel F. Collier of the Manchester Mission finds its counterpart in the work in Edinburgh. George Jackson was called to Edinburgh in 1888, shortly after his ordination. He was called as pastor of a Wesleyan Methodist congregation in Nicolson Square, but it was not many months until he discovered that there were thousands of people on Edinburgh's streets who never entered a church of any kind. Congregations of the State Church and of the Free Church were numerous, and they had their imposing places of worship and their large attendance on Sunday; and yet thousands of people were without church connection.

The young pastor of Nicolson Square Church resolved to establish a mission congregation on the West Side, and to attempt to reach the unchurched population in that part of Edinburgh, as Nicolson Square Church was reaching them on the East Side. The new preaching station was opened, and was called the West End Mission. The Albert Hall in Shandwick Place, not far from Free St. George's Church, was their first place of worship. Growth was slow at the outset, yet at the end of two years Mr. Jackson secured the use of the United Presbyterian Synod Hall in Castle Terrace for Sunday evening services. Almost from the start the wisdom of this decision was evident, and it was but a matter of weeks until "George Jackson's Synod Hall" became one of the best known places of worship in Edinburgh. The membership increased from 50 to 100, then to 200, then to 290, and at the end of three years it numbered 357. After that it grew more rapidly, and Synod Hall was filled every Sunday evening. The people of Edinburgh flocked to hear the keen, incisive preaching of the young missionary, who had become one of Edinburgh's leading clergymen.

A man of friendly personality, George Jackson soon gained the good will of his many Presbyterian neighbors, who praised him for his success in reaching the unchurched people of the West Side. Jackson made it clear that there must be no proselyting. "We are not here to make Methodists out of Presbyterians," he declared. "From the first day of our existence we have set our faces like flint against proselyting in any form. Christ's army is not any the stronger merely because one hundred of His soldiers are persuaded to change their regiment, although, of course, there may be individual cases in which the change is an advantage all around. I often tell my people that if ever a day should come (which God in His mercy forbid!) when all we can do is to lead saints to change their *ism,* they will have to look out for a new superintendent." [45] George Jackson soon numbered among his personal friends such men as Alexander Whyte, Marcus Dods, George Matheson, James Denney, John Watson and James Stalker. In October, 1901, the great Central Hall was dedicated. It is a church seating 2000 people, and its cost was $250,000. The church is of the familiar Nonconformist type: a great rectangle with a preaching platform, organ and choir in one end, and galleries running around three sides of the building.

In 1906 Dr. Jackson accepted an urgent call to become pastor of Sherborne Street Methodist Church in Toronto. The people of Edinburgh had welcomed his early writings, and one book in particular had become popular [46] and was looked upon as a good contribution to orthodox Christianity. Hardly had Dr. Jackson left Scotland when the alarming news appeared in print that he had accepted the higher criticism of the Bible that had proved the subject of fierce controversy. Old friends defended him, declaring that all who knew George Jackson were sure that he would be the last to deny verbal inspiration. Among his defenders was Dr. W. Robertson Nicoll. However, when his book on the Old Testament [47] appeared, it was only too evident that Dr.

---

[45]. W. H. Crawford, *The Church and the Slum* (New York, 1908), pp. 74-75.

[46]. Geo. Jackson, *First Things First* (Edinburgh, 1894).

[47]. *Studies in the Old Testament* (London, 1909).

Jackson had yielded to the German critics and their follow-ers in Britain.

"Like most men in middle life," he declared in his introductory chapter, "I was brought up in a belief in the verbal inspiration, the literal accuracy, of every part of the Bible.   To my own unspeakable relief I have parted with that ancient dogma for ever; I could as soon go back to it as an astronomer to the days before Copernicus, or a naturalist to the days before Darwin.   And yet I am here to testify out of a full and glad heart that the Bible was never so much to me, it was never so truly 'the fountain of light of all my day, the master light of all my seeing'; I was never so sure that God is in it." [48]   In this book he declares that he does not believe that Moses wrote the Pentateuch, nor that Genesis gives a trustworthy account of the begin-nings of human life and civilization, nor that the book of Jonah is a sober record of plain fact, nor that the inspiration of the Scriptures is a guarantee of their freedom from error, whether scientific, historic or chronological.   He looked upon much of the Old Testament as anonymous, declaring that Moses did not write the Pentateuch, nor one man the prophecy of Isaiah.   Solomon, he declares, did not write the Proverbs, Ecclesiastes or the Song of Songs, and it can-not be proved that David wrote any of the Psalms.   He looks upon the Old Testament as a composite document, containing law, history, proverbs, prophecy, legend and myth.   Many of the individual books of the Old Testament he considers com-posite in character, and in some of them he speaks of contra-dictions.[49]   The account of Creation he thinks is unscientific, the record of the flood mere legend, the Tower of Babel speculation and the story of Jonah a parable.[50]

Three years later Dr. Jackson published another book,[51] in which he admits that man is a sinner, and yet declares that we know nothing of man's origin, his history or his sin. God's speaking to Israel is disposed of by Jackson as a poetic statement.   The overthrow of Jericho he accepted merely as a picturesque way of saying that the city sur-

---

[48]. *Ibid.*, p. 54.
[49]. *Ibid.*, pp. 13-54.
[50]. *Ibid.*, p. 104ff.
[51]. *The Preacher and the Modern Mind* (1912).

rendered without a struggle.[52] He believed that some time
elapsed between the Crucifixion and the writing of the first
Gospel, giving the account an opportunity to grow with
repetition.[53] He asserts that the Lord Jesus Christ is not the
Author of all the sayings attributed to Him in the Bible.[54]
He makes the astounding statement in both of these books
that the mixture of history, legend, poetry, folk-lore, myth
and superstition is a much richer treasure than the inspired
Bible of previous generations.[55] Dr. Jackson's *The Preacher
and the Modern Mind* provoked much opposition, and it was
answered ably by James Boyd and others.[56]

From 1909 to 1913 Dr. Jackson was professor of English Bible in Victoria College, Toronto; and in 1913 he
returned to England in order to teach at Didsbury College,
Manchester. From 1916 to 1919 he was pastor of Brixton
Hill Church in London, and in 1919 he returned to Manchester to teach English Bible and Literature for the next
decade at Didsbury College.

Dr. Jackson was a popular preacher, especially in his
Edinburgh days. He was gifted with a good voice, clear
and pleasant, an incisive manner of delivery and a cheery
personality. In one of his later books he calls attention to
the fact that evangelical preaching has almost ceased to
exist,[57] and he seems to be at a loss to know why. He quotes
a number of authoritative writers who insist that the preaching of the Cross is all but unknown in recent years. These
men do not realize that when the infallibility of God's Word
is discarded, and it is looked upon merely as a collection of
human writings, including legends and myths, that the very
foundation of one's faith is taken away. Men are not inclined to proclaim evangelical truth if they look upon the
source of that truth as unreliable.

George Jackson was not the only man, in those terrible
days, to turn from a conservative position to the modern
view. Such men grew up at a time when speculation ran
riot, and when it was considered an indication of scholarship

[52]. *Ibid.*, pp. 23-148.
[53]. *Ibid.*, p. 141.
[54]. *Ibid.*, p. 104.
[55]. *Ibid.*, p. 53-54, etc.
[56]. James Boyd, *Can we Believe the Bible?* (Edinburgh, 1912).
[57]. *Reasonable Religion*, (London, 1922).

to defend the Higher Critics and their views. These critics were what some have termed unawakened men, and man's unaided reason was their false god. They blasted the faith of many men who attempted to cling to two conflicting views at the same time, and to reconcile orthodoxy with liberalism. Dr. Jackson lived long enough to see at least the more violent critics discredited, and to see that a false scholarship had been masquerading in the garments of reverence to the truth.

In addition to the four books already mentioned, Dr. Jackson wrote: *The Teachings of Jesus* (1903); *The Ten Commandments* (1898); *Memoranda Paulina* (1901); *A Young Man's Religion* (1900); *The Table Talk of Jesus* (1896); *The Fact of Conversion* (1908); *Guests of God* (1925); *In a Preacher's Study* (1914); and *A Parson's Log* (1927). His biography, *The Life of George Jackson*, was written by Annie Jackson.

P. Carnegie Simpson (1865-1947)

Carnegie Simpson was born in Horsham, Australia, where his father, a Scottish Presbyterian clergyman, was stationed at the time. He attended George Watson's College and Edinburgh University, and upon his graduation with honors, he entered New College, Edinburgh, for his theological studies. There he came to know Principal Rainy, Marcus Dods, A. B. Davidson and other distinguished men of that period of notable scholarship. After his ordination he was called to the pulpit of the Presbyterian church in Wallington, Surrey, near London, where his gifts of clear, incisive preaching soon became known throughout the nearby metropolis. Four years later, in 1899, he was called to the Free Church's congregation at Renfield, Glasgow, where the next twelve years of his life were spent, and where he established his greatest reputation as a forceful preacher. It was while in Glasgow that he was asked by the leaders of his denomination to write a biography of Principal Rainy. The book was started in 1906 and it was published in two impressive volumes in 1909. The great influence of Principal Rainy has declined somewhat as the men who knew him best have died, but Carnegie Simpson's biography of this great leader is still considered a masterpiece of its kind, not only because of its accurate biographical material, but because of the valuable source material that it contains. Carnegie Simpson's great biography of Rainy [58] continues to hold an important place in the vast literature that exists on that stirring period of Scottish history that begins with the Ten Years' Conflict and the Disruption of 1843 and ends with the union of the Scottish churches in 1929, some years after Rainy's death. No student of Church History can understand the peculiar trends of religious thought today unless he is well acquainted with the history of the several Scottish churches during those notable 95 years. It begins with a fierce revolt against Rationalism, a swift revival of rigid Calvinistic orthodoxy, and then the breaking up of the old fashioned, strict form of Calvinism under the impact of speculative science, German Higher Criticism and liberal theology. Although the older conservative leaders opposed the movement tirelessly, yet unionism continued to gain ground in Scotland, and the several groups that had seceded from the old State Church at various times returned once more to the establishment from which their fathers had separated at so great a sacrifice. The relentless progress of church unionism in Scotland attracted attention throughout the world. Although a part of a unionistic movement that appeared in various other countries, yet in some respects it set a pattern for other attempts at church union. The first step of its later phase was taken in 1900, when the Free Church and the United Presbyterian Church united. A very small minority protested, and the matter was taken before the House of Lords, who astonished the world by giving the legal title of millions of dollars worth of church property to the few men of the conservative group. Carnegie Simpson was but 35 years of age at this time, but no man played a more influential part in the struggle of the majority to take away from the little confessional group the vast holdings that Parliament had declared to be theirs by legal right.

In 1911 Dr. Carnegie Simpson, to the surprise and dismay of his Scottish associates, accepted a call to the influential congregation at Egremont, Cheshire, and the remaining 36 years of his life were spent in the Presbyterian Church

---

[58]. P. C. Simpson, *Life of Principal Rainy*, 2 vols. (London, 1909).

of England.   Not long thereafter he was called to the chair
of Church History at Westminster College, Cambridge, where
he remained until his retirement in 1938.   Always active in
church union movements, he served as moderator of the
Federal Council of Free Churches of England.   He was also
moderator of his own General Assembly in 1928.   During
the period in which Sir William Robertson Nicoll gathered
his staff of distinguished writers and caused *The British
Weekly* to become one of the world's most famous religious
journals, Dr. Simpson was a contributing member of the
staff.   His little book *The Fact of Christ* [59] was the most
popular of his several writings, and his biography of Principal Rainy the most scholarly.

Dr. Simpson was a noteworthy preacher, although his
reputation as a church historian and a church leader over-
shadows his earlier high standing in the field of homiletics.
In his earlier ministry it was his "chief desire that Christ's
Gospel should be preached in all its saving power."   One
can only wish, therefore, that he might have prepared and
published a larger number of evangelical sermons.   Other
writings not previously mentioned are: *Facts of Life* (1913);
Church Principles (1923); *Church and State* (1929);
Essentials (1930); and *The Evangelical Church Catholic*
(1934).

George H. Morrison (1866-1928)

Men have been trying for years to explain the popularity
of "Morrison of Wellington," one of Glasgow's most noted
preachers.   Outwardly he appeared to be a quiet man of
average ability, yet long queues of people stood in the streets
before the church whose classic facade looked like a government building rather than a place of worship.   Summer or
winter, morning or evening, the church was always crowded.

George H. Morrison was born in Glasgow in 1866.   After
his university studies he was undecided as to whether he
should enter the theological seminary.   In 1888 he became
one of Sir James Murray's assistants in the preparation of
the great Oxford Dictionary, to this day one of the most
scholarly and exhaustive works of its kind ever attempted.

---

[59]. Edinburgh, 1900; also translations in several foreign languages.

Years later Sir James declared to Dr. Alexander Whyte that of all his assistants, George Morrison was the most method-ical and the most dependable.

Attending the Free Church divinity hall at Glasgow from 1889 to 1893, Mr. Morrison became an assistant for 15 months to Dr. Alexander Whyte, who was feared and respected by all young assistant pastors. He found this great man exacting, yet kindly, and it was a period of train-ing that no young pastor could forget. In 1894 Mr. Morrison was given a congregation of his own, First Free Church at Thurso, the most northerly town in the British Isles. His first sermon at Thurso, "The Two Gardens: Eden and Gethsemane," convinced the congregation that they had called a man of rare ability, and one whom they would never be able to hold for long. While at Thurso a vacancy com-mittee from the Fifth Avenue Presbyterian Church of New York visited Scotland, seeking a pastor of exceptional ability. They submitted to Dr. Rainy the names of two very prominent Scottish preachers. Dr. Rainy assured them that both were good men, yet he could suggest a better one, a young pastor but 30 years of age, in a little town called Thurso.

In 1898 Mr. Morrison was called to St. John's, Dundee, an important congregation. He had established a reputation as an admirable preacher, but like many in Scotland in those days, he was somewhat of a "slave to his paper." It was an American visitor who taught him, without becoming aware of it, to preach without a manuscript. The American was talkative, and it happened to be Wednesday. Mr. Morrison found his visitor interesting, and permitted him to remain until the time of the Wednesday evening service. Then, realizing that he was not fully prepared, Mr. Morrison resolved to preach without his manuscript. His text was, "For ye know the grace of our Lord Jesus Christ, that, though He was rich, yet for your sakes He became poor, that ye through His poverty might be rich." The sermon convinced Mr. Morrison that he was able to preach, and preach ex-tremely well, without his "paper." It was about this time that he became a regular contributor to the *British Weekly*.

that general church periodical that was edited so ably by Sir W. Robertson Nicoll.

In 1902 Mr. Morrison was called to Wellington Church, in Glasgow, his native city. The congregation's place of worship was a large church whose pillared portico resembled a Greek temple with Egyptian detail. The next 26 years were years of undiminished success. Not only was the great church crowded morning and evening, and at the mid-week service, but Dr. Morrison's Round Table for young people became an institution that was copied far and near. It originated when a committee of young people came to him and suggested that a weekly meeting be held at which they could discuss their problems with him. At these meetings utmost freedom of speech was permitted, and the only restrictions were that nothing be repeated to outsiders, and that no reference be made to Wellington Church or its pastor. The young people discussed their problems freely, and Dr. Morrison told them frankly of his own youthful spiritual struggles, and the manner in which he overcame them. He had lived through the period when destructive textual criticism had been the occasion of fierce controversy, and he was equally familiar with the arguments for and against the "new theology" of the early years of the twentieth century.

Dr. Morrison had many of the qualities of the popular preacher, although he was not what is generally termed an orator. His voice was not strong, although it carried well, and was possessed of warmth and flexibility. His sermons were prepared with extreme care, closely reasoned, and expressed in clear, definite language. He arose early in the morning, examined his mail, and then devoted his forenoons to the preparation of his sermons. His desk was always in perfect order, without a scrap of paper in sight. Every book had its place, and was returned to the shelf the moment he was through with it. Information was noted on paper used expressly for this purpose, and filed with painstaking care. Sermons were written with great care, dated and filed. His wife declares that only twice in his lifetime did he ever forget an appointment.

The secret of Dr. Morrison's fame has never been explained. A number of things contributed, and among these is the fact that he looked upon a sermon as a fine piece of craftsmanship. Like Alexander Maclaren, he devoted many hours of honest labor to every sermon that he preached. He was a skilled exegete, and he had a library of useful works on exegesis. He did not, as a rule, allow his finished sermons to show the marks of the craftsman's tools, nevertheless before a sermon was preached, he had devoted many hours of thorough study to its preparation. As a result of his diligent labor, when Sunday came, he had something worth saying, and he said it clearly and with conviction. The Scottish people, at least in his day, were trained to an extent that would astonish an American or an Englishman, in the art of sermon appreciation. They were quick to detect superficial preparation. To the Scotsman a sermon must be closely reasoned, and it must contain solid spiritual food. It was their general habit to refer to the hour or two spent in church as a "diet" rather than a service. They expected solid food, and they responded readily whenever a man appeared who was able to supply this need.

Dr. Morrison may have been disturbed by the claims of the higher critics, but he did not allow their assertions to shake his faith in the Scriptures. Whether the dates and the authors of the sacred writings conformed to tradition did not seem to him so important as the truths that they contained. Where most men allow such things to shake their faith, Dr. Morrison appeared to stand undisturbed. It is to be regretted that he did not bear witness to the inspiration of the Scriptures as did John Smith of Broughton Place Church, Edinburgh, for had Dr. Morrison written such a book, it might have proved a contribution of highest value. He had the ability to do it, and this ability was recognized by all. In 1919 Free St. George's, Edinburgh, attempted to persuade him to become their pastor. Certain prominent American congregations hoped to call him. In 1926 the General Assembly selected him as moderator, the highest honor that comes to a Scottish clergyman.

Five collections of sermons, *The Afterglow of God, Wings of the Morning, Return of the Angels, The Unlighted*

Lustre and *The Wind on the Heath* are typical of a score of books that were written by Dr. Morrison. Two good biographies exist: Mrs. Morrison's *Life of Morrison of Wellington* (1928), and Alex. Gammie's *G. H. Morrison, the Man and his Work* (1928).

John A. Hutton (1868-1947)

John A. Hutton was famous in three countries. He was born in 1868 at Coatbridge, Lanarkshire, was educated at the High School and at the University of Glasgow, and was ordained in 1892. He became pastor of Alyth Church, in Perthshire, going from there to Bristo Church, Edinburgh, in 1898, and to Jesmond, Newcastle-on-Tyne, two years later. His exceptional preaching attracted attention not only in Scotland, but in England as well. In 1906 he became pastor of Belhaven Church, Glasgow. Here he preached twice each Sunday in his own church, but so great was his popularity that there was hardly a Sunday that he was not invited to preach in the afternoon to some nearby congregation. Belhaven Church was wealthy and influential, and their pastor soon became one of Glasgow's most eminent preachers.

After almost twenty years of fame in Scotland, Mr. Hutton was called to Westminster Chapel, Buckingham Gate, in 1923, one of London's most prominent Congregational churches. He met with great success, preaching twice each Sunday to congregations numbering 2,500. From 1925 to 1946 he was editor of the *British Weekly*, to each issue of which he contributed three lengthy articles. His last years were spent in Kent, where every night for six years he carried his invalid wife to the safety of an underground air-raid shelter. He died in 1947 at the age of 79.

Dr. Hutton was gifted with a penetrating analytical skill. The late Dr. J. F. Newton describes a sermon preached by Hutton in City Temple, London.[60] The faces of the great congregation became ashen grey as Dr. Hutton described Antichrist, wearing the robes of the Christian Church and grappling with the Lord Jesus Christ. Dr. Newton declares that his sentences flashed like lightning as he

---

[60]. Jos. F. Newton, *Some Living Masters of the Pulpit* (New York, 1923), p. 42.

crouched in the pulpit, his face livid. Then, rising triumph-
antly, with ringing sentences he described the incredible
love of the Saviour in His death on the Cross for the sin of
the world. Dr. Hutton was a skilled spiritual analyst, able
to search the hearts of his hearers and reveal their sinfulness in a manner almost terrifying. His actual spoken
words often departed widely from the comparatively calm
style of his printed sermons, for he spoke without a
manuscript, and under the excitement of the moment there
was, at times, an energetic fervor that the printed page cannot reproduce. This does not mean that his printed sermons
are lacking in animation, for he was a skilled writer as well
as an eloquent preacher, and his intense personality often
reveals itself in his writings. Dr. Hutton preached widely
in America during his visits in this country, and at Mr.
Moody's Northfield Bible conferences he was known and
admired by thousands. Like Sir William Robertson Nicoll,
Dr. Hutton remained a Scot to the end, sitting calmly in the
cold air-raid shelter with a great tartan shawl about him,
and looking very much like an aged Highland chieftain. At
his funeral the liturgy of the Scottish Kirk was used, and
those who took part in the service were men who spoke with
the rich brogue of the North Country — and that is just as
the vivid old Scotsman would have preferred it.

Dr. Hutton published 30 or more books. It is difficult
to select a few titles, for all are written in his fine literary
style. It is with hesitation that we list a few of them, namely:
Loyalty: the Approach to Faith (1917); *That the Ministry
be not Blamed* (1921); *Fear of Things* (1911); *Pilgrims in
the Region of Faith* (1906); *At Close Quarters* (1913);
Winds of God (1912); *Weapons of our Warfare* (1914);
Our only Safeguard (1918); *There they Crucified Him*
(1924); *The Authority and Person of Our Lord* (1910); and
Finally, with Paul to the End, (1934). Harper's have included in their well-known series a selection from his writings entitled *The Best of John A. Hutton* (1950). It contains 31 of his sermons, and gives him a place among the
great preachers of recent centuries. It is difficult to describe
the vivid personality of Dr. Hutton, and the hushed awe of a
great congregation in the vast Westminster Chapel. If he

was ever influenced by the negative spirit of the age in which he grew to maturity, this was not apparent in his London days, for he pictured sin in its awful colors, and exalted the risen, crucified Saviour as the only means of escape from sin's havoc. Thousands responded every Sunday, as men always will, when sin and grace are preached with evangelical conviction.

Hugh Black (1868-1953)

Hugh Black, the oldest of three famous brothers, was born in Rothesay, in the Isle of Bute, in the year 1868. He attended Rothesay Academy, Glasgow University (1883-87), and Free Church College, Glasgow (1887-1891). He was ordained in 1891, and served Sherwood Free Church, Paisley, from that year until 1896.

In 1892, before he had completed his first year in Paisley, Dr. Alexander Whyte asked him to become his associate at St. George's Free Church, Edinburgh. The call from St. George's was signed by 901 members; and Dr. Taylor Innes, Dr. Sutherland Black and Dr. Joseph Bell appeared before the Paisley Presbytery pleading for Mr. Black's release. When their efforts failed, an appeal was made to the General Assembly, but the action of the Presbytery of Paisley was sustained. In 1896 another effort was made and this proved successful. For the next ten years Hugh Black was Dr. Whyte's associate. Dr. Whyte was 60 years old at the time Mr. Black was called. From October to May the two colleagues took morning and evening service alternately. In 1905 Dr. Whyte, in a letter to Dr. Taylor Innes, said of his associate: "He has been having amazing congregations all these past Sabbaths. What a spell he holds over the people!" In the same letter Dr. Whyte said that Hugh Black was planning to pay a visit to America. He was little aware that this visit would lead to a call to a professorship in America, where Black was to spend the remaining 48 years of his life. He did not give up preaching by any means, for after the death of Dr. Bradford, Dr. Black served First Congregational Church, Montclair, N. J., for a year and a half. In 1921 his brother, Dr. Archibald Black, began his long pastorate at the same church.

Dr. Black declared that he had no admiration for the form of preaching that is satisfied merely with the familiar vocabulary of religion, while the true inner spirit is lacking. "Men speak with censorious judgment," he declared, "of some as not preaching the Gospel, because their ears have not heard the particular phrases which they are accustomed to associate with the great message of the love of God. They seem to think that the Gospel means a set of formal propositions; whereas it is a question whether you can speak of the Gospel at all apart from the gospeller. A man may have all the facts right, and all the deductions from the facts, may state all the great Christian verities, may formally explain the way of salvation, and make use of all the usual phrases; and yet not preach Christ, not commend the Gospel, never touch the hearts of men by the pity of God and the passion of the Cross." [61]

Among Dr. Hugh Black's many works are: *The Dream of Youth* (1894); *Friendship* (1898); *Culture and Restraint* (1900); *Work* (1902); *The Practice of Self-Culture* (1904); *Listening to God* (1906), which is a collection of 27 sermons preached at Free St. George's, Edinburgh; *Christ's Service of Love* (1907); *The Gift of Influence* (1908), a collection of university sermons; *Comfort* (1910); *Happiness* (1911); *Three Dreams* (1912); *According to My Gospel* (1913), a collection of 26 sermons preached in Montclair; *The Open Door* (1914); *The New World* (1915); *Lest we Forget* (1920); and *The Adventure of Being a Man* (1929). Dr. Black died April 6, 1953, at Glen Ridge, N. J.

Donald Fraser (1870-1933)

During the closing years of the nineteenth century almost every college boy in Great Britain, America and continental Europe knew the name of Donald Fraser. He was an eager young man in those days, touring America, Europe and the British Isles, visiting college after college, seeking to recruit young men for the foreign mission field. His infectious zeal and his glowing eloquence won many a friend for the cause that he held so dear.

---

[61]. Hugh Black, *According to My Gospel* (1913), pp. 18-19.

Fraser was born in 1870 at Lochgilphead, Argyllshire, almost within sound of the whirlpool Corryvreckan. After attending the Glasgow High School he studied at Glasgow University and at the United Free College, Glasgow. While at Free College he became interested in the Student Volunteer Movement, and became their travelling secretary. Possessed of a missionary zeal that nothing could quench, he visited the colleges of the Old World and the New, preaching and delivering addresses everywhere, and urging the cause of the Student Volunteers. His eloquence, his West Coast accent and above all, his enthusiasm for foreign missions, captured the hearts of college and university students in several lands. In 1896 he became identified with Dr. Laws in the Livingstonia mission field. He was ordained and spent some time in Central Africa. Then he returned to Scotland and continued his work of arousing others. He often attended the General Assembly and kept the cause of foreign missions prominently before them. In 1922 he was elected moderator. His address upon that occasion is remembered to this day. His subject was, "The Supreme Task of the Church," and he proved to his hearers that his zeal for the cause had by no means abated. Much of his life was spent as field secretary, making it necessary for him to compose his sermons in railway trains, aboard an ocean liner, or in a hotel room. Nevertheless he was a preacher of unusual forcefulness, able to think clearly and to deliver his sermons and addresses in a manner that not only convinced his hearers, but aroused within them some of that love for missions that remained his until he died.

Donald Fraser's books are authoritative additions to every clergyman's shelf of missionary works. They are: *The Future of Africa; African Idylls* (1923); *Autobiography of an African* (1925); *Winning a Primitive People* (1914); and a work on Livingstonia. His biography, *Life of Donald Fraser,* was written in 1934 by his wife.

George Erskine Nicol (1872-1936)

George Erskine Nicol, whose preaching stirred the simple fisher folk at Nairn, the Tommies on the West Front and the holiday makers on the Riviera, was born at Clackmannan. He received his education at the divinity hall of the United Presbyterian Church, served as missionary at Stonehousemills, Edinburgh, and then as an assistant to Dr. Mair at North Morningside Church. In 1897 he was called to Rosebank Church, Nairn, where he spent seven years working among the fishermen of that place. Pastorates followed at Withington, Manchester, Westcliffe-on-Sea and Muswell Hill, London. During the first World War he was a chaplain at the casualty clearing stations on the Western Front. He attained the rank of captain, and was awarded the OBE decoration because of his significant record. After the war he was a missionary of the Church of Scotland at Biarritz, Bordighiera and Cannes. He preached for six months at a Presbyterian church at Pretoria, South Africa, and he engaged in preaching tours in America and New Zealand.

"He was a powerful and eloquent preacher of scholarly attainments and widely read, and he was up to date in his thinking and exegesis. He had a particularly fascinating way of speaking to children. It was not alone his sympathetic voice and the living message he so faithfully delivered, but also his winning personality and cheerful outlook on life which made him so attractive and successful as a minister of Christ." [62] He died in Edinburgh April 16, 1936.

James Black (1879-1949)

Dr. James Black was one of three brothers who won distinction in the Scottish and American pulpits. He was born in Rothesay, in the Isle of Bute, and he was a son of the late Hugh Black, Sr. After attending the academy at Rothesay he continued his education at Glasgow University, at Marburg in Germany and at the United Free College in Glasgow. He was ordained in 1903, and from 1907 to 1921 he was pastor of Broughton Place Church, Edinburgh, where John Brown of Edinburgh had been pastor during the three middle decades of the nineteenth century. While at Broughton Place, Mr. Black became one of the most prominent preachers in Edinburgh. His pulpit ability brought him a number of important calls, one of which was from the Marble

---

[62]. *British Weekly*, April 16, 1936.

Collegiate Church in New York. However, he chose to remain in Scotland, even though his brothers Hugh and Archibald had accepted important calls in and near New York City. During the World War of 1914-18 he served with distinction as chaplain to the 15th and 16th Royal Scots and the Second Seaforth Highlanders, attaining the rank of Major, and receiving commendation in the dispatches. In 1921 he was called to Edinburgh's most prominent pulpit, Free St. George's, which had been filled with exceptional ability by Robert Candlish and Alexander Whyte.

Dr. Black was well known in America, and during the summer months he was often heard in some of the most prominent pulpits in New York and other large cities. He delivered the Warrack Lectures on Preaching in 1922-23, the Sprunt Lectures at Union Seminary in Richmond in 1923, the Turnbull Lectures in Melbourne in 1928, and the Baird Lectures in 1944.

Dr. Black published a number of books. Among those that were widely read are: *The Pilgrim Ship* (1910); *The Mystery of Preaching* (1924); *An Apology for Rogues* (1929); and *New Forms of the Old Faith* (1948). Others, equally well received, were: *The Foes of the Faith; The Dilemmas of Jesus* (1925); *Burthen of the Weeks; The Man on the Other Cross;* and *Around the Guns.* Dr. Black was a contributor to *Harvest and Thanksgiving Sermons,* and a co-author of *Communion Addresses,* (1903). His *An Apology for Rogues,* later called *The Rogues of the Bible,* was a book of considerable influence in its way. It attempts to account for the shortcomings of Cain, Esau, Korah, Balaam, Saul and many other Bible characters, and to find good qualities in them which might have been directed into useful channels. Cain is described as a big, high-spirited, aggressive man, subject to temptations unknown to men of the placid sort. His anger flared, and in a moment he sinned. In his study of Pontius Pilate, Dr. Black declared that he must be judged by the current standards of Roman jurisprudence, and not by our modern standards. The Lord Jesus admitted His Kingship, and in the eyes of the Roman law this was high treason, and the only possible penalty was death. Pilate, according to Dr. Black, was obliged to carry

out the Roman law.	Echoes of Dr. Black's book were heard
in many a pulpit, and men who had condemned the conduct
of the prodigal son's elder brother, and of Ananias and of
Demas, went far beyond Dr. Black in attempting to discover
mitigating circumstances for their conduct.

Dr. Black was a master of a simple, vigorous literary
style, and his books can be read with ease.	Some of his
sermons and essays are factual and psychological, and without an extended condemnation of sin or detailed exposition
of the doctrine of grace.	Where his predecessor at Free St.
George's would have found in Jezebel and Gehazi and the
Pharisees an awful proof of the universal dominion of sin,
Dr. Black attempted to account for it after the manner of
the religious psychology of the twentieth century.	This is
but an evidence of the change that came over preaching in
the comparatively short time that elapsed between the days
of Alexander Whyte and those of James Black.

CHAPTER XI

PREACHING IN WALES

WHEN the Celts reached the British Isles, after having
occupied a large part of continental Europe, they found
Britain inhabited by a dark-haired race, sometimes called the
Iberians. The newcomers pushed the older inhabitants into
the western parts of Britain, including the mountains of
Wales. The earliest Celts may have arrived in the British
Isles as early as 800 B.C., while the last wave of Celtic
invaders, called the Brythons, seem to have come between
the first and fourth centuries B.C. The blood of the ancient
inhabitants of Britain flows in the veins of the Welshman of
today, who differs in language and in racial characteristics
from the Saxon Englishman, his neighbor.

Christianity did not come to Wales with the Romans,
who arrived shortly before the opening of the Christian era.
It came from the East, probably by way of St. Honorat, Arles
and Tours. It was at Tours that St. Martin established his
great missionary training school from which workers went
forth to Scotland, Ireland, and no doubt to Wales.

"This early Celtic Christianity was, in many respects,
an exceedingly beautiful thing," says one well-known
authority. "Never has the world beheld more perfect missionaries than the spiritual and tender-hearted preachers
who took the Gospel across stormy seas, amid countless
perils, to Britain, Ireland, Scotland, parts of Germany, and
even distant Iceland. To Christians of the West, Iona ought
surely to be a spot scarcely less sacred than Rome itself.
But little priestly pomp pertained to these early preachers;
gentleness, simplicity and faith were their most pronounced
qualities. Their meekness overcame every obstacle, from
the ferocity of wild beasts to the more dangerous ferocity
of savage men. They knew little or nothing about rules
and discipline, and there is hardly a trace of Latin order and
love of law perceptible in their genius. As saints they were
superb; but their churchmanship was indifferent. It was
the Roman and the Teuton who built the splendid edifice of
the mediaeval Catholic Church. The Christian communities
of the Celts were too mystical and too spiritual to attempt
to compress the Almighty into human formulas; they could

produce holy men, and they could produce heretics, but defenders of the Faith they could not produce. To appreciate the immense difference it is only necessary to contrast the generous and genial character of Columba with that of the hard, grasping and narrow Augustine. From the year 664, when the famous Synod of Whitby met, the Celtic Church in Wales and the Roman Church in England each went its own way, until the sword of the Norman accomplished that which the eloquence of Augustine had failed to do, and the two Churches were merged into one. It is unfortunate that our knowledge of the famous Celtic Christians of the fifth century is so scanty. It was eminently an age of saints — Dewi, Cybi, Padarn, Illtud, Dyfrig, Cadog — and a host of others whose names have been perpetuated in hundreds of churches up and down the countryside. In the Celtic schools, too, were found scholars who represented the very flower of the culture of the period, far finer than anything that the England of the day could show." [1]

If it be true that St. Dewi, or David, founded 53 churches in South Wales before his death in 601 A.D., then the impulse must have come from *Candida Casa* rather than from Iona. St. Dewi was a pupil of Paul the Aged, a blind teacher who formed a living link with St. Ninian, a pupil of St. Martin of Tours. Dewi studied later at Rosnat, an old Irish name for Whithorn, where Ninian's *Candida Casa* was located. The early history of Welsh Christianity is identified with the great Celtic Church, an account of which may be found in our opening chapters of volume I and need not be repeated at this place.

Giraldus Cambrensis, who itinerated throughout Wales with Archbishop Baldwin, as they preached the third crusade in 1188 A.D., has left an excellent account of the Wales of the twelfth century. In this *Itinerarium Cambrense* we have an account, by a keen observer, of the people of his time, and their way of living.

In the year 1277 the Welsh prince was betrothed to the daughter of Simon de Montfort. She was living in France at the time, and on her journey to Wales, she was captured by Edward I of England. He held her as a ransom until the

---

[1]. W. Watkin Davies, *Wales* (London, 1925), pp. 43-44.

Welsh prince not only agreed to a heavy indemnity, but promised to visit England once a year in order to do homage to the English king. When the people of Wales arose in revolt, the English monarch sent an army against them, and the Welsh prince was eventually slain, and his brother captured and put to death with torture in Shrewsbury. In 1284 A.D. Wales became subject to England.

The influence of the Reformation was slow in reaching Wales, cut off as it was from the main stream of events. It was not until the year 1563 that the English Parliament passed an act which decreed that "the Bible, consisting of the New Testament and the Old, together with the Book of Common Prayer and the Administration of the Sacraments, should be translated into the British or Welsh tongue — should be viewed, perused and allowed by the Bishops of St. Asaph, Bangor, St. David, Llandaff and Hereford — should be printed and used in the churches by the first of March, in the year 1566, under a penalty in case of failure of forty pounds, to be levied on each of the above bishops." It was further enacted that at least one printed copy of this Welsh Bible should be provided for every cathedral, collegiate church, parish church and chapel of ease throughout Wales, and should be read at the time of the church service, and at other times, for the benefit of the people.

Four years later, in 1567 A.D., a Welsh New Testament and a Welsh liturgy were published. The translation of the New Testament was largely the work of William Salesbury, a noted linguist. The liturgy and several of the Epistles were translated by Richard Davies, one of the Welsh bishops, while the Apocalypse was translated by Thomas Huet. A dispute between Salesbury and Davies, said to have been over the etymology of one word, delayed the work for a number of years. Realizing the need of a complete Bible, William Morgan, vicar of Llanrhaiadar-ym-Mochnant, after eight years of laborious effort, published a complete Welsh Bible in the year 1588. Unfortunately the edition was a small one, and soon exhausted. In 1620 Dr. Richard Parry, assisted by Dr. John Davies of Mallwyd, the latter a noted lexicographer, published a new edition of the Welsh Bible. In his preface Dr. Parry says: "The former impression of the Bible being exhausted, and many, or most of our churches being either without any, or having only worn out and imperfect copies; and nobody, as far as I could learn, so much as thinking of a republication; in these circumstances of this matter, and induced by these considerations, I set about revising our translation."

Toward the end of the seventeenth century, and during the early years of the eighteenth, a religious decline was felt throughout Wales, as well as in many other parts of the world. Of this period Christmas Evans says: "Nothing was to be seen in almost every parish but young men and young women flocking together into the churches and churchyards and engaging in different gambols and pastimes, such as ball playing, foot ball, leaping, fighting and such like frolics, as if Wales had been changed into an Olympic mountain, and old paganism restored again.

"Common preaching," says the same authority, "will not do to rouse sluggish districts from the heavy slumbers into which they are sunk. Indeed, formal prayers and lifeless sermons are like bulwarks raised against these things in England; and this evil genius has also entered the Principality under the pretence of order. Five or six stanzas will be sung as dry as Gilboa, instead of one or two verses like a new song, full of God, of Christ, of the Spirit of grace, until the heart is attuned to worship. The burying grounds are kept in fine order in Glamorganshire, and green shrubs and herbs grow on the graves, but all this is of little value, for the inhabitants of them are all dead — so is every form of godliness where its power is not felt. Order without life is exceeding worthless."

The fearful spirit of spiritual deadness, so widespread in other countries, had reached the mountains and deep valleys of Wales. Any suggestion of spiritual fire had come to be regarded, even by the emotional Welsh people, as unbecoming in the house of God. "You are content," said Christmas Evans, "with a preacher speaking so lifelessly and so low that you can hardly understand the third part of what he says; and you will call this decency in the sanctuary." In their outward lives any show of the fruits of faith came to be looked upon as sanctimony, and a thing

to be concealed with care. A studied disregard for upright-
ness of life was the fashion, and where Christian virtues still
lingered, it was considered proper to hide them behind a
pretended sophistication. One is reminded of Joseph Trapp,
who preached a series of sermons in Christ Church, St.
Lawrence Jewry and St. Martin's in the Fields, in London,
on "The Nature, Folly, Sin and Danger of Being Righteous
Overmuch." The same spirit had invaded Wales. The brief
awakening of spiritual life in the days of Vavasor Powell
was soon forgotten, and Wales lapsed into spiritual slumber
until the trumpet calls of such men as Griffith Jones, Daniel
Rowland and Howel Harris. When the great awakening
came, Wales was to enjoy a century or more of religious
zeal such as few nations have known. It was a part of a
movement that arose almost simultaneously in places widely
separated. It came at almost the same time as the Evangelical Awakening in England under Whitefield and Wesley
and the Great Awakening in the American colonies under
the Tennents and Jonathan Edwards. For more than a
century the little principality of Wales, with an area one-
sixth that of the State of Pennsylvania and a population at
that time of perhaps a million people, gave the world a great
number of famous preachers. Due to the fact that many
of them preached in the Welsh language, their sermons and
their printed biographies have remained locked up in that
language, and comparatively few have been translated into
English. Welshmen throughout the world know the story
of these remarkable men, and the fame of some of them is
well known to people of other countries.

Welsh preaching has a character of its own. It is
simple, direct, and generally within the experience of the
people. The Welsh preacher and his hearers are fond of
illustrations, but they are not interested in allusions to
ancient Greek and Roman history. They prefer familiar
incidents. Their own mountains and narrow valleys furnish
the preacher with many a remarkable illustration. They
are possessed of lively imaginations, and to the preacher
everything suggests a spiritual truth. A stream of water
trickling from a stagnant pool would hardly be noticed by
an Englishman or an American, but to the quick imagination

of the Welsh preacher it suggests the fact of original sin — humanity contaminated at its very source through the fall of Adam. The Welsh preacher describes the slimy pool and the sluggish stream in vivid language and drives home his spiritual lesson with startling effect. The sight of a gnarled oak tree on an exposed headland, wrestling with the storm, yet standing secure, suggests to him the Christian whose faith is rooted and grounded in the Lord Jesus Christ. When an old woman thrust a lantern into the hands of a Welsh clergyman one dark night, saying, "It is only a little lantern, and very old, but it will light you safely home," this homely incident suggested to the famous Herber Evans the theme for one of his most powerful sermons, namely the value of the old Bible of the cottager as a sure source of light in his spiritual pilgrimage. The Welsh people are not particularly interested in close reasoning, and even less in speculation, but a striking illustration means much to them.

The great Welsh preachers knew the value of proof texts, and they used them continually. The great sermon of Christmas Evans on "The Fall and Recovery of Man" is rich in proof texts and parts of texts. Perhaps much of the preaching of our own day bears but little fruit because it is often barren of quotations in the very words of Scripture, which things are "spirit and life."

The older Welsh preachers were dramatic. They did not hesitate to put into the mouths of Bible characters words that are not to be found in the Scriptures. Thus, when the Saviour commanded His disciples to go and teach all nations, the Welsh preacher of a century ago would not hesitate to say: " 'Lord, shall we go and seek the scribes and Pharisees who despised Thee? Shall we seek out the men who platted the crown of thorns, and pressed it down upon Thy sacred brow; and the men who mocked Thee and buffeted Thee, and those who spat upon Thee and reviled Thee? Shall we preach to the very multitudes who cried out to Pilate to crucify Thee, and who declared before all that they have no king but Caesar?' To these questions of Simon Peter the Lord answered, 'Go ye into all the world, and preach the Gospel to every creature. He that believeth and is baptized

shall be saved; but he that believeth not shall be damned.'
'But Lord,' said Peter, 'surely it is not Thy will that we
should go to the Roman soldiers who drove the cruel nails,
and to the men who derided Thee because Thou didst not
come down from the cross and save Thyself?' The Lord
looked at Peter and said, 'Preach the Gospel to every
creature.' "

Not only did some of the famous Welsh preachers add
such details, but they did it with much dramatic action. We
are told of men who visited the church before the congregation arrived, and selected with care the very spot where the
Lord was to stand in their description of a Biblical scene,
and where the Disciples were to stand, and where the scribes
and elders were to be. If the sermon was to be upon Blind
Bartimaeus, a spot would be selected in advance at one end
of the preaching platform, and the blind man would be
described so dramatically that every eye in the congregation
would be fastened upon the spot where he was supposed to
be. Even the candles, or the kerosene lamps, would be
arranged in advance in order to enhance the dramatic effect.
Such things might prove distasteful to an Englishman or an
American, but to the imaginative Welsh people, it contributed to the vividness of the sermon. One must not judge
the Welshman by Saxon standards. He must be taken as
he is. All this dramatic action is but a part of the Welsh
temperament, for who has not seen a Welshman of the old
generation, when relating even a simple incident, pick up
a stone and place it carefully on the ground, then another
stone and another. "He stood here. I stood right there.
The other man stood over here," etc. It is his natural
manner of adding realism to the story he is telling, and the
same characteristics were to be found in the Welsh pulpit
in olden days.

The Welsh preacher is noted for his fiery delivery. A
quiet, conversational tone is not a part of the Welsh temperament. He speaks with animation. A quiet Welsh
preacher is almost a contradiction of terms. He may begin
quietly — and usually does — but it is not long until he takes
fire. "As he advances in his sermon," writes Kilsby Jones,
"and fairly gets into the *hwyl,* he nearly exhausts the

variations of the gamut. Now there is the shrill startling alarm; and then the deep, sepulchral tones of solemnity. Now we have the dash of defiance; the shout of triumph; the dance of joy; and then the tremulous accents of tenderness; the earnest tones of remonstrance and the muttering of the thundering denunciation. Now we have the plaintive melancholy of bereavement's soliloquy — the wail of sorrow and the cry of despair; and then the wild, ecstatic notes of the Christian pilgrim, as with a tear in his eye he sings of the dawning of the morn that will set him in Heaven's bowers of repose. Now we have the loud voice rending the the sky and awakening the echo; and then the 'still small voice' and the whisper of confidence. In short, there is all the variety both of manner and tone that disinterested love or friendship would employ in private, in attempting to dissuade a person from pursuing a suicidal course, or to persuade him to look after things in harmony with the tremendous destiny of an immortal creature." [2]

The Welsh language itself is unusually expressive. It lends itself readily to the major, rather than to the minor key. Its structure produces a slight waviness that is not apparent in most other languages, and an agreeable musical lilt that comes as a surprise to those who are accustomed to the more level progression of the English language. Moreover, the Welsh people are aware of the value of a well-trained voice, and the attention given to the art of public speaking by the theological student and the ordained pastor is considered time well spent. Where many speakers fall into the habit of employing a range of but five or six notes of the scale, a Welsh preacher will often have a normal range of a full octave, and may at times exceed an octave. The Welshman's volume of tone is changing constantly, ringing forth at full strength one moment, and then reduced almost to a whisper, as the subject matter may require. All of this is natural, and it is a rare thing to hear a Welsh preacher who gives one the impression that he is striving artificially for effect. Like other branches of the Celtic race, the Welsh are an emotional people, and it is but natural that

---

[2]. J. R. Kilsby Jones, *Characteristics of Welsh Eloquence* (1862).

this characteristic will reveal itself in their preaching and in their great love for music.

More important by far than any of the characteristics that we have mentioned was the evangelical content of the sermons of the great century of Welsh preaching. A sermon may be illustrative in style, it may even contain proof-texts, Bible incidents may be described with vivid detail, and the delivery of the sermon may be animated, but if the subject matter is limited to an exposition of conventional morality it will prove to be as cold as a festoon of icicles. J. R. Kilsby Jones says: "So well established is the character of the Welsh pulpit for *evangelicalism* that it is not deemed necessary to dwell upon it in this paper. Suffice it to say that is absence would soon entail upon the hapless preacher the dismal task of addressing himself to empty seats and echoing walls."[3] Their evangelical preaching was, of course, of the old-time "reformed" type. They looked upon the Bible as a verbally inspired Book, to be interpreted literally. They laid stress upon the fall of man, and the contamination of the whole human race by reason of the sin of our first parents. They preached Christ crucified, as the one hope of the sinful world, and faith in His righteousness and atoning death as the condition of salvation. They had the Calvinistic conception of the Sacraments, and their attitude toward the Sunday question was that of the reformed theologian. In olden times all preparation for Sunday was made on the previous day, wood was cut for the fire, food prepared as far as possible, shoes polished and clothing laid out. Sunday was given over to church attendance, and only work of the strictest necessity was performed.

Preaching was by no means confined to Sunday. If a famous Welsh preacher were invited to speak at some important gathering, such as a meeting of the Association, he prepared his sermon well in advance. Then he arranged a preaching tour, notifying the pastors in every village through which he was to pass. Not only did he preach his sermon every evening in the various villages, but there were noonday and afternoon services along the way. A famous preacher, of which there were many between the years 1780

[3]. J. R. Kilsby Jones, *op. cit.*,

and 1890, could always depend upon a large gathering of people. Regardless of the time of day, the farmer, the weaver, the blacksmith and the tailor laid aside their usual tasks, and the housewife banked her kitchen fire, and all hastened to the village church, the market square or the open fields. These descriptions, found so often in the biographies of the great Welsh preachers, are not exaggerated, for all writers are in full agreement that just such things took place. For a century religion was the great topic of conversation in Wales, and one reads again and again of the doctrinal awareness of the people. Many a writer of those days has described the informal gatherings in the evening, in the smithy, the shoemaker's shop or in a farm cottage, when men would gather in order to discuss religion. The older men would describe in detail the great pulpit orators of their boyhood days, and many of them were proud of their ability to quote a long paragraph or two of a notable sermon. They added as far as possible the dramatic action and tone of voice of the original. Welsh literature is full of such descriptions of evenings in the blacksmith's shop or the village tailor's. Again, there was a discussion of controversial matters. The Calvinistic Methodist schoolmaster, perhaps a lay preacher himself, was well able to defend the doctrinal position of his denomination. The Baptist squire, a diligent Bible reader, whose book shelf was filled with commentaries and the lives and printed sermons of Christmas Evans, Rhys Davies and John Williams, was always prepared to set forth the Baptist teachings. The Congregational shoemaker and the Episcopal tailor knew well the distinctive doctrines of their denominations, and did not hesitate at all to explain them. They differed in regard to the doctrine of election, they argued with animation the subjects and mode of Baptism, and they were not at all agreed in regard to church government, but they all had one thing in common: a profound respect for the Bible and its inerrancy. Were a stranger to set forth the views of the Higher Critics, Methodist, Baptist, Congregationalist and Welsh Episcopalian would unite as a man, and the newcomer would be silenced quickly enough.

The Association meetings were always notable gatherings. They were not revivals, nor were they preaching missions of the English kind. They might be compared to a conference, where the time was devoted to preaching rather than to committee reports and discussion of business matters. For a week there were local services in all the churches. References were made in the sermons to the coming Association meeting, and prayers were offered for it. Every house in the village was put in order: rooms swept, windows washed, the exterior walls whitewashed, the thatched roof mended and flower beds weeded. Thresholds were scoured, hearthstones were whitened with chalk, and furniture was polished with beeswax. Every home was ready to welcome either the visiting clergy or else friends from nearby communities. A speakers' platform was built in a place where the sloping ground formed a natural amphitheatre. The best choirs in the village, and in the surrounding communities, had been practicing for days.

On the opening day of the Association meeting, every tradesman's shop was closed. The curious little railway trains, with their piping whistles, brought crowds of people from places as far distant as 40 or 50 miles. Wagons, carriages and farm carts filled the village market square, and the fields surrounding the village. Other people came on horseback, and many came afoot. A preacher such as John Jones of Talsarn, Herber Evans or William Davies could be depended upon to attract the entire population for miles around. It was not at all unusual to find three or four such preachers at an Association meeting, and people walked as far as 20 miles to hear them, if a horse was not available. At 6 a.m. there were often 10,000 to 20,000 people gathered at the preaching grounds. The Welsh people have been famous for their singing for centuries. As early as the twelfth century Giraldus Cambrensis was surprised to hear entire congregations singing in four-part and eight-part harmony, and in his writings he expresses astonishment that "they do not sing in unison, like the people of other countries, but in different parts."

As the sun rose, and with the great mountains as a background, their tops hidden by long trailers of morning mist, the all-day service began.   A choir of 60 trained singers on the platform led the great congregation.   In no other country can such singing be heard.   In England the boy trebles dominate the singing, and in Scotland and America the voices of the men are obscured by the strong voices of the women.   It is otherwise in Wales, for there the men's voices predominate.   A Welsh choir contains fully as many men as women, and their powerful voices create a solid foundation of first and second bass that reminds one of the great Pedal Diapasons of a cathedral organ.   Several Welsh chorales are sung as the last of the people arrive.   A group of 40 or 50 clergymen, in their black coats and white ties, sit on the platform with the choir.

There are three sermons, any one of which may be a full hour in length.   After an intermission at noon, there are three more sermons in the afternoon, and two or three more in the evening.   Such men are heard as Robert Roberts, David Davies, Kilsby Jones, Edward Matthews of Ewenni, Owen Thomas of Liverpool and Dr. Hugh Jones, President of Llangollen College.   Younger and less noted men are also heard.   These Association meetings were often union-istic, and Calvinistic Methodist, Baptist and Congregational clergymen all took active part.   During the two days of the Association the people have listened to about fifteen sermons, and have sung scores of Welsh hymns.   At the end of the second day the people return to their respective valleys, many of them afoot and singing in four-part harmony as they walk along in the moonlight.   It is to be feared, how-ever, that such scenes are becoming things of the past.   The National Eisteddfod still draws thousands, but Association meetings remind one nowadays of the pastoral conference rather than the preaching festival.   One may still meet old men, here and there, who are able to spend an entire evening describing some of the last of the great preachers, quoting with surprising accuracy long extracts from notable sermons, adding vividness to their narrative by means of gesticulations and modulations of voice.   Their generation, however, is fast becoming extinct.   The radio and the cinema have found their way to the Welsh valleys, and Wales is no longer a secluded country.   There was a day, not so long ago, when the chapels of the village and open countryside were the centers of community life. Each chapel had at least two Sunday services, and the Sunday-school was attended by old and young, and each lesson was studied seriously. Children were taught to read, and a book of simple Bible stories was their only text book. The older men came, often with standard Bible commentaries under their arms. Then there was the chapel literary society, devoted largely to religious subjects, and every chapel, and in South Wales every colliery had an excellent singing society. Music has suffered but little from the influence of the outside world, and at a National Eisteddfod one can still hear the bards and poets, the splendid choral societies and the choruses of harpers; but the two-day preaching festival of bygone years is largely a thing of a vanished generation.

Edmund Prys (c. 1541-1624)

While there were excellent preachers during the period of the Welsh Reformation, yet the great age of preaching was not to come until that remarkable period that began about the year 1780 and ended about 1880 or 1890. Among the noted preachers of the sixteenth and seventeenth centuries one finds the name of Edmund Prys. He was born about the year 1541, and the place of his birth is said to have been Tyddyn Du, in the vale of Maentwrog. Not much is known of his early life until he appeared on the records of Cambridge University as a sizar. This seems to have been during the time that the great Puritan, Thomas Cartwright, was professor of theology at Cambridge. Edmund Prys appears again when he was ordained deacon at Conington, Cambridgeshire. In 1568 he became an ordained clergyman at Ely, and in 1572 he received the presentation of Ffestiniog and Maentwrog. He does not seem to have taken his parish duties very seriously, for he continued to live in Cambridge, where he was appointed Preacher to the University in 1574, and seems to have fulfilled his duties with a certain degree of distinction.

However, Prys was a pluralist. He was made rector of Ludlow, but after paying a brief visit to his new parish, he seems to have lost interest. During the same year, 1576, he was made Archdeacon of Merioneth, Canon of Bangor, and then Prebend of Bangor. Four years later he received the presentation of Llanenddwyn and of Llanddwywe. In 1602 he was made Canon of St. Asaph. He relinquished Ludlow, but it appears that he held no less than eight livings at one and the same time. It is said that he tried to the best of his ability to perform his duties, going from parish to parish, preaching everywhere and visiting the sick and dying.

Edmund Prys is described as a man of superb scholarship. He was master of eight languages, and able to preach with equal fluency in Welsh and English. William Morgan respected his scholarship, and Prys was one of a group of learned men to whom Morgan submitted his translation of the Bible before publishing it. Edmund Prys's great gift to the Welsh nation was his fine metrical translation of the Psalms, which he published in 1621. No nation in the world can excel the Welsh in singing, and it was not long until Prys's metrical Psalms were heard in every Welsh chapel. Shepherds and farmers sang them in the fields, and groups of people returning from church and from market, sang these Psalms as they walked along the roads. It was Edmund Prys, more than any other man, who laid the foundation for Welsh hymnody. He who has never visited South Wales and listened to a hundred miners, returning at evening from the coal pits, and singing hymns in magnificent harmony, has never heard sacred music at its best.

William Morgan (c. 1545-1604)

Dr. William Morgan, who gave the people of Wales the Bible in their own language, was born about the year 1545 in the parish of Penmachno, Carnarvonshire. He received his education at St. John's College, Cambridge, where he was graduated M.A. in 1571. In 1575 he became vicar of Welshpool, and in 1578 he received the appointment of Preacher to the University. During the same year he became vicar of Llanrhaiadar-ym-Mochnant, Denbighshire. He performed his duties faithfully, preaching to his people in a day when many Welsh clergymen did not trouble themselves with such things as preaching.

As he visited the homes of his people, William Morgan found much ignorance and superstition among them. He became convinced that the greatest need of Wales was a complete Bible in the language of the people. Portions of the Bible had been translated into Welsh; and Richard Davies and William Salesbury had published a Welsh New Testament in 1567. William Morgan began the task of translating the Old Testament into Welsh, and revising the Davies-Salesbury New Testament. Hardly had he begun his work when opposition arose. There were men who declared that a comparatively unknown young vicar was not competent to undertake so important a project. The Archbishop of Canterbury summoned Morgan, and after a careful investigation decided that he was qualified to do the work, and gave him permission to continue. After eight years of laborious effort, William Morgan's complete Bible was published in 1588. Unfortunately the edition was a small one and the supply was soon exhausted. William Morgan did not live to see his great ambition fulfilled, namely a Bible in the language of the people in every Welshman's cottage; yet he laid the foundation upon which other men were soon to build, and his Welsh Bible established the language in the same manner that Luther's translation had done this in Germany. Before its final publication Mr. Morgan submitted his translation to a number of excellent scholars, whose valuable suggestions he mentions in his preface. The Old Testament is entirely his own work, while in translating the New Testament he gives much credit to the previous translation of Salesbury and Davies. In 1583 Cambridge University awarded him a doctor's degree, and in 1595, seven years after the publication of his Welsh Bible, William Morgan was made bishop of Llandaff, and in 1601 bishop of St. Asaph.

Dr. Morgan was a preacher of ability. While he never won the distinction in the pulpit of such men as Christmas Evans, Daniel Rowland or John Elias, yet his name is honored by every Welshman because of his translation of the Bible. It was not by an act of Parliament, nor by royal command, nor at the suggestion of the bishops that this great work was done. A country vicar, almost unknown at the time, realized the spiritual needs of his people and was aware that only the Bible in their own language could meet these needs.   In spite of the opposition of his fellow clergymen he continued his task with determination.   When one recalls the fact that Dr. William Hughes, bishop of St. Asaph, was accused in 1587 of holding no less than 16 of the richest livings in Wales, we can realize that such shameless pluralists were not likely to be interested in giving to the Welsh people the Scriptures in their own mother tongue.

John Penry (1559-1593)

John Penry, a Welsh martyr, was born in 1559 at Cefnbrith, in the parish of Llangammarch, Breconshire.   In 1578 he entered Cambridge University, and it is generally believed that he was a Roman Catholic at the time.   However, he made the acquaintance of several Puritans, and became a Puritan and an extreme Calvinist.   He took his degree in 1584 and proceeded M.A. at St. Alban's Hall, Oxford, two years later.   At Cambridge and at Oxford he attracted attention because of his eloquent preaching, although it is doubtful whether he was ever ordained.

In 1587 Penry returned to Wales, and was grieved because of the great religious destitution there.   He published a pamphlet calling attention to the spiritual needs of the Welsh people, declaring that there were thousands in Wales who knew nothing of the Saviour, and who had barely heard His name.   He insisted that there were many places where preaching was unknown, and other places where the clergy preached but four times a year.   He called attention to the fact that many clergymen were non-residents, unwilling to preach, ignorant of the teachings of God's Word, unacquainted with the Welsh language, and irregular in their habits.   Some he accused of drunkenness and more serious faults.   He appealed in his pamphlet for clergymen of the right kind, suggesting that devout Welshmen be trained for the ministry, and that in some cases properly qualified laymen be given a license to preach.

The pamphlet created a sensation.   At first it was praised, and its author was looked upon as a brave reformer, who sought only the spiritual good of his own people.   However, when the attention of the notorious Whitgift, Archbishop of Canterbury, was called to the pamphlet, he condemned it as a scurrilous attack on the bishops and clergy of Wales. He summoned John Penry before the High Commission, and he was tried and sentenced to prison, but after twelve days he was released and allowed to return to Wales.

In 1588 Penry published his *Exhortation*, directed to the people of Wales and their rulers. In it he condemned the unfaithful clergy, the bishops, and the Established Church that permitted such conditions to exist. It was a fearless attack on the abuses of the time, but the zeal of the young reformer exceeded his good judgment, and it must be admitted that his language, in places, was rather abusive. However, the gravest wrongs existed, and Penry felt that it was no time for diplomatic language. He applied some hard words to the unfaithful bishops and clergy, and again he pleaded for preachers who would declare to the neglected people the way of life.

It was about this time that the scurrilous Marprelate Tracts appeared in England. To this day it has never been proved fully who wrote them. Penry was accused of their authorship, or at least of knowing who wrote the tracts. He was compelled to flee to Scotland, where he found friends who protected him. However, the sad spiritual condition of his native land haunted him, and in 1592, after two years in Scotland, he determined to return to Wales, telling his friends, "I realize that I go with a hangman's rope about my neck, but if my death will bring about the spiritual liberation of my beloved country, then I go gladly, leaving the outcome to my Lord."

John Penry's fears were realized. In 1593 he was arrested, brought up to London and tried. He was accused of having created ill feeling in Wales against the bishops and the clergy. He was accused of having been implicated in the Marprelate Tracts. Thus it was that in 1593 this courageous young reformer, 34 years of age, was hanged like a common felon by the archbishop and his bishops. His only fault was that he had longed for the spiritual improvement of his beloved country, and had cried out against

history of preaching be
cried out in protest a
tantism, whose bishop
instruct the Welsh peo
Penry was led to the
would raise up others
he laid it down, and th
of God would ring fr

William Wroth (c. 15

When John Penr
was still an undergra
the year 1576 at Ab
graduated from Ch
proceeded M.A. at
1600 he was ordain
mouthshire. There
were soon recogniz
such an extent that
churchyard. Arch
when William Lau
liam Wroth began
high commission,
by the prelates.
gation at Llanfach

William Wrot
as well as the Fa
at Oxford he mu
countryman, Joh
learned from act
of Wales. In or
a group of your
then sent them
was much negl
importance of
As his student
preached to the
the Scriptures,
evident.

When Wil
the threshold

the corruption of
enjoying the rich l
themselves too in
people. In a Prot
was hanged by
Elizabeth, called

John Penry
and a man who
when one reads
this bishops an
very patterns a
defeaters of Go
seasoned and \
and wolves, mi
of all uncleanr
the sacred mii
one reads of tl
spread neglec
clergy in John
possessed of i
ful men respe

Certain i
ful scholarsh
author of th
highly impor
lish in recer
than not, ta
with writin
written a b
and a numl
them those
no proof v
times, to
entirely p
printing
literature,
Marprelat

4. William
5. Albert I
6. Champl
   gationa

faithfully for almost forty years. By his faithfulness he set
an example to the unfaithful clergy of his generation. He
preached himself, and he preached well; and in order that
the Gospel might be heard in places where it had been so
seldom proclaimed before, he established his own school and
trained men, and succeeded in stirring up within them some
of the zeal that he himself possessed.

Rees Prichard (1579-1644)

As John Penry, the Welsh martyr, was led to the
scaffold, he said to the multitude that had gathered to see
his execution: "I leave the success of my labours to such
of my countrymen as the Lord is to raise after me for the
accomplishing of that work which, in the calling of my
country to the knowledge of Christ's blessed Gospel I began."
The people of Wales had not long to wait. The man who
was to carry on the crusade for the preaching of God's Word
was a lad but fourteen years of age when Penry met his
martyrdom. Rees Prichard was his name. He was born in
1579 at Llandovery, where his father was a man of position.
He took his degree at Jesus College, Oxford, in 1602, nine
years after John Penry's execution. He was ordained the
same year to a living at Witham, Essex, but before the year
was ended we find him back in his native Wales, and vicar
of Llandingat, near his birthplace. He was made chaplain
to the Earl of Essex, holding the rectory of Llanedi as well
as the vicarage mentioned.

It was not long until Prichard realized that John Penry's
eloquent protests were only too true, for Rees Prichard found
a shocking lack of religious knowledge and spiritual life
among the people of his two congregations. The people
were ignorant of some of the most familiar parts of the
Bible, and for the reason that the former rectors and vicars
rarely preached. Catechetical instruction had been neglected
altogether. Prichard was an eloquent preacher, and not
only did he make clear to his people the teachings of the
Bible, but he made it a point to weave as many Scripture
verses as possible into his sermons, repeating them frequently so that his hearers might become familiar with them.
He was faithful in instructing both children and older people,
and this by means of the Welsh language.

Prichard realized that people throughout Wales were suffering from the same lack of spiritual knowledge, either because of the fact that few sermons were preached, or because many of the clergy were ignorant of the Welsh language. In order to give the truths of God's Word circulation far beyond the bounds of his own parish, Prichard began to write verse. He was quite aware of the Welshman's love for poetry, and he set the teachings of Scripture to rhyme and meter, and published his poetry. His writings were circulated widely during his lifetime, and in 1672, about 28 years after his death, his poems were collected and published in a book, *Canwyll y Cymry*, or *The Welshman's Candle*. This book became a classic. "Next to the Bible, nothing has been read so much or has proved so great a blessing as these sacred songs. In every cot throughout the land they are known, and often on the field as well as by the fireside, in the smithy as in the sanctuary, those grand, inspiring words are repeated, and never without producing a powerful and hallowing influence." [7] In one of the first poems of the series, Prichard declares that not one Welshman in a hundred is able to read his Bible for the reason that there were so few Welsh Bibles in print. They were so scarce that even many of the rich people were without a copy. He says that the clergy were indifferent to this condition, and both rich and poor were spiritually ignorant. They grew to maturity, grew old and died, ignorant of the simplest teachings of the Bible. No piety was to be found in the clergyman, the farmer, the laborer, the artisan, the bailiff, the judge or the nobleman. [8]

Rees Prichard did not leave the Established Church. He remained a conformist and a royalist throughout his life, but in his religious views he was strongly inclined toward Puritanism. His preaching attracted wide attention. He attacked the worldliness and the spiritual indifference of his time, and with it all he was diligent in setting forth the fundamental teachings of the Scriptures, as he understood them. Strangely enough his testimony against the slothful clergy did not send him to prison or to the gallows, as had

---

[7]. David Davies, *Echoes from the Welsh Hills* (London, 1883), p. 189.
[8]. *Ibid.*, p. 172.

been the case with John Penry. On the contrary, Rees
Prichard was made prebendary of the collegiate church of
Brecon in 1614 and chancellor of St. David's in 1626. He
died, after 42 years of faithful witness-bearing.

Walter Cradock (c. 1606-1659)

One of the men who took a prominent part in the
evangelization of the neglected people of Wales was Walter
Cradock. He was born about the year 1610 at Trevela, in
the parish of Llangwmucha, in Monmouthshire, of a family
of land-holding gentry. After his education at Oxford he
was ordained about the year 1628 as curate of Peterson-
upon-Ely, Glamorganshire. A little later he was curate at
St. Mary's Church, Cardiff. In 1633 he was ejected by the
bishop of Llandaff, who declared him to be "a bold, ignorant
young fellow." The bishop's accusations proved unfounded,
however, and a short time after his ejection he was made
curate of the famous parish church at Wrexham, Denbighshire, where he remained for about a year.

Mr. Cradock's difficulties, and his frequent changes, were
due to no wrong-doing on his part, but rather to his great
zeal for preaching. He journeyed throughout the surrounding country, meeting with a remarkable response, and the
non-preaching clergy, of whom there were far too many in
his day, resented this.

In 1639 he assisted William Wroth, whose great zeal for
preaching had led him to establish an independent congregation at Llanfaches. He became Wroth's assistant, and in
1642 his successor. He acted as chaplain to Sir Robert
Harley, of Herefordshire, and in 1646 he went to London
where, among other activities, he preached before Parliament.

David Davies says that Cradock "was a man of very
exceptional gifts and much fervour, and did more than any
other, save perhaps Vavasor Powell, for the evangelization
of his country." [9] When Walter Cradock began his ministry,
William Wroth and Rees Prichard were going throughout
Wales preaching to great congregations of people, some of
whom had never before heard the Gospel preached, and none

---

[9]. David Davies, *Echoes from the Welsh Hills* (London, 1883), p. 191.

of whom had heard Law and Gospel proclaimed in the
manner that these men preached it. Early in his life
Cradock caught the spirit of these fearless men, whose
jeremiads regarding the unfaithfulness of the clergy had
aroused the lax bishops and the indolent clergy. Cradock
was well aware that he could expect no favors from the
bishops, were he to make common cause with such men as
Wroth and Prichard. Filled with missionary zeal, and with
flaming desire to make known the truths of God's Word to
his neglected countrymen, he gave up all thought of advance-
ment, but took the course that meant only ejectment. William Wroth, Rees Prichard and Walter Cradock are held in
highest veneration in Wales today, while the bishops and
clergy who opposed their so-called irregularities are all but
forgotten.

Vavasor Powell (1617-1670)

Shortly before the death of William Wroth in 1642 and
of Rees Prichard two years later, a new voice was heard in
Wales. It was the voice of Vavasor Powell, whose extraordinary gifts and commanding eloquence were to captivate
Wales for the next thirty years. Vavasor Powell was born
in 1617 at Cnwcglas, in the parish of Heyop, in Radnorshire.
His parents were people of humble circumstances, but there
is no reason to believe the tale of Powell's enemies, who
circulated the report that the father of this eloquent preacher
had kept an ale shop, and that Vavasor Powell himself had
been a stable boy. Even more outrageous is the slander,
sometimes mentioned in biographical works, that Powell
began his ministry on the basis of forged ordination papers.

His early life was entirely honorable, for his uncle,
Erasmus Howell, vicar of Clun, sent the lad to Jesus College,
Oxford, where he gave a good account of himself. Then,
returning to Wales, he taught school; later going to Clun to
teach in his uncle's parish school, and to act as lay curate.
While yet unordained, he was standing one Sunday afternoon watching some games that were being played by the
young men of the village. A Puritan stepped up to him and
asked how he, a parish schoolmaster, and a candidate for
holy orders, could by his presence give consent to Sunday

sports. This admonition made a deep impression upon the young man. He went to hear William Wroth preach, and the sermon convinced him that he was not at all free of worldly ideas. In that sermon Wroth described the service of Jesus Christ as a hard service, a costly service, a derided service, and a forlorn service. The young candidate was greatly disquieted, for, measured by the standards set up by William Wroth, he felt himself a worldly and an unworthy man. He describes his long struggle in his writings, admitting that at this time he knew very little of the teachings of the Scriptures. He read a book *The Bruised Reed*, by Dr. Sibbs, as well as other devotional writings, and still he found himself as one groping in the dark. Then he heard Walter Cradock preach a sermon on St. Mark 16, 15: "Go ye into all the world, and preach the Gospel to every creature." Cradock's exposition of the meaning of the word "Gospel" drove young Powell to an intensive study of his Bible. First he was convinced of the lost estate of his soul by nature, and of the futility of his many acts of penance and self-denial. "Whilst I was in this agony," he writes, "the God of all grace . . . did about noon present to me that Scripture, John iii, 36, 'He that believeth on the Son hath everlasting life,' which words were then revealed to me, and opened thus: First, that there is nothing necessary to salvation but only believing in Christ; Secondly, that to such as did believe in Christ there is certainty of salvation." [10]

In 1639, while still unordained, he began to preach. His success came almost at once, and great congregations gathered wherever he went. He was arrested for preaching in a house, and on another occasion for preaching in the open fields, for such things were looked upon as irregular and illegal in those days. He sought ordination, but was refused on the ground that he had been guilty of irregularity in preaching in unconsecrated places. This rebuff did not silence him, for he preached wherever opportunity offered, and to increasing multitudes. His name soon became famous throughout Wales, and his congregations numbered thousands. At the height of his fame he often preached three to four times in a single day, and five days a week.

---

[10]. David Davies, *Vavasor Powell* (London, 1896), p. 40.

His chief fields of labor were Radnorshire, Cardiganshire and Montgomeryshire.

In 1642 he went to London where he preached for two years, and from London he went to Kent, where he gave his services heroically during a plague. In 1646 he returned to Wales, and a year later an excellent living, the rectory of Penstrowed, was offered to him, but he declined it for reasons of conscience. In 1649 he was invited to preach before the Lord Mayor, the Lord High Sheriff and the aldermen of London, and in 1650 he preached before Parliament. By the year 1654 he had identified himself with the Baptist movement, and when bitter persecutions broke out against the Baptists at the time of Charles II, Powell shared with the others of his denomination the indignities that they suffered.

Many incidents might be recorded of the overwhelming power of his eloquence. On one occasion he was stopped in the highway by a Mr. Trevor, a great Flintshire gentleman who lived near Treuddyn. Not aware that he was speaking to none other than Vavasor Powell himself, the nobleman informed him that he was on his way to a church service where he intended to kill the preacher. When they reached the place where the service was to be held, Mr. Trevor was amazed to see his companion mount the pulpit. So astonishingly did he preach, that his would-be murderer rushed up to him at the close of the service, confessed his great sin and begged forgiveness.

On another occasion Vavasor Powell was arrested for preaching outdoors, and was led to the house of the local justice. That official was not at home. A great crowd gathered before the house, and while awaiting the return of the justice, Vavasor Powell preached to the multitude, and among those who were deeply impressed were the daughters of the justice.

During his active ministry Powell was imprisoned thirteen times. One of his foremost persecutors was Hugh Floyd, high sheriff of Radnorshire, and a near relative of Mr. Powell. On one occasion Mr. Powell was taken to London and imprisoned for two years in Fleet prison. At an-

other time he was imprisoned for five years at Southsea
castle dungeon, near Portsmouth. He died in Fleet prison.

Vavasor Powell had inherited a modest estate, and one-
fifth of his income was devoted to charity. His hospitable
home was always open to friends, and it was he who is the
author of the well-known saying that he was able to entertain
twelve friends in his home, fifty more in his stables and a
thousand in his heart. He published a number of writings,
and yet he said, "I would not neglect the preaching of one
sermon for the printing of a thousand books."

After his short stay in London it was said, "He returned
to Wales and became a most indefatigable instrument of
propagating the Gospel in those parts. He preached in most
of the churches and chapels, and often in the mountains, at
fairs and in market places. . . . He was of an unconquered
resolution, and of a mind unshaken under all his troubles." [11]

Vavasor Powell lies buried in Bunhill Fields, London,
the "Westminster Abbey of Nonconformity." Over his tomb
is the following inscription: "Vavasor Powell lyes here
enterred, who was a successful teacher of the past, a sincere
witness of the present, and a choyce example to future ages;
who, in the defection of many, found mercy to be faithful;
for which, he being called to several prisons, he was there
tryed and found faithful, would not accept deliverance, expecting a better resurrection, in hope of which, he finished
his life and testimony together, in the eleventh year of his
imprisonment, and in the 53rd year of his age, October 27,
1670."

Griffith Jones (1683-1761)

Even in days of great apostasy, the Lord has His faithful
witnesses here and there. In an age of spiritual torpor,
there was an eminently gifted clergyman of the Church of
England, Griffith Jones of Llanddowror, who never ceased to
bear courageous witness to the Saviour.

Griffith Jones was born in 1683 in Carmarthenshire. He
was educated in the grammar schools, and in 1711 a church
at Llandilo was given him. Five years later he was made

---

[11]. Edmund Calamy, The Nonconformists's Memorial (Saml. Parker's
edition, London, 1775), vol. 2, p. 639.

vicar of Llanddowror. This faithful man was grieved deeply when he observed the spiritual laxity of the lay people. He began to preach repentance and faith with a fervor that had seldom been known in Wales.

Educational opportunities were primitive in many parts of Wales in those days, and Griffith Jones was surprised to find that few people read their Bibles for the simple reason that many of them could hardly read or write. He organized catechetical classes for both children and grown people in his own parish, but it was not long until he discovered that many were so poorly educated that something else was needed. Then it was that he organized a series of schools throughout South Wales, in which were taught the usual secular subjects, and religion as well. So successful was the venture that by the year 1760 there were 215 such schools in South Wales, and in them was enrolled about one-third of the population of all Wales, or 158,237 children and older people.[12] He appealed to the Society for the Propagation of the Gospel, and 30,000 Bibles were printed in the Welsh language, so that the older people, who found it difficult to learn English, might have the Word of God in a language that they could understand.

This was but a part of the activity of this extremely useful man. He preached Sundays and weekdays in his own parish church, and in various other places. He was an unusually fine preacher, and great numbers of people came to hear him. T. R. Roberts said of him: "He was an able and impressive preacher, and often his churches were quite inadequate to contain the immense crowds that flocked to hear him."

Once he noticed a very young, somewhat arrogant clergy-man among the congregation. This was Daniel Rowland, a youthful curate, who had come out of curiosity. As the older pastor preached, Rowland realized as never before his own sin, and his need of a Saviour. The young visitor went away a changed man, determined from now on to go among the people of Wales preaching repentance and faith in Jesus

---

[12]. E. Middleton, *Evangelical Biography*, vol. 4, p. 337.

Christ. Thus did the preaching of Griffith Jones kindle a light that was soon to shine from Anglesey to Glamorgan.

Griffith Jones is often called "the morning star of the great spiritual awakening in Wales," for it was his forceful preaching that day that caused a careless young curate to see clearly his duty. Soon there were to be many faithful witnesses: Daniel Rowland, Howel Harris, David Charles, Thomas Charles, John Elias, Lewis Rees, William Williams of Pant-y-celyn, William Williams of Wern, Christmas Evans and many others, whose eloquent preaching roused the people of Wales to the most remarkable period of spiritual life in their history, and made the mountains and valleys ring once more with their fervent hymns of praise.

Griffith Jones was a remarkable preacher. Here is a contemporary account of his manner of preaching: "His sermons were well composed and digested. He entered into the very heart of whatever subject he undertook. His divisions were obvious and perspicuous; his deductions natural; his matter solid, striking, lively and judicious. These advantages, set off by an agreeable delivery, a musical voice, and a proper action, soon made him famous as a preacher, and great multitudes flocked to hear him wherever he went.

"In the explication of his text, or of any divine truth, he was clear and pertinent. As he advanced, his subject fired him more and more. One while he glowed with ardent love to his fellow saints and fellow sinners: anon, he flamed with holy indignation against all ungodliness and unrighteousness of men; then melted into tenderness and grief, lest the means of grace might not be rendered effectual to his hearers. On these occasions, every feature and every nerve seemed intensely animated. There was a noble pomp in his descriptions, clearness and strength in his reasonings. His appeals to conscience were close and pointed. A surprising force and abruptness sharpened his interrogations. A sacred pathos distinguished his address. He spoke naturally, for he spoke feelingly. Everything he uttered bore the stamp of sincerity, which art may mimic, but cannot reach. In refuting, remonstrating and reproving, he assumed the tone of conviction and majestic authority; but when he came to the application, he gave way to a still superior burst of religious vehemence, which, like the impetus of an irresistible torrent, mightily carried all before him. Great was the power of the Divine Spirit that accompanied the Word. The prayerless cried for mercy, and the ignorant were made wise unto salvation." [13]

Nevertheless Griffith Jones's great power was based upon something more fundamental than his perfervid eloquence. The same eyewitness says of him: "He enforced the necessity of doing good works, and at the same time displayed the madness and impiety of trusting in them. Christ was all in all to him; and it was his greatest delight to publish and exalt the unsearchable riches of his Redeemer's righteousness." [14]

Middleton describes the fearlessness of Griffith Jones. He hated sin, and denounced it emphatically. He did not hesitate to rebuke the sins of the wealthy and influential members of his parish, nor did he at any time ever hesitate to denounce sin because of the fear that people might be offended at his words. Often he made them angry, but the earnestness of this great preacher was so well recognized that those whom he rebuked, publicly and in private, knew that he did it solely for the good of their souls.

Daniel Rowland (1713-1790)

Daniel Rowland, often spelled Rowlands, was one of the most wonderful of all the great Welsh preachers. The Countess of Huntingdon, one of the most discriminating judges of preaching of the eighteenth century, declared that only George Whitefield could excel him. Rowland was born at Pant-y-beudy, Llancwnlle, near Llangeitho, in Cardiganshire, where his father, Daniel Rowland, was a clergyman of the Church of England. At the age of three, young Rowland had a narrow escape from death. Welsh fireplaces are often five feet or more wide, five feet high and three feet deep. The fire is kept in an iron grate in the center, and within the fireplace, at each end, are low stools. People literally sit within the fireplace. The young lad was sitting on one of these stools, but for some reason he arose

---

[13]. E. Middleton, *Evangelical Biography*, vol. 4, pp. 334-335.
[14]. *Ibid.*, p. 335.

quickly and ran out into the room. Hardly had he vacated the chimney when a enormous piece of stone fell with such force from the top of the chimney, that the heavy oak stool on which he sat, was crushed.

Daniel Rowland was sent to a grammar school at Hereford, on the English border. It is not certain whether he attended college, but if he did, his studies were cut short at the age of 18, when his father died. In 1733, at the age of 20, he was ordained deacon. His father's death had left the family in poor circumstances, and the young man walked 200 miles to London, and 200 miles in return, to receive ordination. This was not due entirely to religious zeal, for at the time of his ordination Daniel Rowland was a worldly young man, much more interested in the Sunday afternoon cock-fights and wrestling matches of his companions than in religion. He became curate to his brother at Llangeitho. He was a gay, careless young man, with no serious interest in his duties, and he seemed destined to become one more of the many pleasure-loving parsons who preached drowsy sermons to dwindling congregations on Sunday, and spent the remainder of the week in hunting, fishing and drinking with the neighboring squires. Rowland preached dull sermons, entirely without evangelical truth of any sort, and the congregation continued to dwindle.

The awakening of Daniel Rowland was due to two circumstances. He discovered that many of his own church members were attending a nearby Dissenting chapel where a man named Pugh was preaching. This chapel was always crowded, and people stood outside listening at the open windows. Upon questioning his parishioners, Rowland was told that Mr. Pugh preached most eloquently of man's sinfulness and his need of the cleansing blood of Jesus Christ. Rowland considered this mere fanaticism, nevertheless it caused him much concern.

About this time the famous Griffith Jones, of Llanddowror, preached in nearby Llandewibrefi. Rowland considered him a fanatic, and yet he went out of curiosity to hear him. He found the church crowded, and people standing in the churchyard outside. Some one recognized him, and he was admitted through the sacristy door and he managed to find a place to stand, which was directly beneath the pulpit. Looking down during his sermon, Griffith Jones saw the young man, and so conceited was his appearance, and so evident the sneer of derision on his face, that Griffith Jones paused in his sermon and offered a prayer for the young man's conversion. Rowland was angry, but at the same time deeply troubled, for in his arrogance it had never occurred to him that he himself might be a great sinner. Griffith Jones preached the Law with great severity, and at the same time pointed his hearers to the Crucified Lord. Rowland returned to Llangeitho with the sermon ringing in his ears. He began to preach in a manner that he thought was that of Griffith Jones. Laying aside his former quiet manner of delivery, he began to preach with great vehemence. However, his early efforts did not go beyond an impassioned condemnation of sin. He had not yet learned to preach the Gospel together with the Law. His empty church filled quickly, but there were no evidences of spiritual growth. The people only grew sullen under the weekly condemnation of their manner of living. Daniel Rowland was accustomed to spend his Sunday afternoons with a group of young men of his own age, who engaged in games and cock-fighting. Shortly after hearing the sermon of Griffith Jones, he surprised his former companions by appearing one Sunday afternoon and preaching an indignant sermon on Sunday amusements. He called upon his Dissenting neighbor, Mr. Pugh. "Preach the Gospel, Mr. Rowland," said Pugh. "You have been preaching only the Law, but you must preach Gospel as well, and apply the balm of Gilead, the blood of Christ, to their spiritual wounds, and show them the necessity of faith in the crucified Saviour."

Rowland studied his Bible with diligence, day and night. Mr. Pugh assisted him during his days of spiritual concern. His preaching improved from Sunday to Sunday, and people in growing numbers were brought to a knowledge of the way of salvation. Rowland was a devout Anglican Churchman, and he had a dislike for outdoor preaching. This dislike was overcome through the influence of a simple farmer's wife from Ystradffin, Carmarthenshire. She had walked 21 miles over the hills to visit her sister, and on

Sunday she attended the parish church. After the service she was heard to say that "the minister is daft." Nevertheless she returned on the following Sunday, and for the next six months she walked the 21 miles every Sunday to hear Rowland. Finally she came to him and begged him to visit Ystradffin and preach to the people there, for many of them were in utmost spiritual ignorance. Rowland told her of his prejudice against preaching outside the parish to which he had been called, but he promised to come if she could get the permission from her own pastor. "If that farm woman is willing to walk 21 miles to Llangeitho, and 21 miles in return, every Sunday for half a year, perhaps it is my duty to go there, for others may get some little benefit from my poor efforts."

Daniel Rowland visited Ystradffin, and this was the beginning of his week-day preaching. He was always in his own pulpit on Sunday, but during the week he often preached in nearby places. If he could get permission to preach in a parish church, he would do so, but when men often closed their pulpits to him, he preached in the open fields. The people, lulled to spiritual indifference by the wretched preaching of their day, responded quickly to Rowland's forceful preaching of sin and saving grace. They found him to be a man of genuine piety, brilliant, possessed of imagination and feeling, a wonderful orator, but above all, a man who preached the great truths of evangelical Christianity without fear. There was a parish church at one place that seated 3,000 people, and this was always filled to the very pulpit steps. People came for as many as 100 miles to hear him. When he celebrated Communion, his communicants numbered 1,500 and 2,000, and one eye-witness says that he counted 3,000 people who received Communion at a single service.

It is not surprising that these things created much enmity on the part of the neighboring clergy. He was accused of disorder in that he preached in unconsecrated places, and within the parishes of other clergymen. Complaint was made to the bishop, and Daniel Rowland was formally ejected from his curacy. A deputy from the bishop read the announcement on a certain Sunday in 1763, just as Row-

land was about to begin the service. Stepping from behind
the altar rails, Rowland told his congregation that he would
not oppose his bishop. He was ejected from the church and
its property, but the bishop had no jurisdiction beyond that.
The service would proceed outside the churchyard gates.

After Rowland's deprivation, the people of his parish
built him a large chapel where he preached weekly for the
remainder of his days. Rowland's remarkable popularity
never diminished. For more than half a century he preached
in Llangeitho and throughout the neighboring country to
great gatherings of people. It was not mere curiosity that
drew them, for he received scores of letters telling him of
the lasting spiritual benefit that his hearers had received.
People who had grown up in total religious ignorance had
been instructed; men and woman who had thought of God
as a bookkeeper, who marked down good deeds and bad
deeds in a great record book, and finally balanced the two
accounts, realized that they had depended upon good works
for their salvation. Broken families were united, sins of
long standing were confessed, family devotions became the
rule, and diligence in hearing the Word and receiving the
Lord's Supper became prevalent. Daniel Rowland's earnest,
evangelical preaching caused a religious awakening that was
felt far beyond his own parish. Other clergymen became
awakened and preached evangelical sermons, and everywhere churches took on new spiritual life.

Eight of Rowland's sermons have been translated from
the original Welsh into English. There is nothing in them to
give one the secret of his extraordinary fame. Like Luther,
like Knox, like Whitefield and like Chalmers, his sermons are
not remarkable when in print. Such men were decidedly
better in the pulpit than when at their desk. The words of
their sermon manuscripts were amplified, and were expressed in a manner far superior to their written style. This
has been the testimony again and again of people who were
familiar with their spoken words. When J. C. Ryle wrote
his valuable *Christian Leaders of the Last Century* in 1868
— a book that ought to be found in every clergyman's
library — there were one or two very old people who had
heard Rowland preach. These, as well as many who left

written accounts, agree that Rowland's spoken discourses were far superior to the sermons that have appeared in Welsh and in English. From the testimony of such people, Dr. Ryle was led to say that the chief characteristic of Rowland's preaching was the prominent place of the Lord Jesus in every sermon. "The blood, the sacrifice, the righteousness the kindness, the patience, the saving grace, the example, the greatness of the Lord Jesus, are subjects which appear to run through every sermon, and to crop out at every turn. . . . His divinity and His humanity, His office and His character, His death and His life, are pressed on our attention in every possible connection. . . . A ministry full of the Lord Jesus is exactly the sort of a ministry that I should expect God to bless. Christ-honouring sermons are just the sermons that the Holy Spirit seals with success." [15]

Christmas Evans, the famous Welsh Baptist preacher, has left us a lengthy and vivid description of Daniel Rowland and his manner of preaching. Rowland was accustomed to appear suddenly in his pulpit, clad in a black preaching robe. After reading his text, Psalm 27, 4 (a single verse) was sung by the congregation. Then the preacher announced a single, striking idea, which Christmas Evans compares to the opening of a box of sweet ointment whose flavor filled the whole church, leading the people to expect more and more from the same box. Evans compares his sermon to the fiery sparks flying in all directions from the smith's anvil. He would begin quietly, but soon his voice would ring with a tone of authority throughout the entire church. His face was exceptionally expressive, and he held the closest attention of his hearers. He carried a scrap of paper into the pulpit, and gave it a quick glance six or seven times in the course of a sermon. He had no applications at the end of the sermon, for he had made practical applications all through the discourse. He concluded with a few very striking ideas, which, Mr. Evans declares, came with overwhelming effect. Then, after a very short prayer, he would disappear through the pulpit door as hastily as he had entered.

---

[15]. J. C. Ryle, *Op. cit.*, pp. 197-198.

Eight sermons of Daniel Rowland were translated into English and published in 1774, and three additional sermons appeared in English in 1778. These have since been reprinted. There are two biographies: J. Owen's *Memoir of the Rev. Daniel Rowlands* (1840) and E. Morgan's *Ministerial Records . . . of Daniel Rowlands* (1840). Dr. J. C. Ryle devotes two full chapters to him in his *Christian Leaders* (1868), and Owen Jones has included a good memoir in his *Some of the Great Preachers of Wales* (1885).

Howel Harris (1714-1773)

Howel Harris, the lay preacher, whose name is always linked with that of Daniel Rowland, was born in 1714 at Talgarth, Breconshire, South Wales. He attended school until 18 years of age. He came from an excellent family. Upon finishing school, he decided, without any real seriousness of purpose, to become a clergyman of the Established Church.

On Palm Sunday morning, 1735, while listening to a confessional address before Holy Communion, he realized deeply his sinful nature and his need of a Saviour. Strangely enough, this was the same year that Daniel Rowland had been brought to a knowledge of sin and salvation.

Howel Harris went at once to Oxford and attended for a term at St. Mary's Hall, but because of the lack of spiritual warmth, he soon returned to Talgarth. Eager to speak to others in regard to repentance and salvation, and mindful of the spiritual deadness in his home parish, he visited every family in turn, pleading with them to repent and trust only in the Saviour. In this visitation he met with suprising success, and soon we find him preaching. Often he preached as often as five times a day, and it is interesting to observe that this was a year before either George Whitefield or John Wesley had begun their field preaching.

His pastor was displeased, not especially because Harris preached sin and grace, but because such outdoor preaching, in those days, was looked upon as irregular, and as disorder. He pleaded with Harris to cease his efforts, but with no success. The young man could not be silenced. When he

applied to his bishop for ordination, he was refused because
of his irregularities.

Howel Harris continued to preach, and it was not long
until he had gained a reputation far beyond his home parish
because of his eloquent testimony. Wherever he went,
thousands were stirred. He began to organize societies
within the Established Church. This was not at all unusual
in those days, for societies had been formed for one cause
or another for some time. Within four years he had no less
than 300 such societies.

He even went so far as to attempt to establish a Christian
community at Trevecca, where he had opened a school in
1736. This community experiment was began in 1752, and
within three years it numbered 120 persons.

Wherever he went, Howel Harris attracted thousands.
Not all were friendly, however, for on various occasions he
was attacked by mobs. Howel Harris and Daniel Rowland
were jointly responsible for the beginning of the great
spiritual awakening in Wales, but the two did not meet for
some years, until Harris had a chance to go to Defynog to
hear Rowland preach.

Howel Harris is often called the first lay preacher of
the Calvinistic Methodist church. In doctrine he agreed
with Whitefield rather than with Wesley. He preached in
Whitefield's tabernacle in London in later years. "A man
of extraordinary gifts, but always a lay preacher," one
biographer said of him. Thomas Rees said that Harris was
"the most successful preacher that ever ascended a platform
or pulpit in Wales. . . . He was an extraordinary instrument
raised by Providence, at an extraordinary time, to accomplish
an extraordinary work." T. R. Roberts says of him, "He
stands pre-eminent among the benefactors of his country.
Religious activity in Wales began with him, and through his
efforts the heart of the nation was roused to such a pitch
of religious fervor that from then till now the Welsh have
been known, so far as they are known at all, as a people of
extreme religious enthusiasm." When he died in 1773, at
the age of 59, his funeral was attended by 20,000 mourners.

Throughout his life Howel Harris remained in communion with the Church of England, for during his lifetime

the Calvinistic Methodists were a group within the Established church. He met with considerable opposition from the clergy, and on more than one occasion some local vicar led the mobs who attacked him. On one occasion a justice of the peace was sent with a warrant for his arrest. Pausing on the edge of the multitude to hear Harris preach, the justice was so impressed by what he heard that he thrust the warrant into his pocket, and invited Harris to enjoy the hospitality of his home. On another occasion an attempt was made on his life, but the musket ball went wide of its mark.

There are three biographies of Howel Harris: "B. T.", *A Brief Account of the Life of Howel Harris* (1791); T. Jackson, *The Life of Howel Harris* (1837), in the *Library of Christian Biography* series; and H. J. Hughes, *Life of Howel Harris* (1892). He was a man of tireless evangelical zeal, and his sermons, like those of Daniel Rowland, were centered upon the redeeming work of the Lord Jesus Christ.

William Williams of Pant-y-celyn (1717-1791)

The name of Williams of Pant-y-celyn is known to Christians everywhere because of his fame as a hymn-writer. Throughout Wales, and wherever Welshmen have migrated, his fame as a preacher is equally well known. He was born in 1717 at Cefn-y-Coed farm, Llanfairar-y-bryn, Carmarthenshire. His father, a Calvinistic Methodist, had encouraged his son to be a physician, and had sent him to Llandovery and Llwynllwyd, in Breconshire, for his education.

Having heard Howel Harris preach, young Williams gave up all thought of the medical profession. He was ordained deacon in 1740, and became curate of Llan Wrtyd and Llanddewi Abergwessin. Soon after this, through the famous George Whitefield, he became interested in the Calvinistic Methodist movement. His preaching tours took him throughout Wales. He travelled 3,000 miles a year for 50 years. Although he never attained the fame of Daniel Rowland, Howel Harris and Christmas Evans, yet he has always been given his rightful place among the group of exceptional men who played so important a part in the great spiritual awakening of Wales.

William of Pant-y-celyn wrote 800 hymns in English and in the Welsh language. Perhaps the best known of these is his "Guide me, O Thou Great Redeemer." Unfortunately this has been altered, and is known best in America as "Guide me, O Thou Great Jehovah." In its original form it reads:

> Arglwydd, arwain trwy'r anialwch
> Fi bererin gwael ei wedd, etc.

It is an unfortunate fact that many vigorous hymns have been altered from time to time. Such alterations almost always have weakened the hymns theologically, so as to make them acceptable to people of every shade of belief.

William Williams of Pant-y-celyn was a man whose theology was not of a vague, colorless sort. He called sin by its rightful name, and he directed men to the one sure Source of Salvation, Jesus Christ. Wales had suffered greatly through the long years of spiritual sloth, when pastors without evangelical zeal either performed their duties in a perfunctory manner, or else neglected them altogether. Preaching had sunk to a low level, and sermons were as lacking in the truths of Redemptive Christianity as were those of Germany in the heyday of Rationalism. Williams of Pant-y-celyn, with his Christ-centered sermons and his devout hymns, did much to arouse the people of Wales, and to further the work begun by Daniel Rowland and Howel Harris. His great hymn, "Guide me, O Thou Great Redeemer," is almost the Welsh national anthem to this day. John Hughes wrote a fine musical setting in true Welsh choral style to which the hymn is sung by Welsh people throughout the world. It is known as *Cwm Rhondda,* and should by all means be used, rather than the popular melody to which this fine hymn is sung in America. He who has not heard a large congregation of Welsh people sing William William's great hymn in their own language, and in four-part harmony with a foundation of magnificient bass, has not yet heard congregational singing at its best. The story of William Williams's life and work is found in E. Morgan's *Ministerial Records . . . of William Williams, Pant-y-celyn* (1847).

Peter Williams (1722-1796)

Peter Williams, an eminent preacher and Bible scholar, who put family Bibles, commentaries and concordances into every Welsh home, was finally expelled by his denomination when almost 70 years of age, and compelled to spend the last four or five years of his life on a farm.

Williams was born at West Marsh, near Laugharne, Carmarthenshire, in 1722. His parents died before he was 12, and he was brought up by an uncle on a farm. From 1740 to 1743 he attended the grammar school at Carmarthen. In 1743, George Whitefield preached in his town, and Peter Williams went to hear him, and came away greatly impressed. After teaching school for a year, he was ordained in 1744, and began to preach. He became curate at Eglwys Cummin and master of the parish school. After a year he was dismissed because of his Methodist views.

After serving several brief curacies, he became identified, in 1746, with the Welsh Calvinistic party, but retained his connection with the Church of England. He spent a dozen years on preaching tours throughout Wales, and in nearby parts of England, taking an active part in the work which led to the great awakening. He shared in the persecution directed against Howel Harris, Daniel Rowland and others of his time.

He resolved to continue a work so well begun by Griffith Jones, and between 1767 and 1770 he published a Welsh family Bible and commentary, issuing it at first in separate parts, which were sold at a price within the reach of every family. In time the "Peter Williams Bible" went through more than a dozen editions, and no Welsh household was considered complete without it. In 1773 he published his *Mynegeir Ysgrythurol,* a Welsh concordance written for the common people as an aid to their Bible study. In 1790 he published John Canne's Bible, with his own marginal notes and foot-notes.

These books were used widely throughout Wales, and met with favor everywhere. It was not until almost 20 years later, in the year 1791, that Peter Williams was brought to trial on heresy charges, because of a statement made in his family Bible, in connection with his notes on the first

chapter of St. John. Here he attempted to explain the
doctrine of the Holy Trinity by means of mysticism. A new
generation had grown up in Wales, and some of them were
not friendly to Peter Williams. The exact nature of their
internal difficulties is not known today, but they used his
comments on St. John 1, and brought charges of Sabellian
tendencies. Williams protested vigorously, and with all his
power as a public speaker he insisted that he had never
for a moment departed from the teachings of the New
Testament.

There are many people who insist that the Williams
heresy trial is a blot on the record of the denomination to
which he belonged, and for whose teachings he suffered so
much persecution in his younger days. They look upon it
as a factional quarrel, in which the young men tried to break
the rule of an older generation. Peter Williams was
declared ineligible and suspended from membership in the
Calvinistic Methodist church. He succeeded in remaining
at Water Street Chapel, Carmarthen. At the age of 70 he
moved to a farm, but served his congregation until his death,
in 1796, at the age of 74.

In addition to his Bible, concordance and commentary,
he published several other books, including a hymnal.

David Jones (1735-1810)

David Jones was born in 1735 in the parish of Llanllueni,
Carmarthenshire, Wales. He was educated in the schools of
his town and in Carmarthen college. After serving a curacy
for ten years, he became rector, in 1768, of Llangan parish.
His coming is said to have wrought wonders in Llangan. So
fervent was his preaching that his church was crowded at all
times, and there were many occasions when it was necessary
to make use of the churchyard, so great were his congregations. Spiritual life was reawakened.

Although an Anglican, Jones leaned strongly toward
Methodism, and his sermons were decidedly evangelical. He
preached far and wide throughout Wales and England, often
going on extended tours. His coming always attracted
enormous congregations. Like William Haslam of a century
later, David Jones drew a sharp distinction between an

external religious life which satisfies itself in mere outward faithfulness to the means of grace, and a spiritual life which concerns itself with the facts of repentance and a living faith in Jesus Christ as man's only Saviour.

David Morris (1744-1791)

David Morris, one of the great preachers and hymn-writers of Wales, was born in Llendrod, Cardiganshire, in 1744. His baptismal name was Dafydd Morys. He began to preach in the Welsh Methodist chapels at the age of 21. Once, when preaching at a place near Wrexham, the senior deacon demanded of him, "And who are you? Are you worthy of a congregation?" After the service the people crowded around the young preacher to congratulate him because of his excellent sermon. Among them was the senior deacon, who exclaimed, "Dafydd Morys, *bach!* I hope you will forgive my conduct to you before the service." "Man," said Morris, "before the sermon you showed your teeth, but after the service you are wagging your tail."

David Morris was called to a congregation in Twrgwyn, and in connection with it he served several chapels in nearby villages. He served these congregations until his death in 1791, when he was succeeded by his gifted son Eben. David Morris was one of the most popular preachers of his day. Wherever he went the congregations were so great that he was obliged to preach in the open air. He had all the fire and the dramatic action of the Welsh preachers of his generation, and many tales are told of his oratorical powers. He published a collection of hymns in 1773, and these include some that are favorites in the Welsh churches to the present day.

Thomas Charles of Bala (1755-1814)

This noted Calvinistic Methodist preacher, commonly called Charles of Bala, was born in 1755 at Llanfihangel, Carmarthenshire. He was educated at Llanddowror and at the academy at Carmarthen. He entered Jesus College in 1775, and was ordained in 1778. His first curacy was in Somerset, and in 1784 he became curate of Llanymawddwy in his native

Wales. A year later he withdrew from the Church of England and became a Calvinistic Methodist.

Not only was he a diligent and unusually able preacher, but he continued the work of the famous Griffith Jones of a generation previous to his time, by interesting himself in providing the Welsh people with Bibles in their own language. He prepared two editions of the Welsh Bible for publication.

Like many other eminent Welsh preachers of his day, he journeyed throughout his native principality, attracting great congregations wherever he went. He was an exceptionally able preacher, and he did his full share toward keeping alive the great wave of spiritual fervor of his day.

Thomas Charles lived at Bala from 1783 onward, and he became one of the leaders of the Calvinistic Methodist movement in Wales. He interested himself in the circulating schools, and did much to make them successful. In 1807 he went to Ireland on a preaching tour. Not only was he one of the founders of the British and Foreign Bible Society, but he himself established a religious publishing house in Bala, preparing a number of books and tracts for publication, and writing a catechism in Welsh, which was translated into English and enjoyed wide circulation.

In the headquarters of the British and Foreign Bible Society is an old Welsh Bible that is one of their most valued treasures. It was once owned by a little Welsh girl, Mary Jones, 16 years of age. Her father was a poor weaver who lived in a small village at the foot of Cader Iris. Mary wanted a Bible to read, but found that there was not a copy in the village. However, a family living two miles away possessed a Bible, and to their home Mary Jones went two or three times a week, in order to read the Bible. Then she learned from a Methodist preacher that Thomas Charles, of Bala, might have two or three copies of the Welsh Bible, for he had ordered some from London.

Bala was more than 25 miles away, but the 16-year-old girl set out on foot early one morning, and walked to Bala. She returned, the proud possessor of a Welsh Bible. That was in the year 1800, when a Bible in the Welsh language was somewhat of a rare book. Thomas Charles was asked to preach in London two years later, and he told the story of Mary Jones, and her walk of more than 25 miles to Bala, and the same distance home again, in order to own a Welsh Bible. Great interest was aroused. Joseph Hughes, of the Religious Tract Society became interested; and C. F. A. Steinkopf, pastor of a Lutheran church in London, appealed for Bibles for continental Europe. In 1804 a meeting was held, attended by 300 people. An executive committee of 36 was appointed, 15 representing the Established Church, 15 representing Nonconformity, and six from the foreign language congregations of London. This was the beginning of the British and Foreign Bible Society, which has supplied the world with almost 500 million copies of the Bible.

In the village of Bryn Crug, in Wales, is a monument erected to the memory of the 16-year-old Welsh girl, who walked more than 50 miles in order to become the owner of a Bible. Lengthy inscriptions, in Welsh and in English, tell of this incident which led to the founding of the British and Foreign Bible Society, and the distribution of many millions of Bibles.

It is difficult to realize that as recently as the year 1800, printed Bibles were comparatively few, and so costly that the poorest people could not afford to buy a copy. Thomas Charles of Bala was one of the men who became interested in providing the cottager with a Bible in his own spoken language, and his eloquent pleas, and the story that he told of Mary Jones, led to a movement that has supplied Bibles in hundreds of languages to people in every part of the world. Bibles are inexpensive today, and the supply is plentiful. It was a few men such as Thomas Charles of Bala who made this possible.

Morgan J. Rees (1760-1804)

Morgan J. Rees, sometimes called the Father of Religious Freedom, was born in 1760 at Graddfa. As a young man he became interested in the establishment of night schools and Sunday-schools. Not only did he teach young and old in these schools, which were held in chapels, barns and private homes, but in some cases he provided books so that the poorer people might learn. He attended an academy in Bristol, and in 1787 he began to preach in Baptist churches. He urged his denomination to establish Sunday-schools throughout Wales. These were not organizations in which children were taught a brief lesson. They were schools in which both children and their elders devoted several hours to diligent study. Many of the poorer people could hardly read or write, and Morgan Rees realized that they must be taught to read in order to be able to understand their Bibles. In his schools he taught reading, writing and the Bible. Going from place to place he aroused interest in his project, and did much to encourage the study of the Bible in Wales.

Morgan Rees was a man of tireless missionary spirit. In 1792 he had an active part in the founding of a Bible Society whose object it was to supply the Scriptures to the French people. He visited France, but his work was stopped in 1793 by a war. Returning to Wales, he took up the cause of religious and political liberty. He believed that the United States Constitution contained the principles of freedom that would serve admirably as a model for Wales. He founded a periodical, Cylchgrawn, in which he set forth his principles. His good intentions were misunderstood, and a warrant was issued for his arrest. When an officer came from London to arrest him, he was compelled to flee to Liverpool. Later he emigrated to America and made his home in Philadelphia. In 1797 he led a group of Welsh immigrants to Cambria County, Pennsylvania, where he established a congregation. He died seven years later at the age of 44.

Morgan Rees was a forceful preacher, an able writer and a man of tireless missionary spirit. Like Charles of Bala, he had an important part in a movement which brought religious education into homes throughout Wales. Before the days of these men, and others of like minds, there were schools in the larger cities and towns, but the small villages and the populous valleys had but meagre opportunities for education. Morgan Rees, Charles of Bala and their associates founded their schools, used the Bible as the chief text book, where people of all ages were to be found "discussing almost every question pertaining to this world and the next. Sunday-schools were quickly adopted by all the Nonconformist bodies, and by the Episcopal Church as well; and among the former at least church membership implied membership of the school. Owing to this the minds of the people of Wales became saturated with the Scriptures. The geography of Palestine was more familiar to them than that of England. Bible stories, Bible arguments, and Bible metaphors were become interwoven with the very texture of their thought."[16] The Sunday-schools of those days were places of serious study, and not, as is often the case today, a mere half hour of superficial instruction.

David Charles (1762-1834)

David Charles, a brother of the noted Charles of Bala, was born in 1762 in St. Clears, Carmarthen, South Wales. He was educated in the schools of his village, and then apprenticed to a flax dresser. In 1780 he went to Bristol, in England, to continue his education. Three years later he returned to Wales and engaged in secular business, at the same time devoting much attention to religious work. He became known as an able speaker, and often was called upon to address religious gatherings.

When 40 years of age, he felt the call to devote all his time to preaching, and he was ordained in the Calvinistic Methodist church. From that time onward, his life's story reads much like that of many other prominent Welsh clergymen, for "he went throughout Wales preaching with great power, and attracting multitudes wherever he went." This experience, so common to most of the famous Welsh preachers, is not hard to understand. Noncomformity was spreading rapidly throughout Wales, and preachers were relatively few. It became necessary for the abler men to spend much of their time traveling from place to place. The principal scenes of the labors of David Charles were Carmarthenshire, Pembrokeshire and Glamorganshire. He was able to preach effectively both in the Welsh and the English languages, and from 1803 to 1828 he was widely known and

---

[16]. W. W. Davies, *Wales* (London, 1925), p. 223.

eminently successful. Christmas Evans said of him, "I feel holy sparks emanating from him, as from a great star, and melting the frost of my soul." He visited London on several occasions, and preached at least twice for Rowland Hill in Surrey Street Chapel. In 1828 he suffered a stroke of apoplexy, and for six years lay speechless until his death in 1834.

His well-known sermon, "Christ All, and in All," delivered in the Welsh language, but translated into English, is remarkable. It is a long sermon, but there is hardly a sentence in it that does not speak of the Lord Jesus. It is Christo-centric to a degree, and one marvels at the scores of proof texts that he was able to weave so naturally into the discourse. In our day, when the Saviour is often not mentioned in a sermon until the closing paragraph, this sermon of David Charles is well worthy of study.

Robert Roberts (1762-1802)

Robert Roberts, whose preaching contributed much toward the spiritual awakening of Wales, was born in 1762 in Llanllyfui, Carnarvonshire. As a young man he worked in a stone quarry, and while there fell into evil habits. In 1778 he went to hear the Rev. David Jones, and became convinced of sin. In order to be free of the bad influence of his former companions, he gave up his work in the quarry and became a farm hand. He studied diligently, and in 1787, when 25 years of age, he began to preach. Not long afterward he became pastor of Chapel House, Clynnog.

Robert Roberts died at the early age of 40, after having preached but 15 years, but during that time he exerted a great influence throughout his part of Wales. New life was infused into many indifferent congregations, and he is said to have made a lasting impression on the spiritual life of Wales.

"In choice of language, flights of imagination, eloquence of speech, and the irresistible power of conviction, he was second to none," declares one of his fellow countrymen.[17]

---

[17]. T. R. Roberts, *Eminent Welshmen*, p. 475.

The same writer adds that his great power as a persuasive preacher lay not in his human oratory, but in the fact of his close communion with his Lord.

Robert Roberts was not a scholarly man, but he was a preacher who knew his Bible, realized the sad havoc wrought in the world by sin, and who pleaded eloquently with his fellow men to repent and put their trust in the atoning work of the Saviour. He was a Calvinistic Methodist, and knew thoroughly the teachings of his denomination, and bore witness courageously.

Christmas Evans (1766-1838)

Wales has produced many able preachers, but none greater than Christmas Evans. At the height of his fame, no chapel in Wales was large enough to hold the thousands who flocked to hear him. It is not an exaggeration when writers of his time say that many people followed him from village to village, for twenty to thirty days. Were it not for the fact that his sermons exist largely in the Welsh language, barring a few that were translated into English in 1859, his fame as a preacher would be second only to that of Wesley and Whitefield.

Christmas Evans was born on Christmas Day, 1766, at Ysgaerwen, Cardiganshire, South Wales. His father, Samuel Evans, was a shoemaker of humble means, who died when the lad was nine years old, leaving the family destitute. A relative named James Lewis took the boy into his home, where he was allowed to grow up with absolutely no religious training. His new home was not a happy one, and he was made to work hard, and not permitted to go to school. He was eighteen years old before he learned to read and write, but by this time he had learned to drink heavily. Once, when he was attacked by ruffians, he lost the sight of his right eye.

A Welsh Presbyterian preacher named David Davies took an interest in the boy's spiritual welfare, and persuaded him to join the Presbyterian church. He was not satisfied, however, and at 22 he united with the Baptist church. in which denomination he spent the remainder of his life.

Just how much theological training he received, we cannot say, but, like William Bray, he was largely self-taught, and the Bible was his most important text book. At 23 he was ordained at Lleyn. From 1792 to 1826 he lived in Anglesey, where he served many congregations and preaching stations. These became so numerous that he placed resident pastors in charge of some of them, yet continued to act as their overseer. He was a man of considerable determination, and some of the pastors and congregations did not take kindly to his oversight. Their unwilling attitude caused him to leave the district in 1826, and go to Glamorganshire. Two years later we find him in Cardiff, and four years later in Carnarvoran. He died in Swansea in 1838, aged 72.

Robert Hall says that Evans was "the tallest, the stoutest, the greatest man I ever saw; he had but one eye, if it could be called an eye; it was more properly a brilliant star; it shined like Venus." Old engravings show him to be a man of powerful physique, yet not stout. One well-known engraving shows him in a high cylinder-like pulpit, with a large congregation filling all the benches and the aisles on every side — the men sitting on the right side of the church and the women on the left.

Most of his preaching, however, was done outdoors, because of the great congregations that were attracted wherever he went. He usually preached seventeen times a week, five times on Sunday and twice on each week day. In his younger days he often walked twenty miles in a single day, in order to fill his appointments. Later in life he was able to buy a horse and trap, and the sight of the old white horse and the two-wheeled trap, was a familiar one throughout Wales; with the big, one-eyed preacher talking to the old horse as though it were a human being.

As a preacher, Christmas Evans was idolized by the Welsh people. He was a man of fiery eloquence, and with his full share of the religious fervor for which the Welsh people have always been noted. He was a man of lively imagination. He was not content to tell a Bible story. He dramatized it, describing minutely the appearance of those of whom he spoke. If authentic detail was lacking, his lively Celtic imagination supplied it readily enough. Thus Nicodemus was not merely a man of the Pharisees, a ruler of the Jews, but Evans gave him a flowing white beard, a wealth of snow-white hair and a purple robe; and described him making his way furtively at midnight through wind and driving rain to the upper room at Jerusalem.

One incident is repeated throughout Wales to this day, whenever the name of Christmas Evans is mentioned. He was preaching to a great audience in the open country, and his subject was the Parable of the Prodigal Son. He described the wretched, ragged boy coming home to his waiting father. "There he comes!" he cried, pointing suddenly to a distant hill. Thousands of people turned quickly and gazed at the distant hill, fully expecting to see the boy on his homeward journey.

Christmas Evans preached, as a rule, in the Welsh language. He insisted that the English language lacks fire and fervor, and is fit only for those who would make their sermons quiet and lifeless things. On one occasion, just as he had announced his text in the Welsh language, he saw in the congregation a clergyman who objected to the fiery sort of delivery so dear to the Welsh people. Turning suddenly to English (which he could speak only with a rich brogue), he tried to preach with moderation, in deference to his visiting friend. Even so, his word-picture of the suffering Saviour was so stirring that the moderate preacher cried out, "In Heaven's name, brother, lead me to know Him!"

Christmas Evans lost his fire for a brief time. It was in 1796, when the strange Sandeman movement was sweeping Wales. Two Scottish preachers, Glas and Sandeman, had started a peculiar sect. They favored separation of church and state, complete autonomy for each local congregation and a mild religious communism. Stress was laid on the Lord's Supper, foot-washing was practiced, and its followers were not permitted to take part in games of chance, nor to cast lots. An eminent Welsh preacher, J. Jones, became a convert to the new religion and soon it was being preached in many places in Wales. For a brief time Christmas Evans was influenced by it, but he found to his dismay that his old fervor was growing cold. Weeks of great distress followed, but finally he was overjoyed when he was freed of the hold which the strange new religion had had upon him.

Few men have had such an endless store of Scripture verses at instant command as he. In some of his sermons there are long paragraphs that are made up largely of proof-texts, or portions of proof-texts. He could mingle these with his sermon with rare skill, supporting every sentence at times with one or more portions of a verse of Scripture. The effect upon his congregations was tremendous. He preached sin and grace continually, and had a rare gift of personifying his dogmatics, sometimes going a bit too far for the people of our day; for he would give a lively description of the Law, picturing it as the stern Angel of Justice, thrusting in the face of the trembling sinner a scroll upon which were written the demands of the Law. His description of the Angel of God's Mercy and Grace was equally realistic.

The printed sermons of Christmas Evans are excellent reading today, for their style is that of the twentieth century rather than of the nineteenth. His printed words stir one today with their warmth, almost as much as his spoken words aroused the people who gathered more than a century ago on the hillsides of Wales. Without doubt this is due to the fact that Christmas Evans knew how to preach sin and grace. Weaving in scores of proof-texts from the Holy Scriptures, he pictured sin in all its hideousness, and the grace of God in Christ Jesus in so attractive a manner, that it is not hard to realize what an irresistable impression he must have made on his great outdoor congregations.

Even his homiletical style is striking. His introductions were generally brief, and his main divisions more often than not were but two in number, and expressed in a few definite words. His subdivisions lead one on and on, progressively and with fine logic. In his well-known sermon on Romans 5, 15, he pictures first the terrible corruption of man, and then his restoration through the grace of God in Jesus Christ. In the first half of the sermon he leads one on, step by step, and the account of man's natural depravity becomes more and more terrible. Beginning with the Fall of Man, he reminds his hearers that pure water cannot be expected to flow from such an unclean fountain. With entire verses from Scripture, but more often by weaving in but three or four striking words of a Scripture verse, he proves that man's depravity is universal. His inward corruption shows itself in outward actions. With rapid, fiery words, often brief extracts of Scripture, he mentions cursing, hatred, poisonous words, robbery, drunkenness, gluttony, persecution and various other proofs of man's fallen state.

Then, through several terrible paragraphs he pictures the wrath of God that awaits the sinner. Reaching a climax, he cries out:

"Behold the wretched fallen creature! The pestilence pursues him. The leprosy cleaves to him. Consumption is wasting him. Inflamation is devouring his vitals. Burning fever has seized upon the very springs of life. The destroying angel has overtaken the sinner in his sins. The hand of God is upon him. The fires of wrath are kindling about him, drying up every well of comfort, and scorching all his hopes to ashes. Conscience is chastizing him with scorpions. See how he writhes! Hear how he shrieks for help! Mark what agony and terror are in his soul, and on his brow! Death stares him in the face, and shakes at him his iron spear. He trembles, he turns pale, as a culprit at the bar, as a convict on the scaffold. He is condemned already. Conscience has pronounced the sentence. Anguish has taken hold upon him. Terrors gather in battle array about him. He looks back, and the storms of Sinai pursue him; forward, and hell is moved to meet him; above, and the heavens are on fire; beneath, and the world is burning. He listens, and the judgment trump is calling; again, and the brazen chariots of vengeance are thundering from afar; yet again, the sentence penetrates his soul with anguish unspeakable, — 'Depart from me, ye cursed, into everlasting fire, prepared for the devil and his angels!' " It is not hard to realize the terror that swept through his great congregations as they listened to such words.

Then, in the second half of his sermon, his lively imagination pictured a vast graveyard surrounded by a lofty wall. Within it were all the children of men, suffering from the frightful disease of sin. Open graves yawned, ready to swallow them. Then came the Angel of God's Mercy, weeping over the awful scene, and seeking to relieve the dying children of men. However, the Angel of Justice barred the gate, and would not permit the Angel of Mercy to enter. He declared that mankind had broken the Law, and the wages of sin is death. Then came God's own Son, and offered to take upon Himself the guilt of sinful mankind, and pay fully the penalty for the evil deeds of a fallen race. In vivid language he pictures the Lamb of God ascending the hill called Calvary and cancelling the awful debt by means of His death upon the cross. This He did freely, out of the abundance of His grace; and He sent forth throughout all the world the triumphant message of victory, "By grace are ye saved, through faith; and that not of yourselves; it is the gift of God; not of works, lest any man should boast."

In eloquent language Christmas Evans pictured the glories of that grace which "hath abounded unto many," crying out to his hearers to cast away their weapons of rebellion, and throw themselves at the Saviour's feet, and He will look upon them as though they had never sinned, and give them the Holy Spirit to apply the work of Redemption to them. It is a stirring sermon, and except for the fact that the active obedience of our Lord was given but little notice, it may be regarded as a most effective sermon. His word-picture of the Angel of Justice and the Angel of Mercy, while dramatic, will be questioned by those who are not ready to accept St. Anselm's teaching that the prompting cause of man's salvation is to be found in the wrath of God, rather than in His love. This theory would have us believe that the Lord God, since He is just, will not permit His Law to be violated. His offended justice must in some manner be satisfied, for sin is a debt, and brings guilt. Somebody must suffer for this guilt. Thus it was, according to Anselm, that the Lord Jesus Christ became man's Substitute, in order that justice might be satisfied. Evangelical preaching of today, while admitting God's justice, nevertheless would find the basic cause of man's redemption in the grace of God and merit of our Saviour Jesus Christ. His merit includes both His perfect obedience to the Law (for the Law demands perfection), as well as His suffering, death and resurrection.

In His keeping of the Law He became our Substitute in respect to the Law; and God the Father accepted this obedience as though it were ours. Since the wages of sin is death, our Lord Jesus became our Substitute in regard to the penalty of the Law as well; and God the Father accepted this as though we had paid the penalty. Thus would evangelical preaching of today lay stress upon the grace of God and the merit of our Saviour, rather than to give outraged justice so important a part in the plan of Salvation.

Few men have preached a flawless way of Salvation. Christmas Evans did not always distinguish clearly between the uses of the Law, nor did he always seem entirely clear in regard to the importance of our Saviour's perfect obedience to it. It was precisely this perfect obedience that made His work complete, so that nothing remains for man to do but to make use of His God-given faith. Any holiness of life is a result of salvation, not a cause of it.

It is not enough to say that the stirring eloquence of men such as Christmas Evans, nor their dramatic presentation of their subject, was the cause of their success. These things were valuable external aids; but, after all, such men used their gifts merely as means of presenting the great truths of sin and Salvation. Wherever this is done, the people will be attracted, they will be brought to true repentance, and they will be pointed to the way of eternal Life.

Evans was too honest a man to indulge in bursts of oratory merely to hear people call him the "golden-mouthed Chrysostom of Wales." His matchless eloquence was as much a part of him as were his rugged face and his powerful body. Eloquence is a natural attribute of every true Cambrian, — this and a fervent love for good choral singing. When those qualities depart from a Welshman, he ceases to be a Welshman.

Christmas Evans began life as the child of a very poor family, and at 18, he was still illiterate. However, at 40 he had mastered Hebrew and Greek, and was able to read the Holy Scriptures in the original. He was a grown man before he learned to speak English, and this he did so as to be able to preach in either language. When 65 years of age, he contributed a series of 200 sermons to the press.

His unparalleled description of the graveyard of sin, and the Angels of Mercy and of Justice, and the Saviour's rescue of the sinner, is familiar to everybody old enough to remember the days of the school reader, where this description was printed under the title: "A Specimen of Welsh Eloquence." It exists in slightly different forms, for Evans used it in more than one sermon.

A good collection of the sermons of Christmas Evans, in English, was published by Joseph Cross (Philadelphia, 1859). This volume is prized by public libraries and by rare book dealers, and is kept in locked cases. It is well worth the price asked for it, because of the attractive manner in which Mr. Evans is able to present familiar truths. Among the biographies of Christmas Evans are: David Phillips, *Memoirs of the Life, Labors and Extensive Usefulness of Christmas Evans* (1843); J. Davis, *Memoirs of Christmas Evans* (1840); E. P. Hood, *Christmas Evans, the Preacher of Wild Wales* (1883); and biographies by D. R. Stephens (1847) and by D. M. Evans (1863).

Ebenezer Morris (1769-1825)

Ebenezer Morris, one of the great Calvinistic Methodist preachers, was a son of the Rev. David Morris (1744-1791). He was born at Henbant, Lledrod, Cardiganshire. He received his education at a grammar school in Troed-yr-aur, and at the age of 17 he taught a day school at Trecastle, Breconshire. In 1788 he began to preach. So quickly did he attain fame that in 1790, when but 21 years of age, there were some who considered him one of the great pulpit orators of Wales. He was ordained in 1791, and became assistant to his father at Twrgwyn. His father died the same year, and Ebenezer Morris became his successor, serving until his death in 1825.

Samuel Breese (1772-1812)

Samuel Breese was born in Llandinam, Montgomeryshire, Wales, in the year 1772. In his early years he was a school master. In 1795, when 23 years of age, he began to preach. In time he became "one of the most popular and powerful preachers of the day." He was noted for his vivid

powers of description. In this respect he might be compared
to Christmas Evans, for Samuel Breese had the gift of
making his Bible characters live and act in a most realistic
manner. He lived in a time when there was a shortage of
preachers, and thus it was necessary for him to do much
traveling. He was equally versatile in Welsh and English.
In 1803 he went to Aberystwyth, where he was associated
with John James, a celebrated preacher of the day. Later
he was associated with Newcastle Emlyn. Breese was a
Baptist preacher. He died in 1812 at the age of forty.

John Elias (1774-1841)

Of all the great preachers of Wales, few can excel John
Elias. He deserves a place second only to such men as
Christmas Evans and Daniel Rowland. John Elias was born
in 1774 in the parish of Abererch, near Pwllheli, Carnarvonshire. At the age of 16 he heard a sermon by Daniel Rowland, at that time a man of 77. Rowland died shortly afterward, not aware of the lasting impression that he had made
upon a youth who was to become one of the greatest
preachers of the century. Having become a Calvinistic
Methodist, John Elias began to preach at the age of 20,
itinerating throughout Carnarvonshire, preaching in his
native language. By diligent study under the guidance of
the Rev. Evan Richardson, of Carnarvon, he became proficient in English, Hebrew and Greek.

Mr. Elias was ordained in 1811, after having served for
some years as a lay preacher. In 1823 he was one of the men
chosen to draw up the articles of faith of his denomination.
In addition to his itinerating, he served congregations at
Llanfechell and at Llangefni, Anglesey.

"He had a strong, tall body," says the Rev. David Davies,
"and a noble and commanding appearance. His face and
eyes beamed with an unearthly earnestness and solemnity,
and he had a strong voice, which was fully at his command.
Thousands at a distance could hear his words distinctly. He
gained attention at once, then riveted it, and roused it into
enthusiasm by degrees. He worked one theme after another
into a series of climaxes, each one enhancing the interest of
the hearer up to the last climax, which generally and fully

captivated every heart in his audience. Every attitude, every look and every cadence were natural as life. People felt the electric effect of his earnest heart to such a degree that they forgot his oratorical power. There was a kind of mesmerism in his oratory which put his audience *en rapport* with him. It seemed as if some invisible, subtle spirit, which no one could define or explain, went forth with his words, that made them to possess a peculiar charm and power, which they had not when uttered by ordinary preachers. I heard him preach once at Bala Association from the words: 'Shall the prey be taken from the mighty?' etc. He looked with scrutinizing gaze right into the heart of the vast congregation and asked if there was anyone present who could answer the question. The vast throng stood breathless. Then he turned to his brethren in the ministry who sat around him, and asked if one of them could give an emphatic reply to the audience — their lives dependend upon the answer. There followed a profound silence. Then, reaching out his hand and pointing with his finger toward the heavens, he said, 'Oh, Heaven, what hast thou to say to us — hast thou no hope? No one here on earth can answer the question. Gabriel, thou mighty archangel and messenger of the Most High, thou who seest Him face to face and dwellest in the ineffable brightness of His presence. Canst thou give a reply to the anxious throng?' The silence during these pauses was almost unbearable. At length the preacher exclaimed, "There is only One more that we can ask; we will pass by Gabriel and go to Gabriel's God, and say, 'O Lord, Who art our only hope, wilt Thou in mercy answer Thine own question?' 'Shall the prey be taken from the mighty, or the lawful captive delivered?' The preacher paused, looking into the heavens; then, as if catching the Divine answer from the skies exclaimed with the full compass of his voice — a voice like that of an archangel — 'Even the captives of the mighty shall be taken away, and the prey of the terrible shall be delivered: for I will contend with him that contendeth with thee, and I will save thy children.' The vast multitude who had all but fainted in the fearful suspense that he created, now broke forth into torrents of praise, so that Elias was silenced. He sat down to let the people rejoice over their escape, like the Israelites of old on the banks of the Red Sea." [18]

On one occasion John Elias went to Rhuddlan. It was just before the harvest, and although the day was Sunday, there were many booths in the market square, and crowds of people were buying scythes and sickles. Like George Whitefield, who often preached at fairs and carnivals, John Elias ascended several steps and began his outdoor service with a prayer. This attracted the attention of the people, and a great crowd gathered about him. Then he began to preach, reminding the people that Sunday should find them in their churches and chapels, rather than engaged in buying and selling. At first a hush fell upon the crowd, and as Elias rose from climax to climax, first one and then another was filled with a strange sense of impending danger. Scythes and sickles were hidden, and the musicians in one of the booths became silent. More than one was seen to fling away the sickle that he had bought. It is said that this one sermon ended the Sunday harvest fair for almost 80 years.

On another occasion John Elias was asked to preach in Anglesea at a convention of the Bible Society. On the platform sat the Marquis of Anglesea, one of the heroes of Waterloo. In the course of his sermon, John Elias mentioned the battle of Waterloo, declaring that even as he spoke, a critical battle was being fought in Wales between the legions of Jesus Christ and the legions of Belial. "I think I can hear the Lord saying of the Marquis of Anglesea, 'I want him to lead an army that shall carry the Word of Life to every country, and tongue, and people, and nation over the face of the earth.' What see we now? The enemy is bound, but the Word of God is not bound." The Marquis, who was not sufficiently acquainted with the Welsh language to understand all that had been said, leaned over to a friend and asked what had caused the tenseness that was so apparent throughout the congregation. Upon learning the reason for it, the old soldier, who had not flinched before Napoleon's armies, wept openly before all the people.

---

[18]. David Davies, *Echoes from the Welsh Hills* (London, 1883), pp. 341-342.

The Rt. Hon. David Lloyd George, who lived at Bryn-
awelon, Criccieth, a few miles from the birthplace of John
Elias, was often asked by his friends to describe the famous
sermon on the Feast of Belshazzar. "This was more than a
sermon, it was a theatrical performance, and the stage had
to be set for it. John Elias, visiting the chapel before the
service, directed that the candles should be so arranged that
his outstretched hand, while preaching, should cast a shadow
on the whitewashed wall of the chapel. 'Place that one
there,' L. G. would depict him as saying to the verger. 'And
this one here — no, a little farther back.' The arrangements
were completed with the greatest care, and then the
preacher would embark upon his famous sermon — the
Writing on the Wall — in relation to the sins of the present
generation. L. G. would describe the terror of the congregation when, at the psychological moment, the awful message
was actually written on the wall. And no matter how often
the sermon was repeated, and it was repeated often, and by
request, John Elias was able to produce the same effect
upon his audience." [19]

It is an easy matter to dismiss such preaching lightly
and to call it sensationalism, but the fact must not be overlooked that there is a difference between the Celt and the
Saxon. The Welshman, the Scottish Highlander, the Islander
and the Cornishman are emotional, and their preaching is
inclined to be dramatic. To such people the preaching of
the Englishman and the German seem cold and intellectual.
Especially distasteful to them is the Englishman's habit of
reading a sermon from a manuscript. On this subject John
Elias once declared: "In order to reach the hearts of the
people a sermon must have warmth. There must be spiritual
fire in it, and a paper manuscript is a poor thing in which
to carry fire." When H. P. Hughes, the famous Welsh pulpit
orator who stirred London for 15 years, was criticized by a
man whose liberal religious views were little short of
atheism, Hughes declined to engage in a public debate.
"Instead of that," said Price Hughes, "I am willing to bring
to the platform of St. James Hall, Piccadilly, one hundred

---

[19]. Frances, Countess of Dwifor, in *The British Weekly*, May 26, 1949,
p. 7.

men whose lives have been completely transformed by the Word of God as I preach it, if you are willing to bring in the same number of men who have been brought to repentance and faith by your kind of teaching."

It is said that an English visitor once suggested to John Elias that the excellent sermons that he had heard in Wales might be still more effective if there were less dramatic action. "You described the stoning of Stephen so realistically that I found it difficult to keep my seat. I felt that I was an actual spectator, and I felt as though I should cry out in protest. Such things, if you will pardon me, mar a sermon that is excellent in all other respects." Without a word of direct reply John Elias led his friend to the top of a nearby hill and called his attention to the chapels that could be seen throughout the valley. "There are still old people who can remember when all those chapels were empty on Sunday, and their doors creaked on rusty hinges. The people of Wales spent their Sundays at drinking in the taverns, cock-fighting, hunting, fishing, buying and selling. Today every chapel as far as your eye can see, whether it be Methodist, Baptist, Independent or Anglican, is filled to overflowing, not only on Sunday, but often on weekday nights as well. Our Association preaching festivals attract thousands who stand from early morn, while the dew is yet wet on the grass, until the moon comes up over Snowdon. Today, when the farmers return to their homes on market day, instead of the obscene, drunken songs of a generation ago, they walk along in a company making the eternal hills echo with the hymns of Zion."

The sermons of John Elias contained much more than dramatic description of Bible narratives. "He was a man of very acute, as well as vigorous and sublime genius," says one of his biographers. "His strong intellect and solid judgment were clearly developed in his compositions, speeches and sermons. Perhaps no mathematician could arrange his ideas better, and no logician could draw more correct and proper inferences from them, and no orator could bring them to bear on the people in a more commanding and influential manner, by the instrumentality of voice, manner and eloquence. . . . His discourses possessed amazing depth, solidity and power."

"In his day he was the greatest pulpit orator in Wales. There were many other great preachers — equal to him, perhaps, in some respects — but Elias took the palm as an orator: he was the Demosthenes of the Principality." In theology John Elias was a conservative Calvinist, and an opponent of Arianism.

John Evans (1779-1847)

John Evans, a celebrated Calvinistic Methodist clergyman, was born in 1779 at Cwmgwen, Pencader, Carmarthenshire. With the help of his devout parents he was able to read the Bible when four years of age. Hoping that he might become an Independent (Congregational) pastor, his parents sent him to good schools, where he studied Latin, Greek and Hebrew at an early age. Later he attended a Presbyterian college. When 14 years of age he heard David Jones, of Llangan, an Episcopal clergyman who leaned strongly toward Methodism. The preaching of David Jones made a lasting impression upon the boy, and two years later he became a Calvinistic Methodist.

In 1808 he was ordained deacon at Llandaff, for at that time many men held Methodistic views and yet had not severed their connection with the Established Church. He served several curacies, and attracted attention because of his unusual gifts as a preacher. Not satisfied with weekly sermons, he began to preach outdoors whenever the opportunity arose, and thus brought upon himself the admonition of his spiritual superiors, who regarded his activities as irregularities. When Calvinistic Methodism became a clearly defined denomination he remained with that group. He became known in Wales as John Evans, Llwynffortun, in order to distinguish him from other men who bore the name John Evans. He is described as "a man of princely presence, his figure tall and commanding, his features regular and well-defined, his eyes large and lustrous, and his voice unusually rich in the melodies of the minor key. His temperament was intensely melancholy, and his face and voice were in perfect harmony with his habitual pensiveness."

Whenever a prominent clergyman died, whether an Anglican, a Calvinistic Methodist, a Baptist or an Independent, John Evans mentioned the fact in his sermon, predicting that before the year was ended, he himself might be wrapped in his winding sheet. Evans died at the age of 68, of melancholia.

Although John Evans's sermons were of a sombre tone, yet he was a preacher who never failed to attract large congregations, and whose words were remembered and quoted long after his death. Like many other Welshmen, he was able to use everyday incidents with surprising effect. In one of his sermons he describes a field of wheat encountering the winds of a bleak Welsh winter, the nipping frosts, the howling gales and the deluging rains. Will it ever survive and be fit for the sickle of the reaper? Yes, "for did I not hear the earth, the sun and the clouds enter into a solemn league and covenant that they would take charge of it until it was fit for the reaper? 'I will nestle it in my bosom,' said the earth; 'and I,' said the mist-cloud, 'will spread a counterpane of white driven snow over it to keep it warm'; 'and I,' said the sun, 'when the balmy spring shall set in, will visit it with my fructifying beams,' 'and we,' said the clouds, 'will water it with showers'; and thus, through the joint agencies of earth, sun and shower, that field of wheat, which has only now just sprouted, shall become a waving, golden-eared crop, gladdening the heart of the hard-working husbandman." [20] Then, by means of a number of Scripture verses, Mr. Evans assured his hearers that the true Christian will be made ripe for Heaven, "and shall be gathered in amidst the triumphant shoutings of gladsome reapers." The entire quotation, more than a page of print in length, was a favorite with the old people of Wales, many of whom were able to quote it accurately from memory whenever their conversation turned to the great preachers of early days. A short account of the life of John Evans, Llwynffortun, was written by T. J. Williams, and Dr. Lewis Edwards, who devoted 16 pages to Evans in his *Traethodau*

---

[20]. David Davies, *Echoes from the Welsh Hills* (London, 1883), p. 266.
   Ibid., p. 349.

Llenyddol, considers him one of the greatest of the Welsh preachers of his time.

William Williams of Wern (1781-1840)

Of the eighteen Welshmen named William Williams who have attained fame, one of the most illustrious was Williams of Wern, as he is commonly known. He was born in 1781 at Llanfachreth, near Dolgelly. His father, although a man of upright character, was not an active chapel-goer. His mother was a devout Calvinistic Methodist. Before he was 14, William Williams joined the Independent church at Trawsfynydd, Merionethshire. He began to preach at the age of 19. He attended school at Newtown, and the Congregational grammar school at Wrexham. He was ordained in 1808, at the age of 27, and became pastor of the Independent chapel at Wern, four miles from Wrexham. With the exception of two years spent at Great Crosshall Street chapel in Liverpool, his 31 years of active service were spent in Wern.

His biographer, James Rhys Jones, says of him: "Never, perhaps, since the days of the Great Teacher, did any preacher lay the objects of nature and the pursuits of men under greater contributions for the exposition and enforcement of religious truth. All things seemed to whisper something to him which had never been disclosed before, and to point out for his occupation new and highly advantageous points of observation. . . . Williams seemed to look at everything from unfrequented points that commanded fresher and broader views. . . . His mind was of too masculine a cast, and too solemnly pledged to a usefulness in all pulpit engagements to admit of his dallying with the mere ornaments of oratory. His use of comparisons was sufficient to convince anyone that he attached no value whatever to them, except so far as they subserved the explanation or application of truth. Unlike certain showy and weak-minded preachers, who are so enamored of tinsel and glare that they often employ even religious truths only as pegs on which to suspend a fine simile, he, on the contrary, with almost instinctive severity of taste, allotted to figures only a subordinate department in expounding the great verities of the Bible." [21]

William Williams had a voice that was not especially strong, but it was good. He adhered honestly to the truths of God's Word, as he understood them, and preached salvation through the cross of Calvary.

Thomas Rhys Davies (1790-1859)

One of the colorful pulpit orators of Wales was Thomas Rhys Davies. He was born in Cilgerran, Pembrokeshire, and became a Baptist in his youth. He began preaching in 1812, and was ordained two years later. In 1818 difficulties arose in regard to the title of a chapel, and Mr. Davies preached for seven years in Wesleyan chapels, although he made it clear that he still clung to his Baptist views. In 1825 the matter of the chapel seems to have been settled, and Mr. Davies returned to the Baptist Church. After preaching for a time in Liverpool, he returned to Wales and preached at Cilgerran in Pembrokeshire, and at Conway in Carnarvonshire. He itinerated widely, and during the 47 years of his active ministry he preached 13,145 sermons: an average of five a week.

Mr. Davies was a man of striking appearance. He was a tall, broad shouldered man with all the bearing of a chieftain. Since he was subject to colds, he wore a velvet skull cap in the pulpit, hence his nickname, "Black Cap." He was an unusually popular preacher. His sermons were expressed in simple language, often colloquial, and he was famed for his shrewd sayings and for his illustrations drawn from the daily incidents of the Welsh village and countryside. Like Whitefield, he preached the same sermon again and again, and congregations often asked him to return and preach once more a sermon that had impressed them. One of these was based upon the text, "And upon this Rock I will build My church." In the course of the sermon he asked various notable people the question, "Who is this Rock?" Among others, he asked the Pope, who answered him, "St. Peter." Describing the fine paintings of Simon Peter that hang in

---

[21]. J. R. K. Jones, *Memoir of William Williams of Wern* (London, 1846).

the Vatican, and the great church of St. Peter's in Rome, the preacher seemed to hesitate for a moment. Finally he cried, "Who shall decide the matter between us? Shall St. Paul? I am willing. . . . 'Paul, what hast thou to say about the Rock upon which the church is to be built?' 'Other foundation can no man lay than that is laid, which is Jesus Christ'." Then, with a triumphant burst of oratory, Mr. Davies declared that the Lord Jesus Christ had won the day.

In his old age he continued to accept invitations to preach in distant parts of Wales. He declared that he had but two ambitions insofar as earthly things are concerned: to be able to bear witness to Jesus Christ to the end, and then to be buried in the same grave as Christmas Evans, whom he considered the greatest preacher since the days of the Apostles. While on a preaching tour in South Wales, he preached his last sermon in Morriston, near Swansea. On the following Sunday he died, and in respect to his wishes he was buried in Christmas Evans's grave.

John Jones (1796-1857)

One of the great preachers of the eighteenth century is a man about whom the world knows too little. His name was John Jones, and he is generally called John Jones of Talsarn. He lived and died in Wales, his biography exists in the Welsh language for any who can read it, and his printed sermons and hymns are in Welsh. John Jones was born in Tanycastell, Dolwyddelan, Carnarvonshire, the eldest of nine children. His father died when John was a mere lad, and he had to seek employment first on a farm and later in a stone quarry. He became acquainted with the Rev. Evan Evans (Glan Ceirionydd), who encouraged him in his desire to study, and who supplied him with the necessary books.

In 1820, after much diligent study, directed by clergymen with whom he became acquainted, Mr. Jones began to preach at the age of 24. After serving as a lay preacher for nine years, and continuing his studies meanwhile, John Jones was ordained, and in time he became one of the foremost preachers of Wales. He was a man of enormous physical strength, gifted with a superior mind, a lively imagination, and a mastery of the Welsh language that few men could excel. Eloquent to a degree, he is often compared to Thomas Chalmers in vigor of mind, command of forceful language, creative imagery and originality of expression. His sermons are considered models of good taste. Prime Minister Lloyd George, who had made almost a lifelong study of the great preachers of Wales, and who had collected material for a great work on Welsh preaching which was not yet ready for the publisher when he died, is said to have considered John Jones of Talsarn almost equal to such men as Christmas Evans, John Elias and William Williams of Wern. Lloyd George was able to speak at length of John Jones, and to quote paragraphs from his sermons.

Like the other great preachers of Wales, John Jones of Talsarn was dramatic, and like Evans, Williams and Elias, he studied in advance the exact effects that he intended to produce. If he preached on the Pharisee and the Publican, he visited the church before the congregation had assembled, selected a spot where the Pharisee was to stand, and another spot, far in the rear of the congregation, where the publican was to stand. In delivering the sermon, he was able to describe the Pharisee so dramatically that every one of his hearers looked intently at the spot that the preacher indicated. When he described the publican, this was done so realistically that the congregation would turn in their seats to a man, and gaze at the far end of the church.

With the great Welsh preachers these things were not mere showmanship. They did it with tremendous earnestness, and their one motive was to impress as vividly as possible upon their hearers the incidents mentioned in the text. Then, in ringing tones, they would drive home in emphatic language the spiritual lesson of the incident. There were old men in Wales a few years ago who were able to quote long passages from the sermons of John Jones of Talsarn and Edward Matthews of Ewenni, and to accompany it with all the dramatic action of these great preachers themselves. Jones of Talsarn was one of the men that they seldom failed to quote, and whose manner in the pulpit they would describe with great detail.

The best biography of John Jones of Talsarn was written by Dr. Owen Thomas, himself an eminent pulpit orator, and is entitled *Cofiant y Parch. John Jones, Talsarn.* It was published in Wrexham in 1874. After his death a volume of his sermons, *Pregethau y Parch. John Jones,* was published in Denbigh. In the collection are 53 sermons that are declared by Welsh people to be of a high degree of excellence. John Jones also composed hymn and Psalm tunes, and in the hymnal edited by Morris Davies are some 40 melodies attributed to Jones of Talsarn.

Henry Rees (1798-1869)

Henry Rees, a book-binder, who became one of the famous Calvinistic Methodist preachers of the nineteenth century, was born in 1798 at Llansannan, Denbighshire. He began to preach in 1818, supporting himself by daily labor. In 1821 he went to Shrewsbury, where he worked for a book-binder and preached on Sunday. In 1827 he was ordained in Bala. He was a diligent student, and found time to read the works of the old Puritan writers, as well as the theological and homiletical writings of various men of evangelical views. In 1836 he went to Liverpool, where he immediately became recognized as a pulpit orator of superior gifts. He was made superintendent of the Calvinistic Methodist congregations of that district, and served in this capacity for almost 33 years. In addition to his work in Liverpool, he preached throughout Wales, and was often one of the principal speakers at Association meetings. "He quickly attained great popularity as a preacher, and, for ability to bring his hearers face to face with the truth in all its native power, he stood pre-eminent. Though great in the pulpit, he was greater still at the Lord's Table; some of his communion services are even more memorable for their chastening, holy influence than his sermons. There were others who equalled, and even surpassed him in their eloquence of power and delivery, but as a sermon-maker he was, undoubtedly chief among the mighties." [22] These searching Communion addresses were long remembered by the Welsh people, and the Rev. David Davies, in whose writ-

---

[22]. T. R. Roberts, *Eminent Welshmen* (Cardiff, 1908), p. 446.

ings are preserved the testimonies of a wholly unique generation of men who memorized some of the more striking sermons of the great Welsh preachers, tells of a Bible class of forty men, varying in age from 20 to 70 years. It was taught by the shoemaker of the village, and among its members were two blacksmiths, the village tailor, the schoolmaster and other men of various callings. These men brought their Bibles to the class, and they owned and studied the commentaries of Dr. Lewis and of Robert Ellis, Welsh translations of Albert Barnes's *Notes* and of Matthew Henry's *Commentary*. In their discussion of the lesson, these men were in the habit of quoting Christmas Evans, Williams of Wern, John Elias, Henry Rees and others. The shoemaker told of having heard a sermon by Henry Rees, in which he used the text, "Beginning at Jerusalem." He described the surprise of Simon Peter:

" 'Jerusalem!' he exclaimed, 'Good Master, the chief priests and scribes, and those who crucified Thee are there!' 'Yes,' replied the Saviour, 'go and tell *them* that God so loved the world that He gave His only begotten Son, that whosoever believeth in Him should not perish, but have everlasting life.' 'But,' said Peter, 'Pilate is there. He gave Thee over to be crucified when he knew that Thou wast innocent.' 'Yes,' answered the gracious Lord in the tenderest of tones, 'Go to *Pilate*; tell *him* there is enough virtue in My blood to wash away his sins, and tell him further that if he refuses to believe this that he will pierce My heart with a thousand wounds worse than any I received upon the Cross'." [23]

The biography of Henry Rees was written by Dr. Owen Thomas,[24] and shorter accounts of his life are to be found in several biographical works, such as those of T. R. Roberts and of T. Mardy Rees.

William Rees (1802-1883)

William Rees, one of Wales's greatest bards, as well as one of her famous preachers, was born in 1802 on a farm near Llansannan, Denbighshire, North Wales. His early

---

[23]. David Davies, *Echoes from the Welsh Hills* (London, 1883), p. 218.
[24]. Owen Thomas, *Cofiant Henry Rees*, (1870).

educational opportunities were limited, for as a lad it was necessary for him to secure work as a shepherd. Like the famous Scottish preacher, John Brown of Haddington, William Rees bought books and studied as he watched his sheep. At the age of 24 he took part in a Welsh eisteddfod, and won distinction for a poem that he had written. Two years later he appeared at another eisteddfod, and added further to his honors.

Much as he liked to write poetry, William Rees was determined to become a preacher. He was 27 years old when he preached his first sermon. A year later, in 1830, he was licensed to preach. In 1831 he became pastor of a Welsh Congregational church at Mostyn, Flintshire, and in 1837 he was called to Swan Street Church in Denbigh. In 1843, the congregation worshiping in Great Cross Hall, Liverpool, called him as their pastor, and here he won a wide reputation as a preacher of superlative talents. In 1853 he was called to Salem Chapel, Liverpool, and so great was his success that in 1867 a large, imposing new church was built in Grove street, where he served for eight years, until he retired at the age of 73.

William Rees (sometimes spelled Rhys), is well known for his biography of William Williams of Wern, but his greatest distinction came because of his poems. One of these *Emmanuel,* is often cited as the greatest literary product of the Welsh nation. It is an epic poem filling two volumes, and is considerably longer than Milton's *Paradise Lost.* William Rees wrote a number of Welsh hymns, only one of which became famous, namely his *Dyma gariad,* greatly beloved by the Welsh people.

In addition to his great reputation as an eloquent, evangelical preacher, and as a poet, William Rees won distinction as a newspaper man. With all his other activities, he found time to found and edit a Welsh newspaper, and to act as one of its chief contributors. He has often been mentioned as one of the most famous Welshmen of the nineteenth century. As a bard in the national eisteddfod, he stands almost without an equal. He was a man of many talents, and able to do a number of things extremely well, and without neglecting any of his duties.

As a preacher it has been said that "his self-possession, intonation, attitude, fluency, eloquence and elevated sentiments render him one of the most renowned orators of the day." [25] He was a man of imposing appearance, despite the fact that, like Christmas Evans, he had lost his right eye. This was due to small-pox, when he was but three years of age. He had a fine speaking voice, and wherever he went, people came from afar to hear him preach.

William Roberts (1809-1887)

William Roberts, of the Calvinistic Methodist church, was well known both in Wales and America. He was born in Llanerchymedd, Angelsey. As a boy he was deeply impressed with I John 1, 8-9, while reading that Epistle aloud with his mother. The eighth and ninth verses gave him a realization of sin, and of the fact of forgiveness. He attended the schools of his village, and at 16 he studied the classics and English with the Rev. W. Griffith, of Holyhead. At 20 he entered the Presbyterian Collegiate Institute in Dublin.

Two years later, while still a student, he founded a Calvinistic Methodist congregation in Dublin. In 1831 he was licensed to preach. In 1835 he founded an academy in Holyhead, for young men with the ministry in view. William Roberts preached throughout Angelsey for 18 years. From 1849 to 1855 he was pastor of an English congregation at Runcorn, which belonged to the Countess of Huntington's Connexion.

About the year 1860 he came to America and became pastor of a Welsh Calvinistic church in New York City. In 1869 he became pastor of a congregation in Scranton, and in 1875 of another congregation in Utica.

William Roberts must have been a preacher of extraordinary ability, for his name is mentioned frequently together with those of William Charles and John Elias. He was able to present the plan of salvation simply, practically and logically, as may be seen by reading his sermon "Christ the Mighty Saviour," [26] said to be one of his most character-

---

[25]. H. C. Fish, *Pulpit Eloquence of the Nineteenth Century*, p. 795.
[26]. *Ibid.*, p. 786ff.

istic discourses. He discusses man's lost condition first. Man is ruined by sin, he is powerless to save himself, he does not realize his lost condition. Then he discusses Christ's power to save. He has the personal and official qualifications to save man. He saves him from the curse of the Law, from the dominion of sin, from the power and malice of Satan, from death, the grave and Judgment. He saves all ranks and stations of men, He saves sinners of every character, He saves in all circumstances and emergencies.

A simpler and more logical treatment of this subject could hardly be found, and he presents it in language that is marvellously simple and practical. Toward the end of the sermon he mentions the names and occupations of a score or more Bible characters in a manner that is convincing beyond all question. Like Alexander Maclaren of Manchester, William Roberts had the gift of presenting the fruits of painstaking preparation in language of fascinating simplicity.

Owen Thomas (1812-1891)

Owen Thomas was born in 1812 at Holyhead, Anglesey, Wales. After an education in the elementary schools of his native village, he was apprenticed at the age of 13 to a stone cutter. At the age of 21 he felt the urge to preach, but it was not until he was 29 years of age that he was able to attend the University of Edinburgh. He was ordained in 1844, at the age of 32. He was pastor of congregations at Penmount, Pwllheli, as well as at Newton, London and Liverpool. He was a Calvinistic Methodist.

Owen Thomas was possessed of a remarkable voice. W. W. Davies says that on one occasion when he preached at Bangor, he could be heard distinctly in Anglesey, across the Menai Straits.

"He was the last of the Welsh pulpit celebrities of the 19th century. He remained for some years as the only living typical preacher of a generation of preachers who have passed away. His eloquence and power at times were simply marvellous." [27]

---

[27]. T. R. Roberts, *Eminent Welshmen* (Cardiff, 1908).

We have selected a few examples out of many that might have been cited. W. W. Davies says that Wales has contributed comparatively little in poetry, painting and sculpture, "but between 1780 and 1880 it produced successive generations of preachers, who brought pulpit oratory to a point that has never been surpassed, even if it has been equaled, by any other nation before or since." [28]

"Even today," says the same observer, "when oratory has declined, and when there are so many competing attractions, there is nothing that the Welshman loves so well as a Preaching Meeting. Five thousand people will still come together eagerly to the village green on one of these great occasions. At six o'clock in the morning two sermons, averaging each an hour in length, will be delivered. These will be followed, at ten o'clock, by two others of the same length. In the afternoon two more will be delivered. The day will close with yet another two, or sometimes three, such sermons; and the multitude will disperse over hill and moor to their scattered homes, discussing the great feats of oratory to which they have listened, quoting and conferring with discrimination, and singing, for the twentieth time that day, some favourite hymn." [29]

The golden age of the Welsh pulpit began with Griffith Jones and ended with Herber Evans. It found a race of people largely unchurched and burdened with inherited superstition, and out of them it made a race famed throughout Christendom for its evangelical fervor. It found a slumbering church which few took the trouble to attend, and in its place it left churches and chapels everywhere. It found a group of worldly, slothful clergy, and in place of them it produced men who not only stirred all Wales with their mighty preaching, but it gave to other countries many of their most noted preachers. It found a race of people meagerly educated, and it gave them one of the finest educational systems in the world.

---

[28]. W. W. Davies, *Wales* (London, 1925), p. 214.
[29]. *Ibid.,* pp. 214-15.

J. R. Kilsby Jones (1813-1889)

J. R. Kilsby Jones, a noted Congregational preacher and writer, was born in 1813 at Penylan, Llandovery, Carmarthenshire. His father was an Independent clergyman, and the family claimed descent from the ancient Britons who dwelt in the British Isles long before the coming of the Celts, the Romans and the Saxons. J. Rhys Jones, as he was then known, attended Neuaddlwyd and other grammar schools, and the Presbyterian College in Carmarthen. At the time of his ordination in 1840, he was pastor of an Independent congregation at Kilsby, Northants., and he became known among the people of Wales as Kilsby Jones, and in his later writings he often used this name. After serving congregations at Kilsby, Birmingham and Bolton, he returned in 1857 to his native Wales, where his most important work was done, and his lasting fame achieved. He served a congregation at Rhayader, and later he became pastor at Llandrindod, where he spent the remainder of his years.

J. R. Kilsby Jones was a large, powerful man. "His hair bore traces of having been bleached by the heat of life's day, but there was scarcely a sign of his having borne its burden, for he still stood as stalwart and erect as an ancient Briton, from which race he proudly claims descent. His massive, powerful countenance revealed in a humanized form the same rugged reality and volcanic strength as the everlasting hills and hoary mountains among which he was bred. When he spoke his words and thoughts flowed out in torrents, shocking men with the suddenness with which they leaped from point to point, and then charming them with the grandeur of their erratic course." [30]

Kilsby Jones was often among those who preached at the Associations, those remarkable gatherings once held in Wales at which eight or nine clergymen preached in turn to outdoor assemblies that numbered from 5000 to 15,000 or more people. One of his famous sermons was entitled "Away with Him," and he was asked to repeat it again and again. The following selection, made from Mr. Jones's notes

---

[30]. David Davies, *Echo from the Welsh Hills* (London, 1883), p. 329.

(not from the complete sermon), may convey a slight idea of his unusual style:

"Away with Him? Can you do without Him? You may, till you are convinced of sin, till the Law thunders in your ears, till the weight of guilt presses on the conscience. When the heart is faint and the spirit fails can you do without Him? When the hour arrives when man can do nothing for you — what and how then? Away with Him? Let the thirsty man with his lips parched and his tongue cleaving to the roof of his mouth say to the sparkling stream, 'Away with it!' The hungry man to bread, 'Away with it!' The naked to clothing, 'Away with it!' The lost wanderer to the guide, 'Away with him!' The helpless infant to his mother, 'Away with her!' The parched and thirsty earth to the cloud bearing refreshing rain, 'Away with it!' The dead and dreary winter to the reviving spring, 'Away with it!'

"Away with Him? Very well; if you are prepared to brave the consequences. Do not turn cowards; quit you like men; stand your ground without flinching. The Jews invited God's judgments. Suppose He were to take some of you at your word. I see another day. A white throne is set up in the heavens. Ten thousand angels herald the coming of the Judge. The trumpet sends forth a long, loud blast, and earth and sea give up their myriad dead. 'Open unto us, open unto us' is the cry, but the ear, once the quickest to hear, and so quick that the sigh of penitence does not escape it, is now deaf. 'Away with you — depart from Me!' The multitudinous throng begins reluctantly to move. Ah! it is gone forever! Its wail fills the air. My erring brethren, recall the words. It is not too late. God be thanked for that." [31]

Kilsby Jones lectured widely, and on the platform he was famed for his wit, which at times was inclined to sharpness. One of his serious lectures was on John Penry, who was hanged in 1593 because of his religious views. One of J. R. Kilsby Jones's most famous writings, *Characteristics of Welsh Eloquence,* appeared originally in 1862 in *The Homilist.* In colorful language he describes the dramatic preaching of the great Welsh pulpit orators. This essay has

---

[31]. *Ibid.,* pp. 447-8.

been printed and quoted many times. Mr. Jones edited the complete works of William Williams of Pant-y-celyn (Glasgow, 1868); he translated Bunyan's *Pilgrim's Progress* into Welsh (Glasgow, 1869); he published a new edition of the Peter Williams Bible (Glasgow, 1869); a Welsh translation of John Brown's *Biblical Dictionary* (Glasgow, 1869-70); and an English translation of Rhys's *William Williams of Wern* (London, 1846).

Charles J. Vaughan (1816-1897)

While many of the eminent preachers of the later period in Wales were Nonconformists, yet the Episcopalians are to be credited with a number of eminent men. Perhaps the most distinguished of these was Charles J. Vaughan, dean of Llandaff. He was born in Leicester, where his father was vicar of St. Martin's. Taught by his father, he was sent to Rugby at 13, where he had the privilege of attending during the days of the great Dr. Arnold. He went from Rugby to Trinity College, Cambridge, graduating B.A. in 1838 and M.A. in 1841. He was senior classic and chancellor's medalist. In 1845 he received his D.D. degree.

Mr. Vaughan was ordained in 1841 and became vicar of St. Martin's, Leicester. In 1844 he was made headmaster of Harrow, the famous school just out of London. He found a school with but 60 students, but within two years the enrollment had increased to more than 200. Mr. Vaughan sought to make his school second to none in its scholastic standing, and in order to do so he gathered one of the most remarkable groups of masters of the 19th century. In 1859 he was named bishop of Rochester, but unwilling to leave his school, he declined this office. However, a year later, he accepted the appointment as vicar of Doncaster. In 1869 he was made Master of the Temple, where his exceptional preaching attracted favorable notice.

Dr. Vaughan was not to remain an English educator and preacher for many years, although during the first period of his notable career he prepared over 450 men for ordination. In 1879 he was made bishop of Llandaff, Glamorganshire, and he accepted it with the understanding that he could retain a connection with the Temple. His tenure at Llandaff was a notable one. Perhaps his most important work was his part in founding the University College of Cardiff in 1883-1884, of which he became president in 1894.

Both at the Temple and in Llandaff Dr. Vaughan preached the sermons that were to bring him more lasting fame than even his successful work as headmaster at Harrow and president of University College, Cardiff.

"The influence of Dr. Vaughan as a preacher," says a writer in *The Guardian* (1871), "is an unusual, and, in some sense, a remarkable influence. At the Temple Church his preaching seems to have inaugurated a new era in spiritual life; a congregation, perhaps the largest intellectual and educated congregation in England, hangs upon his lips, Sunday after Sunday, in hushed and earnest attention. At Cambridge while from many causes (for some of which the College authorities are responsible), the usual attendance of undergraduates at St. Mary's has greatly diminished, the galleries are always thronged to listen to Dr. Vaughan; nor does the verdict of the older members of the University seem to differ materially from that of the younger men. And yet . . . . we could not place him on the level of Robertson . . . . What is the secret of his great and most valuable influence? Why does he so firmly hold and powerfully direct the thoughts of his hearers? Why is it all but universally considered to be a subject of thankfulness that he should have been placed in that high position which no man in England could better fill?

"Much, no doubt, is due to the known disinterestedness and seriousness of the preacher's character; much to the remarkable vigor and manliness of his tone; something to the great felicity and precision which marks his language. The knowledge, moreover, that he acts and thinks for himself, belonging to no distinctly marked party or school, and apparently caring very little whether he and his teaching are popular or not, is another great influence which gives force to his words and drives each of them home. But the true secret lies deeper than any of these things, and is full of instruction and encouragement. It is, we believe, simply the fact that Dr Vaughan never forgets that he is a preacher of Christ, and is therefore keenly alive to the all-important difference between oratory and preaching. It is obvious to every hearer that he speaks of that which he knows and feels — neither less nor more — and that he speaks it because he believes that it is a message of God, and not the imagination or thought of man. This it is which gives an unaffected solemnity, and a real, though most unobtrusive, authority to his words."

This tribute was written during Dr. Vaughan's earlier years in England. Much the same may be said of his later career in Wales. Some humorist has said that the surest way to diminish the excellency of a great preacher is to make him a bishop or a college president. Such was certainly not true of Dr. Vaughan. The large congregations that filled the cathedral and the university chapel not only admired his unusual preaching, but they profited by it. The British Museum catalogue of books lists some 120 titles under his name, many of them books of sermons, or in some cases single sermons in booklet form. These are not books that are soon forgotten, and sold in the sidewalk bins of secondhand dealers in old books. They are still read and prized by discriminating men.*

Although it is possible that Dr. Vaughan came under the influence of the liberal views of his days regarding the inspiration and canonicity of certain Books of the Bible, yet he held firmly to the facts of original sin and the need of salvation solely through the unmerited grace of God in Jesus Christ, and its application to the sinner through the work of the Holy Ghost. In a sermon on St. Matthew 28, 19, to be found in his *Ten Discourses on Public Worship,* he speaks of Holy Baptism, and does not hesitate to bear witness to the fact of Original Sin. He begins by giving a beautiful word picture of the parents and sponsors standing with an infant child at the baptismal font in a parish church:

"But that little child — what has he to do with sin?" he asks. "It must be a mere dream of the theologian, to

---

* Dr. Wilbur C. Smith, in the *Moody Monthly,* January, 1955, recalls the fact that Dr. B. F. Westcott, the noted commentator and New Testament scholar, read one of Dr. Vaughan's sermons every Sunday afternoon for 30 years.

conceive of that beautiful, that perfect little being, lying there asleep in the arms of its mother, as tainted already with anything that can want, or is capable of, spiritual cleansing.

"We can scarcely blame shortsighted man if he speaks thus. It needs faith, doubtless — and yet I will venture to say, something far short of the Christian faith; only just that foresight of a very near future, which is given to every reflecting person by experience of the past; it needs that we should just be able to imagine that little infant developed into a child of four or five years, into a boy of fourteen or fifteen, into a man of forty or fifty years; and then we shall perceive that even in this new-born babe there dwelt by nature no good thing (Romans 7, 18), nothing, that is, which could be trusted, apart from inward and outward influences not always to be reckoned upon, to grow up into a maturity undefiled and upright; we shall perceive that, left to himself, not good will spring forth from it but evil; in a very short time there will be tempers working there, and dispositions, and desires too, self-willed, self-indulgent, selfish continually, let alone, these will develop into faults, into sins, into vices, into crimes; let alone, that beautiful infancy will become in a few years a hell of passion first, and a hell of misery afterwards; and what man can only deplore in its fulness, God sees already in its spring. There is something, call it what you will — the Church calls it Original Sin — some flaw, some taint, some evil bias, in all that are born into this world of Adam's offspring; some influence, which, let alone, will work itself out not in good but in evil; not in holiness, not in gentleness, not in love to God and love to man, but in the opposite of these things: Christ knows this, and has taught it to His Church: and therefore it is that that little infant, ignorant as yet of evil, innocent as yet of the very power of sinning, is brought hither to be sprinkled with that lustral water which is the symbol and the type and the sacrament of cleansing." [32]
Dr. Vaughan's words are quoted as they stand, even though the reader may observe that the words "innocent as yet of

---

[32]. Charles J. Vaughan, *Ten Discourses on Public Worship* (New York, 1872), pp. 166-168.

the very power of sinning" cannot be reconciled with the inspired Psalmist's "Behold, I was shapen in iniquity, and in sin did my mother conceive me," and the inspired St. Paul's "That which is born of the flesh is flesh, and that which is born of the Spirit is spirit," and "I know that in me (that is, in my flesh) dwelleth no good thing." Then, Holy Baptism is much more than a symbol and a type of cleansing, for St. Paul says, Titus, chapter third: "By the washing of regeneration, and renewing of the Holy Ghost, which He shed on us abundantly through Jesus Christ, our Saviour, that, being justified by His grace, we should be made heirs according to the hope of eternal life."

Of the 120 or more printed works of Dr. Vaughan, mention may be made of the following: *St. Paul's Epistle to the Romans* (1859); *St. Paul's Epistle to the Philippians* (1862); *Lessons of Life and Godliness* (1862); *Lectures on the Revelation of St. John,* 2 vols. (1863); *Words from the Gospels* (1863), which are sermons preached in Doncaster; *Epiphany, Lent and Easter* (1865); *Christ the Light of the World* (1866); *Twelve Discourses Connected with the Liturgy and Worship* (1867); *The Wholesome Words of Christ* (1867); *Sundays in the Temple* (1871); *Foes of Faith* (1873); *Words of Hope* (1874); *Words from the Cross* (1874); *The Two Great Temptations* (1875); *Temple Sermons* (1881); and *The Epistle to the Hebrews* (1890). A 43-page biography of Dr. Vaughan is included in F. D. How's *Six Great Schoolmasters* (London, 1904).

Edward Matthews (1813-1892)

Edward Matthews, Ewenni, as he is called by the Welsh people, was born at St. Athan, near Cowbridge, Glamorganshire, in 1813. He preached his first sermon in 1830, when but 17 years of age, although it was not until 1841 that he was ordained. In 1850 he was invited to preach before the Llangeitho Association. The sermon was one that was long remembered and quoted by the thousands who heard it, and it established the place of Edward Matthews among such famous contemporaries as John Jones of Talsarn, Owen Thomas, E. Herber Evans and Kilsby Jones. He was pastor at Pontypridd from 1849 to 1852. During the ten years that followed he served a church at Ewenni, and so widely was he known throughout Wales that the people called him Edward Matthews, Ewenni, long after he was called to Canton, Cardiff, in 1862, and then to Bonvilston, near Cardiff, in 1875. He was chosen moderator in 1857, and later he distinguished himself because of his successful efforts in raising an endowment fund for Trevecca College. Aware of his exceptional ability, an American university awarded him a doctor's degree, which he declined.

Edward Matthews was a preacher of great originality, and his empathic declaration of evangelical doctrine, as understood by the Calvinistic Methodist Church, never failed to make a lasting impression because of its freshness of treatment. He was an excellent writer as well. One of his ardent admirers was the Rt. Hon. David Lloyd George, who sometimes named him as second only to Christmas Evans, John Elias and William Williams of Wern. Lloyd George, a superb orator in his own right, never grew tired of telling his friends of a sermon by Edward Matthews on the Lost Sheep. With the lively imagination so often found among the Welsh preachers, the sermon was dramatic.

"The speaker, as he told the familiar parable over again, held his congregation, mostly farmers and their families, spellbound as he took them over hill and dale, across torrents and through thickets in search for the missing animal. " 'Is she there?' he called. 'No, she is not there.' 'But she must have come this way: here is wool from her coat on the brambles' (holding up an imaginary strand). And again, 'Is she there?' The search continues, till the congregation themselves seem to be joining in it, and their excitement rises. At last, with a great cry, and with the movement of hoisting the animal on to his shoulders: 'She is found,' he shouts — 'Glory be to God,' shouts the congregation with him." [33] This vivid type of preaching was characteristic of the famous Welsh preachers between the years 1780 and 1880, and it appealed to the lively imagination of the people. The preacher who had something worth saying,

---

[33]. Frances, Countess of Dwifor, in *The British Weekly*, May 26, 1949, p. 7.

and who said it in a dramatic manner, never failed to attract great congregations. A biography, in Welsh, was written by D. G. Jones in 1893; and another account of the life of Edward Matthews, Ewenni, by Dr. J. C. Jones, appeared about the same time.

Evan Herber Evans (1835-1896)

Evan Herber Evans, who is usually known as Herber Evans, was born in 1835 near Newcastle Emlyn, Carmarthenshire. His father, a blacksmith, gave the boy a good general education, hoping that he might decide to become a clergyman. Young Evans worked for a time for a draper, and in 1854 he went to Liverpool where he was employed as a draper's apprentice. He continued his education at Normal College in Swansea, and at Memorial College, Brecon. He preached a sermon at Tabernacle Chapel (Welsh Congregational), and gave evidence of exceptional homiletical gifts.

In 1862 he was ordained as pastor of Libanus, Morriston, not far from Swansea. The valley, once famous for its natural beauty, has become one of the most desolate spots in the British Isles because of copper smelteries which have destroyed every form of vegetation except a small, creeping yellowish plant of the camomile family. In 1865 Mr. Evans became pastor of Salem Congregational Church in Carnarvon, where he remained for over 30 years. In 1891 he became lecturer on homiletics at Bala-Bangor Congregational College, and in 1894 he was made principal of the institution, but continued to serve his congregation.

Herber Evans was a man of attractive appearance and personality. He was one of the most eloquent preachers of his generation, and he had received his full share of the vividness of language for which the Welsh are famous. He was an emphatic believer in the integrity of the Bible, and had little patience with the critics who professed to find scientific and historical inaccuracies in it. He was called upon again and again to preach a certain sermon on the infallibility of God's inspired Word. The Welsh people called it "the sermon of the little lantern." In the course of this sermon he told of an old Welsh preacher who had come a long way to preach to a congregation. It was necessary that he return to his home that night, although his way led down a narrow valley and along an unlighted footpath where a misstep would have meant certain death on the rocks far below. As he was leaving the church, a woman thrust an old lantern into his hand and said, "It is only a little lantern, Mr. Evans, *bach,* and it is very old. My father and my grandfather used it — but it will light you home." The old preacher took the little lantern. Heber Evans described his dangerous journey down the crooked path through the steep *cwm* (valley), and the joy of the old man when he finally reached his home and saw the light in the window. Then, holding the open pulpit Bible high above his head, he would cry out in a ringing voice: " 'Thy Word is a lamp unto my feet, and a light unto my path,' and it may be depended upon to light you home."

In another sermon on the same subject, he described a scientist looking at the sun through a telescope, and then announcing in triumph that he had found small spots on the sun. These proved to be slight flecks in his telescope. Describing the incident dramatically, Mr. Evans would declare that critic after critic had professed to find flaws in the Bible, but such spots were due to the imperfection of the apparatus of human reason, and not with the Bible itself. The sun shines on in all its splendor, unmindful of the man who thinks that he sees minute flaws in it; and in the same manner does God's Word send forth its warm rays to all mankind, undimmed by any claim that any scientist or textual critic may see fit to make.

Herber Evans delivered lectures on David Livingstone and on Oliver Cromwell, and these were heard in many parts of Wales. For 18 years he edited Y *Dysgedydd* (The Instructor), and for a time he served as chairman of the Congregational Union of England and Wales. The manner of his preaching may be realized in a small degree by reading his *True and False Aims,* a book of sermons published in 1897. The story of his life is told in Elvet Lewis's *Life of Herber Evans* (1897), in Lewis Probert's *Memoir of Evan Herber Evans* (c. 1898), and in *Welsh Religious Leaders of the Victorian Era.*

John Evans (1840-1897)

John Evans of Eglwysbach was born in 1840 at Tydu farm, near Eglwysbach, Denbighshire. He was educated in the National School and at 17 he preached his first sermon. Ordained in 1865 at Mold, Flintshire, he served a congregation in Liverpool, going from there in 1862 to Bangor; returned to Liverpool in 1872, then went to London in 1878, returning to Bangor in 1886, and once more to London in 1890. While in London he attended King's College, and eventually became an Associate.

John Evans was a Welsh Wesleyan, and his unusual oratorical gifts caused him to become known as the "Spurgeon of Wales." It was he who organized and directed the forward movement in Glamorganshire, with which he was identified from 1894 to 1897, after his second London ministry. He published a life of Howel Harris, a Welsh biography of John Wesley (1880), and a short biography in English of the same man. He translated Wesley's sermons into Welsh (1887), and his *Life and Epistles of St. Paul* appeared in 1889. Four volumes of the sermons of John Evans were published during his lifetime and a fifth appeared the year after his death.

Howell Elvet Lewis (1860-1953)

One of the most noteworthy names in the recent period of Welsh preaching is that of Dr. H. Elvet Lewis, hymn-writer, poet, archdruid and eloquent preacher. He was born in the parish of Conwil Elvet, Carmarthenshire, and after his education at the Presbyterian College at Carmarthen he was ordained and served Congregational churches at Buckley, Hull, Llanelly, Harecourt, and in his later years the Welsh Tabernacle at King's Cross in London.

Dr. Lewis's fame as a hymn-writer and poet won for him the award of the bardic crown at the National Eisteddfod of 1888, and six years later of the chair. From 1923 to 1927 he was archdruid of Wales, at the *eisteddfodau*. In 1926-27 he was president of the Free Church Council, in 1927-28 president of the Welsh Union of the League of Nations, and in 1949 chairman of the Union of Welsh Independents.

The *eisteddfod,* with which the name of Dr. Lewis will long be associated, is at least as old as the 4th century. It is a great national gathering, the purpose of which is to encourage good music, poetry, hymn-writing and prose compositions. I recall a visit to the Welsh border, when every village was all but deserted. When the reason for this was asked, an old Welshman asked in surprise, "Do you not know of the *eisteddfod* at Machynlleth? All but the very old and the bedridden are there this week." At such great gatherings the singers, the harpers and the poets compete with one another, and in the evening the superb choruses from all over Wales are heard. Even the collieries of South Wales have their grand male choruses, and they sing their Welsh hymns and secular songs to audiences that include thousands of people. It is not unusual for Welsh choruses from America and the colonies to compete. One may converse with men from the coal pits, their fingers bent from hard labor, and one may discover in just such men an amazing technical knowledge of the world's great choral works. It was at just such gatherings that Elvet Lewis competed as a young man, and over which he presided in his later years. Meanwhile at Buckley, Llanelly and in the Welsh Tabernacle in London he was making for himself an enduring reputation in preaching. He wrote over 200 hymns, many of which are sung by Welsh congregations throughout the world. Blindness came upon him, but this did not interfere seriously with his work in the pulpit. He died December 9, 1953, at the age of 93.

Among the numerous writings of Dr. Lewis are *The Sweet Singers of Wales* (1889), which is an account of famous Welsh hymns and their writer; *With Christ among the Miners* (1906), the story of the Welsh revival of 1904-06; *Pattrwm y gwir Cristion* (1908), a Welsh translation of the *Imitation of Christ; Dr. Herber Evans: Life and Letters* (1897); *The Book of the Prophet Jeremiah* (1924), a commentary; *By the River Chebar,* on Ezekiel; *Howel Harris,* a biography; *Gwilym Tel* (1924), a Welsh translation of Schiller's well-known work; *The Approach to Christ* (1940); *The Book Still Speaks* (1943); *The Book Speaks Again* (1947); *Homes and Haunts of the Pilgrim Fathers* (1920), based upon a book of the same title by Alexander Mackennal; and several books of poems and hymns.   Dr. Lewis refused to accept any royalties derived from his 200 or more hymns.

CHAPTER XII

PREACHING IN IRELAND

IRELAND lies directly west of England and Scotland. It is separated from these countries by a body of water that varies from 13½ to more than 100 miles in width. Not only is Ireland clearly visible from Scotland, but one may stand on the Kintyre peninsula on a clear day and distinguish moving objects on the Irish coast. Ireland is irregular in shape. Its greatest width, from east to west, is hardly more than 180 miles; while its diagonal length, from southwest to northeast, is 300 miles. Its area is 32,375 square miles, which is a little larger than the State of South Carolina but not as large as Indiana.

Ireland is composed of Eire, also known as the Irish Free State, with a population of 2,989,700; and Northern Ireland, with a population of 1,279,745. Eire has a Roman Catholic population of 2,773,920 and a Protestant population of 182,746. Among the Protestants, the Episcopal Church numbers 145,030 communicants, the Presbyterians number 28,067 and the Methodists 9,649. Northern Ireland is strongly Protestant. Its Roman Catholic population is 428,290, as compared to 851,455 Protestants. Here the Presbyterians lead with 390,931 communicants, followed by the Episcopalians with 345,474, the Methodists with 55,135 and miscellaneous denominations with a total of 59,915 communicants.

Ireland was inhabited long before the coming of the Celts, as the many stone monuments that exist today will verify. Its definite history begins with the Celts, a race of people who inhabited large areas of western and northern Europe at the opening of the Christian era. They began to form colonies in Ireland as early as 400 B.C. The Celts enjoyed a fairly high degree of civilization, and were not the rough barbarians that Caesar describes. To the Roman, with all his pride, any other race was considered barbarian. The Celts established small districts in Ireland, each of which was ruled by its chieftain, or petty king. There were two assemblies: one composed of ordinary freemen, and the other of the nobles. Five major provinces, or "fifths" came

618   A HISTORY OF PREACHING

into being, and eventually these became Ulster, North
Leinster, South Leinster, Munster and Connach. As time
went on, we find a high-king presiding over the lesser kings
in an annual assembly at Taillte. The five provinces became
seven in number. One must not overlook the fact that
ancient writers called the people of Ireland the Scoti, or
Scots.

Christianity was introduced into Ireland at an early
date, but its precise time of coming remains a subject for
conjecture. Attempts have been made from time to time to
prove that Joseph of Arimathea visited England in the year
63 A.D., and first preached the Gospel in Glastonbury. This
conjecture is based partly upon an ancient tradition, and
partly upon the supposition that Joseph was a merchant.
The British Isles, as we call them today, were a part of the
Roman Empire, and it is a fact that the Phoenicians, and
perhaps the Jews as well, came to Cornwall seeking the tin
that was mined there. Traces of a wattle-and-daub building
have been found in Glastonbury, and several books have
been written by archaeologists, and articles have appeared in
printed reports of several societies, all attempting to prove
that a chapel was built there by Joseph of Arimathea. It is
possible that there was some contact between the British
Isles and Palestine during the early part of the Christian
era. In the absence of definite documentary evidence one
may only say that Christianity was known at an early date
in Ireland. However, it is possible that it came through the
Celts, rather than through others. They did not come to
Ireland as raiders, as a certain school of historians would
have us believe. There was a constant pressure upon the
Celts of the European continent, and it is known that some
of these people went to Ireland, seeking to establish new
homes where they would be free from the constant struggle
with other races. As they grew numerous in Ireland, the
Celts began to establish colonies along the west coast of
Scotland, and in England, Wales and Cornwall. Thus it is
that Wales, Cornwall and parts of Scotland are Celtic to this
day. Pressure from the Germanic tribes who invaded England from the east, pressed the Celts into the peninsulas of
Wales and Cornwall, and in the north the same Teutonic

tribes drove the Celts of Scotland into the Highlands and
the Islands. Today we find the two races in Scotland, and
the Celts of the Highlands and Islands still speak of the
Englishman as the *Sasunnach*, or Saxon. The Irish use the
same term.

The language of Ireland is the Gaelic. It differs somewhat from the Gaelic of the Scottish Highlands and Islands,
but the Gaelic-speaking Irishman and the Gaelic-speaking
Scot have no difficulty in understanding one another. Gaelic
was a dying language in Ireland, but in recent years there
has been a revival of interest in it. Various textbooks exist,
such as a series prepared by Brian Mac Giolla Pádraig, O.S.,
M.A., and published under the general title of *Bun-Čúrsa ar
Ceapadóireačt Gaeďilge*. Thus if one were to go to Ireland
today and greet a native in the Gaelic language, he would
receive a prompt response from the young people more often
than the older ones. Even in such places as Boston and
New York, Irish Gaelic has become a popular study. In
Boston, the University Extension courses offer instruction
in elementary and advanced Gaelic, while in New York
there are groups of people of all ages who meet in night
classes and receive instruction from competent Gaelic-
speaking teachers.

The difference between Irish Gaelic and Scots Gaelic
may be illustrated readily enough by comparing the Lord's
Prayer as it exists in these two languages. The Irish version
is as follows:

*" Ar n-Athair atá ar Neamh, go naomhuighthear t'ainm;
go dtigidh do ríoghacht; go ndeantar do thoil ar an talamh
mar a deantar ar Neamh; tabhair dúinn indiu ár n'arán
laetheamhail, agus maith dhúinn ár bhfiacha mar mhaith-
imid dár bhfiachannaibh féin; agus ná leig sinn i gcath-
ughadh, ach saor sinn ó olc. Amén."*

In Scots Gaelic it is somewhat different:

*"Ar n-Athair a tha air nèamh; gu naomhaichear
d'ainm; thigeadh do rìoghachd; deanar do thoil air an
Talamh, mar a nithear air nèamh; Tabhair dhuinn an diugh
ar n-aran laitheil, argus maith dhuinn ar fiachan, amhuil
mar a mhaitheas sinne d'ar luchd-fiach, agus na leig 'am*

buaireadh sinn; ach saor sinn o olc; oir is leatsa an rìoghachd, agus an cumhachd, agus a' ghlòir, gu sìorruidh. Amen."

It will be seen that the Irish version ends with the words "but deliver us from evil. Amen." The Scottish Presbyterian adds "for Thine is the kingdom, and the power, and the glory, forever and ever. Amen."

The visitor to Ireland is interested in the forms of greetings used there. These are expected of the newcomer, and their use opens up the way for congenial conversation, while the absence of such greetings is silently noted. The usual form of greeting is *"Go mbeannuighidh Dia dhuit,"* which means "May God bless (everything) for thee." The customary reply of the Irishman is, *Go mbeannuighidh Dia agus Muire dhuit,"* or "May God and Mary bless (everything) for thee." If he is a Protestant Irishman he will probably omit the word "Mary." Upon entering the home of an Irishman one is expected to say, *"Go mbeannuighe Dia annso,"* or "May God bless all (who dwell) here." The Irishman will reply as above, and to this he may add, *"Céad míle fáilte,"* or "a hundred thousand welcomes," which is a very common Irish expression. Such greetings are expected of everybody, and particularly of the stranger, who is looked upon as uncivil if he meets others with a mere "How are you?" which is quite proper in Scotland. In Munster is it quite proper to shorten the greeting to *"Dia dhuit!"* that is, "May God be with you!" and to this one's host will reply, *"Dia's Muire dhuit!"* or "God and Mary be with you!" However, in the South of Ireland one is more likely to hear *"Dia's Muire dhuit's Padraig!"* that is, "God, Mary and Patrick be with you!" Other familiar greetings are, "God save you!" with the reply, "God save you kindly!" In bidding the time of day one may say in English, "Morrow to you!" and the reply will be, "Morrow kindly!" Other common greetings are, *"Dia do bheatha!"* or "May God guard thy life!" *Mora's Muire dhuit!"* which means, "Morrow, and Mary be with thee!" *"Go mairir!"* or "Mayest thou live!" One must be careful in Ireland not to omit the customary "God bless you!" The Irishman will say to the newcomer, "And it's from America that you've come, God bless you!" Even in speaking of animals he will say, "That's a fine cow, God bless her!" This is not affectation, it is the usual way of speaking, and nothing "lets down" a stranger so surely as to neglect these daily expressions. If one has occasion to mention illness or mishap, one must always add, *"Dia edruinn is gach olc is urchoid!"* and this means, "May God be between us and all evil and harm!"

Gaelic is a highly expressive language, and admirably suited to both sacred and secular oratory. This, together with the exceptional gift of persuasive eloquence for which the Celt is famous, may account for the fact that one finds exceptional preachers in those countries where the Celt predominates. These men have never been given their just due. The preachers who use the Gaelic language, whether in Ireland or in Scotland, have been overlooked; and the same is true of their racial cousins in Wales. In the Gaelic-speaking days of a few generations ago the preaching of the Irishman and the Scottish Highlander was often in that language. Histories of preaching have been written by Americans, Scottish Lowlanders, Germans and Englishmen, none of whom had a working knowledge of Gaelic. Too often the books of sermons of the noted Gaelic preachers were not translated into English, but remained locked up in a language that the Englishman and the American could not read. The same was true in Wales, although some of Christmas Evans's sermons have been translated into English.

Racial differences are responsible in part for the disregard shown toward the Gaelic preacher. The Englishman and the Scottish Lowlander are taught to subordinate their emotions, rather than to give free expression to them; and when he hears a sermon by a Gaelic preacher, he is too ready to declare that the latter is a crude man who shouts his highly emotional sermons at sentimental congregations. It is true that the Gael is emotional, but his emotionalism differs from that of, for example, the German Pietist. It takes the form of persuasiveness, and often there is a strong vein of pathos. Theobald Mathew possessed it to a high degree. Although his voice was high pitched, and although he preached with a vehemence that was entirely strange to the quiet Englishman, yet on his English preaching tours he was well received everywhere; while in America his preaching filled the largest assembly halls. John Summerfield, although born in England, was a young Irishman, and no man with the possible exception of George Whitefield, has caused such a sensation in America as did Summerfield on the preaching tour that proved to be his last. Bernard Vaughn was of Irish ancestry, and while on a preaching tour in Italy, people declared, "Of course he is an Irishman, for no Englishman ever gesticulated as he does; also he is never at a loss for a word." To this a very famous Church dignitary replied, "He was born in Vesuvius and sent to England to cool."

Some Irish preachers have been accused of an exaggerated fondness for pathos, and a spirit of national martyrdom. However, it must not be forgotten that the Irish people have suffered greatly. Even though one may differ from them in doctrine, yet it cannot be denied that the treatment of Ireland has been extremely unkind, to say the least. They suffered much under Henry VIII and Elizabeth. When James I came to the English throne, it was not long until the Irish clergy were ordered to leave the kingdom, and were driven from place to place, and even put to death for refusal to do so. The Act of Supremacy and the Act of Uniformity were enforced rigorously in Ireland, and English laws and customs were forced upon the people. The lands in the province of Ulster were confiscated, their owners driven out, and Northern Ireland was colonized with English and Scottish settlers. Charles I continued this policy of confiscation until at last the Irish people rebelled in 1641. The Penal Laws excluded the native Irishmen from engaging in the legal profession, from serving as judges or as members of Parliament. They were not allowed commissions in the Army or Navy, nor could an Irishman hold a civil office or serve as an official of a corporation. He could not inherit land, nor could he be given a lease-hold. He was not allowed to have arms or ammunition, nor could he own a horse that was worth more than $25. The observance of Roman Catholic religious festivals was forbidden, and even the Irish Presbyterian was restricted in many ways. Marriage between Irish Catholics and Protestants was forbidden, and any priest or Protestant clergyman who performed such a marriage made himself liable to the death penalty. Roman Catholic churches were not permitted to have towers or spires, and the ringing of bells was forbidden. They were treated as Dissenters, and their places of worship were known as chapels, regardless of their size. All Irish clergymen were obliged by law to register as Dissenters, and members of monastic orders were ordered to leave the country. These severe laws remained in force for half a century, and even then they were modified but gradually, and some restrictions remained for generations. When one bears these things in mind, one is not so surprised to hear that the Irishman looks upon his race as an oppressed one, and that an injured note is evident at times in his sermons. The English House of Stuart and their successors did not hesitate to use force to stamp out what they considered Dissent, and their harsh treatment of Scottish Presbyterians and of Irish Nonconformists of all kinds, are dark pages in Church History.

Jonathan Swift (1667-1745)

The unpleasant details of the life of Dean Swift are known to all, and need not detain us long. He was born in Dublin in 1667, of English ancestry. Dryden was his cousin, and Thomas Swift, the vicar of Goodrich was a near relative. Although able to read the Bible at the age of three, his school record was not at all brilliant. He had a fine intellect, but an aversion to study. At the Kilkenny grammar school he completed his studies only by a special act of charity on the part of his masters. He entered Trinity College, Dublin, in 1682, was often disciplined because of his absence from chapel and classes, his insolent spirit toward his professors, and his indifference toward his studies. His record in Greek is marked *bene,* theology *negligenter* and philosophy *male.* He went up to Oxford in 1692, entered Hart Hall, and after idling his way through the university he managed eventually to get a master's degree *"ad eundem."*

He was ordained in 1694, and it is but a sad example of the low estate of the Protestant Church at the time that a man of his personal character and lack of the fruits of faith, should have orders conferred upon him. That he was not at all averse to pluralism and absenteeism is seen by the fact that he was given the livings of Laracor, Agher, Rathbeggan and the prebend of Dunlavin in St. Patrick's, with a combined living of about 230 pounds annually. There is little evidence that he sought seriously to improve the spiritual life in these places, for a year later we find him in London, where he spent the greater part of the next three years. Even though he returned to his congregations in Ireland now and then, his visits to London were frequent and his absences prolonged. He had been the nominal incumbent of Kilroot as early as 1695, but had spent most of his time in Belfast. In 1704 his *Battle of the Books* gave evidence of his literary genius. The satirical *Tale of the Tub* soon followed. In London he made the acquaintance of Addison, Steel, Pope and other literary men, and began to take part in politics. The writing of satirical pamphlets seemed to interest him much more than Christian doctrine. Living sometimes in Belfast, but more often in Dublin and in London, he soon gained fame in the literary world, where his unquestioned genius compensated partially for his unpleasant personal character and conduct.

In 1713 Dr. Swift was made Dean of St. Patrick's Cathedral, Dublin, which position he held for the next 32 years. He showed a certain amount of zeal for the Established Church, and his efforts in behalf of the poor of Ireland, as well as his attempts to rid the Irish people of the oppression which they suffered, seem entirely sincere.

As a preacher, Dean Swift won a certain degree of recognition, chiefly because he lived in an age when standards were deplorably low. He assumed an appearance of loyalty to Christian truth, but his preaching, although brilliant in some respects, was wholly lacking in conviction. With Laurence Sterne and a few others, Swift is an example of the "unconverted" type of clergyman against whom William Haslam carried on a crusade a century or so later. His collections of sermons, which have been printed from time to time, are of a high intellectual and literary quality, but plainly the products of a man to whom the spiritual meaning of Christian truth is as a foreign language. English Rationalists and Scottish Moderates might have received these sermons with enthusiasm, but in reality they are merely moral essays, such as any self-respecting editor of a secular magazine might write. One of his most popular sermons is a satirical admonition against sleeping in church. As a man of letters, Dean Swift holds a lasting place in the realm of English literature, and his writings are edifying to those who do not object to a form of satire that ranges from merry humor to undisguised ill-nature. His poems are not of the highest merit, and are marred at times with coarseness.

Of his private life, not much need be said. Even the high school boy is familiar with some of its details, such as his baffling conduct toward two women who had so important a part in his life, his dementia, which appeared as early as 1738, his final insanity and his burial at midnight in his own cathedral in the same grave with one of these women, who had died some years previously. Jonathan Swift, in spite of his high reputation as a literary man, is no credit either to Ireland or to the Church of Ireland. "Without unction, without fervor, without sentiment," says one of his biographers, "he leaves us with the impression that he neither sought nor found in the Gospel which he accepted and delivered so faithfully, anything that illuminated or anything that cheered." [1] Even this is an over-statement, for there is little evidence that he really preached evangelical truth.

John Abernethy (1680-1740)

The same disregard for evangelical truth that was known as Moderatism in Scotland, had its equivalent in Ireland and England. John Abernethy is not an extreme example of this tendency, but in his preaching one finds a disproportionate attention to the ethical and a neglect of the evangelical element. Abernethy was the son of a Presby-

---

[1]. J. C. Collins, *Life of Swift* (1893). Other biographies include: J. C. Collins, *Jonathan Swift, a Biographical and Critical Study* (1893); Sir Henry Craik, *Life of Jonathan Swift* (1882); W. H. Dilworth, *Life of Jonathan Swift* (1758); Thos. Sheridan, *Life of Swift* (1784); John Forster, *Life of Jonathan Swift* (1875); Lord Jeffery, *Jonathan Swift* (1853); Sir Walter Scott, *Memoirs of Jonathan Swift* (1814); G. P. Morairty, *Dean Swift and his Writings* (1893); and Deane Swift, *Essay upon the Life, Writings and Character of Dr. Jonathan Swift* (1755); Samuel Johnson, *Lives of the Poets*, vol. III.

terian pastor, and was born in 1680 at Brigh, in County Tyrone. During the unsettled political conditions of his boyhood, he was sent to Scotland, where he lived with relatives. He attended the elementary schools, and then Glasgow University. Later he continued his studies at Edinburgh.

Abernethy was ordained in 1703 and became pastor of a Presbyterian congregation at Antrim. He served here without particular distinction. In 1717 he was translated to Dublin, but after three months, and against the expressed wishes of his synod, he returned to Antrim. Such a procedure was without precedent, and it led to a synodical investigation. Abernethy insisted upon his right of freedom of action, while his synod declared that no man has the privilege of defying the express wishes of his brethren in the ministry. It led eventually to a disruption in the synod, and to the formation of two groups, known as the Subscribers and the Non-Subscribers. John Abernethy was a leader of the opposition group, and in 1726 he and his followers were expelled from synod. In 1730 he became pastor of the Wood Street Church in Dublin, where he remained until his death, ten years later. In 1731 he came into prominence because of his zealous opposition to the Test Act, and to "all laws that, upon account of mere differences of religious opinions and forms of worship, excluded men of integrity and ability from serving their country."

While Abernethy was considered one of the representative preachers of his time, and while he had been given many of the outward graces of the pulpit orator, yet one reads his sermons today without spiritual edification.[2] Several volumes of these sermons exist,[3] and while correct in literary and homiletical form, yet one wonders how these essays, with their lack of evangelical warmth, could have created so favorable an impression in the eighteenth century. He does not question Christian truth, but like the Moderates of Scotland he sets aside those truths that are so vital to the

---

[2]. John Abernethy, *Discourses on the Being and Perfections of God,* 2 vols. (London, 1740-43).

[3]. *Sermons on Various Subjects,* 4 vols. (London, 1748-51); *Tracts and Sermons* (London, 1751).

growth of Christian life, and devotes much of his effort to moralizing. It is the significant absence of certain definite Christian teachings that mars his sermons, and disqualifies him for a place in the evangelical succession.

John Leland (1691-1766)

John Leland, the great foe of the Deists, was born in Wigan, Lancashire, in 1691, but was brought up in Dublin. He became pastor in Dublin, serving first as associate pastor of a chapel in New Row, and later as pastor of a congregation in Eustace Row.

His fearless preaching won him renown. He attacked Tindal, Morgan, Dodwell, Bolingbroke and other Deists. He was possessed of a remarkable memory and of great learning. During his lifetime he published a number of books.

Benjamin McDowell (1739-1824)

Benjamin McDowell, although a prominent Irish Presbyterian, was born in Elizabethtown, N. J., of Irish parents. He received his education at Princeton and at Glasgow University. He joined the Established Church, was licensed to preach in 1766 and ordained later in the same year. For a time he served a congregation at Ballykelly, near Londonderry, Ireland. In 1778 he was called to the Capel Street Church in Dublin. It was at about this time that the Capel Street Church was rebuilt and renamed St. Mary's Abbey, although why a Presbyterian congregation should select such a name is not clear. When Mr. McDowell went to Dublin, his congregation numbered but six families, but he remained there to see it increase to 2,000 communicants. In 1791 he was appointed inspector of the Presbyterian congregations in the western and southwestern parts of Ireland. He had served as moderator of his synod in 1786. In 1791 he attracted attention because of his observance of Christmas Day.

Benjamin McDowell was one of the illustrious preachers of Irish Presbyterianism. He was a defender of the conservative standards of his denomination, and an opponent of the New Lights. He opposed John Cameron and a majority of the members of the Presbytery and Synod of

Ulster, charging them with teaching unsound theories in regard to the doctrine of the Person of Christ. His defense of the position that he looked upon as Scriptural was fearless, and at times one notes a polemical spirit in his preaching. Dr. McDowell's writings are often of a controversial character.

Walter B. Kirwan (1754-1805)

W. B. Kirwan, the famous Irish pulpit orator, noted for his charity sermons, was born in 1754 at Gortha, Galway. After attending the Jesuit College at St. Omar, he spent six years at St. Croix in the West Indies with a relative, a landed proprietor. Returning to Europe he went to the College of St. Anthony of Padua at Louvain, was ordained and became professor of natural and moral philosophy. In 1779 he returned to the British Isles and became chaplain to the Neapolitan embassy in London. He took a lively interest in the sessions of Parliament, attending the debates and studying the style of the noted orators. His own sermons meanwhile were beginning to attract wide attention.

In 1787 he declared himself a Protestant and united with the Church of Ireland. His first sermon, preached in St. Peter's, Dublin, caused a great sensation and revealed him as a pulpit orator of singular power. He became famous for his charity sermons, often raising $5,000 to $6,000 as a result of a single appeal. He was made prebend of Howth and was given the living of St. Nicholas Without, Dublin, and in 1800 he was made dean of Killala.

One of his most famous charity sermons [4] was based upon St. Luke 16, 25, "Son, remember that thou in thy lifetime receivedst thy good things, and likewise Lazarus evil things: but now he is comforted, and thou art tormented." It was an appeal for charity, and not only did the great congregation assembled to hear him cast into the plates all the money that they had brought with them, but many placed their watches and jewelry in the offering plates.

Dean Kirwan's last public appearance was upon the occasion of the annual charity sermon at St. Peter's, Dublin.

---

[4]. W. Kirwan, *Sermons by the late Walter Blake Kirwan* (Phila., 1816), pp. 43-63.

He was ill at the time, but he insisted upon rising from his bed and going to the church. He read the service and then announced his text. Pausing, he waved his hand toward the orphans who had been brought to the service, and who were crowding the galleries. "My poor children," he said, "I am unable to plead your cause." He was assisted to his home and died soon afterward.

Henry Grattan, the orator, said of him: "He called forth the latent virtues of the human heart and taught men to discover in themselves a mine of charity of which the proprietors had become unconscious. In feeding the lamp of charity he almost exhausted the lamp of life. He came to interrupt the repose of the pulpit, and shake the world with the thunder of the other. The preacher's desk becomes a throne of light." [5]

He was a man of attractive presence, yet almost stern of countenance. His voice was not particularly melodious, but is said to have been marvellous in its persuasive qualities. Thirteen of his sermons were published after his death,[6] and have been reprinted. Easy in style, and at times almost careless, they lack the close logical continuity that one might expect. Too often the spirit of evangelical urgency is lacking, and the appeal is made to less noble instincts in man. Mr. Kirwan is conscious of this defect, and expresses regret that he is compelled to resort to the tricks of the orator and appeals to mere sentiment in order to accomplish his purpose. In one of his sermons he utters these words of reproof:

"If there be any just ground for such a thought, why has it become necessary to prostitute, in some degree, the most sacred of all functions for the purpose of moving and inspiring us to the practice of this virtue? Why has the pulpit been obliged to descend to the very language of flattery, in order to extort from your vanity what it is hopeless of obtaining from a principle of religion? Why is it become necessary to hold out, on almost every occasion of this nature, the too dangerous doctrine 'that Charity

[5]. From an address before the Irish Parliament, June 19, 1792.
[6]. Op. cit.

covereth a multitude of sins'; and thus run the hazard of misleading you on the subject of your own salvation, in order to force you to become the instrument of salvation to others? Why are we obliged to use the arts and coloring of profane eloquence to make appeals to your passions; to search and probe the great body of human misery to the bone; to bring it, I may say, before your hearts, naked and expiring, quivering and disjointed; to expose all its miseries and horrors; to mingle our own tears with the tears of the unhappy objects that invoke us? And after all, why do we often fail? Yes, most deplorably fail? Why does misery often perish in the horrors of famine? or, what is infinitely worse, shoot up in swarms of infamy and guilt?" [7]

Alexander Carson (1776-1844)

An Irish Baptist is somewhat of a rarity, although that denomination has about 100 congregations in Ireland. One of the most famous preachers in Ireland's history was a Baptist. His name was Alexander Carson, and he was born in 1776 at Annahone, County Tyrone. He attended Glasgow University and was graduated as highest honor man in 1796. He was ordained a year later and became pastor of a Presbyterian congregation at Tobermore, in Londonderry. He did not remain long in the Presbyterian Church, for a year or so later we find him serving a group of independent people. They had no place of worship, and Mr. Carson often preached in private homes, then in large barns and finally in the open air. He was an exceptional preacher, and his followers increased in number. In 1814 a stone church was built. In 1831 Alexander Carson became a Baptist, and most of his congregation followed him. He served them until 1844, when he died as the result of a fall.

It is difficult to describe Alexander Carson's eloquence. It has been called a "burning, blazing, volcanic eloquence," that few could resist. However, his reputation as a preacher of first rank does not rest upon mere eloquence, for he was a man of exceptional scholarship. At one time he was offered a professorship at Glasgow University because of his thorough knowledge of the Greek language and liter-

---

[7]. *Op. cit.*, Sermon 2.

ature, but when he found that he must pledge himself to the Westminister Standards, he declined the overture. Perhaps no Irish preacher has ever equalled him in exegetical gifts, and not many men in other countries have excelled him in this respect. He was a tireless student, and he labored for days over a single sermon; but he seldom wrote his sermons before preaching them. He made copious notes and then preached extemporaneously. On the following day he wrote out his sermon carefully. His printed sermons are interesting reading even today. His style is admirable, and it conveys to a considerable extent the majestic character of his oratory. Very few highly gifted preachers have been able to convey an impression of their remarkable gifts by means of the printed page. Even such men as George Whitefield and John Summerfield seem almost commonplace when their sermons are reduced to type. This is not the case with Alexander Carson, for there are fine passages in his sermons that give one at least a suggestion of the moving eloquence that once attracted thousands. There are times when he reminds one of Ebenezer Brown, and again his literary style has suggestions of that of Dr. Chalmers. His printed sermons do not arouse one to the extent that those of Christmas Evans do, yet few people can read Carson wthout feeling the warmth of his evangelical zeal. Whether so majestic a style would appeal to the average congregation of today is a question, accustomed as we are to a simpler, more colloquial mode of expression.

Alexander Carson was a master of expository preaching. Expository preachers such as Campbell Morgan are skilled at making clear the language of the text. Alexander Maclaren expounded the truths contained in the text. Alexander Carson was able to do both. Even though he seldom wrote his sermons before preaching them, yet their logical progression of thought leaves little to be desired. Whatever his theme may be, it is centered upon Jesus Christ and His work of redemption.

Although Alexander Carson awakens one's admiration because of his majestic sermons, yet the fact must not be overlooked that he was a theological writer as well. His work on plenary inspiration was valued highly by Dr.

Thomas Chalmers, who used it as a textbook in his classes. Mr. Carson published a work on Baptism that was long a classic among Baptists.[8] Another of his important writings is on the doctrine of the Holy Trinity. Some men have said that it is strange that a man who could express himself so graciously when in the pulpit, was able to indulge in sharp polemics when discussing a controversial subject in his doctrinal writings. However, Mr. Carson was a man of strong convictions, even though there were times when he defended error, or a partial truth, with the same dogmatic force that he used when defending truth. Whether one may agree with all he says or not, yet it cannot be denied that he deserves a place among Ireland's most influential preachers. Two biographies exist,[9] and his collected works have been published in six volumes.[10]

James W. Doyle (1786-1834)

James W. Doyle was born in 1786 near New Ross, Wexford. His early education was received from his mother and then in a school at Rathnarague. At the age of 11 he was a spectator at the battle of New Ross, at the time that an attempt on the part of Ireland to establish a republic was put down with much bloodshed. In 1800 he entered a seminary at New Ross, and five years later he began his novitiate in a convent at Grantstown. He made his profession and took his vows in 1806, and then went to Portugal, where he entered Coimbra University. While there the invasion of Napoleon took place, and the work of the University was interrupted. James Doyle joined the army, and served for some time. In 1808 he returned to his home in Ireland, was ordained in 1809 and returned to his convent as a teacher of logic. He was transferred to Carlow College in 1813, where he taught rhetoric, humanity and theology. His inaugural address was a notable one, and established his reputation as a master of eloquence.

[8]. A. Carson, *Baptism in its Modes and Subjects Considered* (Edinburgh, 1831).

[9]. John Douglas, *A Biographical Sketch of Alexander Carson* (London, 1884); George C. Moore, *Life of Alexander Carson* (New York, 1851).

[10]. *Works of Alexander Carson,* 6 vols. (Dublin, 1847-64).

In 1819, when but 33 years of age, he was made Bishop of Kildare and Leighlin. Deeply interested in education, he established schools in every parish where these were lacking, and strove to improve those that existed. The times were still in an unsettled condition, and he made several preaching tours, speaking in churches and in the open air, his eloquence and his gift of persuasion doing much to restore quiet. He became engaged in a controversy with William Magee, the Protestant Bishop of Dublin. Magee was a pronounced anti-Catholic, and the controversy attracted wide attention. James Doyle's controversial writings, which he signed "J. K. L." were as vigorous as his preaching, and he did not hesitate to attack the Church of England and her attitude toward the Irish question.

Bishop Doyle was a tall, stately man, very definite in his likes and dislikes. When he preached there was an authoritative ring to his words, and a precision of thought that left no doubt in the minds of his hearers that he proposed to defend the rights of the Irish people. His attitude toward strangers was reserved, and his oversight of the priests in his diocese was strict. He held very definite views in regard to the language question, and not only preached in the English language himself, but admonished his priests to learn to use English effectively. He is generally believed to be the first Irish preacher of prominence to preach in the English language. He was equally proficient in Gaelic, and whenever the circumstances demanded it, he could use that language in the pulpit with marked effect. He held firmly to the doctrines and practices of the Roman Catholic Church, and left the impression in the minds of his hearers that these teachings were the correct ones, and that he proposed to defend them against Anglicans, Presbyterians or whoever else might question them. As a forceful preacher he was held in highest esteem by his countrymen, who considered him one of the strongest men of his time.

Henry Cooke (1788-1868)

Henry Cooke, known among Irish Presbyterians as "the Champion of Orthodoxy," was born in 1788 on a farm near Maghera, in County Derry, Ireland. He entered Glasgow

University in 1802, but did not remain to receive his degree. In 1808 he was ordained by the Presbyterian Church and became assistant pastor of a congregation at Duneane, in County Antrim. In 1811 he was called to a church in Donegore, in the same county. While there he sought to complete his studies, going finally to Glasgow in 1815-17 and to Trinity College, Dublin, in 1817-18, and studying theology and medicine. In 1818 he became pastor of a congregation at Killyleagh, County Down; and in 1829 he went to the May Street Church in Belfast, which he served for almost 40 years. He was moderator of the General Assembly in 1841 and again in 1862.

Dr. Cooke was the leader of the conservative group in the Irish Presbyterian Church. He took an active part in the Arian controversy of 1824-29, opposing Henry Montgomery, another powerful leader. Dr. Cooke fought Arianism relentlessly until the liberal group were forced to leave the synod in 1829, and until every evidence of Arianism was driven out of the presbyteries, the congregations, the seminaries and colleges. In 1841 he challenged Daniel O'Connell, known as the Irish Liberator, but for some reason the debate never took place. When the subject of voluntaryism agitated the Presbyterian Church, Dr. Cooke met Dr. Richie of Edinburgh in a debate that extended over two entire nights. In 1847 he was made professor of sacred rhetoric and catechetics at the General Assembly's college in Belfast, performing his duties there in addition to his congregational and synodical work. He died in 1868 at the age of 80, and in 1875 a statue was erected in Dublin to his memory.

Dr. Cooke was one of Ireland's great preachers. He was tall, slender, with an aquiline nose, and a voice of great range and power. His fierceness in debate made him feared by all who opposed him, yet in private life he was a mild, friendly, mirthful man, with a genial word for all, and with no suggestion of the polemical spirit that was so evident in his church's assemblies. His sermons were doctrinal and expository. He was a careful exegete, he edited a Bible to which he had added some 20,000 exegetical notes; and he prepared a concordance to the Bible that was destroyed by fire in a London hotel shortly before its delivery to the publishers.

His printed sermons are often strongly doctrinal, and the Person and Work of the Saviour are given careful attention. He was able to preach doctrine in a clear, simple and even an exuberant manner. He was strongly opposed to synergism, and was at some pains in his preaching to oppose the idea that "if I repent God will pardon me." This, he declared, makes repentance a good work that is found in man, and in view of which God pardons him. He declares that man is not saved on account of his repentance, for if this were true, then salvation is by works and not by grace. Pardon of sin, he declares, is the cause of repentance, not its effect. A laudatory biography of Dr. Cooke was written after his death by his son-in-law.[11]

Theobald Mathew (1790-1856)

One of Ireland's most distinguished sons was the Rev. Theobald Mathew, the great friend of the poor and the "apostle of temperance." He was born in 1790 at Thomastown Castle, five miles west of Cashel, in Tipperary. His father was the adopted son of a family of wealthy landowners. Theobald Mathew was educated at the Catholic Academy at Kilkenny, and in 1807 he went to Maynooth College. After finishing his schooling he joined the Franciscan friars at Dublin. Ordained in 1814, he became assistant to a remarkable man, the Rev. Fr. Donovan, of Cork. Father Donovan was in charge of a little chapel hidden in a narrow street in one of the poorest sections of the city. The chapel was but 43 feet in length, and the congregation was so poor that the chapel did not have so much as an organ.

Father Donovan was famed throughout Cork because of his singular devotion to the poor. He served as chaplain to a local prison, and in a day when laws were severe and men were executed for comparatively trivial offenses. Father Donovan spent much of his time with condemned men, seeking to bring them to repentance, and he always accompanied his men to the gallows. He insisted that these men go to the gallows in clean clothes, and it was his custom to give those

11. J. L. Porter, *Life and Times of Henry Cooke* (Belfast, 1875).

who could not afford it a clean shirt. Stories are told in Cork to this day of times when Father Donovan was compelled to receive callers while in his bed, because he had but one shirt left, and this was in the hands of the laundress. It was by such a man as this that young Theobald Mathew received his early training, and in the years that followed, his devotion to the poor exceeded that of his superior. The stories told in Cork of Father Donovan and Father Mathew are many. Unwilling to celebrate Christmas without music, Father Donovan paid an organ-grinder to bring his barrel-organ into the little chapel, for he found that the man owned two cylinders, one of which played "O Come, all ye Faithful," and the other "Lord, Dismiss us with Thy Blessing." The organ-grinder was concealed back of a curtain that formed the sacristy, and the people of Cork declare that Father Donovan's eyes were filled with tears of joy when his congregation sang these hymns with organ accompaniment. However, the organ-grinder, anxious to do more than he was paid to do, concluded the service with a third number. It was a popular Irish number, "Mol in the Wad"; and the joy of the two priests was turned to consternation.

The Irish people were under severe restrictions in 1814, and the infamous Penal Laws of 1702-15 had not been entirely repealed. The children of the poor were not yet given the advantage of state aid in their education. One of Theobald Mathew's first steps, upon coming to the Little Friary Chapel, as it was called, was to rent an empty store next to the chapel and open a parochial school. He prevailed upon kindhearted women to teach, since the congregation could not support a school. Father Mathew served as principal. Within ten years the school grew until it had 500 enrolled pupils. Among other evils of the day were the prohibitive burial rates, or taxes, which made it next to impossible for a poor man to be given a decent burial. The clergy of another denomination insisted upon the right to bury the dead in their own churchyards. As a relief from this abuse, Father Mathew secured a part of the old Botanical Gardens, laid it out in plots and granted free burial to any one who was a professing Christian, whether Roman Catholic, Presbyterian, Anglican or Methodist.